Rethinking Criminal Law

Rethinking Criminal Law

George P. Fletcher

OXFORD
UNIVERSITY PRESS
2000

OXFORD
UNIVERSITY PRESS

Oxford New York
Athens Auckland Bangkok Bogotá Buenos Aires Calcutta
Cape Town Chennai Dar es Salaam Delhi Florence Hong Kong Istanbul
Karachi Kuala Lumpur Madrid Melbourne Mexico City Mumbai
Nairobi Paris São Paulo Singapore Taipei Tokyo Toronto Warsaw

and associated companies in
Berlin Ibadan

Published by Oxford University Press, Inc.
198 Madison Avenue, New York, New York 10016

Library of Congress Cataloging-in-Publication Data
Fletcher, George P.
Rethinking criminal law / George P. Fletcher.
p. cm.
Originally published: Boston : Little, Brown, c1978.
Includes bibliographical references and index.
ISBN 0-19-513695-0
1. Criminal law. 2. Criminal liability. I. Title.
K5018.F57 2000
345—dc21 99-086719

1 3 5 7 9 8 6 4 2

Printed in the United States of America
on acid-free paper

To Fanny Fletcher Naxon
a woman of valor

Contents

Chapter Nine: The Theory of Mistake 683

Preface

Criminal law is a species of political and moral philosophy. Its central question is justifying the use of the state's coercive power against free and autonomous persons. The link with moral philosophy derives from one answer to the problem of justifying the use of state power. If the rationale or a limiting condition of criminal punishment is personal desert, then legal theory invariably interweaves with philosophical claims about wrongdoing, culpability, justifying circumstances and excuses.

A number of factors have inhibited the refinement of Anglo-American criminal law and its underlying theory. First, for over a century the prevailing philosophy of criminal law has been the utilitarian theory of sanctions inspired by the work of Beccaria, Bentham, Holmes, Stephen and, in our time, Herbert Wechsler and the Model Penal Code. Though the utilitarians have sharpened our sensitivity to the social costs and benefits of punishment, this emphasis on goals has distracted our attention from the problem of justice to the individual accused. The question whether a sanction is in the social interest has overshadowed the more basic inquiry whether the punishment of the accused is morally justified.

The emphasis in much recent thought is on the use of the criminal law to identify and confine potentially dangerous offenders. This is the explicit rationale in the Model Penal Code for assessing liability in cases of criminal attempts. The good of the whole is furthered by isolating a dangerous person in prison. And this is all that is thought necessary to justify the suffering of the individual confined.

The shift in emphasis from guilt to dangerousness betokens a movement to merge the criminal law with the administrative process of civil commitment. The confinement of the dangerously insane was once radically distinguished from punishment of the guilty. But the fashion now is to view both processes as aspects of one mechanism of social control. Even the requirement of culpability is reinterpreted as an evidentiary index of dangerousness. That the wicked are punished and the insane confined, is no longer taken to be an ordering distinction of the law. Not surprisingly, this emphasis on social control has inhibited refinement of the basic principles of criminal law. The emphasis on interrelated instruments of social control calls into question the identity of criminal law as a distinct field of inquiry.

Another factor inhibiting study of the theoretical foundations of criminal liability is the progressive legitimation of discretionary judgments within the formal criminal process. Insensitive laws are no evil if we can rely on the "good sense" of prosecutors. If there are important differences among offenses and offenders, we can rely on judges and parole boards to individualize punishment under systems of discretionary and indeterminate sentencing. Thus the criminal law may have a function in warning the public about conduct that might be punished, but the fine discriminations in the level of punishment are left to discretionary judgments.

If this has been the general drift of the criminal law, there are nonetheless signs that the tide may change. The revival of normative ethics and political theory signals the retreat of utilitarian influence. The sustained critique by Rawls, Nozick, Dworkin and Unger—all writing from the perspective of different moral philosophies—has expanded the potential of normative theory. Our minds are coming unstuck from the calculus of utility and groping toward new theories of justice and of the good. More than a decade ago, H. L. A. Hart helped to stimulate this search, first, by limiting the principle of utility to the justification of the criminal law as a whole; and further, by demonstrating that the criminal law lends itself to rigorous philosophical analysis. In more recent years, the search for justice in the criminal law has revived retribution as the rationale of punishment. There is also growing concern that moral culpability function as a necessary condition of liability. In the openness of the present climate and with the groundbreaking philosophical work of the last decade, the times may be right for a major commitment by many scholars to reworking and refining the substantive criminal law.

There are in fact urgent practical reasons for taking the criminal law seriously as a body of principles bearing on the just punishment of offenders. The mood of the country has suddenly shifted against indeterminate sentencing. Whatever the stimulus for this shift, the future may well lie with determinate sentencing schemes of the type recently enacted in California. The new scheme prescribes a standard penalty for each offense, with a permissible variation of one year upwards or downwards. If a sentencing judge elects the more serious or the more lenient sentence, he or she must justify the deviation in a written opinion. Parole is limited to time earned for good behavior.

The turn toward determinate sentencing means that the drawing of close distinctions can no longer be avoided by the exercise of judicial discretion. The burden falls on the criminal law to state the criteria that ought to be sufficient for the standard sentence and which should point in favor of aggravation or mitigation. If there is an important difference between the perpetrator who fires the fatal shot and the accessory who supplies the weapon, the distinction should be articulated and defended in principle. If there are good reasons for recognizing excuses, such as mistake of law, the claims should be recognized openly in the criteria defeating liability, not covertly in the process of prosecutorial or sentencing discretion. If determinate sentencing is going to work, then we must pay closer attention to the criteria that justify prescribed sentences.

This book does not propose a detailed set of criteria defining criminal liability; rather it provides the groundwork for others to carry forward the enterprise. If there is a contribution, it lies in reworking the apparatus with which we think about criminal liability.

Two methodological guidelines shape the argument of the book. First, as often as possible, the method of analysis is comparative, with primary attention to German law. German legal theory suggests alternatives to Anglo-American law; first, because the dominant strain of the German literature has remained relatively insulated from utilitarian legal theory, and secondly, because the system has long regarded prosecutorial discretion as an impermissible solution to substantive legal issues. Ironically, as the mood is changing in the United States, so it is in West Germany. As we rediscover the virtues of retribution, younger German scholars press for rehabilitation as the proper focus of the criminal law. As Kant and Hegel are exhumed in the United States, they are interred in the land of their birth. These ebbs and flows of intellectual history do not undermine the lessons we can derive from the German experience and they, from ours. But the two legal cultures' being out of phase requires us to be conscious of our historical situation. The next step for us, as for the Germans, may be to cultivate ideas that are in eclipse in their country of origin.

The second methodological premise reveals my debt to the Anglo-American legal tradition. As the common-law judge eschewed abstract principles for concrete precedent, we begin by embracing the details of the law—concrete and technical details about larceny, burglary, attempts and homicide. General propositions emerge from these details, but slowly. The first set of general claims seeks to organize the major criminal offenses in three patterns of liability—the patterns of manifest criminality, subjective criminality and of harmful consequences. The thesis of the first five chapters is that the criminal law is a polycentric body of principles. Each of the major patterns of liability must be appreciated on its own terms. We must resist the temptation to reduce the criminal law to a single formula for determining when conduct ought to be treated as criminal.

It is only in the second half of the book that we take up general themes that cut across the three patterns of liability. In Chapter Six, we explore the conceptual bases for formulating general principles of criminal liability and then seek to defend the distinction between wrongful acts and personal accountability for wrongdoing. What we find, however, is that the theory of wrongdoing is buffetted by the three conflicting patterns of liability and that one's view of the criminal law is influenced by which of the three patterns one takes to be representative of the whole.

Chapter Seven carries the process of distinction one step further and explores the internal structure of wrongful conduct. In Chapter Eight, we turn away from structural issues and seek to develop a general theory of derivative liability, uniting the seemingly disparate fields of omissions (failing to avert harm) and accessorial liability. This chapter rounds out the basic claims for organizing our thoughts about criminal liability. In Chapter Nine, we apply the results of our investigation to the problematic field of mistake, and in Chapter Ten, we return to the study of wrongdoing and accountability, but from the more conventional perspective of the theory of justification and excuse.

This book builds heavily on the work of common law as well as Continental theorists. My regret is not being able to document more fully my debts to prior writers. Early in my work on the book, Susan Laemmle Fletcher made me realize that I was writing neither a hornbook nor a treatise, but a reformist, critical work. The titling of the book is her doing. From this conception of the enterprise, one can derive, with some charity, a policy of footnoting that leaves some important sources unmentioned.

I am indebted to many people for helpful suggestions about this draft of my ideas as well as earlier papers reworked in the book, specifically, to Hans-Heinrich Jescheck and Albin Eser, for useful critical suggestions about German law; Pat Hanlon, then of the *Harvard Law Review*, for insights about the history of larceny; Bruce May and Cole Durham, for valuable assistance and criticism in the summer of 1977; Fred Parnon, for working on the index; Paul Brest, for thoughtful comments about Chapter Six. The manuscript would not have taken shape without the assistance of Paul Kahn, Susan Krinsky, Irene Jensen, Sandra Mullings, Fran Richtman and Antonia Turman. Above all, I am indebted to my students without whose audience and patient criticism these ideas would never have matured. Neither they nor my colleagues could save me from the mistakes that careful readers will discover and which I trust they will call to my attention.

A grant from the American Council of Learned Societies provided me with the free time necessary for thinking through this book and writing the first draft.

George P. Fletcher

Santa Monica, Calif.
March, 1978

Table of Abbreviations and Short-Form Citations

Baumann	J. Baumann, Strafrecht: Allgemeiner Teil (7th ed. 1975)
Bay. OLGSt.	Decisions of the High State Court (*Oberlandesgericht*) in Bavaria, Criminal Cases
BGB	German Civil Code (*Bürgerliches Gesetzbuch*)
BGHSt.	Decisions of the German Supreme Court (*Bundesgerichtshof*), 1951 to present
Blackstone	W. Blackstone, Commentaries on the Law of England (1765--69) (4 volumes)
Bouzat & Pinate	P. Bouzat & J. Pinatel, Traité de droit pénal et de criminologie (2d ed. 1970) (2 volumes)
Bracton	Bracton on the Laws and Customs of England (S. Thorne trans. 1968) (4 volumes)
BVerfGE	Decisions of the German Supreme Court in Constitutional Cases (*Bundesverfassungsgericht*), 1952 to present
Caljic	California Jury Instructions: Criminal (3d ed. 1970)
3 Coke	E. Coke, Third Institute (1644)
First Report	*First Report from His Majesty's Commissioners on Criminal Law*, 26 Parliamentary Papers: Criminal Law (1834)
Foster	M. Foster, A Report of Some Proceedings of the Commission for the Trial of the Rebels in the Year 1746 in the County of Surrey and of other Crown Cases (1762)
GA	Goltdammer's Archiv für Strafrecht

Hale	M. Hale, History of the Pleas of the Crown (1736) (2 volumes)
Hall	J. Hall, General Principles of Criminal Law (2d ed. 1960)
Hawkins	W. Hawkins, Pleas of the Crown (1716) (2 volumes)
Holmes	O. W. Holmes, The Common Law (1881)
Jescheck	H. H. Jescheck, Lehrbuch des Strafrechts: Allgemeiner Teil (2d ed. 1972)
JS	Juristische Schulung
JZ	Juristenzeitung
Kurs (GP 1968)	Criminal Law: The General Part (eds. H. Belaev & M. Shargorodsky 1968) (in Russian)
Kurs (GP 1970)	Course in Soviet Criminal Law: The Criminal Offense (eds. A. Piontovsky, P. Romashkin & V. Chkhikvadze 1970) (volume 2 in series) (in Russian)
Kurs (GP 1972)	Soviet Criminal Law: The General Part (eds. M. Gel'fer et al. 1972) (in Russian)
Kurs (GP 1974)	Soviet Criminal Law: The General Part (eds. V. Men'shagin et al. 1974) (in Russian)
Kurs (SP 1968)	Criminal Law: The Special Part (eds. I. Zagorodnikov & V. Kirichenko 1968) (in Russian)
Kurs (SP 1973)	Course in Soviet Criminal Law: The Special Part (ed. M. Shargorodsky 1973) (in Russian)
Lambert	L. Lambert, Traité de droit pénal spécial (1968)
LaFave & Scott	W. LaFave & A. Scott, Criminal Law (1972)
Maurach GP	R. Maurach, Deutsches Strafrecht: Allgemeiner Teil (4th ed. 1971)
Maurach SP	R. Maurach, Deutsches Strafrecht: Besonderer Teil (5th ed. 1969)
MDR	Monatsschrift für deutsches Recht
Merle & Vitu	R. Merle & A. Vitu, Traité de droit criminel (2d ed. 1973)

MPC	Model Penal Code (Proposed Official Draft 1962)
NJW	Neue Juristische Wochenschrift
Packer	H. Packer, Limits of the Criminal Sanction (1968)
Perkins	R. Perkins, Criminal Law (2d ed. 1969)
Proposed Federal Criminal Code	S. 1437, 95th Cong., 1st Sess. (1977)
Prosser	W. Prosser, Law of Torts (4th ed. 1971)
RGBl.	Reichsgesetzblatt (German session law prior to 1945)
RGSt.	Decisions of the German Supreme Court (*Reichsgericht*) in Criminal Cases, 1880 to 1944
RGZ	Decisions of the German Supreme Court (*Reichsgericht*) in Civil Cases, 1879 to 1944
Rudolphi in SK StGB	See SK StGB *infra.*
Samson in SK StGB	See SK StGB *infra.*
Schmidhäuser	E. Schmidhäuser, Strafrecht: Allgemeiner Teil (2d ed. 1975)
Schönke-Schröder-Cramer, Schönke-Schröder-Eser, Schönke-Schröder-Lenckner, Schönke-Schröder-Stree	P. Cramer, A. Eser, T. Lenckner, & W. Stree, Kommentar von Schönke-Schröder zum Strafgesetzbuch (18th ed. 1976) (each segment of the *Kommentar* cited to the author responsible for that segment)
SGP	Soviet State and Law (periodical in Russian)
SJZ	Süddeutsche Juristenzeitung
SK StGB	H. J. Rudolphi, F. Horn, E. Samson, H. L. Schreiber, Systematischer Kommentar zum Strafgesetzbuch (1975) (each segment of the *Kommentar* cited to the responsible author)
Smith & Hogan	J. Smith & B. Hogan, Criminal Law (3d ed. 1973)

Stefani & Levasseur	G. Stefani & G. Levasseur, Droit Pénal Général (9th ed. 1976)
Stephen	J. F. Stephen, History of the Criminal Law of England (1883) (3 volumes)
StGB 1871	The former German Criminal Code, in force from 1871 to 1975
StGB	German Criminal Code (current)
StPO	German Code of Criminal Procedure
Stratenwerth	G. Stratenwerth, Strafrecht: Allgemeiner Teil I (2d ed. 1976)
Ugol. kod.	Criminal code in force in a republic within the Soviet Union, cited to the particular republic; e.g., Ugol. kod. (RSFSR) refers to the code in force in the Russian Soviet Federal Socialist Republic.
Welzel	H. Welzel, Das Deutsche Strafrecht (11th ed. 1969)
Williams	G. Williams, Criminal Law (2d ed. 1961)
ZStW	Zeitschrift für die gesamte Strafrechtswissenschaft

Part One
Rethinking Specific Offenses

Chapter One
The Topology of Theft

§1.1. *Introduction*

The field of theft offenses displays a variety as rich as the imagination of those who seek dishonest gain. There are crimes committed in cashing bad checks, misusing credit cards, eating at a restaurant without paying, joyriding in another person's car, appropriating someone else's electricity—the list goes on and on. In this book we could not canvass all of these crimes of dishonest acquisition even if we were so inclined. Our objective will be to elicit the basic structure of theft by focussing on three types of crime that have crystallized in all Western legal systems. The traditional pattern in France, Germany and the Soviet Union as well as Anglo-American jurisdictions is to recognize a crime of *larceny* committed by taking the goods of another, a crime of *embezzlement* committed by improperly keeping goods entrusted to the actor, and a crime of *fraud* or *false pretenses,* committed by fraudulently inducing another to part with his property.

In general terms, we could identify the voluntary participation of the victim as the source of the distinctions among these three classic offenses. Larceny is committed against an involuntary victim. Embezzlement is committed against a victim who voluntarily entrusts possession of his goods to the defendant, but who is an involuntary victim of the defendant's subsequent appropriation. The crime of obtaining property by false pretenses is committed against a victim who nominally consents to the transfer of his goods to the defendant. Yet his nominal consent is induced by fraud and therefore does not reflect the owner's true preference. In a fourth type of offense, extortion, the owner again nominally consents to the surrender of property. But in this variation the consent is induced by improper threats rather than fraud.

One reason for concentrating our efforts on three core offenses of larceny, embezzlement and fraud is that the working out of the contours of these crimes, individually and in contrast with each other, has proven to be a task with rich jurisprudential overtones. By studying the difficulties attendant to refining these offenses, we find much to learn that is of general application to the theory of criminal liability.

§1.1.1. Larceny and Embezzlement. As we seek to be more precise about larceny and embezzlement we should keep in mind that larceny is one of the primordial crimes of Western culture.[1] Its roots extend back to the earliest stages of legal thought. Embezzlement, in contrast, is almost always a later statutory refinement of the original common-law crime of larceny. In English legal history, embezzlement is engrafted onto the crime of larceny in a series of eighteenth-century statutory enactments,[2] which typically took the form of extending larceny to encompass cases now called embezzlement. In the early nineteenth century, the English courts began to hold that the most far-reaching of these eighteenth-century statutes, that of 39 George III (1799), created a new offense of em-

§1.1. [1] See Watkins, *Studies in Indo-European Legal Language, Institutions, and Mythology*, in Indo-European and Indo-Europeans 321 (G. Cardono et al., ed. 1970); D. Daube, Studies in Biblical Law 235–305 (1947). See §2.2 *infra*.

[2] 15 Geo. II, c. 13, §12 (1742) (clerks of the Bank of England); 24 Geo. II, c. 11, §3 (1751) (clerks of the South Sea Company); 5 Geo. III, c. 25, §17 (1765) (clerks of the Post Office); 39 Geo. III, c. 85 (1799) (servants and clerks generally).

bezzlement.[3] At about the same time, the French National Assembly recognized a comprehensive French crime of embezzlement in the Napoleonic Penal Code of 1810.[4]

This basic difference in historical genesis accounts for several problems in defining larceny and embezzlement. In Anglo-American law, larceny received its first authoritative definition in the English Larceny Act of 1916.[5] In the course of history, judges have punished larceny on the assumption that they knew what it was.[6] When the common-law writers and judges turned to a definition of larceny, the terms that most often appear in their accounts are (1) a trespassory taking and (2) *animus furandi.* Today we would say that the former was an objective element; the latter a subjective dimension of the offense. The term "trespassory taking" stood for a complex of three elements:

a. a physical movement of the object,[7]
b. a taking from the possession of another,[8] and

[3] Regina v. Headge, 168 Eng. Rep. 613 (1809) (held that the essence of the offense was "breach of trust"; therefore indictment properly founded on statute rather than common law).

[4] Code Pénal §408.

[5] Larceny Act 1916, 6 & 7 Geo. V, c. 50, §1; the act defines the offense of "stealing" to apply to anyone "who, without a claim of right made in good faith, takes and carries away anything capable of being stolen with intent, at the time of such taking, permanently to deprive the owner thereof." This definition has been superceded by Theft Act 1968, c. 60, §1 ("dishonestly appropriates property belonging to another").

[6] See §2.2 *infra.*

[7] This element was known at common law as the requirement of asportation; the indictment had to allege that defendant *felonice cepit & asportavit.* See 3 Coke 108; 4 Blackstone 231; Perkins 263–65. It followed from this requirement that larceny could not be committed against immovable property. The element is carried forward in the Larceny Act 1916, as the requirement of "carrying away." See note 5 *supra.*

[8] This requirement is fundamental, but it is not mentioned in the common-law texts as part of the definition of larceny. Bracton 150b; 3 Coke 107; 1 Hale 504; 1 Hawkins 134; 4 Blackstone 229. Nor is it in the definition given by the Larceny Act 1916, *supra* note 5. The requirement of a taking from possession tends to be discussed in the context of the rule that if the actor receives possession by delivery, he cannot commit larceny in subsequently appropriating the goods. E.g., 1 Hale 505–06; 4 Blackstone 230–31.

c. an act contrary to the will of the owner.[9]

Though the first element of physical movement is as straightforward as the law can be,[10] the second issue of "taking from possession" has posed innumerable conundrums. The problem is that except in very early stages of the common law, possession has sometimes been more and sometimes less than what meets the eye. A person may look as if he has possession of an object and not have it. Someone else, who is not even near the object, might have legal possession. The concept of possession has matured (or degenerated, depending on your taste) from a natural to a legal fact. When someone looks as if he has possession but does not, under the law, we say that he has mere custody over the object. It may be some consolation to know that all leading Western legal systems have struggled with the metaphysics of custody and possession, and later we shall look at these efforts in abundant detail.[11]

In addition to these three standard objective elements of a trespassory taking, a major dispute arose in the nineteenth century about the intangible quality of trespass in the act of taking. The question was whether the word "trespass" meant the same thing in larceny as connoted by the early common law of trespass *vi et armis*.[12] Did the act of stealing have to be tinged with stealth or force? Or could one steal in a harmless, unobtrusive sort of way? This dispute, as we shall see, has never been completely resolved and, indeed, invites us to consider the deeper underpinnings of the law of larceny.

[9] The element *invito domino* is mentioned continuously after Bracton 150b. E.g., 3 Coke 107; 1 Hale 504. Yet it is abandoned in the Theft Act 1968, c. 60, §1 which omission generates problems in distinguishing larceny from false pretenses. See note 37 *infra*. Note that the Model Penal Code also fails to mention this self-evident element of larceny. MPC §223.2.

[10] Some complications are possible. See Williams v. State, 63 Miss. 58 (1885) (*D* shot a hog and turned it over, but this was insufficient for asportation).

[11] See §§1.2.5, 2.2.1 *infra*.

[12] The phrase *vi et armis* became standard after the Statute of Gloucester in 1278. Yet there are doubts whether the phrase imparted any specific meaning. See S. Milsom, Historical Foundations of the Common Law 247 (1969).

The requirement of *animus furandi*[13] meant that in the course of the trespassory taking, the actor have the "spirit of one thieving." The common-law writers, Coke, Hale and Blackstone,[14] were never more precise about the intent required for larceny. In the nineteenth century, we begin to find courts referring to "an intent to steal"[15] as a specification of the *animus furandi* and sometimes more precisely to "an intent to deprive the owner permanently of his property."[16] This latter set of words found its way into the 1916 Larceny Act which, as noted, proposed the first legislative definition of larceny in the English-speaking world.[17]

While the common law of larceny builds on a shared understanding of what larceny is,[18] embezzlement is a creature of legislative will that varies from jurisdiction to jurisdiction. The legislative schemes typically require (1) that the offender have been entrusted with the object by the owner, or at least have possession at the time of the offense, and (2) a subsequent act of deprivation, usually termed conversion or fraudulent appropriation. The differences among legislative schemes turn primarily on whether they are comprehensive or whether they are limited to specified relationships of trust. The generative English Statute of 1799 was lim-

[13] The phrase *animus furandi* is introduced in Bracton 150b as a substitute for the Roman *lucri causa faciendi*. Blackstone later revived the phrase *lucri causa* (for the sake of gain) and said it was the equivalent to acting *feloniously*. 4 Blackstone 231–32. This caused some difficulty in nineteenth-century litigation, until the courts returned to the view that the motive of pecuniary gain was irrelevant to *animus furandi*. See, e.g., The Queen v. Jones, 169 Eng. Rep. 205 (1846) (defendant stole letter to suppress report regarding his character; held, guilty of larceny, but the opinion is muddled by the question whether this was a motive of gain); Rex v. Cabbage, 168 Eng. Rep. 809 (1815) (defendant took horse and killed it in order to destroy evidence against friend; held, motive sufficient for larceny).

[14] *But cf.* Blackstone's view on *lucri causa*, *supra* note 13.

[15] Rex v. Holloway, 172 Eng. Rep. 1082 (1833) (jury acquitted on ground defendant had "no intention of appropriating [the gun] to his own use"); State v. South, 28 N.J.L. 28 (1859) ("felonious intent to convert [the goods] to his own use and make them his property, without the consent of the owner").

[16] People v. Brown, 105 Cal. 66, 38 P. 518 (1894); Delk v. State, 64 Miss. 77 (1886).

[17] See note 5 *supra*.

[18] The comparative analysis of larceny is postponed to §1.2 *infra*.

ited to "servants and clerks";[19] the French Code of 1810, to two specific types of entrustment.[20] Persons not included under these headings were simply not criminally liable for misappropriating an entrusted object. Yet the inclusion of some and the exclusion of others, particularly in Anglo-American jurisdictions, has never seemed to be backed by convincing arguments of principle, and therefore the historical pattern has been to expand the categories of persons subject to liability. In the English Statute of 1812, coverage was extended to bankers, merchants, brokers, attorneys and "agents of any description whatsoever."[21] Parliament fashioned the new crime of larceny by a bailee[22] which encompassed all persons receiving chattels by delivery. Similarly, in the development of French law, the pattern of development has proceeded by statutory accretion;[23] the number of protected entrustments has increased from two to at least six, now including relationships generated by leases, deposits, commissions, pledges, lending for use, and unsalaried as well as salaried employment.[24]

The California Statute of 1872 represents one of the early Anglo-American efforts to define embezzlement comprehensively to include all persons "fraudulently appropriating property which has been entrusted to [them]."[25] The provision of the German Criminal Code, also enacted in the 1870s, applies comprehensively to anyone who has possession of the object.[26] When embezzlement is defined comprehensively, without regard to the particular status

[19] 39 Geo. III, c. 85 (1799).

[20] Code Pénal §408 *(à titre de dépôt ou pour un travail salarié).*

[21] 52 Geo. III, c. 63 (1812).

[22] 20 & 21 Vict. c. 54 (1857).

[23] See statutory modifications of 1832, listed along with contemporary laws and decrees modifying the crime, in Code Pénal §408, at 235 (Dalloz 63d ed. 1966).

[24] Code Pénal §408.

[25] Cal. Penal Code §484. For analogous provisions, see, e.g., Hawaii Penal Code §830(4).

[26] StGB §246. The German provision divides the crime of *Unterschlagung* in two degrees. The lesser crime, punished by a maximum of three-year imprisonment, requires only that the defendant have had possession of the object prior to the appropriation; the more serious, punished by a maximum of five years, requires in addition that the chattel be "entrusted" (*anvertraut*) to the defendant.

of servants, clerks and the like, there is obviously no need to introduce a supplementary crime of larceny by a bailee.

The contemporary trend in Anglo-American jurisdictions is to merge larceny and embezzlement in one overarching offense committed by anyone "who dishonestly appropriates the property of another."[27] This is the language of the 1968 English Theft Act,[28] which has been incorporated as well in the 1973 Crimes Act in Australia.[29] The Model Penal Code, which was written a decade earlier, retains the distinction between taking and exercising unlawful control over the property of another.[30] The economy of the merger represented by the 1968 English innovation is that it dispenses with the distinction between taking from possession and taking while in possession. Lost in the process of merger is the crisp, directive language of "taking" and "trespass." It is true that both German[31] and Soviet law[32] treat the concept of "appropriation" as the element common to the distinct crimes of larceny and embezzlement. What makes the 1968 English Statute different is the attempt to abolish the two offenses and to rely exclusively

[27] Theft Act 1968, c. 60, §1. This reform was inspired, in part, by the recurrent demand in the literature for statutory simplification. See, e.g., Edwards, *Possession and Larceny,* 3 Current Legal Prob. 127 (1950); Goodhart, *The Obsolescent Law of Larceny,* 16 Wash. & Lee L. Rev. 42 (1959); Turner, *Larceny and Trespass,* 58 L.Q. Rev. 340 (1942); Williams, *Reform of the Law of Larceny: An Urgent Task,* 21 Mod. L. Rev. 43 (1958).

[28] For commentary on the concept of "dishonest appropriation," see E. Griew, The Theft Act 1968, 19–22 (2d ed. 1974); J. C. Smith, The Law of Theft 8–33 (2d ed. 1972).

[29] Crimes (Theft) Act 1973, No. 8425, §72(1) (Victoria, Australia). See Elliott, *Three Problems in the Law of Theft,* 9 Melb. Univ. L. Rev. 448 (1974).

[30] MPC §223.2. This provision has been adopted in a number of states. See, e.g., Colo. Rev. Stat. §18-4-401; Del. Code Ann. tit. 11, §841.

[31] The concept of *Zueignung* appears both in the definitions of larceny and embezzlement. StGB §§242, 246.

[32] Soviet criminology distinguishes carefully between *pokhishchenie* and *khishchenie;* the former is characteristic of larceny in its various forms; the latter term applies to all offenses of dishonest appropriation. See Ugol. kod. (RSFSR) §§89, 90, 92, 93, 93[1]. 3 Kurs (SP 1973) at 344–49. The distinction is of great practical importance; §93[1], enacted in 1962, imposes the death penalty for crimes of *khishchenie* of state property in "especially large quantities." As to whether this provision could be properly applied to the attempted hijacking of a state-owned airplane, see T. Taylor (with Dershowitz, Fletcher, Lipson and Stein), Courts of Terror 152–54 (1976).

upon the murky concept of appropriation[33] as the criterion of criminality.

§1.1.2. Obtaining Property by False Pretenses. Though the generative statutes had little to say on the matter,[34] the eighteenth-century English courts found that a necessary condition for the crime of fraud was that the defendant's false pretense induce the victim to part with title in his goods. Thus in this judicial refinement, the offense does not apply where the pretense merely induces the owner to part with possession, but not title—as in a transaction of lease or pledge. This restriction on the offense, coupled with some expansion of larceny,[35] has generated particular difficulties in distinguishing larceny from the crime of false pretenses. A good example of problems at the intersection of the two crimes is Graham v. United States,[36] in which the victim gave the defendant, a lawyer, $2,000 that the lawyer was to use in bribing the police on the victim's behalf. In fact, the defendant was honest about bribing but not about stealing; he kept the money for himself. On appeal from the defendant's conviction for larceny, the dispute was whether the victim had parted with title or merely possession in the sum of money. The appellate court affirmed the conviction on the ground that the owner had not intended to part with title, but merely possession and that therefore, the appropriate charge was larceny rather than false pretenses. It is obvious that one could have maintained that the victim had parted with the $2,000 with no intention of ever seeing it again, and that is an intent to pass title if anything is.[37]

[33] The concept is defined in Theft Act 1968, c. 60, §3(1) as "any assumption by a person of the rights of an owner. . . ." The Criminal Law Revision Committee identified "appropriation" with the concept of "conversion" in tort, but this equation is rejected by the commentators, Griew, *supra* note 28, at 19; Smith, *supra* note 28, at 8.

[34] 33 Hen. VIII, c. 1 (1541), 30 Geo. II, c. 24 (1757).

[35] The expansion is the development of "larceny by trick" considered *infra* in §2.3.1.

[36] 187 F.2d 87 (D.C. Cir. 1950), *cert. denied,* 341 U.S. 920 (1951).

[37] Cf. People v. Noblett, 244 N.Y. 355, 155 N.E. 670 (1927) (title to money held to have passed). The Model Penal Code maintains the distinction between theft by ap-

The German law of fraud (*Betrug*) has never shared this limitation and therefore would apply in cases in which the victim intended merely to part with possession or use of the object.[38] Thus the kind of close distinction that troubled the court in *Graham* simply would not arise under German law. Graham would have been guilty of fraud rather than larceny. Contemporary efforts at law reform in Anglo-American jurisdictions point as well toward looser boundaries in the law of false pretenses. The English Theft Act of 1968 casts the net of fraud wide enough to include anyone who obtains "ownership, possession or control" of property by a fraudulent deception.[39] This definition would obviously include *Graham* as well as many other cases of larceny. The Model Penal Code takes a more conservative line, insisting upon the transfer of "property"[40] as an element in theft by deception.

Another area in which the Anglo-American law of false pretenses is enjoying a relaxation of earlier restraints is in the requirement of the pretense itself. The earlier rule was that the actor had to induce the victim to transfer title by deception about the external world—about, say, the defendant's credit status or the quality of the goods offered for sale.[41] In the 1954 case of People v. Ashley,[42] the California Supreme Court boldly swept aside the requirement of an objective misrepresentation and held that a mis-

---

propriation and theft by deception. MPC §§223.2, 223.3. The nominal difference in the Theft Act 1968, c. 60, between §1 and §16, has tended to collapse in litigation. In *Lawrence*, a cab driver took an excessive amount from a foreigner who laid his wallet open to the driver and allowed him to take out the appropriate fare. The Court of Appeal argued that this could be either theft by appropriation (§1) or theft by deception (§16). Regina v. Lawrence, [1971] 1 Q.B. 373; the House of Lords affirmed with some reservations about the collapse of the two offenses into one. Lawrence v. Metropolis Police Commissioner, [1971] 2 All E.R. 1253. See Elliott, *supra* note 29, at 451–56.

[38] German law in fact goes much further. See §1.2, at note 3; §1.3.3 *infra*.

[39] Theft Act 1968, c. 60, §15(2). *Cf.* additional crime of obtaining a "pecuniary advantage" by deception. *Id.* §16.

[40] MPC §223.3.

[41] See Chaplin v. United States, 157 F.2d 697 (D.C. Cir. 1946); Commonwealth v. Drew, 36 Mass. (19 Pick.) 179 (1837); Rex v. Goodhall, 168 Eng. Rep. 898 (1821).

[42] 42 Cal. 2d 246, 267 P.2d 271 (1954), *cert. denied*, 348 U.S. 900 (1954).

representation about one's intention could be a false pretense.[43] That precedent has not garnered a following in other common-law courts. But the trend of contemporary legislation is to drop the traditional requirement of an objective, documentable lie[44] and embrace the potential punishability of routine credit transactions.[45] It is now possible to commit the crime of false pretenses in many jurisdictions by borrowing money with the intent not to repay it. Receipt of the money satisfies the element of acquiring title. Though the borrower falsely promises to repay the loan, he engages in no deception about the external world that is subject to proof at the time of his act. His deception, if any, is about his plans for the future, and the best evidence of that is what he does when the debt falls due. Though the crime is technically committed at the time the loan is received, the critical evidence of liability is furnished by his failure to repay at some future time.[46]

This relaxation of the Anglo-American law of fraud conforms to the rules both of German[47] and Soviet law.[48] Under both of

[43] *Cf.* Commonwealth v. Green, 326 Mass. 344, 348, 94 N.E.2d 260, 264 (1950) (defendant's various unkept promises to use money collected to form an investment trust held to be false "statement of fact as to the intention").

[44] See Minn. Stat. §609–52, subd. 2(3)(b); N.Y. Penal Law §155.05(2)(d); Crimes (Theft) Act 1973, No. 8425, §81(4) (Victoria, Australia); Theft Act 1968, c. 60, §15(4); MPC §223.3.

[45] The court in *Ashley* thought that abuses would be prevented by the corroboration rule in Cal. Penal Code §1110. See 42 Cal. 2d at 259, 267 P.2d at 275. Yet the courts appear to be satisfied with corroboration of the representation rather than of defendant's consciousness of its falsity, People v. Phillips, 64 Cal. 2d 574, 414 P.2d 353, 51 Cal. Rptr. 225 (1966) (false pretenses used as basis for charge of felony-murder; the false pretense was that defendant believed he could cure cancer of the eye; no corroboration of his knowingly misrepresenting his ability; conviction reversed on other grounds). *But cf.* People v. Randono, 32 Cal. App. 3d 164, 108 Cal. Rptr. 326 (1973) (alleged pretense was false promise to pay for liquor; corroboration found in concealment of the liquor after delivery).

[46] *Cf.* Del. Code Ann. tit. 11, §844.

[47] The German view, strictly speaking, is that the "intent to pay" is a present fact and may be fraudulently misrepresented. Schönke-Schröder-Cramer §263, note 15, at 1519; Judgment of the High State Court (*Oberlandesgericht*) in Celle, February 27, 1957, 1957 GA 220 (intent not to pay in installment sale).

[48] Kurs (SP 1973) at 803; B. Nikiforov, The Protection of Private Property by the Criminal Law in USSR 133 (1954) [in Russian] (criticizing pre-revolutionary Russian writers for insisting on an externally verifiable pretense).

these latter systems, a false promise about the future is sufficient to satisfy the required element of a fraudulent misrepresentation. Indeed, both systems go so far as to treat silence—the failure to disclose something that ought to be disclosed—as sufficient for liability.[49] French law, in contrast, insists that the offender's fraud be manifested in the use of a false name, the allegation of a false property, or a fraudulent maneuver.[50] Of course, in all of these systems for defining the crime of fraud, there must be a causal nexus between the actor's fraud and the voluntary participation by the victim in surrendering his property interest.

§1.2. *Points of Stress in the Topology of Theft.*

The preceding outline of theft offenses suggests that larceny, embezzlement and fraud have the same contours in all the major Western legal systems. This mapping from Anglo-American law onto Continental legal systems is roughly accurate, but the fringes of each offense reveal problematic cases that are resolved differently under the four legal systems that concern us. The divergence among Western legal systems is best appreciated by considering four points of stress in the topology of theft. The following four cases of dishonest acquisition have taxed the ingenuity of courts and scholars across the Western world:

I. The suspect *D* hires a horse from *X* with the intent to steal it and later does appropriate the horse to his own use. The same type of case is raised by anyone who, with a fraudulent purpose, receives the chattel from a prior possessor.

II. The suspect *D* finds a ring on the street that is apparently

[49] Schönke-Schröder-Cramer §263, note 21, at 1520; Kurs (SP 1973) at 804; Nikiforov, *supra* note 48, at 126-27. *But cf.* W. Nauke, Zur Lehre vom strafbaren Betrug 106-10 (1964).

[50] Code Pénal §405; F. Goyet, Droit Pénal Spécial 667 (8th ed. by Rousselet et al. 1972) ("the fraudulent maneuver must consist in a manifest act *(acte apparent)* . . . that renders the fraud tangible and . . . concrete").

lost. He picks it up and keeps it without reporting the finding to the police or taking other measures to locate the owner.

III. The suspect *D* requests the withdrawal of funds from his account; *X*, a bank teller, mistakenly delivers excess funds to *D*, who knows of the mistake and leaves the bank with the intent to keep the money.

IV. A customer enters a bank, hands a note to the teller *D* with the intent of depositing it. *D* pockets the note without putting it in the customary cash drawer.

All four of these cases are instances of dishonest, immoral behavior and for that reason, there is considerable pressure in virtually every legal system to bring them within the ambit of one of the theft offenses. Yet because they all lie at the boundaries among the three offenses, each of the leading Western legal systems classifies these problems differently. And not all systems punish all four forms of dishonest acquisition. The remarkable feature of Anglo-American law is that the courts concluded that the first three of these problematic cases were to be resolved by distending the law of larceny.[1] The systematic preference for larceny in Anglo-American law was a driving force behind the reconceptualization of larceny in the late eighteenth and nineteenth centuries. A detailed study of the metamorphosis of larceny must await Chapter Two. This section provides a comparative background for that study by indicating the points of stress at which the common law of larceny diverged in its development from European conceptions of the crime. This comparative background is important in demonstrating that these problematic cases admitted of a variety of solutions. There was no logical necessity in Anglo-American law's choosing larceny as the solvent for absorbing the first three of these cases into the field of punishable behavior.

In comparing Anglo-American law with French, German and

§1.2. [1] See The King v. Pear, 168 Eng. Rep. 208 (1779) (case I); Regina v. Thurborn, 169 Eng. Rep. 293 (1848) (case II); The Queen v. Middleton, L.R. 2 Cr. Cas. Res. 38 (1873) (case III). The fourth case was resolved by developing the law of embezzlement. See §1.1, at note 2 *supra*.

Russian solutions to these cases, we have to keep in mind the three distinct stages of the common law's evolution:

stage I: common-law larceny as explicated by the leading commentators and cases, prior to the end of the eighteenth century.

stage II: common-law larceny as it developed primarily in the nineteenth century and as embodied in the English Larceny Act of 1916.

stage III: the movement, typified by the English Theft Act of 1968, to abolish the distinctions among the three types of theft offenses.

For the purposes of the present comparison, we shall take the law of stage II as our base point. This stage still predominates in the United States, even in states that have followed the recommendations of the Model Penal Code. With regard to contemporary French, German and Soviet law, we need not enter a similar qualification. Though these systems have evolved over time, there is no stage analogous to the English Theft Act of 1968. There is no comparable movement to abolish the distinctions among larceny, embezzlement and fraud. At the conclusion of this comparative study, we shall append a guide for systematically analyzing cases in the common law of stage II.

§1.2.1. Receiving the Chattel with a Fraudulent Purpose. Consider the problem raised by the first case. Someone acquires nominal possession with a fraudulent purpose and then decides to keep the acquired goods. The German courts would deal with this problem either as a case of embezzlement or of fraud, but not as a case of larceny. Embezzlement is appropriate, for the situation is one in which the suspect misappropriates goods entrusted to him.[2] The crime of fraud would also cover the case, for the defendant induces the transfer of possession with a fraudulent purpose, and under German law, the transfer of possession is sufficient to satisfy the required element of harm.[3] In the case of

[2] StGB §246.

[3] StGB §263; see Judgment of January 16, 1963, 18 BGHSt. 221 (defendant

horse stealing as it actually arose in the common law,[4] the defendant lied about his address as he negotiated hiring of the horse.[5] It is significant that under German law, this overt lie would not be necessary. His failure to disclose his fraudulent purpose would be sufficient.[6] German courts would not convict for larceny, for there was no taking of possession in the initial acquisition by delivery from the stablekeeper, and there was no taking of possession when the defendant appropriated the horse to his own use. At the later moment, according to German doctrine, he would already have possession and therefore would not be in a position to take from the possession of another.[7]

French courts would balk at treating this case either as larceny or as fraud. Larceny would be problematic for essentially the same reasons that would influence German courts. The voluntary delivery by the stablekeeper would transfer possession and preclude a finding of the required trespassory taking (*soustraction*).[8] Fraud would not come into play, for the French law of fraud (*escroquerie*) requires that the fraudulent intent be manifested in the use of a false name, the allegation of a false property, or the use of a fraudulent maneuver.[9] It is questionable whether the use of a false address

---

acquired the use of another's car from a garage attendant on the implicit misrepresentation that he was authorized to use the car. *Id.* at 222. The German Supreme Court reversed the larceny conviction, holding that the crime should have been classified as fraud).

[4] The King v. Pear, 168 Eng. Rep. 208 (1779).

[5] *Id.* at 209.

[6] See §1.1, note 49 *supra*.

[7] See Bittner, *Zur Abgrenzung von Trickdiebstahl, Betrug und Unterschlagung*, 1974 JS 156.

[8] Code Pénal §379; Larceny (*vol*) is committed by anyone who "*a soustrait une chose qui ne lui appartient pas*" [who has taken an object that does not belong to him]; on the requirement of *soustraction* and its functional equivalents, see Lambert 211–27; Berr, *Aspects actuels de la notion de la soustraction frauduleuse*, 1967 Revue science criminelle et de droit pénal comparé 49, 88 (noting that the concept of *soustraction* no longer is in the process of expansion). In cases of consumer installment sales, the French recognize an exception to the principle of transferring possession by voluntary delivery; in this limited context the seller retains possession and thus is protected by the law of larceny, *id.* at 63.

[9] Code Pénal §405; for a sampling of the extraordinary attention devoted to this point in French law, see Lambert 349–412.

would qualify under this standard.[10] The most likely classification under French law would be embezzlement; although the French provision on *abus de confiance* is limited to six specified relationships, it does encompass misappropriation by the lessee of a chattel.[11]

The same considerations that shape the French and German conceptions of larceny would presumably prevail in Soviet thinking.[12] Embezzlement poses a special problem in Soviet law, for in many Republics, including the RSFSR, the embezzlement of private property is not a crime.[13] The most likely category of liability under Soviet law is criminal fraud, for the statute explicitly proscribes the acquisition of possession by means of fraud.[14] The intention not to perform a contractual agreement is sufficient to constitute the required element of fraud.[15]

If this first problematic case were to come before the California courts today as a case of first impression, the judges would have no difficulty classifying it as a case of embezzlement.[16] Yet when a series of cases of this type came before the common-law judges in the late eighteenth century,[17] neither of these options was open to them. Embezzlement by lessees had not yet been penalized and indeed would not be covered by the expanding law until the mid-nineteenth century.[18] The crime of false pretenses

[10] *Ibid.*

[11] Code Pénal §408 (*à titre de louage*).

[12] See generally Kurs (SP 1973) 754–82.

[13] *Cf.* Ugol. kod. (Uzbekistan) §130 (punishing the embezzlement of private property). Embezzlement of Socialist property is punishable in the RSFSR as well as the other republics, Ugol. kod. (RSFSR) §92.

[14] Ugol. kod. (RSFSR) §147.

[15] See Kurs (SP 1973) at 809; in a dispute that reached the Supreme Court of the USSR, the defendant received money from customers as payment for garages that he promised to build. He drank away the money. On appeal from his conviction for fraud, the Supreme Court of the RSFSR reversed the conviction on the ground that the matter was merely a breach of contract. The Supreme Court of the USSR reinstated the conviction; the evidence supported a finding of a false promise. See 1955(3) Decisions of the Supreme Court of the USSR 24 [in Russian].

[16] Cal. Penal Code §484.

[17] In addition to The King v. Pear, 168 Eng. Rep. 208 (1779), see The King v. Semple, 168 Eng. Rep. 312 (1785); The King v. Charlewood, 168 Eng. Rep. 306 (1786).

[18] 20 & 21 Vict. c. 54, §4 (1857).

appeared to be precluded because—for reasons not entirely clear—the judges insisted that the crime applied only if the victim were induced to part with title to his goods.[19] Thus the choice was between denying liability and extending the contours of larceny. The judges chose the latter[20] and thus began a process of distending larceny beyond the scope the analogous crime enjoys in French, German and Soviet law.

§1.2.2. **The Problem of Finders.** The problem of finders' keeping their unexpected windfall raises a set of different issues. The problem is circumscribed because there is no element of fraud that induces the loser to part with his legal interest and therefore the only prospects for penalization are larceny and embezzlement. Some states have passed special statutes to penalize finders who do not take reasonable steps to locate the owner of lost property.[21] Yet the more typical experience of legal systems is to attempt to squeeze the case of finders within the scope of either larceny or embezzlement.

Serious problems attend the classification of dishonest and irresponsible finders as embezzlers. First, there is no act of entrustment from the loser to the finder; even if there were, by fictitious extension of the concepts of bailment and delivery,[22] many embezzlement statutes would fail to apply for want of a statutorily prescribed relationship of trust. Even if these problems were surmounted, the notion of embezzlement would not readily extend to a case in which the finder had the intent to keep the object at the moment he picked it up; embezzlement typically requires that the actor form the intent to appropriate while he is in possession of the object.

Surmounting all these hurdles, German theorists have devel-

[19] Joseph Beale argued that the judges in *Pear* erred; they should have opted for the expansion of false pretenses rather than of larceny. Beale, *The Borderland of Larceny*, 6 Harv. L. Rev. 244 (1892).

[20] *Cf.* the failure to extend liability for larceny in case IV, *infra* at §1.2.4.

[21] See, e.g., Cal. Penal Code §485.

[22] *Cf.* Burns v. State, 145 Wis. 373, 128 N.W. 987 (1910) (*D* convicted of "larceny by a bailee"; the bailment was found in *D*'s taking possession of a money-roll from a third party, who picked it up after an allegedly insane suspect, fleeing from the police, threw it down).

oped the doctrine that a dishonest finder can be guilty of embezzlement. The argument is that embezzlement constitutes a general offense of appropriation;[23] larceny is a specific form of the offense applicable to cases in which the actor breaks possession in the act of taking. If there is no taking from the possession of another, there may nonetheless be an appropriation, and the residuary concept of embezzlement will cover the case. Picking up a lost object without taking reasonable measures to return it is an instance of appropriation without taking possession and therefore, according to German theory and practice, it may be treated as a case of embezzlement.[24] It is immaterial whether the actor forms the intent to appropriate while picking up the object or after he is already in possession. Soviet writers seem to follow this analysis and classify the case of finders as embezzlement.[25] In the RSFSR, this means that the conduct of irresponsible and dishonest finders of private property is exempt from punishment altogether.[26] The finding and nonreturn of Socialist property is subject to punishment as embezzlement.[27] In one type of case, Soviet writers appear to favor extending larceny to cover the finding and appropriation of private property. This is the situation, typified by passengers leaving a box or a trunk in a taxicab, in which the finder knows who the owner is and where to find him.[28]

French, English and American courts have never seriously entertained the option of punishing finders as embezzlers. These systems either lack a comprehensive notion of appropriation or, as is the case in English law, the notion was wanting in the critical stage of history when the courts moved to punish dishonest finders. The doctrinal move was to distend the notions of "trespass" and "taking" (*soustraction*) to cover cases of picking up and keeping a lost object. In the first set of cases that came to the courts,

[23] Schönke-Schröder-Eser §246, note 9, at 1434; Welzel 345 ("every appropriation in the absence of breaking possession is a case of embezzlement").

[24] *Ibid.*

[25] Kurs (SP 1973) at 758–59.

[26] See text at note 13 *supra*.

[27] Ugol. kod. (RSFSR) §92.

[28] Kurs (SP 1973) at 758.

the finder knew who the owner was and what means might be taken to return the mislaid or forgotten object. In 1786, the English courts extended liability to a case like the Soviet example of larceny by a finder: a passenger left a box in a taxicab, and the driver appropriated its contents.[29] In a leading French case, decided in 1817,[30] a domestic servant found a diamond ring in her mistress's home. In response to the latter's questions, the maid denied having seen it. The French court held that this complex of acts was sufficient for larceny. In a later case, in which the goods were found abandoned on the highway, the French court denied liability for larceny.[31] In the English courts, this form of finding, where the owner could not readily be located, did not come under the sanctions of the criminal law until late in the nineteenth century.[32]

§1.2.3. **The Problem of Mistaken Delivery.** The problem of mistaken delivery and receipt is the third of the points at which the common law felt pressure in the course of the nineteenth century. In the typical case, the suspect passively and quietly receives a mistaken remittance from a bank teller. Though he leaves the bank with a fraudulent intent to keep the funds transferred to him, he does nothing except take advantage of someone else's mistake.

Though nineteenth-century English and American courts extended the crime of larceny to cover this type of dishonest acquisition,[33] the French and German systems still balk at subjecting this conduct to any form of criminal liability.[34] French writers steadfastly maintain that the dishonest depositor who takes advantage of the teller's mistake is exempt from all criminal liability.[35]

[29] The King v. Wynne, 168 Eng. Rep. 308 (1786) (note that the case was not identified as one of imposing liability on a finder).

[30] Judgment of June 5, 1817; Recueil Sirey 1815-18.1.326 (*Cour de Cassation*).

[31] Judgment of September 2, 1830, Recueil Sirey 1828-30.1.582 (*Cour de Cassation*) (the court reasoned that the defendant's intention to keep the goods crystallized after he picked them up). Note that larceny committed on a public highway is an aggravated offense, Code Pénal §383.

[32] See §2.4.1 *infra*.

[33] The Queen v. Middleton, L.R. 2 Cr. Cas. Res. 38 (1873); Wolfstein v. People, 6 Hun 121 (N.Y. Super. Ct. 1875).

[34] See Lambert 213–14; Berr, *supra* note 8, at 84–85.

[35] See Berr, *supra* note 8, at 86 (arguing that civil remedies are sufficient to protect the public).

The crime of larceny does not apply because the voluntary delivery precludes the requisite taking (*soustraction*). Embezzlement is precluded, for it appears that the teller intended to part with title as well as possession of the excess funds. The crime of fraud would not apply, for there is no fraudulent maneuver.[36] The French stand on this case reflects a strong commitment to the literal and restrictive interpretation of criminal statutes.

Relying on the same reasoning, German judges would decline to punish the depositor's acquisition as either larceny or embezzlement. Fraud remains an option, for German law recognizes a broadly defined crime of fraud that covers implicit misrepresentations by conduct as well as explicitly fraudulent maneuvers.[37] The precise facts of this problematic case came before the German courts in 1968 and the trial court convicted the depositor of fraud. The appellate court reversed the judgment.[38] It is worth noting the reasons why.

The analysis of the depositor's interaction with the teller requires that one distinguish between two moments of time: (1) when the depositor puts the check on the counter, and (2) when the teller hands the mistaken amount to the depositor. If the depositor expects the mistake when he submits the check and then has the intent to deceive, there would be no problem in finding liability. The problem is that the teller's mistake is unexpected and it first comes to the attention of the suspect when the cash is delivered. The depositor may have a dishonest intent when he receives the funds, but this intent obviously does not induce the teller's mistake. The German crime of fraud (like the common-law crime of obtaining property by false pretenses) presupposes that the fraudulent act induce a transfer of wealth to the suspect.[39] If both the fraudulent act and the transfer of wealth occur simultaneously, it is impossible to say that the former induces the latter.

The German appellate court concluded that the only path for

[36] See note 9 *supra*.

[37] See §1.1, at note 49 *supra*.

[38] Judgment of the High State Court (*Oberlandesgericht*) in Düsseldorf, August 23, 1968, 1969 NJW 623.

[39] See §1.3.4 *infra*.

imposing liability for fraud was to view the crime as fraud by omission—namely, the failure to advise the teller that he was transferring excess funds. As we shall see when we take up the general subject of commission by omission, there is no liability for failure to prevent a criminal harm unless the actor is duty-bound to prevent the harm.[40] If there was a duty in this case, it could have been the general commercial duty of good faith and fair-dealing (*Treu und Glauben*).[41] But the appellate court decided that imposing a duty of good faith, without the support of a criminal statute, would raise problems under the principle of *nulla poena sine lege*.[42] Good faith was too vague a standard for purposes of the criminal law.

Soviet writers concur that that mistake must induce the transfer and therefore the crime of fraud is inapplicable in the case of mistaken delivery.[43] But under specified conditions the Soviet version of embezzlement will apply. First, the property must be public or state property, and secondly, the recipient of the property must be a state official.[44] If the first condition is satisfied, but the recipient is either a private person or acting outside of his official capacity, the retention of the mistakenly delivered proceeds might be punishable under a special provision applicable to the appropriation of "lost or accidentally received property known to belong to state or public organization."[45]

§1.2.4. The Problem of Delivery from a Third Party. The one case of the four in which the common-law courts balked at expanding the crime of larceny is the last situation in which the de-

[40] See §8.3 *infra*.

[41] *Cf.* BGB §242.

[42] See Deubner, *Anmerkung zur OLG Düsseldorf*, 1969 NJW 623.

[43] See G. Kriger, Classifying the Misappropriation of Socialist Property 163 (1971) [in Russian].

[44] Ugol. kod. (RSFSR) §92(1). *Cf.* Kriger, *supra* note 43, at 164.

[45] Ugol. kod. (RSFSR) §97. This is no comparable provision concerning the appropriation of lost private property. For an example of the difficulties of classification under Soviet law, see the case of "G.," an official who received and pocketed an overpayment of 2,000 rubles. He was initially convicted of embezzlement under §92(1); the crime was reclassified as fraud under §93(1); and appeal was brought on the ground that §97 (misappropriating accidentally acquired goods) was the appropriate classification. The Supreme Court agreed with the trial court that §92(1) (embezzlement) was the correct classification. See Kriger, *supra* note 43, at 164.

positor hands a note to the suspect for the purpose of deposit. The situation arises if a customer in a store pays for a purchase by handing money to the employee. The teller or employee appropriates the note. In this type of case, the German courts have no particular difficulty punishing for larceny.[46] The actor takes from the possession of his employer by appropriating the note.

The English courts in the eighteenth century refused to accept this simple expansion of the crime of larceny. The argument was that if given the note by a third party, the teller received possession and therefore could not be guilty of larceny by subsequently appropriating it. A charge of larceny would lie only if the teller transferred possession to the employer's domain (a safe or cash box) before he appropriated the money.[47] A famous acquittal of a teller named Bazeley[48] led to parliamentary intervention and the Statute of 39 George III, which a decade later came to be thought of as the first general embezzlement statute.[49]

The introduction of embezzlement as a crime carried forward the complexities of discerning when the employee had possession and when he transferred it to his employer. If the employee takes the note, puts it in the safe and later takes it out with the intent to steal, is he guilty of larceny or embezzlement? It all depends on whether his putting the note in the safe transfers possession to the owner. If it does, then the subsequent taking is a trespassory deprivation of possession; if not, the taking is an appropriation while in possession. Of course there is no sure method of determining whether the act of putting the note in the safe does or does not transfer possession.[50] As a result, Justice Holmes sug-

[46] Judgment of May 3, 1897, 30 RGSt. 88.

[47] Determining when this transfer occurred raised some subtle problems. *Compare* The King v. Spears, 168 Eng. Rep. 512 (1798) (possession transferred to employer), *with* The King v. Waite, 168 Eng. Rep. 117 (1743) (possession not transferred).

[48] The King v. Bazeley, 168 Eng. Rep. 517 (1799).

[49] See §1.1, note 3 *supra*.

[50] See, e.g., Morgan v. Commonwealth, 242 Ky. 713, 47 S.W.2d 543 (1932) (embezzlement because no transfer had occurred); Commonwealth v. Ryan, 155 Mass. 523, 30 N.E. 364 (1892) (possession not transferred); Rex v. Sullens, 168 Eng. Rep. 1212 (1826) (possession not transferred).

gested toward the end of the nineteenth century that the matter should turn on the employee's intent at the time that he deposited the note.[51] The entire inquiry became so formalistic that thoughtful observers began to doubt the rationality of the applicable distinctions.[52]

The course of legal history would have been different if the eighteenth-century courts had expanded the crime of larceny to cover the case of appropriations by employees who receive objects from third parties. The courts could have minimized the metaphysics of transferring possession by holding that the employer always receives possession of goods transferred to the company, with the consequence that a subsequent taking would be larceny. The courts could have held, for example, that a bank teller acts as a conduit through which possession passes from the depositor to the bank. This notion does not seem far-fetched, yet the eighteenth-century courts presumably would have balked at disengaging the transfer of possession from the physical transfer of the object. Possession might not always run with the chattel,[53] but it is another matter to treat possession-in-law as a disembodied spirit that springs from one person to another without a physical nexus. Of course, one might also buttress this reluctance with a humanistic theory of the employee's personality; to treat him as a mere conduit would be to deny his individual personality and treat him as one pipe in the corporate plumbing. Yet it is doubtful that this concern for the integrity of the working man influenced the courts as much as their inability to conceive of possession springing about as though it were a disembodied spirit. Nonetheless, there is something unsatisfactory about arguing that the courts resisted this innovation simply because they lacked imagination.

Another solution would have been to hold that the employer

[51] Commonwealth v. Ryan, 155 Mass. 523, 30 N.E. 364 (1892).

[52] See the comments by Justice Cardozo in Van Vechten v. American Eagle Fire Ins. Co., 239 N.Y. 303, 306; 146 N.E. 432, 433 (1925) (no "essential difference" between larceny and embezzlement) and Justice Holmes in Commonwealth v. Ryan, 155 Mass. 523, 527, 30 N.E. 364, 364–65 (1892) (technical rules derived from "historical accidents").

[53] See §2.1.1 *infra*.

and employee received joint possession over objects received in the hands of the latter. This suggestion requires that we clarify the "taking" required for the commission of larceny. In the course of a trespassory taking, need the actor acquire possession and simultaneously deprive the victim of the same interest? Or is it sufficient merely to deprive the victim of possession? If the former is true, then someone in joint possession could not commit larceny by taking the object from his joint possessor. On the other hand, if the deprivation of possession is sufficient, then a joint possessor is subject to the law of larceny. Though the matter has not been discussed often, the common law seems to have accepted the view that joint possessors are not liable for stealing from each other.[54] German law, in contrast, recognizes liability for larceny if one joint possessor takes from another.[55] This doctrinal position of German law facilitates the extension of larceny to cases of employees who appropriate goods received from third parties. They are guilty of larceny whether they receive mere custody or joint possession over the goods.

It is not entirely clear why this possibility for extending the scope of larceny never appealed to the same judges who readily inflated the crime of larceny to cover the other three problematic cases. The reason for this judicial restraint might have been that the courts conceived of possession as the interest protected by the crime; accordingly, the crime was committed only by deprivation and acquisition of the protected interest. As we shall see when we turn to this theme below,[56] German jurisprudence has had different reasons for cultivating the requirement of taking from possession.

This survey of four points of stress in the topology of theft has sought to underscore the fluidity of legal analysis at the fringes of the three offenses: larceny, embezzlement and fraud. Different solutions are possible; the logic of the law compels none of them. To see the variety of possibilities, let us review our discussion in the

[54] 2 East 558.
[55] Schönke-Schröder-Eser §242, notes 24–25, at 1403; Maurach SP at 203–04.
[56] See §1.3.2 *infra*.

following graph. Let *L* represent larceny; *E*, embezzlement; *F*, fraud; and *O*, the principled rejection of liability under all three headings. The chart is left blank in those places where the solution in the respective system is unclear.

The Problem	Solutions			
	French	*German*	*Soviet*	*Anglo-American*
I. fraudulent acquisition and subsequent conversion	*E*	*E,F*	*F*	*L*
II. finders	*L*	*E*	*E,L*	*L*
III. mistaken delivery	*O*	*O*	*E*	*L*
IV. appropriation by employee after receipt from a third party		*L*		*E*

The unanswered question is why the common-law systematically preferred larceny where Continental systems opted for alternative crimes or chose to leave the conduct unpunished. This is the deeper problem raised by our study of the metamorphosis of larceny in Chapter Two.

§1.2.5. **A Guide to Analyzing Theft Offenses.** The expansion of common-law larceny in the nineteenth century plagued the courts with serious problems of distinguishing larceny from embezzlement and obtaining property by false pretenses. In this section, I shall propose a roadmap for winding one's way through a set of facts and determining the appropriate classification. The common-law courts complicated the process of classification by assuming that each set of facts is subject to prosecution under one and only one offense.[57] The quest for the right classification often generated appellate reversals in cases where it was clear that the defendant was guilty of one of the three offenses.[58]

[57] This assumption is not shared by German law. For a recent discussion of close cases that recognizes the possibility of multiple classification, see Bittner, *supra* note 7.

[58] A good example is People v. Nichols, 17 N.Y. 114 (1858). Defendant was initially charged with larceny and acquitted. He was then charged and convicted of

The distinction that runs through common-law theft offenses is between two-party and three-party cases. As we noted in the last section, the three-party case, in which an employee receives goods from a third party and appropriates them to the detriment of his employer, sits astride the distinction between embezzlement and larceny. The proper classification depends on whether the employee transfers possession to the employer before he takes the goods. That issue, as we noted, does not lend itself to ready determination.

The two-party cases, in which the suspect receives the goods directly from the owner, raise all three possibilities of classification. Depending on the facts, a dishonest recipient of the goods might be guilty of larceny, embezzlement or false pretenses. The difficult cases of this variety are those beset by two possible moments of criminal conduct. Consider the first three hypothetical cases that guided our discussion in the preceding section. Each of them reveals two moments of possible criminality: T_1 and T_2. The following chart traces the structural similarity of the three cases:

	T_1	T_2
I.	receiving and mounting the horse	appropriating it, possibly by selling it
II.	picking up the ring	failing to take measures to return it
III.	receiving funds from the teller	failing to return the excess

The common element in T_1 is the receipt of the chattel; in T_2, a subsequent act of dishonesty. The basic rule for analyzing theft offenses is that there must be a union of the required act and intent at either T_1 or T_2.[59] If, for example, the act at T_1 constituted a tak-

embezzlement; on appeal, defendant argued that the proper charge was larceny after all, and not embezzlement. Yet jeopardy had presumably attached on the charge of larceny. The doctrinal issue was the scope of the "breaking bulk" exception to possessorial immunity. See §2.1.2 *infra*.

[59] The required union of act and intent in theft offenses provided one stimulus for the maxim *actus non facit reum, nisi mens sit rea*. 3 Coke 107.

ing from possession, there could be no crime of larceny unless the actor also had the requisite intent at T_1. It does not do for the act to occur at one moment and the intent to crystallize at another.

The way to analyze these and similar cases is first to determine the legal interest the recipient acquires at T_1. That interest might be either custody, possession or title to the goods. The determination of that threshold question shapes all subsequent legal implications. As to all three cases, let us consider what follows from assuming that the transaction at T_1 vests the suspect with custody, possession, or title.

A. Custody Acquired at T_1. The implication of this assumption is that no crime is committed at T_1. The mere receipt of custody is insufficient to constitute the act required for any of the three offenses. Thus attention shifts to T_2 as the possible moment of criminality. If we assume that the lessee of the horse in the first case merely acquired custody at T_1, liability turns on the interest acquired in appropriating the horse at T_2. In analyzing the events at T_2, the preliminary question again is whether the actor retains custody, acquires possession, or acquires title. There is a criminal offense only if he acquires possession or title. The latter is implausible, but he might acquire possession in appropriating the horse; and if so, the act at T_2 would satisfy the requirement of a "taking from possession." The actor would be guilty of larceny at T_2 if at that moment he also had the intent permanently to deprive the owner of his property.[60]

B. Possession Acquired at T_1. The owner might part with possession either voluntarily or involuntarily. This distinction is usually expressed by calling the former a "delivery" of the chattel. Thus there are two lines of analysis:

1. *No delivery.* This is the typical case of forcible taking. The taking is larceny if coupled with the requisite intent.

2. *Delivery.* If the owner voluntarily parts with the goods, there are two possible lines of conviction. The resolution of case

[60] This was the original understanding of the reasoning in *Pear's Case*, 168 Eng. Rep. 208 (1779). See §2.3.2 *infra*.

III, where the delivery is prompted by a mistake, is that the recipient commits larceny at T_1.[61] Apart from this case, the delivery effects a transfer of possession, which means that the actor can be guilty of embezzlement at T_2. This is an alternative analysis of case I.

C. *Title Acquired at T_1*. This classification precludes conviction for larceny and embezzlement; the only possible charge is obtaining property by false pretenses.

These optional lines of analysis reveal the structure of common-law theft offenses in the nineteenth and twentieth centuries. The following diagram summarizes the lines of analysis.

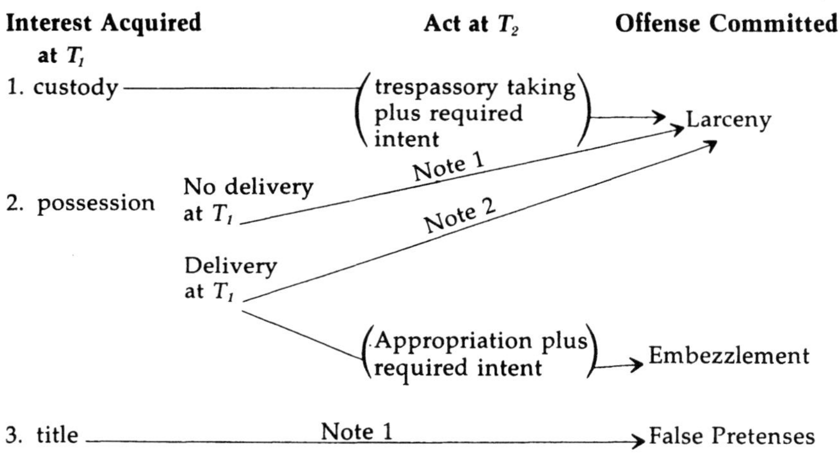

Note 1: it is assumed that the required intent is present at T_1
Note 2: this is the special case of mistaken delivery, coupled with the required intent at T_1.

This summary reveals the extent to which the entire structure of theft offenses turns on the nature of the interest acquired at T_1. Determining this issue is, of course, the most difficult step in the entire analysis. Whether the use of an object represents acquisition of custody, possession or title raises subtle legal problems. The weakness of the system may well be that controversy about what happens at T_1 infects all further efforts to classify the case.

[61] The Queen v. Middleton, L.R. 2 Cr. Cas. Res. 38 (1873). See §2.4.2 *infra*.

§1.3. *The Interests Protected by Theft Offenses.*

Given the backdrop of penal legislation in the last century, we are accustomed to thinking about particular offenses as governmental efforts to protect identifiable interests. Homicide is punished in order to protect life; rape, in order to protect sexual integrity; treason, in order to protect the government. In this frame of reference, it is plausible to think of larceny, embezzlement, and false pretenses as crimes designed to protect private interests in property. Yet this way of thinking about theft offenses is a relatively modern manner of classification. It is not to be found in the classic common-law texts of Coke and Hale. It comes to life in the eighteenth century, particularly in the work of Blackstone, and reflects efforts in the Enlightenment to find reason in the structure of the common law. In Germany, too, the conceptualization of larceny as a crime against property arrives late on the scene. The great German criminalist, Anselm von Feuerbach, writing in 1801,[1] is credited as the first German scholar to identify larceny as a crime against the single interest of property.[2]

The curious aspect of this reduction of all theft offenses to assaults upon the single interest of property is that it equates all three offenses in their gravity. Yet we have reason to believe that the offenses should be differentiated in their seriousness. How else can we explain why larceny dates back to the beginning of recorded legal history, while embezzlement is born of legislative command in the late eighteenth century? How else can we explain the tendency at various stages of history to regard one of the offenses as worthy of greater condemnation? Larceny was a capital offense in the eighteenth century—at least when the value of objects stolen was greater than twelve pence.[3] According to the Stat-

§1.3. [1] A. Feuerbach, Lehrbuch des gemeinen in Deutschland geltenden peinlichen Rechts §§312, 315 (1801).

[2] See H. Mayer, Die Untreue 25–32 (1926). My thinking about theft offenses generally is heavily indebted to the work of Hellmuth Mayer.

[3] 3 Coke 108–09. The penalty for petit larceny, or larceny of goods worth less than twelve pence, was whipping. *Ibid.*

ute of 39 George III, embezzlement was punished by 14 years' transportation to the colonies. By the Statute of 1757, a finding of false pretenses was also punished by transportation.[4] Yet in the course of the eighteenth century, death sentences for larceny were often commuted to a sentence of transportation[5] and therefore it might be misleading to rely on statutory language.

Contrary to the practices of the common law, Dante reasoned in his master work that fraud and embezzlement were the more heinous offenses. The embezzler not only takes the goods, but by betraying trust "snaps the ties of close regard."[6] These comments should give us pause in assuming that the relative gravity of theft offenses can be resolved simply by noting that all acts of larceny, embezzlement and fraud endanger property interests. Something seems to have been lost in the modern reduction of theft offenses to parallel attacks on a single interest, and therefore it would be worth our while to try to understand how lawyers and others thought about larceny prior to the emergence of the modern manner of classification.

§1.3.1. **An Earlier Understanding.** In the early stages of history there were no clearly marked boundaries among burglary, larceny, and robbery. All were collapsed in the single image of the thief coming at night, breaking the close and endangering the security of the manor. It is obvious that there was no single interest jeopardized by this invasion, but rather a multitude of interests, including the security and well-being of the community.

According to both Roman[7] and Biblical law,[8] the manifest thief, the *fur manifestus*, particularly the thief caught at night, was subject to execution on the spot. If a thief was caught with the goods in his possession, he was subject at most to the payment of multiple damages.[9] In Roman and Biblical law, these multiple

[4] 30 Geo. II, c. 24 (1757).

[5] 1 Stephen 471. *Cf.* note by J. Coleridge in 4 Blackstone, Commentaries on the Laws of England 229 (16th ed. 1825).

[6] Dante, The Divine Comedy, Canto 11, lines 50–60 (R. Bottrall trans. 1966).

[7] 3 Gaius, Institutes ¶189, in 1 F. de Zulueta, The Institutes of Gaius 215–17 (1946).

[8] Exodus 22:1 (*ganav bamachteret*).

[9] According to The Twelve Tables, all cases of "theft . . . [where] the thief is

damages varied from double to five-fold the value of the object allegedly stolen.[10] Thus the crime of larceny consisted of two wholly independent branches. A thief caught in the act was killed without trial; a thief caught with the goods was subject to a trial and at most to the payment of monetary damages. What is now prosecuted as crime was treated as an occasion for self-help or as a basis for recovering in a private law suit.

It is commonly held that the distinction between crime and tort did not exist in the early stages of legal history, and therefore it might not be fruitful to ask whether larceny was conceived of as a crime in Roman and Biblical law. Yet the question is of some importance in attempting to establish whether the killing of manifest thieves was taken to be an act of private justice or an act of self-defense. An act of private justice would presuppose that the thief deserved execution as a criminal; the theory of self-defense, in contrast, would stress the execution as a response to the danger manifested to the owner and his family. The consensus seems to be that the execution of the manifest thief began in Roman law as an act of private justice.[11] The Twelve Tables specify that the killing of the thief was "lawful."[12] Similarly, the structure of the Book of Exodus indicates that the killing of the thief "digging under" should be seen as a penal response to larceny rather than as an exception to liability for homicide.[13] In the course of legal history,

---

[not] caught in the act . . ." were subject to a penalty of double damages. Table VIII, §16, in 2 Ancient Roman Statutes 11 (A. Johnson, et al. ed. 1961). If it was a case of "detected" theft, the judgment was for triple damages; apparently, this form of liability presupposed finding the goods on the accused's premises after a search with witnesses. See H. Jolowicz & B. Nicholas, Historical Introduction to the Study of Roman Law 167 (1972). Gaius notes that at a later stage the penalty for *furtum manifestum* became fourfold damages in cases of *rapina* (robbery). See 3 Gaius, *supra* note 7, at ¶209. *Cf.* Exodus 21:37 (fivefold for stealing and then killing or selling an ox; fourfold for doing the same to a sheep); *id.* 22:3 (double damages if the stolen animal is found alive in the defendant's possession).

[10] See note 9 *supra*.

[11] See Watkins, *Studies in Indo-European Legal Language, Institutions, and Mythology*, in Indo-European and Indo-Europeans 338 (G. Cardono et al. ed. 1970); T. Mommsen, Römisches Strafrecht 751 (1899).

[12] Table VIII, §12, in 2 Ancient Roman Statutes 11 (A. Johnson et al. ed. 1961).

[13] That Exodus 22:1 should be seen as providing a penalty for theft rather than a rule of self-defense is suggested by its being located among rules pertaining to

however, this act of private justice came to be seen as a claim of self-defense. This was the progression both in Roman[14] and post-Biblical Jewish law.[15]

In the early English common law, we begin to find a divergence of the concept of manifest thievery from the criteria for the lawful killing of thieves. Bracton extends the Roman concept of the *fur manifestus* to include all persons "apprehended, seized of the stolen property, that is, *hondhabbende et bacberende.*"[16] Thus Bracton's manifest thief is not exactly one caught in the act, but rather a person apprehended with highly incriminating evidence on his person. On the other hand, manifest thieves were not subject to immediate execution as they were under Roman and Biblical law.[17] In a distinct passage on the wrongfulness of homicide, Bracton indicates that the slaying of thieves was no longer to be treated as a form of private execution. He refers to the received understanding that "he who kills a thief, either a day thief or a night thief, is not liable."[18] but adds the qualification that the slayer is exempt only "if he could not otherwise escape danger."[19] Stressing the element of danger to the slayer made it clear that killing the thief was an act of defense, rather than punishment of the thief. It had to be justified by appealing to the needs of the slayer rather than the desert of the thief.

The slaying of thieves lies at the core of modern notions of justified rather than excused killing.[20] This is true partly because

---

theft and punishment by multiple damages. There is some dispute whether this provision is an interpolation in the text. *Compare* A. Phillips, Ancient Israel's Criminal Law 92 (1970) (arguing that provision belongs with early rules pertaining to homicide), *with* B. Jackson, Theft in Early Jewish Law 206 (1972) (arguing against interpolation and in favor of the provision's being seen as punishment for theft).

[14] See H. Jolowicz & B. Nicholas, *supra* note 9, at 169 n.9.

[15] See B. Jackson, *supra* note 13, at 155; D. Daube, Studies in Biblical Law 242 (1947).

[16] Bracton 150c (the Old English phrase is translated "hand-having and back-bearing").

[17] The procedures for prosecuting the manifest thief are discussed in Bracton 150d, e. *Cf.* 1 Britton, On the Laws of England 56 (F. Nicholas trans. 1865 ed.).

[18] Bracton 155a.

[19] *Ibid.*

[20] If a killing was merely excused, the slayer suffered a forfeiture of goods; if justified, he was acquitted outright. See §§5.1.1 and 5.1.3 *infra*. The general theory

there is an historic progression from the notion of private justice in Rome and the Ancient Middle East to the concept of justified killing in modern legal systems.[21] There seems also to be something fundamental in the danger posed by thieves to the social order. When seventeenth-century writers sought to defend the notion of killing as a matter of right, their examples tended to gravitate to the killing of thieves rather than rapists or even murderers. Coke insisted that no "man shall [ever] give way to a thief, etc., neither shall he forfeit anything."[22] The Statute of 1532 recognized that homicide was justifiable when committed in defense against murderous assaults as well as against robbers and burglars.[23] Yet in the history of killing as a matter of right, the thief, particularly the nocturnal burglar, stands out as the paradigmatic threat, as the wrongdoer who should be killed on the spot.[24]

If larceny in earlier stages of development could not be seen simply as an attack on property, nor could the moral and legal offense of embezzlement be so considered. Of course, in the period that we are considering, embezzlement was recognized as an offense neither in England nor in France.[25] When the common-law courts explain why it is not an offense, they describe the act of embezzlement as a "mere breach of trust."[26] The evil perceived was primarily in the betrayal of the master's trust rather than in the acquisition of the chattel. And that harm, like breach of con-

---

of justification and excuse recurs throughout the book. See §10.1 *infra* for clarification of the distinction.

[21] For another example of domesticating private punishment, *compare* Deuteronomy 22:22 (If a man be found lying with a woman married to a husband, then they shall both of them die . . .) *with* encountering adultery as a basis for provocation and mitigation. See §4.2.1 *infra.*

[22] 3 Coke 55. *Cf.* J. Locke, Treatise of Civil Government 14 (Sherman ed. 1937).

[23] 24 Hen. VIII, c. 5 (1532). *Quaere.* Is it significant that the statute refers only to robbers and burglars and not thieves? It should be noted that the concept of the burglar is closer to the *fur manifestus* and the *ganav bamachteret* subject to execution under Roman and Biblical law. See notes 7 and 8 *supra.*

[24] One historical study appears to be very puzzled by the centrality of robbers and burglars in the evolving law of justifiable homicide. Green, *The Jury and the English Law of Homicide, 1200–1600,* 74 Mich. L. Rev. 414, 452–53 (1976).

[25] See §1.1 notes 2–4 *supra.*

[26] The King v. Pear, 168 Eng. Rep. 208, 209 (1779); The King v. Bazeley, 168 Eng. Rep. 517, 521–22 (1799) (argument by counsel).

tract, was thought to be a private complaint remediable under the common-law writs, rather than a public wrong to be corrected by official punishment. The law's focus on breach of trust is captured in the French term *abus de confiance* used to identify embezzlement as a crime in the Code of 1810.[27] The German tradition is illuminating on this point, for it subjected embezzlement to criminal punishment as of the sixteenth century and treated it as an offshoot of the ancient crime of *Untreue* (disloyalty).[28] Thus in all of these Western legal systems, embezzlement has its roots in a breach of faith rather than in the harm of impermissibly acquiring property.

If larceny had retained its status as a crime disturbing to the entire community, and embezzlement, its status as a penalized breach of trust, it would be hard to imagine the contemporary movement to unify the two offenses under one heading of "dishonest appropriation."[29] It is obvious that some transformation has occurred in the way lawyers, particularly in Anglo-American jurisdictions, think about the two offenses. The crimes have been brought into line as parallel thrusts at a common value. The critical aspect of this transformation was the reconceptualization of both crimes as assaults upon the single personal interest in holding private property.[30] The dishonest displacement of property from one person to another has come to be thought of as the concern of all and therefore a proper subject of criminal punishment. In the course of modern history, larceny and embezzlement have become variations on a common theme, and it eventually became difficult for judges[31] to understand why a distinction was ever recognized between them.

§1.3.2. Larceny as a Crime Against Possession. If the contemporary view is that theft offenses are assaults upon private property, the matter remains subject to subtle controversy. With

[27] Code Pénal §408.
[28] Constitutio Criminalis Carolina §170 (1532).
[29] Theft Act 1968, c. 60, §1.
[30] This argument is developed brilliantly in H. Mayer, *supra* note 2, at 20–22.
[31] See the comment by Justice Cardozo in Van Vechten v. American Eagle Fire Ins. Co., 239 N.Y. 303, 306, 146 N.E. 432, 433 (1925).

respect to larceny, the major problem is how the requirement of a taking from possession is to be reconciled with the view that the crime is one against property. Is the victim the one who has been deprived of possession? Or is it the owner who suffers the loss even though the object was taken from the possession of another? There are several points of doctrine that make it plausible to hold, as does Perkins,[32] that larceny is an "offense against possession."[33] First, larceny builds on the concepts implicit in the writ of trespass, which lay on behalf of everyone who was deprived of possession, either of land or of chattels.[34] At the earlier stages of history, the concept of possession was not so clearly distinguished from ownership, and therefore it is sensible to think of trespass as a writ lying to protect the interest in peaceable possession.[35] Secondly, the classic common-law writers held that an owner can commit larceny against someone to whom he has transferred legal possession.[36] Though there might be many accounts of this rule, one explanation is that the interest protected by the offense is peaceable possession and that the owner must respect this state of affairs as much as would anyone else. Thirdly, and most significantly, there is the hard fact that the crime is committed only by acquiring possession in the act of taking.[37] It seems implicit in this requirement that the interest protected by the offense is possession itself.

Against these three points there are equally powerful considerations suggesting that if there is a single interest protected by the crime of larceny, it is property rather than possession. First, when the intent requirement for larceny finally received clarification toward the end of the nineteenth century, the required intent was often stated as the "intent permanently to deprive the

[32] Perkins 238.

[33] This expression is obviously a shorthand expression for the human interest in maintaining possession over objects already in one's possession.

[34] 2 F. Pollock and F. Maitland, History of English Law 510–41 (1911).

[35] See Prosser 68, 78.

[36] 3 Coke 110; 1 Hale 513; 2 East 654.

[37] This rule is expressed in the exemption of joint possessors from liability. See §1.2.4, at note 54 *supra*.

owner of his property."[38] If the interest protected was indeed possession, it would have been more appropriate to hold that the intent required was merely to deprive the possessor of his possession. Suppose that a hypothetical actor, *A* finds a mislaid ring and picks it up with the intent to keep it. *B* regards *A*'s failure to advertise the finding as immoral and illegal and therefore forcibly takes the ring from *A* in the hope of finding the true owner and returning the ring. *A* is in possession at the time of the taking and therefore *B*'s taking would be larcenous if the required intent were merely to deprive the possessor of his possession. Yet the consensus today is that larceny is not committed unless the taker intends permanently to deprive the owner of his property—an intent which *B* surely did not have. In view of this type of case in which the intentional deprivation of possession is not punishable as larceny, it is difficult to maintain that the offense is designed to protect possession.

With regard to the liability of owners for taking from the possession of others, there are other, more satisfactory explanations of this policy of the common law. The theory developed by Coke and East was that bailees and others holding by license of the owner had a "special property" in the chattel.[39] The deprivation of this "special property" satisfied the requirement that there be an intent to deprive the owner (of the "special property") permanently of his special interest. An alternative theory, advanced by Hale, was that the owner was liable only if his intent was to hold the bailee liable in detinue for the loss of the chattel.[40] Under neither of these theories would the owner be liable if he took from a mere possessor—say, a finder—who had no license from the owner to maintain possession. Yet if the claim were that the deprivation of possession was sufficient, the owner would also be liable for taking forcibly from the finder. It is extremely doubtful that the liability of owners at common law ever went beyond the cases of taking

[38] See §1.1 note 16 *supra*.
[39] 3 Coke 110; 2 East 654.
[40] 1 Hale 513; *cf*. 4 Blackstone 231.

from those who held under their license, and therefore this point of law does not adequately support the theory that the crime is one committed against possession.

Even if these points be persuasive, there remains the undisputed fact that the doctrine of the common law requires that larceny be committed by a taking from possession. How is that element to be explained without positing that the interest protected by the offense is possession itself? Common-law writers have never considered an alternative explanation, but a good account is to be found in the German literature. The definition of larceny under German law imposes the same requirement. The prevailing interpretation is that "breaking-possession" (*Gewahrsamsbruch*) is a required feature of the way the taking is accomplished rather than a reflection of the interest protected by the offense.[41] The "breaking-of-possession" is a way of taking from another—a forcible or stealthful taking, rather than merely a peaceable taking in the ordinary course of affairs. There is also considerable support for the view that prior to the mid-nineteenth century, the common law also insisted on a "breaking of possession" as a feature of larcenous takings. This insistence was captured in a rule that larceny was committed not merely by taking, but by a trespassory taking. That additional intangible element of "trespass" pointed to the same features of forcible or stealthful taking that are expressed in the German requirement of a "breaking of possession." As we shall see in Chapter Two, this implicit requirement of the common law accounts in part for many puzzling doctrinal features of larceny as it was defined in the eighteenth century.

What we have discovered is that the analysis of the interest protected by larceny conceals a contradiction. After Blackstone it became commonplace to think of larceny as an assault upon private property. At the same time, the rule requiring a "taking from possession" lent support to the view that the crime was designed to protect possession. This contradiction could be resolved if we interpret the required taking from possession as a quality or feature of the taking, as a way of acting, analogous to the German re-

[41] Schönke-Schröder-Eser §242, notes 28, 29, at 1404–05.

quirement of "breaking possession." So long as the crime required a trespassory taking, that interpretation of "taking from possession" was plausible. But the rule of trespassory taking came into eclipse in the nineteenth century. And thus we are left today with the alternative thesis that "taking from possession" serves to protect possession.

§1.3.3. Protecting Objects and Protecting Economic Interests. Theory has never been the strong point of the common law, and so we are beginning to discover in this discussion of the interests protected by punishing larceny. A good deal of judicial attention has always been devoted to distinguishing between chattels subject to the law of larceny and those things that, for various reasons, were exempt from the law's coverage. Some things were exempt because they were too closely associated with realty;[42] other things, because they were not quite chattels.[43] Animals not ordinarily eaten were exempt, as were dead bodies.[44] Filling in this array of loopholes has kept legislatures busy and accounts, in part, for the patchwork design of legislation on larceny.

Even given the breakthrough of the last hundred years, that all personal property of value should in principle be subject to the law of larceny, there is surprisingly little attention to the question whether it is the interest in holding the object or in the value of the object that we seek to secure by punishing thieves. The conflict between these two ways of interpreting the interest protected in larceny cases has generated considerable controversy in the German literature and in the courts. To begin our own theoretical inquiry, let us survey some of the problems that have proved troublesome in the German courts:

A. *D* steals a passbook that entitles the bearer to withdraw funds from an account; his intent at the time of taking is to with-

[42] Vegetation, crops and minerals could not be stolen directly. However, if they were severed first and allowed to come to rest, they could then be stolen. See *First Report* 22–23; Perkins 234–36.

[43] Intangible rights cannot be "stolen." People v. Ashworth, 220 App. Div. 498, 222 N.Y.S. 24 (1927) (conviction of conspiracy to steal use of plant machinery, reversed).

[44] *First Report* 12–14.

draw a small sum of money and then to return the passbook. Is *D* guilty of stealing the passbook?[45]

B. Waitresses in a beer hall use a system of chits to keep track of the number of drinks sold and their debt to the house. By taking more chits than she is entitled to, a waitress is able to misrepresent the number of beers she has sold and thus to keep payment for an excess number. Is she guilty of stealing the additional number of chits?[46]

C. At the completion of his tour of duty a soldier is required to turn in the equipment issued to him. Yet he cannot find his boots. For fear of being charged for the boots, the soldier takes his neighbor's boots and turns them in in place of his own. Is the soldier guilty of stealing the boots?[47]

D. *D* takes coke bottles from the back of a grocery store and takes them around to the front, where he collects a deposit of 10 cents apiece. Is *D* guilty of stealing the coke bottles?[48]

E. *D* takes a new book from a bookstore with the intent to read it and return it. Is he guilty of stealing the book?[49]

The traditional Anglo-American approach to these problems would probably be to deny liability in all variations of the problem. In all of them the defendant lacks the "intent permanently to deprive the owner of his property." One could argue that in the passbook case, the defendant has the intent to deprive the owner of his property in the funds withdrawn from the account. Yet the intent required in larceny is presumably the intent to deprive the owner of his property in the very item taken, not in some related asset such as the money in the account. A problem similar to cases

[45] This is the famous *Sparbuch-fall;* Judgment of the Supreme Court, May 1, 1884 10 RGSt. 369.

[46] This case came up twice. Judgment of the Supreme Court, February 23, 1893, 24 RGSt. 22 (no liability); Judgment of the Supreme Court, February 19, 1907, 40 RGSt. 10 (liability for larceny).

[47] Judgment of the High State Court (*Oberlandesgericht*) in Hamm, March 26, 1964, 1964 NJW 1427.

[48] Judgment of the High State Court (*Oberlandesgericht*) in Bavaria, August 5, 1960, 1960 Bay. OLGSt. 187.

[49] Judgment of the High State Court (*Oberlandesgericht*) in Celle, March 16, 1967, 1967 NJW 1921.

B and *C* arose in the English case, *Holloway*,[50] which proved to be an important precedent of the mid-nineteenth century. The defendant was paid according to the number of dressed skins submitted at the end of each shift. The defendant surreptitiously took some skins from his employer's stock and submitted them as his own work. All of the judges were opposed to his conviction for larceny. Baron Parke complained that the "books do not give a full definition of [larceny]."[51] Yet he managed to mount an argument against conviction on the ground that larceny requires that the defendant "take entire dominion over the object",[52] the requirement is expressed in the rule that the actor intend "to deprive the owner wholly of his property."[53] All Holloway intended was to hold the skins temporarily in order to receive wages he did not deserve; this, in the court's view, was not the same as "stealing" the skins.

It might be thought that so long as we stick to the firm definition of "an intent permanently to deprive the owner of his property," we should be able to stay free of conceptual snares and complex issues. Yet that may depend on our tolerance for inconsistency. Consider the fact that the defendant taking coke bottles need not intend to keep them himself. Suppose he took them to a store down the street and cashed them in there. If this were not larceny, it would be hard to imagine a case of stealing and selling that would be. Yet if he cashes them in at the same store from which he takes them, this is not larceny! In that case he would not then have the intent permanently to deprive the owner of his property. It seems flatly absurd to hinge liability on the store where the defendant intends to cash in the bottles. Yet if we do not do that, we should have to reverse the result in *Holloway*. If the defendant there took the skins with the intent to sell them to a competitor, he would unquestionably be guilty of larceny; it seems to follow that he should be guilty if he takes the skins with the intent to sell them to his own employer. If the particular store is not

[50] The Queen v. Holloway, 169 Eng. Rep. 285 (1848).
[51] *Id.* at 287.
[52] *Ibid.*
[53] *Ibid.*

relevant in the coke-bottle case, the identity of the intended purchaser should not matter in *Holloway*.[54]

This discussion brings into focus the two conflicting theories that have been worked out in the German literature. According to one theory, the point of the law of larceny is to protect the holding of the object, and in particular, to protect it against permanent deprivation.[55] According to this view, the impact of the deprivation of the holder's total wealth is not important. It should be larceny to take an object against the owner's will even though one leaves the fair market value in its place. But it should not be larceny to take an object temporarily, even if the temporary taking results in monetary injury to the owner. Accordingly, the actor's purpose of self-enrichment is irrelevant; what counts is whether there is an intent to deprive the owner of control over the particular object.[56] This theory dovetails well with the view that larceny is a crime essentially against possession.[57]

The difficulty with this theory is that it leads to the precious distinctions we noted in the discussions of *Holloway* and the coke-bottle case. The alternative to which one is led by the inadequacies of the first theory is that the law of larceny should protect owners from the economic loss that results from thievery.[58] It is not control over the thing that matters, but the economic loss that results from taking the thing. If we defined larceny as taking an object for the

[54] Later we propose a distinction between *Holloway* and the coke-bottle case, *infra* text at note 72.

[55] This is known as the *Substanztheorie*. See, e.g., Schönke-Schröder-Eser §242, notes 45–47, at 1408; Maurach SP at 209–10; Welzel 341, noting that it would be appropriate to call the theory the *Eigentumstheorie*, implying the law of larceny should be limited to those concrete things that can support a claim of ownership. A. Eser, Strafrecht IV, 39–41 (2d ed. 1976).

[56] The theory suggests an analogy with child abduction. The evil in larceny derives from the abduction of the object, regardless of the harm to the former possessor.

[57] *Cf.* the discussion *supra* §1.3.2.

[58] This is known as the *Sachwerttheorie*. It is designed to supplement rather than replace the *Substanztheorie*. See Schönke-Schröder-Eser, *supra* note 55. A. Eser, *supra* note 55, at 41–43. The theory is captured in the formula devised by Rheinhard Frank: the essence of appropriation is that "the object itself or the value embodied in it is incorporated into the actor's estate." See Eser, *id.* at 39.

purpose of gain or the purpose of inflicting an economic loss on another, we could easily support a conviction in the five cases above as well as in *Holloway*. Yet there are many who might regard this definition as far too comprehensive, and therefore seek to limit the "economic theory" to specified instances supplementing the primary theory that larceny protects the possessor against permanent loss of the object.[59]

The common law of larceny has enjoyed radical expansion in the last two centuries, as we shall see when we turn to a study of the metamorphosis of larceny. Yet *Holloway* typifies an aspect of larceny that has evidenced little movement. Even the expansive English Theft Act of 1968 appears to be committed to the principle of non-liability in *Holloway*.[60] We have to admit that there is so little discussion of the matter that one does not know what would happen if the issue were litigated as actively as it was in Germany in the early decades of this century. The theory that the law protects possession of the thing rather than economic interests leads to so many fragile distinctions that it is doubtful today that courts would remain committed to protecting possession rather than economic interests.[61]

German law starts from many of the same assumptions as the common law of larceny. There must be a taking from possession and there must be an intent to take permanently.[62] *Furtum usus*, or the temporary use of another's goods, falls outside the scope of lar-

[59] Maurach SP at 210-12; Welzel 341; A. Eser, *supra* note 55, at 41, note 20.

[60] J. Smith, The Law of Theft 20, 52 (2d ed. 1972).

[61] See United States v. Bottone, 365 F.2d 389 (2d Cir. 1966); the charge was receiving stolen goods, but the critical issue was whether taking documents describing trade secrets with the intent to make a xerox copy and then return the originals was larceny. Copying the documents with the intent to disseminate the copy obviously constituted an appropriation of their economic value. The court ruled that the taking was larcenous even though "the intangible information that was the purpose of the theft was transformed and embodied in a different document." *Id.* at 393. *Cf.* Nimmer, *National Security Secrets v. Free Speech: The Issues Left Undecided in the Ellsberg Case*, 26 Stan. L. Rev. 311, 316 (1974) (arguing that Ellsberg's taking, xeroxing and returning the Pentagon papers did not constitute larceny of the papers).

[62] See Judgment of January 26, 1968, 22 BGHSt. 45 (the distinction between larceny of a car and joyriding, StGB §248b, is that the former requires an intent permanently to deprive).

ceny, as it does in all of the legal systems under study.[63] Yet a distinguishing feature of German law makes it more receptive to expanding the law of larceny to include takings that entail an economic loss. The German Code of 1871 describes both larceny and embezzlement as crimes of "appropriation" (*Zueignung*). Some writers even identify embezzlement as the basic crime, with larceny singled out as a special form of the crime committed by taking the object and breaking possession.[64] Both larceny and embezzlement require the same intent, namely, the intent wrongfully to appropriate the goods. Focussing on the notion of "appropriation" rather than on "deprivation" of the object is the critical feature that renders the German law of larceny more receptive to the view that criminalization functions to protect economic interests as well as the maintenance of possession over specific objects. We shall pause to see why this is so; Anglo-American developments point to similar tendencies and therefore there is much to learn from the inner logic of German law.

In contrast to larceny, embezzlement cannot plausibly be defined solely as some act coupled with an intent to appropriate. The mere holding or exercising unlawful control over a chattel does not signal the formation of a prohibited intent. To insure that the crime not be defined solely by holding the object with an unmanifested intent to retain it, the emphasis in the definition of embezzlement—in all legal systems—is on the occurrence of some external result. This emphasis on an external result leads to the requirement that the chattel actually be appropriated, not merely that there be an unexecuted intent to appropriate. The requirement of actual appropriation could not mean permanent appropriation of the chattel, for waiting to see whether that would occur would be time-consuming, if nothing else. Therefore, embezzlement turns

[63] *Furtum usus* was actionable as a delict under Roman law. T. Mommsen, Römisches Strafrecht 735 nn.2, 3 (1899).

[64] Welzel 339. See §1.2.2 *infra*. This position seems to be based on a distortion of larceny. Welzel describes embezzlement as a parallel instance of "appropriation" (*Zueignung*). Yet larceny does not require an appropriation, but merely a taking with intent to appropriate. StGB §242. Embezzlement requires an actual appropriation. StGB §246.

on a notion of appropriation that, in the logic of the crime, must fall short of permanent deprivation. And yet not every interference with the owner's rights would seem to warrant criminal punishment. Thus the standard must lie some place between total deprivation at one extreme, and a contractual breach at the other.[65]

There appear to be two different ways of approaching the requisite harm in embezzlement cases. One is typified by the Model Penal Code; the other, by the English Theft Act of 1968, and both are found in German law. The Model Penal Code defines embezzlement (within its consolidated offense) as "exercis[ing] unlawful control over the movable property of another with the purpose to deprive him thereof."[66] At first blush this appears to be an adaptation of the standard for larceny to the field of embezzlement. Yet the notion of depriving property is recast in the Code to include any appropriation of "a major portion of [the object's] economic value."[67] This standard is unhappily vague, for it is not clear whether what is at stake is the resale value of the object or its economic significance in a particular transaction. The significance of this ambiguity will become clear when we seek to apply the standard to the five cases drawn from the German experience.

The English Theft Act of 1968 approaches the problem in a radically different manner. Instead of assaying economic harm, the Act focusses on the behavior of the appropriating party. The critical definition is that "any assumption of the rights of an owner" constitutes an appropriation.[68]

The premise of a consolidated theft offense is that so far as there is a conflict in the criteria of larceny and of embezzlement, one must prevail over the other. We have already shown that the permanent deprivation of the chattel cannot be adapted to the con-

[65] In the Anglo-American law, the notion of appropriation closely follows the concept of conversion in tort cases. LaFave & Scott 645; Nimmer, *supra* note 61, at 317–19. In tort, the concept of conversion requires a substantial or serious invasion of the owner's rights. One reason for this high threshold of liability was that the standard of damages was not actual harm but the full value of the chattel. See Prosser 80, 93.

[66] MPC §223.2(1).

[67] MPC §223.0(1).

[68] Theft Act 1968, c. 60, §3(1).

text of embezzlement. Thus the criteria of economic appropriation must prevail and generate the basis for a rationalized union of the two offenses.

Now we can see why German law permits a more flexible approach in the five cases mentioned above and why consolidation in Anglo-American law is likely to have the same effect. First, the harm required for embezzlement is defined in terms either of economic harm[69] or the assumption of the rights of an owner. Secondly, the intent to inflict this harm becomes the standard for committing larceny. Thus we have generated a more expansive view of larceny that would permit convictions in some, if not all, of the five problematic cases. Under the Model Penal Code, it seems fairly clear that the waitress' use of the chits or the soldier's turning in someone else's boots would constitute theft by "taking with a purpose to deprive."[70] The argument against this interpretation would be that the concept of deprivation (appropriation of a major portion of the economic value) is designed merely to cover cases where the taking and use of the object reduces its fair market value. If this view were controlling, it would be difficult to say that the intent required for larceny was present in "depriving" the beer hall of the chits or the fellow soldier of his boots.

The English consolidated theft offense raises a host of different problems. How do we go about deciding whether the defendant has "assumed the rights of an owner"? And in addition, how do we apply the requisite test of intent, namely, to "treat the things as his own to dispose of regardless of the other's rights"?[71] In the cases of *Holloway*, of the waitress and the chits, and of the

[69] There is a problem in the Model Penal Code that we are concededly gliding over. The standard of economic deprivation is introduced to define the purpose of "depriving" the owner of his goods. MPC §223.0(1). Strictly speaking, the harm required for the portion of the consolidated offense relating to embezzlement is merely the act of "exercising unlawful control." MPC §223.2(1). The implication is that even momentary unlawful control would be sufficient provided there is an intent "to deprive." Thus embezzlement becomes like larceny—a crime in the nature of attempted rather than consummated appropriation. *Cf.* Theft Act 1968, c. 60, §1, requiring actual appropriation for all variations of "theft."

[70] MPC §223.2(1).

[71] Theft Act 1968, c. 60, §6(1).

soldier and the boots, the actor does not purport to be the owner. He does not treat the thing as his "own to dispose of regardless of the other's rights."[72] On the other hand, the coke-bottle recycler (he recycles them from the back of the store to the front) does hold himself out as the owner, and therefore he would be guilty under the standard of the Theft Act. Though we argued earlier that there was no significant difference between *Holloway* and the coke-bottle recycler, the Theft Act builds squarely on a distinction that runs between these two cases.

It seems odd to place so much weight on the question whether, say, the soldier returning boots holds himself out as the owner or treats the boots as though they were the pair issued to him. The standard of assuming the rights of an owner makes sense in cases of embezzlement, for the victim in these cases is typically, if not always, the owner. The embezzler's assuming the rights of an owner is thus an appropriate test of economic harm. Yet the economic harm in the case of the beer chits or the soldier's boots has nothing to do with anyone's acting like an owner, and therefore it is not clear why this standard, imported from the law of embezzlement, should be controlling.

The German law on these cases is so difficult, primarily because both standards—economic harm and assuming the rights of an owner—interweave in the debate about whether the taking constitutes an appropriation. In the passbook case, the former *Reichsgericht* acquitted the defendant where his intent was to use the book to withdraw a sum and then to return it.[73] This decision still invites criticism, even by those who might not resort to a standard of economic harm. It is argued, for example, that presenting a book at the bank is to act as though one were the owner.[74] The case of the beer chits came before the *Reichsgericht* twice. The first time the court acquitted the waitress;[75] the second time, the court held that the elements of larceny were satisfied.[76]

[72] *Ibid.*
[73] Judgment of May 1, 1884, 10 RGSt. 369.
[74] See Maurach SP at 212; Rudolphi, *Der Begriff der Zueignung*, 1965 GA 33 ff.
[75] Judgment of February 23, 1893, 24 RGSt. 22.
[76] Judgment of February 19, 1807, 40 RFSt. 10.

The rationale was that "it suffices for a wrongful appropriation that the actor intends to exploit another's personal property and thus to use it to one's own benefit."[77] This decision has become a leading precedent in support of the theory that taking an object in order to exploit it for its economic value supplements the traditional forms of larceny.

In recent years German appellate courts have affirmed convictions both in the cases of the coke-bottle recycler[78] and the dishonest soldier.[79] The latter decision has generated considerable criticism,[80] for the extension of liability to the soldier breaks faith with the principle that the thief must intend to dispose of the object as though he were the owner. When the question was put to one of the chambers of the Supreme Court whether the law of larceny should encompass a soldier's turning in someone else's issued goods, the answer was that the activity should not be regarded as larceny, but perhaps as fraud.[81]

The more flexible German approach to the harm required for larceny has generated particular difficulties in cases of takings with the intent to use temporarily, as in the fifth case of the avid reader who takes the new book with the intent to read and return it. The problem is that the thing to be returned (a used book) is not exactly the same as the thing taken (a new book). The gap between these two represents economic harm to the bookstore that goes beyond the harm resulting from the book's temporary absence from the shelves. In principle, German law excludes *furtum usus*, or takings for temporary use, from the scope of larceny. Yet the purpose of economic appropriation was sufficient for conviction in a recent German case,[82] as it might well be under the

[77] *Id.* at 13.

[78] Judgment of the High State Court (*Oberlandesgericht*) in Bavaria, August 5, 1960, 1960 Bay. OLGSt. 187.

[79] Judgment of High State Court (*Oberlandesgericht*) in Hamm, March 26, 1964, 1964 NJW 1427.

[80] See A. Eser, *supra* note 55, at 46, note 10.

[81] Resolution of January 21, 1964, 19 BGHSt. 387.

[82] Judgment of the High State Court (*Oberlandesgericht*) in Celle, March 16, 1967, 1967 NJW 1921. For a discussion of this case and the difficulty of distinguishing between this instance of appropriation and *furtum usus*, see A. Eser, *supra* note 55, at 44–45.

Model Penal Code's standard of taking with an intent to appropriate "a major portion of [the object's] value."[83] Yet it is highly doubtful that a conviction could have been had at common law, and the English Theft Act appears to cleave to this highly conservative posture in cases of taking for temporary use.[84] The technical bar to conviction is that the actor does not have the intent "to treat the thing as his own to dispose of regardless of the other's rights."[85] This interpretation presupposes that the reader does not "dispose" of the book by using it and converting it into a less valuable, secondhand item.

The point worth stressing in this comparative analysis is the extent to which the contours of larceny are affected by the conceptualization of a comprehensive crime of "appropriation" including both larceny and embezzlement. We have attempted to show that while the traditional posture of the common law would presumably have been to deny convictions in all the cases listed at the outset of this section, German law was sufficiently supple to generate convictions in most, if not all, these cases. The reason for this adaptability in German law is a more flexible posture toward economic harm as the gravamen of larceny, and that flexibility derives, in turn, from the influence of criteria of embezzlement and appropriation on the intent required for larceny. The argument is that with the tendency to bring larceny and embezzlement under a common rubric of appropriation, similar developments can be expected in Anglo-American law.

§1.3.4. The Interests Protected in Punishing Fraud. The common theme in crimes of fraud is that the victim is induced by the offender's fraudulent pretense to part with a legal asset. Yet legal systems vary considerably about the kind of legal asset protected under the law of fraud. As soon as the crime of obtaining property by false pretenses took its modern form in the Statute of 1757,[86] the English judges became wedded to the principle that the

[83] MPC §223.0(1).

[84] See J. Smith, *supra* note 60, at 51; see Regina v. Feely, [1973] 2 W.L.R. 201 (Crim. App. 1972) (defendant took cash from company safe with intent to pay it back; his conviction for theft was reversed).

[85] Theft Act 1968, c. 60, §6(1).

[86] 30 Geo. II, c. 24 (1757)

only interest protected was full legal title to a chattel.[87] The types of chattels covered by the law and the extension of protection to other assets, such as real property, came to depend upon the particular statutory form.[88] Most of the disputes in Anglo-American cases turn on whether the victim has parted with title to goods obtained by the defendant. Even though the common-law courts started with a restrictive principle limiting the scope of false pretenses, they interpreted the principle even more conservatively and generally held, in disputed cases, that the defendant did not pass title.[89] This pattern of restrictive definition of the common law had a significant impact upon the development of other theft offenses. It meant, in particular, that in many cases the only offense sufficiently flexible to accommodate the judges' impulse to extend the criminal law was the crime of larceny. This is one reason why the common law of larceny underwent a radical expansion in the nineteenth century.[90]

If there is a problem in larceny about whether the law is designed to protect possession or economic value, there is an analogous issue in the law of false pretenses. The question is whether any transfer induced by fraud, contrary to the subjective preference of the owner, is sufficient to constitute the required element of harm. Suppose that a wholesaler demands security on installment sales. The defendant wishes to buy two television sets, each worth $150; as security he offers a chattel mortgage on his automobile worth $3,000 and assures the seller that the title to the car is unencumbered. After the defendant acquires the television sets, it becomes known to the seller that the car was in fact encumbered by a lien of $2,000. The seller insists that he was defrauded of title

[87] The King v. Pear, 169 Eng. Rep. 208 (1779). The misdemeanor created by the Statute 30 Geo. II was insufficiently important to warrant discussion in Blackstone. See 4 Blackstone 229–250 (offenses against private property).

[88] E.g., Cal. Penal Code §484 (money, labor, or real or personal property).

[89] E.g., Hufstetler v. State, 37 Ala. App. 71, 63 So. 2d 730 (1953) (a gas station attendant pumped gas into defendant's tank; title retained pending payment); Bourbonnaise v. State, 96 Okla. Crim. 28, 248 P.2d 640 (152) (the victim gave defendant money to purchase whiskey; defendant absconded; title retained). *Cf.* §1.1, at notes 36, 37 *supra*.

[90] See §1.2 *supra*.

in the two television sets even though the sale of $300 was secured by $1,000 residual value in the car. If it is sufficient that the seller was induced by fraud to enter into a transaction he would otherwise have refused, he was indeed defrauded. On the other hand, there was no objective economic harm to the seller in the transaction, and it is not clear that the criminal law should protect his subjective preferences. On facts similar to these, a divided Court of Appeals in the District of Columbia upheld the conviction for obtaining property by false pretenses.[91] The decision is not surprising, for if the common law never managed to develop a theory of economic harm in larceny, there is no reason why it should have made a breakthrough in the field of false pretenses. The analogue to thinking of the harm in larceny as simply depriving the possessor of a possessed object is to see the harm in false pretenses as inducing the victim to engage in a particular legal transaction, namely, transferring title to an asset, that he, but for the fraud, would not have ventured.

It would follow from this theory of the crime that a merchant would be guilty of obtaining property by false pretenses if he sold an object at its fair market value and yet misrepresented the goods in order to induce the buyer to believe that he was getting a bargain. On the assumption that the particular buyer would have purchased and paid cash for the goods only if the bargain was what the seller claimed it to be, the merchant's fraudulent conduct induces the buyer's payment; this combination of elements satisfies the technical definition of the offense. If the buyer paid by using a credit card, on the other hand, it might be more difficult to establish that he was induced to part with title to a chattel in making payment.

The German law of fraud concurs in its basic structure with the Anglo-American offense, yet there is an important and profound difference. The points of similarity are that (1) the suspect's misrepresentation, (2) must induce the victim (3) to transfer wealth

[91] Nelson v. United States, 227 F.2d 21 (D.C. Cir. 1955) *Accord:* People v. Talbott, 65 Cal. App. 2d 654, 151 P.2d 317 (1944), *cert. denied sub nom.* Talbott v. California, 324 U.S. 845 (1944). For a critical review of the holding in *Nelson,* see Comment, 65 Yale L.J. 887 (1956).

to the suspect or another party.[92] Further, (4) the suspect must act with the intent to enrich either himself or another.[93] The profound difference arises from a radically different approach to the concept of "transferring wealth."[94] As we have already noted, this notion is interpreted in Anglo-American law to require a transfer of property, and traditionally, this means a transfer of title. Contemporary German law starts from different premises about the nature of the interest protected by punishing fraud. The protected interest is not the victim's interest in good title; nor is it his autonomy to direct his assets without being deceived by another's fraud. German law and legal theory conceive the crime of fraud to be directed against the victim's "net wealth"—the sum of his legal interests minus his obligations.[95] This notion is so foreign to the approach of the common law that there is no word in English that corresponds to the German concept of *Vermögen* and the notion of a crime against *Vermögen*.[96] The term "estate" comes close, yet with different connotations and therefore we have to make do with the constructed analogue "net wealth."

Grounding the crime of fraud in the concept of the victim's "net wealth" generates an offense that is both broader and narrower than the traditional Anglo-American crime of obtaining property by false pretenses. The crime is obviously broader, for a variety of legal interests other than title are protected against fraudulently induced transfer. This additional range of interests includes not only possession,[97] but even incorporates claims that one

[92] *See generally* Schönke-Schröder-Cramer §263; A. Eser, *supra* note 55, at 122–23; Welzel 368–77.

[93] In the American literature, the required intent is typically labelled "an intent to defraud." LaFave & Scott 667-68. This is distinguishable from the German *Bereicherungsabsicht*, see generally authorities cited *supra* note 92, which implies an intent not only to harm the victim, but to benefit someone else.

[94] *Vermögensverfügung* in German.

[95] This is the standard definition of *Vermögen*. See Resolution of July 18, 1961, 16 BGHSt. 220, 221 (*"Summe aller geldwerten Güter nach Abzug der Verbindlichkeiten"*).

[96] The category of crimes against "net wealth" includes fraud, §263, but significantly excludes larceny, robbery and embezzlement, which are categorized as crimes of "appropriation." See A. Eser, *supra* note 95, at 111.

[97] *Id.* at 114. Even the possession acquired by a thief is protected, except as against the owner. *Ibid.*

might be fraudulently induced to forego.[98] In one case that might surprise lawyers in the mold of the common law, an impoverished man falsely confessed to several theft offenses in order to be taken into preventive detention and thus to secure protection against cold winter nights. Because he fraudulently induced the state to give him shelter, he was subsequently convicted of fraud.[99] Other examples include the attempt by some commentators and lower courts to find the crime of fraud in a shoplifter's failing to disclose his goods as he passes through the checkstand.[100] The harm to the shopkeeper's "net wealth" arguably consists in fraudulently inducing the clerk not to assert the shop's interest either in compensation or in holding onto the goods. The better argument seems to be, however, that the shoplifter is guilty merely of larceny and not of fraud.[101]

Though the German crime of criminal fraud has this potential sweep, it is also narrower than its Anglo-American analogue. The principle that there is no liability without harm to the victim's "net wealth" implies that merely interfering with the victim's commercial autonomy is insufficient for the crime. In a case in which the defendant misrepresented synthetic goods as "pure wool," but nonetheless gave the buyer value for his money, the Supreme Court held that there was no offense.[102] If the buyer receives value for his money, then his "net wealth" is not affected and though he was tricked into buying something he did not want, the harm is insufficient to support a criminal charge. The underlying principle is expressed negatively: the criminal law does not protect *Dispositionsfreiheit*—namely, the freedom to dispose of one's property as one sees fit.[103] The common law, in contrast, does protect this freedom—or commercial autonomy, as we might call it—as an end in itself.

[98] Schönke-Schröder-Cramer §263, note 41, at 1525.

[99] Judgment of March 11, 1960, 14 BGHSt. 170. The defendant could arguably be convicted under Cal. Penal Code §484 (defrauding the state of "labor").

[100] This extension of the crime is disputed. *Compare* Schönke-Schröder-Cramer §263, note 41, at 1525 *with* Welzel, *Anmerkung*, 1961 GA 350.

[101] Resolution of April 13, 1962, 17 BGHSt. 205.

[102] Resolution of July 18, 1961, 16 BGHSt. 220.

[103] Schönke-Schröder-Cramer §263, note 1, at 1516; A. Eser, *supra* note 55, at 112.

The striking difference between the Anglo-American and the German approaches to punishing fraud is that the Anglo-American approach of protecting commercial autonomy does not require a substantive judgment about whether the victim received value for his money. The aversion to making substantive judgments about the comparative value of exchanged goods is deeply rooted in Anglo-American law; it finds expression as well as in the law of contracts and the principle that even nominal consideration will render a contract binding.[104] German law, in contrast, obviously does not abjure substantive judgments about the fairness of market exchanges, both in the law of contracts[105] and in the law of fraud. Underlying this divergence in attitudes lie differing degrees of faith in the market as the arbiter of commercial justice. A culture that puts its faith in the market is not inclined to second-guess a buyer's judgment to determine whether he received value when he would not have not made the deal had he known the true nature of the goods. Yet the market can work only so far as commercial autonomy is unrestricted, and therefore the task of the criminal law becomes the protection of this autonomy rather than the safeguarding of substantive commercial justice.

A law of fraud that, like the German offense, seeks to protect "net wealth" rather than commercial autonomy can generate subtleties that go far beyond the relatively straightforward common-law rules. The subtleties derive from the recognition that substantive commercial justice depends not only on the market value of the goods, but on the particular economic situation of the victim. In a 1962 decision,[106] the German Supreme Court had to decide whether a salesman was guilty of several counts of fraud in selling milking machines to farmers under the pretense that they were receiving the machines at a substantial discount. In fact the farmers paid the full list price for the machine, and arguably none would have purchased it had they known the truth about the

[104] See Horwitz, *The Historical Foundations of Modern Contract Law,* 87 Harv. L. Rev. 917 (1974).

[105] BGB §138(II). *Cf.* Code Civil §1674 (land sale transactions).

[106] Resolution of August 16, 1961, 16 BGHSt. 321.

price. The latter fact would presumably have been sufficient to convict under the Anglo-American principle of protecting commercial autonomy. Yet the German court would not convict on this fact alone. The court balked at treating the salesman's fraud as exempt from the scope of the law simply because the farmers received a milking machine that was worth the price they paid for it. The question was whether the particular farmers, under their particular economic conditions, were affected in their "net wealth" by the purchase.[107] One farmer apparently had seized what appeared to be an extraordinary opportunity to buy at a discount even though he thereby jeopardized his liquidity. Another was required to take a loan in order to support the purchase. And a third purchased the machine even though it did not meet his needs: he required a machine that would milk ten cows, and the machine available at the supposed bargain would milk only two or three. The Supreme Court reasoned that these additional facts supported the conclusion that the farmers were injured in their "net wealth." A minor purchase induced by misrepresentation, such as the purchase of dry goods misrepresented as "pure wool," might not injure the purchaser in his "net wealth."[108] But in the case of a major purchase such as the milking machine, the court readily finds the additional facts to support the inference that it was not only commercial autonomy, but "net wealth" that was infringed by the salesman's fraud.

The analysis of "net wealth" proceeds on the basis of "economic realities" rather than a consideration of legal rights and duties. If the latter perspective were assumed, the courts would have to consider the implications at private law of the farmer's right to rescind the fraudulently induced transaction or to receive compensation for breach of warranty. If rights acquired under the civil law were considered, a fraudulent transaction would hardly ever affect the victim's net wealth, for his claims of rescission and compensation theoretically make up the loss due to the defendant's fraud. Merely considering the victim's legal rights would ig-

[107] *Id.* at 325.
[108] See text at note 102 *supra*.

nore the expense entailed by the process of asserting legal rights in order to rectify the loss induced by fraudulent sale.[109]

This perspective of economic reality generates a subtle distinction in a case very much like the District of Columbia case in which the defendant fraudulently acquired credit by giving his car as security.[110] In the German[111] as in the American case, the security was sufficient to cover the credit and therefore, there was arguably no economic damage to the creditor who was fraudulently induced to enter into the transaction. Yet the German Supreme Court drew the distinction between a chattel mortgage and a security interest, such as a pledge, that could be liquidated without the cooperation of the debtor. A chattel mortgage entailed risks—the debtor might wreck the car or illegally dispose of it—and therefore, regardless of its amount, this form of security was insufficient to prevent an injury to the "net wealth" of the creditor.[112] Though it started from different premises, the German Supreme Court concurred with the American court that a debtor was criminally liable for fraudulently acquiring credit, even though the debt was secured by a technically sufficient chattel mortgage.

The English Theft Act of 1968 nominally suggests a movement in the direction of the German theory that the crime of fraud protects economic interests rather than commercial autonomy. According to §16 of the Act, a person commits a variation of criminal fraud if "by any deception [he] dishonestly obtains for himself or another any pecuniary advantage."[113] Yet this is but a nominal movement toward the language of economic interests, for the Act defines the scope of §16 narrowly to encompass only three types of pecuniary advantage.[114] The more general provision is §15, which

[109] See Resolution of July 16, 1976, 23 BGHSt. 300 (victim was fraudulently induced to subscribe to a magazine. She cancelled after receipt of the first issue. Although she suffered no out-of-pocket loss, the risk of loss was sufficient to justify a conviction). See generally A. Eser, *supra* note 55, at 146, 152–55.

[110] See text at note 91 *supra*.

[111] Judgment of June 3, 1960, 15 BGHSt. 24.

[112] *Id.* at 26. The court left open the question whether a different result would be reached in the cases of a pledge in sufficient amount to cover the indebtedness.

[113] Theft Act 1968, c. 60, §16(1).

[114] Theft Act 1968, c. 60, §16(2). The three defined instances of "obtaining a

defines the crime of "obtaining property by deception" in the mold of the common law, with but a few amendments in favor of broader coverage.[115] There is no commitment in the new Theft Act to analyze both sides of a commercial transaction in order to determine whether the victim is injured in his "net wealth." The basic principle is still the protection of commercial autonomy.

pecuniary advantage" are, in brief (a) reducing, evading, or deferring a debt, (b) borrowing by way of overdraft or acquiring an interest under an insurance policy or annuity contract, and (c) earning money by labor or betting. These are the only possible categories of self-enrichment under §16. See J. Smith, *supra* note 60, at 91.

[115] "Obtaining property" is defined to include obtaining "ownership, possession or control." Theft Act 1968, c. 60, §15(2). *Cf.* MPC §223.0(6), defining "property" to include "anything of value" which presumably encompasses "possession" and "control" although the examples given in MPC §223.0(6) are types of personal and real property rather than ways of holding an object.

Chapter Two
Common-Law Larceny and Its Metamorphosis

§2.1. *Enigmas of the Common Law.*

Though we have developed some familiarity with larceny as interpreted in the nineteenth-century English and American courts, we have yet to assay the original conception of common-law larceny that prevailed until the late eighteenth century. This body of law consists of an array of puzzles that have baffled commentators and judges for the last 200 years. Justice Holmes and other distinguished writers have dismissed the rules of larceny as the imprints of historical "accidents."[1] Jerome Hall has written an influential book maintaining that social and economic forces can be summoned to explain the mysterious tracks of larceny in the legal sand.[2] Somehow in the total confusion about the history of larceny, these two views have coexisted. Larceny is thought to be both the expression of freakish accidents and the predictable prod-

§2.1. [1] Commonwealth v. Ryan, 155 Mass. 523, 527, 30 N.E. 364, 364–65 (1892).
[2] J. Hall, Theft, Law and Society 14–33 (2d ed. 1952) (discussing the Carrier's Case).

uct of social and economic forces. An adequate theory would find a course between these extremes. It would neither succumb to the aimless currents of historical accidents nor founder on the simplistic shoals of historical determinism.

There are three recurrent enigmas in the early common law of larceny: (1) the rule that someone in possession could not commit larceny, (2) the doctrine of "breaking bulk" as an exception to the first rule, and (3) the practice of acquitting some persons on the ground that their taking, however dishonest, lacked the element of "trespass." Constructing a theory to account for these three enigmas is of central importance in the overall plan of this book. The theory that we develop in §2.3 introduces us to the notion of a "pattern of criminality." This first pattern, which we call the pattern of manifest criminality, accounts for the puzzling features of common-law larceny and at the same time poses a general theory of criminal liability that accounts as well for other criminal offenses.

The pattern of manifest criminality is but the first of three patterns that will emerge in the first half of this book. Taken together, the three patterns of liability generate an interpretive mode for understanding commonalities and contrasts among a wide range of specific offenses. Thus our descent into the historic details of larceny is but a first step toward transcending larceny and understanding the general pattern of manifest criminality.

The second half of this chapter charts the eclipse of the original understanding of larceny and the expansion of the crime in the late eighteenth and nineteenth centuries. This process of expansion expressed the second of our three patterns of criminality, a pattern that we shall call "subjective criminality." The emergence of this theory of criminality accounts for two important phenomena: (1) the systematic preference for the crime of larceny in resolving points of stress at the intersection of the three theft offenses, and (2) an unwitting reinterpretation of the common law that expressed nineteenth-century criteria of rationality but incidentally generated a screen of misunderstanding about the early history of larceny. What made sense to Coke, Hale and Blackstone came to resemble a jumble of technical rules. Thus the emergence of the new view of larceny traded on a reinterpretation of the past—a reinterpretation that has beclouded the early history of larceny as well as the general principle of manifest criminality. The transition from the early pattern of manifest criminality to the nineteenth-century commitment to subjective criminality, with the attendant reinterpretation of the tradition, is what we mean by the metamorphosis of larceny.

Our first task is to cut through the camouflage that conceals the inner coherence of the common-law approach to larceny. That requires, first, that we review the problematic doctrines that gradually fell into disrepute in the nineteenth and twentieth centuries.

§2.1.1. Possessorial Immunity. We have already noted the explicit rule of the common law that those who acquire possession over chattels are not subject to criminal liability—at least prior to the end of the eighteenth century and the enactment of embezzlement as a distinct offense. Those who had possession over movable objects enjoyed immunity from prosecution for misappropriating them to their own use.[3] This possessorial immunity was typically conferred by the prior possessor's delivering the chattel to a new possessor. Yet it could also be acquired by taking possession of a lost or mislaid object. Possessorial immunity lasted until the possessor returned the object to its owner or passed it on and conferred immunity upon another possessor. If the possessor was a carrier, this meant that the entrusted goods had to be carried and deposited at their destination.[4] If the possessor was an employee and he received money or chattels from a customer, he retained possession until he deposited the chattels in his employer's cash drawer or other receptacle indicative of the employer's dominion.[5]

The striking feature of possessorial immunity is that it emerged in all the leading Western jurisdictions, in French,[6] Ger-

[3] R. Glanvill, The Treatise on the Laws and Customs of the Realm of England 13–14 (G. Hall ed. 1965) ("Clearly he is not guilty of theft, because he initially had possession from the owner of the thing.").

[4] 3 Coke 107–08; Blackstone 230.

[5] See §1.2.4 *supra.*

[6] Lambert 214–15.

man[7] and Russian law[8] as well as the English common law. The contemporary universality of the rule is even more striking in view of its absence from ancient legal systems.[9] In cases neither of manifest nor of non-manifest larceny was possession a significant boundary. We might describe the modern rule of possessorial immunity as expressing a shared Western understanding about the kind of relationships that ought to be exempt from the scope of the criminal law.

Possessorial immunity presumably emerged in Western jurisprudence as an institution that facilitated privately structured understandings about the management of money, tools, animals and other chattels. If one of these privately ordered relationships miscarried in a dishonest misappropriation, the harm was apparently felt to be private rather than public. It was an injury compensable, to be sure, under the common-law writs of detinue and later trover,[10] but it was not a matter for the criminal courts. It is very tempting to argue that the law respected such privately structured relationships and treated them as autonomous and exempt from the jurisdiction of the courts. Yet this form of explanation will hardly do unless we take a closer look at the cases in which possessorial immunity attached and those in which it did not. This, we shall see, is where the puzzle emerges.

At early stages of the common law, the concept of possession coincided with actual dominion over an object.[11] In the course of the law's evolution the courts gradually recognized, and then widened, a gap between actual control and legal possession. As of the fifteenth century, the judges recognized that a guest in an inn did

[7] Schönke-Schröder-Eser §242, notes 14, 24–25 at 1401, 1403; Welzel 347–48. Yet note that under German law, someone in joint possession of an object may commit larceny, §1.2.4, at note 55 *supra*.

[8] Kurs (SP 1973) at 429.

[9] See H. Jolowicz & B. Nicholas, Historical Introduction to the Study of Roman Law 169 n.2 (1972); T. Mommsen, Römisches Strafrecht 735 n.5 (1899); and Biblical jurisprudence, see Exodus 22:7. See generally 2 B. Cohen, Jewish and Roman Law: A Comparative Study 409–32 (1966).

[10] F. Maitland, Equity and the Forms of Action at Common Law 356–57, 365 (1913).

[11] See 3 W. Holdsworth, A History of English Law 336 (6th ed. rev. 1934).

not acquire possession of eating utensils or bed linen.[12] In the fifteenth and sixteenth centuries there was considerable controversy whether servants enjoyed possessorial immunity for misappropriating goods acquired from their masters. After some vacillation[13] it was settled that a servant's custody did not amount to possession as long as the servant was on the master's premises or in the master's company.[14] Parliament intervened in this development in 1529 with a statute that subjected servants to the law of larceny as to all valuable property entrusted to them by their masters.[15] In due course, however, this statute was interpreted not to apply to the goods that servants received from third parties.[16]

In these disputes about the scope of possessorial immunity, the underlying transaction typically involves only two parties.[17] The owner hands the suspect an object or the suspect picks it up with the owner's permission; the question is whether the acquisition of the physical object is sufficient to acquire legal possession. In the cases of crockery and linen in another's inn, the user would not expect eventually to acquire full control or property in the chattel. The problem is more subtle if the transaction is of the sort in which the user normally expects to acquire the object as his own. This more difficult variation was posed in the mid-seventeenth-century case of *Chisser*,[18] in which the defendant bolted

[12] The Carrier's Case, Y.B. Pasch. 13 Edw. IV, f. 9, pl. 5 (1473), 64 Selden Soc. 30, 33 (1945) (opinion of Nedeham).

[13] *Compare* Y.B. Mich. 3 Hen. VII, pl. 9 (1488) *with* Y.B. Hil. 21 Hen. VII, pl. 21 (1506), translated in C. Kenny, A Selection of Cases Illustrative of the English Criminal Law 216 (8th ed. 1935); see 3 W. Holdsworth, *supra* note 11, at 363–64.

[14] See Kenny, *supra* note 13, at 216; 3 W. Holdsworth, *supra* note 11, at 365 & n.2.

[15] 21 Hen. VIII, c. 7 (1529). The statute does not formally alter the concept of possession; it provides that servants who "go away" with "caskets, jewels, money, goods, or chattels" which had been "delivered to them by their master or mistress . . . to the intent to steal the same . . . shall be deemed and adjudged [to have committed] felony. . . ." In time, larceny by servants was molded into the conceptual system by holding that in this class of cases servants did not get possession. See The King v. Bass, 168 Eng. Rep. 228 (1782); 2 East 555–60.

[16] See Anon., 73 Eng. Rep. 12, 12–13 (K.B. 1533) (opinion by Englefielde).

[17] See the analysis of two party transactions *supra* §1.2.5.

[18] 83 Eng. Rep. 142 (1678).

from a store without paying for two cravats that the shopkeeper handed him for inspection. The Court of Exchequer found the taking to be felonious; despite the handing over of the cravats, the owner retained legal possession and was therefore protected until actual sale of the ties.[19] In this situation, as well as in the case of the guest and the servant, drawing the line of possession short of physical control meant that one could commit larceny by carrying off an object already in one's hands. Thus the widening of the gap between legal possession and actual control functioned as a way of restricting possessorial immunity.[20]

If the point of possessorial immunity was that privately ordered relationships ought to be exempt from the jurisdiction of the criminal courts, it is by no means easy to explain why bailees enjoyed immunity, but servants and customers in shops did not. The philosopher William Paley attempted to explain these rules on the ground that the "law will not interpose its sanctions to protect negligence and credulity, or to supply the place of domestic care and prudence."[21] This is a way of saying that the owner assumed the risk of misappropriation by handing over possession of his goods to another. Yet it is hard to see why a master should have assumed the risk of misappropriation by a carrier whom he might know only distantly, and yet not assume the risk of defalcation by a servant, whom he would presumably know more intimately. The paradoxical fact is that the less control the owner had over the goods and persons using them, the less protection he enjoyed un-

[19] There is a conflicting interpretation of the case, taken up §2.3.3 at notes 40–42 *infra*.

[20] The case law in France, Germany and the Soviet Union is equally sensitive to the problem of restricting possession to some subset of cases of physical control. See, e.g., Judgment of March 6, 1968, 1968 Recueil Dalloz 395 (*Cour de Cassation*) (salesgirl who took home and converted clothes from her shop guilty of larceny); Judgment of June 11, 1965, 1966 GA 244 (German Supreme Court) (customer who took ring after having tried it on with the shopkeeper's permission guilty of larceny); Kurs (SP 1968) at 272 (reference to person asked to watch luggage in train station, guilty of larceny when he took it). The formal ground of all these decisions was that the degree of control imparted by the owner was insufficient to establish possession (*possession, Gewahrsam, vladenie*), and that therefore the rule of possessory immunity, recognized in all of these systems, see note 17 *supra*, did not apply.

[21] W. Paley, Principles of Moral and Political Philosophy 408 (1821 ed.).

der the criminal law. The innkeeper retained possession over his crockery; the shopkeeper over goods handled by customers. Even before the Statute of 1529 the master retained possession over goods used by his servant on his premises or in his presence. Yet as to strangers acting in the commercial world, the owner was deemed to have assumed the risks of misjudgment.

We are likely to do better in assaying this enigma of the common law if we leave aside assumption of risk and focus instead on the possible reasons for protecting commercial relationships from criminal sanctions. Possessorial immunity typically protected relationships defined solely by contract, in which the visible face of the other looked solely upon the chattel that bound the parties together. Immunity did not attach in more complex relationships occurring under the roof of the owner, in which there were either expectations of continuing interaction or a relationship of authority and dependence. Though we find the principle of possessorial immunity as early as the thirteenth century,[22] it may be that the institution was well suited for a form of commercial life in which relationships with strangers were seen as private matters, subject to autonomous regulation by contract and therefore properly exempt from the jurisdiction of the criminal courts.

This admittedly speculative analysis provides a hypothesis for understanding the puzzling institution of possessorial immunity enjoyed by servants receiving goods from third parties.[23] We noted earlier that the Statute of 1529 did not alter the status of servants and employees relative to depositors in banks and customers in stores.[24] There were particular conceptual impediments to the argument that the third party passed possession directly to the master or employer.[25] A supplementary account emerges if we focus on the kinds of relationships involved. The relationship between the third party and the servant was precisely the kind of limited interaction, defined solely by the transfer of the object, that triggered possessorial immunity. Yet the relationship between master and

[22] See note 3 *supra*.
[23] See the analysis of three-party transactions, *supra* §1.2.4.
[24] See note 16 *supra*.
[25] These are surveyed in §1.2.4 *supra*.

servant was the paradigm of the more complex, ongoing relationship in which the transfer of the object failed to confer immunity.

These considerations help us make some sense of the rules of the common law defining the contours of possessorial immunity. Later we shall propose a broader hypothesis that will shed some light on the importance of possession as a boundary on liability, and serve to unite the analysis of this problem with that of other puzzling developments of the common law that await our attention.

§2.1.2. Enigmas of the Common Law: The Carrier's Case. The Carrier's Case,[26] decided in the Star Chamber in 1473, was a major event in the history and theory of larceny. It was the first and only judicial effort to pierce the veil of possèssorial immunity and subject a bailee to liability for larceny. The rule of the case, namely, that a bailee is liable if he "breaks bulk" in taking the goods in his possession, has taxed the explanatory powers of commentators for nearly five centuries. Any adequate theory of common-law larceny must begin with due regard for this seminal and provocative case.

The facts are straightforward. A carrier had made a bargain with a merchant to carry some bales of dyer's weed to Southampton; instead he took them to another place, broke open the bales and took the contents.[27] All or part of the goods thus taken appeared to have fallen into the hands of the sheriff of London, who was sued by the original owner—an alien merchant who had come with a royal safe conduct covering his goods—for the return of his property.[28] The sheriff's defense was that the goods were forfeit to the King as waif, because the taking had been a felony.[29]

The impediment to treating the taking as a felony was the rule

[26] Y.B. Pasch. 13 Edw. IV, f. 9, pl. 5 (1473), 64 Selden Soc. 30 (1945) [cited hereafter to the Selden Society reprint and translation].

[27] See *id.* at 30 (reporter's note).

[28] See *id.* at 34 (reporter's note).

[29] *Id.* (reporter's note). Waifed goods are those feloniously taken and then abandoned; these are normally forfeited to the Crown. See 1 Blackstone 296–97 (explaining the rule as an inducement to owners to pursue thieves and recapture stolen goods before they are abandoned).

of possessorial immunity. Chief Justice Brian took this rule to be decisive: the bailee, having lawfully taken possession of the goods, could not take them *vi et armis,* and therefore the taking could not be said to be felony or trespass.[30] Yet in the end the judges were of the opinion that the taking had been a felony. They could not concur on a rationale,[31] but Lord Chokke's opinion developed the argument that eventually became the rule of the case.[32] Chokke argued that[33]

> [T]he things which were in the bale were not given [to the bailee], but the bales as chose entire . . . , in which case if he had given away the bales or sold them, it would not be felony, but when he broke open [the bales] and took out of [them] what was inside he did this without warrant [and it is felony].

This is the language that generated the rule of "breaking bulk," which remained a prominent exception to possessorial immunity until the mid-nineteenth century.[34] It was only after all

[30] 64 Selden Soc. at 30–31 (opinion of Bryan, C.J., C.P.).

[31] The various justices advanced several theories on which the bailee's taking could be considered a larceny. Huse, for example, thought that a felony was committed when the carrier "claim[ed] the goods feloniously without cause from the party with intent to defraud him to whom the property belongs. . . ." *Id.* at 31. The Chancellor and Molyneux also seem to have held this position. Vavasour and Laken sought to distinguish between a bailment, in which there is actual delivery and possession in the bailee, and a bargain to carry, which was thought to give only a limited warrant to take the goods. Thus, if the carrier by his conversion revealed an intent not to comply with the terms of the warrant, his initial taking was felonious. See *id.* at 31 (Vavasour), 33 (Laken, J.K.B.). Nedeham took this argument a step further and maintained that possession determined when the carrier went outside the purpose for which he had been given the bales. See *id.* at 33 (Nedeham, J.K.B.). This analysis would have assimilated the case to those in which the taker had custody merely, and not possession.

[32] See 3 Coke 107; M. Dalton, The Country Justice 324 (1655); 1 Hale 504–05; 4 Blackstone 230.

[33] 64 Selden Soc. at 32. This principle does not appear to have been without precedent. Chokke gives an example: "[I]f a man is given a tun of wine to carry, if he sells the tun, it is not felony or trespass, but if he took out twenty pints it is a felony, for the twenty pints were not given to him. . . ." *Cf.* Rattlesdene v. Gruneston, Y.B. Pasch. 10 Edw. II, pl. 37 (1317), 54 Selden Soc. 140 (1935).

[34] The Carrier's Case was viewed as establishing two different circumstances in which a carrier or bailee could be found guilty of larceny. In the first, the culprit

bailees were brought within the scope of either embezzlement or larceny by a bailee[35] that the exception of "breaking bulk" lost its significance.

No one in the last century, so far as I know, has uttered a kind or even charitable word for the rationale of the Carrier's Case.[36] The assumption has been that the rule of "breaking bulk" was an arbitrary legal form, a manipulation of the law that must have been the reflection of deep-seated social and political forces. In the late nineteenth century, Fitzjames Stephen argued that the case was a concession to the royal policy of protecting alien merchants.[37] Unsatisfied with this account, Jerome Hall adds a detailed account of commerce in the fifteenth century and contends that economic conditions helped shape the decision of the case.[38] All of these claims prove to be inaccurate. Instead of responding to what was actually decided in the dispute over the carrier's goods, Stephen and Hall engage in *a priori* arguments about the necessary influence of social and political forces in shaping the law. A closer look at the legal problem actually posed in the case reveals how misleading it is to assume that the law always responds to the "felt necessities of the time."[39]

What Hall and Stephen have in mind is that it was important that the bales should be returned to the foreign owner and shipper. Yet the plain fact is that if this had been the point of the po-

---

breaks bulk and carries away the contents *animo furandi.* This was a felony at the time of the breaking and taking, not at the time of initial receipt of the goods. See M. Dalton, *supra* note 32, at 324; 3 Coke 107; 1 Hale 505; 1 Hawkins 135; 4 Blackstone 230. In the second set of circumstances, the carrier, having received the pack and "carr[ied] it to the place appointed, . . . take[s] the whole pack *animo furandi* . . ." 3 Coke 107. See 64 Selden Soc. at 33 (opinion of Nedeham, J.K.B.); M. Dalton, *supra* note 32, at 324; 1 Hale 505; 4 Blackstone 230.

[35] 20 & 21 Vict. c. 54, §4 (1857). Regarding similar American legislative revisions of the rule of "breaking bulk," see 2 J. Bishop, Criminal Law 479 (6th ed. 1877).

[36] Stephen treated the rule of "breaking bulk" as an "obscure distinction resting on no definite principle." 3 Stephen 140; *accord,* Perkins 261 ("absurd distinction"); T. Plucknett, A Concise History of the Common Law 424 (4th ed. 1948) ("devious reasoning"); L. Weinreb, Criminal Law: Cases, Comments, Questions 304 (2d ed. 1975) (akin to "Humpty Dumpty's doctrine").

[37] 3 Stephen at 139, *accord,* T. Plucknett, *supra* note 36, at 424.

[38] See J. Hall, Theft, Law and Society 14–33 (2d ed. 1952).

[39] Holmes 1.

litical and economic pressures of the time, the judges could have reached that result directly, simply by holding that the taking was not felonious. The goods would then have been returned to the merchant as his property. Holding that the taking was felonious meant that they were waif, which in turn meant that they were forfeit to the King and therefore properly retained by the sheriff of London.[40] Holding that the goods were waif, therefore, required an additional legal innovation, namely, the principle that the ordinary law of waif would not apply in the case of an alien merchant who had been given a safe conduct by the King.

Further, it is difficult to maintain, as does Jerome Hall, that the decision served the interests of the rising merchant class.[41] There was some protection to be gained in extending the scope of the criminal law to carriers who "broke bulk." But this gain has to be offset against the risk that their goods would be declared waif—as feloniously taken and then abandoned—and therefore subject to forfeiture to the King. In view of the civil remedies already available, it is a close empirical question whether the interests of the merchants were in fact served by adding a criminal sanction and yet depriving them of their right to recover abandoned goods. Sociological explanations of legal phenomena must obviously begin with the facts, not with claims about what must have been the influence of economic conditions.

Even if Hall and Stephen were right, their hypothesis would have little explanatory power. Their theory of political and economic forces might, if the facts supported it, explain the expansion of liability in cases of "breaking bulk," but they could not explain the corollary of the case, that if the carrier converted the goods without breaking bulk, he remained behind the shield of possessorial immunity.[42] If the point of the decision was to protect merchant shippers by deterring larceny, then why not protect all of them against all risks of larceny? Why should the law artificially create an incentive to convert bales without opening them? It is

[40] 1 Blackstone 296–97.
[41] See J. Hall, *supra* note 38, at 31–32.
[42] 3 Coke 107; 1 Hale 504; 4 Blackstone 230.

unilluminating to argue that the judges "had to stop some place," for, again, what we should wish to know is why they stopped at the juncture of "breaking bulk." Indeed, if some cases were to be included arbitrarily, why should "breaking bulk" not have been an argument for exclusion rather than inclusion? One problem in searching for the social and economic causes of judicial decisions is that these "causes" can explain, at most, why a particular party won the case; they do not provide an account of particular doctrinal forms of the law.[43] An adequate theory of larceny would explain not only why the merchant received his goods, but would account for the judicial intuition that "breaking bulk" should constitute an exception to the principle of possessorial immunity.

In proposing a general theory of common-law larceny below, we shall attempt to explain the particular appeal of the phrase, "breaking bulk," and relate the conundrum of Carrier's Case to other puzzles in the law of larceny. Before turning to this theory, we should complete our agenda of data to be explained by turning to a more recent problem in the judicial shaping of larceny as a crime.

§2.1.3. The Problem of Staged Larceny. In the two preceding sections, we encountered problems in extending liability for larceny, either by restricting possessorial immunity or by piercing the veil of immunity with the doctrine of "breaking bulk." In this section we address ourselves to a relatively modern line of cases in which the law's puzzle is presented by a judicial propensity to acquit obviously dishonest and dangerous people.

The cases we shall examine follow a recurrent pattern. The suspect seeks to steal from the owner by enlisting the aid of the latter's employee. The employee in turn informs the owner, who then instructs his employee to feign cooperation in order to catch the suspect in the act. The owner or the police keep watch as the suspect goes through the motions of stealing; then they apprehend him. There is a surprising number of decisions in this vein of case

[43] For some illuminating comments on these problems of method, see M. Douglas, Purity and Danger 48–50 (1966) (rejecting causal and instrumentalist explanations of taboos in Jewish law).

law,[44] and the opinions interweave a number of nearly appropriate doctrines in an attempt to explain why the conviction should be affirmed or reversed. Some sense that the issue is entrapment.[45] Yet apart from the traps being staged by private parties rather than the police, these are typically cases in which the would-be thief initiates the plan.[46] Admittedly, entrapment might be a factor in some extreme cases of overbearing inducement.[47] The more interesting precedents are those that acknowledge that the issue is not the defendant's voluntariness or culpability,[48] but nonetheless struggle with an intuition that something is awry when the crime is acted out on a stage manipulated by the owner of the goods.

To express their intuition that something is amiss, the courts deploy a variety of doctrinal gambits. Sometimes they say that the element of "trespass" is missing in the taking. Sometimes they hold simply that there is no liability because the owner "consented" to the taking or because the owner "delivered" the goods to the would-be thief. None of these doctrinal rationalia is adequate to the task of explaining why these convictions of dishonest and dangerous people should be reversed. To demonstrate their inadequacy, we shall closely examine one appellate opinion that uses all of these arguments to frame the judges' intuition that

[44] See the cases collected in Annot., 10 A.L.R.3d 1121 (1966).

[45] Entrapment is typically raised and rejected as a defense. See, e.g., Jarrott v. State, 108 Tex. Crim. 427, 1 S.W.2d 619 (1927) (phrasing issue as one of entrapment and rejecting the defense); Lowe v. State, 44 Fla. 449, 32 So. 956 (1902) (rejecting the defense); Pigg v. State, 43 Tex. 108 (1875) (jury instruction in language of entrapment; conviction reversed on other grounds).

[46] See, e.g., People v. Rollino, 37 Misc. 2d 14, 233 N.Y.S.2d 580 (Sup. Ct. 1962); Rex v. Turvey, [1946] 2 All E.R. 60 (Crim. App.). On the defense of entrapment generally, see §7.3.2 B *infra*.

[47] A good example is Love v. People, 160 Ill. 501, 43 N.E. 710 (1896), in which a hired detective had repeatedly plied the defendants with liquor and proposed they together commit a series of burglaries. When the defendants were intoxicated, the detective led them through a burglary that had been arranged in advance with the owner who had hired him. The reversal in this case was rendered easier because the conviction was for burglary rather than larceny. See note 64 *infra*.

[48] E.g., People v. Rollino, 37 Misc. 2d 14, 233 N.Y.S.2d 580 (Sup. Ct. 1962); Rex v. Turvey, [1946] 2 All E.R. 60 (Crim. App.); Regina v. Lawrance, 4 Cox Crim. Cas. 440 (1850).

something is awry if the stealing is staged by the owner of the goods.

Topolewski v. State[49] came to the Wisconsin Supreme Court on a set of facts that richly illustrate the typical pattern in cases of staged larceny. In an effort to acquire meat products from a packing company, Topolewski sought the cooperation of one Dolan, recently employed by the company and personally indebted to him. Dolan informed the manager of the company of Topolewski's criminal intentions. The manager instructed Dolan to feign cooperation, which he did in meeting repeatedly with Topolewski. The plan that emerged was that Dolan would arrange to have four barrels of meat placed on the loading dock of the plant and Topolewski would be identified as the party to whom they were consigned. Topolewski arrived in his own truck and, acting like any other customer, he loaded the barrels in his truck and drove off. Though the platform boss apparently did not know of the trap, the company manager had set a watch over the barrels. Topolewski was presumably arrested shortly after he drove off.[50]

In reversing Topolewski's conviction, the Wisconsin Supreme Court carefully separated out matters that were not in dispute. There was no question about Topolewski's intention to steal the barrels of meat.[51] Nor was there any dispute about whether entrapment provided a rationale for reversing the conviction. The court specifically said that it is wrong to justify reversals in this sort of case on the ground that the owner's deception excused the would-be criminal, or, alternatively, that the owner's improper behavior should preclude a criminal prosecution.[52] The proposition recurs repeatedly in the opinion that regardless of the actor's criminal intent there could be no conviction unless his conduct satisfied the objective elements of larceny. The central objective requirement was a trespass. All of the court's doctrinal arguments were

[49] 130 Wis. 244, 109 N.W. 1037 (1906).
[50] See *id.* at 246–47, 109 N.W. at 1038.
[51] See *id.* at 247, 109 N.W. at 1038.
[52] See *id.* at 255, 109 N.W. at 1041.

designed to prove that the taking of the barrels with the intent to steal was not sufficient to constitute a "trespass."[53]

Three subsidiary arguments emerged to demonstrate the absence of a trespassory taking: first, that the conduct of the manager and the platform boss meant that the company had "consented" to the taking; secondly, that the transaction at the loading dock amounted to a delivery; and thirdly, that the company had gone too far in facilitating Topolewski's taking of the barrels. Though popular in this line of cases, none of these three arguments provides an adequate ground for reversal.

The claim that the victim consents to the taking is a recurrent theme in these cases. But one can only be puzzled that the claim is so appealing. Surely there is no consent in the ordinary sense. The goals of the would-be thief and victim hardly converge as they do in cases of consent to sexual contact or to a medical operation. In these cases of staged larceny, the would-be thief intends to steal the goods; the victim lets him do it in order to catch him in the act. It is very odd to call this a form of consent. Would one say that a woman consents to battery or to rape if she walks in Central Park in order to lure a suspected rapist into attacking her? Would one say that a homeowner consents to burglary if he suspects that burglars are casing his home and, in order to trap them, he lets his newspapers pile up and leaves his lights off at night until the suspects break in? It would be counter-intuitive to treat these two cases as a matter of consent. Accordingly, one can only wonder why it might strike the Wisconsin judges as "consent" to have four barrels of meat left on a loading platform to see whether a suspect would attempt to steal them.[54]

Perhaps it is not actual consent that the court has in mind, but apparent consent. The facts of *Topolewski* suggest the appearance of an ordinary commercial transaction; and this, one might say, is a form of apparent consent. But Topolewski was not deceived by

[53] The issue of "trespass" is the refrain of the opinion. See *id.* at 250, 252, 254, 255, 256, 109 N.W. at 1039, 1040, 1041.

[54] There is the additional problem whether consent should constitute a defense if the defendant is unaware of the intended victim's desires; see §7.4.1 *infra.*

appearances; he thought he was stealing the barrels. Apparent consent makes sense of a defense only so far as it negates the actor's culpability in acting as he does.[55] But Topolewski was unequivocally culpable in executing his plans to get the barrels. Indeed the thrust of the court's argument is not that the circumstances of the taking excused Topolewski, but that they precluded the finding of the requisite criminal act.

A German case supports the conclusion that "consent" is not a suitable rationale for acquittal in cases of staged larceny. In a case that came before the German Supreme Court in 1953,[56] a policewoman, apparently dressed in plain clothes, left her purse exposed in an effort to trap a suspected thief. The suspect took it and was convicted of larceny. The Supreme Court reversed the conviction, yet it rejected "consent" as the appropriate rationale on the ground that the suspect "knew nothing" of the alleged consent and "assumed under the circumstances that his act was consummated larceny."[57] The same reasoning should commend itself to common-law judges who might consider consent as the appropriate ground for reversal in cases like *Topolewski*.[58]

The discussion of "delivery" in the Court's opinion adds little to the argument of consent.[59] Both concepts are deployed in an effort to assimilate this case to one in which there is a fully voluntary transfer of possession. The Court recognized that there was no actual delivery, for it used such phrases as conduct "practically amounting to a delivery"[60] and a delivery "in practical effect."[61]

[55] The claim of apparent consent is analogous to a claim of putative self-defense: the defendant reasonably thinks he is being attacked when he is not. That this is properly analyzed as an excuse bearing on culpability, see §10.1.2 *infra*.

[56] Judgment of April 30, 1953, 4 BGHSt. 199.

[57] *Id.* at 200.

[58] The German case, *supra* note 56, held that a charge of attempted larceny would be appropriate on the facts. The problem with regard to charges of attempt in cases like *Topolewski* is whether the impossibility of consummating the offense precludes a conviction for attempt. For a detailed discussion of this problem, see §3.3.3 *infra*.

[59] The concept of delivery is introduced in the discussion of Regina v. Lawrance, 4 Cox Crim. Cas. 440 (1850), which is cited as a case illustrating the line between consent and non-consent; see 130 Wis. at 251, 109 N.W. at 1039.

[60] 130 Wis. at 251, 109 N.W. at 1039.

[61] *Id.* at 256, 109 N.W. at 1041.

The rhetorical effect was to confer an image on this transaction that rendered it parallel to a case in which voluntary delivery actually transfers possession to the recipient.

An independent line of argument was that Dolan and the company manager had unduly facilitated the theft and therefore they—instead of the defendant—had done "some act in the transaction essential to the offense."[62] This language evokes association with a well established rationale for denying criminal liability in burglary cases. Suppose one night Dolan, the would-be accomplice, had met Topolewski outside the plant in pursuit of a plan to obtain the barrels by burglary. While the latter kept watch, Dolan climbed through a window, which he and the manager had arranged to leave open. It is well recognized that the pseudo-burglary by Dolan could not be imputed to Topolewski.[63] In speaking of the owner's doing the act "essential to the crime," the Court apparently sought to assimilate *Topolewski* to this type of case. Yet the meaning of "essential act" is different in the staging at the company's loading dock. Neither Dolan nor the company manager committed the trespass, as the would-be accomplice performed the act of breaking-and-entering by climbing through the window.

What the Wisconsin court had in mind was that the "design to trap a criminal" went too far, because the company's facilitation prevented the "taking of the property from being characterized by an element of trespass."[64] The reference to "essential acts" helps us little in understanding why the "design . . . went a little too far." The "essential act" wanting is the trespass, and "trespass" in the context of larceny is not an act in the ordinary sense. It is a quality or an attribute of taking property. The difference between a trespass and a mere taking lies in the manner of acquisition. As we shall argue more fully in the next section, a trespass has to invoke associations with the ancient form of taking *vi et armis*. A taking that appeared to be in the ordinary course of business would lack the required tinge of force and thus not be trespassory.

[62] *Id.* at 254, 109 N.W. 1040.

[63] See State v. Hayes, 105 Mo. 76, 16 S.W. 514 (1891) (burglary conviction reversed when the feigned accomplice was the only party to enter the building).

[64] 130 Wis. at 254, 109 N.W. 1040.

This view of the requirement of a trespassory taking would lead to an acquittal in other cases in which the suspect receives the goods under conditions of apparent normalcy. A good example is the problem of mistaken delivery in which the bank teller remits too much money and the depositor knows of the mistake when he receives the excess cash.[65] Our analysis of *Topolewski* would suggest that this receipt would not be trespassory. So far as trespass is an indispensable element of the offense, the law of larceny should not apply to the dishonest receipt by the depositor.

The underlying claims of *Topolewski* have far-reaching implications for restricting the scope of larceny. And yet still wanting is an account of why the intangible quality of "trespass" should be so important in the crime of larceny. Does it relate to any interests protected by the crime? Does it further any of the policies of the criminal law? The fact is that the requirement of "trespass" leads to acquittal in cases of obviously dangerous people threatening interests generally protected in the criminal law. Accounting for this baffling element of trespass and for results like *Topolewski* is a task for any general theory of common-law larceny.

§2.2. *A Theory for Resolving the Enigmas of the Common Law.*

There are several items of data that press for an explanation. First, we should want to know why there is so much similarity among Western legal systems in their structuring of theft offenses, particularly when the Western concept of larceny diverges so radically from the earlier systems found in Rome and the Ancient Middle East. The leading Western legal systems (and perhaps all) concur that larceny may be committed only against someone in posses-

[65] This is the problem posed in The Queen v. Middleton, L.R. 2 Cr. Cas. Res. 38 (1873). The outcome of the case was at odds with *Topolewski*. See §1.2.3 *supra;* §2.4.2 *infra*.

sion of the chattel.[1] This requirement is absent in Roman and Biblical discussions of larceny.[2] Further, the same contemporary legal systems concur in limiting larceny to cases in which the taker intends to deprive the owner permanently of his property.[3] *Furtum usus*—or taking for temporary use—was included within the Roman conception of larceny.[4] Yet it is implicitly rejected in the modern requirement of an intent permanently to deprive the owner of his property. There is indeed something strange about the convergence of modern legal systems in counter-distinction to the practice of the ancients. It is almost as though some time in the Middle Ages, the older conception of larceny died out and a totally new one was born.

The second set of data that concerns us is the set of puzzles in the common law that we examined in the preceding section. All of these puzzles are shared by or at least are consistent with French, German and Russian law. All of these foreign systems face the problem of defining the boundaries of possessorial immunity. None of them has had a precedent with the influence of the Carrier's Case. Nonetheless, the famous case of the carrier's "breaking bulk" is compatible, I shall argue, with the general theory underlying all Western legal systems. The problem of staged larceny has arisen in the case law of Germany and has similarly resulted in reversing a conviction for larceny.[5] Therefore, in proposing a theory to account for these enigmas of the common law, we are in fact doing more. The theory provides a basis for understanding the historical core of a common Western theory of larceny.[6]

The thesis is that the common law of larceny—as well as other

§2.2. [1] See Lambert 214–15 (French law); Schönke-Schröder-Eser §242, notes 14–26a, at 1401–04 (German law); Kurs (SP 1973) at 429 (Soviet law).

[2] See B. Cohen, Jewish and Roman Law: A Comparative Study 409–32 (1966); H. Jolowicz & B. Nicholas, Historical Introduction to the Study of Roman Law 169 n.2 (1972); Exodus 22:7.

[3] See §1.1, at notes 5, 16 *supra;* A. Eser, Strafrecht IV, at 44-45 (1976).

[4] T. Mommsen, Römisches Strafrecht 735 nn.2, 3 (1899).

[5] See §2.2, text at note 56 *infra.*

[6] Yet the theory does not overcome the divergence between German and Anglo-American law on the interests protected by the law of larceny. See §1.3.3 *supra.*

Western conceptions of the crime—derives in a continuous line of development from the ancient crime of *furtum manifestum.* Not only has there been no break in the historical development of the crime, but the line of development runs to the earliest periods of legal consciousness. The important point implicit in this thesis is that only *furtum manifestum* survives in the modern evolution of larceny. *Furtum nec manifestum* never became a public offense. The distinction between the two branches of larceny, it will be recalled, is between the case of the thief caught in the act (*manifestum*) and that of the person found in possession of stolen goods. The former was subject to immediate execution; the latter to a judgment, after trial, to pay multiple damages.[7]

The distinction between these two branches of larceny is one of the primordial organizing principles of Indo-European legal thought.[8] The principle that manifest thieves are subject to private execution is found in ancient Hindu and Greek law as well as in the more familiar Roman and Jewish systems.[9] The transition from the earlier to the modern European systems of larceny was shaped by the gradual domestication of this private right of execution. The private killing of the nighttime thief caught in the act gradually became the process of trial and punishment that we know today.[10] One of the early steps in this development was the qualification of private execution by the preliminary duty of the outcry.[11] The function of the outcry was to communicate the impending execution to the rest of the community; it provided assurance that the slayer was not going to be treated as a criminal.[12] In Roman law,

[7] See generally §1.3.1 *supra.*

[8] See Watkins, *Studies in Indo-European Legal Language, Institutions, and Mythology,* in Indo-European and Indo-Europeans 321, 338 (G. Cardono et al. ed. 1970).

[9] *Id.* at 342–45. *Cf.* Plato, The Laws ¶874 ("He that slays a thief entering the house by night with intent of robbery shall be guiltless").

[10] In later Roman law, the penalty for *furtum manifestum* was mitigated by the praetor's edict to fourfold damages. See 3 Gaius, Institutes ¶189, 1 F. de Zulueta, The Institutes of Gaius 217 (1946).

[11] Watkins, *supra* note 8, at 339–40; Pugsley, *Furtum in the XII Tables,* 4 Ir. Jurist (N.S.) 139, 151 (1969). *Cf.* the early common-law institution of the "hue and cry," 3 Coke 116–18.

[12] H. Jolowicz & B. Nicholas *supra* note 2, at 169 n.9 (distinguishing between

the institution of the outcry functioned to broaden the concept of *fur manifestus* to include daytime thieves who offered resistance.[13]

Medieval English common law carried forth the concept of the *fur manifestus,* but with gradual recognition that a trial had to precede execution.[14] By the time of the thirteenth century the right of private execution had become a public right of execution after a summary trial in the field.[15] It is doubtful that in medieval English law, the legitimate slaying of thieves went beyond the limited cases of necessary defense.[16]

The important corollary of the thesis is that only *furtum manifestum* found its way into the modern law of larceny. The body of law supporting the levying of multiple damages against persons found in possession of stolen goods died with the legal systems of which it was a part. This explains why *furtum usus*—or larceny for temporary use—never became punishable in European legal systems. This was a form of larceny compensable as a delict in Roman law and not considered as a form of behavior that warranted criminal punishment. As larceny became synonymous with capital execution ordered by the courts, the rules and forms associated with delictual recovery were left behind.

The general law of *furtum manifestum,* shared by all early legal systems, found its primary expression in two characteristics. First, the law invested extraordinary interest in the significance of enclosures and boundaries. It was critical that the thief take from an enclosure. The Bible refers to the thief as one "digging under."[17] According to Gaius, the better view of Roman law is that the thief actually had to be caught inside the enclosure to be subject to exe-

---

two distinct functions of the outcry: (1) a call to neighbors to witness the act, and (2) a declaration that the defender was prepared to justify his act).

[13] Table VIII, §13, in 2 Ancient Roman Statutes 11 (A. Johnson et al. ed. 1961).

[14] Note Bracton's broadening of the concept of the manifest thief and the corresponding restriction on the justifiable slaying of thieves, *supra* §1.3.1 at notes 16–20.

[15] See 1 Britton, On the Laws of England 56 (F. Nichols trans. 1865 ed.)

[16] Compare the Anglo-Saxon sources that recognized a right to slay thieves who attempted to escape. 2 Aethelstan 1.2; The Laws of the Earliest English Kings 127 (F. Attenborough trans. & ed.); Ine 12, *id.* at 41.

[17] Exodus 22:1.

cution[18] or the later surrogate of fourfold damages.[19] This significance of enclosures emerges as well in ritualized searches of well-defined places which, as described both in the Bible and in Roman law, functioned as the equivalent to a trial on guilt or innocence. According to Roman law, if the goods were found after the ritual of a search *cum lance et licio*, the owner of the place was taken to be equivalent to a *fur manifestus*.[20]

The second feature of the law of *furtum manifestum* is that a characteristic form of conduct came to be associated with the act of thieving. Thieves could be seen thieving; they could be caught in the act. This feature was implicit in the institution of private execution. There could be no private killing with impunity if there were doubts in the community whether the slain man was a thief. If there was not to be a blood feud, the facts on which the slayer relied to vindicate the deed had to be highly public—either visible to others or readily invoked. That the thief was slain in another's enclosure was doubtless important, but it seems also to have been critical that people could readily agree on when persons breaking the close were acting like thieves. A system of private execution is not one that can tolerate mistakes.[21]

If there was a characteristic form of thieving, what was it? There is no doubt that the dominant motif was furtive or stealthful conduct, as the etymology of these adjectives suggests.[22] Yet the image of furtive conduct was blended in some cases with an ele-

[18] See 3 Gaius, *supra* note 10, at ¶184. *Cf.* Watkins, *supra* note 8, at 338.

[19] See 3 Gaius, *supra* note 10, at ¶189.

[20] Watkins, *supra* note 8, at 336; 3 Gaius, *supra* note 10, at ¶186–187 (discussing *furtum conceptum* for cases in which the object is found on the thief's premises and the injection of new action called *actio furti oblati* when the owner of the premises is not actually the thief). See D. Daube, Studies in Biblical Law 264–65 (1947).

[21] Gaius insisted that *furtum manifestum* was a natural fact, not subject to legislative modification: " [S]tatute can no more turn a thief who is not manifest into a manifest thief than it can turn into a thief one who is not a thief at all, or into an adulterer or homicide one who is neither the one nor the other." 3 Gaius, *supra* note 10, at ¶194.

[22] The word "furtive" derives from "*fur*," meaning "thief" in Latin, 4 Oxford English Dictionary 620 (1933). The word "stealth" derives from the same root as "steal." 10 *id.* at 884, 887.

ment of force. Larceny at common law presupposed a trespass, and trespasses were done *vi et armis*. In most legal systems, however, forcible takings from the person eventually crystallized as the separate offense of *rapina*,[23] *Raub*,[24] or robbery.[25] Yet forcible seizures in the absence of the owner continued to be seen as part of the compositive image of manifest thievery. In referring henceforth to the principle of manifest criminality, we shall have in mind this prototypical case of the thief caught *in flagrante delicto*.

To summarize, the two critical features of *furtum manifestum* were that, first, the thief had to tread on a significant boundary and enter a forbidden area; and, secondly, that the act of thieving had to manifest a form of behavior that could readily be identified as thieving. It was not essential to the crime that the thieving occur at night, as the development in Roman law itself indicates. The thesis is that these two elements underlay, shaped and guided the common law of larceny. Now we shall demonstrate the explanatory power of the thesis by seeking to account for the three enigmas of the case law.

§2.2.1. **Possessorial Immunity.** The emergence of possessorial immunity in Western legal thought may be interpreted as a continuation of the early legal preoccupation with boundaries and the crossing of boundaries in committing larceny. The Western law

[23] According to the law of the Twelve Tables, the concept of *furtum* apparently included larceny coupled with violence. See T. Mommsen, *supra* note 4, at 737 n.6. Gaius notes that the praetor introduced a new action for fourfold damages against those who rob—i.e., commit theft by violence. See 3 Gaius, *supra* note 10, at ¶209.

[24] Prior to the Constitutio Criminalis Carolina §157 (1532) the major distinction in the German law of theft was between a secret taking and an open taking; *Raub* was the latter. R. Eckardt, Controversen in der Lehre vom Diebstahl 35 (1899). After the Carolina, *Raub* stood for the offense of taking from a person with force or the threat of force. See K. Dickel, Der Tatbestand des Diebstahls nach deutschem Recht (1877). StGB §249.

[25] In the early common law, robbery was an open taking; theft, a secret taking. See F. Pollock & F. Maitland, History of English Law 494 (1911). By the time of Coke, the felony had received its present definition. See 3 Coke 68–69. The distinction between secret and open theft is retained in the current codes in the Soviet Union. Ugol. kod. (RSFSR) §144 (defining *krasha* as the "secret taking of the personal property of another"); *id.* §145 (defining *grabjesh* as the "open taking of personal property of another"); *id.* §146 (Soviet analogue to robbery).

of larceny expanded beyond the original notions of taking from an enclosure so as to include takings directly from the person. Yet the principle of breaking a boundary survived in the rule that the actor had to break possession or take out of the possession of the victim. It followed that if the actor were already inside the magic boundary—if he already had possession—he could not commit the offense. There are, no doubt, other explanations of the rule of possessorial immunity; and we have already alluded to several.[26] Yet there is doubtless appeal to the structural similarity between the boundaries of the earlier law and the boundaries of modern Western law. In both sets of legal rules, the thief must cross a significant perimeter that sets the victim off from the rest of the world.[27]

The requirement of taking from possession is also closely tied to the principle of manifest criminality. Those who take from possession, and "break possession" in the German phrase, tend to look much more like thieves in the act. This connection between possession and the rule of manifest criminality sheds new light on the problem of drawing the contours of possession and restricting the scope of possessorial immunity.

The principle of manifest criminality supported the expansion of the law to include all acts of taking that conformed to the shared paradigms of stealthful and forcible taking. A guest sneaking out with his host's dining utensils looked as much like a thief as any then punished. So, too, the customer that runs from the store with the shopkeeper chasing after him. And the servant who made off with his master's tools might typically have conformed to the same shared image of stealing. In other situations, the user's scope of control was so widely defined that his conversion and personal use did not appear to be the slightest bit suspect. If someone hired a horse, he could ride it and use it in a wide variety of ways without coming under suspicion. Even his selling would be suspect only if we should assume general knowledge of his status as a temporary possessor. Of course, this general approach of asking

[26] See §2.1.1 *supra*.

[27] Watkins considers perimeters or enclosures to have been a structural form in the prototypical Indo-European form of larceny. See Watkins, *supra* note 8, at 336.

whether conduct is manifestly criminal requires a stipulation about the knowledge attributable to ideal observers. If everything is known about a person selling someone else's horse at market, then of course his conduct is manifestly criminal. In most cases the question of suspiciousness and manifest criminality turns on the conventional acceptability of the behavior under the circumstances. In the clear cases, we can readily perceive particular forms of conduct as suspicious and others less so. The concept of possession and the rule of possessorial immunity were adjusted in the course of history so as to fit only those cases in which the taking was relatively ambiguous. Possession was curtailed and immunity denied in those cases in which the taking typically conformed to the shared image of thieving.

This theory, it should be noted, does not explain all the cases in which the courts agonized about possession and custody. It does not explain the cleavage between cases in which servants received goods from their masters and those in which they received them from third parties.[28] For this distinction, we need to turn to other principles already discussed.[29] Despite the limits on the thesis, the influence of manifest criminality in drawing the contours of possession is sufficiently strong to make the rules of possession coherent and to help us sense the inner dynamic of the development of the common-law rules.

§2.2.2. **Carrier's Case.** The thesis that larceny should encompass all, and only manifestly criminal cases of thieving provides a powerful tool for interpreting the Carrier's Case and the stable rule that emerged from the case that "breaking bulk" provided an exception to possessorial immunity. It is here that we find the principle of manifest criminality most clearly at work. One characteristic of the thief is his taking swiftly and violently. That aspect of thieving is captured in the moment of breaking of the bales; the judges were less likely to sense thievery in the acts of selling or giving away the bales. Consequently, these other forms of misappropriation remained within the protection of possessorial im-

[28] See §1.2.4 *supra.*
[29] *Ibid.*

munity.[30] Further, the entry into the bales constituted the crossing of a prohibited line and thus invoked associations with breaking into a protected enclosure. This feature of the crime is expressed in the seemingly technical argument that the carrier received possession over the bales but not over their contents.[31]

It is significant that in the opinions expressed by the judges in the Carrier's Case, we find an explicit reference to the principle of manifest criminality. In the reported words of Nedeham:[32]

> [I]t has been held that a man can take his own goods feloniously. For instance, if I give goods to a man to take care of, and I come *secretly like a felon* because I want to recover damages against him by writ of detinue, and I take the goods *secretly like a felon,* it is felony.

The critical factor in this example is the manner of taking, and in the case of the carrier who broke bulk it is the same. In the former situation, the taking is secret; in the latter, forcible. But in both cases the taking conforms to the shared image of furtive behavior.

The significance of the Carrier's Case is that it was received into the tradition as holding that manifest criminality should prevail over the principle of possessorial immunity. The shared image of the thief proved to be more influential than the practice of exempting the conduct of bailees from the law of larceny.[33] This suggests that indeed the principle of possessorial immunity was subsidiary, and that the controlling vision of the courts was that all manifest thieves should be brought within the scope of the offense.

In this discussion we have attempted to demonstrate the expansive effect of the principle of manifest criminality. The judges interpreted the principles of possessorial immunity so as to encompass manifest thieves, and the principle of "breaking bulk" prevailed as another rubric for punishing those whose taking

[30] See §2.1, at note 34 *supra.*

[31] 64 Selden Soc. at 32 (opinion by Chokke).

[32] 64 Selden Soc. at 33 (emphasis added).

[33] Blackstone was apparently the first commentator to explicate the rule of "breaking bulk" as an instance of manifest criminality. See 4 Blackstone 230.

peaked in a moment of stealth or force. To avoid misunderstanding, we should note that there is no connection between the principle of manifest criminality and what is often called strict liability. *Animus furandi* has always been an independent dimension of liability—at least as long as the courts rather than private parties have administered the law of larceny. Yet is is important to understand how the notion of *animus* functioned in the law of larceny prior to the end of the eighteenth century, for its status in the structure of the common-law crime differs markedly from the place of intent in contemporary criminal theory.

The purpose of raising an issue of *animus* was to challenge the authenticity of appearances. Someone who looked like a thief in the act of taking might not have been one in fact. In the ordinary case the issue of *animus* did not have to be litigated, for someone who looked like he was thieving typically was doing just that. Thus there was a close evidentiary tie between the requirement of manifest thievery and the proof of *animus furandi.*[34] Yet it is misleading to think of manifest thievery as a presumption for establishing criminal intent. If it were merely a rule of evidence, the absence of manifest thieving could be remedied by the equally persuasive evidence of intent—such as an admission or a confession. The requirement of manifest larceny was an independent substantive requirement. If it could not be established, there was no point in inquiring further about the actor's intent.

The link between manifest larceny and *animus furandi* was conceptual as well as evidentiary. The issue of intent in larceny was not thought of separately from the manifestation of that intent in the external world.[35] The problem was not how the judges

[34] *Cf.* Blackstone's linking the two concepts. *Ibid.*

[35] The one exception to this generalization appears to be the set of cases in which the defendant fraudulently invoked the legal process in order to acquire the victim's goods. These were called cases of larceny *in fraudem legis.* See 3 Coke 108; 1 Hale 507. The leading case is Farre's Case, reportedly tried at Old Bailey in April 1665. See 84 Eng. Rep. 1074 (1665). According to the facts found at trial, Farre and his mistress Chadwick fraudulently brought a writ of ejectment against Mrs. Stanyer (Steneer). Having had her ejected and arrested, they then rifled her house, breaking open cupboards and trunks, and carried off a variety of valuable goods. The defendants were convicted of larceny and executed. One could interpret this

should prove intent, but whether appearances were a reliable guide to reality. The primary inquiry was the act of larceny, and only in extraordinary cases might there have been a dispute about whether someone who acted like a thief had the "spirit" or *animus* of a thief. Thus the law was structured so as to render intent a subsidiary issue. It was a basis for defeating the implications of the primary element of acting manifestly like a thief.

§2.2.3. **Staged Larceny.** The place of manifest criminality in the common law of larceny meant that if there were no manifest act of thieving, there could be no conviction. The taking was not manifestly criminal if it appeared to be a routine business transaction, in which all parties participated voluntarily in the transfer of goods. This is the perspective from which we should seek to understand the puzzling exemption from liability in *Topolewski* and other cases of staged larceny.[36] We have already noted that the doctrinal gambits of "consent" and "delivery" do not adequately account for the disposition to acquit in these cases.[37] The appropriate way to interpret these doctrines is that they approximate the central intuition that a taking should be criminal only if it bears the mark of a forcible or stealthful act of thieving. Routine business transactions, deliveries and takings by consent do not bear this imprint of larceny, and therefore it is effective rhetoric to assimilate the cases of staged larceny to these other situations that lack the features of manifest thievery.

The concept of "trespass" is well suited to expressing the element of manifest thievery. This function of trespassory taking is demonstrated by the Wisconsin Supreme Court's analysis of cases of staged larceny in which they would be willing to convict. A

---

case as one of manifest thievery, with a subsidiary question whether the defendants could rely on a fraudulently acquired writ of ejectment as a defense. On this view the issue of fraud served to deprive the defendants of a defense, not to ground a conviction. However, in cases of burglary, fraudulently acquired entries are called *in fraudem legis* and treated as the equivalent of a forcible entry. See Le Mott's Case, 84 Eng. Rep. 1073 (1665); 3 Coke 64 (proposing a hypothetical case of fraudulently inducing a constable to open someone else's door).

[36] See generally §2.1.3 *supra.*

[37] See text §2.1.3 at notes 54–64 *supra.*

prominent example is The King v. Egginton,[38] where a servant, a putative accomplice, let a band of thieves into his master's house. He stood by as the thieves broke into a large desk and took silver ingots. Though the servant was acting under his master's instructions and though the thieves could not have reached the ingots without the servant's aid, a majority of judges perceived the taking to be trespassory. The Wisconsin Supreme Court endorsed this decision as an illustration of the "trespass" that was missing in *Topolewski.*[39] The labels used to express the difference between the two cases are that in *Egginton* there was no consent and no delivery, but in *Topolewski* there was. These terms are best seen as expressing the perception that in *Egginton,* the servant's participation did not undercut the manifestation of thievery.[40] In *Topolewski,* however, the dissembled cooperation converted the taking into one that appeared to be in the ordinary course of business and that was enough to warrant the conclusion that the barrels were "delivered" to the defendant.

If this account of acquittal in cases of staged larceny demonstrates the explanatory value of our hypothesis, it also raises some serious problems. The scope of these problems can be seen by examinating a variation of the facts in *Topolewski.* Suppose that Dolan and Topolewski had conspired to steal the barrels of meat and the taking of the barrels that transpired precisely as it did. The appearance of criminality would have been exactly the same, yet without the element of staging there is no doubt that both Topolewski and Dolan would have been found guilty. If that is true, we can hardly maintain that a manifestly criminal act is an essential condition for committing larceny. It is best to concede that this hypothetical case of a conspiracy between the insider Dolan and the

[38] 168 Eng. Rep. 555 (1801).

[39] 130 Wis. at 251–52; 109 N.W. at 1039–40.

[40] The critical fact in *Egginton* was apparently that the servant merely stood by and let the thieves carry out their plan. *Cf.* Rex v. Turvey, [1946] 2 All E.R. 60 (Crim. App.); Regina v. Lawrance, 4 Cox Crim. Cas. 440, 442 (1850) (directing acquittal if the servant handed the would-be thief a deed, but suggesting that conviction would be permissible if the servant laid the deed down).

outsider Topolewski is a genuine counter-example to our thesis.[41] It demonstrates that the principle of manifest criminality cannot account for all variations of larceny.

Once we recognize this counter-example, we can think of others. Suppose someone contrives a manner of taking that appears to be totally innocent. Indeed this ingenuity is reflected in the common technique of daytime burglars who don the disguise of furniture movers. What distinguishes these counter-examples from *Topolewski* is that in the egregious cases of staged larceny, the owner participates in the image of an innocent taking. This is the point the court was trying to capture in its discussion of the owner's having facilitated the trespass.

§2.2.4. The Rationale of Manifest Criminality. The counter-examples of the Dolan-Topolewski conspiracy and the disguised burglars are embarrassing to the requirement of manifest criminality. It would be irrational to acquit in these cases—and thus we receive our first indication of the law's need to expand and to adopt alternative theories of liability. Yet before we abandon the principle of manifest criminality and turn to the emergence of subjective criminality in the nineteenth century, we should seek to appreciate the inner logic of manifest criminality. As we shall see in Chapter Three, manifest criminality continues to inform the law in a range of offenses, including burglary, criminal attempts and possession offenses.

The principle of manifest criminality embodies a way of thinking about liability that many theorists have since identified as characteristic of legal thought. The mode of thought requires a two-stage progression in the analysis of liability. The first stage consists of objective facts; and the second, of subjective criteria related to the actor.[42] Further, the external facts are typically in-

[41] This concession is preferable to the strained argument in Fletcher, *The Metamorphosis of Larceny*, 89 Harv. L. Rev. 469, 497–98 (1976). There is little value in diluting manifest criminality to the point that "the thought . . . of falling prey to thieves" supplies the element of public apprehension characteristic of manifest criminality. *Id.* at 497.

[42] Thus many theorists have argued that in contrast to moral principles, the law is based on external and objective facts. See, e.g., R. Stammler, The Theory of Justice

criminating; and the subjective facts, exculpatory. The case for liability moves from the objective to the subjective, the external to the internal, the act to the actor. This way of thinking is deeply embedded in the law. It shapes not only the pattern of manifest criminality, but also the third pattern of harmful consequences, most notably in the law of homicide.[43] The one pattern from which it is absent is the subjective theory of liability that arose in the nineteenth century. This pattern of liability took the actor's intent to be the central question in assessing liability and thus dispensed with the preliminary finding of public, incriminating facts.

The value implicitly protected in the pattern of manifest criminality is the privacy of criminal suspects. Judges may not inquire about the accused's mental state, self-control and culpability unless they find preliminarily that the accused's conduct meets an objective standard of liability. The objective standard is the manifestly criminal act. The Carrier's intent was irrelevant unless his breaking open the bales constituted an act sufficient for common-law larceny. Topolewski's intent was irrelevant unless his taking the barrels satisfied the objective standards of a trespass in the taking.

The principle of manifest criminality gave full expression to the maxim that no one should be punished for thoughts alone. Thoughts, intents, beliefs—none of these subjective elements can incriminate a suspect unless his conduct meets an objective standard of manifest criminality. The argument is not that the principle of manifest criminality crystallized for the sake of protecting privacy. Rather, as Friedrich von Hayek would express it, the protection of privacy was the "result of human action, but not of human design."[44] It was an incidental benefit of the court's carrying forward criteria of criminality that originated in the private slaying of manifest thieves. Though this pattern of liability might not cover all cases of larceny that ought to be punished, it expresses an at-

---

41 (Husik transl. 1925); H. Kantorowicz, The Definition of Law 43 (1958); Holmes 50. This thesis is modified in the text to hold that the first stage of legal analysis is based on objective, external facts.

[43] See §5.3 *infra*.

[44] F. von Hayek, Studies in Philosophy, Politics and Economics 96–105 (1967).

tractive, minimalist theory of criminality that repeatedly asserts itself in larceny and in other offenses.

§2.3. *The Metamorphosis of Larceny.*

The total transformation of larceny was an integrated social and legal process, in which the courts, Parliament and the scholarly community all played a significant part. The courts expanded the law of larceny by interpreting the law of larceny to encompass the first three problematic cases discussed in §1.2. The scholarly community provided the intellectual foundation for the metamorphosis by reinterpreting the common-law tradition in order to support the new conception of larceny. Parliament played its part by deferring to the courts and the scholars and, finally, by incorporating the judicial developments in a statutory definition of larceny.

The relevant historical periods divide roughly into the period from the late eighteenth to the mid-nineteenth century and from the latter date to the present. The first period was marked by qualified steps in the case law and, more importantly, by the scholars' laying the foundation for the judicial expansion of the law in the second half of the century. In the course of the twentieth century, the initiative in developing the law of larceny has passed gradually from the courts to the legislature. In this section we review the developments of the late eighteenth and early nineteenth centuries—a period that is of significance for the intellectual history of the common law as well as for the metamorphosis of larceny.

§2.3.1. **The King v. Pear.**[1] The famous conviction of Pear, who hired a horse and then sold it, proved to be an important transitional development. It nudged the law of larceny in a new direction; more importantly, it provided modern grist for the scholarly mills churning the law of larceny into new forms. Nomi-

§2.3. [1] 168 Eng. Rep. 208 (1779).

nally, the case was no more important than other horse-stealing cases of the late eighteenth century. Yet in the course of the history, *Pear's Case* came to be canonized as the source of a new form of larceny, which in this century has garnered the title: "larceny by trick."[2] There is still disagreement about the case, and therefore it is worth a close examination. Eventually we shall see how the reinterpretation of *Pear* became one of the scholarly endeavors of the early nineteenth century.

The prosecution of Pear posed a recurrent eighteenth-century phenomenon of horse theft. Pear had hired a horse from one Finch and said he was going to ride to Surrey; in fact he rode to Smithfield and sold the horse. It appeared also that he lied about his residence. In Pear's trial for larceny the barrier to conviction was that he had acquired the horse by delivery from Finch, and thus presumably he had acquired possession. There was no "breaking of bulk" and therefore the case did not come under the limited exception of the Carrier's Case.[3]

The problem was an old one: Is an intent to steal sufficient to override the immunity provided by acquiring possession? The traditional answer, as we have seen, was always negative.[4] Yet the factual pattern represented by *Pear* and similar horse-stealing cases was an appealing one for moving the law in a new direction. When someone who borrows or leases a horse rides off with it, there is no single moment of time in which the actor's dishonesty peaks in a recognizable point of manifest thievery. Yet in the facts

[2] The origin of this expression is obscure. Hall uses it, see J. Hall, Theft, Law and Society 40 (2d ed. 1952), but it is not to be found in earlier studies of *Pear's Case*. See Beale, *Borderland of Larceny*, 6 Harv. L. Rev. 244 (1892); 2 J. Bishop, Criminal Law 451–52 (6th ed. 1877). The term is used in other legal systems, but without the specific technical meaning acquired in English.

[3] See §2.1.2 *supra*. In some cases, a conviction could be justified if the lessor and lessee agreed in advance about the number of hours or miles the horse was to be ridden. The leading example is the conviction of John Tunnard at Old Bailey in 1729. Tunnard borrowed a horse to ride three miles, but rode to London and sold it. He was convicted. The reported rationale was that after he exceeded the agreed-upon limit, his privity lapsed and his taking was felony. That theory did not apply in *Pear*, for Pear sold the horse on the same day and apparently did not breach any well-defined limit as to time or distance. See 168 Eng. Rep. at 209, note (a).

[4] See §2.1.1 *supra*.

of *Pear* itself there were other objective data, such as his lie and his subsequent selling of the horse, which revealed a course of conduct that only a thief would undertake. Why, then, should one insist on so narrow a view of what it is to act like a thief?

Presumably influenced by reasoning of this sort, Justice Ashhurst instructed the jury that if Pear had the intention of selling the horse at the time he mounted it and rode off, he was guilty of larceny,[5] but if he formed the intent later he was not guilty.[6] Pear's subsequent conviction generated controversy among the judges. They met several months later and the majority of them confirmed Ashhurst's instructions as sound. If Pear's intention was fraudulent at the outset,[7] they reasoned, he never acquired legal possession. Thus conversion of the horse (presumably at some moment on the ride to Smithfield or at the time of the sale) became equivalent to the taking and carrying away characteristic of common-law larceny.[8]

The interpretation of *Pear* has generated considerable controversy, largely because there are two published versions of the judges' opinion. The first report, published in 1789,[9] holds that the crime occurred at the time of the subsequent conversion, and not when Pear mounted and rode off. A second version of the opinion,

[5] 168 Eng. Rep. at 208.

[6] *Id.* at 209.

[7] It is important to distinguish between a "fraudulent intent" and *animus furandi.* The former, but not the latter, would be satisfied by an intent to take temporarily. But see State v. Coombs, 55 Me. 47 (1867) (interpreting the rule to require merely a fraudulent or tortious taking). On this view, the relevant moment for the *animus furandi* is the subsequent conversion, not the initial acquisition of the chattel.

[8] The requirement of a conversion has led to some acquittals and appellate reversals. See, e.g., Regina v. Brooks, 173 Eng. Rep. 501 (1837) (offering a hired horse for sale insufficient to constitute a conversion); Blackburn v. Commonwealth, 28 Ky. 96, 89 S.W. 160 (1905) (no conversion of hired horse and buggy if defendant pledged it with the intent to redeem it). The occurrence of the crime at the moment of conversion suggests that *Pear* stands for an offense more like embezzlement than larceny. Compare the solution in French and German law, §1.2.1 *supra.*

[9] This is the report of the case reprinted at 168 Eng. Rep. 208, initially published in 1 Leach 211 (1789 ed.). In 1787, prior to the publication of this volume, Leach reviewed several applications of *Pear* in his annotation to Hawkins. He con-

published in East, *Pleas of the Crown* in 1803,[10] has the judges saying that the crime occurs at the moment of riding off,[11] which presumably implied that no subsequent conversion was necessary.

It is important to see how these two versions of *Pear* affect the moment of criminality and the time at which the criminal suspect could be properly arrested. According to Leach's report in 1789, the function of Pear's fraudulent intent at the time of mounting the horse was merely to prevent the acquisition of possession. It followed that this intent need not have been the full *animus furandi* required for larceny. For example, if the rider merely intended to use the horse for several extra days without paying for the hire, his intent would be fraudulent and presumably prevent the acquisition of possession. If he later changed his mind and decided to appropriate the horse permanently to his own use, his appropriation would constitute the taking from possession that would trigger a conviction for larceny.[12] According to East's version of the case, the reference in *Pear* to a fraudulent intent at the time of mounting the horse meant the full *animus furandi* required for larceny. In our example of the dishonest rider who intends at first merely to keep the horse temporarily, there would be no liability; for the intent at the moment of initial acquisition would be insufficient, and the later intent to keep the horse would be irrelevant, the requisite taking having occurred at the time of mounting and riding off.

The difference between these two versions of *Pear* has an impact beyond this one illustrative case. The earlier version by Leach stood for a view of the crime that was at least partially compatible with the traditional conception of larceny as manifest thievery. The moment of thieving was displaced by the subsequent conversion

---

cluded that the case stood for the proposition that fraud at the time of the initial acquisition prevented transfer of possession and thus made the subsequent conversion felonious. See 1 W. Hawkins, Pleas of the Crown 135 n.1 (6th ed. T. Leach 1787).

[10] 2 East 685–89.

[11] The critical line attributed to the judges is "that in all these cases the intention was the thing chiefly regarded, and fraud supplied the place of force." *Id.* at 688.

[12] See note 7 *supra*.

and selling of the horse, which manifested the purpose of misappropriation. Viewed in this way, the extension of larceny was merely a judicial anticipation of the statutory crimes of embezzlement and larceny by a bailee.[13] In contrast to this minor readjustment of the traditional crime, East's version of the case is a radical innovation. If larceny can be committed at the moment of mounting and riding off with the horse, then a routine act such as a lessee's laying hands on a horse becomes criminal if at that moment the lessee is visited with the wrong kind of intention. This means that Pear could have been arrested as soon as he mounted the horse, particularly if he had confided to a police informant that he intended to steal the horse.

It is difficult to appreciate the original meaning of *Pear's Case*, for East's version of the opinion began a process of reinterpretation that distorts our understanding of the eighteenth-century background to the case. Many contemporary writers tend to rely on East and other nineteenth-century commentators and therefore misconceive the original significance of the decision.[14] Yet there is ample authority indicating that the original understanding of the case has not been totally lost.[15]

East's report of *Pear's Case* was one of several factors converging in the early nineteenth century and reflecting the consensus that the crime of larceny should be extended to encompass takings that appeared to be outwardly innocent. This movement to dispense with the principle of manifest criminality was the driving spirit of the metamorphosis of larceny. An essential feature of this movement was that a new interpretation of the common law be found that would support the extension of liability.

§2.3.2. Reinterpreting the Tradition. Every revolution brings

[13] Compare solutions in other legal systems, §1.2.1 *supra*.

[14] Perkins 246; L. Weinreb, Criminal Law: Cases, Comments, Questions 315 (2d ed. 1975); Packer 82–83; Pearce, *Theft by False Promises*, 101 U. Pa. L. Rev. 967, 970–71 (1953).

[15] LaFave & Scott 627; F. Pollack & R. Wright, An Essay on Possession in the Common Law 219 (1888); 3 Stephen 160; Scurlock, *The Element of Trespass in Larceny at Common Law and Under the Statutes*, 22 Temp. L.Q. 12, 21–22 (1948); Turner, *Middleton's Case and the Larceny Act* 1916, 7 Camb. L.J. 337, 339 (1941).

with it a rewriting of history, and the transformation of larceny into a new form of criminality is no exception. Not only did East generate a view of *Pear* that made the crime depend on the actor's intent in receiving the horse; other writers of the early nineteenth century began to reinterpret critical events in the evolution of common-law larceny. Using the conceptual lens of their time, they took another look at the older cases as well as the rules governing temporary takings and takings under color of right. Instead of a pattern of manifest criminality, what they found in the past was primarily an inquiry about felonious intent.

The reinterpretation of the exemption for temporary takings illustrates the new approach. The traditional writers concurred that in the common law, as distinguished from Roman law,[16] a temporary taking was not felonious. As Blackstone put it, "if a neighbor takes another's plow that is left in the field, and uses it upon his own land, and then returns it . . . [cases like this] are misdemeanors and trespasses but no felonies."[17] When Archbold returns to this hypothetical case in 1812, in the first edition of his influential manual on criminal evidence, it is apparent to him that the issue is not whether the goods are in fact returned, but whether at the time of the taking there was an intent to return.[18] The relevant act of returning, or not, is seen as evidence of the intent at the time of the antecedent event of taking.[19]

Another issue reinterpreted from the perspective of the actor's intent was the phenomenon of taking under color of right. As that doctrine developed in the common-law texts, the issue of color of

[16] See T. Mommsen, Römisches Strafrecht 735 nn.2, 3 (1899).

[17] 4 Blackstone 232.

[18] J. Archbold, A Summary of the Law Relating to Pleading and Evidence in Criminal Cases 119 (1822 ed.). This view is anticipated in 1 Hale 509 (selling a horse instead of returning it "is declarative of his first taking to be felonious").

[19] Focussing on the intent at the time of taking rather than the fact of the subsequent return generated the possibility of acquitting someone who had not, in fact, returned the thing taken. Several acquittals and reversals are recorded in cases in which the defendant took a horse and later abandoned it. See, e.g., Rex v. Crump, 171 Eng. Rep. 1357 (1825) (acquittal on charge of horse-stealing); Dove v. State, 37 Ark. 261 (1881); 2 East 662 (discussion of the *Phillips & Strong Case*, apparently decided in 1801); 2 W. Russell, Crimes and Misdemeanors 1037 (discussion of

right speaks to the problem of convicting someone whose taking is rendered ambiguous by a dispute between the parties arising from objective circumstances, such as "color of arrear of rent,"[20] that would raise in the mind of a third-party observer a question of who had the better title to the goods. Hale insists on a "pretense of title,"[21] and the examples he gives indicate uneasiness about prosecuting someone who takes goods "openly in the presence of the owner, or of other persons that are known to the owner."[22] The doctrine was one readily implied by the requirement of a manifestly criminal taking.[23]

When nineteenth-century writers begin to discuss the issue, they gravitate to the phrase, "claim of right," as an equivalent to "color of right."[24] Though the earlier writers of the century, like East, are careful to explain that by "claim of right" they mean a "fair pretense of property or right in the prisoner,"[25] the view slowly takes hold that any claim of right will prevent a conviction for larceny. Thus Chitty argues in 1816 that any claim of right will do, "however unfounded."[26] Later in the century one finds Bishop summing up the doctrine as one that would be available to the de-

---

Phillips & Strong); *cf.* People v. Brown, 105 Cal. 66, 38 P. 518 (1894) (defendant took bicycle in spat with playmate with intent to return it; conviction reversed). Yet as the case law developed, it became difficult for the defendant to avoid conviction in cases of abandonment. See State v. Davis, 38 N.J.L. 176 (1875); State v. Ward, 9 Nev. 297, 10 P. 133 (1886); *cf.* Rex v. Trebilcock, 7 Cox Crim. Cas. 408 (1858) (defendant impermissibly took an object and pawned it, allegedly with the intent to redeem and return it; conviction affirmed).

[20] 4 Blackstone 232.

[21] 1 Hale 509.

[22] *Ibid.*

[23] Yet in Hale's analysis, it is fair to say that doctrine was thought of as a basis for presuming an innocent intention, rather than a criterion of an objectively criminal act. Hale continues: ". . . yet this may be but a trick to colour a felony, and the ordinary discovery of a felonious intent is, if the party doth it secretly, or being charged with the goods denies it." *Ibid.*

[24] 2 J Bishop, *supra* note 2, at 474; H. Roscoe, A Digest of the Law of Evidence in Criminal Cases 537 (2d American ed. 1840). This is the phrase used in the Larceny Act 1916, 6 & 7 Geo. V, c. 50, §1(1).

[25] 2 East 659.

[26] 3 T. Chitty, A Practical Treatise on Criminal Law 920 (1816).

fendant, "however puerile or mistaken the claim may in fact be."[27] Yet framing the issue as a "claim" rather than "color" of right furthered the tendency to conceptualize the issues of larceny as subjective rather than objective. It brought the issue into the same medium of analysis as East's version of *Pear* and Archbold's theory of temporary takings.

The Carrier's Case became a focal point in the process of reinterpreting the common-law tradition. So far as Blackstone reflects the sentiment of his time, lawyers in the 1760s still found the case coherent and plausible.[28] This was no longer true in the early nineteenth century. Beginning primarily with East in 1803,[29] one finds two new readings of the case, both of which ignored the traditional understanding that breaking bulk was important because at that moment, as Blackstone put it, the "*animus furandi* is manifest."[30] One new interpretation of the case was that breaking bulk "determined" the bailment and thus caused the possession in the contents to spring back to the bailor.[31] This reading of the case reflected a preference for mystifying "breaking bulk" and thinking of the rule as an elaborate fiction. The theory that possession in the contents sprang back to the bailor had little to do with the traditional notions of determining a bailment according to the terms

[27] 2 J. Bishop, *supra* note 2, at 474. This formulation of the defense found its way into the case law in People v. Hillhouse, 80 Mich. 580, 45 N.W. 484 (1890). Compare the equally extreme but stylistically different statements of the rule in State v. Sawyer, 95 Conn. 34, 110 A. 461 (1920), and People v. Eastman, 77 Cal. 171, 19 P. 266 (1888).

[28] See §2.1.2 *supra*.

[29] 2 East 697.

[30] 4 Blackstone 230.

[31] See J. Archbold, *supra* note 18, at 124; 2 East 697; 2 W. Russell, *supra* note 19, at 1093; *First Report* at 7; *accord*, Commonwealth v. James, 18 Mass. (1 Pick.) 385 (1823); Regina v. Cornish, 169 Eng. Rep. 790 (1854). It was apparently East who devised this argument, supposedly on the authority of Hale's having argued that "the privity of contract is determined by the act of breaking the package. . . ." 2 East 697. In fact, Hale invoked the notion of possession's being "determined" exclusively to explain the distinct rule emerging from the Carrier's Case, that if the carrier carries the bales "to the place, and delivers or lays them down . . ." and then takes the bales, he is guilty of larceny. 1 Hale 505.

of the original agreement.[32] Yet there was no longer an effort to see the case as an expression of a plausible conception of larceny. Treating the case as one rooted in fiction was an important phase in the process leading to skepticism about the rule of breaking bulk and the eventual decision, in 1857, to extend larceny to all conversions by bailees.[33]

More important for our present purposes was the simultaneous tendency to read the Carrier's Case as a holding about intent at the time of initially acquiring the bales.[34] This view derived from Kelyng's argument,[35] antedating Blackstone, that "breaking bulk" was significant only as evidence of the intent at the time of receipt of the bales rather than as a manifestation of thievery at the moment of breaking. Though this view was ignored by Blackstone and later dismissed by Holmes as an argument that "hardly can be accepted,"[36] it reflected a view of larceny whose time, in the early nineteenth century, had clearly come. The view, generally, was that the manifestation of thievery or dishonesty should not be seen as the moment of criminality, but merely as evidence of a crime occurring earlier at the time of initial acquisition. This shift in emphasis from the later to the earlier event was the fuel that powered the engine of reinterpretation. It also affected the reasoning of *Pear* and analogous horse-stealing cases by making it seem more plausible that the crime occurred at the moment of initial taking.

The new preference for relating manifest thievery to an earlier moment of intending to steal found expression as well in a reinterpretation of Chisser's Case.[37] The plausible reading of *Chisser* is

[32] See note 54 *infra*.

[33] 20 & 21 Vict. c. 54.

[34] The leading advocates for this view were East and Russell. See 2 East 696–97; 2 W. Russell, *supra* note 19, at 1093.

[35] See Kelyng 82–83 (1789 ed.).

[36] Commonwealth v. Rubin, 165 Mass. 453, 455, 43 N.E. 200, 201 (1896). For earlier rejections of Kelyng's argument, see State v. Fairclough, 29 Conn. 47 (1860); First Report 7. The primary difficulty with Kelyng's view, as history, is that it fails to explain why taking the entire bale did not provide as much evidence of the antecedent intent as breaking it open and removing the contents.

[37] 83 Eng. Rep. 142 (1678).

that when the shopkeeper hands Chisser the cravats for inspection, the shopkeeper retains possession; when Chisser bolts from the store, he deprives the shopkeeper of possession and commits larceny.[38] This is the way the problem of theft in a self-service store would be analyzed today in the leading Continental jurisdictions.[39] Yet there is a hint in the opinion in *Chisser* that his conviction should be based on his intent when he first received the two ties.[40] This reading of the case is advanced by East,[41] who argues that the judges in *Pear* so interpreted the case in relying on it as an authority for their decision.[42]

In all three of these reinterpretations, the moment of criminality shifts from a moment of manifest taking to an earlier moment when the defendant first lays hands on the goods. The pattern becomes apparent in the following diagram:

	Initial Acquisition	**Manifestation of Thievery or Dishonesty**
Carrier	laying hands on the bales	breaking open the bales
Chisser	laying hands on the tie	bolting from the store
Pear	mounting the horse	selling the horse in Smithfield

The new view of the common law carried with it a number of

[38] This reading is supported by the third paragraph of the opinion: "although these goods were delivered to Chisser by the owner, yet they were not out of her possession by such delivery. . . ." *Id.* at 142–43. This interpretation of the case is shared by Leach, see 1 W. Hawkins, *supra* note 9, at 135 n.1; and by F. Pollack & R. Wright, *supra* note 15, at 140.

[39] See §2.1, note 20 *supra.*

[40] See the second paragraph of the opinion, 83 Eng. Rep. at 142.

[41] 2 East 687.

[42] For another opinion on similar facts, that similarly interweaves the issues of antecedent intent and the objective transfer of possession, see The King v. Sharpless, 168 Eng. Rep. 148 (1772).

critical jurisprudential implications. First, it thrust forward the idea that conduct might be criminal even if it appeared outwardly to be innocent, as in the acts of receiving bales for delivery, mounting a horse after hiring it, and nonchalantly picking up a necktie in a shop. Secondly, it created a situation in which the old rules of the common law suddenly came to appear formalistic and arbitrary. Why should it matter whether the carrier breaks bulk or converts the entire bale? Both actions are indicative of an earlier intent to steal. What sense does it make to say that Chisser does or does not get possession of the tie? The metaphysics of possession has little to do with proving his intent when he enters the store or takes hold of the tie. Thus we can begin to see that the contemporary view that the law of larceny is a briar patch of arbitrary distinctions is itself the outgrowth of a new theory of history sown in the early nineteenth century.

§2.3.3. **The Intellectual Background.** There is, of course, no intimation intended that Chitty, East, Russell and Archbold sought purposefully to rewrite history. Their craft was not so much history as the creation of a more rational law of larceny. When they looked at the old cases, they perceived what the intellectual currents of the time permitted them to see. These loyal laborers of the law did not fashion the enlightened rationality of early nineteenth-century England. But their work clearly reflects a new climate of opinion that was then taking hold of social and legal thought.

The reinterpretation of the old tradition served to bring the criminal law in line with the rationalist and utilitarian theories made popular by Bentham and the English translation of Beccaria.[43] In the early nineteenth-century intellectual culture, the view was gaining ground that punishing the guilty was not an end in itself, but a means of protecting society and promoting human happiness.[44] Pun-

[43] See C. Beccaria, On Crimes and Punishments (2d ed. 1769) (first published in 1764); 2 J. Bentham, An Introduction to the Principles of Morals and Legislation (1823 ed.) (first published in 1789). In his lectures on law, delivered at the University of Pennsylvania in 1790–91, James Wilson noted the importance and sweep of the investigation into the theory of criminal law prompted by Beccaria's work. See 2 J. Wilson, Works 614–16 (McCloskey ed. 1967).

[44] See C. Beccaria, *supra* note 43, at 7–9; 2 J. Bentham, *supra* note 43, at 1; 2 J.

ishment could no longer be accepted unreflectingly or justified simply on the ground that the guilty deserved it. The infliction of pain, even on convicted criminals, had to be justified as a means serving well-defined social goals, such as the prevention of harm and the deterrence of crime.[45] Against the background of these theories, it would no longer do to argue that larceny should be regarded as criminal if, and only if, the act of larceny was manifested in a socially unnerving act. Knowing that in primitive legal systems certain forms of conduct met with immediate execution might be of antiquarian interest, but it had little to do with the movement toward a rational criminal law.

The new utilitarian emphasis on an efficient use of criminal sanctions supported the emergent theory that crime should be defined in order to protect particular social interests. The criminal sanction could serve as a means of social protection only if the law identified the interests worthy of protection and then took the necessary measures to protect those interests.[46] The focus on the interests protected by the criminal law led to the conceptualization of larceny as a crime against property.[47] The criminal, it turned out, was rational like the rest of us; he sought wealth and would steal so long as the benefit of theft outweighed the cost of prospective punishment.[48] The breakdown of the social order into specific interests and the conceptualization of crime as an intrusion against those interests provided the conceptual background for the emerging school of protectionalist criminology. At a single stroke, this view of crime generated a theory of criminal motivation and enabled legislators to calculate a rational response to crime by measuring the punishment against the social interest at stake and the strength of the motive inducing criminal behavior.

Wilson, *supra* note 43, at 611. On this point Blackstone concurred, see 4 Blackstone 11–12.

[45] See C. Beccaria, *supra* note 43, at 12; 2 J. Bentham, *supra* note 43, at 14–15.

[46] See, e.g., C. Beccaria, *supra* note 43, at 29–33; W. Paley, Principles of Moral and Political Philosophy 46–47 (1821 ed.).

[47] See, e.g., C. Beccaria, *supra* note 43, at 83–84; 2 J. Bentham, *supra* note 43, at 139–40; 2 J. Wilson, *supra* note 43, at 639.

[48] See, e.g., 2 J. Bentham, *supra* note 43, at 16.

If the function of the criminal law was to protect social interests, it seemed pointless for the police and the courts to stay their hand until damage occurred. The most socially protective measure was to intervene prior to the occurrence of harm.[49] Thus the late eighteenth century witnessed the first cases recognizing the doctrine of criminal attempts.[50] By like token, larceny should be subject to police intervention as soon as the actor acquired the goods with intent to steal. Therefore in cases like the Carrier's Case, *Chisser* and *Pear,* the police should be able, in principle, to intervene as soon as the actor laid his hands on the goods with the intent to steal. If preventing crime is the supreme value of the criminal law, there is no reason to wait until the actor manifests his criminal design in a moment of violence or stealth.

Another major influence of the period was the quest for well-defined, rationally consistent rules of criminal liability. Theorists like Montesquieu, Beccaria and Bentham insisted on clear and definite rules as the foundation for a rational system of law that would provide a well-tooled mechanism for deterring criminal conduct.[51] These ideas were to come to fruition in the early nineteenth century, which in virtually all Western legal systems was a period of intense legislative activity. Legislation imposes demands of generality, definition and consistency that are hardly satisfied by appeals to a shared image of thievery. The first parliamentary report on the criminal law, published in 1834, takes the law of larceny to be the best illustration of the newly felt chaos of the common-law rules.[52] If the criminal law was to come under legislative control, it seemed that there would have to be a new methodology for identifying criminal conduct.

[49] The eighteenth-century theorists of criminal law heavily emphasized prevention, see, e.g., C. Beccaria, *supra* note 43, at 164, which avoids both the evil of the offense and the evil of punishment. Blackstone relied on the sentiment that "*preventive* justice is . . . preferable in all respects to *punishing* justice," 4 Blackstone 251, in praising the English system of requiring those who gave just ground of apprehension of future misbehavior to find pledges and securities for keeping the peace, *id.* at 251–52.

[50] See §3.3. at notes 9, 10 *infra.*

[51] See 1 Montesquieu, The Spirit of the Laws 108–10 (1750 ed.); C. Beccaria, *supra* note 43, at 13–14; 2 J. Bentham, *supra* note 43, at 267–73.

[52] See *First Report* 4–9

The early nineteenth century witnessed the birth of the theory that "breaking bulk" is to be explained by the magic phenomenon of determining the bailment and causing possession to spring back to the bailor.[53] There was no prior discussion of this theory in three centuries of commentary on the case. And there is no evidence, so far as one can tell, for the general proposition that a breach of contract or a tortious act could "determine" a bailment. The precedents on determining bailments all held that bailments terminated if the bailee performed an act, such as riding a specified time or distance or delivering the goods, which, according to the original agreement, was designed to mark the outer limits of the bailment.[54] Yet it is not surprising that in the mood of the early nineteenth century, the judges would play with the doctrines of the common law as though they were meaningless forms of the past. In an era bent on legislative reform of the criminal law, the judges quite expectedly found less meaning in the rules of their own tradition.

§2.4. *Judicial Expansion of the Common Law.*

Though proposals to revamp the law of larceny date back to the 1830s,[1] parliamentary intervention in the nineteenth century was limited largely to expanding the scope of embezzlement as a crime.[2] The rationalization and expansion of common-law larceny

[53] See note 31 *supra.*

[54] By the end of the eighteenth century, there were two types of case in which the bailment was thought to be "determined." The first was by delivery to destination in accordance with the agreement. See 4 Blackstone 230; Coke 108; 1 Hale 505. The second was by reading an express limitation on the duration of the bailee's possession or the distance he was permitted to take the bailed object. The latter category emerged in the early eighteenth century. The leading case is Tunnard's Case, discussed in note 3 *supra.* This second means of terminating a bailment, which permitted termination prior to delivery, encountered criticism. See Rex v. Banks, 168 Eng. Rep. 887 (1821).

§2.4. [1] See *First Report* 2-9.

[2] See §1.1.1 *supra.*

fell to the courts. The call for legislation created a climate in which lawyers regarded the newly felt "chaos" of the common law as properly subject to amendment and reform. It was only a matter of institutional efficiency whether the courts or the Parliament would carry out the revision of the law. In two major expansionary moves, the courts penalized takings by finders and takings after a mistaken delivery. Both of these developments in the nineteenth century led to the punishment of conduct that was outwardly innocent and unthreatening. They both contributed, as well, to a crime of larceny with contours different, in these two areas of dispute, from their counterparts in France, Germany and the Soviet Union.[3]

§2.4.1. Liability of Finders. According to the traditional texts, finders could not be guilty of larceny.[4] The rationale, presumably, was that they did not take from the possession of anyone—a lost object was one possessed by no one. Alternatively, the finder's immunity may be explained by the objectively ambiguous nature of taking an unpossessed object, a taking not readily recognized as that of a thief. Yet the frontier between taking an unpossessed object and taking from the possession of the owner could hardly be staked out by appealing to the image of the thief. There were too many ambiguous cases where possession dissolved into loss of control. Consider the case that Hale devised: "A man hides a purse of money in his corn-mow, his servant finding it took part of it. . . ."[5] Is this a taking from the owner's possession? To determine whether the owner still has possession, one is drawn toward considering the owner's intention in laying down the purse. Yet if one considers the owner's state of mind, why not also look to the finder's understanding of the situation? Thus one is drawn to construing the case as larceny or not, according as the finder knows of the owner's point in putting the purse in the corn-mow. Hale con-

[3] See §1.2 *supra*.

[4] 3 Coke 107; 1 Hale 506; 1 Hawkins 134. But note that the finding of a treasure trove (valuables buried in the earth), and the failure to turn the valuables over to the King subjected the finder to a penalty of imprisonment for misprision. 1 Blackstone 295–96; 4 *id.* at 121.

[5] 1 Hale 507.

tinues: "[I]f by circumstances it can appear he knew his master laid it there, it is a felony."[6] Evidently in these cases in the borderland of possession, the principle of objective criminality yielded to an inquiry about the special knowledge of the taker; and even ambiguous takings, coupled with an incriminating subjective state in the putative finder, might well support convictions for larceny.

One of the reasons that finding is a special case is that the finder's wrong typically has little to do with the act of acquiring physical control over the object. His wrong is failing to take proper steps to locate the owner and return the object.[7] Picking up a wallet lying in the middle of the street is a responsible act—hardly a basis for a capital offense. Yet if the finder's behavior thereafter falls short of community expectations, one might have a sound reason for blaming and punishing him as a criminal.

Though the two sets of problems were of a different order, early nineteenth-century commentators had little difficulty assimilating the case of finding and improper keeping to the cases of forcible and other felonious takings. With little authority[8] other than Hale's comments in the late seventeenth century,[9] East,[10] Chitty[11]

[6] *Ibid.*

[7] Frankel treats this body of law as an example of liability for omissions. See Frankel, *Criminal Omissions: A Legal Microcosm,* 11 Wayne L. Rev. 367, 406–10 (1965). See generally §8.3 *infra.*

[8] One case that helped shape the new doctrine of larceny by finders was The King v. Wynne, 168 Eng. Rep. 308 (1786), in which a coachman was convicted of larceny for unwrapping a box that a passenger left behind and selling the contents. The problem was that the defendant apparently obtained possession without fraud on his part, *id.* at 309; therefore *Pear* would not apply. According to Leach, the trial judge instructed the jury that it was felony only if the coachman "uncorded the box, not merely from natural though idle curiosity, but with an intention to embezzle any part of its contents." *Id.* The holding makes little sense except as an application of the principle of "breaking bulk." The court did not treat the problem as an instance of liability of finders.

[9] See text at notes 5–6 *supra.*

[10] East discusses *Wynne, supra* note 8, as a finder's case and repeats Hale's example of the "purse-in-the-corn-mow," stressing that even in that case the circumstances must be "pregnant; otherwise it may be reasonably interpreted to be a bare finding. . . ." 2 East 664.

[11] 3 T. Chitty, A Practical Treatise on Criminal Law 920 (1816) (discussing *Wynne* as an example of liability by a finder).

and Russell,[12] writing from 1803 to 1819, developed a doctrine that a finder could be guilty of larceny if he failed to exercise due care to locate the owner and return the object. These facts occurring after the taking were assimilated to the traditional analysis of larceny on the theory that they tended to prove felonious intent at the time of the initial receipt.[13] This technique of analysis obviously conforms to the theories developed in reinterpreting the Carrier's Case, *Chisser* and *Pear*. The category of evidentiary facts began to swell as the relative substantive issues contracted. Though the act of improper keeping was the core of the offense, the theorists of the time treated it as merely an evidentiary factor bearing upon an earlier criminal intent.[14]

Though this doctrinal development came early in the century, the courts were slow in creating precedents to incorporate the new learning. The first major case was Regina v. Thurborn, decided as a Crown Case Reserved in 1848.[15] The defendant had come across a note that someone accidentally dropped on the highway; he picked it up allegedly with the intent to keep it. At that time there was no indication who the owner was or that the owner might be able to find it again. The following day, however, Thurborn was informed of the owner's identity. Though he apparently believed this information, Thurborn kept the note. The judges ruled that on these facts that Thurborn could not be guilty of larceny.[16]

What is interesting for our purposes is Baron Parke's analysis of the question whether the initial taking of the note was larcenous. The gist of the problem, according to Baron Parke, was to determine the circumstances as they appeared to the prisoner at the time of the taking. The judge's statement of the rule that

[12] Russell cites *Wynne, supra* note 8, as showing "that the taking *animo furandi* of goods which have been *found* by the party may amount to larceny." 2 W. Russell, Crimes and Misdemeanors 1042 (emphasis in original).

[13] See Russell's view, *ibid.*

[14] The liability of finders could be added to the chart, *supra* p. 99. The shift in emphasis is from the culpable failure to return the goods to intent at the time of picking up the lost object. Compare the French cases, §1.2.2, at notes 30-31.

[15] 169 Eng. Rep. 293 (1848).

[16] His subsequent intent to retain the note was protected by the principle of possessorial immunity. *Id.* at 297.

should govern the finder's liability reflects the new conception of larceny:[17]

> "[I]f a man find[s] goods that have been actually lost, or are reasonably supposed by him to have been lost, and appropriates them, with intent to take the entire dominion over them, really believing when he takes them, that the owner cannot be found, it is not larceny. *But if he takes them with the like intent, though lost, or reasonably supposed to be lost, but reasonably believing that the owner can be found, it is larceny.*"

Thurborn was not guilty under this rule, and although English judges initially responded skeptically to Baron Parke's dictum,[18] the theory advanced in *Thurborn* guided subsequent litigation both in England[19] and the United States.[20]

§2.4.2. **The Problem of Mistaken Delivery.** The evolving law of finder's criminal liability provided a precedent for thinking of outwardly innocent takings as criminal if they should be accompanied by a prohibited state of mind. Yet the problem of finders could be thought of as a separate branch of the law, artificially engrafted onto the central trunk of larceny. For the centrality of intent to displace the requirement of manifest criminality in an ordinary case of stealing, one had to await the outcome of a line of cases centering around the liability of persons receiving goods by mistake. The critical case, The Queen v. Middleton,[21] decided in 1873, posed a paradigmatic instance of outwardly innocent taking. The accused, one Middleton, maintained a savings account at the post office; he submitted an application to withdraw ten shillings from his account. When he presented himself at the clerk's window for payment, the clerk mistakenly remitted the wrong

[17] *Id.* at 296 (emphasis added).

[18] See The Queen v. Glyde, L.R. 1 Cr. Cas. Res. 139, 143–44 (1868) (opinions of Cockburn, C.J., and Blackburn, J., criticizing *Thurborn* as unsound); Regina v. Deaves, 11 Cox Crim. Cas. 227, 230 (Crim. App. 1869).

[19] The rule in *Thurborn* was eventually incorporated in the Larceny Act 1916, 6 & 7 Geo. V, c. 50, §1(2)(i)(d) (finder takes goods "where at the time of the finding the finder believes the owner can be discovered by taking reasonable steps").

[20] See, e.g., State v. Levy, 23 Minn. 104, 110 (1876) (citing *Thurborn* approvingly in a case where the defendant apparently saw the owner leave the goods behind).

[21] L.R. 2 Cr. Cas. Res. 38 (1873).

amount, overpaying the accused by about eight pounds. Middleton, obviously knowing of the mistake, left the post office with the excess and kept it. The case is more difficult than that of finding and keeping, for here the clerk's handing the money to Middleton bears all the earmarks of a delivery—a surrender of possession, if not title;[22] and thus one is hard pressed to see the case as a felonious taking. Nonetheless, the courts could have approached the problem on analogy to *Pear* and reasoned that Middleton acquired only custody over the excess payment and therefore his subsequent conversion constituted a criminal taking.

Without adverting to the limited egress offered by *Pear,* the judges of the time opted for a radical extension of the law of larceny. Eleven of the fifteen judges hearing the case concluded that Middleton was guilty of common-law larceny.[23] Their reasoning was simply that Middleton took the surplus with the intent to keep it, and that was all that was required to convict.

Justices Martin and, in particular, Bramwell, sensed that there was something fundamentally wrong about convicting for larceny in the absence of a manifest act of thievery. Yet they had few doctrinal gambits with which to mount an attack on the majority view. They insisted, as did the Wisconsin Supreme Court in *Topolewski,* that larceny requires a "trespass"[24] and not merely a taking and, further, that there could not be a trespass if the victim consented to delivery.[25] Yet these arguments meant little to judges who failed to respond to Bramwell's claim that larceny should be limited to a "privy (i.e., clandestine), or forcible taking."[26] Nor did

[22] The major dispute in the opinions was whether the post office clerk transferred title to the excess funds. *Compare* the opinion of Justice Brett, *id.* at 59–66 (arguing that there was a transfer of both title and possession), *with* that of Justices Bovil and Keating, *id.* at 46–49 (contending that because the clerk lacked authority to convey title to the authorized funds, there was no transfer). *Cf.* the German and French view, §1.2.3 *supra.*

[23] For a harbinger of this extension, see Regina v. Mucklow, 168 Eng. Rep. 1225 (1827) (recognizing the possibility of convicting in a case of acquisition by mistake where there is *animus furandi* at the time of initial receipt).

[24] L.R. 2 Cr. Cas. Res. at 41, 48, 49 (1873).

[25] *Id.* at 53, 58 (Martin, J.).

[26] The thrust of Bramwell's opinion was that the taking was not *invito domino*—

these arguments gain much weight as a result of Bramwell's attack on the judges voting for conviction as being among those who believed that "the prisoner was as bad as a thief . . . and being as bad, ought to be treated as one. . . ."[27] Bramwell raised some troubling points,[28] but alas, they went unnoticed by the majority of the judges, who saw little impediment, in policy or principle, to affixing criminal liability to routine and unincriminating acts that became criminal only by virtue of the actor's intent at the time.

If *Middleton* was a landmark case in the growing influence of the new theory of larceny, it was nonetheless a case that retained the requirement of a taking as an objective phenomenon. Twelve years later, in The Queen v. Ashwell,[29] that requirement, too, would come to be seen through the lens of a subjective theory of larceny. In *Ashwell* the accused had borrowed a coin from a compatriot; both initially thought that the coin was a shilling while in fact it was a sovereign. Upon discovering the mistake Ashwell appropriated the coin. Even under the newer cases—*Pear, Thurborn* and *Middleton*—the accused should have been protected by the rule of possessorial immunity. He had no felonious intent at the time of acquisition, and it was hard to see why he did not acquire full legal possession of the coin. Nonetheless, seven of the fourteen judges (enough to affirm the conviction) held that Ashwell did not get possession until he discovered the mistake and therefore, at

against the will of the owner. As in *Topolewski,* one finds an interweaving of the concepts of trespass and the absence of consent, see §2.1.3 *supra.* Bramwell offers no account of why he favors a broad view of "consent"—one that would imply that the clerk "consented" because he "intended to do the act he did." L.R. 2 Cr. Cas. Res. at 55. It was not important to Bramwell that the clerk made a mistake in intending to part with the money. Bramwell's reasons include the claim that if the defendant "was led into temptation[,] the prosecutor [i.e., victim] had very much himself to blame . . ." *Id.* at 56.

[27] *Id.* at 56.

[28] Bramwell clearly realized the broader implications of rejecting the requirement of an objectively criminal act. He repeatedly refers to the case as one in which "great and important principles are involved." *Id.* at 54; see *id.* at 59. He obviously had in mind something of greater moment than the doctrines of passing title and consent. In conclusion, he criticizes those who believe: "The prisoner was as bad as a thief . . . and being as bad, ought to be treated as one. . . ." *Id.* at 59.

[29] 16 Q.B.D. 190 (1885).

that moment, "took" the coin from the owner's possession.[30] Some courts later reacted against hitching the phenomenon of taking to the actor's subjective state.[31] But now that takings which to all appearances were innocent could be punished, there seemed to be no good reason for insisting that the "taking" be an objective rather than a subjective phenomenon.[32] From the perspective of the theory of larceny based on subjective states, it seemed picayune to insist that the felonious intent crystallize exactly at the moment that the actor first touches the object he later steals. As a result, the subjectification of "taking" eventually prevailed in English law.[33]

American courts adhered closely to the pattern of subjectification that occurred in England. At about the same time that *Middleton* was decided, a New York court had little difficulty reaching the same result on similar facts.[34] Though American courts have not followed the development marked by *Ashwell*,[35] they have concurred since the end of the nineteenth century that an outwardly innocent taking could be felonious if the intent at the time was one prohibited by law.

§2.4.3. Legislative Consolidation. The gains wrought by the metamorphosis of larceny found a stable footing in the first Anglo-

[30] See *id.* at 203 (opinion of Cave, J.) ("Ashwell did not consent to the possession of the sovereign until he knew that it was a sovereign"). But see *id.* at 206 (Stephen, J., dissenting in a careful and scholarly opinion).

[31] See, e.g., Regina v. Hehir, 18 Cox Crim. Cas. 267 (1895); The Queen v. Flowers, 16 Q.B.D. 643 (1886). Note that in cases of mistaken taking, the defendant might arguably be guilty of larceny as a bailee under 24 & 25 Vict., c. 96, §3 (1861). In *Ashwell* this argument was rejected on the ground that a recipient who does not take on the condition that he return the specific object is not a bailee. 16 Q.B.D. at 199 (opinion of Smith, J.).

[32] Compare the subjective theory of attempts, §3.3.5 *infra.*

[33] See, e.g., Russell v. Smith, [1957] 3 W.L.R. 515; Rex v. Hudson, [1943] 1 K.B. 458. The opinion in *Hudson* consists largely of a lengthy quotation from the opinion of Cave, J., in *Ashwell.* For a critique of the trend toward subjectification of the concept of "taking," see Kerr, *The Time of Criminal Intent in Larceny,* 66 L.Q. Rev. 174 (1950); Scurlock, *The Element of Trespass in Larceny at Common Law and Under the Statutes,* 22 Temp. L.Q. 12, 14 (1948).

[34] Wolfstein v. People, 6 Hun 121 (N.Y. Sup. Ct. 1875).

[35] See, e.g., Mitchell v. State, 78 Tex. Crim. 79, 180 S.W. 115 (1915) (holding that there is no larceny if the recipient discovers the mistake after physically

American legislative definition of larceny—the English Larceny Act of 1916. The terms carefully chosen in this formulation reflect a century of litigation that brought larceny into patterns of behavior that in other legal systems go unpunished or are treated under the headings of fraud or embezzlement. It is significant, for example, that the word "trespass" is deleted from the definition of larceny as encompassing any person:[36]

> "Who without the consent of the owner, fraudulently and without a claim of right made in good faith, takes and carries away anything capable of being stolen. . . ."

This casting of the crime by the legislative mint did not totally ban the coin of trespass from circulation. The concept retained currency in American decisions on the problems of staged larceny;[37] and it took on different forms in English decisions supporting the same conclusion of non-liability.[38]

The experience of nineteenth-century English courts made its impact on the definition of a "taking" in §2(i) as "obtaining possession

a. by any trick
b. by intimidation
c. under a mistake on the part of the owner with knowledge on the part of the owner that possession has been so obtained
d. by finding, where at the time of the finding the finder believes that the owner can be discovered by taking reasonable steps."[39]

---

receiving a mistakenly drawn check); Cooper v. Commonwealth, 110 Ky. 123, 60 S.W. 938 (1901). For American criticism of *Ashwell*, see W. Clark & W. Marshall, A Treatise on the Law of Crimes 849 & n.69 (7th ed. M. Barnes 1967); Perkins 259 n.91.

[36] Larceny Act 1916, 6 & 7 Geo. V, c. 50, §1(1).

[37] See §2.2.3 *supra* and the discussion of Topolewski v. State, 130 Wis. 244, 109 N.W. 1037 (1906).

[38] See Rex v. Turvey, [1946] 2 All E.R. 60 (Crim. App.) (focussing on issue of "delivery," reversing conviction).

[39] Larceny Act 1916, 6 & 7 Geo. V, c. 50, §2(1).

It is easy to detect the trace of *Pear* in subsection (a); of *Middleton* in subsection (c); and of *Thurborn* in subsection (d). The Parliamentary Report of 1834 called for a systematic legislation in the field of larceny, yet it took nearly a century of litigation to generate the contours of the new offense.

It would be difficult to maintain that the metamorphosis of larceny in the nineteenth century led directly to the consolidation in 1968 of larceny and embezzlement in one offense called theft, covering anyone who "dishonestly appropriates property belonging to another with the intention of permanently depriving the other of it."[40] Yet the metamorphosis of the offense, complete by 1916, stood for a conceptual reorientation of both larceny and embezzlement that made unification highly attractive as a legislative program.

The central point of the reconceptualization was the shift in both crimes to a focus on improper and intentional acquisition. With the demise of "trespass," larceny ceased to be a crime manifested in stealthful or forcible conduct. Embezzlement shifted over, in time, from a breach of trust to a crime expressed in the intrusion on property rights. If all crimes had to be thought of as violations of specific quantifiable interests, then embezzlement had to shed its moral overtones of betrayal and become like larceny—a crime of acquisition.[41] Thus, with the crimes brought into the same conceptual harness, there appeared to be little reason to maintain their identity as separate grounds of prosecution.

Though German law also recognizes the unity of larceny and embezzlement under the general heading of "appropriation," the distinction between them is maintained by requiring that larceny be manifested in a "breaking of possession."[42] Soviet law also recognizes a general unifying concept of "appropriation"; yet the notions of "secret" and "open" continue to mark off the ancient forms of larceny.[43] Unless the taking from possession is thought of

[40] Theft Act 1968, c. 60, §1(1).
[41] For further discussion of embezzlement, see §3.2.1 *infra*.
[42] See StGB §242.
[43] Ugol. kod. (RSFSR) §89 (secret taking of socialist property), §90 (open taking

as "trespass," as a manifestation of the larcenous purpose, there is little sense in retaining the common-law baggage of "taking" and "acquiring possession."[44] Though the metamorphosis of larceny might have been only one condition for unification, it is significant that no comparable metamorphosis has occurred in Continental jurisdictions. This may explain why none of these jurisdictions evidences a trend toward abolishing the boundary between larceny and embezzlement.

Having worked our way through these details, we are now in a position to reflect, in Chapter Three, on the broader conflict implicit in the history of larceny.

---

of socialist property), §144 (secret taking of private property), §145 (open taking of private property).

[44] See the halfway solution proposed in MPC §223.2 (retaining a distinction between "taking" and "exercising unlawful control" over the movable property of another).

Chapter Three
Two Patterns of Criminality

§3.1. *Abstracting from the History of Larceny.*

The metamorphosis of larceny permits us to abstract two general patterns of criminality that find expression in a variety of crimes in addition to larceny. The common law of larceny up to the time of Blackstone reflected what we may call the pattern of manifest criminality; the modern law of larceny, emerging in the late eighteenth century, stands for a pattern of subjective criminality. By generalizing the features of these two conflicting patterns of liability, we shall find that we have a powerful interpretative mechanism for understanding disputes in the law of burglary, attempts and other inchoate offenses, treason, and even a central dispute in the theory of constitutional arrests under the Fourth Amendment. The tension between the pattern of manifest criminality and the pattern of subjective criminality is one that pervades a wide field of the criminal law.

§3.1.1. The Pattern of Manifest Criminality. The critical feature of this basic pattern of liability is that the commission of the crime be objectively discernible at the time that it occurs. The assumption is that a neutral third-party observer could recognize the activity as criminal even if he had no special knowledge about the offender's intention. Now it may be true that there is no activity—with the exception perhaps of prohibited sexual copulation—that can always and reliably be identified as criminal. What one sees may be a performance of guerilla theater: even a rape might be simulated in order to make a political point.[1] Yet to focus excessively on these problems at the fringes of the pattern ignores the simple fact of experience, namely, that we can tell when a crime is occurring. In the vast majority of cases what we perceive to be a mugging, a rape, a bank robbery, a house-breaking or safe-cracking is in fact just that. It is from this simple fact of experience that we derive the idea of catching someone in the act, *in flagrante delicto*.

Two important features of crimes follow from this distinguishing mark of manifest criminality. First there is a sense in which the crime itself crystallizes as the product of community experience, rather than being imposed on the community by an act of legislative will. The contours of what we perceive to be larceny spring from a shared experience with thieves. It is incorporated in our language as well as our legal judgments. We have distinctive conceptions of furtive and stealthful behavior, largely because these terms trade on our shared image of the way thieves act. This element of natural connection between a concept of criminality and community experience is highlighted in Gaius' comment that the contours of *furtum manifestum* were not subject to legislative manipulation:[2]

> [S]tatute can no more turn a thief who is not manifest into a manifest thief than it can turn into a thief one who is not a thief at all, or into an adulterer or homicide one who is neither one nor the other.

§3.1. [1] On the problem of imputing knowledge to third-party observers, see the discussion of selling a borrowed horse in an open market, §2.2.1, pp. 82–83 *supra*.

[2] 3 Gaius, Institutes ¶194, in 1 F. de Zulueta, The Institutes of Gaius 217 (1946).

There is no doubt that this way of looking at crime and criminals is foreign to the modern view that the criminal law is imposed on the community by the courts or the legislature. Yet the sense that the criteria of criminality are rooted in social experience is a basic feature of a large segment of the early common law as well as of ancient legal systems.

The second feature born of the principle of manifest criminality is the subsidiary position of intent in the analysis of liability. The issue of non-intent arises primarily as a challenge to the authenticity of appearances, rather than as a basis for inculpating the actor. It is only after the manifestly criminal quality of the act is established that intent can conceivably become an issue. In this way of thinking the required intent is linked conceptually to the commission of certain acts. It is not thought of as some mysterious inner dimension of experience that exists independently from acting in the external world.

The pattern of manifest criminality may be understood as a theory about the appropriate jurisdiction of the criminal courts. The premise is that the courts should stay their hand until the actor manifests discernible danger to the community. Thus the criteria for judicial intervention resemble the ground for the private execution of thieves in ancient legal systems. The incidental benefit of this jurisdictional premise is the protection of individual privacy. Judges have no warrant to inquire about subjective states unless the threshold of manifest criminality is satisfied.[3]

To avoid misunderstanding, we should state carefully what the pattern of manifest criminality is *not*. It is not a theory of criminal types. It does not represent a rejection of the discipline of legality for the sake of isolating persons who conform to a psychological profile of thieves, rapists or political assassins. The orientation in this cut of the law is toward criminal acts, not criminal actors. The rule implicit in this pattern of liability is that the state will proceed against an individual only if his conduct objectively manifests danger to the community. A criminal law de-

[3] For further development of this point, see §2.2.4 *supra*.

signed to pick out criminal types abandons the discipline of assessing criminal acts as a condition for further inquiry.[4]

§3.1.2. **The Pattern of Subjective Criminality.** The contrasting pattern of liability begins with the radically different assumption that the core of criminal conduct is the intention to violate a legally protected interest. A crime in this pattern may presuppose the occurrence of a particular event, such as the "taking from possession" required for larceny. But this result is often not incriminating, as indicated by the cases of finders and those who receive a chattel by mistaken delivery. The function of the criminal act is to demonstrate the firmness rather than the content of the actor's intent. If, in addition, the act provides some evidence of the required intent, so much the better; but there are other acceptable means of proving intent, such as confessions, admissions against interest and evidence of prior as well as subsequent conduct.

This pattern of liability presupposes a notion of intending that treats intent as a dimension of experience totally distinct from external behavior. Intending is conceived as an event of consciousness, known to the person with the intent but not to others. Thus the relationship of intending to action is dualistic rather than monistic. The intent exists in the realm of the mind, the act in the realm of the body.

This dualistic way of thinking about intent has undergone philosophical criticism in recent years;[5] yet it retains a powerful grip on the way lawyers think about the criminal law. Its power derives in part from its dovetailing with an appealing theory of criminality. The criminal law should begin, this theory holds, by identifying interests that are worthy of protection. The next step should be preventing conduct that threatens those interests. The reasons that humans sometimes threaten those interests is either that they intend to do so or that they take risks that subject the

[4] A system of *Täterstrafrecht* (actor-oriented criminal law) won considerable currency as a National Socialist theory of social control. See, e.g., G. Dahm, Der Täterstrafrecht (1940); Lange, *Täterschuld und Todesstrafe,* 62 ZStW 175 (1944).

[5] See generally G. Ryle, The Concept of Mind 11–24 (1949); N. Malcolm, Problems of Mind (1971).

protected interests to danger. Therefore the purpose of the criminal law should be to prevent people from embarking on courses of behavior that threaten these worthy interests. The way to deter people from embarking on these courses of conduct is to punish those who intend to violate the interests. The only reason we require that offenders act on their intention is to make sure that the intention is firm and not merely fantasy. Additionally, where the offense presupposes a result like the deprivation of property, the actor must execute his intent in order to bring about the requisite state of affairs.

One key concept in understanding the difference between the patterns of manifest and subjective criminality is the distinction between substantive and evidentiary rules. Manifest criminality requires, as a substantive rule of law, that the act betoken danger to the community. The subjective criminality of intending harm invites a variety of means of proving the required intent, and one of these may be an act manifesting danger. In a particular case of manifestly criminal, punishable conduct, it may be impossible to determine whether the fact fulfills a substantive requirement or whether it functions merely as evidence of intent. The distinction has a concrete impact only in cases where the conduct of the accused is outwardly unincriminating. If manifest criminality is a substantive requirement, no surrogate proof of intent will suffice; if, in contrast, it fulfills an evidentiary function, the absence of manifestly criminal conduct may be corrected with surrogate proof of a criminal intent.

Thus the difference between the two patterns may be simply stated as turning on whether a manifestly criminal act is a substantive requirement. In the pattern of manifest criminality, it is; in the theory of subjective criminality, it is not.

§3.1.3. Maxims Common to Both Patterns of Liability. These two patterns of liability—the manifest and the subjective—interweave in contemporary thinking about criminal law. Yet they remain camouflaged by a common stock of legal maxims that create an image of unity in criminal theory. It is generally said that criminal liability presupposes (1) an act, (2) an intent, (3) a union of act and intent. In addition, it might be asserted that

(4) a danger to the community, and (5) an intrusion upon the public sphere are general features of criminal conduct. Though the requirement of these elements is nominally common to both patterns of criminality, the concepts of act, intent, union, danger, and public sphere acquire different meanings and significance, as they are interpreted in one pattern of liability or the other.

In the pattern of manifest criminality, the requirement of an "act" means an act manifesting the criminal plan. In the pattern of subjective criminality, the point of the act requirement is not to establish the *content* of the actor's intent, but merely the *firmness* of the actor's resolve. While only some acts are manifestly criminal, any voluntary act can establish the actor's commitment to do harm. Similarly, the requirement of intent means in the former pattern, a basis for thinking that appearances are true in reality; in the latter pattern, intent refers to an event in the subject's consciousness that provides a basis for predicting that the actor will violate a legally protected interest.

In the former pattern, the required union of act and intent expresses a conceptual point. One cannot properly think of criminal intent apart from its manifestation in criminal conduct: therefore it is natural to say that act and intent are conjoined in criminal acts. Yet in the pattern of subjective criminality, it is quite plausible to think of acts and intents as occurring at distinct moments of time. Nonetheless, the conceptual point of the older pattern of liability carries forward as a maxim of criminal justice. Analyzing larceny in cases like *Pear, Thurborn* and *Middleton*,[6] the common-law judges paid a great deal of attention to whether the intent occurred at the same time as the required act. This is a very curious requirement to insist upon in the pattern of subjective criminality, for when the intent is not overtly manifested, only the actor knows exactly when he intends to steal. Yet there is no doubt that the courts sought to retain this maxim, even though the claim that the actor entertained his unmanifested intent at one moment rather than at another began to take on the quality of fiction.

[6] See §§2.3.1, 2.4.1, 2.4.2 *supra*.

The element of danger to the community is shared under the two patterns, but with differing significance. The danger in manifest criminality is reflected in the act itself; in subjective criminality, the locus of the danger is the intent to violate a protected interest. The former is perceived danger; the latter, actual though concealed danger, engendered by a decision to commit a crime. Both patterns share the principle that purely private conduct should be immune from the criminal law. Yet the "purely private" in the case of manifest criminality encompasses all routine, unthreatening conduct; in the theory of subjective criminality, the realm of the private is reduced to the world of fantasy, belief and other purely subjective experience; as soon as thoughts are translated into action, they come within the purview of the state's authority.

There are some deeper points to be brought out in contrasting the two patterns of liability, but first we should seek to demonstrate the influence of these two patterns in a wide variety of offenses in addition to larceny. Before we turn to the details of these crimes, we should be clear about the kind of claim we are making. We shall refer to the influence, the rise and the fall of these conflicting patterns of liability. Yet we should be careful about reifying these patterns and treating them as though they possess a reality beyond the data they explain. The value of these abstract patterns is their explanatory power. They bring order to the dispersed data of the criminal law and help us to see the underlying unity in a wide array of disputes about doctrinal rules. In many situations, the pattern will be expressed only imperfectly. It is worth measuring these imperfect cases against the abstractly defined patterns as a way of gauging elements of diversity in the criminal law. Also, we should be aware of the danger of over-generalization from larceny and the other offenses to which we now turn. It is only a segment of the criminal law that reflects the imprint of these two patterns of criminality.

As we shall see in Chapters Four and Five, homicide stands for a different pattern of harmful consequences. The distinguishing feature of homicide and related offenses is neither the manifest danger of threatening to kill nor the intent to kill. The central feature of homicide is the death of one person at the hands of another.

This concrete harm stimulates the quest for persons accountable for bringing it about. In contrast to this response to an accrued harm, the pattern of manifest criminality begins with a particular kind of *act;* subjective criminality, with a particular *intent* to do harm. The task immediately before us is to trace this tension between act and intent, manifest and subjective criminality, in a range of offenses other than larceny.

§3.2. *Related Theft Offenses.*

To complete our discussion of theft offenses, we should note how embezzlement, false pretenses and burglary display the tension between theories of manifest and of subjective criminality.

§3.2.1. **Embezzlement.** The English crime of embezzlement emerged by legislative command in the same period in which the common-law commentators and courts began to expand liability to include non-manifest takings as larceny.[1] In one respect, subjecting embezzlement to criminal sanctions may be viewed as part of the expansion that we have termed the "metamorphosis" of larceny. It is difficult to think of embezzlement as a crime that peaks in a single moment of stealthful conduct. There are so many subtle ways that a bank teller might appropriate a note deposited by a customer that in many cases it would be difficult for an Olympian observer to discern the act of acquisition. In other cases it is highly problematic to specify the precise moment that an appropriation occurs. Suppose that a mechanic decides to take a car left in his possession on a trip across the country. This would clearly exceed the bounds of permissible use, and in the standard definition of appropriation, it would constitute the "assumption of the rights of an owner."[2] Yet when does the appropriation occur? If the mechanic sets out from Los Angeles, the appropriation would

§3.2. [1] For supplementary notes on embezzlement, see §1.1.1 *supra.*
[2] Theft Act 1968, c. 60, §3(1) (English definition of "appropriation").

presumably occur some place before the Mississippi River, but there is no way of fathoming whether it occurs in Nevada or in Kansas. The intent to appropriate surely is not enough to trigger the appropriation, for the latter purports to be an independent element of the offense. Though there are many cases that conform to this example of the mechanic driving across the country, there are no doubt other instances of embezzlement in which the appropriation is discernible as the sudden and unjustified assumption of the rights of an owner.

Because the act of appropriation lends itself to consideration as a manifest act in some cases, there is a dispute about the nature of appropriation that reflects the tension between the two patterns of liability. The question is whether the appropriation should be thought of as the act required for the offense, even though criminality is at best mutely manifested in many cases of embezzlement. Or should the appropriation be thought of as the element of harm comparable to the loss of possession in larceny? There is considerable support in the German literature for the view that embezzlement is a characteristic form of conduct expressed in specified types of appropriation.[3] This opinion reflects an effort to keep the principle of manifest criminality intact in the law of embezzlement. Whatever the ambiguities of the mechanic's appropriating the car left in his possession, there is some sense to thinking of "the assumption of the rights of an owner" as an open and notorious act. In this respect the standard of appropriation is reminiscent of the claim of open and notorious use necessary to establish an allegation of adverse possession to real property.[4]

This way of looking at embezzlement has made no impact on the opinions of common-law scholars, who appear content to think of appropriation in criminal law as equivalent to conversion in tort law.[5] The latter, it seems, is conceived primarily as the element of harm to be compensated by civil recovery. Thus the crime of embezzlement is reduced to the elements of harm, and intending to

[3] Maurach SP at 241; Bookelmann, Book Review, 65 ZStW 569, 588–89 (1953).
[4] See 3 American Law of Property §§15.3 and 15.4 (A. J. Casner ed. 1952).
[5] LaFave & Scott 645; Prosser 79–97.

harm; the act of appropriation has no independent significance. This is a way of thinking about embezzlement that brings it into line with the metamorphosed crime of larceny, cast in the mold of subjective criminality.

§3.2.2. **False Pretenses.** The major issue in the law of false pretenses is whether the crime must be objectively discernible at the time of commission. This problem is expressed, doctrinally, in the question whether misrepresentations of future facts or even silence may satisfy the required element of a fraudulent misrepresentation. If a misrepresentation about one's willingness to repay a loan is sufficient to constitute the required pretense, then it is obviously possible to commit the crime at a moment at which one's conduct appears to be in the ordinary course of business. Penalizing these unmanifested intentions to defraud is the clear trend of the law, in Continental as well as Anglo-American jurisdictions.[6] As such, the trend conforms neatly to the pattern of subjective criminality, for the essence of fraud then reduces to the twin elements of fraudulent intent and the harm suffered by the deceived victim.

Though the modern trend conforms to the principle of subjective criminality, it is not so clear that the older rule reflects the principle of manifest criminality. Requiring a pretense about a past or present fact provides an external anchor for the crime. Yet the offender's lie is not immediately discernible as false; if it were, we should regard the victim as a fool and personally at fault in suffering his loss. This externalized false pretense resembles the falsehood in libel per quod rather than libel per se.[7] The lie is documentably false, but only after researching the true state of affairs, say, of the offender's credit situation or of the quality of the goods. It is external criminality, but not manifest criminality. Thus we see that our two patterns of criminality do not fit perfectly in accounting for this dispute about the required false pretense.

§3.2.3. **Burglary.** As a crime closer in its roots to *furtum manifestum,* the evolution of burglary more precisely reflects the

[6] See §1.1.2, at notes 41–46 *supra.*
[7] See Prosser 763–64.

tension between the patterns of manifest and of subjective criminality. Burglary received its classic definition early in the common law: it is committed by (1) nocturnally[8] (2) breaking and entering,[9] (3) a dwelling house,[10] (4) with a felonious intent.[11] The burglar obviously bears close resemblance, particularly with the emphasis on nocturnal house breaking, to the *fur manifestus* and the thief "digging under" penalized under Biblical law.[12] Yet the recognition of burglary as a distinct offense appears to be a distinguishing feature of Anglo-American law. Continental systems typically recognize the crime of forcible entry[13] and sometimes treat theft in an inhabited dwelling as an aggravated form of larceny.[14]

One significant feature of common-law burglary is that it was an inchoate offense recognized and punished centuries before the recognition of liability for attempts at the end of the eighteenth century.[15] The offense is committed in the act of breaking and entering, with the intent to commit a further felony inside the dwelling house. The offense is inchoate, relative to the felony inside the building, for the full plan need not be consummated in order for the offender to be guilty of burglary. Thus the proper analysis of burglary requires that judges think about two different facets of the burglar's intention. The intent to break and enter is obviously manifested in the acts of breaking and entering, but the intent to commit the felony inside is unexecuted and need not be manifested in the commission of an act that indicates the particular felony planned. Blackstone insisted that this inchoate intent be "demonstrated by some attempt or overt act,"[16] but this effort to

[8] 3 Coke 62; 1 Hale 550; 4 Blackstone 224.

[9] The common-law term was *fregit and intravit*. See 3 Coke 64; 1 Hale 550; 4 Blackstone 226.

[10] 3 Coke 64 ("mansion house"); 4 Blackstone 225 ("mansion or dwelling house").

[11] 3 Coke 65; 4 Blackstone 227–28 (intent need not be executed).

[12] See pp. 32, 79 *supra*.

[13] StGB 123 (unlawful entry).

[14] Code Pénal §386(1) (aggravated larceny if committed at night in an inhabited house); StGB §243(1)(1) (aggravated larceny if committed by entering a "building, apartment, service or business establishment or other enclosed quarters").

[15] See §3.3, at notes 9–13 *infra*.

[16] 4 Blackstone 227.

retain the principle of manifest criminality has never made an impact on formal definitions of the crime. The inchoate intent in burglary has emerged as an example of an intent that need not be incorporated in a manifestly criminal act, and therefore it has provided powerful evidence for the way of looking at intent that is characteristic of subjective criminality.

The significant battle between the two patterns of liability has played itself out in analyzing the requirement of a "breaking." In its original conception, the requirement of a "breaking" was designed to insure that the entry was a manifestly criminal act. All the classic writers held that the breaking must be "actual," not merely "constructive" as in cases of trespass.[17] Blackstone wrote that there must be a "substantial and forcible interruption."[18] The requirement is resonant with the tinges of manifest thievery that we found in the rule of "breaking bulk."[19] As in the experience with the requirement of a manifestly criminal act in larceny, the determination when a breaking occurred for the purposes of burglary led to some close distinctions. It was generally thought that opening a window was a "breaking" as well as lifting up the latch on a door.[20] Going through an open window was not a breaking,[21] but going down the chimney was.[22] The formal rationale for treating entry by the chimney as a "breaking" was that a chimney "is as much closed as the nature of things will permit."[23] Yet to make sense of these distinctions we should think of them not as inferences from the nature of things, but as judgments designed to capture the manifest criminality in breaking and entering. In our ordinary experience, entering by the chimney is far more incriminating than entering by an open window.

Despite this general rule of manifest criminality, it is important to note that from the time at least of Coke, the common-law

[17] E.g., 3 Coke 64; 1 Hale 551; 4 Blackstone 226.
[18] Blackstone 226.
[19] See §2.2.2 *supra*.
[20] 1 Hale 552; 4 Blackstone 226.
[21] *Ibid.*
[22] 1 Hale 551–52; 1 Hawkins 160–61; 4 Blackstone 226.
[23] *Ibid.*

writers and judges recognized that a fraudulent entry could provide a surrogate for a forcible entry. Coke gives the example of thieves who raise the hue and cry and thereby induce a constable to search their intended victim's house. Following the constable inside, they subdue both him and the owner and then effectuate their larcenous plan.[24] Cases of this sort were denominated *in fraudem legis.* Hawkins broadened the rule to include all fraudulent entry.[25] This broader version of the rule was supported by the leading case of Le Mott, who, together with his cohorts, gained admittance to the victim's house at night by pretending to wish to speak to the owner and then, once inside, carried out an allegedly pre-planned robbery.[26] It is important to note that in these cases of fraudulent entry, the thief typically consummates a full larceny or robbery. The offense is not treated as inchoate and incomplete as in the standard instance of burglary. Nonetheless, the possibility of substituting an act of fraud for an act of force had a substantial impact on the principle of manifest criminality. These cases of liability *in fraudem legis* were later cited by those who sought to stress the subjective dimensions of larceny.[27] They provided respectable authority for the interpretation of *Chisser* and *Pear* as cases in which a fraudulent, unmanifested intent provided an adequate substitute for force in the taking.[28]

If we leave aside these cases of fraudulent entry, with all their special features, it is clear that the ancient common-law crime is rooted in the pattern of manifest criminality. The expression of criminality came in the "breaking," yet the remarkable fact is that the modern legislative trend is to dispense with the requirement of an actual breaking. This is already established law in about half the jurisdictions in the United States,[29] in the English Theft Act of

[24] 3 Coke 64.

[25] 1 Hawkins 161; *cf.* 1 Hale 552.

[26] Kelyng 64 (3d ed. 1873) (as related by Wylde).

[27] An intermediate stage was the doctrine of *in fraudem legis* in larceny. The leading case is *Farre's Case,* discussed in §2.2, note 35 *supra.*

[28] See §2.3.2 *supra.*

[29] LaFave & Scott 710 n.23 (listing 22 jurisdictions that have dispensed with the breaking requirement). See generally, Wright, *Statutory Burglary—The Magic of Four*

1968,[30] and it is also supported by the recommendation of the Model Penal Code.[31] This means that in many jurisdictions any entry into one of a set of enumerated structures, if done with a felonious intent, satisfies the elements of burglary.[32] This means that if an actor enters a store with an unmanifested intent to commit larceny, he is guilty of burglary as soon as he sets foot in the store.[33] One could hardly imagine a clearer instantiation of the pattern of subjective criminality. The English Theft Act of 1968 and the Model Penal Code have balked at this extreme and have introduced the rule that the entry must be at least unlicensed[34] or trespassory.[35] This retains at least a trace of the traditional rule that the entry must be manifestly suspicious.[36]

§3.2.4. New Offenses Akin to Burglary-Without-Breaking. Once it became tenable to think of burglary as a crime committed by a nominally innocent and unthreatening entry into a building, legislators began to sense the potential of a whole new model of

---

Walls and a Roof, 100 U. Pa. L. Rev. 411 (1951); Note, *A Rationale of the Law of Burglary,* 51 Colum. L. Rev. 1009 (1951).

[30] Theft Act 1968, c. 60, §9(1)(a).

[31] MPC §221.1(1).

[32] See People v. Barry, 94 Cal. 481, 29 P. 1026 (1892) (defendant entered store during business hours with intent to commit larceny); Pinson v. State, 91 Ark. 434, 121 S.W. 751 (1909) (defendant entered saloon during business hours with intent to steal whiskey); Commonwealth v. Schultz, 168 Pa. Super. 435, 79 A.2d 109 (1951), *cert. denied,* 342 U.S. 842 (1951) (defendant entered tavern during business hours with intent to steal vending machine).

[33] This doctrine is particularly insidious when coupled with the felony-murder rule. See People v. Earl, 29 Cal. App. 3d 894, 105 Cal. Rptr. 831 (1973) (store guard apprehended defendant shoplifting; in the ensuing struggle defendant killed the guard; conviction for first-degree murder in the course of a burglary upheld on the theory that defendant entered the store with intent to shoplift).

[34] MPC §221.1(1) (no burglary if building is "open to the public or the actor is licensed"). *Cf.* Proposed Federal Criminal Code §1711 (burglary committed by one who at night and "without privilege . . . enters . . . a dwelling" [of another] with "intent to engage in conduct constituting a crime").

[35] Theft Act 1968, c. 60, §9(1)(a) (". . . enters a building or part of a building as a tresspasser . . ."). *But cf.* Regina v. Jones and Smith, [1976] 3 All E.R. 54 (Crim. App.) (holding that entering with intent to steal makes one a tresspasser).

[36] *Cf.* Proposed Federal Criminal Code §1711, which treats the act of "remain[ing] surreptitiously" within a dwelling or building as equivalent to entering it.

criminality. Recent years have witnessed a spate of new offenses penalizing various acts of "entering" buildings, trains, or other structures.[37] It is too early to assess whether this liberalized conception of burglary will generate large numbers of convictions where the entry is unincriminating. Yet the potential is undoubtedly there.

A recent decision in New Jersey reflects the extent to which the courts now take the pattern of subjective criminality to be a normal and sound framework for thinking about criminal liability. In State v. Young,[38] decided in 1970, the defendant was charged and convicted of violating a statute that prohibited any person other than a specified list of those with ordinary school business from entering any "place used for any educational purpose" with the "intent . . . of interfering with the peace and good order of the place. . . ."[39] The defendant, a lay minister, had entered a school building and had participated with students in a sit-in. On the assumption that this activity was designed to interrupt the "peace and good order" of the school, the jury had merely to find that at the time of entry, the defendant had the intent to participate in a sit-in. Though there was no manifestation of the defendant's thoughts or feelings at the time of entering the school, the jury apparently found beyond a reasonable doubt that he entertained the prohibited intent at that point of time.

The defendant's challenge to his conviction proved to be a constitutional attack on the entire pattern of subjective criminality. His claim was that his act of entry was "innocent" and that it "was beyond the power of the state to punish an innocent act merely because of a forbidden purpose."[40] It was to the appellant's credit that he attempted to articulate a new constitutional theory requiring a manifestation of criminal purpose. Yet there was no authority for him to build on; the recurrent constitutional question

[37] 18 U.S.C. §1991 (entering or trespassing on train with intent to commit murder or robbery); 18 U.S.C. §2276 (breaking or entering any vessel with intent to commit a felony).

[38] State v. Young, 57 N.J. 240, 271 A.2d 569 (1970), *cert. denied,* 402 U.S. 929 (1971).

[39] N.J. Stat. Ann. §2A: 149A-2.

[40] 57 N.J. at 255–56; 271 A.2d at 576–78.

in the litigated cases is not whether the act is sufficient, but whether the required intent or mental state is sufficient to permit a just conviction. The judges were unsympathetic to the claim that a criminal intent, coupled with some act in execution, was insufficient for a conviction. Their willingness to accept subjective criminality as a normal standard in the criminal law was reminiscent of the sentiments of the majority of the judges in *Middleton,* who remained unperturbed by the searching dissent of Baron Bramwell, protesting the subjectification of larceny.[41] When the issue is raised, whether it is proper to convict in the absence of manifestly criminal behavior, judges today typically respond that the principles of criminal justice are satisfied by an act demonstrating that the criminal plan has moved from the realm of thought to the realm of action.[42] Another standard technique of justification is to list other crimes conforming to the pattern of subjective criminality, thereby dispelling the suggestion that any one of them is an aberration.[43]

The technique of punishing nominally innocent acts has been carried to a fine art in federal criminal legislation. It is now a standard practice to punish the "act of traveling in interstate commerce" if the traveler then entertains a legislatively prohibited intent, such as the intent to avoid federal prosecution or the intent to avoid giving testimony in a federal trial.[44] This technique of definition goes beyond the subjectified burglary statutes, for the act of "traveling" or "crossing a state line" is thought of primarily as a nexus for establishing federal jurisdiction, rather than as a criminal act demonstrating the firmness of the actor's intent.[45]

The most notorious application of this form of federal of-

[41] See §2.4.2, at notes 25–28 *supra.*

[42] See Justice Douglas' opinion in Haupt v. United States, 330 U.S. 631, 644 (1947).

[43] See Justice Traynor's opinion in People v. Ashley, 42 Cal. 2d. 246, 264 n.4; 267 P.2d 271, 282 n.4 (1954) (upholding the principle that a fraudulent intent is sufficient for a false pretense by referring *inter alia* to burglary and larceny).

[44] See, e.g., 18 U.S.C. §1073.

[45] *Cf.* Proposed Federal Criminal Code §1831, which distinguishes carefully between the crime of inciting a riot and the criteria of federal jurisdiction.

ense—travelling with a prohibited intent—is the "Chicago Seven" trial in the aftermath of the riots at the 1968 Democratic Convention.[46] Eight defendants were initially indicted for crossing a state line with the intent "to incite a riot."[47] The case for the prosecution turned heavily on the defendant's political associations and beliefs; these beliefs, taken together with the events that occurred in Chicago, provided the critical proof of the prohibited intent at the time of crossing a state line. This prosecution reveals some of the abuses associated with the pattern of subjective criminality. When guilt or innocence turns on an unmanifested intent, the proof of guilt is likely to turn on an inference from the type of person the defendant is to a probabilistic conclusion about his having the prohibited intent at the relevant moment of time.

Our purpose, however, is not to evaluate the two patterns of liability, but to demonstrate the pervasive tension between them in diverse fields of the criminal law. In this section, we have pursued the traces of this tension in the crimes of embezzlement, false pretenses, burglary and related crimes of "entering" and "crossing." Now we turn to the general field of inchoate offenses, and particularly the punishment of attempted crimes.

§3.3. *Attempts.*

Before turning to a full discussion of attempted, but uncompleted offenses, we should become clear about what we mean either by an attempted offense or, more generally, by the concept of "inchoate" liability.

Attempts are cases of failure. A would-be killer shoots, but his aim is off. A woman bent on robbery enters a bank and pulls a gun, but is arrested before she gets the money. A man tries to rape

[46]United States v. Dellinger, 472 F.2d 340 (7th Cir. 1972) (reversing for procedural errors), *cert. denied,* 410 U.S. 970 (1973).

[47] 18 U.S.C. §2101.

a woman, but she dissuades him by telling him that she is pregnant. A man puts poison into his intended victim's coffee cup, but the latter spills the coffee before drinking it. All of these frustrated crimes are candidates for liability as criminal attempts.

The punishability of specific behavior as an attempt is inferred from a defined offense-in-chief, such as murder, robbery or rape. There are major problems in determining whether the existence of an offense entails the punishability of an attempt to commit it. Many European codes take the restrictive path of penalizing attempts only when the code so specifies in the section defining the offense-in-chief.[1] Anglo-American legislation is lax on this point. As a result, the problem whether an attempt is punishable frequently takes the form of a debate in principle. It is often argued, and usually unsuccessfully, that offenses such as burglary[2] and assault,[3] that are inchoate in nature, cannot themselves generate derivative liability for an attempt. It is obviously preferable for legislatures to specify precisely when attempts are punishable and when they are not.

Liability for an attempted offense is a paradigmatic instance of an inchoate offense. The attempt is inchoate relative to the offense-in-chief. This claim is easily made, for the attempt is defined as an act falling short of the consummated crime. In other contexts, however, it is more difficult to assess whether a defined offense is an "inchoate" or a "consummated" offense. Consider the examples of conspiracy, vagrancy, and disseminating pornography. Are these offenses in the nature of inchoate offenses designed to inhibit a more egregious form of harm?[4] Or is the conspiracy, the occurrence of vagrancy or the dissemination of obscene matter in itself

§3.3. [1] StGB §23(1) (attempted felony (*Verbrechen*) is always punishable; attempted misdemeanors (*Vergenen*), only when the code so provides); Code Pénal §2 (every attempted felony (*crime*) punishable; no reference to lesser offenses); Ugol. kod. (RSFSR) §15 (attempt liability for all offenses); MPC §5.01 (all "crimes").

[2] E.g., People v. Gibson, 94 Cal. App. 2d 468, 210 P.2d 747 (1949) (liability affirmed); State v. Kleier, 69 Idaho 491, 210 P.2d 388 (1949) (liability affirmed).

[3] *Compare* State v. Wilson, 218 Ore. 575, 346 P.2d 115 (1959) (liability for attempted assault) *with* Wilson v. State, 53 Ga. 205 (1874) (no liability for attempted assault).

[4] See §3.4 *infra*.

the harm that the law seeks to prevent? This is an important question; as an aspect of our study of attempts we should seek to determine which other offenses are inchoate and therefore functionally analogous to liability for an attempted offense.

Absent a catalogue of harms that the law seeks to prevent, the distinction between inchoate and consummated offenses proves to be illusive. Murder is a good candidate for a consummated offense, though an isolated act of killing might be seen as inchoate if the killing is the first step in a program of genocide. Conspiracy is commonly treated as an inchoate offense, for the crime is complete at the moment that the actors enter into an agreement to commit some other crime. The agreement is seen as the first step in carrying out the planned unlawful act. Yet can we be so sure that the agreement itself is not the evil the law seeks to prevent? The phenomenon of people forming criminal bands might be regarded as sufficiently unnerving to be prohibited for its own sake.

Similar doubts affect the ancient practice of punishing vagrants, vagabonds, and other dissolute persons as criminals. Though this type of legislation has been declared unconstitutionally vague,[5] there was no doubt a time when people knew precisely who vagabonds were.[6] The modern view of these crimes is that they are inchoate offenses, designed to prevent undesirable and dangerous types from committing serious offenses. The point is clear. Without a general theory of harms that ought to be prevented, one can hardly develop a ranking of offenses as complete and inchoate.

If the theory of harm does not make the matter sufficiently complicated, let us recall the crime of *furtum manifestum,* which provides the basis for Western theories of larceny. The thief breaking the close was subject to immediate execution and it did not seem to matter whether he had his hands on the owner's goods. According to contemporary criteria we would say that the thief

[5] Papachristou v. City of Jacksonville, 405 U.S. 156 (1972).

[6] This perception of a criminal type should not be confused with the shared image of thieving, discussed in §2.2 *supra.* The difference is between concurring on a type of person and concurring on a type of act.

could be executed for attempting larceny or burglary. It is not so clear, however, that the matter was conceived this way in ancient legal systems. The act of stealthful or forcible intrusion may have been sufficient to warrant labelling the actor as a thief. We could adapt the theory of harm to this case and hold that the intrusion was sufficient harm to justify the private act of execution. Yet it may be a distortion to insist upon fitting manifest larceny into the conventional categories of consummated and inchoate offenses.

Despite these objections, it does seem clear that the modern tendency is to restrict the number of relevant harms and therefore to expand the scope of inchoate offenses. Holmes went so far as to argue that what we take to be completed larceny is merely an inchoate offense relative to the risk of permanent deprivation.[7] The extreme application of this reductionist view would be that the only harm that matters is death, and that all offenses, including larceny, arson and treason, should be seen merely as inchoate attacks on the value of life. This view has much to commend it, even though it seems to ignore the common law's effort to protect other interests, such as order, security and liberty as ends in themselves.

Though some arguably inchoate offenses, such as vagrancy and conspiracy, have long been part of the common law, the formal doctrine of attempts did not emerge until the late eighteenth century. English law lagged in this process of development. Continental systems had recognized as early as the sixteenth century that an independent crime of attempting could be derived from an offense-in-chief.[8] Professor Sayre argues persuasively that the common-law doctrine stems from Rex v. Scofield,[9] decided in 1784;[10] in his opinion, Lord Mansfield noted explicitly that the "*completion* of an act, criminal in itself, [was not] necessary to constitute criminality."[11] The defendant Scofield was charged with having put a lighted candle among combustible material in a house that was

[7] Holmes 71.
[8] Constitutio Criminalis Carolina §178; see generally Jescheck 385–86.
[9] Cald. 397 (1784).
[10] See Sayre, *Criminal Attempts*, 41 Harv. L. Rev. 821 (1928); *cf.* Hall 569–74.
[11] Cald. at 400 (emphasis in original).

then in his possession, with an intent to burn it. The intended arson was apparently unconsummated, but Lord Mansfield reasoned that a derivative crime of attempting covered the case.[12]

From the outset there was a strong inclination to think of attempts by analogy to the emerging theory of subjective criminality in larceny. The intent to commit the offense-in-chief would be the core of the offense, and the function of the act of partial execution would be to demonstrate the firmness of the actor's resolve and perhaps to provide evidence of his intent. Even the opinion in *Scofield* contains the comment: "The *intent* may make an act, innocent in itself, criminal . . ." [13] The pattern of subjective criminality eventually did gain the upper hand in the theory of attempts, both in Continental as well as in Anglo-American jurisdictions. Yet in the course of the nineteenth century, and to some extent in our own time, judges and theorists have been deeply concerned about the potentially unlimited scope of liability of those who intend to commit recognized crimes. The struggle against thrusting intent to the core of the offense has been expressed in criteria closely related to the principle of manifest criminality. Thus the history of liability for attempted offenses recapitulates, in part, the tensions we have noted in the history of larceny and of burglary. The emphasis on the actor's intent as the core of the offense stands in conflict with the emphasis on objective criteria as a condition for liability. These tensions have been played out, as we shall see, in two interrelated doctrinal disputes.

§3.3.1. **Two Doctrinal Issues in Attempts.** Of the two recurrent themes in the law of attempts, the first is the problem of pinpointing the time in the unfolding of a criminal plan at which the actor becomes liable for an attempt. The execution of a criminal plan is thought typically to pass through several stages: conceiving the plan, acquiring the materials or firearms necessary for the job, making one's way to the scene of the intended crime, deploying the materials, and then executing the crime. The problem is speci-

[12] The case also stands for the proposition that an attempt to commit a misdemeanor is punishable as a misdemeanor. See *id.* at 402–03.

[13] Cald. at 400 (emphasis in original).

fying the point in this process at which the actor passes the threshold of criminality. This is important not only if the plan is unsuccessful but also if it is interrupted and we wish to know whether the aborted plan itself constitutes a punishable crime. It is also important in determining when the police may intervene in the course of conduct without risking liability for false arrest.[14] Most legal systems define the threshold of criminality as the difference between an attempt and mere preparation. This distinction does not hold in the Soviet Union, however, which subjects both attempts and preparation to criminal sanctions.[15] However, the Soviet court may in its discretion dismiss a prosecution for preparation if the defendant's conduct was a minimal social threat.[16] The legalist sentiments of the nineteenth century recoiled against punishing conduct so far removed from the legislatively defined offense. As a result, most legal systems then held the contrary view that to be guilty of an attempt one must do everything in one's power to effectuate the offense. This latter extreme has now been rejected as incompatible with the policy of early intervention and prevention of harm. Therefore the problem is finding the mean that is compatible with the principle of legislative definition of punishable conduct and yet consistent with the practical value of early police intervention.

The second, and related, theme concerns attempts which, in the nature of things, cannot lead to fruition. Of course, all prosecutions for attempted crime are directed to cases of failure and the failure might be due to a variety of causes. The police might intervene, the victim might resist and escape, a third party might appear at the last minute and scare off the would-be offender. A special class of these failures has been singled out for concern among judges and theorists seeking to subject the crime of attempt

[14] See §3.7 *infra* for a discussion of permissible preventive action by the police and its impact on the substantive law of attempts.

[15] Ugol. kod. (RSFSR) §15. One recent text stresses that liability for preparatory acts should be imposed only for those acts that are "dangerous to the interest of the socialist government, the socialist legal order or the rights and interests of private citizens. . . ." Kurs (GP 1970) at 408.

[16] Ugol. kod. (RSFSR) §7(2); *cf.* Kurs (GP 1968) at 551–52.

to just boundaries. These attempts are conventionally called "impossible" attempts. They are typified by cases of attempting to pick an empty pocket or to kill by shooting at a tree stump, thinking that it is a person. Another type of case that has caused considerable trouble to the courts is receiving goods, thinking they are stolen when in fact they are not. It should be noted in all of these cases that the actor makes a mistake about the effectiveness of his act in executing his criminal intention. Unlike a mistake that excuses an actor for causing harm,[17] these are mistakes in execution that prevent criminally minded persons from realizing their intentions. Thus the problem resembles the issue we encounter in analyzing the cases of staged larceny: is there a good reason for acquitting someone who is obviously dangerous and has done everything in his power to commit an offense?[18]

The issue is sometimes posed as whether "impossibility" ought to be a defense, yet this is highly misleading. With the exception of a short period in the mid-nineteenth century,[19] the courts have never been willing to acquit for all cases of impossibility. As in the cases of staged larceny, the problem is working out a coherent account of those cases in which the courts have been willing to acquit.

Both of these major arenas of dispute pertain to the element of acting rather than the element of intent. It is generally agreed that the intent required for an attempt is the intent to effectuate the offense-in-chief. Attempted larceny requires an intent to steal; attempted murder, an intent to kill. There are in fact some conceptual puzzles in explaining why the intent requirement for attempt is sometimes more demanding than the state of mind required for the offense-in-chief.[20] We shall later have occasion to examine

[17] See generally Chapter Nine *infra*.

[18] See §2.1.3 *supra*.

[19] See text at notes 41–46 *infra*.

[20] See, e.g., Thacker v. Commonwealth, 134 Va. 767, 114 S.E. 504 (1922) (intent to kill necessary for attempted murder, but not for murder); United States v. Short, 4 U.S.C.M.A. 437, 16 C.M.R. 11 (1954) (Brosman, J., dissenting) (arguing that an unreasonable mistake as to victim's consent would not be a defense to consummated rape, but should be a defense to the inchoate offense of assault with intent to rape). Several common-law writers have argued that recklessness as to the result should

these puzzles, but for now our attention is directed to points of controversy in assessing the act required for a criminal attempt.

From the perspective of the major movements that sweep across the terrain of the criminal law, there is a close connection between the two doctrinal problems in defining criminal attempts—distinguishing attempts from preparation and impossibility. The critical question that unites them is the elementary issue whether the act of attempting is a distinct and discernible element of the crime of attempting. To say that the act is a distinct element is to require that the act conform to objective criteria defined in advance. The act must evidence attributes subject to determination independently of the actor's intent. In short, there must be features of the attempt as palpable as the death of the victim in homicide or a trespassory taking in larceny. We shall refer to the set of arguments favoring this approach as the "objectivist" theory of attempts. Though the term "objective" may have a different connotation in some contexts, we shall use the term to mean a legal standard for assessing conduct that does not presuppose a prior determination of the actor's intent.

The opposing school is appropriately called "subjectivist," for it dispenses with the objective criteria of attempting. The act of execution is important so far as it verifies the firmness of the intent. No act of specific contours is necessary to constitute the attempt, for any act will suffice to demonstrate the actor's commitment to carry out his criminal plan.

As we delve more deeply into objectivist and subjectivist theories of liability for criminal attempts, we shall discover that objectivists tend to favor a minimalist approach, and subjectivists, a maximalist approach to liability. As to the two doctrinal issues that we underscored, this means that objectivists tend to draw the line of liability as close as possible to consummation of the offense and

be sufficient for an attempt. See Williams 619 (recklessness as to truth of representation should be sufficient for attempted false pretenses). See generally J. Smith, *The Element of Chance in Criminal Liability*, 1971 Crim. L. Rev. 63, 72–73. Under the German interpretation of the intent required for an attempt, *dolus eventualis* is sufficient, Jescheck 388; for the relationship between recklessness and *dolus eventualis*, see §6.5.2 *infra*.

tend, further, to be sympathetic to claims of impossibility as a bar to liability. This combination of views generates a minimalist approach to liability. Subjectivists, in contrast, tend to push back the threshold of attempting and reject the relevance of impossibility—a stance that yields a maximalist net of liability. In turning to a more detailed study of objectivist and subjectivist theories, we should keep in mind that the watershed between them is the question whether the act of attempting is a distinct element of liability.

§3.3.2. **Objectivist Approaches and the Theory of Attempts.** The nineteenth century witnessed a persistent effort to defend an objectivist theory of attempting. The draftsmen of the French Penal Code of 1810 took the issue to be so important that in §2 of the code they defined the threshold of attempting in a classic phrase that came to dominate European thinking about the crime. The critical threshold was *le commencement d'exécution.* At the point that the execution began, but not before that, the actor became criminally liable. This phrase was carried over in the Prussian Code of 1851[21] and then in the German Code of 1871.[22] An analogous standard found its way into the nineteenth-century English case law.[23] Of course, it is by no means easy to know when the execution has begun. Does bringing a ladder to the scene of an intended burglary commence the execution? Or sterilizing instruments with the intent to perform an abortion? Or burning down a house with the intent to defraud an insurance company? Whether or not the French formula is easy to apply, it does represent a significant ideological effort to link the act of attempting with the definition of the substantive offense. This was a way to vest the act of attempting with substantive content and thereby avoid the dangers of an elastic, discretionary system of justice.

There are many points on the spectrum between preparation and consummation and the easiest point for the objectivist to de-

[21] Prussian Criminal Code §31.

[22] StGB 1871, §43.

[23] Regina v. Eagleton, 6 Cox Crim. Cas. 559 (1855) ("acts immediately connected with [the commission of the offense]").

fend is the extreme closest to consummation. This test is expressed in English jurisprudence as the threshold of the "last step" or the "last proximate step" toward commission of the offense. The actor must take all steps connected with the execution of the offense in order to be guilty of an attempt. If the actor has yet to pull the trigger, to submit a fraudulent claim to his insurance company or to ignite the material prepared for burning, he cannot be guilty of attempted murder, fraud or arson. The primary disadvantage with this extreme point of demarcation is that it insulates all criminal conduct prior to the "last step" from arrest and prosecution. Though Western courts may have defended this extreme end of the spectrum in the mid-nineteenth century, the consensus—even within the objectivist camp—now favors some criminalization of conduct that falls short of the "last step" attempt.

Once objectivist theorists break from the moorings of the "last step," it proves harder than expected to find a secure anchor in the ebb and flow of events leading from preparation to consummation. The most one can do is to isolate a number of different courses plied in the hope of defining a required act of attempting independently of the actor's criminal intention. The approaches break down into theories that emphasize (1) the stages of commission, (2) the danger of the act, and (3) the apprehension felt by the victim. The latter test, as we shall see, invokes a variation of the principle of manifest criminality.

A. Stages of Commission. This approach to the threshold of attempting presupposes a common structure underlying all criminal activity. The argument is that every criminal act consists of a discernable number of discrete acts beginning with conception and terminating in execution. Firing the gun is the last act, aiming the gun is the penultimate act, drawing the gun is the antepenultimate act, and so forth.[24] If this structure of acts did exist in nature, one could measure the required degree of proximity to success by counting back the required number of acts from the last act necessary for execution. Yet it is philosophically questionable to suppose that the number of acts between entering the victim's

[24] See Williams 627.

house and pulling the trigger could actually be counted. Even if this structure of phases were tenable, there would be serious problems of policy in subjecting all crimes to the same test of proximity.

The more general question is whether a sound approach to the act required for a criminal attempt could ignore differences among types of offenses. Is it possible to formulate a test for obtaining property by false pretenses that would apply to killing by poison? When the principle of the "last proximate step" prevailed in Western jurisprudence, it might have made sense to think of a universal test applying to all crimes. Since the retreat from that position, a sensible approach requires that some attention be paid to the problems characteristic of different offenses.[25]

B. The Criterion of Danger. One recurrent objectivist argument is that only those acts should constitute attempts that are "directly dangerous" to interests protected under the law. It is true that this test might lead to a lower threshold of liability for, say, killing by poison than for crimes of fraud. This is a theme particularly prominent in German theory.[26] It is also advanced by Holmes in his sophisticated comment that the line between preparation and attempt should be drawn with a view to the "nearness of the danger, the greatness of the harm, and the degree of apprehension felt."[27] The difficulty with the standard of dangerousness is that the concept admits of infinite variations of degree. How dangerous must the act be in order to warrant criminalization? There obviously can be no precise answer to that question, yet the emphasis on danger brings home the importance of thinking of attempts as relational events, signalling the breakdown of order and the eruption of a threat to the victim.

C. Apprehension and Unequivocal Conduct. The third theory, intimated by Holmes' reference to "the degree of apprehen-

[25] This theme is explored in Arnold, *Criminal Attempts—The Rise and Fall of an Abstraction,* 40 Yale L.J. 53 (1930).

[26] Schönke-Schröder-Eser §22, note 28, at 284; Jescheck 386–87; Horn, *Der Versuch,* 202 StW 309 (1900); for the current state of German law, see text at notes 94–96 *infra.*

[27] Holmes 68; *cf.* Commonwealth v. Kennedy, 170 Mass. 18, 48 N.E. 770 (1897).

sion felt," invokes the principle of manifest criminality. Conduct can generate apprehension only if it is manifestly criminal. Reasoning from the harm of apprehension to the type of conduct that can induce it, we are led to the standard that is conventionally called the requirement of "unequivocally" criminal conduct. The advocate of this approach in the common-law literature was Justice Salmond, who introduced this theory into the law of New Zealand[28] and defended it in his textbook on jurisprudence.[29] According to Salmond a criminal attempt is "an act that shows criminal intent on the face of it."[30] The inverse implication of this standard is that an act, innocent on its face, is not a criminal attempt. The act of attempting is one that must bespeak criminality. One cannot invoke the unmanifested intent of the actor in order to establish the criminality of the act.

Though contemporary academic writers routinely attack this standard,[31] and though New Zealand abolished the test by legislation in 1961,[32] Salmond's theory still enjoys a following in Anglo-American jurisidictions. The concept of "equivocality" has crept into several American legislative formulations of a test for attempts.[33] And in 1967 an English court endorsed a variation of the principle.[34] The arguments against this test rarely, if ever, reach the level of principle. The main complaint is that it is difficult to know whether an act unequivocally bespeaks criminality. After all, as Glanville Williams argues with finesse, a man approaching a haystack with a lighted match may have the intent but to light his

[28] The King v. Barker, [1924] N.Z.L.R. 865, 872 (Ct. App. 1924). *Cf.* Cambell & Bradley v. Ward, [1955] N.Z.L.R. 471 (act of approaching parked car too equivocal to constitute attempted larceny).

[29] J. Salmond, Jurisprudence 404 (7th ed. 1924).

[30] [1924] N.Z.L.R. at 874.

[31] Stuart, *The Actus Reus in Attempts,* 1970 Crim. L. Rev. 505, 507-08; LaFave & Scott 435–36; Hall 581; Williams 630. *But cf.* Turner, *Attempts to Commit Crimes,* 5 Camb. L.J. 230, 236 (1934).

[32] Crimes Act 1961, No. 43, §72(3).

[33] Del. Code tit. 11, §532; Wis. Stat. §939.32(2).

[34] Davey v. Lee, [1967] 2 All E.R. 423 (Q.B.) (attempt to steal metal from storage yard; fence found cut and defendant apprehended in possession of wire cutters; conviction affirmed on the ground that the act could "not reasonably be regarded as having any other purpose. . . .")

pipe.[35] Even shooting with real bullets at someone sitting in a car might bear the innocent purpose of testing the bullet-proof armor and glass recently installed in the car. Yet a preoccupation with borderline cases bypasses the theoretical core of the argument. In the broad range of crimes such as arson, robbery and homicide, the criminal act is patent in observable facts. It is true, however, that the further back one sets the threshold of attempt, the more difficult it is to demand that the preliminary act unequivocally bespeak danger and criminality. Nonetheless, the standard of unequivocality has such persistent appeal that we should put aside the problems of solving borderline cases and consider whether in principle the standard warrants our approval.

The arguments in favor of the principle of unequivocality have never been fully aired. For one, it has never been made clear why, in principle, the act should be "criminal on the face of it." If the argument is that this is a test designed to prevent the conviction of innocent persons, the argument is not likely to persuade those willing to put their trust in other sorts of evidence.[36] The problem is why one should insist on one type of evidence rather than another. The test appears to be more defensible if one thinks of it not as a matter of evidence, but as a theory about the act as an independent substantive element in the definition of a criminal attempt. The principle that the act must bespeak a criminal purpose generates an objective test for the act of attempting. The test both supplies evidence of intent and implicitly rejects proof of the intent by other means. If the act is not "criminal on its face," no extrinsic proof of a criminal intent can render it criminal. Stressing the evidentiary function of Salmond's standard ignores its vital significance as an objectivist theory about the act required to constitute an attempt.

Now one might be properly troubled by two questions. First, why is it important that there be an objective test for the act of attempting? Why not simply determine the actor's intent by any

[35] Williams 630.

[36] Hall 581–83 (apparently willing to rely on confessions as adequate proof of intent).

means available? Secondly, if an objective test if desirable, why should it be this one? The first question must await our systematic study of the implications of objective and subjective theories of attempt liability. The second question finds its answer in the premises of the pattern of manifest criminality. That criminal conduct is unnerving to the community is sufficient to justify either private or official intervention. Private intervention takes the form of defensive force; public intervention, of prosecution for a criminal offense. If the public feels "apprehension" at the suspect's manifestly criminal conduct, that is a sufficient social interest to warrant suppression. The corollary is that if an act is so equivocal that it does not generate apprehension, then it should not be subject to either private or public suppression.

Stated in this fashion, Salmond's criterion of attempting enjoys some appeal. At least it explains to us why the act of attempting should be regarded as an independent element of liability and what the criteria should be for assessing whether a particular act is sufficient. Yet the standard of community apprehension also bears a serious flaw, which derives from grounding liability in a case-by-case assessment of public apprehension. This flaw is suggested by Holmes' discussion of an antebellum conviction for attempted rape in Alabama;[37] a slave had "run after a white woman, but desisted before he caught her."[38] In a more recent case, the Alabama Supreme Court sustained a conviction for attempted assault with an intent to rape in a case in which a black man followed a white woman down the street and said something "unintelligible," but never came within "two or three feet" of her.[39] In working out his theory of attempts, Holmes approvingly cited the former case, presumably as an example of the way in which the "degree of apprehension felt" affects the boundaries of attempts.[40] It seems that, for a like reason, he would have approved of the more recent case. Any theory that is tied to apprehension actually felt or to an in-

[37] Lewis v. State, 35 Ala. 380 (1860).
[38] Holmes 68.
[39] McQuirter v. State, 36 Ala. App. 707, 63 So. 2d 388 (1953).
[40] Holmes 68.

digenous sense of social order might have to concur in this analysis. A majority of Alabamans might then have regarded it as unnerving for a black man to follow a white woman down the street; that, for them, would have been conduct unequivocally indicating a lascivious purpose. Presumably, a white man's chasing a black woman would not unequivocably manifest criminality and danger. In convicting for attempted rape on these racist criteria, the Alabama judges were at least faithful to their fears. Their decisions provide a clear warning of the tyranny implicit in any theory of criminality that surrenders totally to the sentiments of the local community.

It is true that the common law of larceny was grounded in the principle of manifest criminality and the theory of crime as an unnerving event. Yet there was an important difference. The early law of larceny required the breaking of an enclosure; the later law, the "breaking" of possession as a condition of liability. These rules mediated between the theory of liability and the day-to-day decisions of the courts. The courts did not appeal directly to their sense of who looked like a thief; rather they sought to interpret rules that, in turn, were inspired by a shared image of thieving. If the Alabama court had to state a rule of liability, it is unlikely that they would explicitly declare race to be a relevant factor in the definition of a criminal attempt. It is the unmediated appeal to the community's sense of what is criminal and unnerving that permits the covert influence of racist criteria. What is needed to avoid the abuses of responding directly to the community's fears is a two-step decision procedure: first, the articulation of rules based on criteria of manifest criminality; and, secondly, application of the rules in particular cases.

The principle of manifest criminality proves to be a source both of protection and of danger to a criminal suspect. It is a source of protection so far as it sets a standard of criminality that excludes all acts that appear innocent on their face. It is a source of danger so far as it unleashes a standard of liability that is responsive to the community's fears and irrational sentiments. The safeguard against the latter danger is the invocation of manifest criminality as a rationale for rules rather than for individual decisions on liability. Yet the ongoing problem in the law of attempts is how one should formulate those rules in a sound and workable fashion.

§3.3.3. **Manifest Criminality and Impossible Attempts.** We have seen that the principle of manifest criminality is one of several strands in the efforts of judges and theorists to make sense of the criminal act of attempting as a distinct element of liability. Other approaches include the analysis of proximity to consummation and of the danger represented by the defendant's acts. The field of impossible attempts poses a special set of problems. The defendant thinks that a stump is the man he wants to kill and shoots at it. Or he puts sugar in his intended victim's coffee cup and he believes, mistakenly, that the sugar is arsenic. These cases are typical of the enigmas that have befuddled courts and commentators for the last century. These cases of impossibility trouble objectivist theorists because they are situations in which the effort of the defendant is not dangerous to anyone. So far as the concept of attempting is linked with the issues of danger and socially disturbing conduct, totally harmless activity should not qualify as criminal. The challenge for objectivist theory is the clarification of its own premises by working out the distinction between those cases of impossibility where the courts should convict and those where they should acquit on the ground that the required element of acting is not satisfied.

The claim of impossibility reached its peak of influence in the mid-nineteenth century. In 1864 an English court held that it was not criminal to stick one's hand into an empty pocket with an undisputed intent to steal.[41] At about the same time, a Prussian court held that it was not criminal to break into a room for the purpose of stealing if it turned out that the goods sought were not there.[42] There is also a mid-century French case in which administering an innocuous abortifacient was held not to be attempted abortion.[43]

[41] Regina v. Collins, 169 Eng. Rep. 1477 (Crim. App. 1864); *but cf.* Regina v. Goodchild, 175 Eng. Rep. 121 (1846) (liability for administering abortifacient to non-pregnant woman).

[42] Judgment of the Prussian High Court, February 22, 1854, 1854 GA 548.

[43] Judgment of January 6, 1859, Recueil Sirey 1859. I. 362.

In this very brief phase of development, it seemed that any effort to commit a crime that was intrinsically impossible would be exempt from punishment.

It is a point of historical interest that the leading English advocate of this indulgent approach toward impossible attempts was Baron Bramwell[44]—the same learned judge who in *Middleton* fought a rear-guard defense of larceny as a "privy or clandestine taking."[45] Bramwell consistently favored a theory of criminality that elevated the criminal act to an independent dimension of liability. In the case of larceny, his view took the form of insisting that the taking had to be a trespass—a manifestly criminal act. In the field of attempts, his philosophy led to the view that if the act, by its nature, was incapable of producing harm, it could not constitute the kind of act that justified criminal punishment.

As Bramwell's views lost ground in the metamorphosis of larceny, they gradually receded in the English law of attempts. In the last quarter of the nineteenth century, it gradually became clear that the courts were going to subject some impossible attempts to liability. The only question was how far and how fast they would move.[46]

The same trend was noticeable on the Continent. In the late 1870s the French *Cour de Cassation* held that liability was properly imposed on someone who, with the intent to kill, shot into a room where his enemy usually spent the night but which was empty at the time.[47] Similarly, the French court held, contrary to the English precedent, that someone who tried to pick an empty pocket was guilty of attempted larceny.[48] In 1880, the first year of its published decisions, the Supreme Court of the German Reich held that intentionally using an innocuous substance with the intent to abort constituted the crime of attempted abortion.[49] In the same year the

[44] See Bramwell's opinions in Regina v. M'Pherson, 169 Eng. Rep. 975 (1857); Regina v. Collins, 169 Eng. Rep. 1477 (1864).

[45] See §2.4.2, at notes 25–28 *supra*.

[46] *Collins* was overruled in Regina v. Ring, 17 Cox Crim. Cas. 491 (C.C.R. 1892). See generally Hall 587–589; Williams 635–37.

[47] Judgment of April 12, 1877, Recueil Sirey 1877. I. 329.

[48] Judgment of November 4, 1876, Recueil Sirey 1877. I. 48.

[49] Judgment of May 24, 1880, 1 RGSt. 439.

Court also decided that trying to kill a child who was already dead was attempted infanticide.[50]

There were different theories that could have justified this rapid movement toward the criminalization of some impossible attempts. As we shall see, a version of objectivist theory would justify punishment in most of these cases. In the German development, the stimulus was judicial adherence to a subjective theory of attempt liability. Since the Court's aggressive beginning in 1880, the German judiciary has adhered to the view that the defendant's subjective perception is controlling on whether his act constitutes an attempt.[51] If, for example, the defendant believes that sugar is arsenic and he uses it to try to poison another, his belief is the only relevant consideration. This was a remarkable development in German law, for the scholarly community held out against this pattern of subjectification, at least until the beginning of the Third Reich.[52] They argued that these decisions violated basic principles of liability, and they devoted considerable effort to developing theories about when impossible attempts should be punished and when they should be exempt.[53]

With the case law proceeding ahead of theory, courts and theorists on both sides of the Atlantic have struggled to find patterns implicit in the decisions.[54] In taking a closer look at these decisions we shall attempt to determine whether this resistance to sub-

[50] Judgment of June 10, 1880, 1 RGSt. 451.

[51] See generally Jescheck 399–401; Schönke-Schröder-Eser §22, notes 63–64, at 290. For an analysis of the provision in the 1975 code, see text at notes 95–96 *infra.*

[52] For a critique of the collapse of the objective theory, see Spendel, *Zur Neubegründung der objektiven Versuchstheorie,* in Festschrift für Ulrich Stock 89 (1966).

[53] For a clear statement of the objectivist school, see R. Frank, Strafgesetzbuch für das Deutsche Reich §43, I, at 83–84 (18th ed. 1931) (arguing that the ordinary language of "attempting" and the principle *nulla poena sine lege* support the defense of "inaptness"). *Id.* §43, III, at 88–89 (summarizing the literature of the objectivist school).

[54] For some thoughtful recent studies, see Elkind, *Impossibility in Criminal Attempts: A Theorist's Headache,* 54 Va. L. Rev. 20 (1968); Enker, *Impossibility in Criminal Attempts—Legality and the Legal Process,* 53 Minn. L. Rev. 665 (1969); Hughes, *One Further Footnote on Attempting the Impossible,* 42 N.Y.U.L. Rev. 1005 (1967); Smith, *Two Problems in Criminal Attempts Reexamined—II,* 1962 Crim. L. Rev. 212; Strahorn, *The Effect of Impossibility on Criminal Attempts,* 87 U. Pa. L. Rev. 962 (1930).

jectification of the law reflects an intuitive commitment to principles of manifest criminality. The problematic cases tend to group themselves in several recurrent patterns.

A. The Shooting Cases. It is agreed by all supporters of an objectivist approach to attempts that there should be no liability in the case of shooting at a tree stump with the intent to kill.[55] Yet the courts have found liability in closely related situations. A California decision in 1892 imposed liability for attempted murder for shooting at a hole in the roof where the defendant thought his intended victim would be and indeed where the victim had been a few moments before.[56] A few years later, a Missouri court convicted on a charge of attempted murder for shooting at the bed where the intended victim usually slept.[57] Courts have also convicted in cases in which the defendant has gone through all the motions of an attempted killing but the gun proved to be unloaded.[58] It seems obvious that these cases of attempted homicide conform clearly to the pattern of manifest criminality. Although there is no shared image of attempting as there is of thieving, in the facts of all these cases where liability is imposed, we can discern an obvious effort to commit homicide. Shooting at the intended victim's bed and aiming a gun manifest the intent to kill. In shooting at a tree stump, in contrast, there is nothing in the facts to indicate that an attempt is under way. According to objectivist theory, attempting is not just an event of inner experience. It is an effort in the real world to accomplish one's objective. Therefore, when the act is aptly related to the actor's objective, the courts perceive a manifest attempt to commit an offense. Yet when the act is objectively unrelated to the intent, as in the case of shooting at a tree stump, judges and theorists properly balk at positing an act of attempting. The notion of aptness here is obviously

[55] Holmes 69; Regina v. M'Pherson, 169 Eng. Rep. 975 (Crim. App. 1857).

[56] People v. Lee Kong, 95 Cal. 666, 30 P. 800 (1892).

[57] State v. Mitchell, 170 Mo. 633, 71 S.W. 175 (1902). *Cf.* the comparable French decision, *supra* note 50.

[58] State v. Damms, 9 Wis. 2d 183, 100 N.W.2d 592 (1960) (interpreting the fact that the gun was unloaded as an intervention of an "extraneous factor" under the applicable statute; for analogous decisions, see LaFave & Scott 441, nn.28–30.

closely related to the principle of manifest criminality. An apt attempt is one that manifests danger to the surrounding environment.

A careful application of this theory of aptness[59] requires that one be able to describe the case in a manner abstracted from the particular incident. Once the description is at hand, the problem of aptness is one of assessing whether in the long run the type of conduct involved is likely to produce harm. If the type of conduct would produce harm in the long run, then the defendant's act is apt and a punishable attempt, even though it is impossible under the circumstances. The critical stage in the analysis is the description of the case. If, for example, we import the fact into the description that the intended victim is *not* in his bed, then it is clear that when extrapolated over the long run, the type of conduct involved—shooting into an empty bed—is not likely to produce harm.

The test for whether facts should be incorporated into the description is whether the fact is likely to be known to objective observers of the event. The test is admittedly not precise, though it does provide a rule of thumb for distinguishing between a tree stump and the bed of the intended victim. The former is readily observed for what it is, and therefore our description of the stump case includes the fact of the stump. Yet the bed of the intended victim is likely to be thought occupied at night and therefore it seems less plausible to include the victim's not being there in abstracting the case to a type of activity.

A good example of a borderline case in this sort of analysis came before the Missouri courts a few decades ago. A hunter shot at a stuffed deer with the intent to kill a live deer. An appellate court reversed his conviction for attempting to kill a protected animal out of season.[60] The decision is highly debatable. If the case is described as shooting at a stuffed deer, there is no doubt that the

[59] The general term in German and Russian to refer to an impossible attempt (*untauglicher Versuch, negodnye pokushenie*) is better translated as "inapt attempt." Thus the terminology of these systems incorporates the theory advanced here. French terminology (*le crime impossible*) is the same as English.

[60] State v. Guffey, 262 S.W.2d 152 (Mo. App. 1953).

conduct would not be dangerous. Yet if the activity is described as shooting at what appears reasonably to be a deer, then shooting under the circumstances is dangerous; in the long run some of these appearances will prove to be authentic and deer will suffer. Whether the factor of appearance should be incorporated in the description of the case depends on how deceptive the dummy was. If everyone in the vicinity would have taken the dummy to be just that, then the case begins to resemble that of the tree stump and liability should be denied.

In this particular case there was another factor that, paradoxically, would have converted the deceptiveness of the dummy into an argument for acquittal. Because the dummy was set up by forest rangers in order to catch those with a proclivity to hunt out of season, the court might have been subliminally influenced by a concern that the defendant was entrapped.[61] The claim of unfairness in being entrapped by the dummy would be more persuasive the more deceptive the dummy was. Thus a very deceptive dummy, which everyone would take to be a real deer, would tend to make the act of shooting appear dangerous and thus support conviction. Yet from the perspective of entrapment, a dummy that looked real would generate a better argument that the hunter was unfairly deceived. We see that in cases of this sort we have to be careful in interweaving arguments that bear now on the required act, now on the required culpability. The two levels of argument often point in opposite directions.

The general analysis of aptness is borne out in a recent military conviction for attempted rape. The defendant forced intercourse upon a woman he thought had fainted; it turned out that she had died minutes before penetration.[62] If this case is described as forcing intercourse on a woman who appears to be alive, there is no doubt that over the long run, the type of conduct is likely to result in rape. The attempt was apt and therefore, even according to an objective theory of attempting, the conviction was justified.

[61] For the claim that impossibility sometimes functions as a defense of entrapment, see in MPC §5.01, Comment at 37 (Tent. Draft No. 10, 1960).

[62] United States v. Thomas, 13 U.S.C.M.A. 278, 32 C.M.R. 278 (1962).

But if the defendant sought to have intercourse with a corpse in a funeral parlor (in the mistaken belief that she was alive), the general theory of aptness would readily lead to an acquittal of an attempted rape (though other charges might lie for desecrating a dead body).

What we may conclude from this discussion of shooting, raping and other forms of overtly aggressive behavior is that an objective theory can well support convictions for attempt in cases in which the behavior is an apt effort to accomplish the actor's intent. Whether the defendant's act is apt is closely connected with the criteria of manifest criminality. If the conduct manifests danger, it is the type of conduct that can be analyzed as dangerous in the long run. Thus we have arrived at a definition of the kind of act that can, under the objective theory, subject a defendant to liability for attempt. The act must be a manifestly apt effort to commit a proscribed offense.

B. The Poisoning Cases. Several authorities support the view that an inapt effort at poisoning with an innocuous substance is insufficient to support a conviction for criminal attempt. To offset our earlier indictment of Alabama jurisprudence,[63] we should note another antebellum decision in Alabama, in which the court reversed the conviction of a slave charged with attempting to kill her master. There was no evidence that the "Jamestown weed" she added to his food was a deadly poison.[64] A leading case in England in 1919 held that a physician's prescribing an innocuous substance as an intended abortifacient was insufficient to support a conviction for attempted abortion.[65] The principle that inapt efforts should be exempt from liability readily explains why the courts do not discern an act of attempting in the giving of an innocuous substance as an intended poison or abortifacient.

The difficult problem in these cases is drawing the distinction between giving the intended victim an innocuous substance and giving him too small a dosage of a noxious poison. It is the dis-

[63] See notes 37–39 *supra*.

[64] State v. Clarisa, 11 Ala. 57 (1847).

[65] Regina v. Osborn, 84 J.P. 63 (1920).

tinction between trying to kill by putting sugar in his coffee and trying to kill by administering a harmless dosage of cyanide. In the latter cases, the courts have been willing to convict,[66] and as a result we are put to the challenge to explain why sugar makes the attempt inapt but a harmless dosage of cyanide makes it apt. As we discovered in our analysis of the shooting cases, the standard of aptness does not apply to isolated events, but rather to types or classes of acts. Apt attempts belong to a class of acts that are likely to generate harm. If the class is defined as administering a dosage of cyanide or other deadly poison, there is no doubt that the class of acts is likely to generate harm, and therefore we can regard every instance of the class as an apt attempt.

The problem with this entire mode of analysis is that there is no rigorous way of defending a classification of events. As a matter of logic, the relevant class could be defined as administering a dose of poison large enough to kill. If that were the relevant type of dangerous activity, then administering too small a dosage of poison would not be thought of as an apt attempt. Yet particularly in the context of poisoning, the definition of the relevant class is influenced not by principle, but by everyday fears and taboos. In life as we know it, the event that signals danger is putting poison—even too small a dosage of poison—in someone else's food. There appears to be no way of avoiding the sensibilities of ordinary people in trying to decide the class of events into which the defendant's particular act falls. Holmes appears to be the only common-law theorist who ever evidenced much sensitivity to this problem of allocating acts to classes of dangerous events, and eventually he became skeptical of satisfactorily defining the relevant categories of events.[67]

As a substitute for theory, one English judge coined a colorful metaphor to capture the problem of aptness. As Rowlatt, J., put it

[66] Commonwealth v. Kennedy, 170 Mass. 18, 48 N.E. 770 (1897); State v. Glover, 27 S.C. 602, 4 S.E. 564 (1888).

[67] *Compare* Holmes 69 ("[A]n act which could not have effected the crime . . . cannot be an attempt. . . . At some point or other, of course, the law must adopt this conclusion. . . ." *with* his later skepticism in Commonwealth v. Kennedy, 170 Mass. 18, 20, 48 N.E. 770, 771 (1897).

in the case of the accused abortionist who prescribed an innocuous abortifacient: there is no liability if the actor is "not on the job," "not on the thing itself at all." [68] Trying to poison with an innocuous substance is not on the job at all, but trying to poison with too little cyanide is. This makes intuitive sense and perhaps that is all that one can expect from a system of categorization rooted in indigenous fears.

C. The Empty Receptacle Cases. Another set of cases that have troubled the courts is defined by attempted larcenies, frustrated by the absence of goods to be stolen. The intending thief tries to pick an empty pocket or break into a house or safe that has no bounty to offer. The courts once had considerable difficulty with these cases,[69] but as of the late nineteenth century the pattern uniformly favors conviction.[70] There is nothing inapt about these efforts. They are well calculated to provide a thief's income, even if it turns out that in the particular situation the bounty is not there.

Similarly, a manifestly apt effort to gain property by deception[71] or intimidation[72] will support an attempt conviction even though the victim is unaffected by the defendant's conduct.

D. Receiving Stolen Property. Another specialized set of cases that have proved irksome to the courts consists of those typified by someone's buying goods in the mistaken belief that they are stolen. In the leading case of *Jaffe,* the police had recovered stolen cloth and sold it to the defendant, a suspected "fence." The New York Court of Appeals reversed the conviction for attempt to receive stolen property.[73] In the mid-1960s, after the California Supreme Court had reached the opposite results and affirmed the conviction,[74] it seemed that *Jaffe* had been overtaken by an ascendant principle of subjective criminality. If the defendant believed

[68] Regina v. Osborn, 84 J.P. 63, 64 (1920).

[69] See notes 41–44 *supra.*

[70] For recent decisions, see Gargan v. State, 436 P.2d 968 (Alaska 1968); State v. Meisch, 86 N.J. Super. 279, 206 A.2d 763 (1965).

[71] Commonwealth v. Johnson, 312 Pa. 140, 167 A. 344 (1933); Regina v. Hensler, 22 L.T. 691 (C.C.R. 1870).

[72] People v. Camodeca, 52 Cal. 2d 142, 338 P.2d 903 (1959).

[73] People v. Jaffe, 185 N.Y. 497, 78 N.E. 169 (1906).

[74] People v. Rojas, 55 Cal. 2d 252, 358 P.2d 921, 10 Cal. Rptr. 465 (1961).

the cloth to be stolen, that was arguably sufficient to justify conviction for an attempt. Though the subjective approach may now mean there is liability in the tree stump case and in the trying-to-poison-with-sugar case, the problem posed by *Jaffe* is far from settled. As recently as 1973, the House of Lords reversed a conviction for attempted receiving when the goods were no longer in fact stolen goods.[75]

If we try to apply our distinction between apt and inapt attempts in this type of case, we would be led to inquire whether the cloth appeared to be stolen under the circumstances. This line of argument closely resembles the analysis whether the dummy appeared to be a deer or the raped woman appeared to be alive.[76] If the cloth in *Jaffe* appeared to have been stolen, repeated purchases under similar facts would tend to generate the result prohibited by statute—namely, the acquisition of stolen goods. Yet there is a fundamental difference between this type of case and the previous discussions of shooting, raping, poisoning, and stealing from an empty receptacle. In all these other instances, the attempted crime is derivative of one of the central harms that the criminal law seeks to prevent. There is no comparison, I wish to argue, between these core cases of attempting harm, and the problem of attempting to receive stolen property.

Receiving stolen property is itself a derivative offense; receivers were initially punished as accessories after the fact of larceny.[77] It was not until the late eighteenth century that receiving emerged in English law as an independent misdemeanor, subject to prosecution regardless whether the thief was caught and convicted. Suppressing the business of receiving is an indirect way of controlling thievery. There is no harm that arises merely as a result of buying goods known to be stolen. A single incident, or even repeated incidents of receiving are hardly disturbing or unnerving events. This is an important point, for our theory of aptness was worked out in cases where the attempt could be seen as a form of

[75] Haughton v. Smith, [1974] 2 W.L.R. 1 (H.L.).
[76] See text at notes 60–63 *supra*.
[77] See generally §8.5.4 A *infra*.

manifest criminality. If receiving itself is not manifestly criminal, then there is no reason to expect that attempted receiving would be. Therefore our test of aptness, which works well in cases of attempted harm, fails to illuminate the analysis of crimes that consist merely in providing collateral support for harmful criminal activities.

Another case that does not lend itself to analysis under the standard of aptness is the recent reversal in United States v. Berrigan.[78] While Father Philip Berrigan and Sister Elizabeth McAllister were in jail on other charges, they communicated with people on the outside by secreting letters back and forth. Apparently the warden knew of this network and allowed the passing of letters to continue. Later they were indicted on charges of attempting to smuggle letters out of prison "without the knowledge and consent of the warden."[79] They were not guilty of the offense-in-chief, for the warden knew of the courier's operation. The question was whether the charge of attempt could hold despite the issue of "impossibility." The Court of Appeals for the Third Circuit held that despite the actor's criminal intent, there was no supportable charge of criminal attempt: the impossibility of completion precluded criminal liability.

In this situation we are at a total loss to apply the criteria of aptness and inaptness. It appeared that the warden had not consented to the delivery of letters; should appearances control this case as they would the analysis of attempting to rape a woman who was apparently alive? The concept of aptness is rooted in the likelihood of harm. But communication by prisoners with persons outside of jail is obviously not a harm in itself; it is an offense presumably designed as a prophylactic against jail breaks and other criminal activity. When a crime is purely inchoate, the gears of manifest criminality and aptness simply idle. The problem of Berrigan's liability cannot be solved merely by inquiring whether it appeared that the warden had not consented to the delivery of the letters.

The cases of *Jaffe* and *Berrigan* require us to think afresh about the problem of attempted crime and to develop an objectivist the-

[78] 482 F.2d 171 (3d Cir. 1973).
[79] 18 U.S.C. §1791; 28 C.F.R. §6.1.

ory of liability that is not tied to criteria of manifest criminality. Any theory supporting exemption from liability in these cases would have to be in the objectivist mold, for subjectivists would be quite willing to convict both Jaffe and Berrigan on the ground that their intent is sufficient for liability.

In the next section we set forth this alternative theory. Upon developing the theory, we shall find that it is so convincing that it threatens to displace the standard of aptness from the objectivist's arsenal of techniques to keep alive the substantive element of acting.

§3.3.4. A General Theory of Attempting. As a prelude to a more general theory of attempting, we should return to the premises of the objectivist program. We have referred several times to the distinguishing claim of objectivist theory that the act of attempting should be taken as an independent element of the crime of attempting. We would do well to clarify what this claim means and why a reputable group of theorists are repeatedly drawn to it.

The ambiguity in the word "attempting" is that it functions both as the name of a crime and the name of an element of that crime. It is the counterpart both to the concept of larceny and to the element of trespassory taking. The objectivist ambition is simply to clarify what one means by "attempting" in its latter role as the required act for the crime of attempting.

The subjectivist's response to all this is that he too insists upon an act in execution of the required intent, and that therefore this supposed difference between the two schools is illusory. This objection requires us to be more precise about the concepts of an element of the offense and why only certain acts will satisfy the objectivist notion of attempting.

The premise underlying objectivist theory is a general proposition about the nature of legal liability, particularly criminal liability. The proposition is that no liability should attach unless, first, the defendant's conduct objectively conforms to criteria specified in advance; and secondly, that his mental state should bear solely on his accountability for this act in violation of the law. In the common-law definition of larceny, this two-staged set of requirements was readily satisfied. The objective dimension was the trespassory taking; the subjective dimension, the *animus furandi.* As we shall see in the next chapter, these criteria are also met in the analysis of homicide; the objective dimension is the causing of death; the subjective, the minimal criteria of personal accountability.

As it is stated, this two-staged inquiry seems to pose no barrier to the subjective theory of attempts; for again the subjectivist may retort that he too insists upon an act as a condition of liability, and that is all that is required at the first stage of analysis. This is the point at which the critical feature of objectivist theory becomes clear. Not any act will satisfy the requirement of conduct in violation of the law. The principle of legality requires that the particular act be one that is prohibited in the definition of the offense. Thus the acts of forcible intercourse, trespassory taking, and causing death readily satisfy this standard, but the acts of putting sugar in someone's coffee and firing at a tree stump do not violate any preannounced standard. The only way to find a dimension of the crime of attempt that is parallel to the criminal acts required for rape, larceny, and murder is to focus on the one required act that constitutes the crime of attempt: namely, the act of attempting. Analyzed in this way, the crime of attempt consists of two elements: an act of attempting and an intent that renders the actor responsible for his act of attempting. Shooting at someone's bed and putting poison in someone's coffee are acts as to which we can sensibly ask: is the actor accountable for his dangerous and unnerving act? If he intended the act, we can fairly hold him accountable. But what is it for which we hold someone accountable for putting sugar in another's coffee or shooting at a tree stump? In these cases the only suspect "event" or "state of affairs" is the intent itself. Thus the subjective approach conflates the test of accountability, namely the actor's intent, with that for which he is held accountable.

One way to understand the act of attempting as a distinct element of the crime is to focus on the function of intent in assessing liability. If the issue of intent is directed to the question of accountability for an act in violation of the law, then the act is conceptually separable from the intent. In subjectivist theory, where the act of attempting is not that for which one is held responsible, the actor's intent, as executed in any act whatever becomes the ultimate inquiry. Intent is no longer raised as an issue of responsibility. It becomes the core element of the crime.

The link between the principle of legality and objectivist theory, then, is the proposition that criminal liability should be imposed only when individuals are fairly accountable for states of affairs that violate the law. In the case of attempts, there are two reasons why this state of affairs cannot be the intent to commit the offense-in-chief. The first reason is that the required state of affairs in violation of the law should be objectively and publicly observable. The second reason is that treating the intent as the state of affairs for which one is accountable requires a standard of accountability other than the intent. One could argue that the "decision" to formulate the intent provides a test of accountability.[80] But the relentless effort of objectivist theory is to avoid this regression into subjective criteria. Its program is to find a dimension of attempting that is separable from the issue of intent and which satisfies the requirement of a publicly observable state of affairs that violates the law.

There is no doubt a good deal of work to be done in defending these premises of the objectivist program. It might be objected, for example, that this interpretation of the principle of legality is simply false. Legality does not require a structuring of issues into states of affairs that violate the law and subsidiary criteria of accountability. Alternatively, it might be argued that if this is what legality does require, perhaps we should not be so legalistic. Whether these objections can be met or not, this is the plane in which the opponents of objectivist theory should conduct their campaign. As we shall later discover, however, the proponents of subjectivist theory wield an entirely different battery of arguments that have little to do with the implicit demands of the principle of legality.

Our present effort is to develop a theory of attempting that is independent of the criterion of manifest criminality, for we have concluded that the latter theory ought not to apply to offenses, such

[80] *Cf.* Welzel 189 (an attempt is the execution of a "decision" to commit the crime).

as receiving stolen property, that in themselves do not threaten the core interests protected under the criminal law. Therefore we should return to the basic question: What does it mean to attempt a crime? The concepts of "trying" and "attempting" are rooted in English usage and therefore we should probe the semantic rules that generate the boundaries of these concepts.[81] The specific cases we are interested in are those in which actors are mistaken about the circumstances surrounding their action, and the question is how their mistakes influence the analysis of what they are attempting to do.

Let us consider a mundane case of acting under a mistaken belief about the date or the day of the week. Suppose that Paul is trying to fix a leaky faucet on Saturday, and while he is working, he happens mistakenly to think that it is Friday. What is Paul trying to do? To fix a faucet on Friday or simply to fix a faucet? Subjectivist theory, as expressed in the Model Penal Code, suggests that Paul's conduct should be judged according to the circumstances as he takes them to be.[82] Thus his mistaken belief about the day should be incorporated in the description about what he is trying to do. It follows that he is attempting to fix a faucet on Friday. Yet this way of proceeding is not only counterintuitive, it generates absurd results. Suppose Paul were mistaken about any number of other things, such as whether there was life on Mars or whether the president was then at work in the Oval Office. Would we say that he was trying to fix the faucet so long as there was life on Mars or while the president was at work? It is obvious that a mistake about *X* is not sufficient to say that one is trying to do *X*. It is little help to say that he must be mistaken about an "attendant circumstance," for until we formulate a general test for the relevance of mistaken beliefs on the concept of attempting, there is no way of specifying which "attendant circumstances" ought to fall within the description of the attempted act.

There are some cases in which a mistake about the date does

[81] This is nothing special about the verbs "try" and "attempt" in English. The same arguments apply to *tenter* in French, *versuchen* in German.

[82] MPC §5.01(1)(a).

bear on an accurate description of what the actor is trying to do. Suppose that a taxpayer is working energetically to finish his income tax forms on Friday in the belief that the date is April 15, and his forms have to be in the mail by midnight on the 15th. In fact it is only April 14. It seems intuitively plausible to say that he is trying to finish his income tax forms by April 15. His mistake about the date proves to be relevant in an account of what he was doing.

On the basis of these examples, we may hazard a general thesis about the relevance of mistakes on attempting. The thesis is this: mistaken beliefs are relevant to what the actor is trying to do if they affect his incentive in acting. They affect his incentive if knowing of the mistake would give him a good reason for changing his course of conduct. If Paul had known that it was Friday rather than Saturday, his being disabused of his mistake presumably would not give him a good reason for postponing his efforts to fix the faucet. Therefore his mistaken belief does not affect his incentive; nor, by like token, his mistaken belief about whether the president is then at work in the Oval Office. On the other hand, if our conscientious taxpayer were told that it was only April 14, he might well decide to relax for the rest of the day and finish the following day. His mistake does bear on his incentive and therefore it should be included in the description of what he is trying to do.

We shall refer to this thesis as the test of rational motivation. Its validity as a theory depends on its providing an account of what ordinary people mean when they talk about "trying" or "attempting" to do something. Within an objectivist theory of attempts, this invocation of ordinary usage is appropriate, for what we are trying to fathom is what the law seeks to prohibit with the crime of "attempting" to do something. When the law itself provides no guidance to the meaning of one of its critical terms, we have to fall back on the source of Anglo-American legal terms—namely, the English language.

Now let us apply the test of rational motivation to the cases that are troublesome in the law. In *Jaffe* and *Berrigan,* the test supports the conclusion of the courts that there is no act of attempting in the respective fact situations. In *Jaffe,* it seems fairly clear that the fact that the cloth was stolen does not affect the actor's incentive in paying the price at which the cloth was offered to him by the police. If he were told that the goods were not stolen, that would not have provided him with a reason for turning down the offer. If they were not stolen, so much the better. It follows, therefore, that it is inappropriate to describe his conduct as attempting to receive stolen cloth. At least it is no more plausible to say that Jaffe was trying to receive stolen cloth than it is to say that Paul was trying to fix his faucet on Friday.

Similarly, it did not seem to be part of Berrigan's system of incentive that the warden knew and tolerated his efforts to smuggle messages to persons outside the prison. If he had known of the warden's implicit consent, his incentive to communicate with persons on the outside would presumably have been the same. Of course, one might imagine a case in which the mere fact of sending out letters with a courier functioned as a signal, and in that case, the warden's knowledge of the activity might provide a reason to desist. This is a variation of the case to which we shall have to attend presently.

Another case readily solved under the test of rational motivation is a hypothetical problem posed in the *Jaffe* opinion. Suppose the accused engages in sexual intercourse with a girl he takes to be under the age of consent; in fact, she is overage. Is he guilty of attempted statutory rape? In the normal case it would not be part of the actor's incentive that the girl be underage (again, one could imagine a variation in which the youth of the girl did bear upon the actor's motivation). If he is just as happy to have intercourse with a girl overage, then his mistake would not bear on his incentive and it would be incorrect to describe his act as trying to have intercourse with a girl under the age of consent.

In all of these cases, the test of rational motivation yields results that are at odds with the subjectivist standard that the circumstances should be taken as the actor believes them to be. On the latter test, Jaffe, Berrigan and the would-be statutory rapist are all guilty.

Our proposed test of rational motivation has some precursors in the literature. J. C. Smith appears to have pursued the same theory in an effort to distinguish between the actor's intention and the actor's purpose.[83] Smith's interpretation of *Jaffe* would be that the defendant intended to receive stolen cloth, but his purpose was to receive the particular piece of cloth at the price offered—regardless of whether it was stolen. The thesis is that there should be liability in a case of impossibility only if the actor fails in his purpose. This analysis moves in the direction of giving an account of what we mean by attempting an offense. But it is misleading to rely on the concept of purpose as the linchpin of the argument. The implication is that liability should turn on some slightly more abstract form of the actor's intent.[84] This fails to account for the hypothetical way that mistakes bear on motivation.[85] The only way to determine whether the actor is attempting an act that includes a particular circumstance, *X*, is to inquire: what would the actor do if he knew that *X* was not so? If he would behave in precisely the same way, we cannot say that his mistaken belief in *X* bears on his motivation; and if it does not, we cannot say that he is attempting to act with reference to *X*.

The arguments in favor of the test of rational motivation are, first, that the test appears to be in tune with judicial intuitions that still reign in the Anglo-American case law; and secondly, that this analysis of attempting, based upon the ordinary usage of the words "trying" and "attempting," carries out the objectivist program of grounding liability in an act of attempting that is conceptually separable from the actor's intent. It is true that this theory of attempting interweaves subjective and objective elements, for one cannot analyze the actor's motivation without inquiring into the

[83] J. Smith, *supra* note 54, at 216–222.

[84] This is reminiscent of earlier efforts to distinguish an abstract from a concrete intent. See Keedy, *Criminal Attempts at Common Law,* 102 U. Pa. L. Rev. 464 (1954); Perkins, *Criminal Attempt and Related Problems,* 2 U.C.L.A.L. Rev. 319 (1955).

[85] Even though Smith's argument is not fully developed, it should have been taken more seriously in the literature. For an example of an unsympathetic reading, see Hughes, *supra* note 54, at 1013–15, who dismisses Smith's argument on the ground that the criminal law is not concerned about the purpose or motive. Even if that were true, *cf.* §4.5.3 *infra,* the question is whether in this context the law ought in principle to be blind to the actor's purpose.

question whether the truth would have affected the actor's incentive. The test is objective in the sense that the question whether the act constitutes an attempt is not settled by an inquiry into the actor's intent.

The unsolved problem is that this engine of analysis appears to idle in the case in which the actor has an unusual incentive that, say, makes it important to him that the warden not know of his passing letters to people outside or that the girl with whom he is making love be of Lolita's age. The question is whether we should add a gear that would abstract the analysis from these particular motivations, and ask whether in general people under these circumstances would have a good reason for acting differently; or whether the analysis should grind more finely and inquire whether the incentive of this particular individual would have been affected by his knowing of the mistake. The dimension of acting appears to be directed to a more general inquiry; and the issue of intent, to an individualized judgment. This provides a tenuous ground for abstracting the analysis of attempting from the particular individual and his possibly idiosyncratic motives; yet the problem admittedly does not lend itself to a compelling solution.

The test of rational motivation displays considerable theoretical power. Not only does it make sense of the outcomes in *Jaffe* and *Berrigan,* but it yields convincing results in two other types of case that have long troubled legal theorists. These other two types of case are illustrated by the following hypothetical situations: (1) Richard engages in private homosexual conduct in the mistaken belief that homosexuality is still penalized in the particular jurisdiction. (2) Samuel lies to a police officer under the mistaken belief that lying to an officer of the law is punishable as perjury.

In these two cases, Richard and Samuel made mistakes about whether their conduct under the circumstances constitutes a punishable offense. In that respect their mistakes are just like those of Jaffe and Berrigan. The aspect that makes them slightly different is that their mistake seems to involve a misapprehension about the law rather than about a "factual" circumstance. Richard is mistaken about whether homosexual activity is still criminal; Samuel, about whether a particular case of lying constitutes perjury. Subjectivist theorists are inclined to think that it is important that these are mistakes of "law" rather than of "fact"; the general view is that these actors should enjoy a defense of so-called legal impossibility.[86] We shall have occasion to examine these claims later; for the time being we should note that the test of rational motivation readily yields acquittals in these cases. And we need not immerse ourselves in the subtle distinction between "law" and "fact" in order to account for this result. In neither case is the actor's mistake relevant to his motivation. Richard would presumably continue his homosexual activity even if informed that it is now legal; and Samuel would have no reason not to lie if informed that he could do so without committing an offense.

The test of rational motivation is powerful not only because it handily solves these hypothetical cases. Relating the concept of attempting to the actor's incentives also poses a serious challenge to the alternative objectivist theory, namely, the standard of aptness. If applied to the cases of shooting at stumps and "poisoning" with sugar, the test of rational motivation leads to convictions where the standard of aptness would favor an acquittal. It is obviously part of the actor's system of incentives that he believe the stump to be a person, or the dosage to be sufficient to kill. If told of the truth, he would presumably change his plans. So far as the standard of incentive is controlling, the person shooting at the stump is undoubtedly attempting to kill. The problem is whether the test of aptness should prevail over the theory of rational motivation in cases involving assaults on the core interests protected by the criminal law. It should be recalled that we developed the test of rational motivation because we found that the standard of aptness did not function outside of these core cases of attempted murder, rape and larceny. Now the question is whether, with the proposed test of rational motivation, we can justify the retention of the theory of aptness.

One reason to believe that the principle of aptness is indispensable in a comprehensive theory of attempt liability is that

[86] LaFave & Scott 442–445; Hall 594–96; Williams 633–635.

there is no other way to solve one case in which virtually everyone agrees that there should be no liability. That is the case of nominal efforts to inflict harm by superstitious means, say by black magic or witchcraft. The consensus of Western legal systems is that there should be no liability, regardless of the wickedness of intent, for sticking pins in a doll or chanting an incantation to banish one's enemy to the nether world.[87] Against the background of the fears and taboos prevailing in modern Western society, objectivist theorists take these cases to be inapt attempts, therefore exempt from punishment. Yet the theory of rational motivation points in the direction of liability. If the intending party knows the truth about black magic (namely, that it does not work), he would have a good reason to change his plan of attack. To account for the consensus favoring an exemption in this type of case, we need the principle of aptness to offset the implications of the competing theory of rational motivation.

The problem that remains to be resolved is determining the relative scope of these two competing theories. We shall return to this problem after we survey efforts to develop a coherent theory of attempting within the framework of subjective criminality.

§3.3.5. The Ascendancy of Subjective Criminality. Apart from the difficult but isolated cases in which common-law judges and theorists have struggled with the problem of impossible attempts, the general thrust of Western legal theory has favored the rise of subjective criminality in resolving the two central issues in the law of attempts. The subjective approach is defined by the rejection of the claim that the act of attempting is a distinct dimension of liability. For subjectivists, it is important that the actor take steps to execute his criminal intent, yet no specifically defined act is required for liability. This means that no conviction should ever founder on the ground that there was something wrong with the

[87] Williams 652; Hall 592–93; Judgment of June 21, 1900, 33 RGSt. 321; Schönke-Schröder-Eser §23, note 13, at 297; Jescheck 401–402; Kurs (GP 1968) at 568; *cf.* People v. Ellmore, 128 Ill. App. 2d 312, 261 N.E.2d 736 (1970) (dictum). *But cf.* MPC §5.01, Comment at 38 (Tent. Draft No. 10, 1960), §5.05(2) (permitting discretionary punishment).

"act" element of attempting. Of course, a conviction might be barred on the ground that there was insufficient evidence of criminal intent, but never solely on the ground that the "act" did not reveal the objective earmarks of an attempt. Thus the two issues of most concern to the objectivists—drawing the line between preparation and attempt, and defining the limits of impossibility as a defense—dissolve, in the hands of the subjectivists, into issues of evidence bearing on the proof of intent.

Since the late nineteenth century, the principle of subjective criminality has been almost unceasingly ascendant. To note the advance of subjectivist theory in defining the threshold of attempting, we should consider a controversial case. If the suspect has reached the scene of his intended victim or the intended larceny, there is little difficulty in finding that the preparation has gone far enough to constitute an attempt. The more problematic case is posed by lying in wait for the intended victim or going out to search for him. In a controversial 1927 decision in New York, the court held that there was no attempt at robbery in cruising about in an automobile looking for a bank messenger who was scheduled to make deliveries at a particular place.[88] However, in a leading case decided in 1913, the French *Cour de Cassation* held that merely lying in wait for a collection agent was sufficient to constitute attempted larceny.[89]

Incidentally overturning the 1927 New York precedent, the drafters of the Model Penal Code set out to overcome all objective impediments to attempt convictions. The Code defines an attempt as "an act or an omission constituting a substantial step in a course of conduct planned to culminate in . . . [a] crime."[90] Instead of defining a "substantial step" the code proceeds to list several categories of acts that "shall not be held insufficient as a matter of law." Among the six categories that are not insufficient, one finds a specific reference to "lying in wait, searching for or following

[88] People v. Rizzo, 246 N.Y. 334, 158 N.E. 888 (1927).

[89] Judgment of January 3, 1913, Recueil Dalloz 1914. I. 41. *Cf.* Comment, 1913 Revue pénitentiaire et de droit pénal 750.

[90] MPC §5.01(1)(c).

the contemplated victim of the crime."[91] This style of drafting is odd in a tradition of lawmaking supposedly concerned about informing the public when their acts cross the boundary into the realm of the criminal. There is no analysis or theory to explain how much preparation is required to constitute a "substantial step."[92] The only safeguard against arbitrary prosecution and conviction is the evidentiary rule that the substantial step be "strongly corroborative of the actor's criminal purpose."[93] The objectivist concern about an act of attempting that stands as an independent element of the offense is thus transformed into a problem in the technique of proving intent. The only limitation on pushing the threshold of attempting further back is the practical problem of proof.

Though the French courts and the Model Penal Code recommend a threshold of attempting sufficiently low to include cases of lying in wait,[94] the German courts do not appear prepared to go that far.[95] In the new code that came into force on January 1, 1975, the standard of attempting is a modified subjective standard which reads: "A criminal act is attempted by an actor who, according to his conception of the act, directly initiates the commission of the offense."[96] This test interweaves objective and subjective criteria. The ultimate standard is the actor's perception of what he is trying to do. Yet he is not "attempting" unless, according to his perception, he has directly initiated the commission of the offense. In the case of lying in wait, there would presumably be no criminal attempt; unless the actor imagined the victim's presence, a court would be hard pressed to construe the act of lying in wait as the "direct initiation of the commission of the offense."

[91] *Cf.* MPC §5.01(2)(a).

[92] *Cf.* the definition of "substantial step" in Del. Code tit. 11, §532 ("an act or omission which leaves no reasonable doubt as to the defendant's intention . . .").

[93] MPC §5.01(2). *Cf.* Proposed Federal Criminal Code §1001(a) (the act must "indicate [an] intent that the crime be completed").

[94] See notes 89, 91 *supra*.

[95] *But cf.* the Soviet codes, which explicitly penalize preparatory acts, e.g., Ugol. kod. (RSFSR) §15.

[96] StGB §22 ("*zur Verwirklichung des Tatbestandes unmittelbar ansetzt*").

If there is some controversy among Western jurisdictions about setting the threshold of attempting, there is relatively more agreement about eliminating the exemption for inapt attempts. For the last one hundred years, German and French courts have consistently applied a subjective theory in coping with cases of inapt attempts.[97] The new German code resolves the problem by permitting discretionary mitigation of punishment where the inaptness of the attempt is due to the actor's "gross misunderstanding" of the means used or the object of the offense.[98] The thrust towards subjectification has come later in English and American jurisprudence, with the initial impetus arising in the academic community. In his influential book, first published in 1953, Glanville Williams argued persuasively against the English precedents recognizing a doctrine of inapt attempts.[99] A decade later, the prestigious Model Penal Code adopted the subjectivist principle that liability should depend on the circumstances as the actor "believes them to be."[100] As an idea whose time has come, this position has been adopted in all of the American states adopting new penal codes.[101]

The remarkable feature of this sweep by the subjectivist position is that there is little case law to support it. There are a few decisions in California that may be cited on its behalf—one affirming a conviction for attempting to receive stolen goods that were not stolen,[102] and another affirming a conviction for the attempted purchase of heroin when the thing purchased was but white powder.[103] Yet the proponents for this position are able to generate an

[97] See notes 47–50 *supra*.

[98] STGB §23(3).

[99] G. Williams, Criminal Law: The General Part 484 (1953).

[100] MPC §5.01(1)(a).

[101] In an abundance of legislative clarity, many states have explicitly abolished the defense of impossibility. See, e.g., Colo. Rev. Stat. §18-2-101 (eliminating both factual and legal impossibility); Ill. Ann. Stat. c. 38, §8–4(b) (ostensibly affects only factual impossibility); N.D. Cent. Code §12.1-06-01 (same language as Colorado statute); Pa. Cons. Stat. Ann. tit. 18, §901(b) (same language as Illinois statute); *cf.* Proposed Federal Criminal Code §1001(c)(1) (eliminating factual and legal impossibility).

[102] People v. Rojas, 55 Cal. 2d 252, 358 P.2d 921, 10 Cal. Rptr. 465 (1961).

[103] People v. Siu, 126 Cal. App. 2d 41, 271 P.2d 575 (1954). *Cf.* United States v.

impressive array of authority for their view. The case law is mustered by lining up as precedents on behalf of the subjective view all cases in which impossible attempts are punished.[104] This means that decisions readily supported under the objectivist theory of aptness, such as the conviction of the man who shot at his intended victim's empty bed,[105] are cited as though the result could be explained only on the subjectivist principle that the facts be taken as the defendant thinks them to be.

The proponents of subjectivist theory, of course, have never rested their claims solely on the case law. The Model Penal Code is a reformist document, based upon a consistent and coherent body of principles. It is time that we assessed those principles.

§3.3.6. The Principles Behind the Subjectivist Theory of Attempts. The dispute about subjectifying the law of impossible attempts is significant for reasons that go beyond the occasional blunderer who might shoot at a tree stump in an effort to kill the president. The conflict between the objectivists and the subjectivists reveals a deep philosophical rift about the nature of a system of criminal law.

The objectivist position is an aspect of a broader theory of criminal justice that we shall call the legalist philosophy. We have already noted the connection between objectivist theory and the principle of legality. Now we shall attempt to deepen the analysis by explicating two broad principles of this general philosophy about the day-to-day operation of the criminal law. The first principle is that the processes of the criminal law are appropriately different and ought to be kept distinct from administrative processes, such as the civil commitment of the dangerously insane. The second principle stands for one of the ways in which these two radically different processes are kept distinct. The law functions by means of preannounced standards of behavior that are interpreted and applied in particular cases. It is important that these standards

Giles, 42 C.M.R. 960 (1970) (defendant held accountable for attempt to use marijuana when he mistakenly believed cigarette contained marijuana).

[104] MPC §5.01, Comment at 32–38 (Tent. Draft No. 10, 1960).

[105] State v. Mitchell, 170 Mo. 633, 71 S.W. 175 (1902).

or rules be interpreted in particular cases without adverting to the overall goals of the system of criminal justice. For example, it is undoubtedly one of the goals of the criminal law to isolate and imprison dangerous persons. Yet in the legalist philosophy, it would be impermissible to consider whether in a particular case a person ought to be held criminally liable according to whether he is dangerous. To allow the overall goal of the system to intrude upon decision-making in a particular case would be like turning to the overall aim of the income tax system—namely, raising revenue for the government—in a dispute about whether a particular taxpayer was entitled to a charitable deduction. The legalist philosophy concedes that personal dangerousness may be the appropriate standard of decision in civil commitment proceedings. The difference between legal and administrative processes is precisely whether the overall aims of the system guide decisions in particular cases.[106]

The movement to subjectify the law of attempts is grounded in a root-and-branch rejection of these principles of legalism. It is true that some of the impulses toward subjectification come from the same factors that shaped the pattern of subjective criminality in the law of larceny, namely, the movement toward legislative definition of the criminal law and the quest for earlier points of intervention.[107] Even if there had been a consensus that the act should be treated as an independent, substantive element of attempting, the issues might have proved too subtle for the legislative craft of Anglo-American jurisdictions.[108] The virtue of the Model Penal Code's ambiguous requirement of a "substantial step" is that, regardless of whether it is right, it is at least simple and suitable to the modern legislative style. The issue of impos-

[106] For additional comments on this distinction see §6.3.2, particularly at note 30.

[107] See §2.3, at p. 102 *supra*.

[108] StGB §23(3) appears to be the first legislative attempt to define a range of inapt attempts that warrant special treatment. This provision appears to be flawed by its failure to distinguish between inapt and superstitious attempts. See Schönke-Schröder-Eser §23, note 13, at 297; Rudolphi in SK StGB §23, note 8, at 182–83; Jescheck 402.

sible attempts is subtle and so badly treated in the literature that no rational legislative committee would attempt to formulate a rule about when impossible attempts are exempt from liability. It is much simpler to adopt the Model Penal Code's view that the circumstances should be treated as though they were as the actor believed them to be.

Like the parallel transformation of larceny, the subjectification of attempts facilitates earlier intervention and thus enhances the preventive work of the police. If the threshold of attempting can be set back to include lying in wait and even acquiring the tools of the offense, then the police should be able to prevent more crimes from coming to fruition.

Yet even more significant than these factors in common with the metamorphosis of larceny is the principled challenge to the philosophy of legalism. This challenge has many different aspects, but the most prominent is the willingness to take the goals of the system as a whole as the guideline of decisions in particular cases. Virtually all the proponents of subjectivity in the law of attempts stress the value of their approach in identifying and convicting dangerous persons. The typical argument is: If the ultimate test is the dangerousness of the actor, then there is no point to exempting inapt attempts from liability.[109] A man who shoots at a tree stump might well be just as dangerous as someone who shoots at his intended victim's bed. So, if the ultimate test is indeed dangerousness, the subjectivists are right. The inquiry then turns to the proposition whether dangerousness ought to be the test of liability in particular cases.

There is no doubt that confining dangerous persons is one of the overriding goals of the system, but it does not follow that systemic goals should influence the outcome of particular cases. Subjectivists characteristically fail to mark the difference between systemic goals and the criteria for decision in individual cases. That

[109] Wechsler, Jones & Korn, *The Treatment of Inchoate Crimes in the Model Penal Code of the American Law Institute: Attempts, Solicitation and Conspiracy,* 61 Colum. L. Rev. 571, 579 (1961). *Cf.* MPC §5.01, Comment at 32 (Tent. Draft No. 10, 1960) ("The basic premise here is that the actor's mind is the best proving ground of his dangerousness").

failure betokens a breakdown of the distinction between legal and administrative processes. One of the features of administrative processes is that there is no cleavage between systemic and particular decisions. The individual case is decided by reference to the goals of the administrative scheme. There are other administrative elements in the criminal process, as in the institutions of discretionary sentencing and indeed in discretionary charging. Therefore it is not startling to encounter the implicit claim that the substantive decision of criminal liability should proceed in the style of administrative decision-making.

This shift from a legalist to an administrative philosophy of criminal law is never directly assayed in the literature or in legal opinions. It is a deep structural reorientation of the system that is barely visible to participants in the process. Even the emphasis on dangerousness does not appear to be a radical break with the tradition of criminal law. Oliver Wendell Holmes, Jr., referred to the "nearness of the danger" in working out the line between preparation and attempt.[110] German theory has long referred to the standard of endangering protected interests as an issue in defining the threshold of attempts.[111] Yet the commonality of the word "danger" obscures a vital distinction. The earlier usage was always directed toward the danger posed by particular acts. The contemporary concern is about danger emanating from particular persons. This shift in usage betokens the reorientation from the legalist concern about whether the act violates the standard of liability to the contemporary concern about whether the actor is the type of person whose confinement will serve the purposes of the criminal law.

The distinction between requiring a dangerous *act* and searching for dangerous *persons* goes to the heart of the dispute. Requiring that the act be dangerous expresses the legalist principle that the act, standing alone, must conform to some objective standard of liability. Apart from the values of legalism, this requirement serves no goal of the system as a whole. It does not maximally fur-

[110] Holmes 68.
[111] See note 26 *supra*.

ther prevention of crime. That goal is better served by shifting, as the subjectivists do, from the dangerousness of acts to the dangerousness of persons; even an act that is not dangerous in itself can reveal the actor to be dangerous. The goal of general deterrence is served equally well, it seems, by focusing either on acts or actors.[112]

In view of the Model Penal Code's aim of isolating dangerous persons, it is surprising that the issue of the actor's dangerousness is not—with rare exceptions—incorporated in the criteria of liability. Perhaps an explicit recognition of personal dangerousness as the standard of liability would be too radical a fusion of administrative and legal processes. It remains preferable to relegate the issue to the less visible halls of prosecutorial discretion. There are other reasons that contemporary theorists are uneasy about a subjectified theory of attempts. This becomes evident if we pause to consider the theoretical difficulties in working out a subjectified law of attempts.

§3.3.7. **The Prospects of a Subjective Theory of Attempts.** At first blush it appears that a subiective theory of attempts greatly reduces the number of categories with which theorists must contend. An adequate objective theory requires attention to the distinctions between apt and inapt attempts; between cases in which belief about attendant circumstances affects the actor's incentive and cases in which it does not; and, further, between the types of case properly analyzed under the standard of aptness and those properly controlled by the test of rational motivation. All of this is swept aside in the subjectivist's simplifying stroke that the attempt should be judged according to the circumstances as the actor believes them to be. Yet the ease of disposing of one set of problems is offset by new difficulties that crop up elsewhere.

There are two types of case in which the subjectivist stumbles in seeking a solution. The first is the largely hypothetical problem of attempting to kill by invoking black magic or some other tech-

[112] For an analysis of these various purposes of punishing crime, see §6.3.2 *infra*

nique that conventionally reasonable people regard as superstitious. For convenience, we shall call this the problem of the superstitious attempt. In the second type of problematic case, the actor thinks that he is engaged in a crime and yet, due to his mistaken view of the law, it turns out that his activity is perfectly legal. This is typified, as we noted in our earlier discussion, by the act of lying to a police officer in the mistaken belief that such lying is perjury. In the Anglo-American literature this problem is labeled the issue of "legal impossibility."

The consensus in Western legal systems is that there ought to be an exemption from punishment for attempts both in cases of superstitious attempts[113] and of legal impossibility, at least where the latter is properly construed.[114] Most subjectivist theorists acknowledge that an adequate theory of attempts would accommodate exemptions in these two types of case. Yet within the framework of the subjective standard that the facts should be taken as the actor perceives them to be, it is by no means easy to explain why superstitious attempts and legally impossible attempts should be exempt from punishment. According to the actor's view of the world, his use of black magic is likely to produce the desired effect, and therefore he should be held accountable. In the case in which he takes his lying to a police officer to be a case of perjury, he believes that he is violating the law, and therefore he should be held accountable as though he were.

The Model Penal Code boldly suggests that cases in which the act is "inherently unlikely to result" in the commission of a crime

[113] See note 87 *supra.*

[114] This type of "attempt" is termed a *Wahndelikt* (illusory offense) in German law. Although the new code is silent as to illusory offenses, the assumption is that they are not punishable. Jescheck 402–03; Schönke-Schröder-Eser §22 note 78–85, at 293–94. See, e.g., Judgment of May 26, 1955, 8 BGHSt. 263, in which the defendant injured himself by driving into a tree. He left the scene of the accident. The court held, absent injuries to other persons, that there was no duty to remain at the scene of the accident under StGB §142. If the defendant thought he had a duty to remain, his offense was illusory. 8 BGHSt. at 269. *Cf.* MPC §5.01, Comment at 31 (Tent. Draft No. 10, 1960) (recognizing requirement that "the result desired or intended by the actor constitute a crime"); Williams 633–35; Hall 586–87; LaFave & Scott 442–44.

should be resolved by a judicial inquiry into whether the actor "presents a public danger."[115] This is an unusual example of a legislative provision that interweaves criteria of personal dangerousness with the standard of liability. By its terms, the provision appears to cover both cases of superstitious attempts and legal impossibility; both are cases in which the act is inherently incapable of realization. For some reason, the commentary to the code concedes that cases of legal impossibility should be exempt from all liability—regardless of whether the actor poses a "public danger."[116] The problem generally for the subjective theory of attempts is whether the theory can accommodate the widespread intuition that superstitious and legally impossible attempts should be exempt from all liablility or whether, as the Model Penal Code suggests, a discretionary inquiry into personal dangerousness is the only means of resolving difficult problems in this borderland of liability.

In attempting to explain why superstitious attempts should not be punishable, subjectivist theorists gravitate toward a few characteristic arguments. It is sometimes claimed that when the attempt is irrational, we have inadequate evidence of the actor's intent. Another move is to modify the rule of liability so as to require that a "reasonable man in the same position as the defendant would believe the circumstances to be as the defendant believes them to be."[117] This test would immediately exclude liability for attempted killings by magic incantations, but it would also exclude liability in cases of attempted "poisoning" with sugar, where the mistaken perception of the sugar was unreasonable under the circumstances. More fundamentally, one is puzzled by the sudden intrusion in this context of the reasonable person. Why should it matter whether the mistake about the efficacy of black magic or the white substance put in the coffee is reasonable or unreasonable? This is clearly an effort to gerrymander the legal rule so as to exclude cases from liability on the basis of an unarticu-

[115] MPC §5.05(2).
[116] MPC §5.01, Comment at 31 (Tent. Draft No. 10, 1960).
[117] See Elkind, *supra* note 54, at 35; *cf.* Sayre, *supra* note 10, at 851.

lated and unanalyzed intuition about why they should be excluded.

A more convincing subjectivist argument is that superstitious actors are not dangerous. This claim at least brings us to the source of subjectivist theory and concern, namely the identification and isolation of dangerous persons. The supposition is that those who try to kill by incantations either know in their hearts that their activity is harmless, or are so out of touch that they could not competently execute a plan to kill by more rational means. We have so little experience with black magic in modern industrial society that it is difficult to know whether this supposition is correct.

The issue of legal impossibility is obviously of greater importance than the hypothetical case of black magic. In a system of criminal law subject to reform and amendment, it might often be the case that people think they are participating in crimes when they are not. It seems relatively easy to dispose of cases like those in which the actor engages in homosexual relationships after the decriminalization of this activity. Even if we were inclined on theoretical grounds to punish this willingness to flout the law, we would not know what to call the offense or how to phrase the indictment. The actor cannot be charged with attempted homosexual activity, for attempts are parasitic on a punishable offense-in-chief. Of course, one could legislate a new offense that would cover all cases in which people act in the belief that they were violating the law. The advantage of such an offense is that it would protect society against people who in their hearts were prepared to violate the law. There is something untoward about hitching criminal liability exclusively to the actor's beliefs about what he is doing. Yet this form of liability would not be different in nature from punishing the act of putting sugar in coffee, if the act is accompanied by a wicked intent.

The more troublesome cases of "legal impossibility" are those that cannot be disposed of simply because we do not know what to call the offense and there is no general prohibition against acting in the belief that one is violating the law. Consider these examples. Someone changes the figures on a check in order to raise the payable amount, but he does not change the verbal statement of the amount; he falsely believes that tampering with the numbers is itself forgery. In fact, this alteration is not considered material, and therefore his conduct does not constitute forgery.[118] Or suppose that someone surreptitiously manufactures a sticker in order to gain admission to a convenient parking lot. She is convinced that parking stickers are the kinds of documents covered by the law of forgery; again she is mistaken and there is no consummated offense.[119] Or suppose that it is not a crime to possess less than one ounce of marijuana. The actor thinks that the amount in his possession is two ounces, which amount, he realizes, would make him liable under the law. In fact, the amount possessed is less than four-fifths of an ounce. In all of these cases there is an offense-in-chief that could be invoked to charge the actor with attempt. Therefore, one is put to the test whether any or all of these cases should be covered by the rubric "legal impossibility."

English and American commentators typically approach this problem by arguing that "unless the intended end is a legally proscribed harm,"[120] no conduct in furtherance of that end can constitute a crime. The claim is that this rule derives from the principle of legality. We might readily concur that certain cases should be exempt from criminal liability, but the question is whether the legality or the illegality of the actor's intended end provides an adequate account of our intuitions.

It is understandable that subjectivist theorists would seek to generate a rationale for exempting certain cases from punishment by relying on the actor's intent. That intent, after all, is the central concern of subjectivist theory. The problem, however, is how do we know what the actor in fact intended? Does the would-be forger in the first case merely intend to change the figures on the check? Or does he intend to alter the value that the check repre-

[118] See Wilson v. State, 85 Miss. 687, 38 So. 46 (1905).

[119] For an analogous case, see Judgment of July 1, 1959, 13 BGHSt. 235 (actor mistakenly assumed that specific ration cards were covered by the law of forgery; held, no liability for attempt).

[120] Hall 586–87; LaFave & Scott 442; Williams 633; Perkins 570–71; Smith & Hogan 207; MPC §5.01, Comment at 32 (Tent. Draft No. 10, 1960).

sents? Does the possessor of marijuana intend merely to possess the amount that he has? Or does he intend to possess two full ounces? The first of these descriptions states an "intended end" that would exempt the actor from liability. The second description states an "intended end" that, if realized, would subject the actor to liability. Both of these descriptions are possible, and there is no apparent method for choosing between them. Without an authoritative description of the actor's intent, there is no way of applying the subjectivist rule of thumb that liability for an attempt should turn on whether the intent, if realized, would constitute a crime.

The problem is not simply one of discerning the relevant facts. Even given a clarified factual situation, we confront the problem of describing the facts broadly or narrowly. The description we choose determines the legal result. This is neither a novel nor a surprising critique of the orthodox view.[121] What is surprising is that the critique is well known and yet the orthodox view remains unshaken. The faith remains firm that by construing the actor's intent we can fathom whether his conduct should amount to an attempted offense.

As an example of the enduring subjectivist reliance on the actor's state of mind, witness the effort by LaFave and Scott to distinguish *Jaffe* from *Wilson*—the case that inspired the first forgery hypothetical. The conclusion the authors try to support is that an acquittal in the altered figures case is justified, but that those who received goods (mistakenly) believing them to be stolen should be convicted of an attempt.

In the forgery case, they argue, the actor is "ignorant of the material alteration requirement of the crime of forgery. In *Jaffe*, on the other hand, what the defendant intended to do was a crime, and if the facts had been as the defendant believed them to be, he would be guilty of the completed crime." [122] This argument is admittedly a shade more sophisticated than straightforward reliance on the actor's intent, but the approach remains true to the subjectivist assumption that legality should turn on what the actor

[121] See, e.g., LaFave & Scott 440.
[122] LaFave & Scott 443.

thinks and believes about the world. If his mistake turns on the interpretation of a legal norm (what it means materially to alter a check), there should be no liability; if his mistake turns on whether a particular object possesses a legal attribute (stolen or not stolen), liability should attach. There is admittedly a distinction between these two types of mistake, but the troubling question is why so much theoretical hope is invested in this precious distinction.

Threading the law through the eye of this distinction is but another way of invoking the rule: unless what the actor intends to do is a crime, the attempt is not punishable. If his mistake is about the legal attribute of a thing rather than about the scope of a legal norm, then we should describe his intent in such a way that were it carried out, the intended act would be punishable. Thus in *Jaffe,* we should describe the intent as the intent to receive stolen cloth. In the marijuana case, we should describe the intent as the intent to possess two ounces. These ends, if realized, would be punishable acts. Yet in our other hypothetical case, in which the actor makes up a phony parking sticker, we should presumably say that her mistake is about the scope of the law of forgery rather than about an attribute of the sticker, and therefore the intent should be described as the intent to forge a sticker—an intent that, under the circumstances, cannot generate a criminal offense. According to LaFave and Scott, this latter case would appropriately be dubbed one of "legal impossibility" and therefore be exempt from liability.

Notice that this approach to the actor's intent turns ultimately on the stability of the distinction between the scope of a legal norm and the legal attribute of a thing. This is but a variation of the theme of distinguishing between mistakes of fact and mistakes of law. As we shall see later in Chapter Nine, this distinction has long plagued efforts to distinguish between the types of mistakes that excuse violations of the law from those that do not. In the context of attempts, however, mistakes of law exculpate rather than inculpate; and mistakes of fact inculpate rather than exculpate.[123]

[123] This statement will do for now; in fact we should be more skeptical about the utility of distinguishing between "fact" and "law." See §9.4 *infra.*

This inverse correlation may appeal to some writers on grounds of symmetry, but the problems that affect the theory of exculpatory mistake are so different that we should be wary of linking the two fields in our thinking about sound criteria of liability.[124]

What is particularly surprising in the subjectivist approach to the problem of "legal impossibility" is the claim that legality demands attention to the actor's intent and the type of mistake he might be making. The first principle of legality is not that the actor's intent be of the wrong sort, but that his conduct conform to the objective description of the offense. The maxim *nulla poena sine lege* requires, at minimum, that the *lex*—the legislated law—specify the objective criteria of liability. If the objective criteria are satisfied, the inquiry should turn to the actor's intent or other required state of mind. If the principle of legality is understood in this classical sense, the conventional rule about the actor's "intended end" has the inquiry inside out. It is not the internal question of intent that should first concern us, but the external issue whether the actor's conduct objectively constitutes "an attempt" to commit a recognized offense.

Thus the principle of legality, if properly construed, does not lead us to focus on the actor's intent, but on the question whether the actor's conduct meets the preannounced definition of a criminal attempt. Fidelity to the principle of legality should lead us to the view that if we punish for attempted murder, attempted burglary or attempted rape, then we must know what it means to "attempt" a crime. This reorientation of the issue takes us back to the objectivist claim that liability for an attempted offense presupposes an act that can properly be called an "attempt."

The theory that we developed earlier is that people attempt to achieve only those ends that affect their motivation in acting.[125] Their mistaken beliefs constitute part of the attempted act only so far as being disabused of their mistakes would alter their course of

[124] This correlation is widely discussed in the German literature. See, e.g., Sax, *Zum logischen und sachlichen Gehalt des sog. "Umkehrschusses aus §59 StGB,"* 1964 JZ 241; Baumann, *Das Umkehrverhältnis zwischen Versuch und Irrtum im Strafrecht,* 1962 NJW 16.

[125] See text at pp. 160–66 *supra.*

conduct. This is an argument, it will be recalled, that is rooted in the ordinary understanding of what it is, in daily life, to try to achieve a particular end.

As applied to the problems of so-called legal impossibility, this analysis of attempting provides a strikingly clear passage through the conundrums of the common law. In most cases, beliefs about the law do not affect motivation and acting. The would-be forger who raises the numerical amount on a check is not interested in committing forgery for its own sake. If he were told it was not a crime to alter the check and deceive an endorser, he would be so much the happier. The same is true about the case of preparing a phony parking sticker. It follows that in these cases the actor is not attempting to commit forgery. He may be attempting to deceive others, but the manner of his attempted deceit does not constitute forgery. That he believes that his conduct is criminal is insufficient to say that he is attempting or trying to commit the particular offense.

The third situation, of the party possessing marijuana, is more subtle. One could imagine a case in which, if the actor were told that the amount he had was only four-fifths of an ounce rather than two ounces, that fact might indeed affect his motivation. He might be preparing a trip and would not set forth on the journey without at least two ounces in his possession. If this were the case, it seems perfectly sensible to describe his activity as attempting to possess two ounces.

Subjectivist theorists, relying on their theory of the intended end, would concur with acquittals in the two forgery cases and a conviction in the marijuana case. The difference between the two approaches emerges in cases like *Jaffe* and *Berrigan* where subjectivists tend to favor conviction and the proposed test supports the judicial disposition to acquit. In *Jaffe,* the actor's motivation is not affected by his belief that the cloth is stolen; in *Berrigan,* the actor's motivation is presumably not influenced by the warden's knowing and tolerating the sending of letters out of prison. Subjectivists would convict in these cases on the ground that the mistakes supposedly relate to questions of fact or of legal attributes rather than the scope of legal norms. The same conclusion may be stated by describing the "intended end" so that, if realized, the end would constitute a crime.

It bears repeating that the test of rational motivation does not focus on the actor's state of mind, but rather on the counterfactual conditional: how would the actor behave if he knew that he was mistaken about particular facts? That difference between simply examining the actor's beliefs and asking how those beliefs affect his motivation is the key to constructing a concept of attempting an offense. It is central to realizing the principle of legality in a definition of attempting, rather than letting liability for attempts turn solely on the actor's beliefs and intents.

The pragmatic virtue of the test of rational motivation is its explaining an array of judicial results as well as uniting and simplifying the categories of analysis. Whether the mistake is one of law, of a legal attribute or of fact is irrelevant, and any doctrinal move to classify cases in this way only distracts us from the question: what is an attempt? What counts is the way the actor's mistaken beliefs influence his decision to act. By proceeding on this theory of what it means to attempt a crime, we can explain the tendency to acquit in cases of so-called "legal impossibility," as well as the persistent judicial conviction that there is no crime of attempting in cases like *Jaffe* and *Berrigan.*

The one type of case that does not readily fit in the analysis is typified by attempts to suborn a witness or a juror. In the leading case of *Teal,*[126] the defendant sought to convince a potential witness to lie about an act of adultery that seemed relevant to a divorce proceedings. As things turned out, the incident of adultery was not alleged in the pleadings and therefore was not a material issue. Thus the attempt to suborn perjury did not relate to a material issue in the proceedings. As a result, he was acquitted on the charge of attempted suborning, and the controlling ground was the impossibility of the attempt. In other cases, the defendant has been acquitted after offering a bribe to someone he thought was a juror.[127] Again, the controlling consideration was the impossibility

[126] People v. Teal, 196 N.Y. 372, 89 N.E. 1086 (1909).

[127] State v. Taylor, 345 Mo. 325, 133 S.W.2d 336 (1939); State v. Porter, 125 Mont. 503, 242 P.2d 984 (1952)

that the bribe would affect the judicial proceedings. It appears that both subjectivist theory and the test of rational motivation falter in these cases. According to their subjective perceptions, these actors were engaged in suborning witnesses and jurors. Thus, according to this test, they should have been guilty. It is also clear that their beliefs influenced their motivations, for it would hardly be rational to offer a bribe to someone who, it was known, would not testify at the proceeding or would not be a juror. Thus, one has some difficulty understanding the judicial inclination to acquit in these specific cases.[128]

An account of these isolated reversals might be found in the theory of aptness that we developed as an aspect of the objective theory of attempts.[129] These cases appeared to be inapt attempts, for there is no evident danger associated with offering money to people who in fact are not going to testify in judicial proceedings. On the other hand, in *Teal,* it appeared that the suborned witness might have to testify at trial, and this factor of appearance could arguably be sufficient. A more basic problem with the theory of aptness in this context is that, as we reasoned earlier,[130] the theory should only apply in cases in which there is an assault on one of the major interests protected under the criminal law. Of course, one could argue that the integrity of judicial proceedings is one of these interests. The notions of aptness and manifest danger appear to be so flaccid at the fringes that one despairs about resolving the problem of their application to this category of case. It may simply be that in these few cases, suborning and bribery cases stand apart and that, for reasons not entirely clear, some courts have been unwilling to convict where the bribe cannot produce a corruption of justice.

§3.3.8. The Problem of Abandonment. Suppose that a man bent on arson pours gasoline on the floor of a warehouse and strikes a match with the admitted intent to set the place ablaze. At

[128] Glanville Williams maintains that the "wrong conclusion" was reached in *Teal,* Williams 635. His argument is that *D* "intended to influence the decision of the divorce court." *Ibid.*

[129] See text at pp. 149–54 *supra.*

[130] See text at p. 156 *supra.*

the last minute he has a change of heart and puts the match out. Even though his acts went far enough to constitute a punishable attempt, there is a persistent effort in Western legal thought to acknowledge a defense of abandonment in this type of case. In its elegant formulation of 1810, the French Penal Code held that there was liability for attempted crime only if the effort "is interrupted or fails to produce the intended effect as a result of circumstances independent of the actor's will."[131] This definition entails a valid defense of abandonment when the attempt fails to come off for reasons attributable solely to the actor's will. The German Code of 1871 included a special section with similar language to provide for the defense,[132] and the provision, with slight alterations, has been carried forward under the 1975 Code.[133] The RSFSR Code of 1960 also recognizes a defense for the good-faith abandonment of criminal attempts.[134] This standard theme in the repertoire of Continental legal theory has never gained a firm audience among Anglo-American judges.[135] Yet today the text writers,[136] the Model Penal Code,[137] and numerous code revisions[138] recognize the defense. It is worth delving into the details of abandonment, or renunciation of purpose, as the issue is sometimes labeled. For

[131] Code Pénal §2 ("*si [la tentative] n'a été suspendue ou si elle n'a manqué son effet que par des circonstances indépendantes de la volonte de son auteur . . .*")

[132] StGB 1871, §46(1).

[133] StGB §24(1). The earlier code used the negative French formulations (abandonment without interference by circumstances "independent of his will"); the new code recasts the standard in affirmative language ("whoever voluntarily abandons further execution . . .").

[134] Ugol. kod. (RSFSR) §16 ("whoever voluntarily abandons further execution . . .").

[135] Fitzjames Stephen was fully aware of the French rule, yet he regarded the doctrine as both "dangerous" and "of little practical importance." 2 Stephen 226–27. For examples of recent cases, affirming convictions, and totally unsympathetic to the doctrine of abandonment, see People v. Crary, 265 Cal. App. 2d 534, 71 Cal. Rptr. 457 (1968); People v. Staples, 6 Cal. App. 3d 61, 85 Cal. Rptr. 589 (1970). *But cf.* the 1916 decision in *Graham,* discussed *infra* note 145.

[136] LaFave & Scott 450; Williams 620–21; *cf.* Perkins 588–90.

[137] MPC §5.01(4).

[138] Conn. Gen. Stat. Ann. §53a–49(c); Colo. Rev. Stat. §18-2-401; Del. Code tit. 11, §541; N.Y. Penal Law §40.10(3); Pa. Cons. Stat. Ann. tit. 18, §901(c); Tex. Penal Code §15.04.

though of marginal practical importance, the issue strikes to the theoretical core of liability for attempted offenses.

The impulse to recognize the defense of abandonment derives from a sense that attempts are different from other offenses. In most systems it would be of no avail for a thief to argue that he returned the goods that he stole, or for someone who illegally possessed narcotics at one point of time to argue that he had thrown them away and therefore was no longer guilty. The offenses of larceny and possession are complete in themselves and a subsequent change of heart is irrelevant to liability. If acts of repentance do not cancel liability for these offenses, why should an abandonment of an attempt constitute a reason for not convicting of the completed crime of attempt?

One popular argument is that the promise of immunity from sanctions encourages attemptors to desist and thus serves the law's purpose of preventing harm. These arguments appeal to those who find it helpful to relate every issue to a purpose of the criminal law, yet the claim that this promise is an effective inducement needs far more proof than any of its proponents have offered. Though German scholars and judges once advanced this argument,[139] they now recognize it as naive.[140] Even if it were empirically sound, this argument would not help us understand why there is a disposition to recognize the defense of abandonment in cases of attempts but no parallel inclination to recognize an inducement to return stolen property.

Another argument readily accepted by subjectivist theorists is that the abandonment indicates that the actor is not dangerous and therefore he is not the type of person who should be punished. This claim makes more intuitive sense than the empirically

[139] The argument goes back at least to Anselm von Feuerbach's writings in the early nineteenth century; see Jescheck 406; the pre-war Supreme Court espoused the same theory. See Judgment of June 6, 1882, 6 RGSt. 341. The argument survives in the French and Soviet literature. See 1 Bouzat & Pinatel §210, at 295; Kurs (GP 1968) at 577.

[140] See Judgment of February 28, 1956, 9 BGHSt. 48, 52; Bockelmann, *Wann ist der Rücktritt vom Versuch freiwillig?* 1955 NJW 1417; Schönke-Schröder-Eser §24 note 4, at 300.

shaky principle of inducing attemptors to desist, yet it raises the basic question whether the criminal law should be grounded in case-by-case assessments of personal dangerousness. If this indeed were the rationale for the defense, it would be sound in principle to inquire whether the actor was generally dangerous, even though he abandoned the offense on a particular occasion. This is what the Model Penal Code proposes in cases of superstitious attempts,[141] and it should follow that it would be contrary to the purpose of social control to close one's eyes to those who "present a public danger" just because they happen once to abandon an attempted crime. Further, this argument shares one of the flaws affecting the claim that attemptors might desist if promised immunity; neither is adequate to distinguish attempts from other cases in which the actor's repentance after a crime, say of larceny or illegal possession, indicates a change of character.[142]

The two arguments that we have found unsatisfactory—an incentive to desist and the inference of non-dangerousness—were sufficient to persuade the draftsmen of the Model Penal Code that abandonment should be recognized as a bar to liability.[143] They may well be right, but for the wrong reasons. Any adequate account of the matter would have to explain why attempts as crimes are different from the completed offenses as to which acts of repentance are irrelevant.

When the German courts abandoned the rationale of encouraging actors to desist, they turned to a closer examination of the structure of attempting in order to explain the significance of an abandonment. In a 1956 decision the argument emerged that an abandonment demonstrates that the actor's "criminal intent was not as firm as would have been required for the execution of the offense."[144] This is an illuminating suggestion, for it begins to explicate the peculiar quality of the intent required for an attempt. It

[141] MPC §5.05(2).

[142] The same criticism applies to the argument, Jescheck 407, Baumann 524, that immunity functions as a "reward" for abandoning the attempt. The question is why a thief who returns the stolen goods doesn't deserve the same "reward."

[143] MPC §5.01, Comment at 71–72, 144 (Tent. Draft No. 10, 1960).

[144] Judgment of February 28, 1956, 9 BGHSt. 48, 52.

is worth noting that the argument here is not that the abandonment raises doubts about the actor's intention up to that time. The principle that can be derived from this argument of the German court is that the intent required for an attempt is not merely a firm resolve up to the time the attempt is complete as a punishable act. The intent required is one to carry through.[145] Whether the actor has an intent of this degree of firmness can be determined only by waiting to see whether in fact he carries out the plan.

This point may be put more neatly by using the language of conditions. Attempts are different from other crimes in that implicit in each punishable attempt is the assumption that the actor will carry through with his plan. The condition subsequent to each completed attempt is that the actor will not desist in his efforts. When this condition subsequently fails—and the actor does desist—the concept of attempting in itself yields the conclusion that there ought to be no liability.[146]

The difficulty with this analysis is that it suggests that there should be liability only in cases in which there is no doubt about whether the actor will carry through with his plan. If we recall that attempts are cases of failure, where the plan does not succeed, this would mean that liability should attach only where the actor has done everything in his power and no longer has the capacity to

[145] See People v. Graham, 176 App. Div. 38, 162 N.Y.S. 334 (1916) (defendant spilled gasoline on bed and then told his son, "I won't do it; God has stayed my hand").

[146] If the actor has done everything in his power to reach his result (e.g., put poison in the coffee, pulled trigger on gun), the attempt is called a "finalized attempt" (*beendigter Versuch*) in German law, and the implicit condition subsequent is that the actor not intervene to prevent the harm from occurring (spilling the coffee, warning the victim). On the distinction between the two types of attempt (finalized and unfinalized), see Jescheck 407–09; Schönke-Schröder-Eser §24, notes 58–72, at 309–12. According to StGB 1871, §46(2), the actor had to intervene prior to the discovery of a "finalized attempt" with affirmative efforts that effectively prevented the harmful result. The new code, StGB §24(1) consolidates two changes previously advocated in the case law and the literature. First, an abandonment is possible even after discovery of the deed, provided the abandonment is nonetheless voluntary. See Schönke-Schröder-Eser §24, notes 50–51, at 308; Rudolphi in SK §24, note 29, at 191. Secondly, the new code provides a defense even in cases where the defendant's "earnest effort" to prevent the result is not the factor that causes the attempt to fail. StGB §24(1)(2).

prevent the harm from occurring.[147] The paradigm case would be shooting at the intended victim and missing. It would not be irrational to limit attempt liability to this type of case; paradoxically, however, when the attempt goes this far and yet fails, one might properly wonder if the actor was subconsciously conflicted in his goals.[148]

If we limit liability to these extreme cases where we are nominally certain of the actor's firm resolve, we ignore the value of permitting police to intervene early in order to prevent harm from occurring. Of course, we need not link the issue of police intervention to the definition of substantive offenses.[149] Yet in the history of attempt liability, the value of early intervention was surely one of the factors that informed the contours of liability. As a result, the law of attempts in every jurisdiction includes cases in which the actor's attempt is interrupted before he has taken all the measures necessary to complete the offense.

When the crime is interrupted by external factors, such as arrest or the resistance of the victim, there is no way of knowing whether the actor would have carried through with his plan. Nonetheless, the courts are willing to convict of criminal attempt. The fact remains, however, that if the plan had not been interrupted, he might have changed his mind at some moment before consummation of the offense. The condition subsequent, implicit in the concept of attempting (namely, that the actor carry through), is neither satisfied nor refuted. Our willingness to convict in the face of doubt about the actor's resolve may seem contrary to the general principle of favoring the accused in cases of doubt. Yet this compromise is the only way to structure the law of attempts in order to permit the police to prevent the consummation of criminal plans.

Within the field of abandoned attempts, the critical doctrinal question is whether the abandonment is "voluntary." This is the word typically seized upon in all legislative formations of the is-

[147] This is the standard of "last-step" attempting. See text at notes 23–24 *supra.*

[148] See Note, *Why Do Criminal Attempts Fail? A New Defense,* 70 Yale L.J. 160 (1960).

[149] See §3.7 *infra.*

sue.[150] The standard reliance on the concept of voluntariness tells us, correctly, that the issue posed by the abandonment is whether the actor had the resolve to carry through.

Yet the concept of voluntariness should not mislead us into thinking that this field of problems has anything in common with the other areas in which the law puts its faith in the distinction between voluntary and involuntary conduct. Consider the problems of voluntary consent to sexual intercourse, voluntary waiver of Fourth Amendment rights, voluntary confessions, and the problem of voluntary conduct under conditions of duress or necessity. Though all of these difficult issues are controlled by the standard of voluntariness, it would be a mistake to think that the criteria sufficient for involuntary conduct in one context would be sufficient in another. In the same breath an actor might waive his rights under the Fourth Amendment and confess to a crime. The former might be seen as voluntary, and the confession (in the absence of *Miranda* warnings) as involuntary.[151] The payment of money does not render an employment contract involuntary, but it does certainly undercut the voluntariness of a constitutional waiver. The issue of voluntariness is obviously not an observable fact, but is a framework for inquiring whether the external pressures influencing the actor's decision are sufficiently great to say that he should neither be held accountable for his decision nor take credit for it.

In the context of abandonment, the problem is whether the actor should get credit for his decision to renounce his criminal purpose. The problem is deciding which external factors should deprive him of this credit and which should not. It seems clear that the external factor of detection by the police, or by someone who

[150] See statutes cited note 138 *supra; but cf.* Code Penal §2 (the attempt must fail for reasons independent of the actor's will); Wis. Stat. Ann. §939.32(2) (the attempt would have succeeded "except for the intervention of another person or some other extraneous factor").

[151] See Schneckloth v. Bustamonte, 412 U.S. 218 (1973) (holding that police warnings are not necessary for the "voluntary" waiver of Fourth Amendment rights).

is likely to inform the police, is sufficient to deprive him of any benefit that might derive from a decision to desist.[152] Let us consider some more subtle cases. Suppose the actor enters a gallery with the intent of stealing an artifact he admires. When he gets to the artifact, he discovers that the gallery owners have substituted an imitation in its place that is worth about ten percent as much. He could steal the imitation without being detected, but he sees no point to it and leaves. Or suppose that he is about to rape a woman and she persuades him to desist with the promise that if they meet later in the evening she would be delighted to have intercourse with him. On these and other subtle borderline cases, there is much to be learned from German jurisprudence. Having worked with the defense of abandonment for more than a century, the Germans have accumulated a vast body of case law as well as a sophisticated theoretical literature.

The consensus of German theory and practice is that if a would-be thief desists because the bounty is not large enough, she is nonetheless guilty of an attempt.[153] This might make sense in the case in which the thief expects a valuable art object and finds a cheap one. Yet it seems counterintuitive in the case in which a mugger approaches an ostensibly rich man on the street, demands his "money or his life," and then discovers that the man is carrying only ten dollars. If the disappointed mugger then tells the victim to "forget it," one finds it hard to think of his activity as attempted robbery. Of course, if the victim had no money at all, the would-be thief would be guilty; the attempt would have been aptly related to its purpose, although the execution was objectively impossible. One could assimilate the case of the discriminating mugger to the category of punishable apt attempts by defining his activity as the attempt to steal at least ten dollars, which turned

[152] Judgment of February 28, 1956, 9 BGHSt. 48, 51; Rudolphi in SK, note 25, at 190; Schmidhäuser 633. *But cf.* the argument that abandonment due to shame or a general fear of punishment is voluntary. *Ibid.*

[153] E.g., Schönke-Schröder-Eser §24, note 48, at 307; Jescheck 409. See Judgment of February 20, 1953, 4 BGHSt. 56.

out to be impossible under the circumstances.[154] The line between the cases of disappointment and the category of impossibility proves to be not as firm as one might initially think.

In the second case in which the actor is persuaded by the victim's promises to desist, one leading German case[155] holds that this abandonment is voluntary and that there should be no liability for attempted rape. This is a surprising result, for it seems odd to give the would-be rapist the benefit of a situation in which his threatening conduct yields a promise of intercourse from his intended victim. The case warrants our close attention, for the curious result can be explained only by reflecting on the theory of liability for attempted crime.

The leading German case on this problem arose in 1955 on facts inspiring our hypothetical problem. The defendant accosted a girl whom he had not previously known, threw her to the ground and tried to kiss her. His intent to coerce intercourse seemed apparent, but the girl did not offer resistance. Instead she induced the defendant to desist with the promise that she would later submit voluntarily. They both stood up and at that moment the girl saw two evening strollers to whom she called for help.[156] At trial the defendant was convicted of attempted rape, his defense of abandonment being rejected on the ground that it was not "voluntary."

The German Supreme Court reversed the conviction in a carefully reasoned opinion. The Court began by defining the problem as the determination of the motive that prompted the defendant to desist. The written opinion of the trial judge was deficient, the Court reasoned, for failing adequately to analyze the defendant's motives.[157] It was significant that the victim did not know the defendant personally. This implied that the actor rationally had little reason to fear apprehension by the police. If so, it would follow that his abandonment was probably not motivated by a sudden fear

[154] See, e.g., Jescheck 409; Schmidhäuser 628.
[155] Judgment of April 14, 1955, 7 BGHSt. 296.
[156] *Id.* at 296–97.
[157] *Id.* at 298.

of apprehension and punishment. The trial judge had mistakenly concluded in his opinion that the fear of prosecution had prompted the abandonment.[158]

The underlying assumption of this discussion is that the fear of immediate apprehension and prosecution renders the abandonment involuntary. There seems to be a strong consensus on this point. Yet the fear of external reprisal is distinguished from the unanalyzed fear of going through with the crime, which is not thought to render the abandonment involuntary.[159]

The subsequent discussion in the opinion assays the question whether the victim's persuasion undercut the voluntariness of the defendant's decision. In language reminiscent of the definition of attempt in the French Penal Code, the Court says that the issue is whether "the execution of the crime is interrupted by factors that are independent of the actor's will."[160] The actor can still be "master of his decision" even if he considers the victim's entreaties and promises. And now comes the critical point:[161]

> The law does not require that the motive of the abandonment be commendable or even of merit . . . the exemption from punishment in cases [of abandonment] is granted not as a reward for good behavior, but because in these cases the criminal project did not reach a harmful stage.

This is undoubtedly a bold and forthright stand and one that would not have been possible without a solid grasp of the connection between abandonment and the concept of attempting. If the defense of abandonment were thought of as a supervening defense, recognized only because the actor's repentance had "erased" or somehow compensated for the initial criminal act, it would be plausible to demand that the decision be prompted by a commendable motive. Though this latter theory has some support,[162] the prevailing view in German law is that the exemption from

[158] *Ibid.*
[159] *Cf.* note 152 *supra.*
[160] 7 BGHSt. at 299.
[161] *Ibid.*
[162] See Bockelmann, *supra* note 140; Baumann 524.

punishment, as the Court said, "is not a reward for good behavior."

Abandonment is accepted as a defense because it reveals that the actor's criminal will was insufficiently resolute to carry through. In a 1967 decision,[163] the German Supreme Court recognized the defense of abandonment in a case in which the defendant's partner in an attempted burglary talked him out of going through with it. Both the would-be burglars were on probation, and as they were about to jimmy open the door, one of them became apprehensive of being held in violation of probation and convinced the other to give up the plan. Is it so different if a rape victim persuades the aggressor to stop? And why should it matter whether the technique of persuasion is an appeal to the defendant's moral sensibility or to the promise of a later assignation? In both the burglary and the rape cases, the defendant desists from a plan that is still patently subject to execution. And he desists without being afraid that he is going to be apprehended and punished. So far as attempt liability is reserved for culprits of stronger resolve, it should not matter whether it is the victim or a partner in crime that persuades the defendant to desist. And it follows, as German theory holds, that the moral quality of the actor's motives should be irrelevant to his coming under the protection of the defense.

If this line of reasoning seems convincing, we should consider a few other cases to see how precious the theory of abandonment can be. In another recent German case, the Supreme Court held that the abandonment of an attempted rape was not voluntary; the consideration inducing the defendant to desist was not the promise of a later assignation, but the discovery that the intended victim was then menstruating.[164] That the defendant lost interest in carrying out the rape implied that he was no longer acting as the "master of his decision."[165] He revealed no strength of will in desisting, for he had no desire to carry through. The distinction be-

[163] Judgment of October 11, 1967, 21 BGHSt. 319.
[164] Judgment of October 5, 1965, 20 BGHSt. 279.
[165] *Id.* at 280 (*"Herrseiner Entschlüsse"*).

tween this and the earlier case of the promised assignation is philosophically defensible, for there is a difference between being persuaded to give up one's criminal plan and being influenced by independent circumstances to lose interest in the crime.[166] Yet the realization of this distinction in practice requires not only philosophical subtlety,[167] but a well-nigh omniscient finder of fact.

In these cases of persuasion, where the defense is operative, it is critical that the actor definitively abandon his criminal plan. If the would-be rapist accepts the promise of a latter assignation under the implicit threat that if necessary, he will accost the girl again, the abandonment is hardly complete.[168] Also it should be noted that in these cases in which the victim persuades the attemptor to desist, the attemptor may well be guilty of extortion. If a thief is induced to desist from taking a family heirloom by the owner's giving him cash instead, he may not be guilty of attempted larceny; but he surely is guilty of extortion in taking the cash under the threat of larceny.

It seems that the defense of voluntary abandonment will eventually become a standard feature of American penal codes.[169] But it is highly unlikely that the courts will emulate German teaching on the issue. There are important differences between Anglo-American and German law that are likely to generate a divergent development on an issue of this degree of moral refinement.

First, it is important to note that German appellate courts can exercise a much greater scope of review on cases involving close

[166] *Cf.* LeBarron v. State, 32 Wis. 2d 294, 145 N.W.2d 79 (1966) (defendant abandoned attempted rape after discovering that his intended victim was pregnant; conviction affirmed on the ground that the pregnancy was an "extraneous factor," i.e., independent of his will).

[167] This subtlety was obviously absent in People v. Crary, 265 Cal. App. 2d 534, 71 Cal. Rptr. 457 (1968), in which the victim, a gas station proprietor, talked a group of boys out of committing a robbery· the conviction for attempted robbery was nonetheless affirmed.

[168] 7 BGHSt. at 297. *Cf.* MPC §5.01(4) ("Renunciation is not complete if it is motivated by a decision to postpone the criminal conduct to a more advantageous time . . .").

[169] For a partial list of states that have already enacted the defense, see note 138 *supra*.

questions of fact. The German trial judge must write an opinion setting forth the reasons for his finding of guilt or innocence. If he or she fails adequately to analyze the factors bearing on the voluntariness of the attempt, the decision is subject to reversal. In contrast, the only issue that is likely to trigger a reversal in an Anglo-American court is a prejudicial error in the jury instructions. If the judge correctly instructs the jury on the issue of abandonment, the jury's finding of guilt is not likely to be upset on appeal. It is hard to imagine a case of voluntary abandonment that would be so clear that an appellate court would hold that there was insufficient evidence to support the jury's finding of involuntariness. This difference in the mode of appellate review enables German appellate judges to inquire into fine points of motivation; that there is a written opinion subject to their scrutiny means that they may direct their critical attention to the essay written by the trial judge rather than to the inscrutable events of the case.

The acute question for Anglo-American law is whether the jury instructions should incorporate the fine distinctions that have evolved in German theory. It is possible that the courts will someday so hold, yet skepticism seems warranted. First, it is uncharacteristic of Anglo-American criminal trials to probe so deeply into the actor's motivation. More significantly, drawing the necessary distinctions in the instructions requires a degree of philosophical sophistication that is not readily mustered in the heat of trial. Trial judges would have to struggle with the differences between being persuaded and being influenced by external factors. They should have to ponder the difference between incorporating reasons offered by others into one's own decision and losing interest in a crime as a result of objective circumstances. Intelligent lawyers and lay persons would be forgiven for not understanding these subtle points.

An even more decisive consideration is that the distinctions as drawn in German law would meet considerable resistance from scholarly quarters in the United States. We should remember that the Model Penal Code adheres to the view that the defense should be recognized either because it is an inducement to desist, or because an act of abandonment reveals that the actor is not dangerous.[170] Neither of these rationalia would generate an acquittal in the case of the would-be rapist who stops because he has extorted a promise of a later tryst. As for the theory of providing an incentive to desist, it would seem that no motivation should be adequate for the defense unless it includes an interest in enjoying the law's promise of immunity. Even if the defense were construed more broadly, it is impossible to tell whether on the basis of this rationale, the court should acquit someone who is persuaded, either by the victim or by a cohort, to give up the plan. As to the rationale that the abandonment reveals a lack of personal dangerousness, it is doubtful that this perspective would lead to the fine-grained distinctions that have emerged in German law. The man who desists from rape because the promised assignation appears more attractive is hardly someone to be trusted in the future. Nor is there much reason to think that the would-be burglar who desists because his partner gets "cold feet" is unlikely to plan another burglary at another time and another place. What the draftsmen of the Model Penal Code must have had in mind is the case in which the actor experiences a sudden and overwhelming change of character in the course of committing a crime. If that should ever happen in the world as we know it, it would be a pity to be caught without an appropriate provision of the penal law. Yet so far as this is the underlying theory of the defense, the claim of abandonment is likely to remain an elegant artifact of criminal codes, viewed with admiration, yet rarely employed in the day-to-day affairs of the courts.

§3.4. *Possession Offenses.*

There are many disquieting features of the law of attempts. One of these that is subject to legislative remedy is the imprecise and fluid boundary between preparation and attempt. It may not be an

[170] See text at notes 139–43 *supra.*

important value that would-be criminals know precisely when their behavior crosses the line into the realm of the punishable, for if they voluntarily abandon their attempts they are still exempt (or arguably should be exempt) from punishment. Yet it is important to be able to assess whether judges decide in accordance with the law rather than in response to improper considerations. Thus the constantly shifting definition of criminal attempting is a proper source of concern. Legislators have responded to this concern by singling out a specific type of behavior, namely, acquiring the instruments of crime, and subjecting it to special legislation.

In English legal parlance, these offenses are grouped under the general heading of "possession" offenses. The crime is committed by knowingly possessing a prohibited item. The objects most typically prohibited are specified types of weapons, obscene materials and narcotics. This technique of legislation is known, in varying degrees, in virtually all modern legal systems.

The virtue of these offenses is the relative precision gained by casting the crime in the elementary criteria of possession and knowledge. Yet the problem that these offenses pose is that a conviction is possible without proof that the defendant intended to harm anyone with the materials possessed. It may be that the possession is motivated by an entirely innocent, even socially acceptable purpose. This was the claim of a defendant in California who was indicted and convicted for possessing a pair of brass knuckles—a weapon prohibited by the statute.[1] He explained his possession by saying that the brass knuckles were a family heirloom.[2] The court was unsympathetic to the claim, yet it reserved judgment about a case in which a museum keeper possessed a prohibited item.[3]

The issue of innocent purpose becomes more acute as this legislative technique is extended to objects that lend themselves to non-harmful uses. A good example is the controversial crime of

§3.4. [1] People v. Ferguson, 129 Cal. App. 300, 18 P.2d 741 (1933).

[2] *Id.* at 302; 18 P.2d at 742. Note, however, that in the facts of the case, there was substantial evidence that *D* grabbed the brass knuckles immediately prior to his arrest. *Id.* at 301; 18 P.2d at 741.

[3] *Id.* at 305; 18 P.2d at 742.

possessing burglary tools. The issue posed by these statutes is not so much the problem of vagueness, for the prohibited tools can be rather precisely defined as any "key, picklock, jimmy, jack or bit."[4] Even if the statute includes the catch-all phrase "or any other instrument of housebreaking,"[5] the specified items provide a good guide to the scope of the offense. Even assuming that these instruments can be precisely defined, the courts remain troubled by the blanket prohibition of possession. A lower court in Germany refused to enforce a German statute prohibiting the possession of thieves' tools *(Diebeswerkzeuge)*[6] because it was based on a legislative presumption of guilt;[7] the statute, in the court's view, violated the general requirement of culpability in all criminal offenses.[8] In a strikingly similar opinion,[9] Judge Bazelon reasoned that a statute in the District of Columbia, prohibiting the possession of any tool that "reasonably may be employed in the commission of any crime,"[10] was unconstitutional. As in the German case, the critical defect was the legislative presumption of guilt.[11] Now the presumption of guilt in these cases does not relate to the mental state required for conviction, namely, knowledge that the tools are in the actor's possession. The defective presumption goes to the intent to use the tools in committing larceny or burglary—an intent not even mentioned in these statutes. Thus the critique of these statutes involves two stages of analysis: first, that they cannot stand as crimes unless the definition includes an element of intent

[4] See the former Conn. Gen. Stat. §53–71, discussed in State v. Nales, 28 Conn. Sup. 28 (Sup. Ct. 1968). This statute was patterned after 24 & 25 Vict. c. 96, §58 (1861) ("picklock Key, Crow, Jack, Bit, or other Implement of Housebreaking"); Larceny Act, 1916, c. 50, §28(2) (same language as 1861 act). *Cf.* Theft Act 1968, c. 60, §25 ("any article for use in the course of or in connection with any burglary, theft or cheat").

[5] See 1861 and 1916 English statutes, *supra* note 4.

[6] StGB 1871, §245a.

[7] Judgment by the State court (*Landgericht*) in Heidelberg, October 3, 1958, 1959 NJW 1932.

[8] *Ibid.* (citing provisions in international conventions on human rights).

[9] Benton v. United States, 232 F.2d 341 (D.C. Cir. 1956).

[10] D.C. Code §22–3601.

[11] *Id.* at 344 (the legislative presumption of an intent-to-use failed to satisfy the test of "rational connection" under Tot v. United States, 319 U.S. 463 (1943)).

to use the tools for a criminal purpose; and secondly, that the burden of proof on this issue of intent may not be shifted or eliminated by the use of a legislative presumption.[12]

The intriguing question is why statutes prohibiting the possession of weapons, obscene materials and narcotics do not generate analogous judicial anxieties. There seem to be two explanations for this discrepancy, and one of them invokes the familiar theme of manifest criminality, as contrasted with subjective criminality. Judge Bazelon concedes that some possession offenses might be perfectly acceptable, even without proof of an ulterior intent. But they would have to be cases, he suggests, in which the mere fact of possession gives "rise to sinister implications."[13] And further that "such implications properly arise from articles like opium or lottery tickets which experience teaches are generally held for illicit purposes."[14] This manifestation of "sinister implications" or an illicit purpose is presumably found in the possession of prohibited weapons, narcotics and obscene materials, for these items are not likely to be used for innocent purposes. On the other hand, master keys and other tools for entering locked houses might well be used for legitimate purposes. The problem is not the ambiguity of these terms in determining whether the prohibited articles are in fact possessed; the problem is rather the ambiguity of the purpose implied by the act of possession.

Another account of the difference between weapons, narcotics and obscenity, on the one hand, and burglary tools, on the other, is that the former are dangerous or thought to be dangerous to all those who might come in contact with them. Prohibited firearms can discharge accidentally. The danger latent in obscene materials (if danger there be) would presumably affect anyone who came into contact with the materials. Similarly, the mass distribution of restricted drugs entails a general danger of se-

[12] Note that the earlier English statutes, 24 & 25 Vict. c. 96, §58 (1861) and Larceny Act 1916, c. 50, §28(2) both provide for a defense of "lawful excuse" and stipulate that "the proof [of the excuse] shall lie on . . . the person [in possession]." See §7.3 *infra*.

[13] 232 F.2d at 344–45.

[14] *Id.* at 345.

duction and addiction. On the other hand, the tools of burglary cause harm only if someone undertakes to use them with a criminal purpose. The risk of the tools falling into the wrong hands is not comparable to the risk that guns might discharge or that narcotics might fall into the hands of teenagers with a yearn for experimentation. Thus one may think of the former category of possession offenses as justified partly on the ground that the act of possession manifests danger to the community, even if the possessor has no criminal purpose. It would be difficult to make the same claim about the possession of wire-cutters or jimmies. Even if this factor of general danger is only part of the story, it accounts for why an inference of criminal intent is thought to be less objectionable in cases of possessing prohibited weapons and narcotics. The inference of intent is less objectionable because there is another factor—the risk represented by the objects falling into the wrong hands—that generates at least a partial justification for the prohibition.

This theory of general risk to the community does not account for all the cases in which Judge Bazelon reasons that mere possession gives rise to "sinister implications." Prohibiting the possession of lottery tickets would not make sense on the ground that the lottery ticket, by its very existence, posed a risk comparable to the mass distribution of narcotics or guns. Therefore there seems to be some warrant for finding a constitutional foothold for the pattern of manifest criminality in these decisions holding that the categorical possession of burglary tools is unconstitutional. This foothold would not be strong enough to help the Reverend Young who attempted to mount a constitutional argument against criminal liability for the unincriminating act of entering a schoolhouse.[15] The response to the problem of innocent or ambiguous possession is to insist that the possession be supplemented by an intent to commit a harmful act. The statute in *Young* required such an intent in addition to the unincriminating act of entering the building. Thus the proper interpretation of Judge Bazelon's opin-

[15] State v. Young, 57 N.J. 240, 271 A.2d 569 (1970), *cert. denied,* 402 U.S. 929 (1971). *Cf.* §3.2, at note 38 *supra.*

ion and succeeding cases[16] is not that they support a constitutional requirement of manifest criminality, but rather that they support a constitutional requirement of an intent to do harm, and that cases of possession giving rise to "sinister implications" serve only to create an exception to the general requirement that this intent be proved at trial.

§3.4.1. Possession Offenses as a Form of Discretionary Social Control. The technique of prohibiting possession per se is often aimed at special classes of people who are regarded as especially dangerous. Thus the German prohibition against possessing larceny tools applied only to those who had once been convicted of aggravated larceny, receiving stolen property or similar offenses.[17] The California Penal Code prohibits the possession of concealable firearms by convicted felons, but not by citizens never convicted of a felony.[18] If this kind of legislation is justified, the argument would be that the possession of certain items by convicted felons is both more incriminating and more dangerous than the same act of possession by ordinary citizens. This rationale for the German provision led a trial judge in Heidelberg to attack this form of legislation as the expression of a National Socialist legal philosophy.[19] The fact is that the German provision was introduced in 1933 as part of a National Socialist campaign to combat crime by taking special measures against the "criminal class." Despite judicial circumvention and academic criticism, this provision remained in force until 1969, when it was finally repealed by the German legislature.

Enacting special prohibitions against convicted felons is the culmination of the subjectivist philosophy that the purpose of inchoate crimes should be to identify and isolate dangerous persons. If convicted felons who possess concealed weapons are likely as a class to commit more crimes than other persons possessing such weapons, then it makes sense to impose this additional disability

[16] For cases in accord with *Benton,* see State v. Nales, 28 Conn. Supp. 28 (Sup. Ct. 1968); State v. Edwards, 269 Minn. 343, 130 N.W.2d 623 (1964).

[17] StGB 1871 §245a(1).

[18] Cal. Penal Code §12021 (applies as well to aliens and narcotic addicts).

[19] See case cited note 7 *supra.*

on convicted felons. This style of reasoning is an invitation to a class-oriented criminal law. It could even support the introduction of racist criteria into the definition of offenses, provided statistics supported the inference that one race tended to commit more crimes than another. The California Code actually does prohibit aliens, but not citizens, from possessing concealable weapons.[20] Even apart from the constitutional issues under the equal protection clause, there is something obviously wrong with this style of legislation. The defect does not rest entirely with the subjectivist philosophy that the purpose of the criminal law is to isolate dangerous persons.[21] From a regulatory point of view, the defect is that these measures are too heavy-handed in the pursuit of dangerous individuals. Obviously some aliens are not dangerous, even though they possess concealable weapons. Even apart from this vice of overinclusiveness, there is something more basic at issue.

It is unlikely that the California legislature would limit offenses like embezzlement, credit card fraud, or bigamy to one group within the society.[22] Even if 99 percent of the bigamist marriages in California were contracted by hippies living in Big Sur, it would be unthinkable to legislate a crime limited to hippies (even if this group could be unambiguously defined). Yet apparently it is thinkable to prohibit aliens, but not citizens, from possessing concealable weapons. When possession offenses are used in this way, it appears that the act of possession is not thought of as a crime comparable to any of the traditional offenses. What is involved is a systematic effort to use the nominal forms of the criminal law in order to prevent harm and weed out dangerous people. The effort is not unlike the programs of insurance companies to identify classes of dangerous

[20] Cal. Penal Code §12021. *Cf. id.* §12020, which universally prohibits the possession of specified weapons ("blackjack, slingshot, billy . . .").

[21] In People v. Lovato, 258 Cal. App. 2d 290, 65 Cal. Rptr. 638 (1968), the Court of Appeals said that "it may be reasonable to include aliens within the ambit of §12021 for regulatory purposes. . . ." *Id.* at 295–96; 65 Cal. Rptr. at 642; the case held, however, that §12021 would not support a conviction for second-degree felony murder if the alien should kill another with the illegally possessed weapon. See §4.4.4 *infra*.

[22] Apart from cases of voluntarily assumed, special responsibilities. See, e.g., Cal. Penal Code §800 (acceptance of bribe by public official).

drivers. If actuarial methods are appropriate for insurance companies, they are presumably appropriate for the legislative definition of crimes designed to prevent harm. As insurance companies deny coverage to age groups with high accident rates, the state may deny the right to possess concealable firearms to persons who, as a class, display dangerous tendencies.

In this context we can see the importance of Judge Bazelon's insistence that the prohibition of burglary tools could not stand as a crime unless the prosecution established an intent to use the tools. The requirement of a harmful intent counteracts the actuarial mentality and reconstitutes the offense as a criminal act directed, in the particular case, to the commission of harm. The significance of intent in this context is not that it converts the offense into one requiring a culpable mental state. The fact of possession does not generate liability unless it is *knowing* possession. Nor is it the significance of intent that it converts a class-based judgment into an individualized judgment of dangerousness. The latter type of judgment could be secured as well by the use of refined statistical predictors. The important point about the intent-to-do-harm is that it brings the offense of possession into line with a developed theory of criminality, namely, the theory of subjective criminality. If the offense conforms to a pattern of criminality, then the sanction imposed against the act may properly be seen as punishment, rather than as a regulatory or preventive mechanism directed against a class of dangerous individuals.

The deep problem raised by possession offenses is whether the apparatus of the criminal law may be used for regulatory purposes, with the implication that the offense may be directed at special classes of persons. The best argument for this use of the criminal sanction is the positivist thesis that if the law is well defined and the individual has fair warning of conduct that is punishable, there is no substantive objection that the individual can make against his falling under the sovereign's power to punish. Thus the positivist thesis takes the procedural value of fair warning to be sufficient to justify criminal punishment. In sharp contrast to the positivist thesis, the patterns of manifest and of subjective criminality represent substantive assertions of criteria for justifying criminal punishment. It is a mark of ambivalence in the current state of legal theory that while we are receptive to positivist theories of law, judges balk at applications of the theory in the field of possession offenses. Both in Germany and in the United States, as we have seen, judges have refused to carry out legislative mandates to punish persons found in possession of burglary tools. It is only when the act of possession manifests a "sinister purpose," as Judge Bazelon reminds us, that the state may dispense with proving an intent to harm a legally protected interest. For it is only in the presence of manifest criminality or an intent to harm that we can treat possession offenses as contemporary forms of the traditional patterns of liability.

§3.5. *The Overt Act in Treason.*

The conflict between the principle of manifest and subjective criminality has surfaced as well in the debate over the meaning of the constitutional phrase: "No person shall be convicted of Treason unless on the testimony of two Witnesses to the same overt Act. . . ." [1] The variety of plausible interpretations of this requirement of an overt act for treason replicates many of the views that we have encountered in the fields of larceny, attempts and possession offenses. First, there is the position most closely identified with the principle of manifest criminality, which holds that only those acts are overt that are "consistent only with a treasonable intention." This theory, once advanced in dissent by Mr. Justice Murphy,[2] is reminiscent of Judge Salmond's theory of the act required for a criminal attempt.[3] Secondly, there is the opposite extreme, advocated energetically by Mr. Justice Douglas, that the function of an overt act is merely to make certain that a treasonable project has

§3.5. [1] U.S. Const. art. III, §3, cl. 1.
[2] Haupt v. United States, 330 U.S. 631, 647 (1947) (dissenting opinion).
[3] See §3.3.2, at notes 28–36 *supra*.

moved from the "realm of thought into the realm of action."[4] Finally, there is a middle position, argued ambiguously and later abandoned by Mr. Justice Jackson, which suggests that the overt act has to be incriminating and therefore evidentiary of the actor's purpose.[5] This array of views came to the surface in two major constitutional cases litigated in the aftermath of World War II.[6] They both pertained to the meaning of the overt act requirement in determining a charge of treason, based upon the constitutional definition that treason is committed by "adhering to the . . . Enemies [of the United States], giving them Aid and Comfort."[7]

The problem of determining what is a sufficient overt act in treason is a matter of long-standing historical dispute. An historical survey of the problem is intriguing for its own sake, and the historical perspective will also be useful in analyzing the opinions of the Supreme Court decisions. Yet a caveat is in order. The historical context in which Coke, Hale, Kelyng and Foster debated the significance of overt acts is different from the constitutional framework that generated the divergent opinions we have noted. The classic discussions of the issue of overtness centered on treason by "compassing the death of the King" or one of the other persons enumerated in the Statute of 25 Edward III (1351).[8] Though the Constitution incorporates other grounds of treason that are engrained in the common law, the framers of the Constitution deliberately dropped the controversial ground of "compassing the death" of the nation's leaders. Thus in the American constitutional context, the discussion about the sufficiency of overt acts has centered about a totally distinct ground of treason: adhering to the enemy and giving them aid and comfort. One of the problems that must be kept in mind is whether the analysis of overt acts of "compassing the death of the King" may be properly applied in

[4] Cramer v. United States, 325 U.S. 1, 61 (1945) (dissenting opinion).

[5] Cramer v. United States, 325 U.S. 1 (1945); Haupt v. United States, 330 U.S. 631 (1947).

[6] *Ibid.*

[7] U.S. Const. art III, §3, cl. 1.

[8] 25 Edw. III, stat. 5, c. 2 (calendar year disputed).

analyzing overt acts of adhering to the enemy and giving them aid and comfort.

§3.5.1. **Compassing Death and Overt Acts.** Even though the Statute of 1351 explicitly punishes the mental state of "compassing the death of the King," no one ever seriously contended that the mental state alone was criminal. All the commentary on the crime of compassing recognizes that the plan to kill the King must be manifested in an overt act. It is true that Coke and those following him associate the crime of compassing with the maxim *voluntas reputabatur pro facto*,[9] and it is tempting to interpret this maxim to hold that the "intent is equivalent to the act." On this reading, the function of the overt act is to provide evidence of the intent.[10] If stressing this evidentiary connection implies that the crime was in the compassing, and requiring proof of the overt act was merely a procedural requirement, the interpretation would be misleading. In the context in which Coke uses the term, it is more plausible to read *pro facto* to refer to the consummation of harm, rather than to the phenomenon of acting out an intent. Coke uses the maxim several times in the context of cases that we today would obviously regard as instances of attempted murder.[11] All he could mean by *voluntas reputabatur pro facto* is that an attempt to kill one's lord could constitute treason even though the attempt was not consummated.[12] We should recall that this maxim was influential in the common law before the concept of a criminal attempt was worked out, and therefore writers using the maxim failed to distinguish between the want of a harm and a want of an act.[13]

[9] 3 Coke 5.

[10] Sayre, *Criminal Attempts*, 41 Harv. L. Rev. 821, 822 (1928) ("Again, in discussing high treason, Coke lays it down that in the early law criminal liability might be based on mere intent if the intent were evidenced by some overt act").

[11] 3 Coke 5.

[12] *Cf. id.* at 69, holding that the maxim *voluntas reputabatur pro facto* did not apply in cases of robbery to justify conviction in the absence of the consummated harm; "somewhat must be taken; for the assault only to rob . . . is no felony."

[13] Sayre traces the maxim to Staunford, Pleas of the Crown (1557), see Sayre, *supra* note 10, 823–827. The passages from Staunford support the thesis that the element replaced by the actor's *voluntas* was not the act, but the result.

Coke held that the overt deed required for treason by compassing had to be "an open deed tending to the execution of [the actor's] intent."[14] The overt act had to "manifest" or "declare" the actor's intent.[15] The word "evidence" is not used. This language clearly intimates a link between overtness and the principle of manifest criminality. Acts innocent on their face could not constitute overt acts because they could not "declare" the actor's intent to harm the King. According to Coke, the connection between the compassing and the overt act appears to be conceptual and substantive rather than evidentiary. The crime consisted in the overt act declaring the intention, not in the intention "evidenced" by the overt act.[16] This is an important point, for it illustrates the conceptual link between acting and manifesting intent that provides the foundation for the objective theory of attempts and indeed for all the crimes in the pattern of manifest criminality.

If this were all, we might justifiably read the principle of manifest criminality into the constitutional requirement of "two witnesses to the same overt act." But the theory of treason after Coke took a different turn. As we trace the development, we find a transition from manifest to subjective criminality remarkably similar to the metamorphosis of larceny.

The history of treason is dominated by a recurrent concern about punishing verbal expressions of disloyalty. Coke had written that spoken words could never constitute treason, though written words might.[17] Yet shortly after Coke's death in 1634[18] this distinction came under sharp scrutiny and, indeed, in a curious way, the controversy had repercussions for the concept of an overt act in treason.

[14] 3 Coke 5.

[15] *Ibid.*

[16] This reading of Coke is overlooked in the literature. The leading work, W. Hurst, The Law of Treason in the United States (1971), lists only two interpretations of Coke: either (1) the act provides evidence of intent or (2) it demonstrates that the defendant's guilt had moved from the realm of thought to the realm of action. *Id.* at 28.

[17] 3 Coke 14: "And it is commonly said, that bare words may make a Heretic, but not a Traitor, without an overt act."

[18] The Third Institute was published posthumously in 1644.

The case that began to undermine Coke's views was the conviction of an Irish priest named Crohagan in the year of Coke's death.[19] The defendant was reported to have said in Portugal, "I will kill the King [of England] if I may come upon him." Two years later, he came to England, allegedly to carry out his intention and he was apprehended, tried and convicted for compassing the death of the King. The problem for subsequent commentators was how this decision could be worked into the extant body of legal principles. On the assumption (1) that the case was rightly decided and (2) that "compassing" required embodiment in an overt act, the commentators faced two unappealing prospects for locating the overt act in Crohagan's activities. The overt act was to be found either in Crohagan's speaking in Portugal or in setting foot on English soil. The problem with the former is that it ran afoul of Coke's principle that spoken words alone could not constitute the overt act necessary for treason. The problem with the latter view was that the act of setting foot on English soil did not manifest or declare a treasonous intent.

These alternatives posed a choice between evils, and for Hale, the lesser evil lay in treating an unincriminating act as the overt act of "compassing." Hale conceded that the act of coming to England was "indifferent in itself."[20] Yet taking an indifferent, unincriminating act to be an overt act was the price of upholding Coke's proposition that "regularly words, unless . . . committed to writing are not an overt act within this statute" (i.e., the Treason Statute of 1351).[21] Kelyng, in his inimitable fashion,[22] dissented from this view and argued that Crohagan's words spoken abroad were the overt act sufficient to constitute the treason of compassing the King's death.[23] "Words," Kelyng reasoned, "are the natural way for a man whereby to express the imagination of the

[19] Crohagan's Case, 79 Eng. Rep. 891 (K.B. 1634).

[20] 1 Hale 116.

[21] *Id.* at 111, 114.

[22] *Cf.* Kelyng's views on Carrier's Case and the foundations of the law of larceny, §2.3.2 *supra*.

[23] Kelyng 15. *Cf. id.* at 15 n.1 (editor of 1789 edition dissents from Kelyng's view in favor of Hale and Foster).

heart."[24] One would think that there would be a jurisdictional problem in indicting Crohagan for an overt act committed in Portugal,[25] but this did not stand in the way of Kelyng's effort to expand the law of treason to punish acts of speech.

In this dispute over the interpretation of Crohagan's Case, Hale's view eventually prevailed. Foster attacked Kelyng for ignoring the priest's overt act of setting foot in England.[26] That this act was "innocent in itself,"[27] was no impediment to treating it as the event that rendered a "treasonous purpose" subject to capital punishment. Thus the problem of spoken words declaring a treasonous purpose provided the wedge for disengaging the concept of "overtness" from the manifestation of a criminal purpose. It was far better, in Foster's view, to interpret the law so as to insulate spoken words from liability than to follow Kelyng in treating spoken words as an incriminating overt act.

If this was their view of the required overt act, Hale and Foster could readily claim that "compassing" was a form of treason that consisted and had always consisted in an "act of the mind"[28] or, in a different idiom, in "the imaginations of the heart."[29] The overt act was a form of evidence required by the Statute of 1351, but it was not linked conceptually to the nature of "compassing or imagining the death of the King." It is possible that this expansive view of treason, which took hold only after the turbulence of revolution and the Restoration, captured a truth that Coke never expressed.[30] Yet there is some evidence of historical reinterpretation.

[24] *Id.* at 15.

[25] *Cf.* Lord Preston's Case, 4 State Trials 406 (1690), discussed at Foster 196, where the defendant claimed that he had committed no overt act in the county where the indictment was brought. Boarding a ship with the intent to sail to France, there to confer about plans to invade England, was held to be a sufficient overt act of compassing the King's death as well as adhering to the enemy.

[26] Foster 202–204.

[27] *Id.* at 202.

[28] 1 Hale 108.

[29] Foster 194.

[30] The best support in Coke for the view that treason is consummated in the mind is his statement that the "compassing, intent or imagination, though secret . . . [is] to be discovered by circumstances precedent, concommitant and subsequent. . . ."

Foster took the maxim *voluntas pro facto* to stand for the proposition that even in the fourteenth century, treason was actually committed in the heart.[31] Yet the most that can be inferred from earlier texts is that a criminal act, manifesting the *voluntas*, might be criminal even if it remained an unconsummated attempt.[32]

If there was a progression in the law of treason by compassing, from manifest to subjective criminality, that movement correlates well with other immanent trends. It anticipates the parallel movement in the law of larceny, burglary and attempts. In Foster's work, in particular, the subjectification of treason dovetails with his laying the theoretical foundation for the law of felony-murder. Foster was the first to argue that an independent felonious purpose to steal could convert an accidental killing into the felony of murder.[33] The actor's wickedness of heart as to one felony should be sufficient to convict of the more heinous crime of murder.[34]

It appears that Foster was also the first commentator to develop a systematic alternative theory for insisting on an "overt act" as a condition of criminal liability. After all, if the crime is consummated in the heart, why should the law insist on an act in execution? Why should a confession not be enough?[35] The answer is not simply a matter of evidence and fair procedure. Though Foster conceded that "the law . . . considereth the wicked imaginations of the heart in the same degree of guilt as if carried into actual execution . . . ,"[36] he was quick to add that these imaginations are criminal only "from the moment *measures appear to have been taken to render them effectual.*"[37] The required overt act, then, is but a measure that

---

3 Coke 6. Yet this discussion occurs in a paragraph that treats "compassing" as the *mens rea* of a crime for which there is an act or *actus reus* as well.

[31] Foster 194, 203.

[32] See notes 12 & 13 *supra*.

[33] Foster 258–59.

[34] This thesis is subject to a thorough critique in §4.4.1 *infra*.

[35] *Cf.* U.S. Const. art. III, §3, cl. 1 ("Confession in open Court" equivalent to "the Testimony of two Witnesses to the same overt Act").

[36] Foster 195.

[37] *Ibid.* (emphasis in the original).

translates the actor's intent into the realm of action.[38] The overt act need not declare or manifest the intent, but it must be an act "in prosecution" or "in effectuation" of the criminal intent.

In the controversial field of punishable speech, the implication is that neither written nor spoken words should constitute acts of treason unless they are articulated in furtherance of a treasonous design. Merely saying, "I will kill the King when I come upon him" does not further the actor's intent and therefore these words cannot constitute overt acts of treason.[39] The same is true of written words.[40] In his critique of several convictions for possessing seditious papers,[41] Foster argued that unless the papers are written and distributed in furtherance of treasonous purposes, the mere act of writing cannot constitute an act sufficient for treason. "[W]hile they remain in the hands of the author unpublished . . . [writings, unrelated to specific treasonous purposes] will not make a man a traitor."[42]

A second implication of Foster's thesis is that a conspiracy to kill the King would be sufficient to convict of "compassing" the death of a sovereign.[43] Coke had argued that even a conspiracy to levy war against the King could not be punished as treason without a "levying of war *in facto*."[44] The mere meeting and agreeing to act would not constitute an overt act of compassing or any other form of treason. Yet after the upheavals of the mid-seventeenth century, the disposition to punish treasonous conspiracies gained ascendency.[45] Hale and Kelyng[46] argued that assembling together

[38] *Cf.* Justice Douglas in Cramer v. United States, 325 U.S. 1, 61 (1945) (dissenting opinion).

[39] Foster 203.

[40] Foster attacked Kelyng for seeing "no difference between words reduced into writing and words spoken." *Id.* at 204; in fact, however, Foster's theory also minimizes the distinction.

[41] See the critique of Sidney's Case, *id.* at 198, and of Peachum's Case, *id.* at 198–99.

[42] *Id.* at 198.

[43] *Id.* at 195.

[44] 3 Coke 9.

[45] 1 Hale 108–111, 119 ("assembling together" as an overt act).

[46] *Ibid.;* Kelyng 18.

could be a sufficient act to support a charge of treason.[47] According to Foster,[48] the acts of "meet[ing] and consult[ing] how to kill the King" were sufficient measures to support a charge of treason by compassing. They were to be taken as overt acts, even though they were but spoken words and the acts of consultation occurred in private. The important point as of the mid-eighteenth century was that the act further the treasonous purpose. Verbal consultation could satisfy this test as well as a manifest attempt on the King's life.

In Foster's theory of overt acts, we find a critical premise in the general theory of subjective criminality. The crime inheres in the formulation of the intent, and the function of the act is to demonstrate merely that the act has passed from the realm of thought into the realm of action. This is the same theory of criminality that emerges later as the foundation for the subjective theory of attempts.[49] What the theory lacks, however, is a perspective for gauging how far the act must go in order to constitute "a measure in effectuation of the criminal purpose." How do we know that consultation among conspirators or setting foot in England should be sufficient for treason? The reason that Foster's theory lacks this perspective is that he has no general theory for requiring an act in effectuation of the crime that has already transpired in the actor's disloyal heart. If the only issue is proving guilt, then a confession or an admission to a friend should be sufficient to supply the necessary evidence.

Foster's theory of treason reveals the ambivalence that pervades the subjective theory of criminality. The crime is in the intent, and yet the legacy of the older pattern of manifest criminality retains its grip on eighteenth-century thinking. An act of execution is necessary, but for reasons that Foster and his contemporaries can no longer adequately explain.

§3.5.2. Overt Acts and Treason Under the Constitution. As

[47] *But cf.* 1 Hawkins 55, who attributes this possibility to the temporary legislation of 13 Eliz. and 13 Car. II.

[48] Foster 195, 220.

[49] See §3.3.5 *supra.*

we shift our focus to the types of treason recognized under the United States Constitution, we find a radical shift in the function of the required overt act. The Constitution recognizes only two categories of treason: waging war against the United States and adhering to its enemies by giving them aid and comfort. Both of these headings of treason existed under English law prior to the Constitution, and the procedure for framing indictments required that an overt act be alleged in these cases as well as in the instance of treason by compassing.[50] Yet there is a significant difference between compassing, on the one hand, and waging war and giving aid and comfort to the enemy, on the other. The latter categories of treason are completed offenses in the sense that the suspect's treasonable purpose must register on the external world in a discernable result. War must be waged; aid and comfort must be given. Absent these results, there can be no treason. Now what does it mean to talk about an overt act in these contexts? If we were discussing attempted treason, rather than treason itself, the overt act would be an act tending toward the waging of war or the rendering of aid and comfort. There is obviously something anomalous in using the concept of the overt act, typically used in analyzing inchoate offenses, to describe a necessary feature of a completed offense. Perhaps that explains why the common-law writers barely discuss the issue of overtness in connection with the latter categories incorporated in the United States Constitution.

The distinction between overt acts of treason and treasonous results is illustrated by Foster's analysis of "adhering" to the enemy—one of the conditions for treason by "adhering to the enemy, giving them aid and comfort." In discussing a case in which a seditious letter was intercepted at the post office, Foster reasoned that although it was questionable whether the act of sending the letter was an overt act of adhering, that question need not be reached, "since the letters never came to the enemy's hands and consequently no aid or comfort was actually given."[51] Even more illuminating is Foster's concession that the act of dispatching

[50] Foster 194.
[51] *Id.* at 218 (discussing *Gregg's Case*).

the letters was "undoubtedly an overt act" of treason by compassing.[52] Taken together, these comments permit the inference that the notion of "overt acts" applies only in assessing whether subjective dispositions, such as "adhering" and "compassing," are adequately expressed in external acts. The notion of overtness has nothing to do with whether the treasonous result (giving aid and comfort) has accrued.

If we take Foster's analysis as a guide to the constitutional language, a number of important propositions come into focus. First, we see that the issue of overtness was distinct from the question whether aid and comfort has been given. Further, as a practical point, the inquiry into the required act would not be relevant unless the result—the giving of aid and comfort—were first established.

When this range of issues was presented to the Supreme Court in Cramer v. United States,[53] Justice Jackson interpreted the constitutional definition of treason in conformity with Foster's proposition that aid and comfort must be given to the enemy. The subjective attitude of "adhering" would not be sufficient;[54] there would, in addition, have to be the objective result of aid and comfort. The factual problem in *Cramer* raised difficulties under both headings. The suspect had met and "conferred" for several hours in a restaurant with two German saboteurs under observation by the FBI. This incident provided the basis for the overt acts alleged in the indictment. The acts were supported by the testimony of two witnesses. The constitutional question was whether the act of meeting and talking was an "overt act" in the constitutionally required sense.

Though Justice Jackson accepted one facet of Foster's analysis, he turned the other proposition on its head. Writing for the majority, Jackson accepted the proposition that there was no need to

[52] *Ibid.*

[53] 325 U.S. 1 (1945).

[54] Note that Hale discusses treason by "adhering to the enemy" without requiring the giving of aid and comfort as a condition of liability. 1 Hale 159–69. There was some consideration of defining treason this way in the Constitution, but the "aid and comfort" clause settled the matter. See Hurst, *supra* note 16, at 126–45.

consider the issue of "adhering" if "aid and comfort" were not actually given to the enemy. Yet in contrast to Foster, he disengaged the requirement of an overt act from proof of "adhering" and tied it instead to "finding that the accused actually gave aid and comfort to the enemy."[55] On the issue of "aid and comfort," the Court concluded that Cramer's acts of "social intercourse" and "mingling normally with the citizens" of an enemy country did not meet the constitutional standard. Therefore, the acts charged in the indictment could not constitute "overt acts" of treason.

If there was an ambiguity in *Cramer,* it derived from Justice Jackson's analysis of acts rendering aid and comfort as "incriminating" acts. At one point he suggests that if acts are "trivial and commonplace," it would be doubtful "whether they gave aid and comfort to the enemy."[56] This analysis suggests an interweaving of the criteria of manifest criminality with the concept of giving aid and comfort to the enemy. As a general matter, it is probably true that acts of aiding the enemy are objectively incriminating. This contingent connection was put to the test two years later in Haupt v. United States,[57] in which the alleged overt acts consisted in a father's providing his son with various forms of assistance, none of which would have been suspect if the son had not been a German saboteur. The specific overt acts included "harboring and sheltering" the son and helping him to procure a job at a plant engaged in manufacturing military equipment. Justice Jackson had little trouble concluding that the father's acts had the "unmistakable quality . . . lacking in the *Cramer* case of forwarding the saboteur in his mission."[58] Thus it became clear that the critical question was not whether the acts were incriminating, but whether they provided aid and comfort. The opinion in *Haupt* limits itself to that issue and studiously omits the discussion in *Cramer* about the role of the objective act of treason in generating incriminating evidence of a treasonous intent.

The implication of the Court's reading of the Constitution is

[55] 325 U.S. at 34.
[56] *Id.* at 35.
[57] 330 U.S. 631 (1947).
[58] *Id.* at 635.

that the "two-witnesses" rule applies only to the question of "aid and comfort" and not to the more subtle subjective issue of the defendant's "adhering to the enemy." With the ambiguities of *Cramer* finally settled, the meaning of the law was clear but harsh: the issue of "adhering" was a matter to be left to the jury, with no constitutional requirements of proof.[59]

In his two opinions favoring convictions in both *Cramer*[60] and *Haupt*,[61] Justice Douglas argued that the "overt act" requirement had no connection either with "aid or comfort" or "adhering to the enemy." The only point of the constitutional rule, we are repeatedly told,[62] is to assure proof that the treasonous plot has moved from the realm of thought into the realm of action. This is indisputably true about all crimes, as subjectivist theorists tell us in explaining the requirement of human action. What this argument overlooks is that treason requires an external impact—namely, the giving of aid and comfort to the enemy. There is no need for an overt act to demonstrate firm resolve, for a treasonous plan could not remain in the realm of thought and still produce this external effect.

In the single dissent in *Haupt*,[63] Justice Murphy argued in the vein of manifest criminality that the overt act should tend to establish the treasonable posture of "adhering to the enemy." Perhaps Justice Murphy went too far in vindicating this thesis urged earlier by Foster. Justice Murphy claimed that a sufficient overt act would have to be "utterly incompatible" with decent motives such as familial devotion and religious charity.[64] It must be an act, he argued, "consistent only with a treasonable intention."[65] It would have been more persuasive to retreat to a position analogous to

[59] This point was left unsettled in *Cramer*, 325 U.S. at 29–30, but made explicit in *Haupt*, 330 U.S. at 635.

[60] 325 U.S. at 48 (dissenting opinion, joined by Justices Black and Reed and Chief Justice Stone).

[61] 350 U.S. at 644 (concurring opinion).

[62] 325 at 61; 330 U.S. at 645.

[63] 330 U.S. at 646.

[64] *Id.* at 647.

[65] *Ibid.*

the Model Penal Code's rule that the act of attempting must be "strongly corroborative" of the actor's intent.[66] If the framers were concerned about perjury, as they allegedly were, it would be sensible to insist upon safeguards in the vague subjective realm of adhering; this is the issue on which the suspect is particularly vulnerable to perjured testimony.[67] If a friend or undercover agent testifies that the suspect made confidential admissions of disloyalty to the United States, there is very little that the defendant can do to prove that his heart is loyal and pure.[68]

The great common-law writers were acutely aware of the dangers of using the crime of treason to suppress speech. Yet the way the law of treason has evolved in the United States, a major source of evidence of "adhering to the enemy" are the admissions that the defendant allegedly makes to others. The judges could have interpreted the overt act requirement so as to insure that the defendant's own incriminating conduct would be an indispensable item in the government's proof of emotional adherence to the enemy. Yet in *Cramer* and *Haupt* the Supreme Court went its own way, and it is unlikely that it shall ever return to any version of the manifold possible connections between manifest criminality and the constitutional requirement that there be "two Witnesses to the same overt Act."

§3.6. *An Excursus on Conspiracy.*

A criminal conspiracy is defined today as an agreement to commit a crime, and sometimes, more broadly, as an agreement to engage in any unlawful act.[1] It is often said that the gist of the crime con-

[66] MPC §5.01(2).

[67] See Hurst, *supra* note 16, at 133–34.

[68] Note the incriminating admission by Cramer to Norma Kopp, 326 U.S. at 52–53.

§3.6. [1] See LaFave & Scott 453; Williams 663–678; *Developments in the Law—Criminal Conspiracy*, 72 Harv. L. Rev. 920, 925–40 (1959). MPC §5.03.

sists in the agreement. A narrower definition of the crime requires an overt act in execution of the agreement.[2] These elementary points raise two issues of importance in this chapter on the tensions between manifest and subjective criminality. First, how can the punishability of a mere agreement be reconciled with the higher threshold of liability we find in the law of criminal attempts? Secondly, does the notion of an overt act, when required to supplement the agreement, reflect the ongoing influence of manifest criminality? Or is the notion of overtness at work here akin to the subjective rendering of the constitutional requirement in treason?[3]

Before we turn to these two issues, we should note a totally distinct context in which the concept of conspiracy figures prominently in criminal theory. The issue that will engage us in the second half of Chapter Eight is when accomplices may be held liable for the crimes of their principals. This is the intricate subject of complicity, which the common law has vastly simplified by using conspiratorial agreements as a standard for complicity.[4] In a large number of cases at common law, the issue in fact is complicity in the substantive crimes committed by one of the conspirators, not liability for conspiracy as an inchoate offense. We must obviously keep these uses of conspiracy doctrine distinct, for the issue of inchoate liability is radically different from the problem of complicity. In the former case, conspiracy is the charge laid in the indictment; in the latter, a theory for holding confederates reciprocally liable for their respective crimes.

A third topic that must be kept distinct is whether executed agreements may be punished even though the objective is not a legislated criminal offense. There is a great deal of writing about the aims that render agreements conspiratorial.[5] Many cases at common law support the punishability of conspiracies to defraud

[2] LaFave & Scott 476–478; 18 U.S.C. §371; Cal. Penal Code §184.

[3] See 3.5.2 *supra*.

[4] See §8.5.4 B *infra*.

[5] This is the primary concern in Sayre, *Criminal Conspiracy*, 35 Harv. L. Rev. 393 (1922); *cf.* Williams 687–710; R. Wright, Criminal Conspiracies 23–52 (1887 ed.). Goldstein, *Conspiracy to Defraud the United States*, 68 Yale L.J. 405 (1959).

and conspiracies to corrupt public morals.[6] These cases admittedly render some activities criminal only when they are undertaken by two or more persons.[7] Though further research is needed, it appears that this doctrine is applied to completed ventures, rather than inchoate plans.[8] There is no way to traverse the pitfalls of the conglomerate doctrine of conspiracy unless we distinguish sharply among the fields of the doctrine's application.[9] The only field that we assay at this juncture is the use of conspiracy as an alternative form of inchoate liability—the crime of making particular kinds of agreements and at most an agreement supplemented by an overt act.

§3.6.1. Inconsistent Criteria of Inchoate Liability. At first blush it seems clear that punishing agreements reflects a lower threshold of liability than the doctrine of attempted crime. Under the current German definition of criminal attempts, the actor must go so far toward execution that, at least according to his perception of the facts, he commences final execution of the deed.[10] The mere act of making an agreement obviously does not meet this test. The Anglo-American view is admittedly more controversial. Justice Holmes conceded some time ago that the mere agreement to murder a man 50 miles away could not possibly be treated as attempted murder, but it might be indictable as conspiracy.[11] Yet with the rise of the subjective theory of attempts, particularly as embodied in the Model Penal Code,[12] there might be an argument in favor of treating an agreement as the "substantial step" required for an attempt.[13] The curious argument that comes into play

[6] See cases cited in R. Wright, *supra* note 5, at 9–10.

[7] See, e.g., Director of Public Prosecutions v. Shaw, [1961] 2 W.L.R. 897 (publishing ladies' directory held to be conspiracy to corrupt public morals); Commonwealth v. Donoghue, 250 Ky. 343, 63 S.W.2d 3 (1933) (lending money at high interest rates held to be conspiracy "to injure the public").

[8] Of all the cases discussed in Williams 688–710, there is no reference to an unexecuted plan. Yet the proposition of the text must remain a conjecture until a full-scale review of the cases is made.

[9] The distinct functions of conspiracy laws are well analyzed in Johnson, *The Unnecessary Crime of Conspiracy*, 61 Calif. L. Rev. 1137 (1973).

[10] StGB §22.

[11] Hyde v. United States, 225 U.S. 347, 387–88 (1912) (dissenting opinion).

[12] MPC §5.01(1)(c).

[13] See Johnson, *supra* note 9, at 1163.

in this context is that the verbal act of agreement "declares" and "corroborates" the criminal purpose of the conspirators.[14] Thus the doctrine favoring unequivocal evidence of intent can be turned on its head to favor penalization at this preliminary stage of execution. It will be recalled that this argument, now invoked by the drafters of the Model Penal Code, was devised by Kelyng to justify treating verbal acts as the "overt act" required for compassing the death of the King.[15]

The conglomerate doctrine of conspiracy, with all its diverse functions, is unique to the common-law world. Yet the use of conspiracy as inchoate offense finds a precise counterpart in the German law of attempted solicitation. According to an 1876 amendment to the former German code, the following acts are punishable as though they were cases of attempted felony:

1. agreeing to commit a felony;
2. accepting the offer of another to commit a felony;
3. declaring oneself available to commit a felony.[16]

Though this provision is treated as a variation of solicitation, the specific details of the prohibition have the same impact as the crime of conspiracy;[17] point (3) even goes further in punishing acts prior to the reaching of an agreement. The same provisions are carried forward in the new German code.[18]

This lowering of the threshold of criminality under German law was apparently prompted by an incident in which a Belgian named Duchesne made himself available to the Bishop of Paris to assassinate Bismarck for a specific sum.[19] Unfortunately, the origins of the analogous common-law doctrine are not so readily determined. Indeed there seems to be considerable mystery about the development of conspiracy as a general inchoate offense. At the early stages of the common law, the concept of conspiracy was

[14] MPC §5.03, Comment at 97 (Tent. Draft No 10, 1960).

[15] See §3.5, at notes 21–24 *supra*.

[16] StGB 1871, §49a.

[17] *Cf.* the definition of solicitation in MPC §5.02(1) ("commands, encourages or requests another person" to commit a crime).

[18] StGB §30(2).

[19] Jescheck 531.

limited to the specific civil offense of conspiring falsely to accuse and convict an innocent person.[20] It is true that this offense became criminal in the seventeenth century,[21] but the punishment was comparatively light (forfeiture of goods,[22] the pillory, imprisonment[23]) relative to the widespread capital execution of felons at the time. It is also true that in the seventeenth century, the courts began to interpret this offense as one committed by making reciprocal commitments to accuse another falsely.[24] Yet these data about one conspiratorial objective in the borderland of the criminal law are hardly sufficient to support the widespread thesis that the current crime of conspiracy dates back to the seventeenth century.[25]

Two remarkable transformations occurred in the period from the early seventeenth century to the full-blown recognition of conspiracy as an inchoate offense in the mid-nineteenth century. First, the doctrine was abstracted from its roots in malicious prosecution and gradually extended so that it eventually applied to inchoate agreements to commit violent felonies.[26] Secondly, conspiracy was converted from a relatively minor offense into a major felony, punished on a par with the felony comprising the objective of the unlawful agreement.[27] Neither of these remarkable processes of trans-

[20] 33 Edw. I (1304). See generally 3 Coke 142–43; 4 Blackstone 136–37.

[21] 2 Stephen 229.

[22] 3 Coke 43.

[23] 4 Blackstone 137.

[24] The leading case is the Poulterer's Case, 77 Eng. Rep. 813 (1611).

[25] This popular dogma is expressed in LaFave & Scott 454 (citing Sayre); Sayre, *supra* note 5, at 400 (citing no authority); *Developments in the Law, supra* note 1, at 923 (but a short step from Poulterer's Case "to the proposition that the agreement to commit any crime was a criminal conspiracy").

[26] This process of abstraction traded heavily on two offhand remarks that were repeatedly read out of context. The first is the statement in 1 Hawkins 348 that "all confederacies . . . wrongfully to prejudice a third person are highly criminal at common law." Hawkins cites a few peripheral examples, yet even these minimal authorities "as has frequently been pointed out . . . furnish little or no support." Williams 703. The second is the dictum by Lord Denman, in a case quashing an indictment, that the allegation should have been of "a conspiracy either to do an unlawful act or a lawful act by unlawful means." Rex v. Jones, 110 Eng. Rep. 485, 487 (1832). For a critique of the uses of this dictum, see R. Wright, *supra* note 5, at 48–52.

[27] Cal. Penal Code §182. *Cf.* Williams 685 (noting that under English law, conspiracy is still punished as a misdemeanor).

formation has received much attention in the literature, and this is not the proper framework for the needed historical analysis. Yet both transformations require additional comment, particularly in view of the conflict in the threshold and theory of inchoate liability.

Both processes of transformation—generalization at a lower threshold of liability and upgrading of the penalty—were out of phase with the law of criminal attempts that emerged in the late eighteenth and nineteenth centuries. The lower threshold of liability was patently inconsistent with nineteenth-century tendencies to mark the point of criminality as close as possible to consummation of the offense.[28] And the principle of punishing conspiracy at the same level as the intended felony violated the general maxim favoring mitigation in cases of unsuccessful attempts.[29]

It would be premature to hazard an explanation of these contradictions in Anglo-American criminal law. Yet one historical pattern is worth noting. The law of conspiracy begins in the borderland of criminal law and gradually takes over the heartland of violent felonies. The law of attempts begins with the core offenses and then radiates outward toward penumbral problems. In the process of development, these two lines of the law passed each other as though they were on entirely different planes. This divergent pattern of development may explain the origin of some of the inconsistencies, but it hardly accounts for the law's prolonged toleration of inconsistent criteria of inchoate liability as well as inconsistent principles of punishment.

§3.6.2. The Requirement of an Overt Act. One way to reconcile the criteria of inchoate liability is to import the requirement of an overt act into the definition of conspiracy. The federal statute requires an "act to effect the object of the conspiracy"[30] and in 1912, the Supreme Court held that this required act is part of the

[28] See §3.3, at notes 21–24 *supra*.

[29] MPC §5.05(1) and the Proposed Federal Criminal Code §§1001(e), 1002(e) seek reconciliation of this inconsistency by punishing both attempts and conspiracies at the same level as the executed offense, with reduction by one grade in cases of the most serious felonies.

[30] 18 U.S.C. §371. *Cf.* Proposed Federal Criminal Code §1002(a) ("with intent to effect any objective of the agreement").

definition of the offense.[31] The repeated reference to this requirement as an overt act might lead one to think the principle of manifest criminality informs this tightening of the definition of conspiracy. The primary concern of the Court in 1912 was the definition of the offense for the purposes of laying venue and applying the statute of limitations. Making the overt act part of the offense implied, to the government's advantage, that venue could be laid in any jurisdiction in which an act was committed in furtherance of the conspiracy, and each additional act set the statute of limitations running anew. In a subsequent decision, the Court made it clear that the issue was not manifest criminality, but the classic concern in the theory of subjective criminality, namely, the demonstration "that the conspiracy is at work . . . [and not] a project still resting solely in the minds of the conspirators. . . ."[32] In line with the pattern of subjective criminality, acts "innocent" or "indifferent" in themselves, such as mailing a letter,[33] or making a telephone call,[34] can constitute the required overt act for a conspiracy. The only requirement is that the act be a step toward the criminal objective.[35]

This subjectivist reading of the overt act requirement in the federal statute suggests there is little likelihood of moving the law of conspiracy into line with an objective theory of criminal attempts. The drafters of the Model Penal Code even recommend the abolition of the requirement as to more serious felonious objectives.[36] Yet there is also strong evidence of a trend not only to retain the requirement of an overt act, but even to interpret the requirement in line with the theory of manifest criminality. The new state criminal codes typically retain the requirement,[37] as does the proposed federal criminal code.[38] The commentary to an earlier

[31] Hyde v. United States, 225 U.S. 347 (1912).

[32] Yates v. United States, 354 U.S. 298, 334 (1957).

[33] Hyde v. United States, 225 U.S. 347 (1912).

[34] Smith v. United States, 92 F.2d 460 (9th Cir. 1937).

[35] *Cf.* Foster's theory of "overt acts" in cases of treason, §3.5, at notes 34–38 *supra.*

[36] MPC §5.03(5).

[37] See statutes cited at LaFave & Scott 478 n.108.

[38] Proposed Federal Criminal Code §1002(a).

draft of the proposed federal code concludes that "the overt act must be such that it manifests a purpose to effect an objective of the agreement."[39] When the issue is stated this way, the concern is no longer venue nor simply the firmness of the actor's resolve. The implicit quest is to mold the substantive law to insure a realm of privacy free of criminal sanctions.

It is still too early to tell whether the law of conspiracy as an inchoate offense will witness a resurgence of the principle of manifest criminality. The relentless criticism of the doctrine of conspiracy invites some retrenchment in the scope of liability. The primary libertarian concern is that the prosecution of political conspiracies trenches too far on protected freedoms of thought and speech. A sensible restrictive measure would be strengthening the overt act requirement. This would insure that the prosecution stay its hand until a politically dissident group manifests palpable danger to the community.

§3.7. *Stop-and-Frisk and Flirtations with Manifest Criminality.*

The last in our studies of offenses that reflect the tension between criteria of manifest and of subjective criminality is not an offense at all, but rather the criteria for police intervention to stop and detain suspects on the street and, if necessary, pat them down to determine whether they possess weapons. In our analysis of inchoate offenses as well as the subjectification of larceny, we stressed the importance of the substantive law in facilitating earlier police intervention in criminal plots. It was traditionally the case in Anglo-American law that the substantive law was controlling on the justification of police intervention. An intervention and detention was an arrest, and an arrest had to be justified by probable cause if the police officer was to avoid tort liability for false arrest and

[39] S. Rep. No. 94–00, 94th Cong., 2d Sess., at 181 (1976).

false imprisonment. It is true that an arrest of a suspected felon might be justified if a felony had not been committed, provided the officer had probable cause (reasonable grounds) to believe that the suspect had committed the felony. Yet it could not be justified where the officer knew that no offense—not even an attempt—had yet been committed, even though the officer was convinced that the suspect was preparing to commit an offense. If following an intended victim around was neither an attempt nor a crime in itself, the police could not legally interfere and detain the suspect engaged in the suspicious behavior.

Though police practice might have deviated from this picture for some time, the Supreme Court did not lend its imprimatur to temporary police detention on the street until 1968. In a series of cases decided that year,[1] the Court cracked the syllogistic connection between the substantive law and police intervention. The premise that gave in was the link between the concept of an arrest and the legitimation of intervention. Under the newly coined constitutional concepts of "stop-and-frisk," the Court approved police detention less intrusive than an official arrest. Even more importantly, the Court made it clear that this newly conceptualized form of intervention could be deployed for the purpose of preventing crime as well as for interrogating persons suspected of having already committed an offense.[2]

If properly assimilated into our thinking about substantive offenses, this procedural development should influence the trend toward lowering the threshold of attempting in order to permit earlier police intervention. Now that the police may legitimately intervene in order to prevent crime, without initiating the process of a criminal trial, the criteria of attempting may be assessed on their own terms. If the threshold of attempting is to be lowered to include preparatory acts, the rationale must be that this inchoate conduct warrants punishment. It is no longer sufficient to justify liability as a means of thwarting nascent criminal plans.

There is another reason why the emergent constitutional law

§3.7. [1] Terry v. Ohio, 392 U.S. 1 (1968); Sibron v. New York, 392 U.S. 40 (1968); Peters v. New York, 392 U.S. 40 (1968).

[2] Terry v. Ohio, 392 U.S. 1, 22 (1968). *Id.* at 34 (Harlan, J., concurring).

of "stop-and-frisk" bears on our study of the tension between manifest and subjective criminality. Though the 1968 trilogy—*Terry, Sibron* and *Peters*—does not explicitly raise the issue, an underlying theme in the Supreme Court's analysis is that the detention of suspects should be justified only when they are engaged in behavior that is manifestly suspicious. In the two cases in which the Court affirmed a "stop-and-frisk" as constitutionally valid, the suspect was engaged in conduct that in and of itself triggered the officer's suspicion and justified the intervention. In *Terry* the officer observed the two suspects walk back and forth in front of a store window and repeatedly look inside; a third man conferred with them, left, and then returned again. The officer took this activity to be a "casing" of the store in preparation for a burglary or robbery.[3] Though the suspicious activity did not amount to a criminal attempt, the officer intervened, approached the three men in front of the store and asked them their names. This incident generated a case before the Supreme Court, because after stopping the men, the officer patted them down for weapons and found a revolver on Terry as well as on one of the others. These two men were charged with carrying a concealed weapon; their primary defense was that the revolvers should have been excluded from evidence as the fruit of unconstitutional searches of their persons.

In *Peters,* the officer similarly observed patently suspicious activity. While off-duty and at home, he heard a noise at the door, peeped through the keyhole and saw "two men tiptoeing out of the alcove through the stairway."[4] After calling the police and arming himself, the officer gave chase, apprehended the suspects and after an appropriate frisk, found an envelope containing burglary tools in Peters' pocket.[5]

These two cases should be contrasted with *Sibron*—in which the officer found heroin on the suspect's person, but the Court held that the stop-and-frisk producing the evidence was constitutionally invalid.[6] The only evidence that the officer had to go on before the stop-and-frisk was that he had observed the suspect in

[3] 392 U.S. at 5–7.
[4] Peters v. New York, 392 U.S. 40, 48 (1968).
[5] *Id.* at 49.
[6] Sibron v. New York, 392 U.S. 40 (1968).

the presence of "six or eight" known heroin addicts at one location in the course of an afternoon and evening.[7] As a statistical matter, the officer's hunch that Sibron possessed heroin was as likely to be correct as the judgment in *Terry* and *Peters* that the suspect was preparing to commit a theft offense. Yet the likely accuracy of the officer's judgment was not the controlling issue. The problem was the type of evidence he relied upon in formulating his judgment. This is the aspect of the case that suggests that the justices were drawn intuitively to the principle that in order to justify a stop-and-frisk, the suspect's own behavior had to reveal criminal activity and support the officer's judgment, preliminary to the frisk, that the suspect was armed and dangerous.

There is much in the language of the opinions to support this suggestion that the principle of manifest criminality lay behind the vindication of preventive police intrusions in *Terry* and *Peters.* First, there is the repeated emphasis in the opinions on "suspicious" behavior as the object of police inquiry. What made Terry's behavior suspicious was that it became "apparent"[8] that the three men had some purpose other than waiting for someone. Further, the Court insisted that the officer be able to point to "specific reasonable references"[9] and "articulate suspicion"[10] that criminal activity was imminent.

All of these criteria are readily applied to manifestations of criminal plans in "casing" a store or tiptoeing about a corridor. Yet none of them seems to be at home in assessing the likelihood that a suspect illegally possesses narcotics or a concealed weapon. It is not impossible for an act of possessing a weapon to be manifested in suspicious behavior (the suspect might nervously adjust the strap on what appears to be a shoulder holster), yet this kind of manifestation of an "apparent" purpose is highly unusual. With regard to possessing narcotics, lottery tickets or burglary tools, the fact of possession remains concealed unless, of course, the suspect openly shows the contraband to the police.

[7] *Id.* at 45.
[8] *Id.* at 23.
[9] *Id.* at 27.
[10] *Id* at 33 (Harlan, J., concurring).

It is hard to see what the "specific inference" or "articulable suspicion" would be that could justify intervention in a case where there was no outward manifestation of criminal activity. In one sense it is an "articulable suspicion" that the suspect was in the company of known addicts for eight hours. Yet, as the Court says: "The inference that persons who talk to narcotics addicts are engaged in the criminal traffic in narcotics is simply not the sort of reasonable inference required. . . ."[11] It is critically important to note that the defect in this inference is not the likelihood that it will be incorrect. Practical experience with addicts suggests that there was good reason to believe that Sibron was carrying narcotics, as in fact he was. The defect in the inference was that there was nothing in Sibron's behavior that revealed the act of acquiring or possessing heroin. It would have been closer to the mark, the Court tells us, if the officer had observed something "pass between Sibron and the addicts."[12] That fact of passing a small package would at least have been incriminating in the context, and it would presumably have provided a reasonable basis for inferring that Sibron was then engaged in an act of acquiring or passing narcotics. It would have been a specific fact about the defendant's behavior that would have justified immediate intervention.[13]

There are illuminating parallels to be drawn between *Sibron* and the type of facts required to support a police stop, on the one hand, and *Cramer* and the constitutional concept of an overt act, on the other.[14] In *Sibron,* the problem was whether meeting with known addicts was an act supporting the inference that the suspect possessed heroin. In *Cramer,* the issue was whether meeting with known saboteurs was an overt act sufficient to support a charge of adhering to the enemy and giving them aid and comfort. In neither case was the Supreme Court willing to accept the evidence of meeting with known addicts or saboteurs as sufficient under the applicable constitutional test. In both opinions, a critical argument was that the meeting with known criminals could have

[11] *Id.* at 62.
[12] *Ibid.*
[13] *Cf. id.* at 73 (Harlan, J., concurring).
[14] See §3.5.2 *supra.*

been a perfectly innocent event. However incriminating such a meeting might be to people engaged in police work, the Court would not accept association with known criminals as incriminating in the required constitutional sense. Despite this similarity in the underlying problem, the two cases rely upon obviously different doctrines to support the reversal of the conviction.[15]

Though our analysis of the 1968 trilogy on stop-and-frisk is suggested by the language of the opinions, there is no frontal assessment of the problem posed in stopping and frisking persons suspected merely of possession. Hopes that the Supreme Court might limit the emergent doctrine of stop-and-frisk to cases of manifestly criminal behavior were dashed four years later in Adams v. Williams,[16] a case that testifies to the danger of disengaging the inference of criminality from the suspect's own behavior. In *Williams,* the officer suspected that a man sitting in a car late at night was carrying narcotics and had a gun at his waist. The officer approached the car, knocked on the window, and then, when the suspect Williams rolled down the window, the officer reached in and found the gun at the suspect's waist. At least this is the officer's report of the way in which the encounter with Williams took place. The only evidence that the officer could furnish in support of his suspicion was a tip by an unnamed informer who had allegedly given the officer a tip in the past. The pistol produced by this stop-and-frisk was admitted against the defendant, and he was convicted of possessing it illegally. On a federal writ of habeas corpus, the Second Circuit affirmed the conviction. In his dissenting opinion, Judge Friendly commented that he had the "gravest hesitancy in extending [*Terry*] to cases like possession of narcotics. . . ."[17] The Supreme Court affirmed; Justice Rehnquist's opinion for the six votes in the majority bears little resemblance to

[15] In *Cramer* the overriding issue was whether the defendant's meeting with the saboteurs was tantamount to "giving aid and comfort to the enemy." See §3.5.2, at notes 55–56 *supra.*

[16] 407 U.S. 143 (1972).

[17] Williams v. Adams, 436 F.2d 30, 38 (2d Cir. 1971) (dissenting opinion). *Cf.* People v. Taggart, 20 N.Y.2d 335, 343, 229 N.E.2d 581, 587, 283 N.Y.S.2d 1, 9 (1967) (stop-and-frisk should not extend to all "contraband or criminal" violations).

the analysis or the language of the 1968 cases. Gone is the discussion of "suspicious" behavior, "apparent" purposes and "specific inferences." Now it appears to be sufficient that the officer rely on an informant rather than observe anything himself; for the frisk to be justified, it is sufficient that the officer have "ample reason" to fear for his safety.[18] It is hard to imagine that if the problem in *Sibron* were to come up again, the Court would decide the issue in the same way. The inference from an observed association with heroin addicts is just as strong as the inference from a tip coming from an informer whose reliability was subject to question.[19]

The major problem generated by breaking the tie between manifest criminality and the justification of stop-and-frisk is that the controlling evidence is now inherently suspect. Even assuming that the tip in *Williams* was reliable, there is no corroboration of the officer's claim that he received the tip. The informer was not named. The officer did not do anything himself that indicated that he was acting on the basis of the tip.[20] Of course, the officer's reference to the informer's tip would not have been admissible at the trial to prove the suspect's guilt. The supposedly procedural nature of search and seizure has led to the tolerance of a variety of evidence that no one would consider admissible at trial. The danger of fabricated, after-the-fact evidence obviously increases when this sort of evidence becomes sufficient to support a police intrusion.

In Adams v. Williams, the Court abandoned the protections implicit in the principle of manifest criminality, but it did not embrace the opposing theory of subjective criminality. This asymmetry is not surprising. In the field of police intervention, we should not expect to find an exact analogue to the metamorphosis of larceny. But is is remarkable, nonetheless, that the principle of manifest criminality finds a foothold in the debates about the scope of the Fourth Amendment. This extension of manifest criminality to the field of procedural protections reminds us that the deprivation im-

[18] 407 U.S. at 147–48.

[19] The informer's prior tip did not lead to a conviction. *Id.* at 156.

[20] *Cf.* Draper v. United States, 358 U.S. 307 (1959) (officers waited at train station in reliance on informer's tip).

posed in a police detention differs only in gravity from deprivations imposed after conviction.[21]

§3.8. *The Two Patterns of Criminality Revisited.*

Having studied the tension between manifest and subjective criminality in a half-dozen different legal contexts, we should restate the essential features of the two patterns and then seek to draw some general inferences from the specific pockets of development.

There are three essential features of manifest criminality and each warrants some clarification. First, the criminal act must manifest, on its face, the actor's criminal purpose. The act must bespeak danger, but it may do so in varying degrees. A criminal purpose might be the only possible inference from the act,[1] or the act might simply be latent with "sinister implications."[2] The type of act that patently does not meet this standard is the one that is "innocent" or "indifferent" in itself. Examples are Crohagan's setting foot in England (allegedly with the intent to kill the King)[3] or the recurrent hypothetical of putting sugar in a friend's coffee (allegedly with the intent to kill).[4] These are acts rendered suspect only by independently acquired proof of the actor's criminal intent.

Secondly, the manifestly criminal act is treated as a substantive condition of liability; it is not merely an evidentiary standard that may be replaced by equally probative evidence of intent. Thirdly, the requirement of manifest criminality is linked to a principle that conduct should fall within the scope of the criminal

[21] This analogy is taken up again in §6.3, at note 16 *infra*, where we compare debates about the nature of punishment with debates about the nature of a search under the Fourth Amendment.

§3.8. [1] See Haupt v. United States, 330 U.S. 631, 647 (1947) (Murphy, J., dissenting).

[2] See §3.4, at notes 13–14 *supra*.

[3] See §3.5, at note 19 *supra*.

[4] See §3.3.3 B *supra*.

law only if it is of a type that is unnerving and disturbing to the community as a whole. The "community" or the "public" is embodied in a hypothetical observer who would be apprehensive of the defendant's conduct. It is a demerit of the theory that the exact nature of this response by the hypothetical observer does not lend itself to precise clarification. It remains unclear whether the typical observer must be frightened or merely suspicious that criminal activity is afoot. It is also a weak point that the community's response might be irrational; popular apprehension might, for example, reflect racial bias or indigenous taboos.[5]

The countervailing theory of subjective criminality takes as its core principles, first, that the purpose of the criminal law is to protect specific legal interests, and, secondly, that those who intend to violate these interests are dangerous to the community. The expression of a criminal intent in an external act is still important. The significance of the act is not that it unnerves the community, but that it demonstrates the firmness of the actor's criminal resolve. Acts innocent on their face can demonstrate this resolve, and therefore there is no particular requirement that the criminal act bespeak danger to the community. The major problems in this pattern of criminality are evidentiary and procedural. Because the core of the crime lies in the inaccessible realm of intention, this theory of criminality generates concern about the dangers of convicting the innocent.

There is no suggestion that these two patterns of criminality account for the whole criminal law. There is no reference in these two patterns to homicide—surely one of the primary offenses in any theory of criminal law. There is no reference to crimes committed negligently and only a nod to the role of risk-creation in the definition of criminal conduct. These topics receive full treatment in the coming two chapters. We need a third pattern of criminality to account for homicide and negligence as a basis of liability. Yet not even this full range of three patterns or theories will account for every single offense, and it would be a mistake to squeeze, say, perjury or kidnapping into one of the three patterns

[5] See §3.3.2, at notes 38–40 *supra.*

that we shall develop. The most we can claim for our theory of the three patterns of liability is that we may illuminate the core offenses of the criminal law.

In our survey of the tension between manifest and subjective criminality, we have noted a conflicting approach to defining criminal conduct, which we have called the positivist thesis. In the field of possession offenses, the positivist thesis justifies punishment with neither manifest criminality nor an intent to violate a protected legal interest.[6] The thesis holds that if the public is fairly advised of the rule governing liability, a transgression of the rule in itself justifies criminal punishment. This thesis is procedural rather than substantive, for it stresses the virtues of well-defined and well-publicized rules, but it ignores the content of these rules defining criminal conduct. If accepted, the positivist thesis explains the entire criminal law. Yet this explanation, if it is one, ignores the substantive contours of the offenses that in fact have crystallized in Western jurisprudence. If we take the content, and not merely the form of the criminal law to be important, we should regard the positivist thesis not as a challenge, but as an alternative that stands outside our realm of discourse.

The laws of larceny, burglary, fraud, attempts, and treason evidence a general drift toward the view that an intent to harm is the core of criminal conduct. The principle of manifest criminality survives in corners of the law, such as cases on staged larceny, and it repeatedly asserts itself in fields such as impossible attempts, the possession offenses and the criteria for constitutionally legitimate detention on the street. We may even witness a resurgence of manifest criminality in the law defining the overt act required for conspiracy as an inchoate crime. Yet the resonance of subjective criminality is surely the dominant theme of contemporary criminal jurisprudence.

[6] See §3.4.1 *supra*.

Chapter Four
Homicide: Three Lines of Liability

§4.1. *Toward a Third Pattern of Liability.*

As the first two patterns of liability crystallized in a detailed study of larceny, the third pattern will emerge from the details of the law of homicide. For the present, however, we shall stress the uniqueness of homicide as a crime and then, in the next chapter, move beyond homicide to a general pattern of harmful consequences, including arson, battery, and other crimes requiring concrete injuries to persons and property. What all these offenses have in common is that the starting point for analyzing liability is not an act manifesting danger, not an intent to harm, but the occurrence of the harm itself; once the harm is established, the inquiry centers on attributing that harm to particular actors and assessing whether they are accountable for bringing it about.

What makes homicide unique is, among other things, the uniqueness of causing death. While all personal injuries and destruction of property are irreversible harms, causing death is a harm of a different order. Killing another human being is not only a worldly deprivation; in the Western conception of homicide, killing is an assault on the sacred, natural order. In the Biblical view, the person who slays another was thought to acquire control over the blood—the life force—of the victim.[1] The only way that this life force could be returned to God, the origin of all life, was to execute the slayer himself. In this conception of crime and punishment, capital execution for homicide served to expiate the desecration of the natural order.[2] The desecration, it is worth stressing, inhered in causing death, regardless whether the actor was fairly to blame for the killing; the expiation for the desecration worked by terminating the violation of the sacred order—namely, the slayer's control over the victim's blood.[3]

Though we are inclined today to think of homicide as merely the deprivation of a secular interest,[4] the historical background of desecration is essential to an adequate understanding both of the history of homicide and the current survival of many historic assumptions. For example, consent is not a defense to homicide, as it is in cases of battery and destruction of property. The reason is that the religious conception of human life still prevails against the modern view that life is an interest that the bearer can dispose of at will. The other ways in which the desecration of killing continues to shape the law of homicide will become clear as the discussion progresses.

If the history of theft offenses is one of expanding liability, the history of homicide reflects an unceasing effort to limit liability.

§4.1. [1] D. Daube, Studies in Biblical Law 72, 122 (1947). A. Phillips, Ancient Israel's Criminal Law 86 (1970).

[2] Genesis 9:6 ("whosoever sheddeth man's blood, by man shall his blood be shed"). *Cf.* the analogous duty to execute an animal who kills a human being. Genesis 9:5; Exodus 21:28.

[3] Expiation by sacrificing a heifer was required in cases of slaying where the culprit could not be found. Deuteronomy 21:1–9. *Compare* the community's paying the *murdrum* fine for the slaying of a Frenchman, 3 Stephen 31; whether this was expiation or not, the fine made it clear that the killing of a Frenchman was the community's responsibility. The fine could be avoided by the "presentment of Englishry," i.e., proof that the slain man was an Englishman. Bracton 135.

[4] Kadish, *Respect for Life and Regard for Rights in the Common Law,* 64 Calif. L. Rev. 871 (1976) (life as the highest secular value—"necessary for the enjoyment of all other goods").

The historic point of departure is the principle that unless a killing is justified (say, by killing a manifest thief), the party causing death is always accountable. This principle was enforced in the Anglo-Saxon system of assessing the *wergild*.[5] It was causing death, not the manner and culpability of acting, that determined liability. When the law of homicide came under the King's jurisdiction in the twelfth century and became a crime punished by death, the general principle of liability began to admit of exceptions.[6] The exceptions crystallized as the excuses for killing by inevitable accident *(per infortunium)* and out of personal necessity *(se defendendo)*. These excuses were not recognized as part of the law, but operated extralegally by way of an institutionalized system of royal pardoning. By the Statute of Gloucester, enacted in 1278, suspects found to have killed under either of these headings were remanded to the King's grace, which was expected to be granted as a matter of course.[7] By the early fourteenth century, pardons were also granted to persons who slew while they were suffering from insanity *(en deverie)*.[8] These excuses of accident, self-preservation, and insanity were the beginning of an ongoing effort to prune back the law to the set of cases in which the slayer had a fair opportunity of avoiding the death of the victim. The progressive recognition of these excuses represented the decline of expiation as the impetus of punishment and a growing commitment to blame as a condition for just punishment.

The tension between expiation and individualized justice pervades the law of homicide and continues to haunt the rules of liability. The conflict between the approaches is expressed in divergent views about relevance of harm and of culpability in assessing liability. Today both elements are necessary for liability, but there is a difference of emphasis in conflicting theories about the essen-

[5] The *wer* was paid to the deceased's relatives; the *wite*, to the King; the *bot*, to the victim as compensation for crime. See 1 Stephen 57. Specifically on the *wergild*, see N. Hurnard, The King's Pardon for Homicide 1–30 (1969).

[6] Green, *The Jury and the English Law of Homicide 1200–1600*, 74 Mich. L. Rev. 413, 428 (1976).

[7] 6 Edw. I, c. 9. See 3 Stephen 26; Hurnard, *supra* note 5, at 281–290.

[8] See 3 Stephen 38; Hurnard, *supra* note 5, at 159–70.

tial wrong of homicide. Pending our refinement of "wrongdoing" and "wrongful conduct,"[9] we should think of the problem as identifying the elements of the prima facie case of criminal homicide. Does that prima facie case consist in simply killing another human being, or does it consist in intentionally or negligently causing death? For the sake of convenience, we shall refer to these modes of thinking about homicide, respectively, as the "harm-oriented" and the "act-oriented" approaches. Each of these modes of structuring liability requires some clarification.

The essence of the harm-oriented analysis of homicide is expressed in Blackstone's influential rule of thumb: killing another human being "amounts to murder unless where *justified* . . . , *excused* on the ground of accident or self-preservation; or *alleviated* into manslaughter. . . ."[10] In this mode of analysis, the prima facie case of murder consists merely in killing another human being. The claims of justification, excuse and mitigation are analogous to private law allegations in confession and avoidance. They concede the wrongdoing of killing and interpose new matter as grounds for acquittal or mitigation.[11] In the Blackstonian scheme, claims of accident and mistake do not negate the prima facie case of homicide; they merely render the homicide excusable.[12]

The act-oriented approach to liability takes intentional or negligent killing as a necessary component of the prima facie case. Most issues of justification and excuse are not affected by this shift,[13] but the claims of mistake and accident cease to function as excuses and become instead denials of the prima facie case. A relevant claim of mistake precludes a finding of intentional homicide; and a claim of accident—if the accident is sufficiently free from fault—negates the alternative allegation of a criminally negligent homicide. This restructuring of the prima facie case testifies to a dif-

[9] See §6.6 *infra.*

[10] 4 Blackstone 201. (Italics in original.)

[11] This point requires a qualification as to claims of mitigation. The allegation of provocation as a mitigation negated the element of malice that was otherwise presumed from the killing. *Id.* at 200.

[12] *Id.* at 182–83; Cal. Penal Code §195(1).

[13] E.g., insanity, duress, self-defense. See generally on excuse and justification, Chapter Ten *infra.*

ferent conception of the conduct that is typically sufficient for liability. It is not merely killing that is typically sufficient for murder (*pace* Blackstone), but killing another intentionally or negligently.

Though the distinction between these two approaches to homicide might appear to be a minor question of organization, the tension between them reverberates throughout the criminal law. It will arise again when we turn to the general theory of wrongdoing and the relevance of harm to the just level of punishment.[14] It crops up as well at the more prosaic level of allocating the burden of persuasion.[15] The glimpse that we have now of the distinction will eventually broaden into a wide-ranging theoretical perspective.

It is worth noting two specific implications of the distinction between harm-orientation and act-orientation on the structure of homicide. First, as expressed in Blackstone's summary statement, the orientation toward harm implies that murder is the basic offense; manslaughter, a mitigated form of murder. In contrast, the act-oriented approach to homicide carries no bias toward murder as the basic offense. So far as the gravamen of the charge rests on the particular act causing death, it is more plausible to regard manslaughter as the basic offense and murder, an aggravated form of manslaughter. If act *X* is sufficient for manslaughter, then *X* plus an aggravating factor would be the way to define murder. We shall encounter some examples of the latter way of defining the two grades of murder when we turn to the French and German experience at the end of the chapter.[16]

The second point worth stressing is that the harm-oriented approach works well without a concept of negligence; the issues now raised under the heading of negligence were subsumed at common law under the rubrics of *per infortunium* and inevitable accident. The act-oriented approach, in contrast, requires both a concept of risk and a theory of excessive risk or negligence in order to state the kind of non-intentional killing sufficient for a prima

[14] See §6.6.5 *infra.*
[15] See §§7.1 through 7.3 *infra.*
[16] §4.5 *infra.*

facie case of liability. It is important to see that the excuse of *per infortunium* and negligence are two sides of the same coin of culpability. An accident could excuse a killing only if it was not culpable; a culpable accident betokens negligence. The harm-oriented approach states the issue negatively as a problem of accident; the act-oriented approach states the same issue positively as a problem of excessive risk-taking.

This correlation illuminates the origins of negligence. The concept of negligence enters the law as a standard for limiting liability in the harm-oriented mode of analysis and eventually becomes an affirmative rationale for liability in the transposed, act-oriented structure.[17]

The history of homicide is characterized by a gradual shift from the harm-oriented to the act-oriented mode of analysis. This general transformation bears some resemblance to the metamorphosis of larceny and the transition from manifest to subjective criminality. In both processes of transition, the denial of intention functioned initially as an excuse; the affirmative assertion of intentionally stealing or intentionally killing later becomes an element of the prima facie case. But there is also a critical difference between the two historical developments. The transition to subjective criminality led to a shedding of elements of manifest criminality and thus to an expansion of liability in cases of innocent-appearing takings. The restructuring of homicide, however, did not find expression in an expansion of liability; if anything, the reconceptualization of *per infortunium* as negligent risk-taking expressed a tightening of the criteria of liability.[18]

There is no event in the history of homicide that parallels the eclipse of manifest criminality. The manifest harm of homicide is the act of causing death. This harm is retained as an indispensable element in both modes of thinking about homicide. It is true that a radical subjectification of homicide would lead one to dispense with

[17] The same transformation is evident in the history of tort liability. See Fletcher, *Fairness and Utility in Tort Theory,* 85 Harv. L. Rev. 537, 556–64 (1972).

[18] Compare Brown v. Kendall, 60 Mass. (6 Cush.) 292 (1850), in which the same transition led to a tightening of tort liability.

the occurrence of death as a factor bearing on the gravity of the crime. Shooting and missing would then be just as egregious a crime as shooting and hitting; the only question would be whether the actor intended to kill. No legal system, so far as I know, has ever adopted this proposal to collapse the distinction between attempted killing and actual killing. But the possibility of doing so is a theoretically engaging question, and eventually we shall have to come to grips with the relevance of causing harm to the grading of offense and assessing the just level of punishment.[19]

The agenda for the ensuing two chapters requires us first to descend into the details of the law before we return to the more abstract features of a third pattern of liability. This immersion carries the risk of drowning in the rapid currents of existing litigation on the contours of homicide. To find a way through these currents, we shall emphasize the law of two prominent jurisdictions: California and England. California—perhaps the only major state with a penal code dating from the nineteenth century—still reflects many features of the common-law approach to homicide. Following its own theories of reform, the current law of England stands in useful contrast. We shall round out this survey by adverting to the provisions of the Model Penal Code and the recently redrafted statutes in the United States. At the end of this chapter, we shall compare this development in the English-speaking world with Continental practice, and in Chapter Five we shall return to the jurisprudential themes of homicide and work our way toward a pattern of harmful consequences that transcends the particularities of homicide.

Our discussion of homicide will be functional rather than doctrinal. There are three standards for grading homicide as manslaughter, murder and first-degree murder. These standards, or lines of liability, as we call them, turn on critical facts for interpreting cases of allegedly criminal homicide. The first critical fact is that the killing be deemed intentional; the second, that the death be caused by excessive risk-taking; the third, that the killing

[19] See §6.6.5 *infra.*

occur in the course of another offense or by particular means. The first two lines of liability reflect the act-oriented mode of analysis; the third, which we call the "formal" method of grading homicide, reflects the residual influence of the harm-oriented theory of homicide. All three lines of liability incorporate a scale of increasing liability. In any of the three, the prosecution can prove manslaughter and then, by proving more egregious circumstances, move up the scale toward murder and first-degree murder.

The advantage of thinking about homicide in these functional tracks is that we forego the traditional effort to define malice as the dividing line between manslaughter and murder.[20] The nature of malice proves to be different in each line of analysis and therefore there is little point in attempting an abstract definition of this elusive concept.

§4.2. *Intentional Killings.*

If it is established that the defendant killed intentionally and there is no valid excuse or justification for the killing, the defendant will be held accountable for at least manslaughter. Whether the offense is taken to be a form of murder turns on the absence rather than on the presence of an additional factor. That factor is provocation or heat of passion; if present, the intentional killing is manslaughter; if absent, it is murder.

§4.2.1. **Provocation.** Though provocation does not enjoy a standard definition, the issue is generally understood to be whether the defendant was substantially impaired in his self-control at the time of the killing. If the killing occurs upon a sudden quarrel,[1] or after the defendant catches his or her spouse in an act

[20] On the origins of malice in the fifteenth century, see Kaye, *The Early History of Murder and Manslaughter II,* 83 L.Q. Rev. 569, 572–76 (1967).

§4.2. [1] For classical sources on provocation and chance medley, see 3 Coke 55 ("upon some sudden falling out"); 1 Hale 453 ("sudden falling out"); 4 Blackstone 184 ("heat of blood or passion").

of adultery,[2] it is generally thought that the actor's self-control is sufficiently impaired to warrant classification as a lower degree of criminal homicide. The issue is plainly normative in the sense that the homicide is not mitigated to manslaughter by a mere factual showing that the slayer was provoked. He must be provoked under circumstances and to such a degree that he is not expected completely to control himself. The standard of adequate provocation is obviously shaped by social convention.[3] In our society it is insufficient for the defendant to argue that his killing his sister was mitigated on the ground that she was sexually promiscuous, though it is conceivable that in some societies a killing under these circumstances would be considered adequately provoked. The difference is that in most Western societies, brothers are expected to control whatever shame or anger they may feel as a result of their sister's promiscuity. Similarly, one could imagine a society—there are no doubt countercultural groups in which it is already true—in which lovers and spouses are expected to control the emotions produced by discovering a spouse in an act of sexual betrayal.

The normative character of mitigation generates the difficult institutional question whether it should be the judge or the common-law jury that decides the question whether the defendant was adequately provoked.[4] The traditional answer to this question is

[2] 4 Blackstone 191; 1 Hale 486; Manning's Case, 83 Eng. Rep. 112 (K.B. 1683–84) ("the Court directed the executioner to burn him gently on the hand, because there could be no greater provocation than this"). Rowland v. State, 83 Miss. 483, 35 So. 826 (1904) (defendant killed wife *in flagrante;* murder conviction reversed); Scroggs v. State, 94 Ga. App. 28, 93 S.E.2d 583 (1956) (defendant killed woman to prevent planned adultery with defendant's husband; conviction for manslaughter reversed on ground that the killing might have been *justified* under provision of criminal code then in force). *Cf.* Holmes v. Director of Public Prosecutions, [1946] A.C. 588 (H.L.) (defendant killed wife after she confessed prior act of adultery; held, as a matter of law, a confession of adultery is insufficient to reduce murder to manslaughter).

[3] See Holmes v. Director of Public Prosecutions, [1946] A.C. 588, 601 (H.L.) (opinion by Viscount Simon: ". . . as society advances, it ought to call for a higher measure of self-control in all cases").

[4] Note that where the defendant has good ground for acquittal, the favored strategy of the defense is to oppose instructions on provocation and manslaughter

that the judge should make a preliminary judgment about whether the circumstances could, as a matter of law, constitute adequate provocation. Thus the courts have generated a number of rules of thumb that eliminate some cases from the province of the jury.[5] Though it is generally recognized that proof of a serious physical blow is sufficient to submit the issue of provocation to the jury,[6] the general rule is that insults and abusive language are insufficient. The premise obviously is that though "sticks and stones may break our bones," we are all expected to maintain a stiff upper lip in the face of verbal aggression.[7] Yet verbal reports of rape and adultery are treated differently,[8] as though hearing about an incident was as provocative as witnessing it.

One rule invoked in an effort to lend formal contours to questions of provocation is the principle that after the provocative incident has occurred, the time elapsed prior to the killing must be sufficiently brief to interpret the killing as the direct result of the provocative incident. If the accused has had adequate time to "cool off," then the killing is not seen as an outgrowth of the provocative event, but as an independent act for which the accused is fully accountable.[9] In the abstract, there is no way to define the amount

and thus force the jury to choose between the extremes of convicting for murder and acquitting the defendant altogether. See, e.g., People v. Harris, 8 Ill. 2d 431, 134 N.E.2d 315 (1956) (defendant opposed to manslaughter instructions).

[5] The English jury has acquired increased control over the litigation of provocation by virtue of Homicide Act 1957, 5 & 6 Eliz. II, c. 11, §3, which provides that issue should be determined by the jury whenever "there is evidence . . . that the defendant was provoked . . . by things said. . . ."

[6] State v. Ponce, 124 W. Va. 126, 19 S.E.2d 221 (1942) (victim struck defendant on the "side of the neck," whereupon defendant threw a brick at him; held not only was there error in the instructions, but evidence was insufficient to support a finding of malice); see generally LaFave & Scott 574.

[7] E.g., Commonwealth v. Cisneros, 381 Pa. 447, 113 A.2d 293 (1959) (racial epithet); State v. King, 37 N.J. 285, 181 A.2d 158 (1962) (sexual insults). Freddo v. State, 127 Tenn. 376, 155 S.W. 170 (1913) (victim repeatedly called defendant a "son of a bitch"), criticized thoughtfully in Comment, *Manslaughter and the Adequacy of Provocation: The Reasonableness of the Reasonable Man*, 106 U. Pa. L. Rev. 1021 (1958).

[8] State v. Flory, 40 Wyo. 184, 276 P. 458 (1929) (defendant's wife told him that her father had raped her; conviction for second-degree murder reversed); Maher v. People, 10 Mich. 212 (1862) (defendant informed of his wife's affair with decedent; conviction of assault with intent to murder, reversed).

[9] LaFave & Scott 579–80; Perkins 67–69.

of time sufficient to hold that the accused was no longer properly influenced by a physical blow or by discovering a spouse in an act of adultery; therefore the issue is one properly left to the jury.[10] In some obvious cases, however, the judges have intervened and ruled as a matter of law that the time elapsed was sufficient to preclude a claim of provocation.[11]

In the normal case, the victim of the killing is the party accountable for the provocation of the accused. Yet the fact that it is the victim who typically strikes the accused before he is killed can mislead one to think that the rationale for provocation is the victim's contribution to his own death. It might be thought, particularly in the case of adultery, that the victim in some measure deserves to die and that therefore the accused's crime should be treated leniently.[12] This view of provocation can lead to some controversial interpretations of the law. It led an English court to hold that provocation was inapplicable in a case in which a father, a soldier on leave, had heard of his wife's adultery and neglect of their ill child, and thereafter, for a variety of motives, killed the child.[13] It is not clear whether the accused was concerned about the child's condition or provoked by the mother's adultery and neglect; therefore it might have been perfectly sound for the court to reject the claim of provocation. In light of the summary opinion in the case, it is difficult to take the decision as a precedent for the view that provocation must be based on something "done by the deceased person."[14] Nonetheless, there is a strong moral inhibition

[10] Maher v. People, 10 Mich. 212, 223–25 (1862).

[11] E.g., State v. Gounagias, 88 Wash. 304, 153 P. 9 (1915) (several days elapsed between provocative incident—the victim's committing sodomy on the defendant—and the killing); In re Fraley, 3 Okla. Crim. 719, 109 P. 295 (1910) (nine or ten months after the victim had killed the decedent's son).

[12] The background for this view is the Biblical rule permitting the slaying of both an adulterous wife and her lover, Deuteronomy 22:22. *Cf.* Richardson v. State, 70 Ga. 825 (1883) (shooting a suspected adulterer justified on the ground of protecting wife from commission of a felony).

[13] Rex v. Simpson, 84 L.J.K.B. 1893 (Crim. App. 1915).

[14] The case is so read in Smith & Hogan 235. *Cf.* White v. State, 44 Tex. Crim. 346, 72 S.W. 173 (1902) (provocation unavailable if defendant thought victim was someone other than person who assaulted him).

against condoning the intentional killing of innocent persons,[15] and this inhibition seems to be relaxed as to persons who engage in provocative conduct.[16]

If, however, a claim of provocation were grounded in the victim's contribution to his own demise—or in the victim's guilt as in the adultery cases—it should follow that the defense would be unavailable where the provocative event has not actually occurred, but the provoked defendant believes that it has. Yet the courts consistently hold that the claim of provocation based, say, on the wife's adultery, is well founded whether the wife is actually engaged in adultery or not.[17] These holdings would be precluded by any theory grounding the dissent on the victim's actual contribution to his or her own death.

In an effort to avoid some of these disputes about the scope of provocation, the Model Penal Code relabelled the issue as "extreme mental or emotional disturbance."[18] This act of renaming makes it clear that the mitigation of homicide to manslaughter is based solely on the actor's partial loss of control, which has to be assessed by looking at the actor's response to the circumstances as he perceived them. This latter way of looking at the issue is important, as we shall see, in the development of the analogous defense of diminished capacity.

The primary source of difficulty in the analysis of provocation derives from the failure of the courts and commentators to face the

[15] See Regina v. Dudley & Stevens, 14 Q.B.D. 273 (1884) discussed *infra* §10.4.1.

[16] It is also significant that the doctrine emerged from the concepts of chance medley and sudden quarrel, which presupposed that the victim was the provocative agent. See authorities cited in note 1 *supra*.

[17] State v. Yanz, 74 Conn. 177, 50 A. 37 (1901) (defendant shot man caught in embrace with defendant's wife; reversible error that the trial court charged the jury that mitigation depended on whether in fact "adultery was going on"); White v. State, 44 Tex. Crim. 346, 72 S.W. 173 (1902) (mistaken belief that the person shot at had assaulted defendant sufficient to qualify the killing as provoked).

[18] MPC §210.3(1)(b); *accord:* Del. Code tit. 11, §641; N.Y. Penal Law §125.20(2); N.D. Cent. Code §12.1-16-02(2). The new Pennsylvania code departs from the Model Penal Code and provides that provocation is available in the killing of a person other than the provocative agent only if the defendant "endeavors" to kill the latter and "negligently or accidentally causes the death of the individual killed." 18 Pa. Cons. Stat. Ann. tit. 18, §2503(a). This follows the rule in Ill. Ann. Stat. c. 38, §9–2.

underlying normative issue whether the accused may be fairly expected to control an impulse to kill under the circumstances. Obviously, there are some impulses such as anger and even mercy (as in the case of the father who killed his neglected child) that we do expect people to control. If they fail to control these impulses and they kill another intentionally, they are liable for unmitigated homicide or murder. The basic moral question in the law of homicide is distinguishing between those impulses to kill as to which we as a society demand self-control, and those as to which we relax our inhibitions.

Courts and commentators seek to evade this moral issue by tying the partial defense of provocation to the likely behavior of the "reasonable person."[19] As a general matter, the invocation of this mythical standard of an exemplary person provides some assistance in analyzing the moral issues of criminal responsibility. By projecting our moral judgments into a prediction of what a reasonable person would do, we generate a standard for assessing the behavior of the accused. Yet in the context of provocation, the reasonable person is hardly at home. First, as everyone is prepared to admit, the reasonable person does not kill at all, even under provocation.[20] Therefore it is difficult to assess whether his or her killing should be classified as manslaughter rather than murder. More serious than this conceptual anomaly is the danger that abnormal personal characteristics of the defendant will not be taken into consideration in assessing whether as to him, the provocation was adequate. Thus there are decisions holding that it is irrelevant that the defendant was suffering from a sunstroke[21] or head injury[22] at the time of the allegedly provocative incident. We certainly do not expect people to control the effects of a sunstroke, and therefore if this fact bore on the accused's excitability under the circumstances,

[19] For an early use of this test, see the summing up of Keating, J., in the trial of Regina v. Welsh, 11 Cox Crim. Cas. 336 (1869). *Cf.* Maher v. People, 10 Mich. 212 (1862), discussed at note 26 *infra.* See generally Williams, *Provocation and the Reasonable Man,* 1954 Crim. L. Rev. 740.

[20] Williams, *supra* note 19, at 742.

[21] People v. Golsh, 63 Cal. App. 609, 219 P. 456 (1923).

[22] State v. Nevares, 36 N.M. 41, 7 P.2d 933 (1932) (but note that provocation was merely verbal).

it is irrational not to consider it in assessing whether his killing was at least partially beyond his control. In the most notorious case of this vein, the accused, one Bedder,[23] killed a prostitute who was allegedly taunting and hitting him in a fracas about his inability to perform the negotiated sexual act. The claim was that the accused was impotent and particularly sensitive about his incapacity. Nonetheless, the House of Lords affirmed the instructions to the jury not to consider the impact of the accused's impotence on his reaction to the prostitute's taunting.[24] It may be that the accused should have controlled himself whether he was impotent or not, yet this is a fact that should have been decided by the jury with full appreciation of all the pressures bearing on the event. One can hardly say that the jury passed judgment on Mr. Bedder if they did not even consider the most significant facts that influenced his loss of control.

It seems that decisions like *Bedder* derive from the court's losing sight of why one uses the test of the reasonable person to assess the mitigating effect of provocation. The underlying question is whether the accused should be able to control the particular impulse or emotion that issues in the killing. Yet the intrusion of this mythical standard sometimes induces judges and legislative draftsmen to think that the issue is whether if the average person would have killed under the circumstances, the killing should be partially excused.[25] The test cannot be whether the average person *would have killed* under the circumstances, for that test should more plausibly generate a total excuse.[26] Further, the average person is not impotent; nor does he have a sunstroke or head injury. Therefore these facts presumably should not bear on the question of provocation.

[23] Bedder v. Director of Public Prosecutions, [1954] 2 All E.R. 801 (H.L.).

[24] *Id.* at 803.

[25] See the Homicide Act 1957, c. 11, §3 ("whether the provocation was enough to make a reasonable man do as he did . . .").

[26] The issue is properly framed by Judge Christiancy in Maher v. People, 10 Mich. 212, 220 (1862); "The principle involved . . . [is] that reason should, at the time of the act, be disturbed or obscured by passion to an extent which *might render* ordinary men, of fair average disposition, *liable* to act rashly . . . from passion, rather than judgment" (emphasis in original). The quality of rashness is essential in explaining why the defense serves only to mitigate, not excuse.

This is a good example of the way in which a legal doctrine can become totally alienated from the moral sentiments that give rise to it.

Part of the problem, no doubt, is the general decline of moral thinking in the analysis of liability for homicide.[27] Therefore, it does not generally occur to analysts of provocation that the central problem is determining those impulses that we expect people completely to control.[28] Even the Royal Commission on Capital Punishment was confounded by the doctrine of the reasonable person; the commissioners recognized that the test was unfair and yet they were apparently persuaded by the judges who appeared before them that if physical disabilities and partial insanity were recognized as relevant, it would follow that a bad-tempered man should also receive special consideration under the law.[29] This non sequitur is typical of the confusion that characterizes the decline of moral sensitivity in the analysis of culpability.[30] Once we forget that the problem is the analysis of those impulses that we are fairly expected to control, it follows that judges would have difficulty distinguishing between a head injury and a bad temper.

Once the moral perspective on provocation is lost, the concern develops that the individuation of the standard might lead to its total collapse. Not knowing where to draw the line, judges would prefer not to include any unusual physical feature of the defendant. Thus the English Homicide Act of 1957 retains the rule that provocation should mitigate the homicide only if "it was enough to make a reasonable man do as he did. . . ."[31] A few years later, the Model Penal Code broke from this pattern and boldly declared that the defense of provocation should be judged "from

[27] Compare the utilitarian theory of excuses, discussed *infra* in §10.3.5 *infra*.

[28] See the opinions in Mancini v. Director of Public Prosecutions, [1941] 3 All E.R. 272 (H.L.), and The King v. Lesbini, [1914] 3 K.B. 1116 (Crim. App.).

[29] Royal Commission on Capital Punishment, Report 52–53 (1949–53).

[30] Note also the argument that harsh verdicts of murder, which carry a fixed sentence, could be commuted by the Home Secretary. *Id.* at 53. The intervention of the executive prevents "any eventual miscarriage of justice." *Cf.* the same point made as a rationale for denying excuses, §10.3.3 *infra*.

[31] Homicide Act 1957, c. 11, §3.

the viewpoint of a person in the actor's situation under the circumstances as he believes them to be."[32] Lest anyone fear that individuation of the inquiry would lead to the indulgent mitigation of all provoked killings, the draftsmen added a proviso: there must be a "reasonable explanation or excuse" for the "extreme mental or emotional disturbance."[33] Thus, for example, the moral issue whether insults should be sufficient to mitigate the killing is framed by the question whether the accused has a "reasonable explanation or excuse" for losing control and killing. The virtue of this shift in wording is that it discourages decisions like *Bedder;* the jury's assessment of his killing the taunting prostitute could not be short-circuited by a judicial determination that reasonable people are not impotent.[34]

The persistent appeal of tests based on the likely behavior of reasonable people is hardly adventitious in Anglo-American law. Whatever the proposal of the Model Penal Code, the "reasonable person" still dominates judicial analysis of provocation in American as well as English courts.[35] And even the Code invokes this mischievous, mythical person in framing the defense of duress.[36] The theme of objective tests and reasonable persons as their standard-bearer is one that we shall take up more fully in our study of the quest for a general theory of criminal liability.[37]

§4.2.2. **Diminished Capacity.** One of the more significant developments in the law of homicide in the last two decades has been the progressive recognition that the impaired psychological condition of the accused, though short of insanity, provides a ground for classifying an intentional killing as manslaughter rather than murder. Parliament introduced the defense by legislation in

[32] MPC §210.3(1)(b); *accord:* Del. Code tit. 11, §641; N.D. Cent. Code §12.1-16-02.

[33] MPC §210.3(1)(b); the Delaware and North Dakota provisions, cited *supra* note 32, are in accord on this point also.

[34] Scholarly opinion in Great Britain favors the same interpretation. Smith & Hogan 241.

[35] The "reasonable person" has reasserted himself in the code revisions that were stimulated in part by the Model Penal Code. See Colo. Rev. Stat. §18-3-104; Ill. Ann. Stat. c. 38, §9–2; Tex. Penal Code §19.04(c) ("person of ordinary temper").

[36] MPC §2.09(1).

[37] See the discussion of individualized attribution in §6.8.2 *infra.*

1957. The statute defines "diminished responsibility" in conclusory terms as an "abnormality of mind . . . [that] substantially impaired [the accused's] mental responsibility for his acts and omissions. . . ."[38] The defense applies only in homicide prosecutions and its effect is to reduce a killing that would otherwise be murder to manslaughter.[39]

An analogous defense has emerged in several American jurisdictions by way of imaginative judicial interpretations of what it means to kill with "malice aforethought." The leading case is People v. Conley, decided by the California Supreme Court in 1966.[40] The defendant had intentionally shot and killed two people—a woman who had jilted him and her husband. The evidence indicated that he had been drinking and that his blood alcohol level at the time of the shooting was probably between .21 and .27—an extraordinarily high level. He had also been taking medication for a back injury. The trial judge's rulings were curious. The bifurcated trial in California was designed to simplify the trial on guilt or innocence by relegating psychiatric testimony and other matters bearing on the accused's psychological condition to a separate hearing.[41] Yet the trial judge allowed a defense psychiatrist to testify that Conley was in a "disassociative state at the time of the killing. . . ."[42] Having gone that far, the trial judge refused to give instructions on manslaughter and the defendant was convicted of first-degree murder. This latter decision, ruled the Supreme Court, was reversible error; prior decisions in California[43] had already intimated that the accused's psychiatric condition bore on whether he could "harbor malice," and therefore the evidence in *Conley* warranted an instruction on manslaughter. In the opinion as well as in the model instruction recommended by the

[38] Homicide Act 1957, c. 11, §2(1).

[39] See Regina v. Byrne, [1960] 3 All E.R. 1 (Crim. App.) (error to withdraw evidence of diminished capacity from the jury).

[40] 64 Cal. 2d 310, 411 P.2d 911, 49 Cal. Rptr. 815 (1966).

[41] Louisell and Hazard, *Insanity as a Defense: The Bifurcated Trial*, 49 Calif. L. Rev. 805 (1961).

[42] 64 Cal. 2d at 315, 411 P.2d at 914, 49 Cal. Rptr. at 818.

[43] People v. Wells, 33 Cal. 2d 330, 202 P.2d 53 (1949); People v. Gorshen, 51 Cal. 2d 716, 336 P. 2d 492 (1959).

Court,[44] it is clear that intoxication alone would be sufficient to reduce the offense to manslaughter. This obviously goes further than the defense recognized by the English Homicide Act of 1957.[45] The test of diminished capacity, according to *Conley,* is whether "because of mental disease or intoxication . . . the defendant is unable to comprehend his duty to govern his actions in accord with the duty imposed by law."[46]

It is important to note that this definition focusses on the mental act of "comprehending" one's duty rather than on the issue of self-control. The English definition more broadly encompasses a variety of "mental abnormalities" that "impair" responsibility. The California test reads surprisingly much like the *M'Naghten* test on insanity,[47] which focusses on the actor's knowledge of what he was doing and on his knowledge of the wrongfulness of his act. Though the *Conley* test is clearly designed to increase the range of relevant psychiatric testimony, a technical reading of the Court's holding would lead us to think that anyone who would qualify as not "comprehending his duty to obey the law" would also qualify as insane for not knowing and appreciating that what he was doing was wrong. It seems fairly safe to assume, however, that the context of decisions has as much influence as the wording of the legal test; if a finding of diminished capacity leads to a compromise verdict of manslaughter, rather than acquittal and civil commitment,[48] this difference in practical consequence cannot but influence the contours of the test. This influence crystallized in 1973 when the California Supreme Court ruled that the issue of "irresistible impulse" properly bore on the analysis of diminished capacity, but not on the question of insanity.[49]

In slightly more than a decade of litigation since *Conley,* the

[44] 64 Cal. 2d at 324 n.4, 411 P.2d at 920 n.4, 49 Cal. Rptr. at 824 n.4.

[45] The act limits the defense to abnormalities of mind that arise from "inherent causes" or those "induced by disease or injury." Homicide Act 1957, c. 11, §2.

[46] 64 Cal. 2d at 322, 411 P.2d at 918, 49 Cal. Rptr. at 822.

[47] M'Naghten's Case, 8 Eng. Rep. 718 (H.L. 1843).

[48] Compare the verdict of not guilty by reason of insanity, §10.4.4 *infra.*

[49] People v. Cantrell, 8 Cal. 3d 672, 504 P.2d 1256, 105 Cal. Rptr. 792 (1973). *Cf.* Caljic §8.78.

major problem in the California courts has been to determine when the defense of diminished capacity should apply. The defense was initially recognized in this first track of intentional homicide. In subsequent decisions it was extended, as we shall see, to the second track of homicide by excessive risk-taking.[50] The major unresolved problems are the extent to which the defense applies in cases of felony-murder (the third track of analysis)[51] and in non-homicidal offenses.

§4.2.3. **Premeditation and Deliberation.** In this first line of analysis, malice is implied unless the killing occurs under provocation or subject to a claim of diminished capacity. Thus the standard case of intentional homicide is murder. In many American jurisdictions, this standard form of murder is now called "murder in the second degree." For in these jurisdictions, it is possible for an intentional killing to meet a standard of aggravated murder called "murder in the first degree." As defined in a series of statutes first enacted in Pennsylvania in 1794,[52] the standard for this more egregious form of intentional killing is whether the murder was perpetrated with "premeditation and deliberation."[53] The historic function of this formula is determining whether the murder is sufficiently heinous to be subject to the extreme penalty of death.

In the tortuous history of homicide, planning and calculating the death of another have always stood out as a particularly heinous form of killing. Lying-in-wait and ambushing stood out even in the early English law as paradigmatic forms of murder.[54] The criteria of rational calculation were linked to the concept of malice aforethought.[55] Though this element of planning beforehand withered in the concept of malice, it was eventually to bloom

[50] People v. Poddar, 10 Cal. 3d 750, 518 P.2d 342, 111 Cal. Rptr. 910 (1974).

[51] See §4.4.7 *infra.*

[52] Act of April 22, 1794, 3 Smith Laws 187, §2 (current version at Pa. Cons. Stat. Ann. tit. 18, §2502(a)). See Keedy, *History of the Pennsylvania Statute Creating Degrees of Murder,* 97 U. Pa. L. Rev. 759 (1949).

[53] See generally LaFave & Scott 563–566; Perkins 91–93; Annot. 96 A.L.R.2d 1435 (1964).

[54] Kaye, *Early History of Murder and Manslaughter II,* 83 L.Q. Rev. 569, 574 (1967).

[55] *Id.* at 572.

again in the formula of "premeditation and deliberation." Yet the problem that has beset this formula is that while planning and calculating represent one form of heinous or cold-blooded murder, premeditation is not the only feature that makes intentional killings wicked. Wanton killings are generally regarded as among the most wicked, and the feature that makes a killing wanton is precisely the absence of detached reflection before the deed. Fitzjames Stephen put the case of a man who "sees a boy sitting on a bridge over a deep river and, out of mere wanton barbarity, pushes him into it and so drowns him."[56] Killing without a motive can usually be just as wicked as killing after detached reflection about one's goals. Thus there is obviously a flaw in the criterion of "premeditation and deliberation." It takes one of several grounds that are sufficient to treat a homicide as among the most wicked, and takes that one ground to be necessary to the exclusion of all others.

As a result of this flaw, the courts are constantly buffetted between two inconsistent pressures in their efforts to lend meaning to the concept of "premeditation." One thrust is to stress the elements of time, reflection and cold-bloodedness as the distinction between first- and second-degree murder. The competing thrust is to interpret the law so as to accommodate all heinous and wanton killings within the definition of first-degree murder. The former thrust leads to holdings such as People v. Anderson,[57] in which the California Supreme Court reversed a conviction for first-degree murder on the ground that the evidence was insufficient to indicate that the defendant had a motive, which, together with the manner of killing, would reveal prior reflection and deliberation about the deed.[58] This literal approach to the law is offset by other

[56] 3 Stephen 94.

[57] 70 Cal. 2d 15, 447 P.2d 942, 73 Cal. Rptr. 550 (1968).

[58] The court enumerated three categories of evidence that could support a finding of "premeditation and deliberation." These facts might bear on (1) what the defendant did prior to the killing, (2) the relationship with the victim, particularly as relates to the defendant's motive, and (3) the manner of the killing. On the basis of prior holdings, the court inferred that a first-degree murder conviction had to be supported either by strong evidence of item (1) or evidence of item (2), supplemented by (1) or (3). *Id.* at 26–27; 447 P.2d at 949, 73 Cal. Rptr. at 557. On the facts in *Anderson,* the court reasoned the evidence of (1) was ambiguous; therefore the

cases, in which courts stress that "no time is too short for a wicked man to frame in his mind the scheme of murder."[59]

The notion that some particular subjective condition is necessary to constitute first-degree murder has generated another version of the defense of diminished capacity. In this context, psychiatric testimony is admissible to prove that the defendant did not "premeditate and deliberate" as required under the definition of first-degree murder. The leading case is People v. Wolff,[60] in which the California Supreme Court reduced a conviction for murder in the first to one in the second degree. In the opinion of the psychiatric experts, the fifteen-year-old defendant, who killed his mother with an axe handle, could not "maturely and meaningfully reflect upon the gravity of his contemplated act. . . ."[61] The court held that the essential question in assessing "premeditation and deliberation" was not the duration but the "extent" of the antecedent reflection.[62] Focussing on the "extent" or "quality" of the reflection leads naturally to the view that a sufficient psychological impairment should prevent a conviction for first-degree murder.[63]

Though the test of "premeditation and deliberation" has been a standard feature of legislative gradings of homicide for the last one hundred years, its influence is likely to decline. The Model Penal Code rejected it[64] and the English, after thoughtful consideration,[65] refused to incorporate the concept in their approach to

---

burden of sustaining the verdict fell on (2) in combination with (3), which was found insufficient. *Id.* at 31–32, 447 P.2d at 952, 73 Cal. Rptr. at 561. This complex analysis has not found its way into standard jury instructions. *Cf.* Caljic §8.20.

[59] Commonwealth v. Carroll, 412 Pa. 525, 533; 194 A.2d 911, 916 (1963) (citing Commonwealth v. Drum, 58 Pa. 9, 16 (1868)); Sandoval v. People, 117 Colo. 588, 192 P.2d 423 (1948) (necessary that time be sufficient for "one thought to follow another").

[60] 61 Cal. 2d 795, 394 P.2d 959, 40 Cal. Rptr. 271 (1964).

[61] *Id.* at 821, 394 P.2d at 975, 40 Cal. Rptr. at 287.

[62] *Id.* at 821, 394 P.2d at 975, 40 Cal. Rptr. at 287. *Cf.* Caljic §8.20 ("the true test is not the duration of time, but the extent of the reflection").

[63] See Caljic §8.77 (1976 rev.) (Diminished capacity applies to reduce the homicide to one in the second degree as well as to manslaughter). See LaFave & Scott 328 n.16 for other authorities in accord.

[64] MPC §210.2.

[65] Royal Commission on Capital Punishment, Report 182–89 (1949–53).

the levels of homicide. The newly drafted criminal codes in the United States have tended to abandon the test.[66]

Two reasons for this shift are evident: first, after over a century of litigation, the courts have not been able to settle upon a consistent interpretation of the test;[67] and secondly, so far as the classification of murder into degrees was designed to isolate cases in which the death penalty was justified, that goal appears to be better served by listing the aggravating circumstances and mitigating considerations that bear on the gravity of a proven murder.[68] Indeed this approach is now constitutionally mandated in capital cases as the only medium for avoiding the vices of capricious sentencing,[69] on the one hand, and inflexible, mandatory sentencing, on the other.[70]

§4.2.4. **Intention in Homicide.** Thus far we have shown that the intent to kill provides an organizing principle for understanding a substantial body of the law of homicide. Intentional killings are ranked in ascending order from manslaughter, to second-degree murder, to first-degree murder. Moving up this scale of liability depends on the presence or absence of mitigating and aggravating factors—provocation, diminished capacity, premeditation and deliberation.

Yet we have done little along the way to clarify the concept of "intending to kill." The notion of intention, as contrasted with knowledge, recklessness and negligence, warrants consideration as a distinct topic and therefore will receive full consideration after we complete our survey of the patterns of liability and turn to the general principles applicable to all offenses.[71] At this juncture, it

[66] Conn. Gen. Stat. Ann. §53a–54; Del. Code tit. 11, §636; Ill. Ann. Stat. c. 38, §9–1; N.Y. Penal Law §125.27; N.D. Cent. Code §12.1–16–01; Pa. Cons. Stat. Ann. tit. 18, §2502; Tex. Penal Code §19.02; Wis. Stat. Ann. §940.01. Proposed Federal Criminal Code §1601. *But cf.* Colo. Rev. Stat. §18–3–102(a) ("premeditated intent").

[67] Michael & Wechsler, *A Rationale for the Law of Homicide,* 37 Colum. L. Rev. 701, 707–09 (1937).

[68] See MPC §210.6(3)–(4).

[69] See Furman v. Georgia, 408 U.S. 238 (1972).

[70] See the 1976 capital punishment decisions discussed *infra* §4.6.

[71] See §6.5 *infra*.

would be useful to highlight the ways in which intention in the context of homicide differs from its counterpart in the patterns of manifest and of subjective criminality.

In the pattern of manifest criminality, a challenge on the issue of intent functions to defease the implications of appearances; someone may act manifestly like a thief or appear unequivocally as though he were attempting a crime, when in fact he is not.[72] In the pattern of subjective criminality the requirement of intent similarly lends itself to clear analysis. In the subjective approach to the law of attempts, the intent required is always the intent to bring about the offense-in-chief. This means that the actor must have it as his conscious object to effectuate the elements of the offense. Similarly in treason prosecutions for giving aid and comfort to the enemy, the defendant must have the rendering of this aid and comfort as his purpose in acting. The significance of this way of framing the required intent becomes clear by contrast with the peculiar situation in homicide cases.

The distinguishing feature of causing death (or bodily injury or property damage) is that the harm is often the by-product of other activities. The recurrent problem that plagues the field of homicide is the case in which the actor engages in some other purposive activity and knows that there is a high risk that death might occur tangentially. The primary object might be criminal, as in committing sabotage on a military installation. Or it might be morally permissible, as in a physician's removing a cancerous uterus with the death of the fetus as the inevitable side-effect of the operation. These are both instances of the doctrine of double effect as refined by Catholic moralists.[73] There are two effects of the act: one desired and the other not. Though the doctrine of double effect holds that the undesired side-effect is not intended, the tendency of Anglo-American legal theory is to encompass both

[72] See §§3.1.1 and 3.3.3 *supra.*

[73] For divergent assessments of the doctrine of "double effect," see G. Williams, The Sanctity of Life and the Criminal Law 200–05 (1957); J. Noonan, The Morality of Abortion 48–49 (1970); Bennet, *Whatever the Consequences,* 26 Analysis 83 (1966); Finnis, *The Rights and Wrongs of Abortion,* 2 J. Phil. & Pub. Affairs 117 (1973).

effects within the ambit of intended killings.[74] This tendency in turn raises several difficult questions:

1. What is the minimal required probability that the side-effect will occur, in order to say that it is "intended"? Is a substantial certainty sufficient? Or need there be "practical" or "virtual" certainty that the harmful side-effect will accompany the primary object of the action?

2. If undesired side-effects are "intended," does it follow that the notion of "desire" is irrelevant to the analysis of the notion of intention?

3. If "desire" is irrelevant to the concept of intention, how do we distinguish intentionally causing from recklessly causing harm?

Even more important than the answer to these troublesome questions is the fact that the questions themselves are characteristic of the pattern of liability in homicide cases; the crimes of larceny, treason, attempt and fraud are not—except in unusual cases—committed as the by-product or as the side-effect of other activities.

The structure of the Model Penal Code bears out the view that these three questions are features of homicide, but not of offenses that we have classified in the patterns of manifest and of subjective liability. Larceny,[75] fraud,[76] treason,[77] inchoate offenses,[78] burglary[79]—all of these require "purposeful" rather than merely "knowing" commission of the offense. This means that the actor, in the language of the Code, must have the elements of the offense as his "conscious object."[80] In cases of homicide, in contrast, knowledge that death is a probable side-effect is sufficient for the

[74] See G. Williams, The Mental Element in Crime 24–25 (1965). LaFave & Scott 197.

[75] MPC §223.2.

[76] MPC §223.3.

[77] Treason is not defined in the MPC, but see §2.02, Comment at 125 (Tent. Draft No. 4, 1955), which identifies treason as a crime requiring "a purpose to aid the enemy."

[78] MPC §5.01 (attempts); §5.03 (conspiracy).

[79] MPC §221.1 (the entry must be with the "purpose to commit a crime therein").

[80] MPC §2.02(2)(a).

highest grade of liability.[81] Therefore, in the field of homicide, but not in the other two patterns of liability,[82] we encounter difficult issues about the required degree of probability and the relevance of desire to the required mental state.

The traditional relationship between malice and intention has tended to inhibit careful judicial elaboration of the notion of intentional killing. There are two other tracks for establishing malice, and one of them—highly reckless homicide—borders contiguously on the field of intentional homicide. If, despite his fervent wishes, a defendant kills by throwing a bomb or shooting into a crowded room, he could be liable for a malicious killing either under the tracks of intentional or highly reckless homicide. Whether his case fits precisely into one line of analysis or the other is usually not important. If the notion of intent were defined more restrictively, the slack would be picked up by a broader category of highly reckless homicide.[83]

§4.3. *Homicide by Excessive Risk-Taking.*

The second track for analyzing liability for homicide borders contiguously on the first. If the degree of certainty that death will occur is insufficient to think of the death as intentional, the party who created the risk may still be liable for manslaughter or murder. It all depends on the unacceptability of the risk and the actor's culpability in creating it.

There are three important factors in assessing the acceptability

[81] MPC §210.2(1)(a) (murder committed purposely or knowingly).

[82] The drafters of the code note, curiously, that "acting knowingly is ordinarily sufficient" [i.e., for most offenses]. MPC §2.02, Comment at 125 (Tent. Draft No. 4, 1955). The commentator to the code obviously had a different conception of the ordinary and routine. So far as the two patterns of liability discussed in Chapters One to Three *supra* make up the core of liability outside the field of homicide, the normal requirement is intention or purpose and not merely knowledge.

[83] Distinct problems affect the analysis of failing to avert death. These are taken up *infra* in §§8.1, 8.2.

and culpability of risk-taking. The first is the likelihood of causing death under the circumstances. If a worker throws a brick from the roof of a project, the likelihood of causing serious harm depends on how high the roof is, the number of people below, and the likelihood that people affected would take precautions such as wearing hard hats on the construction site. This is the dimension of risk-taking that we shall call the "gravity" of the risk. It is obvious that the graver the risk is, the more likely the actor will be held liable for manslaughter and even for murder in the event that the risk materializes in death. The utility of the risk is an equally important consideration. It is of little social value to throw a brick off a rooftop, but other grave risks are socially important. Consider a dangerous operation to save someone's life, or shooting in a crowd to prevent the escape of a felon known to be armed and dangerous. These are cases of grave risks that are offset by counterbalancing benefits. Those who take socially beneficial risks deserve commendation rather than punishment, and therefore it is axiomatic that if the benefit of the risk outweighs the likely harm, there should be no criminal liability. Criminal liability for the result of excessive risks presupposes that the risk be both grave and socially detrimental.

A third factor in the analysis is the actor's awareness of the risk being run, yet in the literature on this point there is a great deal of confusion; writers rarely take pains to distinguish the aspects of the risk of which the actor might be aware. It is important to note the differences among the following aspects of a risk about which the actor might be ignorant or mistaken: (1) whether there is a risk at all, (2) the gravity of the risk, (3) the benefits of the risk, or (4) whether as a matter of social judgment, the costs of the risk outweigh its benefits. The best way to proceed in the analysis of risks is to inquire, first, whether if the actor knew of all the risks implicit in his conduct, the risk would be socially undesirable; if it is, then we might inquire about whether the actor's ignorance or mistake will provide an excuse for taking an undesirable, impermissible risk.

The subject of mistakes in risk-taking is taken up in our general analysis of excuses.[1] For now, we should note the profound difference between being mistaken about whether there is a risk at all and being mistaken about whether the benefits of the risk outweigh its costs. An example of the former would be driving at night, totally unaware that the headlights were not working; an example of the latter would be experimenting with a novel method of medical cure in the belief that the possible benefit outweighed the risk to the patient.[2] The latter mistake is tantamount to a good-faith mistake about the legality of one's conduct, for the mistake relates to the legal permissibility of the risk.[3] The former mistake is more properly thought of as a problem of inadvertence rather than a case of misjudgment in good faith. In both cases, the problem is analyzing the extent to which we can fairly expect that people avoid the type of mistake involved. Culpability for inadvertence might appropriately require an analysis different from culpability for good-faith misjudgments about the legality of risk-taking.

These three dimensions of culpability for risk-taking are suggested in the Model Penal Code's definitions of acting recklessly and negligently. With respect to the gravity and utility of risks, the code uses the term "substantial and unjustified risk" to cover both instances of recklessness and negligence. Taking a risk of death does not even raise a question of liability unless the risk is "substantial"; and further, there is no liability unless the social costs outweigh the benefits of the risk and therefore render it "unjustified." The difference between reckless and negligent risk-taking arises at the level of the actor's awareness of the impermissible risk. In cases of recklessness,[4] the actor "disregards" the risk; in cases of negligence,[5] he fails "to perceive it." In neither is the disregard or the failure to perceive sufficient, by itself, to qualify the

§4.3. [1] See §§9.1.1 and 9.2.3 *infra*.

[2] See Commonwealth v. Pierce, 138 Mass. 165, 54 Am. Rep. 264 (1884).

[3] This point is developed further in Fletcher, *The Theory of Criminal Negligence: A Comparative Analysis*, 119 U. Pa. L. Rev. 401, 431–32 (1971).

[4] MPC §2.02(2)(c).

[5] MPC §2.02(2)(d).

conduct as reckless or negligent. In addition, the disregard or failure to perceive must be a gross deviation from a specified standard of conduct. In cases of recklessness, this standard is identified with the projected conduct of a "law-abiding person"; in cases of negligence, with the conduct of a "reasonable person in the actor's situation." If there is a reason for this shift, it is that the culpability of disregarding a risk derives from a conscious departure from a level of legally permissible risk-taking. In contrast, the culpability of failing to perceive the risk derives not from the choice to violate a legal imperative, but from the failure to meet reasonable standards of attentiveness.

There is one other feature of these definitions that bears notice. They both are designed to apply to cases of mistakes about attendant circumstances as well as to the mistakes involved in causing harm. Thus a mistake in a statutory rape case about whether the girl is over the minimum age of consent would be analyzed under the same criteria of recklessness and negligence, depending on whether the local law requires that the actor be merely negligent or reckless about the age of the girl. It is misleading, as we shall see later,[6] to blend these two kinds of mistakes into one conceptual mold. In our analysis of homicide, we shall be concerned only about the risks of causing harm, not the risk that the world (e.g., the age of the girl) is different from what one thinks it is. Apart from this point of overinclusiveness, the Model Penal Code definitions are elegantly and carefully drawn and deserve to guide our analysis of homicidal liability for excessive risk-taking.

§4.3.1. Liability for Manslaughter. It is well recognized that excessive risk-taking can generate liability for what is inaptly called "involuntary" manslaughter.[7] The major dispute in the case law is about the terminology for defining the threshold of liability. The traditional view is that mere negligence, sufficient for tort lia-

[6] See §6.6.6 *infra*.

[7] This usage is simply an archaic way of referring to "unintentional homicide." *Cf.* Code Pénal §319 (*homicide involontaire*).

bility for wrongful death, is not enough to support liability for manslaughter.[8] This attitude toward the tort standard of negligence seems to be stimulated by the feeling that the concept of negligence, as interpreted in civil cases, is fitted to the conduct of a reasonable person and thus fails to attend to the actual culpability of the defendant.[9] Presumably to compensate for this defect, Anglo-American criminal courts have traditionally demanded either gross negligence[10] or conduct that is "indifferent to risks"[11] or even "wanton and reckless" conduct.[12] There are some writers who are even opposed to punishing homicide on the ground that moral culpability presupposes the conscious disregard of a known risk.[13] Some support for this view is to be found in the *Welansky* decision in Massachusetts, which holds that the actor must at least know of the facts that constitute the risk.[14] The argument against punishing negligence is curious, for it suggests that inadvertence—merely being inattentive to a grave and unjustified risk—cannot properly be regarded as culpable. If ignorance were never culpable, we would face some rather serious difficulties in assessing the excuse of mistake of law.[15] In our daily interaction with other people, we expect friends and associates to remember appointments and to be

[8] At an early stage of development, all acts causing death were punishable. See the analysis §4.4.1 *infra*.

[9] The general subject of objectivity and subjectivity in the theory of negligence is taken up in §6.8 *infra*.

[10] Caljic §8.90(1) (vehicle manslaughter-felony); D. Aaronson, Maryland Criminal Jury Instructions and Commentary §413, at 121 (1975). See generally Riesenfeld, *Negligent Homicide: A Study in Statutory Interpretation*, 25 Calif. L. Rev. 1, 37–40 (1936); R. Moreland, A Rationale of Criminal Negligence 9 (1944) (identifying "gross negligence" as the majority rule of the time).

[11] Andrews v. Director of Public Prosecutions, [1937] 2 All E.R. 522 (H.L.).

[12] Commonwealth v. Welansky, 316 Mass. 383, 55 N.E.2d 902 (1944).

[13] See Hall, *Negligent Behavior Should Be Excluded from Penal Liability*, 63 Colum. L. Rev. 632 (1963), criticized in Fletcher, *supra* note 3, at 416. A more plausible case against punishing negligent homicide would build on Herbert Morris' theory of punishment, see his *Persons and Punishment* in H. Morris, On Guilt and Innocence 31 (1976). The argument would be that inadvertently negligent actors do not arrogate to themselves benefits denied to others and therefore do not deserve to be punished.

[14] See note 12 *supra*.

[15] The theory of mistake of law as an excuse is discussed at length in §9.4 *infra*.

attentive to the impact of their behavior on our lives. If inattentiveness is a fault in social interaction, it is not implausible for inattentiveness to the creation of risks to constitute a form of culpability in the criminal law.

Although doubts remain about the culpability of inadvertent negligence, the trend of the last 40 years has been to expand liability for negligent killing. The movement began in the 1920s and 30s with newly legislated offenses of negligent homicide in the driving of a motor vehicle.[16] The standard of liability was ordinary negligence and the punishment less than that prescribed for involuntary manslaughter. The Model Penal Code then recommended a general offense of negligent homicide,[17] punished less severely than manslaughter.[18] Yet in the adaptation of this provision in state penal reforms, the general pattern has been to qualify the required negligence as "criminal negligence."[19] The tension in the punishability of negligent homicide persists, and it is doubtful that it can be resolved without an adequate theoretical assessment of the culpability of negligent conduct.[20]

§4.3.2. **Liability for Murder.** There appear to be at least three different ways of reaching the conclusion that excessive risk-taking is motivated by malice, and that a resulting death caused thereby should be treated as murder rather than manslaughter. One approach is to translate the concept of malice into highly judgmental language that invites the jury to ponder whether the risk-creating activity is so heinous that it should be adjudged murder. One statutory formula colorfully states the issue to be whether the defend-

[16] See generally Riesenfeld, *supra* note 10. *Cf.* Road Traffic Act 1960, c. 16, §1 (causing death by reckless or dangerous driving).

[17] MPC §210.4.

[18] The recommended maximum for negligent homicide (a felony in the third degree) is five years imprisonment, MPC §6.06(3); for manslaughter (a felony in the second degree), ten years, MPC §6.06(2). *Cf.* Road Traffic Act 1960, c. 16, §1 (maximum penalty five years imprisonment).

[19] Colo. Rev. Stat. §18–3–105; Conn. Gen. Stat. §53a–58; Del. Code tit. 11, §631; N.Y. Penal Law §125.10; Texas Penal Code §19.07.

[20] For efforts in this direction *see* Fletcher, *supra* note 3; Note, *Negligence and the General Problem of Criminal Responsibility*, 81 Yale L.J. 949 (1972); H. L. A. Hart, Punishment and Responsibility, c. 6 (1968).

ant was motivated by "an abandoned and malignant heart." Though this formula appears on the books in California,[21] the courts have rejected it and substituted another formula that is equally judgmental; the California jury is instructed today to inquire whether the defendant "for a base, anti-social motive and with wanton disregard of human life" did an act "that involved a high degree of probability that it would result in death."[22] The Model Penal Code favors another formula that evokes the same concern about the moral gravity of the risk-creating act: reckless homicide should be classified as murder if the risk-creating act is committed under circumstances "manifesting extreme indifference to the value of human life."[23] The cases that juries tend to classify as murder under these formulae are those of killing by socially useless, dangerous activities. These are cases in which the defendant shoots into a house, at a train, or at a moving car with knowledge that he is thereby endangering human beings.[24] In one leading case of the last century,[25] the drunken defendant threw a tumbler at his wife who was then carrying an oil lamp. The blow caused the lamp to catch fire, which then spread to the woman, eventually causing her death. The critical feature of these cases is not only the high probability of harm and the indifference to human life, but the absence of any redeeming social value to the conduct. If a death occurs as a result of excessive risk-taking in the course of socially acceptable activity, such as motor traffic or sporting activity, the killing would most likely be classified as manslaughter rather than murder.[26]

A second approach to the problem of classification, probably more common in the United States than elsewhere, is to treat all

[21] Cal. Penal Code §188.

[22] Caljic §8.31.

[23] MPC §210.2(1)(b).

[24] E.g., People v. Jernatowski, 238 N.Y. 188, 144 N.E. 497 (1924) (crowded room); Banks v. State, 85 Tex. Crim. 165, 211 S.W. 217 (1919) (moving train); Wiley v. State, 19 Ariz. 346, 170 P. 869 (1918) (moving car).

[25] Mayes v. People, 106 Ill. 306 (1883).

[26] But if the deaths are caused by drunk driving, the killings may well be treated as murder, e.g., State v. Trott, 190 N.C. 674, 130 S.E. 627 (1925); State v. Weltz, 155 Minn. 143, 193 N.W. 42 (1923).

killings with deadly weapons presumptively as murder, with the burden on the accused to prove that the crime should be mitigated to manslaughter. This is a variation on the mode of harm-oriented analysis that prevailed in the common law at least up to the time of Blackstone. In an illustrative case,[27] tried under the former Delaware Code, it appeared on the evidence that the defendant was alone in a room with the victim and that he fired a shot, which ricochetted off the bed frame and killed the victim. The defendant claimed that he fired merely with the intent to frighten the victim, which claim was obviously supported by the fact that he did not fire directly at her. Nonetheless he was convicted of murder and the conviction was affirmed. The court did not clarify the concept of malice and preferred to rest its decision on the ground that the burden of proof was on the defendant to show that the gravity of the killing should be mitigated. Though this way of thinking has considerable support in the classic common-law texts, it is now unconstitutional in the United States to require the defendant to disprove malice, even if by only a preponderance of the evidence.[28] In the future, courts will have to think more about the criteria distinguishing murder from manslaughter in cases of risk-taking. It is likely that the approach represented by California and the Model Penal Code will become more attractive as the path for sidestepping the constitutional infirmities of presuming malice and shifting the burden of persuasion.

A third and distinct approach to homicide by excessive risk-taking has crystallized in the English case law. The English appear totally to reject a line of analysis based upon excessive risk-taking. Instead, English judges have approached the problem by redefining the intent or knowledge required for murder. In *Vickers,* the defendant beat up and thus caused the death of an old lady who

[27] Brinkley v. State, 233 A.2d 56 (Del. Sup. 1967).

[28] *Compare* Mullaney v. Wilbur, 421 U.S. 684 (1975) (unconstitutional to require defendant to negate malice with proof of provocation) *with* Patterson v. New York, 432 U.S. 197 (1977) (if state renames provocation "extreme emotional distress" and eliminates the concept of malice, state may shift burden of persuasion to the defendant). See generally §§7.1 through 7.3 *infra.*

attempted to prevent his carrying out a burglary.[29] He was convicted under an instruction that the killing was murder "if done with the intent to do her grievous bodily harm."[30] The lowering of the harm that need be intended (i.e., from death to grievous bodily harm) is part of a complex technique for avoiding a separate track of proving murder on the basis of excessive risk-taking with a "base, anti-social purpose." Though parallel ventures are observable in some American jurisdictions,[31] this technique has been pursued with greatest vigor in the English courts.

The flaw in this alternative to homicide by excessive risk-taking is that the standard of an intent to inflict grievous bodily harm is both overinclusive and underinclusive. It is overinclusive so far as it encompasses cases where there is no culpability or malice relative to the risk of death. One can imagine a case in which the victim was subjected to a controlled, but coercive medical operation to deprive him, say, of a kidney that would be transplanted to someone else. If by unanticipated accident, the victim should die in the operation, the kidney thieves would be guilty of murder. The intent to deprive someone of a kidney presumably constitutes the intent to inflict grievous bodily harm. Under both the California test and the Model Penal Code, it would be more difficult to establish liability for murder, for the conduct of those inflicting the controlled medical operation hardly manifests an attitude of indifference to human life. It is undoubtedly reprehensible to commit an assault with the intent to do grievous bodily harm, yet the wickedness of the assault relates to causing grievous bodily harm, not to the evil of causing death.

The problem that has been of more concern to the English courts is the underinclusiveness of the test. There are many cases of killing that appear arguably to be with malice, yet there is no intent to inflict grievous bodily harm. Indeed, in none of the cases noted above, in which American courts have convicted of murder, is there clear proof of an intent to inflict grievous bodily harm.

[29] Regina v. Vickers, [1957] 2 Q.B. 664 (Crim. App.).
[30] *Id.* at 672.
[31] LaFave & Scott 540 n.2.

The approach that the English courts have taken to correct this perceived underinclusiveness is highly instructive of the orientation of English criminal law. Instead of fashioning judgmental language that would underscore the moral issue at stake in distinguishing between murder and manslaughter, the English judges have preferred to extend the concept of malice by introducing the standard of the reasonable person. Thus in *Ward*,[32] the court confirmed a conviction of murder against a man who, disturbed by a baby's crying, killed the baby by shaking it with full strength. Yet there was no evidence that the defendant intended to inflict any harm, not to mention grievous bodily harm. Nor was the defendant apparently aware of the risk that shaking the baby might result in death. The jury was instructed to decide whether the accused "must as a reasonable man have contemplated that death or grievous bodily harm was likely to result. . . ."[33] Presumably a reasonable person would have realized that shaking the baby so hard might cause grievous bodily harm, and this was sufficient to induce the jury to convict. The appellate court was unimpressed by the oddity of convicting Ward on the ground that some mythical person would have realized that shaking the baby was dangerous. Of course, Ward might also have been convicted of murder under the standard used in California or recommended by the Model Penal Code. The virtue of these latter tests is that they focus directly on the moral quality of the accused's conduct, rather than on the conduct of a hypothetical person.

Integrating the reasonable person into the concept of malice produced a major crisis in the English law of homicide. In 1960 the House of Lords approved a test like that used in *Ward* in a case in which a suspect attempted to shake a policeman from his car by accelerating rapidly; as it turned out, the policeman was thrown from the car and killed by oncoming traffic.[34] The additional disquieting feature of the case is that the defendant Smith was sentenced to death. If his act of killing was murder, it met the test

[32] Regina v. Ward, [1956] 1 Q.B. 351 (Crim. App.).
[33] *Id.* at 352.
[34] Director of Public Prosecutions v. Smith, [1961] A.C. 290 (H.L. 1960).

of capital murder set forth in the Homicide Act of 1957. The English legal community was outraged by a man's being sentenced to death who, according to the evidence, did not intend even to inflict grievous bodily harm.[35]

Most of the debate about Smith's conviction centered on the merits and demerits of an objective approach to the concept of malice. In using the term "objective" the writers apparently referred to any approach that turns on the hypothetical behavior of a reasonable person. English lawyers were obviously more disturbed by the introduction of the reasonable person into the analysis of malice than they were about the retention of that hypothetical person in the standard of provocation.[36] Of course, both the issues of intent and provocation relate to the proof of the same issue of malice. Yet the issue of intent has come to be more closely associated with the prosecutor's case, while the concept of provocation is still thought of as a defense in mitigation. Weakening the intent requirement by inquiring what a reasonable person would have intended under the circumstances apparently went too far. In 1967, Parliament intervened with a statute prescribing that the jury must decide whether the accused himself "intended or foresaw the result" of his conduct.[37]

In 1974 the contours of malice again became the subject of dispute before the House of Lords. In Hyam v. Director of Public Prosecutions,[38] the defendant, a woman jilted by her lover for another woman, set fire to the house where the other woman lived with her children. When she poured gasoline in the letter box and ignited it, her intention, she claimed, was merely to frighten the woman into leaving the neighborhood. As it turned out, the ensuing fire killed two of the woman's children who were then in the house. Ms. Hyam was convicted of murder on an instruction that held it sufficient for malice that the accused knew, when she set fire to the house, "that it was highly probable that she would

[35] See, e.g., Williams, *Constructive Malice Revived,* 23 Mod. L. Rev. 605 (1962); Cross, *The Need for a Redefinition of Murder,* 1960 Crim. L. Rev. 728.

[36] *Cf.* discussion *supra* §4.2.1.

[37] Criminal Justice Act 1967, c. 80, §8.

[38] Hyam v. Director of Public Prosecutions, [1974] 2 All E.R. 41.

cause . . . serious bodily harm."[39] After losing on appeal, Ms. Hyam took her case to the House of Lords.

The five opinions of the Lords merit detailed attention. In their style they are a model of careful legal analysis and craftsmanship; and in their substance they illustrate how far the English law of homicide has come to diverge from the pattern exemplified by the Model Penal Code and the case law of California. In the end, the Lords affirmed the conviction, three votes to two, but only after a highly sophisticated set of disquisitions on the mental state required for murder under English law. All of the judges started from the assumption that the jury properly found that Ms. Hyam knew that her conduct would probably result in grievous bodily harm. The question was whether this mental state was sufficient to constitute malice under the accepted definition of murder.

In order to appreciate the variety of ways in which the issue in *Hyam* might be framed, it is important to distinguish among four states of mind at the time of the killing:[40]

A. An intent to kill.
B. An intent to cause grievous bodily harm.
C. Knowledge that the act would probably cause death.
D. Knowledge that the act would probably cause grievous bodily harm.

The problem of murder under English law is that there are two distinct sets of questions that may be asked about these four states of mind as well as variations of these four. The first question is: Which of these is properly regarded as a form of intentional harm? The second question is: Which of these four (and their variations) are sufficient to constitute malice in the sense required for murder. These two questions interweave in the five opinions of the Lords and compound the complexity of the debate.

[39] *Ibid.*

[40] This analysis of malice into four states of knowledge was initially devised by Fitzjames Stephen in F. Stephen, Digest of the Criminal Law §223(a)–(b) (1877); *id.* §233(c)–(d) covers the field now called "constructive" malice, namely the intent to commit a felony and the intent to use force against a police officer. These latter elements of Stephen's analysis of malice were expressly abolished by Homicide Act 1957, c. 11, §1.

In the leading opinion supporting conviction, Lord Hailsham of St. Marylebone takes the position that the notion of intentional harm is conceptually connected with malice. The intent may be either to kill or to inflict grievous bodily harm, but intent there must be.[41] This is a nominal departure from the body of American law supporting conviction for murder in cases of excessive and wanton risk-taking.[42] It is not that Lord Hailsham considered and rejected the American approach to malice. He assumed that there were only two possibilities: (1) either an intent to harm was necessary for malice, or (2) "foresight of [harmful] consequences could be sufficient for malice." Any test based solely on knowledge or foresight would be defective, Lord Hailsham reasoned, for it would encompass cases in which the actor takes risks for a commendable motive. The hypothetical case that concerned him is that of the surgeon who operates, knowing that there is a high risk of death. It is clear that the surgeon should not be liable for homicide if death results. To account for this intuitive judgment, Lord Hailsham argues: "It is the absence of intention to kill or cause grievous bodily harm which absolves the heart surgeon in the case of the transplant. . . ."[43]

The structure of Lord Hailsham's argument is important. The standard of "foresight" does not account for a difficult case in which our intuitions tell us that there ought to be no liability for murder. Therefore the alternative—that there is no intent—is the only possible explanation for denying liability. What this argument overlooks is all the other possibilities for explaining our intuitions in the surgeon's case. Both the California and Model Penal Code tests of high-risk homicide would exclude the surgeon or anyone else who takes socially justifiable risks for a commendable motive.

Whatever the logic of his argument, Lord Hailsham concluded that the essence of malice consists either in an intent to kill or an intent to do grievous bodily harm. Then, in a perspicacious segment of the opinion, he proceeds to analyze the concept of in-

[41] [1974] 2 All E.R. at 52-54.
[42] See text at notes 24-25 *supra.*
[43] [1974] 2 All E.R. at 54.

tention. He argues first that inevitable side-effects, though not desired, should be included within the scope of intention.[44] If a man places a bomb on an airplane for the sake of collecting insurance money, he should be held to have intended any death that might result from the explosion. Yet it does not follow that all probable side-effects, even those appreciated to a substantial certainty, should be included. Therefore, it would not accord with Lord Hailsham's intuitions to hold that Ms. Hyam's knowing that the burning would probably cause grievous bodily harm was equivalent to her intending to do great bodily harm. From the analysis thus far it seems that Lord Hailsham was laying the groundwork for a vote against conviction. Yet in its denouement, the conceptual analysis shifts and sweeps up the activity of Ms. Hyam.

The *deus ex machina,* needed to sanctify the conviction, comes in further elaboration of the concept of intending grievous bodily harm. The spirit of intending is captured, argues Lord Hailsham, by "decid[ing] to expose potential victims to the risk of death or really serious injury."[45] Or, in slightly different language: "deliberately [doing an act] which exposes a victim to the risk of probably grievous bodily harm."[46] This language appears merely to reintroduce the standard of knowledge of probable consequences under another name. Yet there are two important differences: first, that the risk must be aimed at a particular person;[47] and secondly, that there be "no lawful excuse for the creation of the risk,"[48] that is, the risk must be run "regardless of the consequences."[49] Under this interpretation of what it means to intend grievous bodily harm, Ms. Hyam was properly convicted. She willfully exposed a particular person to the risk and, further, she acted "without lawful excuse" and "regardless of the consequences."

It is important to note how this analysis of intending differs from the California test for murder by excessive risk-taking. The

[44] *Id.* at 52.
[45] *Id.* at 55.
[46] *Ibid.*
[47] *Id.* at 54.
[48] *Id.* at 55.
[49] *Ibid.*

second factor pertaining to "lawful excuse" and the attitude toward consequences run parallel to the language in the California instruction that the risk must be created "for a base, anti-social motive . . . with wanton disregard of human life."[50] The phraseology in California is a little more flamboyant, perhaps in keeping with cultural differences between Hollywood and London. Yet it is unlikely that any case would qualify under the California test that would fail under this aspect of Lord Hailsham's analysis.

The distinguishing feature of Lord Hailsham's test is the limitation of malicious killing to cases of exposing a particular person to danger. It would follow from a strict application of this test that all the cases of shooting into a house, train or moving car known to be occupied would not qualify as killings with malice. Although there is a high risk of death and although the person shoots "with a wanton disregard of human life," the danger is not aimed at a specific person. Perhaps these cases of wanton shooting should not constitute murder so far as murder requires an intent to kill or do grievous bodily harm. Lord Hailsham may well be right that the notion of intentionally harming another person presupposes that there be a conscious objective of subjecting a particular person to peril. Yet the fallacy, as we have already noted, derives from assuming that only cases of intentional conduct can amount to malice. Lord Hailsham's analysis leads us to the unsatisfactory view that it is not murder to cause death by shooting into a house without thinking whether it was occupied, but it is murder to cause a totally unexpected death by punching a known "victim" in the nose.

A consistent application of Lord Hailsham's line of reasoning would lead one to question the sufficiency of an intent "to do grievous bodily harm" in the analysis of malice. The required intent should be one that relates to the risk of death, not the risk of bodily injury. This indeed is Lord Diplock's position in dissent.[51] In a carefully reasoned analysis of the sources and of the Homicide Act of 1957, Lord Diplock concluded that the minimum intent required for murder is the intent to cause a bodily injury which is

[50] See the discussion at *supra* note 22.
[51] [1974] 2 All E.R. at 62–69.

known to the offender to be likely to endanger life. That the actor intends grievous bodily harm would not be enough. This narrower standard would have led to a reduction of Ms. Hyam's conviction to manslaughter, for there was insufficient evidence that she intentionally inflicted an injury that she knew was dangerous to human life. This view advanced by Lord Diplock nearly carried the day.[52] Yet Lord Cross of Chelsea cast the decisive vote for conviction,[53] apparently on the ground that *Vickers*[54] has survived the legislative reform of 1957 and therefore supported the sufficiency of an intent to do grievous bodily harm to convict of murder.

Hyam is the high-water mark of a current that has run long in English law. For the last one hundred years, commentators and judges have sought to reduce malice to specific states of intending and knowing.[55] This is but an example of a more general effort to cleanse the criminal law of its normative overtones.[56] But the normative dimension of malice cannot long remain suppressed. It reenters the analysis in qualifying phrases such as "without lawful excuse" and acting "regardless of the consequences."[57] If the distinction between manslaughter and murder turns on the gravity of the deed, then an adequate legal test must call our attention to the moral issue that makes murder the more heinous way of killing.

§4.4. *Formal Criteria of Liability.*

In the preceding two tracks for analyzing the degrees for criminal homicide, the inquiry focussed on a variety of criteria related to the actor's state of mind and self-control. Thus we have taken up the issues of intent to kill, provocation, diminished capacity, pre-

[52] Lord Diplock was joined by Lord Kilbrandon, *id.* at 72.
[53] *Id.* at 70.
[54] See the discussion of Vickers *supra* at notes 26–27.
[55] The process began with Stephen's account of malice. See note 40 *supra*.
[56] Compare the efforts to reduce *mens rea* to a question of fact, §6.2.1 *infra*.
[57] See text at notes 48–49 *supra*.

meditation and deliberation, negligent and reckless homicide. What remains for consideration is a variety of criteria for assessing homicide that are purely formal. These do not focus on the state of mind of the accused, nor do they require a particularized assessment of personal culpability and the circumstances of the killing.

These formal criteria inform the analysis of manslaughter and the two degrees of murder, at least as the law of homicide is still framed in most American jurisdictions. According to rules that developed late in the common law, liability for manslaughter should attach to killings that occur in the course of committing a misdemeanor; liability for murder should attach to killings that occur in the course of felonies. In addition, some state statutes have introduced formal criteria for determining when murder is first-degree murder. According to the California Penal Code, for example, liability in the first degree attaches to all murder "perpetrated by means of a destructive device or explosive, poison, lying-in-wait [or] torture. . . ."[1] These four means of killing arguably provide a formal basis for classifying murder as one in the first degree without assessing the actor's actual culpability.

All of these formal tests stand in constant tension with the first two tracks for establishing the level of the homicide. A homicide might not qualify under either of the first two approaches as even manslaughter, and yet arguably come out as first-degree murder under these formal standards. Consider an accidental killing in the course of driving from the scene of a robbery. In the absence of an intent to kill and of excessive risk-taking, the killing would not even meet the threshold of manslaughter under the first two tracks. Yet it would be punished as first-degree murder committed in the course of a robbery. Or consider the case of someone who stores a bomb in his garage. Some neighborhood kids break into the garage and, playing with the bomb, they manage to detonate it. If the kids are killed in the explosion, the possessor of the bomb might arguably be held for first-degree murder by means of an explosive device.[2]

§4.4. [1] Cal. Penal Code §189.
[2] As to whether this would be the outcome, see §4.4.6 *infra*.

The formal tests of liability are obviously overinclusive. If taken literally, they extend to many cases of killing that are not as culpable as those identified as manslaughter or murder under the first two tracks of liability. As a result, the overwhelming trend of the law is either to abolish these formal tests or to narrow them to minimize their overinclusiveness.[3] The study of these criteria, therefore, is the study of a style of analysis that is in retreat.

§4.4.1. **The Historical Background.** It is important to be clear about the historical foundation for the emergence of formal tests geared to unlawful conduct. The common law of criminal homicide began with the principle that all people who cause death, whether intentionally or accidentally, are liable for murder. By the thirteenth century, this presumptive liability was subject to royal pardons as a matter of course if the killing occurred accidentally *(per infortunium)* or under the necessity of self-preservation *(se defendendo)*.[4] The early reference to malice served not as a way of making out an affirmative case of murder, but as a formula for expressing the absence of one of these two excusing conditions. The recognition of the excuse of misadventure was expressed by saying that the killing was not *per malitiam excogitatim*.[5] Insanity also provided a basis for a royal pardon, though the proof of insanity was not thought of as an excuse parallel to the other two.[6] This was obviously a simplified structure of criminal homicide, which lacked the crime of manslaughter, the degrees of murder, and all the complexities we have considered. The only issue was whether

[3] See, e.g., Colo. Rev. Stat. §18-3-102(1)(b) & (2)(a)-(f) (felony-murder narrowed by providing a six-element affirmative defense); N.Y. Penal Law §125.25(3) (similar four-element affirmative defense); Del. Code Ann. tit. 11, §636 (felony-murder abolished; recklessness or negligence required). *Cf.* Homicide Act 1957, c. 11, §1 (felony-murder abolished).

[4] The critical development was the Statute of Gloucester, 6 Edw. I, c. 9 (1290). Foster argues that even before this statutory regulation of the pardon, "no man was in danger of death in these cases." Foster 282. See generally Kaye, *The Early History of Murder and Manslaughter*, 83 L.Q. Rev. 365, 569 (1967). N. Hurnard, The King's Pardon for Homicide 68–108 (1969).

[5] Kaye, *supra* note 4, at 373.

[6] On royal pardons for infants and the insane, see Hurnard, *supra* note 4, at 152–170. In clear cases of insanity, the judges, even at an early date, acquitted the defendant. *Id.* at 164–66.

the act of the accused caused death; if so, his life was spared if he could make out a case of *per infortunium* or *se defendendo*.[7]

Until the mid-eighteenth century, the problem of killing in the course of an unlawful act was always considered as a rejoinder to the defensive claim of accidental killing. The principle recognized in Coke,[8] Hale,[9] and Hawkins[10] was that the excuse of *per infortunium* was not available to someone whose hands were soiled by an accident's occurring in the course of an unlawful act. It is not implausible to deny an excuse to someone who has acted wrongfully in creating the situation in which the excuse must be asserted. Indeed, this is the principle underlying the general rejection of voluntary intoxication as a defense. The wrongful act of becoming intoxicated in a situation where one might commit a crime is regarded as a plausible ground for not considering the impact of intoxication or the actor's culpability at the time of the act.

It is important to see the limits of this analogy between rejecting intoxication as a defense and rejecting inevitable accident as a defense. Suppose that the accused commits a rape while intoxicated. We then have the following structure of assertion and response:

1. Prima facie crime	Rape
2. Excuse	Intoxication
3. Rejoinder to the excuse	It should not be recognized because the intoxication was voluntary and wrongful.

In the classical harm-oriented analysis of criminal homicide, the comparable structure is the following:

1. Prima facie case	Causing death (murder)

[7] *But cf.* Bracton 136d which expresses a contemporary emphasis on the subjective side of homicide ("In crimes the intention is regarded, not the result").

[8] 3 Coke 56.

[9] 1 Hale 475.

[10] 1 Hawkins 112; but see the interpretation of Hawkins at notes 22–26 *infra*.

2. Excuse	*Per infortunium*
3. Rejoinder to the excuse	Accident occurred in the course of a voluntary and unlawful act

The principle that causing death states a prima facie case of murder obviously diverges from the premises underlying the first two tracks of analysis, each of which starts on the assumption of the act-oriented approach that causing death is innocent unless additional factors (such as intent to kill, the taking of excessive risk) are adduced to create an affirmative case for liability. In drawing the analogy between intoxication and the unlawful act, we must reason in the harm-oriented mode, that is, the mode that takes all questions of culpability as matters of excuse to be raised by the defendant. Though the general style of analysis has shifted from the harm-oriented to the act-oriented approach, the impact of the death's occurring in an unlawful act has retained its original force. What was once a theory for rejecting an excuse has become a formal test of liability. In the discussion that follows we shall attempt to document how this transformation took place. By explicating the shift from the denial of *per infortunium* as an excuse to a formal test of liability, we might hope to gain the understanding necessary for resolving the tension between formal tests of liability and the more limited lines of liability geared to intentional killing and excessive risk-taking.

Prior to the emergence of manslaughter as a separate offense,[11] the implications of denying the excuse were straightforward: the crime remained murder. Even after the crystallization of manslaughter as the lower crime, Lord Coke held to the view that the denial of *per infortunium* implied that the killing was murder.[12] It is significant that in picking an example of an unlawful act, Coke turned away from arson, robbery, and the dangerous felonies and

[11] The distinction between murder and manslaughter was settled in the late sixteenth century, see Kaye, *supra* note 4, at 587–601. The earliest reported verdict of manslaughter is said to be Salisbury's Case, reported in E. Plowden, Les Commentaries f. 100 (1578). See Green, *The Jury and the English Law of Homicide, 1200–1600,* 74 Mich. L. Rev. 413, 484 (1976).

[12] 3 Coke 56.

instead picked the homely example of shooting a deer in the park belonging to another. "If by glance of the arrow," Coke tells us, the actor "killeth a boy that is hidden in the bush: this is murder."[13] There is no indication that shooting in a park belonging to another was a felony. Nor did it matter in Coke's analysis whether the "unlawful act" was a felony or simply a wrongful trespass. Either would have been sufficient to deny a claim of excuse to the party causing death. It is significant, further, that this discussion appears in the chapter devoted to variations of criminal homicide[14] rather than in the chapter on murder. It bears no relation to Coke's discussion on the criteria either of murder or of malice aforethought.[15]

It is abundantly clear from the text that Coke did not think of the "unlawful act" doctrine as a basis for establishing malice, expressed, implied, or any other variety. If he had been so concerned, he would have framed an example of killing in the course of a dangerous felony. In the section on malice, he does refer to a robber's killing a victim who resists as an example of implied malice.[16] Yet this inference of malice is in no way formal or constructive, and there is no intimation that Coke sees a connection between the robber's killing a resisting victim and the doctrine of the unlawful act as a basis for denying the applicability of *per infortunium* as an excuse.

When Hale picked up the discussion later in the same century, the beginnings of a new way of thinking became evident. Repeating the example of shooting at a deer and killing a boy, Hale reasoned that the killing should be classified merely as manslaughter.[17] The logic of this conclusion is not clear, for if the excuse is denied, the crime should presumably be murder.[18] This is obviously the

[13] *Ibid.*

[14] Suicide, forfeiture of goods, *se defendendo* and *per infortunium* are discussed in 3 Coke, ch. 8, at 54–57.

[15] These are both discussed in *id.*, ch. 7, at 47–53.

[16] *Id.* at 52.

[17] 1 Hale 475.

[18] It would be murder, says Hale, "if a man knowing that people are passing along the street throws a stone, or shoots an arrow . . . with the intent to do hurt to people and one is thereby slain. . . ." *Id.* at 475.

beginning of an assessment of the particular unlawful act in deciding whether the resulting homicide should be classified as murder or manslaughter. Thus Hale's analysis represents a nascent shift to an act-oriented approach to killing in the course of unlawful acts. The unlawful act becomes the ground for establishing the degree of criminal homicide, rather than for denying the excuse of *per infortunium*. Hale's conclusion that the accidental killing was merely manslaughter is further testimony to the independence of the "unlawful act" doctrine from the theory of malice.[19] If there had been some connection between malice and killing in the course of unlawful acts, there would have been no option but to conclude that the killing was murder.

It is particularly important to note that these early discussions of the "unlawful act" doctrine relate exclusively to accidental killings. Thus there was an important conceptual gap between the problem of *per infortunium* in cases of hunting and the problem of the robber's killing a resisting victim. The latter case was not even arguably a case of *per infortunium;* were it not for the robbery, the legal dispute about malice would center on the question of provocation. Therefore, the point of Coke's holding that this case was one of implied malice was to make it clear that provocation could not be a defense on behalf of someone whose robbery induced the victim's provocative act. Hale broadens this theme to include the case of men who "come to steal deer in a park . . . and the parker . . . resists and is killed."[20] This type of killing is murder, Hale concludes; though if the poacher shot at a deer and the arrow accidentally hit the parker, the killing would be but manslaughter.[21] Thus there are two distinct ways in which the act of illegal poaching could be used against a party who killed another. It might be used to deny the relevance of provocation; or it might be used to reject the excuse of *per infortunium*.

These two themes come together in Hawkins' treatise pub-

[19] Note that the conclusion that some accidental killings were murder derived from an "intent to do harm," not from the gravity of the unlawful act. *Id.* at 474–75.

[20] *Id.* at 465 (using Coke's category of implied malice "in relation to the person killing").

[21] *Id.* at 475.

lished in the eighteenth century. For the first time we encounter an analysis of how the type of unlawful act affects the gravity of the homicide. In successive paragraphs, Hawkins brings forth examples of shooting at a deer[22] and robbing a park.[23] The former he lists among dangerous and mischievous activities which, if they issue in death, would support a conviction for manslaughter. Yet the emphasis here is clearly on "endanger[ing] the bodily hurt of some one . . .";[24] the term "unlawful act" does not even appear in the paragraph. "Robbing a park," on the other hand, is given as an example of an "unlawful act, which necessarily tends to raise tumults and quarrels."[25] Only the latter category of dangerous activities will support a conviction for murder.

The emphasis in Hawkins appears to be on the incriminating impact of these unlawful acts, rather than their relationship to the defense of *per infortunium.* Yet their incriminating aspect does not derive from the immorality of acting contrary to law or from any formal theory that the culpability of the "unlawful act" is transferred to the act of killing. The point of Hawkins' analysis is that these acts, which happen to be unlawful, are dangerous in varying degrees and that this relative degree of danger supports the classification of the killing as either manslaughter or murder. If the judges and subsequent commentators had built on Hawkins' important work, the formal criterion of killing in the course of an unlawful act might have merged entirely with the nascent analysis of liability based on excessive risk-taking. This would have been a sound turn of events, but it was not to be the course of the common law.

The doctrine of unlawful acts as a formal criterion of liability took hold in Foster's *Discourse of Homicide* published in 1762. Like his predecessors, Foster begins by assaying the concept of *per infortunium* as an excuse.[26] He then switches quickly to the unlawful act as a standard for gauging the gravity of the killing. Now we

[22] 1 Hawkins 112 (§10).
[23] *Id.* at 112 (§10).
[24] *Id.* at 112 (§9).
[25] *Id.* at 112 (§10).
[26] Foster 258.

find an entirely new approach to the venerable hypothetical of the poacher who kills accidentally. The critical question, as Foster sees it, is whether the poacher shooting at the deer intends to steal it. If he does, then he is guilty of felony, and if he kills someone in the bush, "it will be murder by reason of that felonious intent."[27] Thus was born the doctrine of felony-murder. This doctrine has nothing but a nominal link to the analysis in Coke, Hale and Hawkins of unlawful acts and their bearing on the excuse of *per infortunium*. For Foster, it is essential that the "unlawful act" be a felony, and in view of his rationale of transferred felonious intent, it is presumably immaterial whether the felony is dangerous.

There is no authority whatever for the principle that any felonious intent is sufficient to constitute malice aforethought. Indeed, the principle is incoherent, for if the killing occurs intentionally, but under provocation, the intent to kill is sufficient for the felony of manslaughter. If any felonious intent were sufficient for malice, all cases of manslaughter should be classified as murder. As Fitzjames Stephen aptly comments about Foster's invention of felony-murder: "This, I think, is the only blot upon Foster's treatise. . . ."[28]

The apology for Foster's reconstruction of the law is that all felonies of the time were capital anyway, and therefore there was no great evil in upgrading larceny and other felonies to murder.[29] Yet the fact is that execution rates varied widely among the capital felonies. Radzinowicz concludes that in the year 1810, two-thirds of all executions in England were for burglary, housebreaking, forgery, uttering, and murder.[30] In the same year, of 15 persons convicted of murder, 9 were executed (60 percent); of 39 convicted of robbery, only 6 were executed (15 percent).[31] Further, there were over 200 capital offenses then on the books, but only 25 offenses for which anyone suffered death in the first 75 years of the nine-

[27] *Id.* at 259.

[28] 3 Stephen 75. *But cf.* F. Stephen, A Digest of the Criminal Law §223(c), which repeats Foster's formulation.

[29] 3 Stephen 75–76.

[30] 1 L. Radzinowicz, History of English Criminal Law 155 (1948).

[31] *Ibid.*

teenth century. Here is an example where arguing from the law on the books, rather than the practice of the courts, can easily lead us astray. It is simply false to say that it made no difference whether one was convicted of larceny or of murder and that therefore there was no harm in Foster's upgrading every case of larceny-causing-death to the level of murder.

Blackstone[32] and East,[33] picked up Foster's theory of transferred felonious intent and bequeathed the doctrine of felony-murder to the American state legislatures, who cast it in the black letter of their late nineteenth-century penal codes. The California Penal Code, for example, boldly declares that any murder "committed in the perpetration" of one of six specified felonies, is murder in the first degree.[34] In addition, the courts have interpreted the homicide provisions to incorporate a common-law rule of felony-murder in the second degree.[35] These two rules of felony-murder have generated a complex body of law, mostly in decisions of the last fifteen years. In due course we shall immerse ourselves in this struggle to make sense of the rules of felony-murder.

The English courts managed to keep the rule of felony-murder within tight bounds. Fitzjames Stephen's early and articulate hostility to the doctrine no doubt contributed to this restraint.[36] As trial judge in *Serné* he instructed the jury that causing death in the course of a felony would be murder only if the felonious act "was known to be dangerous to life and likely in itself to cause death."[37] Stated in this way, the doctrine is not a formal test of murder, but rather a variation of murder by excessive risk-taking. In the leading case of *Beard*,[38] the defendant suffocated a girl who resisted his attempt to rape her. His conviction was affirmed on the ground that he killed the girl by "an act of violence done in the course of

[32] 4 Blackstone 200–01.

[33] 1 East 255; *cf.* W. Russell, A Treatise on Crimes & Misdemeanors 540 (7th Am. & 3d Eng. ed. 1853).

[34] Cal. Penal Code §189.

[35] See the discussion *infra* at §4.4.4.

[36] See 3 Stephen 75, but *cf.* F. Stephen, *supra* note 28, §223(c).

[37] Regina v. Serné, 16 Cox Crim. Cas. 311, 313 (1887).

[38] Director of Public Prosecutions v. Beard, [1920] 2 A.C. 479 (H.L.).

a felony involving violence."[39] This case, too, would readily qualify as murder under either the California or the Model Penal Code test of murder by excessive risk-taking that is indifferent to the value of human life. Indeed, under the test proposed by Lord Hailsham in *Hyam,* the act of suffocating the resisting victim would qualify as murder by intentional killing.[40] Even though the English never relied heavily on felony-murder,[41] the opposition to "constructive malice"[42] led to the abolition of the doctrine in the 1957 Homicide Act.[43]

It is important to be clear about the distinction between a formal rule of murder and rules such as those invoked in *Beard* that make reference to dangerous felonies. Numerous felonies, particularly rape, robbery and arson, are obviously dangerous to human life. If the act of committing one of these felonies results in death, the risk run by the actor would generally be sufficient to qualify the killing as murder by excessive risk-taking.[44] In this way of looking at the killing, the fact that the act is a felony is incidental. The killing would be murder even if for some technical reason the actor was not liable for the rape, robbery, or arson. Suppose, for example, that the actor violently rapes a woman who resists; overcoming her resistance, he kills her. This is patently murder even if it turns out that the woman is the actor's wife and therefore he is not technically guilty of rape.[45]

A formal test of liability is one that takes the commission of

[39] *Id.* at 504. For another conviction on similar facts, see Rex v. Stone, 53 T.L.R. 1046 (Crim. App. 1937).

[40] See §4.3.2 *supra,* at notes 41–49.

[41] The high-water mark appears to be Rex v. Jarmain, [1946] 1 K.B. 74 (Crim. App. 1945), in which the defendant was convicted of murder after his gun discharged and killed another in the course of a robbery.

[42] See F. Stephen, Digest of the Criminal Law §264, at 219 (8th ed. by Sturge, 1947).

[43] English Homicide Act 1957, c. 11, §1.

[44] Note the instructions in Rex v. Jarmain, [1946] 1 K.B. 74, 76 (Crim. App. 1945), in which the trial judge described the defendant's holding a cocked revolver in a robbery as a "dangerous and unlawful" act. In this instruction, the element of technical unlawfulness is superfluous.

[45] See Cal. Penal Code §261.

the felony as the reason for treating the killing as murder. Under the harm-oriented mode of analysis that prevailed in the early common law, the commission of an unlawful act was a plausible reason for denying the excuse of inevitable accident. The problem is whether, after the transformation to an act-oriented analysis of homicide, the reason for treating the accidental death as murder remains plausible. Foster was plainly of the view that any felonious intent would suffice for malice. It is not clear why that should be true. If there is a principled moral defense of the rule, perhaps it is that people who commit felonies should be required to assume the risk of deaths that occur in the perpetration of the felonies.[46]

§4.4.2. The Misdemeanor-Manslaughter Rule. Sometime in the mid-nineteenth century, English and American courts began to work with the rule that if a death occurred in the course of an unlawful act not amounting to a felony, the killing should be treated as manslaughter.[47] As it is stated, the rule is a formal test of liability, for on the face of things it does not matter whether the act is dangerous to human life in the abstract or in the particular manner of execution. Suppose someone is driving illegally without a license, his brakes unexpectedly fail, and the careening car kills a pedestrian. Under the formal rule of liability, the killing would be manslaughter. Yet the courts have rarely been as insensitive and unjust as their rules would make them seem. From the outset, judges struggled with this formal test of liability in order to bring out results that conformed more closely to the criteria of criminal negligence.

The underlying problem that has recurred under different doctrinal rubrics is whether it is sufficient for manslaughter that at the time of the death the actor be engaged in an unlawful act. Or more restrictively, is it necessary that the dangerous aspect of the

[46] For an explication and a critique of arguments of this form, see §9.3.3 *infra*.

[47] The rule is asserted as part of the common law in F. Stephen, A Digest of The Criminal Law §223 (1877). On the ambiguity of the rule and particularly of the word "unlawful," see LaFave & Scott 594–96.

unlawful act be the direct cause of the death? The difference is that between a condition of illegality and a culpable cause of death. The conflict is posed in cases of the following sort:

1. *D* drives, practices medicine or cosmetology without a license and causes death.[48]

2. *D* hunts illegally and accidentally causes death.[49]

3. *D*, a police officer, illegally fails to arrest drunks and gamblers; while in this illegal state, his gun goes off and kills a bystander.[50]

4. *D* illegally carries a concealed weapon and the gun discharges accidentally, killing a bystander.[51]

The overwhelming tendency is to reverse convictions in cases of this sort, even though the death patently occurs in the course of an unlawful act not amounting to a felony.[52] A variety of doctrinal maneuvers are deployed to justify these reversals. Sometimes the courts simply hold that the test is limited to unlawful acts that are *malum in se,* and that these acts that provide the background for the killing are merely *malum prohibitum.*[53] Without rejecting this distinction between acts that are wrong in themselves and acts that are wrong merely because the legislature has so declared, we might find it hard to understand the point of the distinction in

[48] Commonwealth v. Williams, 133 Pa. Super. 104, 1 A.2d 812 (1938) (no driver's license, reversed); People v. Penny, 44 Cal. 2d 861, 285 P.2d 926 (1955) (no license to practice cosmetology, reversed).

[49] State v. Horton, 139 N.C. 441, 51 S.E. 945 (1905) (reversed).

[50] People v. Mulcahy, 318 Ill. 332, 149 N.E. 266 (1925) (reversed).

[51] Potter v. State, 162 Ind. 213, 70 N.E. 129 (1904) (reversed); Dixon v. State, 104 Miss. 410, 61 So. 423 (1913) (reversed).

[52] See cases cited notes 48–51 *supra.* The only cases where conviction seems likely are those where the unlawfulness of the act consists in driving while intoxicated. See Rex v. Nickle, 34 Can. Crim. Cas. 15 (1920); Keller v. State, 155 Tenn. 633, 299 S.W. 803 (1927); State v. Kellison, 233 Iowa 1274, 11 N.W.2d 371 (1943); for isolated convictions under other statutory rubrics, see People v. Nelson, 309 N.Y. 231, 128 N.E.2d 391 (1955), (building code violation), criticized *infra in* §8.3.5; State v. Kotapish, 171 Ohio St. 349, 171 N.E.2d 505 (1960) (driving without emergency brakes). With the exception of *Nelson,* these are convictions that could readily have been sustained under a theory of criminal negligence.

[53] E.g., State v. Reitze, 86 N.J.L. 407, 92 A. 576 (Sup. Ct. 1914) (sale of liquor to intoxicated person held to be *malum prohibitum*); *accord,* People v. Pavlic, 227 Mich. 562, 199 N.W. 373 (1924).

this context. It might arguably be relevant if the theory supporting the rule of liability were in fact the principle that those who commit evil deeds have no moral basis to complain about being held liable for unexpected consequences. Perhaps there is an element of this theory of assumption of risk at work in the cases, but the judicial intuition against conviction is probably more adequately expressed in other doctrinal forms.

§4.4.3. **Tort Theory Points the Way.** The problem posed in the above cases recurs in tort litigation as well as in manslaughter prosecutions. The literature of tort theory has done a more able job of explaining why an illegal condition should not be sufficient for liability.[54] The analogous doctrinal problem in tort law is whether liability should be imposed for negligence per se. The latter form of negligence is defined as conduct that violates a criminal statute designed to protect a particular class of persons. In all four types of cases listed above, the actor violates a prohibition designed to protect the public from harm, and therefore the party causing death should arguably be liable in damages on a theory of negligence per se. Yet with the possible exception of the fourth case of carrying a concealed weapon, the courts would not impose liability for wrongful death in any of these situations.[55] There is much to be learned from the reasoning developed in the tort literature to explain why there should be no liability in these cases. The reason for denying liability is usually stated as a defect in the causal link between the unlawful act and the death. The idiom of causality also appears regularly in the judgments reversing criminal convictions.[56] Yet there is a sense in which these unlawful acts obviously do cause death. If the defendant had not, say, practiced medicine or cosmetology without a license, he would not have been in

[54] See, e.g., Prosser 192–202; Thayer, *Public Wrong and Private Action*, 27 Harv. L. Rev. 317 (1914); Morris, *The Relation of Criminal Statutes to Civil Liability*, 46 Harv. L. Rev. 453 (1933).

[55] See, e.g., Brown v. Shyne, 242 N.Y. 176, 151 N.E. 197 (1926).

[56] E.g., State v. Budge, 126 Me. 223, 137 A. 244 (1927) (reversed, question was whether the elements of speeding and driving while intoxicated contributed to the accident); Commonwealth v. Williams, 133 Pa. Super. 104, 1 A.2d 812 (1938) (driving without license did not cause accident).

a position to render the fatal treatment. If the defendant had not gone hunting illegally, she would not have fired the shot that accidentally hit an innocent party. In the sense that the death would not have occurred but for the defendant's act, one can surely hold that the unlawful act caused the death.

What is usually meant by the problem of causation in this context is not "but for" causation, but rather the question whether the negligent or risk-taking component of the illegal act caused the death.[57] The problem is sometimes labeled as an issue of proximate causation. If the illegal act of practicing medicine without a license does not entail the kind of risk that occurred, then one cannot say that the illegal component of the act caused the death. People who practice medicine without a license might be more likely than any others to create undue risks, yet in any particular case the fact that the treatment was rendered without a license is insufficient to infer that the death was attributable to the taking of excessive risks. In the other types of case mentioned, in which the courts balked at imposing liability for manslaughter or for negligent wrongful death, there is a similar problem of attributing the death to an increase of risk brought about by the illegal component of the act.[58]

Carrying a concealed weapon, which accidentally discharges and thereby kills another, is admittedly a borderline case. The problem is whether the illegality under the applicable statute consists in carrying a weapon or in carrying a *concealed* weapon. If the former, it seems plausible to impose liability, either for wrongful death or for manslaughter; the act of carrying the weapon in public entails the type of risk, namely, accidental discharge, that results in death. On the other hand, if the illegality consists in the weapon being concealed, the illegal dimension of the act does not create additional risks of accidental discharge. Whether the weapon is openly visible or concealed, it seems just as likely to discharge accidentally. Thus this latter form of illegal conduct should be insufficient both for manslaughter and for tortious wrongful death.

[57] See R. Keeton, Legal Cause in the Law of Torts (1963).

[58] See cases cited notes 48–51 *supra*.

The cases in which the courts do apply the misdemeanor-manslaughter rule confirm this analysis. The outstanding example is drunk driving, resulting in death.[59] These are cases in which the illegally created risk entails the type of harm that occurs. Yet even in these cases, as the tort theorists well know, there may still be a problem of causation. Suppose someone runs out into the street into the path of a speeding or an erratically driven car and an accident ensues. These are cases in which the accident might well have ocurred even if the driver had been driving with the utmost care. Therefore in criminal as well as tort cases, the jury should be required to find that the death would not have occurred but for the additional risk generated by the unlawful component of the act.

It is curious that these doctrinal points have received more refined consideration in the law of torts than in Anglo-American criminal law. It may be that the criminal cases are too preoccupied with punishing evil to pay much attention to the theory of risk. There is also a widespread sentiment among criminal judges that civil tort liability is "objective" and imposed regardless of fault. Yet the fact is that tort doctrine is at least as sensitive to the problem of just liability as is the law of manslaughter. Witness the incessant opposition to disregarding criteria of personal fault in cases of negligence per se. The courts have either overturned the rule of negligence per se or limited it to cases of unexcused violations of law.[60] This, one would hope, would also be the fate of the misdemeanor-manslaughter rule.

The most sensible apology for the misdemeanor-manslaughter rule is that it provided a rule of thumb for assessing criminal negligence at a time when the theory of negligence had not yet been refined. Now that judges sense that punishment for criminal negligence is the underlying rationale for liability in these cases of

[59] See case cited note 52 *supra*.

[60] New Amsterdam Casualty Co. v. Novick Transfer Co., 274 F.2d 916 (4th Cir. 1960) (violation of statute is merely evidence of negligence); Gill v. Whiteside-Hemby Drug Co., 197 Ark. 425, 122 S.W.2d 597 (1938) (violation is merely evidence of negligence); Martin v. Herzog, 228 N.Y. 164, 126 N.E. 814 (1920) (only unexcused wrongs are negligence per se).

causing death, the mere fact of committing an unlawful act is likely to become irrelevant in the analysis of liability. A leading case that points in that direction is People v. Stuart, decided in California in 1956.[61] A druggist prepared a prescription of sodium citrate and inadvertently used a bottle containing poisonous sodium nitrite; whether his mistake was faultful or not, he incurred liability under the Health and Safety Code for preparing an adulterated drug.[62] He sold the drug as sodium citrate; a child took it and died of sodium nitrite poisoning. The druggist was convicted on the theory that his violation under the Health and Safety Code was an "unlawful act," and the Penal Code expressly declares that all killing by "unlawful acts not amounting to a felony" shall amount to manslaughter.[63] The Supreme Court reversed on the theory that according to a general provision of the code, no liability could be established in the absence of either intentional wrongdoing or criminal negligence.[64] Thus the explicit wording of the provision on manslaughter was found to be nothing more than an approximation of criminal negligence.

If the *Stuart* decision receives the following it deserves, the law of manslaughter will return to the line of development that was nascent in the early eighteenth century and evident in Hawkins' analysis of dangerous acts causing death.[65] In the future, there should be no formal test for liability for manslaughter and no rules of thumb that dispense with an analysis of the actor's culpability for taking a particular risk under particular circumstances.

§4.4.4. Felony-Murder in the Second Degree. Although the courts have consistently undercut nineteenth-century efforts to develop a formal criterion of manslaughter, the record of litigation in the field of felony-murder is far more erratic. The courts have developed doctrines that permit the most wide-sweeping prosecutions for murder if a death should occur in the course of a fel-

[61] 47 Cal. 2d 167, 302 P.2d 5 (1956).

[62] The defendant's liability under Calif. Health and Safety Code §26280 was not subject to the excuse of unavoidable accident or ignorance.

[63] Cal. Penal Code §192 (2).

[64] Cal. Penal Code §20 (no liability in the absence of intent or "criminal negligence").

[65] See text at notes 22–25 *supra*.

ony. At the same time, the case law, particularly in California, displays the application of considerable legal ingenuity to limit the application of the felony-murder rule.

The thrust toward expansive use of the rule is reflected in several doctrinal decisions. First, American courts have held that the doctrine of felony-murder is to be regarded as part of the common law of homicide. It follows that if a statute uses the word "murder," the doctrine of felony-murder may be read into the law of the state. In California, for example, the Penal Code makes no reference to felony-murder in the second degree. A killing in the course of one of six enumerated felonies may support a conviction for murder in the first degree, yet there is no mention of felony-murder if the killing occurs in the perpetration of an unlisted felony, such as abortion, drunk driving, or grand theft. This legislative silence is of little moment, for the statute defining murder in the second degree refers to "all other kinds of murders,"[66] which is interpreted to incorporate the common law of homicide, including the principle of felony-murder.[67]

However well-meaning this interpretation might be, it is simply false to hold that the English common law contained a general rule to the effect that any killing in the course of a felony was murder. The history of the "unlawful act" doctrine need not be repeated here, except to recall that there was no mention of the connection between felonies and murder until Foster's rewriting of the law in 1762.[68] The English case law never supported the rule of law that one finds quoted in the American cases, namely, that any killing, even an accidental killing, would be murder if committed in the perpetration of a felony. Certain dangerous felonies such as rape and robbery were linked for a period with the proof of mal-

[66] Cal. Penal Code §189.

[67] The first case endorsing this doctrine was apparently People v. Wright, 167 Cal. 1, 138 P. 349 (1914) (death resulting from felonious abortion classified as murder). The claim that the term "murder" encompassed the felony-murder rule was accepted uncritically in Pike, *What is Second-Degree Murder in California?* 9 So. Cal. L. Rev. 112, 118–19 (1936). *Cf.* People v. Poindexter, 51 Cal. 2d 142, 330 P.2d 763 (1958) (feloniously furnishing heroin to a minor used to support felony-murder in the second degree).

[68] See the historical survey *supra* §4.4.1.

ice, but the doctrine never encompassed accidental deaths incidental to felonies.[69] Yet it is still the law in most jurisdictions in the United States that if in the course of a robbery, a gun discharges accidentally and kills someone, the bearer of the gun as well as his accomplices will be held guilty of murder.[70] Also, the English law of murder never went so far as to include all felonies—even all dangerous felonies—in the proof of implied malice. If an illegal abortion results in the death of the mother in the United States, the case law would support a conviction for murder.[71] In England, even during the reign of the English version of the felony-murder rule, a felonious abortion supported a conviction for murder only if a reasonable person would have contemplated that death was likely to result.[72]

One of the doctrines employed by American courts to expand the scope of felony-murder is the rule of vicarious liability used to hold all co-conspirators liable for substantive crimes committed by any one of the conspirators in the course of executing the unlawful agreement. In its most defensible form, this rule is but a variation of the principle of complicity, by which aiders and abettors are held accountable for the crimes committed by principals in the first degree. Membership in the conspiracy is taken to be a conclusive test of aiding and abetting the crimes committed by other members of the conspiratorial combination, even though the specific crimes committed are not those that define the objective of the conspiracy.[73] This doctrine shall receive due criticism at the proper place;[74] for now, we are more concerned to note the power and danger of joining this rule of vicarious liability with the rule of felony-murder.

[69] The case closest to the American rule is Rex v. Jarmain, [1946] 1 K.B. 74 (Crim. App. 1945); *but cf.* note 44 *supra*.

[70] See cases cited, note 135 *infra*.

[71] People v. Clapp, 67 Cal. App. 2d 197, 153 P.2d 758 (1944); State v. Crofford, 133 Iowa 478, 110 N.W. 921 (1907).

[72] Rex v. Lumley, 22 Cox Crim. Cas. 635 (1911); Regina v. Whitmarsh, 62 J.P. 711 (1898).

[73] This is the so-called *Pinkerton* rule after the leading case, Pinkerton v. United States, 328 U.S. 640 (1946) (*D* held accountable for crimes committed by co-conspirator while *D* was in jail).

[74] See §8.5.4 *infra*.

An illustrative case is People v. Cabaltero,[75] in which seven men conspired to rob the payroll of a local farmer. In the course of the robbery, one of the men, named Dasalla, got angry at another conspirator named Ancheta for firing two warning shots at some men who approached the premises being robbed; in his anger Dasalla shot and killed Ancheta. The six surviving members of the conspiracy were indicted and convicted of murder. It did not matter that the killing was not included within the object of the conspiracy; nor did it matter that Cabaltero was then waiting in the getaway car and could not possibly have prevented Dasalla from killing Ancheta. The reasoning supporting the conviction of all six was that Dasalla was guilty of murder under the felony-murder rule. He might indeed have been guilty of intentional and premeditated homicide, but it was obviously easier for the prosecution to establish guilt by invoking the felony-murder rule. Liability for the murder was then extended to the other five by use of the principle of vicarious liability based on participation in the conspiracy. The extension of liability is also supported implicitly by the felony-murder rule itself; for as to the other five, the killing did in fact occur in the "perpetration of a robbery." There is nothing in the felony-murder rule that implies that only the party who actually fires the homicidal bullet should be held liable under the rule. It seems that by this latter interpretation, even if Dasalla's gun had gone off accidentally and killed Ancheta, all six could have been liable for felony-murder.

These are but two of the ways in which the courts have contributed to the expansion of the felony-murder rule: first, by reading the rule into the common law of homicide and, secondly, by combining the rule with the principle of vicarious liability. In the conclusion of this section, we shall note some other ways in which the courts have distended the doctrine by means of interpretation. Yet to put the problem in perspective, we should now turn to the conflicting and dominant trend toward limitation and refinement of this sweeping formal standard of criminal homicide.

Felony-murder in the second degree is almost entirely a judi-

[75] 31 Cal. App. 2d 52, 87 P.2d 364 (1939).

cially crafted standard of liability. The first problem in defining this standard of murder is selecting the felonies that will support this formal test of malice. In jurisdictions that have a crime of felony-murder in the first degree, the list is simplified by the exclusion of the most dangerous felonies. In California these dangerous felonies,[76] which support a conviction in the first degree, are robbery, burglary, rape, arson, mayhem, and, less plausibly, lewd acts upon a child under the age of 14.[77] In working their way through the remaining felonies to determine the scope of the felony-murder rule in the second degree, the California appellate courts have repeatedly encountered two basic problems. The first puzzle has been whether the underlying felony is so closely related to the fact of killing that it should be regarded as "merged" with or "included in fact" in the killing. The paradigm for this merger of the felony with the killing is causing death by committing an aggravated assault. In *Ireland,* the California Supreme Court held that assault with a deadly weapon could not support a charge of felony-murder in the second degree.[78] The argument was that the assault was so closely connected with the act of killing that for reasons that are not immediately obvious, the felony-murder rule should not apply. This is a noteworthy result, for the factual situations so excluded from the felony-murder rule would readily qualify as intentional murder under the English rule that takes an intent to do grievous bodily harm as sufficient for murder. An aggravated assault would presumably include an intent to cause grievous bodily harm.

The second type of problematic felony is one that represents a minimal risk of death. Since 1965, the California Supreme Court has held that the felony-murder rule would not apply to cases of death caused in the course of any of the following felonies: (1) a conspiracy to obtain methadrine,[79] (2) obtaining property by false

[76] Cal. Penal Code §189.

[77] This crime of "lewd acts" is defined by Cal. Penal Code §288.

[78] People v. Ireland, 70 Cal. 2d 522, 450 P.2d 580, 75 Cal. Rptr. 188 (1969).

[79] People v. Williams, 63 Cal. 2d 452, 406 P.2d 647, 47 Cal. Rptr. 7 (1965).

pretenses,[80] (3) carrying a concealed weapon as an ex-felon,[81] (4) possessing a sawed-off shotgun,[82] (5) escape,[83] and (6) false imprisonment.[84] The rationale for excluding these felonies from the scope of the rule is that none of them, taken in the abstract, is "inherently dangerous to human life." In some of the cases, the particular manner of executing the felony was indeed dangerous to human life; for example, in *Phillips* the accused was allegedly guilty of obtaining property by false pretenses because he received money from the parent of a cancer-stricken girl on the representation that chiropractic treatment could cure her cancer. As a result, the girl went without conventional medical treatment and died.

It is clear that the court must consider the felony abstracted from the particular factual situation; otherwise it cannot hold the felony-murder rule to be a distinct track of liability independent of the other two. If the particular manner of committing—say, receiving property by false pretenses—is scrutinized for danger to human life, then the felony-murder rule would become an alternative version of murder by extremely reckless conduct. For the felony-murder rule to have a grip as a distinct test of liability, it must be pitched to the felony in the abstract, rather than to the facts of the particular case. The most subtle of these recent decisions limiting the scope of the rule is the holding in *Satchell* that neither an ex-felon's possession of a sawed-off shotgun nor any other possession offense could meet the test of a felony "inherently dangerous to human life."[85] It is relatively easy to conclude that, taken in the abstract, a theft offense is not inherently dangerous to human life. But the possession of concealed weapons by ex-felons is prohibited precisely because the act of possession by this class of persons is thought likely to lead to the dangerous use

[80] People v. Phillips, 64 Cal. 2d 574, 414 P.2d 353, 51 Cal. Rptr. 225 (1966). *Cf.* People v. Morales, 49 Cal. App. 3d 134, 122 Cal. Rptr. 157 (1975) (grand theft from person not inherently dangerous).

[81] People v. Satchell, 6 Cal. 3d 28, 489 P.2d 1361, 98 Cal. Rptr. 33 (1971).

[82] *Ibid.*

[83] People v. Lopez, 6 Cal. 3d 45, 489 P.2d 1372, 98 Cal. Rptr. 44 (1971).

[84] People v. Henderson, 19 Cal. 3d 86, 560 P.2d 1180, 137 Cal. Rptr. 1 (1977).

[85] See note 81 *supra.*

of the weapon.[86] Even if this statistical judgment were accurate, the court would not be swayed. The critical factor in the court's reasoning is camouflaged in the cryptic remark that possession is "essentially neutral in its intentional aspect"[87] and therefore could not justify the imputation of malice. What this means apparently is that if the danger to others depends on an intentional act subsequent to the commission of the felony, then the prosecution must prove the intentional homicide rather than infer it from an antecedent act of possession. A general prediction of intentional conduct cannot provide an adequate substitute for proof in the particular case that the killing was intentional and reflected the necessary feature of malice.

This way of putting the result in *Satchell* invokes broader principles of justice. The reason that the prosecution may not rely on a prediction of intentional conduct is that this manner of proceeding fails to respect the suspect as an autonomous agent. Relying on a statistical prediction of what the suspect will intend to do is to treat him as a natural phenomenon whose behavior conforms to scientific laws. Deep ideological premises of the criminal law resist the conversion of the defendant from a subject of duties to an object of administrative regulation. Criminality based on prediction might be acceptable in the field of "regulatory" possession offenses,[88] but it is not acceptable in prosecutions for homicide. To say that possession is "neutral in its intentional aspect" means that possession cannot be used for predicting how an autonomous, self-actuating individual will act in the future.[89] And if this prediction is impermissible, it follows that possession cannot be regarded as an "inherently dangerous" offense.

Having generated the second-degree felony-murder rule by reading it into the common law of homicide, the California courts are now engaged in a two-front attack on their own offspring. If the felony is either too closely or too distantly related to the risk of

[86] *Cf.* State v. Moffit, 199 Kan. 514, 431 P.2d 879 (1967) (holding that possession of a weapon by an ex-felon was "inherently dangerous" for purposes of the felony-murder rule).

[87] 6 Cal. 3d at 43, 414 P.2d at 1372, 98 Cal. Rptr. at 44.

[88] See §3.4.2 *supra*.

[89] For further discussion of this issue, see §6.4.2 *infra*.

causing death, it will not qualify to support a conviction of murder in the second degree. The question is whether there are any felonies that remain in this middle ground. In one recent case,[90] the Supreme Court upheld a theory of felony-murder in a case of willfully administering a poison; the defendant gave the victim methyl alcohol to drink under the pretense that it was potable; the victim died from drinking the surrogate brew. Apparently there was no intent to harm the victim in supplying him with the alcohol. This is a narrow precedent indeed, for if the purpose of the supplier had been to harm the drinker, the case would have been easily characterized as murder by poisoning—first-degree murder under the statute.[91]

The cases in which the doctrine of second-degree felony-murder seems still to be influential are typified by some recent decisions by the courts of appeal. In one case, the court affirmed a murder conviction on the basis of the felony of driving under the influence of a narcotic;[92] in another, on the basis of supplying heroin.[93] The Supreme Court has upheld the rule in a case of intentionally burning an automobile, with death as the result.[94] Because arson is limited to the malicious burning of a dwelling house or its equivalent,[95] other cases of intentional burning do not trigger the first-degree felony-murder rule.[96] These cases on dangerous substances (poison, narcotics and alcohol) and non-arsonous burning identify felonies that carry a sufficiently distinct risk of death to qualify in the unstable center ground of felonies that are "inherently dangerous" but nonetheless independent of the killing.

§4.4.5. Conflicting Rationalia for Curtailing the Second-Degree Felony-Murder Rule. Whether the center of the rule can hold depends on the reasons for curtailing it at its two extremes. The standard policy rationale offered in the courts' restrictive decisions

[90] People v. Mattison, 4 Cal. 3d 177, 481 P.2d 193, 93 Cal. Rptr. 185 (1971).

[91] Cal. Penal Code §189.

[92] People v. Calzada, 13 Cal. App. 3d 603, 91 Cal. Rptr. 912 (1970).

[93] People v. Taylor, 11 Cal. App. 3d 57, 89 Cal. Rptr. 697 (1970).

[94] People v. Nichols, 3 Cal. 3d 150, 474 P.2d 673, 89 Cal. Rptr. 721 (1970), *cert. denied*, 402 U.S. 910 (1971).

[95] Cal. Penal Code §447a, §448a.

[96] See Cal. Penal Code §§449a, 449b, 449c, 450a, 451a.

derives from language crafted by Justice Traynor in People v. Washington[97]—a decision on first-degree murder that we shall consider below. The felony-murder rule, we are told, "should not be extended beyond any rational function that it is designed to serve."[98] The unknown variable in this formula is the "rational function" that is attributed to the rule. Sometimes it is argued that the felony-murder rule was designed to provide an additional deterrent impact to the rule prohibiting the underlying felonies; yet this argument is generally rejected on the grounds that allowing the fortuity of death to influence the penalty for rape or robbery would "deter haphazardly at best."[99] The preferable theory, according to *Washington,* is that the felony-murder rule is designed "to deter felons from killing negligently or accidently by holding them strictly liable. . . ."[100] The influential opinion in *Washington* also criticizes the felony-murder rule because it "erodes the relation between criminal liability and moral culpability."[101] Though the court does not make the connection, it becomes clear on reflection that the discussion of the rule's "rational function" is simply another way of capturing the judges' concern about a just "relation" between culpability and punishment for murder.

Let us suppose that the court is correct in specifying the "rational function" of the rule to be the deterrence of negligent or accidental killing in the course of a felony. What this means is that the rule is supposed to add a differential deterrent impact to the penalty stipulated for the underlying felony. It is supposed to encourage felons to execute their felonies in a manner designed to minimize the danger to human life. This is a plausible rationale for the rule and it explains the result in *Ireland* that aggravated assaults "included in fact" in the killing should not support the felony-murder rule. The reasoning on behalf of *Ireland* would go like this: The purpose of the felony-murder rule is realized only as to those facts that may be committed in such a way as to minimize

[97] 62 Cal. 2d 777, 402 P.2d 130, 44 Cal. Rptr. 442 (1965).
[98] *Id.* at 783, 402 P.2d at 134, 44 Cal. Rptr. at 446.
[99] *Id.* at 781, 402 P.2d at 133, 44 Cal. Rptr. at 445.
[100] *Ibid.*
[101] *Id.* at 783, 402 P.2d at 134, 44 Cal. Rptr. at 446.

the risk to human life. Assault with a deadly weapon is invariably dangerous to human life; it cannot be committed in a relatively safe way so as to minimize the homicidal risk. Therefore, the purpose of encouraging safety cannot apply to assault with a deadly weapon and the felony-murder rule should not apply.

Though the "rational" purpose of the rule might account for *Ireland*, it helps us little in understanding the power behind the competing flank in the two-pronged attack on felony-murder. What is the connection, if any, between the purpose of encouraging the safe commission of felonies and the conclusion that only "felonies inherently dangerous to human life" may support the rule? If criminal sanctions have an influence on behavior, the threat of a murder conviction would presumably deter quack doctors from committing the felony of obtaining property by false pretenses where the false promise of curative powers might endanger someone's life. It is hard to see how the "rational function" of deterrence is not served where the felony is not inherently dangerous, but only dangerous in some cases. Indeed, the premise undergirding the argument of deterrence is that felonies other than those included in the act of killing may be committed in a variety of ways, some ways more dangerous than others. From this perspective, it is impossible to see the difference in principle between encouraging the safe burning of a barn and encouraging the safe commission of a theft offense.

There is a general point to be learned here about the use of the argument of deterrence in justifying limitations on legal rules. There comes a point where the deterrent efficacy of a sanction is so weak that one might properly think that competing values require that deterrence not be accepted as a justification. This might be the case in the crime of obtaining property by false pretenses, where the deterrent force is likely to matter in fewer cases than in the commission of felonies that typically are dangerous to human life. With other values in mind, judges might contend that it is not "rational" to extend the felony-murder rule. But what are those competing values? The goal of deterrence surely does not specify what they are. It is sometimes argued that the proper limitation on deterrence is to be found in the excessive discouragement of socially useful activities. This might work in some contexts,[102] but it is inapt here. No one would argue that the problem in applying felony-murder to felonies remotely related to the risk of causing death is that the deterrent impact excessively discourages the remote felony. The rationale of this limitation on the rule is more plausibly anchored in a theory of moral culpability that justifies a murder conviction in at most a subset of the felonies that result in death.

When we begin to think about the rationale of moral culpability, we find that a proper theory of differential culpability justifies both limitations on the rule. The theory would be that a conviction for murder is justified only if the felony typically includes a negligent risk of death beyond the risks inherent in the felonious activity. This differential culpability—which goes beyond the culpability implicit in committing the felony—justifies conviction for the more serious crime of murder.[103] In the case of aggravated assault resulting in death, there is no differential culpability beyond the risk to life implicit in committing the assault. If the assaulting felon is held guilty of murder when a death ensues, his liability depends on a fortuity, namely the death, for which he is not incrementally culpable. Liability contingent on a fortuity is precisely the kind of arbitrary rule that, in the language of Justice Traynor, erodes the "relation between criminal liability and moral culpability."

At the opposite extreme, when the felony is too distantly related to the risk of death, the erosion occurs in a different manner. If the felony is not "inherently dangerous to human life," then the mere commission of the felony is not indicative of incremental culpability toward the risk of death. In order to preserve felony murder as a distinct track for establishing murder, the felony must be analyzed in the abstract. Therefore the felony supporting the rule must be one that in the typical case carries with it a high risk of

[102] For example, strict liability for marketing adulterated drugs, United States v. Dotterweich, 320 U.S. 277 (1943), might unduly discourage business people from entering the drug business.

[103] This approach to the rule is explicit in a number of legislative reforms of the felony-murder rule. See MPC §210.2(1)(b) (presumed recklessness); Del. Code tit. 11, §636(a)(2) ("recklessly causes death"); §635(2) ("with criminal negligence").

death. Grand theft and false imprisonment do not qualify,[104] but malicious burning, administering poison, supplying heroin—all of these are indicative of a culpable risk toward human life. Yet, in order to survive attack from the *Ireland* flank, these felonies must be capable of execution in a relatively safe manner. If this option of relative safety is unavailable, the felony is so dangerous that it becomes "included in fact" in the act of homicide. Yet before maliciously burning a haystack, an offender can determine whether there are human beings in the vicinity. If he fails to do this and death results, he is properly blamed, not only for the underlying felony but for the incremental culpability in risking human life. It is true, however, that in felony-murder cases the differential culpability toward the risk of death is presumed from the occurrence of death. This conclusive presumption is justified only in the narrow range of cases in which the felony is "inherently dangerous" but not so dangerous that it cannot be performed with relative safety.[105]

There is one additional point necessary to complete this account of the decisions of the California Supreme Court. The incremental culpability that will justify upgrading the felony causing death must be negligence, and not an intentional killing. If the killing is intentional, as in Satchell's killing with the sawed-off shotgun illegally in his possession, a distinct set of arguments requires prosecution for intentional homicide.[106]

Thus we have generated a theory—we might call it an apology—that makes sense of the complex pattern of decisions in the California Supreme Court. Yet if the theory is sound, it carries with it the germs that will eventually infect the rule that it seeks to sustain. Once we see that the underlying rationale for the felony-murder rule is the incremental moral culpability of the actor, what justification is there for presuming from the mere fact of death that the incremental culpability is present in a particular case? Suppose

[104] See notes 80, 84 *supra*.

[105] This result could be stated in the language of "deterrence" by appealing to the "class of cases that we seek to deter." For the fallacies in this mode of reasoning, see §10.3.5 *infra*.

[106] See text at notes 84–86 *supra*.

that a saboteur reconnoiters a bridge thoroughly before she undertakes to burn it; at the last minute, someone runs onto the bridge and is caught in the conflagration. In this case, the careful saboteur has done precisely what the felony-murder rule is supposed to encourage: she has committed her felony with proper regard for the danger to human life. Convicting for murder exemplifies strict liability and erodes the connection between "criminal liability and moral culpability." If it is objected that a dangerous felony cannot be committed without differential culpability relative to the risk of death, then all of these felonies should fail under the *Ireland* rule: they would be so closely related to the act of killing that they could not justify an aggravated penalty. If the felony-murder rule applies, then it is assumed that the felony may be committed carefully, and there is no excuse for the jury not being required to assess whether in a particular case the factor of differential culpability is absent.

Whatever the merit of this argument, the concept of felony murder in the second degree retains its force in the California case law. From the prosecutorial point of view, it has gained additional importance as the only track of analysis that does not admit of diminished capacity to reduce the offense to manslaughter. Instead of admitting psychiatric evidence to negate the malice necessary for murder, the courts regard the commission of the underlying felony as conclusive on the issue of malice. It is true that the courts will consider intoxication and psychiatric evidence in order to negate the intent required for the underlying felony.[107] Yet the degree of evidence required to negate the underlying intent verges on the proof of unconsciousness. When diminished capacity is used in this latter sense as a defense negating the underlying felony, it resembles the issue of insanity more than it does the question of diminished capacity in other homicide cases.

The tension in the felony-murder rule derives from the effort to maintain a standard of liability that is simultaneously formal

[107] People v. Tidwell, 3 Cal. 3d 82, 473 P.2d 762, 89 Cal. Rptr. 58 (1970); see generally Note, *The Diminished Capacity Defense to Felony Murder*, 23 Stan. L. Rev. 799 (1971).

and indifferent to the facts of the particular case and yet responsive to the required connection between culpability and criminal liability. It is impossible to satisfy these inconsistent desiderata in one rule. If the rule is purely formal, it will invariably be arbitrary in its application and erode the link between culpability and liability. If maintaining that link is essential to justifying conviction for murder, then the formal aspects of the rule will eventually wither away and the test will become identical with liability based upon excessive risk-taking.

§4.4.6. First-Degree Murder: The Means Tests. The statutory definitions of first-degree murder employ two tests that are arguably formal in their application: the first-degree felony-murder rule, and the enumeration of specific means of killing that automatically qualify the murder as one in the first degree. We shall consider the latter problem of specific means first, for the judicial interpretation of these tests reveals the kind of sensitivity that might appropriately be extended to the analysis of murder in perpetration of one of the six enumerated felonies. The specific wording of the California statute is critical:[108]

> All murder which is perpetrated by means of a destructive device or explosive, poison, lying-in-wait, torture, or by any other kind of willful, deliberate, and premeditated killing . . . is murder of the first degree.

The most liberal possible interpretation of this language would lead to the conclusion that if the defendant set off an explosive that unexpectedly and without additional culpability on his part resulted in death, he would be guilty of first-degree murder. Yet there are two features of the wording that stand in the way of this expansive reading. First, the statute reads "all murder" and not "all killing"; therefore the relevance of the particular means should arise only if it is first established that the killing was one with malice and thus properly classified as murder. The element of malice would have to be established in one of the three tracks of analysis already considered. Secondly, the specific means are listed prior to the clause, "or by any other kind of . . . premeditated killing."

[108] Cal. Penal Code §189.

Therefore, the specific means should be read merely as examples of the general requirement that the killing be "willful, deliberate and premeditated"—a requirement which would have to be proven in every case.

The first technique for circumscribing the means test, namely the insistence that this form of murder be based upon a showing of malice, has gradually gained acceptance in the courts. It was first advocated by Justice Traynor in 1951; in his concurring opinion in People v. Thomas,[109] a case of murder by lying-in-wait, the Justice first formulated the famous definition of malice that thereafter rekindled controversy in every corner of the California law of homicide.[110] Wherever the term "murder" or "malice" appeared, Justice Traynor argued, it would have to be shown that the cause of death was conduct entailing a "high probability" of death and done for a "base anti-social motive and with wanton disregard of human life."[111] This definition of malice requires an individualized judgment of culpability. The particular manner of killing, whether by torture, poisoning, lying-in-wait, or explosive device, becomes relevant only if it is first shown that the killing was motivated by malice.[112]

The second argument, namely, that the specifics enumerated are but examples of "willful, deliberate, premeditated killing" has fared less well in the courts. In People v. Wolff[113] the Supreme Court analyzed the structure of §189 and concluded that the specific means, and particularly lying-in-wait, were merely presumptive evidence of premeditation.[114] Yet without decrying *Wolff*, the courts have ignored its analysis. Subsequent prosecutions proceeded as though proof of the particular means was sufficient to

[109] 41 Cal. 2d 470, 475, 261 P.2d 1, 4 (1951).

[110] The language from *Thomas* was employed in two other innovative opinions by Justice Traynor, People v. Washington, 62 Cal. 2d 777, 402 P.2d 130, 44 Cal. Rptr. 442 (1965) (malice in third-party shooting); and People v. Conley, 64 Cal. 2d 310, 411 P.2d 911, 49 Cal. Rptr. 815 (1966) (malice negated by diminished capacity).

[111] 41 Cal. 2d at 480, 261 P.2d at 6.

[112] See People v. Sedeno, 10 Cal. 3d 703, 518 P.2d 913, 112 Cal. Rptr. 1 (1974) (classification as first-degree murder presupposes proof of malice).

[113] 61 Cal. 2d 795, 394 P.2d 959, 40 Cal. Rptr. 271 (1964).

[114] *Id.* at 825, 394 P.2d at 976, 40 Cal. Rptr. at 288.

establish premeditation.[115] The accepted doctrine is that the specified means may provide the "equivalent to premeditation or deliberation."[116]

The subsequent cases on lying-in-wait have ignored *Wolff*, decided in 1964, and relied instead on *Harrison*, decided in 1963.[117] According to the latter case, the criteria of lying-in-wait can be discerned independently of the issue of premeditation and even of intent to kill. All that is required is "concealment and watchful waiting with the purpose of facilitating the attack."[118] The judicially approved standard jury instruction now defines "lying-in-wait" as "waiting and watching for an opportune time to act, together with a concealment by ambush or some other secret design to take the other person by surprise."[119] In a 1954 case,[120] still cited approvingly by the courts of appeal,[121] the defendant merely waited in his car in front of the victim's house until the victim's guests had left; this was held to be sufficient to constitute lying-in-wait. There is no need to prove an intent to kill, no need to prove actual premeditation. The required intent appears to attach to the act of "waiting and watching" rather than to the execution of the killing. Thus the doctrine of lying-in-wait functions as a formal test of first-degree murder. The courts treat "lying-in-wait" as though it were an independent offense that, by analogy to the felony-murder rule, is conclusive on the issue of premeditation and deliberation.

The criteria for murder by poisoning and murder by torture have received more careful judicial elaboration. Though both are interpreted to dispense with proof of intent to kill as well as premeditation, the required intent for each relates to the manner of

[115] See People v. Benjamin, 52 Cal. App. 3d 63, 124 Cal. Rptr. 799 (1975); People v. Dickerson, 23 Cal. App. 3d 721, 100 Cal. Rptr. 533 (1972).

[116] Caljic §8.25 (lying-in-wait).

[117] People v. Harrison, 59 Cal. 2d 622, 381 P.2d 665, 30 Cal. Rptr. 841 (1963).

[118] *Id.* at 630, 381 P.2d at 670; 30 Cal. Rptr. at 846.

[119] Caljic §8.25, approved most recently in People v. Benjamin, 52 Cal. App. 3d 63, 124 Cal. Rptr. 799 (1975).

[120] People v. Byrd, 42 Cal. 2d 200, 266 P.2d 505 (1954), *cert. denied*, 348 U.S. 848 (1954).

[121] See, e.g., People v. Dickerson, 23 Cal. App. 3d 721, 100 Cal. Rptr. 533 (1972); People v. Bush, 177 Cal. App. 2d 117, 2 Cal. Rptr. 29 (1960).

the killing. Both require particularly heinous motives. Murder by poison is committed only if the defendant supplies the poison "for an evil purpose."[122] Murder by torture requires an intent to "inflict extreme and prolonged pain" for one of a variety of evil or sadistic purposes.[123] As already noted, all of these forms of first-degree murder presuppose the proof of a killing with malice.[124]

The cultivation of these conclusive criteria for first-degree murder bears serious implications for the relevance of diminished capacity in mitigating murder in the first to murder in the second degree. It is common ground that evidence of diminished capacity may be invoked to negate any of the following: (1) malice in cases other than felony-murder,[125] (2) premeditation,[126] and (3) the intent required to establish a felony under the felony-murder rule.[127] The question is how these rules may be brought to bear in cases of murder by lying-in-wait, poison or torture. By holding in *Wolff* that lying-in-wait was but evidence of premeditation, the court was free to assess the impact of diminished capacity on the reflection required for first-degree murder.[128] But if the law now is that these specific means function as surrogates for premeditation and deliberation, then the evidence of diminished capacity would have to negate the intent required to establish killing by lying-in-wait, poisoning or torture. The appropriate analogy would be negating the underlying felonious intent in felony-murder cases rather than disproof of the meaningful reflection required for premeditation. It would obviously be more difficult in a murder-by-torture case to show that the defendant did not intend to inflict pain than to

[122] People v. Mattison, 4 Cal. 3d 177, 481 P.2d 193, 93 Cal. Rptr. 185 (1971); *but cf.* Caljic §8.23, which relies on older cases and ignores this requirement.

[123] Caljic §8.24 (listing the purpose as "revenge, extortion, persuasion or . . . any sadistic purpose"); People v. Wiley, 18 Cal. 3d 162, 554 P.2d 881, 133 Cal. Rptr. 135 (1976) (endorsing Caljic §8.24 and holding further that victim need not experience the intended pain).

[124] See text at notes 109–12 *supra*.

[125] Caljic §8.77(3).

[126] *Id.* (2).

[127] Caljic §8.79 (1976 rev.).

[128] People v. Wolff, 61 Cal. 2d 795, 821, 394 P.2d 959, 975, 40 Cal. Rptr. 271, 287 (1964).

show, as is ordinarily required for mitigation, that he could not "maturely and meaningfully reflect" upon the gravity of his act. With matters of such gravity at stake, one might expect California lawyers to rediscover the holding in *Wolff* and argue more vigorously that the specific means described in §189 are but presumptive evidence of premeditation and deliberation.

§4.4.7. First-Degree Murder: Felony-Murder. When the felony-murder rule is used to classify killings as murder in the first degree, the local statute typically enumerates the controlling felonies and prescribes that any killing "committed in the perpetration, or attempt to perpetrate" one of the listed felonies is murder in the first degree.[129] With statutes of this seeming precision, the role of the courts appears to be limited to interstitial modification of the legislative rule. The fact is that until recently, courts in the United States have exercised considerable initiative in expanding the scope of felony-murder. One favored category for expansion are killings in the course of armed robberies committed by two or more conspirators. The courts in the last century have had little hesitation in regarding all the conspirators liable under a rule of vicarious liability for a death occurring in the course of a robbery.[130] At common law, liability was more restrictive in two important respects. First, killings by individuals were denominated murder only as to victims who resisted the felony[131] or as to third parties whose interference was feared.[132] Secondly, liability for murder was imputed to co-conspirators only if committed "in pursuance" of the unlawful act; murders collateral to the conspiracy were not imputed to the others.[133]

[129] Cal. Penal Code §189.

[130] See, e.g., People v. Gilbert, 63 Cal. 2d 690, 408 P.2d 365, 47 Cal. Rptr. 909 (1965), *rev'd on other grounds*, 388 U.S. 263 (1965); People v. Miller, 37 Cal. 2d 801, 236 P.2d 137 (1951).

[131] Director of Public Prosecutions v. Beard, [1920] 2 A.C. 479 (H.L.); Rex v. Stone, 53 T.L.R. 1046 (Crim. App. 1937). Both cases held that killing a rape victim to overcome her resistance was felony-murder.

[132] See the example of burglars who kill someone approaching the house, Rex v. Plummer, 84 Eng. Rep. 1103 (1720). There is no indication, however, that the killing would not be murder absent the burglary. The point of the burglary is that it warrants extension of liability to co-conspirators.

[133] *Ibid.*

Under the modern, more formal interpretations both of felony murder and of conspiratorial liability, it does not matter whether one robber kills another[134] or even whether the gun of one of the robbers unpredictably discharges and kills a bystander.[135] Despite the prosecutorial use of felony-murder and the rule of conspiratorial liability to circumvent the ordinary requirements of malice and premeditation, the pattern of liability was limited for a time to cases in which one of the robbers fired the fatal shot. Yet after the Second World War, the courts broke loose from this mooring and began to apply both rules of formal liability (felony-murder and conspiratorial liablility) where the victim of the robbery or even a policeman fired the fatal shot. These cases bear close examination, for they illustrate the belief, shared by some mystics, that one must experience evil in order to appreciate the good. The experience with this almost limitless theory of felony-murder came as a shock to the sensibilities of many lawyers and thus generated the momentum that today tends toward restriction of the felony-murder rule.

The first prominent series of cases emerged in Pennsylvania in the late 1940s and early 50s.[136] In the first case, the victim of a gas station holdup returned the gunfire of the robber and inadvertently killed the attendant in the station.[137] The theory for holding the robbers liable for this death was that the victim's defensive response was instinctive, and therefore causally tied to the commission of the robbery.[138] The theory of causal connection is less plausible when a policeman arrives at the scene and fires at the fleeing felons; his decision to shoot is less instinctive and he ought to be more cognizant of the danger to bystanders. If an innocent

[134] People v. Cabaltero, 31 Cal. App. 2d 52, 87 P.2d 364 (1939) (six participants in robbery held guilty of first-degree murder after one conspirator got angry at another and shot him).

[135] Rex v. Jarmain, [1946] 1 K.B. 74 (1945); State v. Thorne, 39 Utah 208, 117 P. 58 (1911); Regina v. Elnick, 33 Can. Crim. Cas. 174 (1920), People v. Morlock, 46 Cal. 2d 141, 292 P.2d 897 (1956).

[136] There were admittedly some earlier cases. See People v. Payne, 359 Ill. 246, 194 N.E. 539 (1935).

[137] Commonwealth v. Moyer, 357 Pa. 181, 53 A.2d 736 (1947).

[138] *Id.* at 190, 53 A.2d at 741–42.

person is killed in the shooting, the officer obviously bears a large share of the causal responsibility. Though there is this difference between the instinctive, self-protecting victim and the self-conscious police officer, the Pennsylvania courts extended liability for murder to cover both types of third-party killing.[139] In the 1950s it seemed that the courts could not go far enough in distending the felony-murder rule in order to prosecute robbers and other felons for first-degree murder.[140]

The Pennsylvania Supreme Court balked at this sweeping use of the felony-murder rule only when they could no longer coherently describe the killing as the defendant's unlawful act. The turning point was *Redline,* in which one of the robbers was prosecuted for murder after a policeman fired at him and his confederate as they were fleeing, and killed the confederate.[141] It is significant that when the robbers are fleeing and a policeman fires, the causal tie between the commission of the robbery and the responsive act of shooting is minimal.[142] Yet the point that moved the court in *Redline* was that a confederate was killed rather than an innocent bystander. The policeman's killing the confederate appeared to be justified and, as the reasoning went, no one could be held complicitous in a justified killing. A justified killing was lawful; if there is no liability for one's own lawful conduct, neither should there be for the lawful conduct of another.[143] By implication, other killings in the course of a robbery would still be covered by the felony-murder rule. If one robber killed another for a motive unrelated to the prevention of the robbery, the killing would presumably be unjustified and therefore not excluded by

[139] Commonwealth v. Almeida, 362 Pa. 596, 68 A.2d 595 (1949), *cert. denied,* 339 U.S. 924 (1950).

[140] Commonwealth v. Thomas, 382 Pa. 639, 117 A.2d 204 (1955) (victim of robbery killed escaping co-conspirator; other escaping robber held liable for murder); Commonwealth v. Bolish, 381 Pa. 500, 113 A.2d 464 (1955) (recognizing liability in principle where hired arsonist unintentionally killed himself in a fire).

[141] Commonwealth v. Redline, 391 Pa. 486, 137 A.2d 472 (1958).

[142] Thus the case was not readily subsumed under the holding in Commonwealth v. Thomas, 382 Pa. 639, 117 A.2d 204 (1955), where the party firing the fatal shot was the victim.

[143] See generally §8.7.3 *infra.*

the reasoning of *Redline*. Similarly, if the policeman's bullet struck an innocent bystander, the killing was arguably not justified but rather, as an instance of accidental death, merely excusable.[144] Therefore *Redline* stood for a limited break on the expansion of liability and did little to curtail the existing sweep of the rule.[145]

The court's distinction between a third party's killing a bystander and the killing of a confederate in the robbery has failed to impress either commentators or courts in other jurisdictions.[146] When the problem came before the California Supreme Court in the critical case of *Washington*, the California court readily dismissed the reasoning in *Redline;* that distinction, the court opined, makes liability turn on the marksmanship of the third party.[147]

The facts in *Washington* conform to the recurrent pattern of a holdup that leads to a shooting and, in this case, the death of the confederate. The party shooting was the victim—the owner of the filling station—who was apprised of the holdup and had his gun drawn as the defendant entered the filling station with his own gun drawn. The owner shot without additional provocation. The California court was no more inclined than its Pennsylvania brethren to support a conviction for felony-murder in this type of case. Yet to find sharper shears for pruning back the felony-murder rule, Justice Traynor returned to the language of the statute. The critical language, in his view, was that the murder had to be "committed in the perpetration of, or attempt to perpetrate" one of the enumerated felonies.[148] The notion of "perpetration" implied that the killing had to be committed by the defendant himself; it was not sufficient that it was committed in response to the defendant's

[144] 391 Pa. at 510, 137 A.2d at 483.

[145] *Redline* was extended in Commonwealth ex rel. Smith v. Myers, 438 Pa. 218, 261 A.2d 550 (1970) to cases of third-party killings of bystanders, thus overruling *Almeida*. The law of felony-murder appears to be retained as murder of first degree in the new Pennsylvania Criminal Code, Pa. Cons. Stat. Ann. tit. 18, §2502(b).

[146] LaFave & Scott 551, n. 40; Kadish & Paulsen 294, editorial note. Both critics offer counterexamples illustrating the theory of "perpetration by means." See §8.7.3 *infra*.

[147] People v. Washington, 62 Cal. 2d 777, 780, 402 P.2d 130, 132, 44 Cal. Rptr. 442, 444 (1965).

[148] Cal. Penal Code §189.

provocative acts in perpetrating the robbery. Yet the opinion does not exclude the possibility of convicting for murder where an armed robbery results in the death of a confederate or a bystander. These are cases that could qualify under the second track of liability for murder—namely, high-risk conduct undertaken for a "base anti-social motive and with wanton disregard of human life."[149] Reinterpreting the result in a prior case, the court noted that if the robbers "initiated a gun battle" that results in a fatal shot in response, their conduct might well qualify as murder by excessive risk-taking.[150]

Washington became the driving precedent behind all major murder cases of the late 60s and early 70s. The opinion influenced the law of diminished capacity, the law of high-risk homicide as well as both the first- and second-degree felony-murder cases. In *Washington,* the California Supreme Court, for the first time, endorsed the definition of malice that Justice Traynor had expressed in a concurring opinion in *Thomas.*[151] This definition of malice requiring a "base, anti-social motive" and "wanton disregard of human life" found its way into the *Conley* opinion recognizing diminished capacity a year later,[152] and then became the standard definition of malice in all cases of high-risk homicide.[153] The opinion in *Washington* also articulates the rationale of the felony-murder rule that provided the guideline for all subsequent litigation on the scope of felony-murder in the second degree.[154]

The unfortunate ambiguity of this great opinion derived from the failure of Justice Traynor to mark out the frontier between high-risk homicide and felony-murder in the "perpetration" of a robbery. Of course, the court had the limited task of justifying the reversal of Washington's conviction. Yet an expansive reading of the opinion would suggest that perhaps the court was about to in-

[149] 62 Cal. 2d at 781–82, 402 P.2d at 133, 44 Cal. Rptr. at 445.
[150] *Id.* at 782, 402 P.2d at 134, 44 Cal. Rptr. at 446.
[151] See text at note 109 *supra.*
[152] People v. Conley, 64 Cal. 2d 30, 411 P.2d 911, 49 Cal. Rptr. 815 (1966).
[153] Caljic §8.11 (replacing the statutory language of "abandoned and malignant heart," Cal. Penal Code §188).
[154] See text at notes 97–101 *supra.*

terpret the felony-murder rule to require independent proof of malice in every case. The proof could be made either according to the first track of intentional killing or the second track of high-risk homicide. That holding could readily have been justified by stressing the use of the word "murder" as a statutory precondition of felony-murder. The function of the felony-murder rule would then have been analogous to the use of the means tests; if a killing was shown independently to be murder, the fact that it was perpetrated in the commission of a felony would justify classification in the first degree.[155] The import of such a holding would have been to secure the required "relation between criminal liability and moral culpability" that the court was so concerned about in *Washington.* In People v. Ketchel,[156] decided four years after *Washington,* the court explicitly disavowed this potential line of development. If there was any reasoning for the holding, it was that "the law presumes malice aforethought on the basis of the commission of the felony."[157]

The other question left open in *Washington* was the precise difference between the defendant's firing the fatal shot and the defendant's causing the victim to fire the fatal shot. The former case, the court suggested, was murder in the perpetration of a felony; the latter, murder only if it met the test of malice by excessive risk-taking. After the decision in *Conley* the following year,[158] the distinction took on great practical significance. If the prosecution had to proceed on a theory of high-risk homicide, diminished capacity would probably be admissible on the issue of acting "with a wanton disregard of human life" and a "base anti-social purpose."[159] If, on the other hand, the killing could be treated as felony-murder, the prosecution could probably rely on the doctrine that the underlying felony supplies the malice and thus precludes

[155] See §4.4.6 *supra.*

[156] 71 Cal. 2d 635, 456 P.2d 660; 79 Cal. Rptr. 92 (1969).

[157] *Id.* at 642, 456 P.2d at 663, 79 Cal. Rptr. at 95.

[158] People v. Conley, 64 Cal. 2d 310, 411 P.2d 911, 49 Cal. Rptr. 815 (1966).

[159] This point was admittedly not resolved until People v. Poddar, 10 Cal. 3d 750, 518 P.2d 342, 111 Cal. Rptr. 910 (1974).

proof of diminished capacity.[160] Thus there was considerable incentive to test the distinction proposed in *Washington* between firing the gun oneself (which was clearly felony-murder) and inducing the victim or a police officer to shoot and kill (which might not be). As it turned out, the distinction was too precious to withstand renewed attacks in the courts.

When the problem came before the Supreme Court again in *Taylor*,[161] several intermediate appellate cases had already paved the way for an interweaving of the criteria of malice with the felony-murder rule.[162] The frame for the Supreme Court's decision was a challenge to an indictment against Taylor and Daniels, alleging several acts on the part of Daniels and a third confederate, Smith, that caused one of the victims to shoot and kill Smith. The alleged acts consisted in Smith's pointing a gun at the victims while Daniels threatened that Smith might shoot if they did not cooperate. The court upheld the indictment as sufficient in alleging an "intentional act . . . committed with conscious disregard of life and likely to cause death."[163] The significant phrases missing in this formulation are "wanton disregard of life" and "base and anti-social purpose." It is possible that diminished capacity could be used to negate the element of "conscious disregard of life."[164] Yet it is far more plausible to argue that the defendant's condition of intoxication or psychological disability precludes blaming him for a subjectively "wanton" or "base, anti-social" posture toward the

[160] See note 107 *supra*.

[161] Taylor v. Superior Court, 3 Cal. 3d 578, 477 P.2d 131, 91 Cal. Rptr. 275 (1970).

[162] Brooks v. Superior Court, 239 Cal. App. 2d 538, 48 Cal. Rptr. 762 (1966) (defendant grabbed gun of approaching officer, accidental discharge killed fellow officer); People v. Reed, 270 Cal. App. 2d 37, 75 Cal. Rptr. 430 (1969) (officer accidentally killed hostage being held at gunpoint in car by defendant).

[163] 3 Cal. 3d at 582, 477 P.2d at 13, 91 Cal. Rptr. at 277.

[164] *Cf.* Caljic §8.77 (1976 rev.) which prescribes an instruction that the jury not find malice if they have a reasonable doubt "whether [the defendant] was aware of the duty on him not to commit acts which involve the risk of grave injury or death." This instruction would seem to apply in a case like *Taylor*. At the same time, the Supreme Court steadfastly maintains that diminished capacity does not negate malice in a felony-murder case. People v. Cantrell, 8 Cal. 3d 672, 504 P.2d 1256, 105 Cal. Rptr. 792 (1973).

risk of death.[165] The *Taylor* majority's dispensing with these important qualifying adjectives relating to the degree of the actor's culpability justifies the charge by Justice Peters, dissenting in *Taylor*, that the majority had abandoned *Washington* and reinstituted a variation of the felony-murder rule.[166] By returning in *Taylor* to a formal standard of high-risk conduct "likely to cause death," the court did indeed forsake Justice Traynor's effort to infuse normative content into the concept of malice.

The continuing force of the formal elements of the felony-murder rule are evident as well in the approach of the court to the liability of accomplices in cases like *Washington* and *Taylor*. The court concluded that if Daniels were guilty of the murder of Smith, then his co-conspirator, Taylor, would also be guilty.[167] The guilt of Daniels would be "imputed" to Taylor under a theory of "vicarious liability."[168] It was irrelevant that Taylor did not enter the liquor store where the shooting occurred. Nor would it matter whether he was anywhere near the scene of the crime, nor indeed whether the others had promised him that no shooting would occur. The only requirement for vicarious liability is that murder objectively be "in furtherance of the common design."[169] This is not a standard of accessorial contribution, but of strict liability. It expresses the formal rules of liability that underlie the felony-murder rule and demonstrates that the California courts are still far from

[165] The formal issue is framed by the definition of diminished capacity as the defendant's inability to "comprehend his duty to govern his actions in accord with the duty imposed by law." People v. Conley, 64 Cal. 2d 310, 411 P.2d 911, 49 Cal. Rptr. 815 (1966). For diminished capacity to negate a mental state, the definition of the mental state should presumably include an element of duty to conform one's actions to the law. *Cf.* People v. Poddar, 10 Cal. 3d 750, 758, 518 P.2d 342, 348, 111 Cal. Rptr. 910, 916 (1974) (so defining "wanton disregard" of risk).

[166] 3 Cal. 3d at 585, 477 P.2d at 135, 91 Cal. Rptr. at 279.

[167] 3 Cal. 3d at 583, 477 P.2d at 133–34, 91 Cal. Rptr. at 277–78.

[168] *Cf.* the earlier "clarification" in People v. Gilbert, 63 Cal. 2d 690, 705, 408 P.2d 365, 374, 47 Cal. Rptr. 909, 918 (1965), *rev'd on other grounds*, 388 U.S. 263 (1965), prescribing that the liability of accomplices should be assessed "under the rules defining principals and criminal conspirators."

[169] 3 Cal. 3d at 583 n.1, 477 P.2d at 133 n.1, 91 Cal. Rptr. at 277 n.1.

Justice Traynor's goal of strengthening the link between liability and individual culpability.[170]

As it turned out in the particular case, the defendant Taylor benefited from the rule of vicarious liability. The metaphysics of imputing guilt presupposes that one of the confederates be actually guilty of murder. In the subsequent trial, Daniels was acquitted of murder. Taylor was nonetheless prosecuted and convicted of murder. On a second appeal to the Supreme Court, the conviction was reversed: if Daniels was not guilty, Taylor could not be vicariously liable.[171] This same rule of vicarious liability redounded as well to the benefit of one Antick, who was charged with the felony-murder of his confederate, who initiated the gun battle in which he, the confederate, was killed.[172] The Supreme Court held that murder presupposes the killing of another human being and therefore the dead confederate could not be regarded as guilty of murdering himself. If the confederate was not guilty, there was no guilt to impute to Antick and therefore the conviction was reversed.

When we take up the subject of complicity, we shall see that a rule of accessorial liability might generate liability on the part of the accessory even though the perpetrator is not guilty of the offense.[173] Indeed the common law has struggled for centuries to rid itself of the rule that the accessory is liable only if the perpetrator is liable.[174] But if the theory of vicarious liability is indifferent to the degree of the accessory's contribution, it also provides the incidental benefit of insulating the accessory when there is no punishable crime to be imputed to him.

[170] People v. Washington, 62 Cal. 2d 777, 783, 402 P.2d 130, 134, 44 Cal. Rptr. 442, 446 (1965) (felony-murder rule "erodes the relation between criminal liability and moral culpability").

[171] People v. Taylor, 12 Cal. 3d 686, 527 P.2d 622, 117 Cal. Rptr. 70 (1974).

[172] People v. Antick, 10 Cal. 3d 79, 529 P.2d 43, 117 Cal. Rptr. 475 (1975).

[173] See generally §8.7.3 *infra*.

[174] *Cf.* Cal. Penal Code §972: "An accessory to the commission of a felony may be prosecuted, tried, and punished, though the principal . . . may have been acquitted." It is obvious that if Taylor had been treated as an accessory, he would have been guilty irrespective of the outcome of the prosecution of Daniels.

These reversals in the second *Taylor* case and in *Antick* should not obscure the fact that by the early 1970s the movement to reform the felony-murder in California had run its course. This is particularly evident in related fields of decision. In the late 60s it appeared that the court might systematically undermine the felony-murder rule by applying the criteria worked out in the cases of felony-murder in the second degree. In *Wilson*[175] and *Sears*,[176] the court held that burglary could not support a charge of felony-murder if the killing occurred in a subsequent intentional assault after the burglar was inside the house. The best rationale for this decision would have been the argument articulated later in *Satchell:*[177] when the homicidal risk associated with a felony derives from the likelihood of a subsequent intentional assault and that assault in fact takes place, the prosecution cannot rely on a prediction of intentional killing.[178]

Underlying this theory, it has been noted, is a principle of respect for the offender's power of self-actuation and his ability to decide whether he will engage in the predicted intentional assault. With this theory not yet formulated, the court rested its reversal in *Sears* and *Wilson* on the principle of *Ireland* that the burglary was somehow "included" in the subsequent act of killing.[179] This was a misleading rationale, for it encouraged speculation that the court might be willing to rule that armed robbery could not support a prosecution for felony-murder in the first degree. Robbery is more closely related to the act of causing death than is burglary, and therefore it seemed that the theory of *Ireland* might nullify this most common ground for felony-murder prosecutions.

These speculations were stifled in People v. Burton,[180] decided in 1971; the court held that what was true of burglary was not necessarily true of robbery. The opinion contained some infelicitous

[175] People v. Wilson, 1 Cal. 3d 431, 462 P.2d 22, 82 Cal. Rptr. 494 (1969).

[176] People v. Sears, 2 Cal. 3d 180, 465 P.2d 847, 84 Cal. Rptr. 711 (1970).

[177] People v. Satchell, 6 Cal. 3d 28, 489 P.2d 1361, 98 Cal. Rptr. 33 (1971).

[178] See text at notes 85–89 *supra*.

[179] See text at note 78 *supra*.

[180] 6 Cal. 3d 375, 491 P.2d 793, 99 Cal. Rptr. 1 (1971).

language about the significance of "an independent felonious purpose"[181] as the feature limiting the impact of *Ireland.* Robbery has a different purpose from killing, and therefore it is not "included" in the homicide. By like token, the court reasoned, *Wilson* and *Sears* should be limited to cases in which the felonious intent that renders an entry punishable as burglary is the intent to commit an assault with a deadly weapon. It follows that if the purpose of the burglary is theft or rape, a subsequent assault resulting in death would be automatically classified as first degree murder.

The durability of the felony-murder rule is manifest as well in the tendency broadly to interpret the temporal duration of felonies supporting the rule. If someone is killed miles away from the scene of a robbery and twenty minutes after the robbers leave the scene, can the killing be interpreted as murder "in the perpetration of the robbery"? It is strained to extend the perimeters of perpetration beyond killings that occur in hot pursuit of the felons. Yet the Supreme Court has been willing to expand the ambit of felony-murder to sweep in the killing of a police officer 48 minutes after the robbery, in a situation in which the initial contact between the officer and the suspect had nothing to do with the occurrence of the robbery.[182] In a recent case,[183] the court affirmed these broadly drawn contours of "perpetration" in a case in which the officers took up the pursuit of robbery suspects over a mile from the scene of the robbery and with little evidence to warrant their suspicion, other than the proximity of the suspect's car to the robbery and the fact that the suspect driver and passengers all appeared to be Mexicans; after the police stopped the car, the suspects refused to exit and a gun fight erupted, killing one of the officers. The only nexus between the robbery and the killing derived from the undefended assumption that robbers are likely to kill rather than face arrest. If this dubious assumption is sufficient to make out a case of felony-murder, then it would seem that any

[181] *Id.* at 387, 491 P.2d at 801, 99 Cal. Rptr. at 9.

[182] People v. Kendrick, 56 Cal. 2d 71, 363 P.2d 13, 14 Cal. Rptr. 13 (1961).

[183] People v. Salas, 7 Cal. 3d 812, 500 P.2d 7, 103 Cal. Rptr. 431 (1972).

killing of an officer investigating a robbery would qualify as well. That the investigation was a month or two later would not preclude this distorted conception of killing in the "perpetration of a robbery."[184]

These cases on the scope of "perpetration" indicate that the California felony-murder rule has survived the onslaught that began with Justice Traynor's opinion in *Washington.* The rule is too attractive to law enforcement to be easily surrendered. It provides a formal track of liability, which permits a conviction regardless of the jury's assessment of culpability for causing death and regardless, as a practical matter, of diminished capacity.[185] When it applies, it betokens a high probability of conviction for first-degree murder and therefore, its availability as a threat significantly adds to the bargaining position of prosecutors in negotiating pleas for lesser degrees of homicide. It remains to be seen whether despite these advantages of the rule to law enforcement, the California legislature will follow the lead of England,[186] the Model Penal Code[187] and several other states[188] in abolishing the principle of formal liability.

If the legislature refuses to act, there are intriguing possibilities for a constitutional attack on the rule—particularly in a case in which the formal and arbitrary elements of the rule's application are patent. This would be the case if someone were prosecuted for an accidental death that occurred in the course of an enumerated felony[189] or while driving at a safe speed from the scene

[184] People v. Boss, 210 Cal. 245, 290 P. 881 (1930), held that the *res gestae* of robbery for purposes of the felony-murder rule extended until the felons had reached a point of "temporary safety" and terminated their active escape with the goods. See also People v. Salas, 7 Cal. 3d at 821, 500 P.2d at 13, 103 Cal. Rptr. at 437 (endorsing jury instruction "that a robbery is . . . in progress during the robber's attempt to escape with the loot").

[185] Of course, diminished capacity is admissible to negate the intent required for the underlying felony. People v. Mosher, 1 Cal. 3d 379, 461 P.2d 659, 82 Cal. Rptr. 379 (1969); but see the text at note 107 *supra.*

[186] Homicide Act 1957, c. 11, §1.

[187] MPC §210.2(1)(b) (substituting a rule of "presumed recklessness" for felony-murder).

[188] See note 3 *supra.*

[189] See People v. Morales, 49 Cal. App. 3d 134, 122 Cal. Rptr. 157 (1975) (defen-

of the felony.[190] The most convincing constitutional attack would be made under the equal protection clause. The argument would be that there is no rational basis for treating an accidental homicide as murder in the first degree if it occurs contemporaneously with a burglary, but as non-criminal homicide, totally free from stigma and liability, if it occurs on some other occasion. Of course, the contours of this constitutional attack require refinement. We mean here only to hint at the possibility of bringing constitutional criteria to bear on a problem of justice in the criminal law that the courts and legislatures have not been able to resolve.

§4.4.8. The Institutional Context of Formal Liability. In contrast to their record in criminal cases, courts in California and other states have engaged in unremitting efforts to rid the law of torts of arbitrary, formal elements. The rule of negligence per se is also a formal rule of liability based on causing harm in the course of an unlawful act. Yet the courts seek to refine this harsh doctrine by admitting consideration of the actor's fault under the circumstances.[191] The doctrine of proximate causation has received sophisticated elaboration in the literature of tort theory,[192] but its relevance is hardly comprehended in the cases on the scope of the misdemeanor-manslaughter rule and liability for third-party killings. This is not an adventitious phenomenon. It has roots that run to the very ground soil that nourishes and yet stunts the growth of a theory of criminal law.

---

dant snatched a purse from an old lady; the lady fell to ground, with some dispute about whether the defendant pushed her. She injured her elbow, which led to period of inactivity, resulting in a fatal blood clot in the lung. She died three weeks after the incident. Defendant was convicted of murder in the perpetration of a robbery. Reversed on the ground that the jury was not instructed on the degree of force necessary for a robbery).

[190] Another source of arbitrariness derives from the evolution of the law of burglary to include entries without breaking. See §3.2.3 *supra*. Under California law today, killing in the course of shoplifting (if there was intent to steal upon entering the store) is murder in the first degree, People v. Earl, 29 Cal. App. 3d 894, 105 Cal. Rptr. 831 (1973), while a non-negligent killing incident to a theft on the street is not punished as homicide. See *Morales*, note 189 *supra*.

[191] See Saterlee v. Orange Glenn School District, 29 Cal. 2d 581, 177 P.2d 279 (1947).

[192] See notes 54, 55, 57 *supra*.

The significant fact about tort law is that the system of docrines and rules is taken to be subject to total enforcement. This conception of the law is inescapable, for the enforcement of the tort rules is in the hands of private litigants. It follows that the judges must refine the principles of liability to achieve the closest possible fit between the dictates of the law and what is thought to be just and sound policy. Yet no one except perhaps the uninitiated thinks this way about the law of homicide. When the courts say that accidental homicides occurring in the course of burglaries are subject to liability as murder, that statement must be understood in the framework of a system in which prosecutors screen the cases for those that they think are apt for criminal prosecution. There need not be a perfect fit between the formal body of law and what we regard as properly subject to criminal punishment, because the gap can be corrected by administrative decisions prior to trial. Thus the legitimation of prosecutorial discretion encourages the retention of overly broad rules of liability that on their face seem to be capable of generating great injustice.

The argument may be carried one step further. The allocation of screening powers to the prosecutorial bureaucracy provides a rationale for increasing the severity of the nominal rules of criminal liability. As the legislature sets the speed limit at 55 miles per hour if it desires the public to drive at 60 miles per hour, so they may retain harsh doctrines of felony-murder, and even include the threat of capital punishment, when they expect prosecutors to bargain with suspects and settle cases on the basis of pleas of guilty to manslaughter and second-degree murder. The easier it is to threaten conviction for first-degree murder, the easier it is for a prosecutor to induce a plea of guilty to manslaughter. With the overwhelming percentage of cases resolved by pleas of guilty, the doctrines of first-degree murder have to be thought of not only as expressions of justice, but as counters to be used in the plea-bargaining process. Perhaps this explains why we encounter more rigid, formalized definitions at the level of first-degree murder than in the analysis of manslaughter. This less charitable view of the prosecutorial function suggests that perhaps the courts and legislatures are complicitous in creating an illusion that the suspect who pleads guilty to manslaughter is truly receiving adequate consideration for waiving his constitutional right to a trial by jury. If illusion it be, it derives from institutional collusion in preserving doctrines of the criminal law that are harsher than those we would tolerate if the criminal law, like the law of torts, were subject to potentially full enforcement.

It might be illuminating in this respect to compare the early common law of larceny with the pattern of refinement in homicide. Prior to the metamorphosis of larceny, the doctrines of the crime represented a good fit between the law and the desirable ambit of liability. This fit derived, no doubt, from the early enforcement of the law of theft by private execution. Overstating the rules of *furtum manifestum* would have led to disastrous consequences. Defending property owners would have killed nominal thieves where the community did not share the judgment that the "thief" warranted execution. This delicate correspondence between the law and the community's sense of justice never existed in the law of homicide. As we shall see in the next chapter, even before the legitimation of prosecutorial discretion, the rules of liability for homicide were characteristically overdrawn. At earlier stages of liability, the anticipated corrective was the pardoning power of the King, a power, analogous to prosecutorial discretion, that played an essential role in hewing down the rules of liability to conform with principles of justice.

§4.5. *Comparative Notes.*

The noteworthy, formal difference between the Anglo-American law of homicide and the evolved law of France, Germany and the Soviet Union is that the latter three systems have generated distinct grades of criminal homicide without relying on a unifying concept comparable to malice aforethought. Nonetheless, all three systems evidence a set of graded offenses that correspond roughly to the spectrum ranging from manslaughter to first-degree murder.

In this section we shall explore the varying techniques of Continental legislation in distinguishing among the three primary grades of homicide; in addition, we shall underscore some features of legislative technique on the Continent that might provide guidance to law reform in Anglo-American jurisdictions.

§4.5.1. **Analogues to Manslaughter.** All three systems under consideration recognize a special offense of killing under adequate provocation. Yet in all three, the legislative technique is to define a special crime that is punished less severely than the standard form of intentional homicide. This reduced form of liability enjoys no separate label analogous to manslaughter.

According to French Penal Code §321, homicide is subject to mitigation if the killing was "provoked by blows or gravely violent acts against a human being";[1] analogously, §213 of the German code finds a ground for mitigation in "mistreatment or serious outrage"[2] directed against the actor or his dependents that "inflames"[3] the actor and thus "drives him on the spot to commit the deed."[4] While the German standard would appear to encompass insults and other verbal assaults,[5] the settled case law in France is that the statutory standard of "*violence*" does not encompass purely verbal provocation.[6]

The critical passage in the RSFSR criminal code appears to follow the German rather than the French model. The test is whether the act is provoked by "force of a serious outrage" or "any other illegal activity of the victim."[7] The innovation in the Russian formulation is an explicit reference to "serious mental disturbance" as the cause of the actor's partially excusable response; the disturbance must be triggered "suddenly" by the provocative conduct.[8] This integration of psychological criteria into the analysis of prov-

§4.5. [1] Code Pénal §321 (*provoquée par des coups ou violences graves envers les personnes*).

[2] StGB §213 (*Misshandlung oder schwere Beleidigung*).

[3] *Ibid.*; "*der Tetschläger* [war] . . . *zum Zorne gereizt.*"

[4] *Ibid.*; "*auf der Stelle zur Tat hingeressen worden.*"

[5] Schönke-Schröder-Eser §213, note 3, at 1278.

[6] Lambert 140.

[7] Ugol. kod. (RSFSR) §104.

[8] *Ibid.*

ocation is suggestive of the Model Penal Code's proposed mitigation for an intentional homicide in the actor's "extreme mental or emotional disturbance."[9] Yet the Soviet version of provocation concurs with German and French law in insisting that the provocative acts emanate from the victim. Thus Continental legislators balk at extending the ground of mitigation, as with the Model Penal Code, to cover cases like *Simpson,* in which a father, provoked by his wife's infidelity and neglect of his child, killed the innocent child.[10] Provocation is thus distinguished from the general issue of diminished responsibility.[11]

There is some disagreement in Continental theory about why the provocative acts must emanate from the victim. French practice suggests that the rationale for this limitation is the contributory fault of the victim; if the victim's heirs enter the criminal case and sue simultaneously for tort recovery, as they may under French procedure, a good defense of provocation will reduce the tort recovery as well as the gravity of the criminal conviction.[12] Whether the victim has contributed in fact to the killing does not seem to affect the German analysis, for if the party killing is mistaken about whether the provocative acts have taken place, his killing will nonetheless be mitigated.[13] It is difficult to reconcile the theory of the victim's contributory fault with the recognition of provocation based on mistake as equivalent to provocation in fact. The former stresses the actual interaction of the victim and his slayer; the latter focusses more on the actor's condition of reduced self-control at the time of the killing.

French law recognizes some other intriguing limitations on provocation as a ground of mitigation. According to an explicit statutory provision, provocation can never apply as a partial excuse in cases in which the actor kills a parent (mother, father,

[9] MPC §210.3(1)(b).

[10] See §4.2.1, at note 13 *supra.*

[11] Diminished responsibility is regulated in StGB §21; there is no analogous provision in either Soviet or French law.

[12] Lambert 138; Judgment of May 8, 1967, Gazette du Palais 1967.2.16 (*Cour de Cassation*).

[13] Schönke-Schröder-Eser §213, note 8, at 1279.

grandparent),[14] nor is the defense recognized in cases of killing a spouse unless the slayer's life is put in danger by the provocative acts.[15] These exceptions reveal the normative dimension of provocation; they express a special duty to tolerate provocative blows within the family, particularly in the case of a child suffering the anger of a parent.

All three Continental systems under study recognize the case of killing an adulterous spouse, caught *in flagrante* as a sufficient ground of provocation.[16] The three systems also concur in a maximum of five years imprisonment in cases of homicide committed under provocation.[17] This maximum is low by comparison with the fifteen-year maximum permitted under California law[18] and the ten-year maximum recommended by the Model Penal Code. [19] Of course, the operative significance of these maximum terms is difficult to discern without a detailed study of sentencing and parole practices.

The analogue to involuntary manslaughter in French, German and Soviet law is a separate offense of negligent homicide. The French system is the only one of the three that takes killing in the course of an unlawful act *(inobservation des règlements)* as nominally conclusive on the required element of culpability.[20] The German[21] and Soviet formulations,[22] which took form much later in history, rest simply on the concept of negligent killing.[23] Several features of this simply defined offense of negligent homicide are worth noting. In neither German nor Soviet law is there any anxiety felt about neg-

[14] Code Penal §323 (*Le parricide n'est jamais excusable*); see Lambert 143–45.

[15] Code Pénal §324.

[16] Code Pénal §324 (applicable only as to husband's killing wife and lover if caught in the act in the matrimonial home); Schönke-Schröder-Eser §213 note 3, at 1278; Kurs (SP 1973) at 533–534.

[17] Code Pénal §326; StGB §213; Ugol. kod. (RSFSR) §104.

[18] Cal. Pénal Code §193.

[19] MPC §210.3(2); §6.06(2).

[20] Code Pénal §319; see Lambert 186–88 (arguing that violating a legal rule is a graver form of fault than simple inadvertence).

[21] StGB §222.

[22] Ugol. kod. (RSFSR) §106.

[23] *Cf.* the argument, *supra* §4.4.2, that the common-law doctrine of misdemeanor-manslaughter is evolving toward a standard of negligent homicide.

ligence as a suitable ground for holding someone liable for causing death. Neither system is plagued by the question whether ordinary as opposed to gross negligence will suffice. Nor is there any doubt about inadvertent negligence as a subjective rather than an objective standard of liability.[24] These attitudes toward punishing negligent homicide should stimulate us to consider why there is so much confusion and anxiety in Anglo-American law about negligence as a suitable ground for criminal liability.[25] This is a topic best reserved for independent consideration.[26]

§4.5.2. The Standard Form of Criminal Homicide. In all three Continental systems, the standard form of criminal homicide *(meurtre, Totschlag, ubijstvo)* is defined simply as intentionally killing another human being.[27] Of course it is implicit that the killing be without provocation. The rough analogue to this standard offense in the United States is second-degree murder. The major difference is that this standard form of the crime cannot be established in Continental jurisdictions either (1) on a theory of reckless homicide, or (2) felony-murder. Yet at least as to reckless homicide sufficient to constitute killing with malice in the United States, this nominal difference is highly misleading. Both Soviet and German law take an indirect intention *(dolus eventualis)* to be sufficient to constitute intentional killing.[28] The technical definition of indirect intention is that if the actor engages in life-endangering behavior, his killing is intentional if he "reconciles himself" or "makes peace"[29] with the likelihood of death. Thus, if the killing is

[24] For documentation, see Fletcher, *The Theory of Criminal Negligence: A Comparative Analysis,* 119 U. Pa. L. Rev. 401, 428–430 (1971).

[25] It should be noted that the maximum punishment for negligent homicide in Continental jurisdictions is relatively light. Code Pénal §319 (two years); StGB §222 (five years); Ugol. kod. (RSFSR) §106 (three years); *cf.* Cal. Penal Code §193 (maximum of 15 years for involuntary manslaughter, maximum of five years for vehicular manslaughter with gross negligence).

[26] See §§6.6.6 & 9.2.3 *infra.*

[27] Code Pénal §295 ("*L'homicide commis volontairement est qualifié meurtre*); StGB §212 ("*Wer einin Menschen* [*vorsätzlich*] *tötet* . . .); Ugol. Kod. (RSFSR) §103 ("intentional killing").

[28] Schönke-Schröder-Cramer §15, notes 68–79, at 201–03; Jescheck 222–24; Kurs (GP 1968) at 417–20.

[29] In German: *ob er sich mit dem Erfolg abfindet.* Jescheck 222. See §6.5.2 *infra.*

committed with "manifest indifference to the value of human life," even conduct of minimal risk can qualify as intentional homicide. Thus if the suspect fires at a moving car with people in it and a passenger is hit by the bullet, his killing is likely to be treated as intentional. A large number of killings that would be classified as reckless murder in the United States would meet the Continental criteria of *dolus eventualis.*

The penalties for this standard form of homicide vary widely among Continental jurisdictions. In France, the maximum prescribed by statute is imprisonment for life;[30] in Germany, imprisonment for a maximum of only five years;[31] and in the Soviet Union, imprisonment for ten years.[32]

§4.5.3. Aggravated Homicide. The techniques for defining aggravated homicide vary widely, but the point of all systems of grading is to define the most heinous forms of killing subject to life imprisonment or, in France and the Soviet Union, to the death penalty. The analogue to this offense in the United States is not only first-degree murder, but the newly cast offenses of capital murder—namely, those cases of egregious murder subject to the death penalty.[33] To elicit the underlying patterns in these diverse legislative systems, we shall consider three factors that shape the definition of aggravated homicide.

A. The Motive of the Slaying. The German code contains the most detailed listing of the motives that are sufficient to classify a killing as aggravated homicide *(Mord).*[34] Two of these enumerated motives are unusual features of German legislation: an intentional killing is regarded as aggravated if committed (1) for the sake of the pleasure gained in killing *(Mordlust),* or (2) for the sake of sexual satisfaction.

The latter ground was initially interpreted narrowly to require a perverse sexual interest in necrophilia;[35] in recent years the

[30] Code Pénal §304(3).
[31] StGB §212(2).
[32] Ugol. kod. (RSFSR) §103.
[33] See §4.6 *infra.*
[34] StGB §211(2).
[35] See Judgment of June 8, 1955, 7 BGHSt. 353, in which the killing was so classified. The opinion does not preclude a broader interpretation. *Id.* at 354.

courts and commentators have broadened the interpretation to include cases of killing to overcome the resistance of a rape victim.[36] This relation brings the German standard in line with the theory of felony-murder in rape cases that once prevailed in the English courts.[37] The German courts would say that there is an intent to kill in these cases, but as we have seen, the standard of "intent" is interpreted loosely to encompass dangerous conduct in which the rapist is indifferent to the risk of death.[38]

The third motive mentioned in the German code, killing for a pecuniary motive *(Habgier)*,[39] is widely shared in several legislative schemes. In the RSFSR code, it is specifically listed as an aggravating factor sufficient to warrant the imposition of the death penalty.[40] It also appears prominently as a ground for capital punishment in the United States. For example, in the Georgia statute upheld by the United States Supreme Court,[41] the ten aggravating circumstances include: "The purpose of receiving money or any other thing of monetary value."[42] When the required motive is so defined, the actor must kill for the direct purpose of gain; a killing incidental to a robbery is insufficient. The Georgia provision appears to require a purpose to receive a concrete thing of value.[43] The German provision is interpreted flexibly to include cases of eliminating a competing heir or a creditor.[44]

After listing these three motives, the German statute concludes with a catchall clause covering all cases of intentional killing for "base motives" *(niedrige Beweggründe)*. As elaborated in the case law, these "base motives" include vengeance and jealousy[45] avoid-

[36] Judgment of September 17, 1963, 19 BGHSt. 102 (defendant choked his victim in order to overcome her resistance).

[37] *Cf.* Director of Public Prosecutions v. Beard, [1920] 2 A.C. 479 (H.L.), discussed *supra* in §4.4 at note 131.

[38] See text at note 29 *supra*.

[39] StGB §211(2).

[40] Ugol. kod. (RSFSR) §102(a).

[41] Gregg v. Georgia, 428 U.S. 153 (1976).

[42] Ga. Code Ann. §27-2534.1(b)(4).

[43] *Ibid.*

[44] See Judgment of October 22, 1957, 10 BGHSt. 399 (*D* attempted to kill his pregnant girl friend in order to avoid support payments).

[45] Judgment of September 30, 1952, 3 BGHSt. 180.

ing arrest[46] and racial hatred.[47] The Soviet statute avoids a catchall clause of this sort, but includes another broad consideration that is peculiar to the Soviet legal style. A sufficient ground for classifying an intentional homicide as aggravated, and thus subject to the death penalty, is killing "for hooliganistic purposes."[48] The notion of "hooliganism" in Soviet law is closely associated with violations of public order and the proper mode of Socialist life, and is typified by drunk and disorderly behavior in public. A good example of the USSR Supreme Court's construing this provision is the case of *A*[49] who went to a restaurant with some friends and became drunk and boisterous after having had too much to drink. His friend *G* tried to quiet him down. As they left the restaurant and started down the street, *A* lagged behind the others; then he attacked *G* and stabbed him twice. This was a killing that, in the Court's view, was motivated by "hooliganistic motives." The important criminological significance of this doctrine is that it fashions a framework in which drunkenness serves not to excuse the homicide, but to aggravate it. Soviet criminologists regard the link between intoxication and violent criminality as so strong that it is understandable that especially repressive measures would be taken against drunken killings.[50]

B. The Manner of Killing. Considerable consensus prevails on the manner of killing sufficient to qualify homicide as aggravated and therefore subject to the most serious penalty under the law. Virtually all systems include a reference to killings that are especially cruel or barbaric. French law takes an intentional killing to be subject to the death penalty if it is committed by "torture or barbarous acts."[51] German and Soviet law refer generally to

[46] Judgment of July 14, 1970, 25 MDR 722 (1971) (attempted murder).

[47] Judgment of October 3, 1949, 2 Entscheidungen des Obersten Gerichtshofes für die Britische Zone 179, 180.

[48] Ugol. kod. (RSFSR) §102(b).

[49] 1966 (2) Bulletin of the Supreme Court USSR 28–29, reported in Kurs (SP 1973) at 510–11.

[50] *Id.* at 482 (alcohol regarded as significant factor in 25 percent of all homicides).

[51] Code Pénal §303 (classified as *assassinat*); *id.* §302 (*assassinat* punished by death).

"cruelty"[52] and "special cruelty"[53] as aggravating circumstances. In its listing of aggravating criteria sufficient for capital punishment, the Model Penal Code includes a general clause referring to murders that are "especially heinous, atrocious or cruel, manifesting exceptional depravity."[54] Some states have included this highly emotional language in their listing of grounds sufficient for the death penalty,[55] and the Supreme Court has upheld the clause against a challenge of excessive vagueness.[56]

Another general means regarded as sufficient for aggravated murder is killing by ambush or lying-in-wait. Killing secretively, by exploiting the victim's vulnerability, lies at the core of the English law of homicide.[57] The analogous concept of *guet-apens* is of ancient vintage in the French law of homicide. In the Penal Code of 1810, it appears as one of the two grounds (along with premeditation) for classifying an intentional killing as the capital crime of *assassinat*.[58] German law employs an analogous, but slightly different notion of surreptitious killing.[59] This manner of killing, sufficient for aggravated homicide, includes cases of inducing a victim to enter an ambush (but perhaps not all instances of lying-in-wait).[60] It goes beyond the analogous, common-law and French concepts by encompassing the killing of another person, particularly a spouse, in his or her sleep.[61] The German commentators stress the element of breach of trust as the underlying element that renders *heimtückisch* killings so heinous.[62]

Another common standard for qualifying a homicide as

[52] StGB §211(2) (*grausam*).
[53] Ugol. kod. (RSFSR) §102(d).
[54] MPC §210.6(3)(h).
[55] Fla. Stat. Ann. §921.141(4)(h) (Supp.) ("especially heinous, atrocious or cruel").
[56] Proffitt v. Florida, 428 U.S. 242 (1976).
[57] See §4.2.3 *supra*.
[58] Code Pénal §296.
[59] StGB §211(2).
[60] See Judgment of January 17, 1968, 22 BGHSt. 77.
[61] Judgment of October 8, 1969, 23 BGHSt. 119. For a critique of this decision, see Hassemer, *Die Mordmerkmale, insbesondere "heimtückisch" und "niedrige Beweggründe,"* 1971 JS 626.
[62] Schönke-Schröder-Eser §211, notes 14–16, at 1270; Maurach SP at 35–36.

among the most grave offenses is whether the act of killing endangers a large number of people. This is described in German law as killing by "socially dangerous means";[63] in the RSFSR, as killing by "means dangerous to many people."[64] The same consideration is expressed in California's defining the use of "a destructive device or explosive" as sufficient for classifying a murder as one in the first degree.[65] In addition, several jurisdictions in the United States refer to creating a "great risk of death to many persons" as one of the aggravating circumstances to be considered in assessing the death penalty.[66]

France is the only one of the three foreign systems under study that relies on the notion of "premeditation" as a distinguishing mark of aggravated homicide.[67] This prominent feature, as well as the general de-emphasis of motives in the analysis of aggravated homicide, brings into focus the general similarity of style between the French and Anglo-American laws of homicide.

C. Felony-Murder. The similarity of French and American law is further borne out by their being the only systems among all those under study that maintain a comprehensive rule of felony-murder. French Penal Code §304 provides that intentional homicide should be punished capitally if the homicide "precedes, accompanies, or follows another felony." The only requirement is that of "concomitance," spatial and temporal, between the felony and the homicide. Yet the French rule is less sweeping than the American felony-murder rule, for it encompasses only cases of intentional homicide.

The German and Soviet statutes both contain a clause for classifying an intentional homicide as aggravated if it is committed in connection with another felony.[68] Yet both provisions expressly capture a limitation on the rule that, as I have argued, was implicit in the English common law of felony-murder: the homicide must

[63] StGB §211(2).
[64] Ugol. kod. (RSFSR) §102(e).
[65] Cal. Penal Code §189.
[66] Ga. Code Ann. §27–2534.1(b)(3) (Supp.); Fla. Stat. Ann. §921.141(5)(c) (Supp.).
[67] Code Pénal §296.
[68] StGB §211(2); Ugol. kod. (RSFSR) §102(f).

serve either to facilitate or to conceal the ancillary felony.[69] This limitation presumably excludes all cases of killing by third parties as well as killings committed by one confederate against another unless killing the confederate would serve to conceal the felony. The grounds for capital murder in the United States often include a ground of felony-murder,[70] sometimes with the limitation that the killing must be intentional,[71] yet the connection required between the felony and the homicide is typically only one of temporal and spatial concomitance, as in the French law of capital murder. It would have been far preferable to follow the model of German and Soviet legislation and require, as a condition for the death penalty, that the intentional homicides serve to facilitate or conceal the felony.[72]

The Soviet law of aggravated homicide includes one exceptional case of felony-murder in the sweeping sense characteristic of legislation in the United States. If an intentional killing is committed concomitantly with a rape, then the killing is subject to the death penalty regardless of whether the object of the killing is to further or to conceal the rape.[73]

§4.5.4. Special Features of Continental Legislation. Continental codes contain two variations of criminal homicide that are wanting in Anglo-American practice. The first is a German provision that responds to our ambivalence about voluntary euthanasia. None of the legal systems under study recognizes consent as a defense to homicide and therefore the voluntary euthanasia of terminally ill patients constitutes intentional homicide. Though we do not recognize the legality of mercy killings based on consent of the decedent, most of us are inclined to feel that in particular circumstances such acts of mercy are morally justifiable. This conflict between the traditional legal rule and contemporary moral senti-

[69] As to German law, see Schönke-Schroder-Eser §211, notes 21–22, at 1271–72. *Cf.* Code Pénal §304(2).

[70] Ga. Code Ann. §27-2534.1(b)(2) (Supp.); Fla. Stat. Ann. §921.141(5)(d) (Supp.).

[71] Texas Penal Code §19.03.

[72] It is important to note that the expanded German conception of "conditional intent" (*dolus eventualis*) would treat many cases of homicidal risk as intentional killing. See §6.5.2 *infra*.

[73] Ugol. Kod. (RSFSR) §102(f).

ment might find accommodation in prosecutors refusing to bring charges. Yet if the case does come to trial, the defendant, particularly if he is not a physician, might well be convicted of first-degree murder.

A. Killing on Request. The German code responds to the tension between the traditional rule and our moral sense in particular circumstances by recognizing a special offense of "killing on request."[74] Punished at the same level as unprovoked intentional homicide (i.e., a maximum of five years imprisonment), this offense has two critical elements: (1) that the victim "explicity and earnestly demand" that he be put to death, and (2) that this demand provide a motive for the killing.[75] The rationale for the penalty is that the victim's consent reduces the wrongfulness of the killing.[76]

This offense of "killing on request" should be distinguished from related variations of homicide. First, voluntary euthanasia is obviously distinguishable from involuntary euthanasia, where the victim has not requested or consented to the termination of his life. Secondly, killing by request must be distinguished from assisting another person to commit suicide. The difference between the two types of offense is a matter of degree. Killing by request requires that the suspect be the active party in the termination of another's life; assisting someone else to commit suicide implies that the suicidant is the prime mover in bringing on his own death. If the defendant lays hands on the party wishing to die—he suffocates him or gives him an injection—the case is readily classified as killing by request. If, on the other hand, he merely makes pills available to the suicidant, the degree of participation comes closer to merely aiding in someone else's active decision.[77]

[74] StGB §216. The offense is *Tötung auf Verlangen,* which is literally translated as "killing on demand." That translation raises an infelicitous association with the phrase "abortion on demand."

[75] The better view seems to be that the victim's demand need not be the exclusive motive. G. Arzt, Strafrecht Besonderer Teil: Delikte gegen die Person 61 (1977).

[76] *Id.* at 60; Schönke-Schröder-Eser §216, note 16, at 1281. It follows that an accessory in the act of "killing on request" cannot be punished for a higher degree of wrongful homicide, even if the accessory is ignorant of the victim's request.

[77] For a controversial borderline case, see Judgment of August 14, 1963, 19

Aiding someone else's suicide has encountered an extraordinary variety of legal responses. Because neither suicide nor attempted suicide is punished in the jurisdictions under study, there is a strong tendency to regard aiding in suicide as participation in legal activity and therefore itself legal. This is the current stand, in principle, in France[78] and Germany.[79] Yet in both jurisdictions, there are covert techniques for penalizing assistance in a suicide. French commentators favor the use of the general statute requiring affirmative aid to persons in distress as a medium of punishing those who fail to prevent suicides.[80] Rejecting this view, a controversial German case held that failing to prevent the suicide of a wife (or close relative) may be punished as criminal homicide by omission.[81] Thus we have the paradox that actively assisting a suicide (rather than killing on request) is free from punishment, but failing to intervene in a suicide is punishable as criminal homicide.[82]

Soviet jurists concur that in principle aiding in suicide ought not to be punished;[83] however, the 1960 RSFSR Code does address itself to the more limited problem of "driving" another person to commit suicide.[84] This specially hewn offense is limited to cases in

---

BGHSt. 135, in which two young lovers entered into a suicide pact after the girl's parent forbade their seeing each other. After an unsuccessful try with pills, the two agreed to asphyxiate themselves with automotive exhaust. The young man attached a hose to the exhaust pipe and fed it through the car window. The two were found, unconscious, with the motor still running and the boy's foot on the gas pedal. The girl died. The Supreme Court concluded the surviving lover was guilty of "killing on request." The controlling consideration was that the young man was in control of events. The decision is criticized as "hair-splitting" in Arzt, *supra* note 85, at 71. *Cf.* Lambert 46–47, arguing that under French law the dominant party in a suicide pact should be guilty of murder.

78 Lambert 45.

79 Schönke-Schröder-Eser §211, preliminary note 16, at 1265.

80 Lambert 46, favoring application of Code Pénal §63(2).

81 Judgment of February 12, 1952, 2 BGHSt. 150.

82 For a critique of these developments and a preference for treating the problem as a breach of the duty to render first aid under StGB §330c, see Schmidhäuser, *Selbstmord und Beteiligung am Selbstmord in strafrechtlicher Sicht,* Festschrift für Welzel 801, 809 (1974).

83 Kurs (SP 1973) at 544.

84 Ugol. kod. (RSFSR) §107.

which the victim is dependent on the offender, either materially or in some other way, and the offender "drives" the victim to suicide or attempted suicide by "cruel treatment" or "systematic degradation." Withdrawing the criminal law to the special case of inducing suicide generates a negative implication that merely assisting in someone else's voluntary decision should be exempt from punishment.

By comparison with these Continental developments, English and American lawmakers have yet to follow out the implications of legalizing suicide. Aiding in another's suicide is still murder in many jurisdictions, although there is little modern authority on the point.[85] In Great Britain,[86] California[87] and many other states,[88] a specially enacted offense provides for reduced penalties in cases of aiding and abetting another's suicide. These statutory forms do not raise the distinction that plagues the German courts, namely between non-punishable aid in another's suicide and killing on request. Both are collapsed in the crime of aiding and abetting suicide.

Another important distinction to keep in mind is that between actively rendering aid[89] and passively allowing an illness to take its course. The latter cases of passive euthanasia are exempt from liability unless there is an affirmative duty to intervene and render aid or treatment. This is a problem that we shall take up after considering the general problem of liability for failing to prevent death.[90]

B. Infanticide. Another special feature of Continental legis-

[85] See LaFave & Scott 570–71, n.24 for a list of decisions prior to 1920.

[86] Suicide Act 1961, c. 60, §2 (aiding and abetting suicide punishable by maximum of 14 years).

[87] Cal. Penal Code §401 (aiding and abetting suicide, punishable by maximum of five years).

[88] E.g., Conn. Gen. Stat. Ann. §53-A-57 (form of manslaughter); Wis. Stat. Ann. §940.12 (special offense). *Cf.* MPC §210.5 (causing suicide by "force, duress or deception").

[89] The category of active aid includes, in the German context, both aiding and abetting a voluntary suicide and killing on request.

[90] See §8.3 *infra*.

lation is an expression of indulgence towards mothers killing newborn infants. All the systems under study recognize a special crime of infanticide, carrying a reduced penalty, that applies only to the mother and to a newborn infant as victim. The offense presumably acknowledges the stress incident to childbirth and the reduced culpability of a mother's killing her own offspring.[91] Yet in the German codification (but not the French or Soviet versions) the offense covers only the killing of illegitimate offspring.[92] Thus in the genesis of this special offense of mitigated liability, there may be an implicit assumption that the life of the illegitimate child is less worthy of social protection.[93] Building that judgment into the criminal law would be unconstitutional in the United States[94] and it may well be in Germany.[95]

An interesting feature of the Soviet legislation is worth noting. The Soviet version of infanticide covers all cases of mothers killing their newborn children.[96] Yet as an expression of the legislative independence of the 16 Soviet Republics, some of the republic codes recognize the offense and others do not.[97] In the RSFSR, for example, there is no special offense of infanticide, and therefore the killing of the newborn would be treated like any other case of homicide.

[91] See Code Pénal §302(2), stressing that only the mother should be partially excused; accomplices should be punished for murder.

[92] StGB §217.

[93] The commentators stress that the rationale for the offense is the presumed reduced culpability of the mother; Schönke-Schröder-Eser §217 note 1, at 1281; Arzt, *supra* note 75, at 57. It is not uncommon for an outdated theory of the victim's desert or moral worth to survive as a theory about the actor's reduced culpability. *Cf.* the rule of mitigation for killing a spouse caught in an adulterous embrace, *supra* §4.2.1.

[94] The leading case on the imperative to treat legitimate and illegitimate children equally is Levy v. Louisiana, 391 U.S. 68 (1968).

[95] Grundgesetz art. 6(5) ("Legislation should secure illegitimate children the same conditions for their physical and spiritual development as enjoyed by legitimate children"). This provision of the Constitution is interpreted to confer a right directly upon illegitimate children, Maunz-Dürig-Herzog, Grundgesetz: Kommentar, art. 6, note 49.

[96] Kurs (SP 1973) at 538–39.

[97] E.g., Ugol. kod. (Ukraine) §96; Ugol. kod. (Uzbekistan) §83.

§4.6. *Capital Homicide.*

After the upheavals of 1974[1] and 1976,[2] the constitutional law of capital punishment in the United States has gravitated to a position of semi-stability. It has now become fairly clear that the death penalty may only be used in homicide cases,[3] and the procedures for sentencing must ensure both stability and regularity, on the one hand, and an opportunity for mitigation and individualization, on the other. How the required degree of regularity should be secured is a matter of some disagreement among the justices, but at least we know that statutorily well-defined criteria and procedural checks against irregular decisions contribute to the desired result.[4]

The required degree of flexibility is ensured by permitting the sentencing authority to consider mitigating circumstances. A mandatory death penalty, even for killing a police officer, is unconstitutional.[5] But, if the sentencing authority must consider mitigating circumstances, one should expect a clearer understanding of the criteria that sentencing authorities must consider. The eight mitigating circumstances listed in the Model Penal Code's provi-

§4.6. [1] Furman v. Georgia, 408 U.S. 238 (1972) (declaring existing capital punishment statutes unconstitutional as cruel and unusual punishment).

[2] Three decisions upheld the state sentencing procedure: Gregg v. Georgia, 428 U.S. 153 (1976); Jurek v. Texas,428 U.S. 262 (1976); Proffitt v. Florida, 428 U.S. 242 (1976). For a critique of these decisions, see Black, *Due Process for Death: Jurek v. Texas and Companion Cases,* 26 Cath. U.L. Rev. 1 (1976). Two decisions in the 1976 term invalidated state statutes on the ground that they did not provide sufficient opportunity for mitigation in particular cases: Roberts v. Louisana, 428 U.S. 325 (1976); Woodson v. North Carolina, 428 U.S. 280 (1976).

[3] Coker v. Georgia, 433 U.S. 584 (1977).

[4] *Compare* the opinion of Mr. Justice Stewart in Gregg v. Georgia, 428 U.S. 153 (1976) (stressing "careful instructions" to the jury and the review by the trial judge) *with* the opinion by Mr. Justice White in the same case, *id.* at 207 (stressing the function by the state supreme court as a check against arbitrary sentencing decisions).

[5] H. Roberts v. Louisiana, 431 U.S. 633 (1977). At the state level, see Rockwell v. Superior Court, 18 Cal. 3d 420, 556 P.2d 1101, 134 Cal. Rptr. 650 (1976); People v. Velez, 88 Misc. 2d 378, 388 N.Y.S.2d 519 (1976).

sion on capital sentencing[6] are virtually all variations of excusing conditions or factors,[7] such as the consent of the victim,[8] that qualify the wrong in killing.[9] Must a state recognize all eight of these mitigating circumstances? Could a state recognize only one? In the most recent relevant case, the court listed several categories of mitigating circumstances that the sentencing authority has to consider, but there is no suggestion that any of these specific grounds is constitutionally required.[10] One ground mentioned by the court—that the offender believed he had a moral justification for the killing[11]—provoked a stinging reply by Justices Rehnquist and White.[12] It is clear that if some mitigating circumstances must be considered, the court will eventually have to think more deeply about the particular grounds that warrant constitutional status.[13]

The stabilization of capital homicide means that the highest degree of homicide in the United States is defined by the complex set of criteria that justify the death penalty. There are obviously no rules at this level of liability, for the aggravating grounds that might justify the death penalty must be considered along with the criteria of mitigation. The situation is also complicated by the conceptualization of capital murder as a sentencing decision rather than a category of substantive law. The procedural manifestation of this way of looking at capital murder is that the right to a jury

[6] MPC §210.6(4)(a).

[7] See *id.* (b) (extreme mental or emotional disturbance); *id.* (d) (reasonable mistake as to moral justification); *id.* (f) (duress); *id.* (g) (diminished capacity); *id.* (h) (youth).

[8] *Id.* (c) (victim participated or consented). Cf. *id.* (e) (defendant was an accomplice).

[9] As to the effect of the victim's consent on wrongdoing, see §4.5.4 A *supra;* as to the relationship between accessorial status and the degree of wrongdoing, see §8.6 *infra.*

[10] H. Roberts v. Louisiana, 431 U.S. 633, 637 (1977).

[11] *Ibid. Cf.* MPC §210.6(4)(d).

[12] 431 U.S. at 642, 649.

[13] For example, is a state constitutionally required to consider the defendant's role as an accessory in the crime, as recommended in MPC §210.6(4)(e)? For example of an accessory's being sentenced to death for an apparently unplanned killing in the course of a robbery, see State v. Lockett, 49 Ohio St. 2d 48, 358 N.E.2d 1062 (1976).

trial does not apply; either a judge or a jury may be vested with the sentencing decision.[14] The substantive manifestation is that some grounds bear on capital homicide that we would hesitate to include in the definition of murder. Notable among these are prior convictions for serious crimes and the suspect's status as a prison inmate or escaped convict.

Some of the grounds for aggravating homicide are of the sort that we might well consider in defining first-degree murder, but conventionally do not include in our legislative definitions. A good example is murder for hire.[15] The German[16] and Soviet[17] codes both include a pecuniary motive as substantive standard. Perhaps the Anglo-American aversion against considering motives in defining liability[18] accounts for the noticeable absence of this ground in the substantive law of murder. The magic of labelling capital punishment a matter of sentencing renders the heinous motive an appropriate consideration.

We might also rely on the identity of the victim in defining murder, but we do not. French law recognizes the separate capital offense of *parricide,* which covers the killing of a parent, either natural or adopted, or a grandparent.[19] Both French[20] and Soviet[21] law take the killing of a police officer as ground for capital homicide. One of the most favored grounds for capital murder in the United States is killing a police officer.[22] Perhaps this is a factor that we might appropriately include in the substantive definition of murder. There is arguably an additional wrong against the established legal order in killing a police officer. It is also possible, even likely, that the motivation for using capital punishment in these cases is

[14] Proffitt v. Florida, 428 U.S. 242 (1976).

[15] See, e.g., Ariz. Rev. Stat. §13-454(E)(4)(5) (Supp.); Fla. Stat. Ann. §921.141(5)(f) (Supp.); Ohio Rev. Code Ann. §2929.04(A)(2).

[16] StGB §211(2).

[17] Ugol. kod. (RSFSR) §102(a).

[18] See §6.5.5 *infra.*

[19] Code Pénal §299.

[20] Code Pénal §233, as limited to persons designated in id. §§228, 230.

[21] Ugol. kod. (RSFSR) §102(c) (victim in the "execution of his official or social duty").

[22] Neb. Rev. Stat. §29-2523(1)(g); Ohio Rev. Code Ann. §2929.04(A)(6).

not the rational assessment of wrongdoing, but the greater outrage of the public.

The disquieting grounds for capital homicide are those based on prior convictions[23] or status as a prisoner.[24] We admittedly have some statutes that incorporate criteria of recidivism in the definition of an aggravated offense.[25] The Soviet code unabashedly takes recidivism as a ground for aggravated murder, but the general view in the United States still is that prior convictions should be relevant, if at all, only in the sentencing process. Principles of liability are still geared to the particular act charged against the defendant, not to general criteria of moral worth or dangerousness.

It is not entirely clear why these two grounds—recidivism and status as a prisoner—even bear appropriately on the sentencing process. At a later stage I argue against the view that prior offenses warrant an inference of greater culpability in committing the act charged.[26] There is no doubt that we regard recidivism as an index of dangerousness. Perhaps there is even an argument that, as a class, recidivists and prisoners are not as easily deterred as others and therefore are properly subject to greater threats. Even if these arguments justified an increased term of years, one has the greatest difficulty with the notion of executing people simply because they are dangerous or are members of a class that is not easily deterred. One has the uneasy feeling in these cases that the primary motive for the death penalty is eugenic: the aim of ridding society of its irredeemable defects.

Ours would not be the first society in history to believe in killing those whose lives are regarded as a burden. But even if this motive were not disquieting on its face, there is good reason to exclude these eugenic considerations from the permissible use of capital punishment. The Supreme Court requires that both mitigating and aggravating circumstances bear on the judgment of the death

[23] E.g., Ariz. Rev. Stat. §13-454(E)(1), (2) (Supp.); Fla. Stat. Ann. §921.141(5)(b) (Supp.); Ga. Code. Ann. §27-234.1(b)(1) (Supp.).

[24] E.g., Fla. Stat. Ann. §921.141(5)(a), (e); Ohio Rev. Code Ann. §2929.04(A)(4).

[25] See §6.6.2, at note 9 *infra*.

[26] See §6.6.2 *infra*.

penalty. If criteria of general social worth aggravate a killing and justify the death penalty, then similar criteria ought to count in mitigation. But we would be nonplussed by the proposition that talented or gifted people should receive the benefit of their endowments in assessing the death penalty. Perhaps one might say that a prisoner's being a poet or brilliant physicist does not bear on his dangerousness to society, but it might well bear on our judgment whether the risk of crime emanating from that particular person was socially justified. Is it not clear that the risk of crime in the case of a brilliant and creative person is easier to bear than in the case of one who contributes nothing to society? So far as the judgment of capital punishment in cases of recidivism is based on utilitarian grounds, the utilitarian calculus should include all the relevant parameters. Making the calculus complete requires that we consider the person's virtues and talents as well as his defects and the danger he or she represents. If we are unwilling to do that, then perhaps there is something fundamentally wrong in considering a person's criminal record in assessing the justification of the death penalty.

Chapter Five
The Jurisprudence of Homicide

§5.1. *The Uniqueness of Homicide.*

There are three prominent starting places for thinking about criminal liability. In the pattern of manifest criminality, the point of departure is an act that threatens the peace and order of community life. In the theory of subjective criminality, the starting place is the actor's intent to violate a protected legal interest. In the law of homicide, the focal point is neither the act nor the intent, but the fact of death. This overpowering fact is the point at which the law begins to draw the radius of liability. From this central point, the perspective is: who can be held accountable, and in what way, for the desecration of the human and divine realms?[1] The question is never where to place the point of the legal compass, but how far the arc should sweep in bringing in persons to stand responsible for the death that has already occurred.

That causing death is perceived as a unique desecration ac-

§5.1. [1] For further elaboration of causing death as a form of desecration, see §4.1 *supra.*

counts for two distinguishing features of homicide as a crime. The first is the ongoing tension between a practice that we shall call "tainting" and the quest for criteria to determine who should justly be held accountable for causing death. We noted an aspect of this tension in our earlier discussion of the conflict between the harm-oriented and the act-oriented approaches to analyzing homicide. In this chapter we deepen our understanding of that conflict by providing an account of why causing death might be felt to be an evil in itself.

The second mark of homicide as a crime is reliance on characteristic modes of liability that we do not find in the patterns of manifest and subjective criminality. Homicide is punished if committed negligently, and failing to prevent death is sometimes punished as though it were equivalent to causing death. Neither of these modes of liability arises in the crimes surveyed under the headings of manifest and subjective criminality.

A third distinguishing feature of homicide derives not from the structure of the crime, but from the social fact that killings typically occur as the outgrowth of interaction between offender and victim. The interactional genesis of homicide generated a crime of differing levels of culpability and led, as we shall see, to a refined notion of personal culpability.

In the first two sections of this chapter, we shall pursue these three themes as a way of demonstrating the uniqueness of homicide as crime. In the third section, we shall consider ways of moving beyond the distinguishing features of homicide in order to state a third pattern of liability. This inquiry will lead in conclusion to the formulation of a pattern of harmful consequences, encompassing arson, battery and other crimes that take the occurrence of concrete harm as the starting point of analysis. Given these conflicting directions of the analysis, we must confess an ambivalence about homicide. We seek to demonstrate that the crime is unique and yet, in the end, we take homicide to be an instance of a broader pattern called the pattern of harmful consequences. There is value in perceiving the unique features of homicide, but, as we shall see, there is considerable theoretical power in treating homicide as one of several crimes based on the occurrence of concrete harm to persons or property.

§5.1.1. **Blaming and Tainting.** The act-oriented analysis of homicide finds its warrant in two principles for fairly blaming those who cause death. First, we regard it prima facie sufficient for liability that, first, an actor intentionally cause death; alternatively, that he take an undue risk of death.[2] These principles for fairly blaming those who cause death stand in contrast to a third principle rooted in the harm-oriented analysis of homicide—a principle that continues to affect the course of the common law. We shall refer to this third principle as the practice of tainting persons *merely* because their acts issue in the death of another human being. An object may also be tainted if it is used to cause death. A "tainted" person or object is to be shunned and, further, some procedure is necessary to expiate the taint.

The distinction between blaming and tainting is critical to an understanding both of the early and the modern law of homicide. The practice of blaming is always directed to the individual who causes harm. It raises the question of excuses, personal accountability, and the justice of punishment. The practice of tainting, on the other hand, raises issues neither of excuses nor of justice. Whether an object or a person is tainted depends solely on its or his involvement with evil—in our context, with the evil of causing death.

The practice of tainting in the common law was expressed in two institutions of forfeiture. The first of these was the law of deodands, which prescribed the forfeiture to the Crown of all instruments causing death. The spear, the sword, the carriage—whatever the instrument, it was surrendered to the Crown, the embodiment of transcendental authority.[3] Earlier Anglo-Saxon laws had prescribed the surrendering of the instrument to the victim's

[2] The grounds for blaming are only prima facie, for they do not consider the criteria of excuse and justification, discussed in Chapter Ten *infra*.

[3] Finkelstein, *The Goring Ox: Some Historical Perspectives on Deodands, Forefeitures, Wrongful Death and the Western Notion of Sovereignty*, 46 Temp. L.Q. 169, 185–91 (1973); 1 Hale 419–424.

kin.[4] In either event, the transfer of title effected a cleansing of the tainted instrument and permitted its continued use in secular society. Of course, in both the institutions of the deodand and of Anglo-Saxon surrender to the victim's kin there were covert functions at work. The former represented a means of raising revenue for the Crown, the latter, of compensating the victim's kin. The extent to which we stress this covert function depends on how seriously we, as modern observers, take the surface rationale that surrender effected a cleansing of the tainted object. The institution of the deodand persisted in English law until the surprisingly late date of 1846.[5]

The second common-law institution of tainting lay in the practice of forfeiting the worldly goods of all persons who caused the death of another. This principle of forfeiture encompassed persons who were pardoned and later excused on grounds of inevitable accident (*per infortunium*) or self-preservation (*se defendendo*). The effect of these excuses was to eliminate the capital sanction but to leave the forfeiture of goods as fitting response in a case of blamelessly causing death. One important by-product of this institution, which survived nominally until 1870,[6] was that it provided a coherent social response to suicide. Thus forfeiture permitted the English law to treat the essential evil of homicide and suicide as the taking of the human life,[7] not necessarily the taking of another's life.[8]

The analogy between the forfeiture of the deodand and the

[4] Alfred 13, in F. Attenborough, Laws of the Earliest English Kings 71 (1922) ("If one man kills another unintentionally, [by allowing a tree to fall on him] while they are engaged in a common task, the tree shall be given to the [dead man's] kindred . . .").

[5] 9 & 10 Vict. c. 62 (1846). For an assessment of the evidence on survival of the deodand in the American colonies, see Comment, *Bane of American Forfeiture Law—Banished at Last,* 62 Cornell L.Q. 768 (1977).

[6] 33 & 34 Vict. c. 23 (1870).

[7] 1 Hale 412. *But cf.* the modern view about the nature of homicide as it affects felony-murder cases, *supra* §4.4.7, at note 172.

[8] Stephen claimed that the forfeiture was grounded in the breach of feudal obligations. 1 Stephen 488.

forfeiture of the excused slayer's goods is hardly precise. In the former case, the forfeited object is itself the tainted instrument of death.[9] In the latter case, it is more difficult to maintain that the goods themselves were tainted by their owner's causing death. A better example of tainting the person rather than the object is found in the Biblical institution of cities of refuge. Someone who blamelessly caused death had to flee the community and live in a special sanctuary designated a "city of refuge."[10] In the crisp example of Deuteronomy 19:5:

> As when a man goeth into the forest with his neighbor to hew wood, and his hand fetcheth a stroke with the axe to cut down the tree, and the head slippeth from the helve, and lighteth upon his neighbor and he die; he shall flee unto one of these cities and live.

That the woodcutter caused the death of a neighbor was sufficient to require his separation from the community. In this institution we more clearly see the practice of tainting at work. The tainted person is not necessarily to blame for causing death; he is to be shunned and separated, rather than punished.

The distinction between blaming and tainting can be expressed, at the risk of some simplification, as the difference between viewing the agent of death as a responsible person or as a non-responsible object. We blame people on the assumption that they are responsible and accountable for the harm they cause. If their conduct causing harm is excused, they cannot be fairly blamed. Compassion and mercy are appropriate when we treat the agency of death as a responsible person. Tainting, in contrast de-

[9] There is a tendency to describe the thing "as being primarily liable for the death," G. Williams, Liability for Animals 267 (1939) (speaking of surrender to the victim under Anglo-Saxon laws); 3 Stephen 77 (explaining deodands on the ground that the "thing which caused deaths ought to be punished"). It is, in fact, puzzling that stationary objects, not actively employed, could be declared deodands, 1 Hale 422–23.

[10] *Cf.* Numbers 35:12–28; see generally J. Mendelsohn, Criminal Jurisprudence of the Ancient Hebrews 166–67 (1890); Finkelstein, *supra* note 3, at 186–88; A. Phillips, Ancient Israel's Criminal Law 102–08 (1970).

humanizes the agent and looks solely to contamination by contact. If the person or the object has caused death, that is sufficient contact with evil to warrant the imposition of a taint. Neither compassion nor mercy is appropriate. The only response is to avoid further contamination by cleansing the object or separating it from the community.

The distinction between blaming and tainting is implicit in the Biblical provisions on the goring ox:[11]

> And if an ox gore a man or woman, that they die, the ox shall surely be stoned, and its flesh shall not be eaten; but the owner of the ox shall be quit; but if the ox was wont to gore in time past, and warning hath been given to its owner, and he hath not kept it in, but it hath killed a man or a woman; the ox shall be stoned, and its owner also shall be put to death.

In either event, the ox is to be killed by stoning and the flesh not to be eaten, but the owner is to be punished only if he had fair warning of the ox's propensity to gore. This limitation of the owner's responsibility expresses the principle that the owner of an animal that injures another is fairly subject to punishment only if he was personally negligent. If he did not have fair warning of the danger to others, then he is subject neither to blame nor punishment. Further, if he was not to blame, the killing would not be his doing but the animal's; he would not be tainted and under an obligation to flee to a city of refuge.

The question of the ox's being subject to stoning is more complicated. There is one school of thought that treats the ox as a murderer.[12] An opposing view holds that the ox was tainted by its causing the death of a human being. The stoning is then interpreted as a measure to prevent further contamination of the community, rather than as punishment of a culpable animal.[13] This particular institution as well as the general practice of executing animals for crimes has recently received considerable attention in

[11] Exodus 21:28–29. See generally B. Jackson, Essays in Jewish and Comparative Legal History 108–52 (1975).

[12] Holmes 20–22 (discussing an analogous provision in Scottish law).

[13] B. Jackson, *supra* note 11, at 114.

the literature,[14] and we should not try to resolve the debate here. Neither interpretation, so far as we can tell, calls into the question the conceptual distinction between blaming and tainting. There is a problem, however, in determining which of these practices—or which blend between them—adequately accounts for the execution of animals.[15]

One might be tempted to think that tainting was but a quaint practice of primitive legal systems. Since the late eighteenth century, the tendency of legal scholars has been to regard deodands and other tainting practices as relics of a pre-rational past. Foster set the tone of much modern scholarship when he described deodands as the product of "the ignorance and superstition of antient times."[16]

This effort to distance ourselves from our past appears to be misguided in two respects. First, the fear of association with past institutions confuses our effort to understand exactly what those institutions were. We are tempted to dismiss them as expressions of a "primitive" legal culture, as though the word "primitive" aids our understanding of the past. Further, our concern for distancing ourselves from "pre-rational" legal forms camouflages the contemporary influence of these modes of thought. The notion that tainted objects should be forfeited still generates much of the rhetoric in support of federal and state forfeiture laws. These statutes prescribe the forfeiture of vehicles used to transport contraband or tax-unpaid liquor. In the United States, laws of this form are still interpreted so as to divest the interests of totally innocent parties, such as lessors and vendors with a security interest.[17] Though the opinions in this field are sprinkled with references to deodands

[14] *Compare* Finkelstein, *supra* note 1, at 229 & n. 194 (goring ox not an "early instance of the imposition of 'objective liability' or 'guilt' ") *with* Holmes 22 ("no difficulty was felt [in early legal systems] in treating animals as guilty").

[15] See generally E. Evans, The Criminal Prosecution and Capital Punishment of Animals (1906).

[16] Foster 265.

[17] E.g., Calero-Toledo v. Pearson Yacht Leasing Co., 416 U.S. 663 (1974) (lessor's interest divested for lessee's transporting marijuana on board leased yacht); Goldsmith-Grant Co. v. United States, 254 U.S. 505 (1920) (vendor's security interest in car forfeited after purchaser used car to transport distilled spirits illegally).

and goring oxen,[18] one wonders whether the historical materials are not a bit exploited to buttress a rule of strict liability.[19] If there is a rationale for these harsh decisions against innocent parties, it is probably an abiding faith in general deterrence, rather than an ongoing belief that an automobile used to transport narcotics is itself a "guilty res." In West Germany, where there is deeper commitment to culpability as a prerequisite for criminal sanctions, the courts and legislature have revised the law of forfeiture to protect the interests of innocent owners.[20]

Better examples of current reliance on the theory of tainting are found in the law of search and seizure. First, the law limiting what may be seized in the course of a constitutional search long reflected the distinction between tainted and non-tainted articles. Until recently, the Supreme Court maintained that only the fruits and the instrumentalities of crime could be seized;[21] mere evidence lay beyond the seizure powers of the police. This distinction continues to inform the German law of permissible seizure.[22]

The exclusionary rule even more dramatically illustrates many of the premises underlying a practice of tainting. The popular rationale for excluding unconstitutionally acquired evidence is that the courts thereby deter unconstitutional police practices. But this rationale fails to account for judicial indifference to potential excuses for police violations of the Fourth Amendment. Categories of non-deterrable violations,[23] such as those based on unavoidable mistakes about the legality of searches and seizures, should logically be exempted from the bite of the exclusionary rule. Yet they are not. And the best explanation for this indifference to the culpabil-

[18] E.g., United States v. One 1963 Cadillac Coupe de Ville Two Door, 250 F. Supp. 183, 185 (W.D. Mo. 1966); Goldsmith-Grant v. United States, 254 U.S. 505, 511 (1920).

[19] See Finkelstein, *supra* note 3, at 215, stressing the analogy between forfeiture and the principle of strict liability applied in United States v. Dotterweich, 320 U.S. 277 (1943).

[20] See StGB §§74(2)(1), 74a and 74f.

[21] This rule was rejected in Warden v. Hayden, 387 U.S. 294 (1967).

[22] StPO §97(2) (the fruits and instrumentalities of crime not covered by privileged exceptions to the law of seizure).

[23] On the relationship between excuses and the argument of non-deterrability, see §10.3.5 *infra*.

ity of the police is the courts' own argument that they regard the evidence as tainted and their integrity would be compromised by using tainted evidence.[24] The rationale is not that the police have misbehaved and that their conduct may be properly sanctioned; it is rather that a search and seizure in violation of the Constitution taints the evidence thereby acquired, and the courts should shun tainted evidence. This way of looking at Fourth Amendment violations explains why the courts do not refuse to accept jurisdiction over defendants unconstitutionally arrested and brought before the court.[25] Unlike unconstitutional searches and seizures, an unconstitutional arrest does not generate a tainted object (the defendant himself is not tainted!), and therefore the integrity of the courts is not, in their view, compromised by hearing these cases. Of course, this refusal to extend the exclusionary rule to unconstitutional arrests is buttressed by the high price of quashing the whole prosecution, rather than merely rejecting a single item of evidence.

With regard to the law of homicide, the practice of tainting is in obvious eclipse. Gone are the institutions of deodands, forfeiture of goods and cities of refuge. Though the practice survives nominally in the forfeiture of vehicles used in transporting contraband, and though tainting might inform the exclusionary rule, the modern mind balks at the idea that contact with evil is sufficient to communicate a taint. From the full perspective of history, however, we do not understand whether the taint of causing death was a necessary ingredient in the full set of interrelated views that generated a high regard for human life. To regard life as sacred, one might also have to believe that he who takes life, even by accident, upsets the natural order and becomes contaminated by evil.

§5.1.2. Omissions and Negligence. The practice of tainting provides one perspective on the assumption that failing to prevent

[24] Originally in Mapp v. Ohio, 367 U.S. 643, 659 (1961); Elkins v. United States, 364 U.S. 206, 222 (1960); currently in United States v. Calandra, 414 U.S. 338, 357 (1974) (Justices Brennan, Douglas and Marshall, dissenting) ("The exclusionary rule . . . [enables] the judiciary to avoid the taint of partnership in official lawlessness . . .").

[25] United States ex rel. Lujan v. Gengler, 510 F.2d 62 (2d Cir. 1975), *cert denied,* 421 U.S. 1001 (1975).

death is not ordinarily subject to criminal liability. Only those who affirmatively cause death are tainted. Liability for failing to intervene and to rescue a person in distress generates liability for the ensuing death only if there is a special duty to intervene. Merely suffering another to die is an insufficient connection with death to taint the passive party.[26]

The practice of tainting also brings into focus the nature of negligence as a limitation on liability. As we noted earlier, the issue of negligence is initially framed under the heading of *per infortunium* or "inevitable accident."[27] The absence of fault or negligence is recognized as a basis for denying liability despite the taint of causing death. That negligence came into the law as a limitation on liability, of course, does not automatically justify its use today as an affirmative rationale for punishing inadvertent risk-taking that issues in death.[28]

The practice of tainting may help us understand these two special features of homicide, but tainting is not essential to the genesis of either. The distinction between causing harm and failing to avert harm arises in a number of contexts.[29] Negligence can be used as a basis for liability in causing purely worldly harm, such as battery and the destruction of property.[30] These two modes of liability extend to the general pattern of crimes that we shall explicate later as the pattern of harmful consequences.

§5.1.3. Interaction with the Victim and Culpability by Degrees. Most crimes are committed by strangers; the thief who came at night was the paradigm of the foreign enemy who disturbed the peace and order of the community. Yet homicides typically occur in the context of ongoing human relationships. There are indications that this was true in the Middle Ages[31] and it is docu-

[26] Liability for failing to prevent death is explored in §§8.1 to 8.4 *infra*.

[27] See §4.1 *supra*.

[28] For analysis of the structure and culpability of negligence, see §§6.6.8 and 9.2.3 *infra*.

[29] See §8.2 *infra*.

[30] Though Anglo-American law traditionally limits the use of negligence to homicide prosecutions, compare StGB §230 (negligent battery), §309 (negligent arson), §163 (negligent perjury).

[31] Green, *The Jury and the English Law of Homicide, 1200–1600*, 74 Mich. L. Rev. 413, 414–15 (1976).

mentably true today. Most criminologists estimate that in the United States close to 80 percent of all homicides are committed by offenders who are "acquainted" with their victims.[32] New York City has a relatively high rate of murders by strangers, unknown to their victims; of 1622 murders committed in the City in 1976, 354 or 28.4 percent were attributed to strangers.[33] Though these wanton killings are an important part of the total, the more typical cases are those arising from disputes in the family, among lovers, on the job, and in underworld activities such as narcotics traffic. This long-standing criminological feature of homicide means that killing is not typically a case of one person subjecting another to a unilateral criminal plan. The resort to deadly assault springs rather from the interaction between victim and slayer.

That homicide typically grows out of human interaction accounts for the tendency in the law of homicide to recognize degrees of culpability and, on the basis of these judgments of degree, to grade killings as manslaughter or murder. The slayer's interaction with the victim bred the notion of qualified or mitigated culpability. So far as the killing was the product of human interaction, it was to that extent not fully attributable to the slayer's initiative. This way of thinking marks a radical departure from the concept of culpability in cases of larceny, attempts or treason. In these and in virtually all offenses, the concept of culpability is identified with the intent to commit the offense. If a thief was caught in the act, he was guilty—provided he had the requisite *animus furandi.* In a case of attempted rape or burglary, the critical question is the intent to commit the offense. Of course there may be a possibility of excusing the offense altogether on the basis of insanity or duress. But if there is no defense, and if the actor bears the requisite intent, these factors tend to be conclusive on the issue of culpability. Yet as homicide evolved into its present form, the law began to recognize degrees of liability in order to account for the impact of the situation on the act of killing. While the thief intrudes upon a set stage, he who kills acts in a drama written in part by others. Thus the refinement of liability for homicide meant

[32] M. Wolfgang, Patterns in Criminal Homicide 83 (1958).
[33] New York Times, April 20, 1977, p. 1, col. 1.

that the law should take note whether the killing occurred as a result of a sudden fist fight, as the result of the actor's killing for the sake of his own preservation, or as the result of discovering his wife in an act of adultery. The process of refinement has led to a sophisticated notion of culpability that treats the slayer's guilt for his killing as a matter of relative dependency on the circumstances of the crime.

The legislative and judicial practice of grading intentional killings has generated a spectrum of five distinct degrees of culpability, ranging from total self-actuation to total dependence on the circumstances. First-degree murder is the extreme case of self-actuated killing, minimally influenced by interaction with the victim. This element of self-actuation is expressed in the formula of "premeditation and deliberation"; the autonomy of the actor's decision is manifested in advance planning and preparation.[34] The second point on the spectrum of intentional killings is marked by second-degree murder. These killings lie between the point of total self-actuation and the partial dependency on circumstances that we note in the third and fourth stations of diminished culpability.

The third station is the familiar case of killing under provocation; and the fourth is killing where there is no practical alternative but to kill as an act of self-preservation. This latter killing as a matter of necessity was excused in the early common law as *se defendendo.* While the impact of provocation was to mitigate the killing to manslaughter, the effect of a valid claim of self-preservation was to excuse the killing but subject the slayer to a forfeiture of goods. According to the thirteenth-century Statute of Gloucester,[35] killings in self-preservation, like killings committed *per infortunium,* were to be pardoned as a matter of course. Killings in self-preservation were still human acts tainting the slayer and therefore the sanction of forfeiture remained appropriate. The courts and commentators eventually had to clarify the subtle difference between provocation and the case of necessity sufficient for a plea of *se defendendo.* The difference was patently a matter of degree. A minor assault was sufficient for provocation; a major assault, putting the

[34] See §4.2.3 *supra.*
[35] 6 Edw. I. c. 9 (1278).

defendant in fear of his life, might generate the excuse of *se defendendo*. An important mark of the distinction eventually appeared to be whether the slayer at first retreated to a wall or a ditch and resorted to killing only when he had no further options of retreat.[36]

It seems appropriate to identify a fifth point in the spectrum, which would represent a case of killing in total dependence on the circumstances. In a case of *se defendendo*, there is at least a human act and a choice to kill. But one could imagine a case in which a third party put a knife in the defendant's hand and then forced the hand down on the victim's chest. Though there is little learning on this type of case, it follows from general principles that killing under insuperable pressure would not be considered an act of killing at all and would not incur even the minimal penalty imposed for killing *se defendendo*.[37]

At the risk of some exaggeration, we should regard the evolution of this spectrum of culpability as one of the more important jurisprudential developments in the history of the criminal law. The spectrum of culpability teaches us that culpability is not only a matter of cognitive foresight, but of self-control. The issue of self-control, we learn, requires subtle judgments of degree. In some cases of intentional homicide the actor exercises greater control, and in others, lesser. The grading of homicide disabuses us of the view that voluntariness and freedom of the will are black-and-white issues. Rather the shading develops by perceptible degrees from total dependence on circumstances to total independence of external influence.

We are not likely to have learned the principle of graduated culpability from any other offense. It is true that many contemporary statutes recognize degrees of larceny and robbery. But the differentiation in these offenses turns on the scale of the wrong, rather than the degree of culpability.[38] Stealing more may make

[36] 1 Hale 479–80; Foster 277.

[37] Another rationale for outright acquittal was justifiable self-defense, discussed in §10.5 *infra*. So far as self-defense is justified, however, it may be freely chosen and therefore is not a claim dependent on the influence of circumstances.

[38] The law of homicide also reveals some distinctions according to the quality of the wrong. Killing on request, see §4.5.4 A *supra*, is arguably a lesser wrong, as is

one liable for a greater punishment, but this manner of grading hardly carries a broader message about the nature of criminal accountability.

The spectrum of self-control underlying the five degrees of culpability provides the structure for understanding the contemporary use of psychiatric evidence to mitigate responsibility for homicide. Corresponding to each point in the spectrum, we now find a defense based on internal psychological abnormality rather than the external pressure of circumstances. The following chart compares the grounds of psychological mitigation with the traditional claims based upon external pressure:

Level of Offense	*Traditional Ground*	*Psychiatric Ground*
1. First-degree murder	None	None
2. Second-degree murder	Absence of premeditation	Diminished capacity
3. Manslaughter	Provocation	Diminished capacity or extreme emotional disturbance
4. Excused felony subject at common law to forfeiture of goods and, in the case of insanity, to civil commitment.	*Se defendendo*	Insanity
5. Acquittal	*Vis major*	Automatism or hypnotism

The difference between insanity and automatism runs parallel to the difference between *se defendendo* and *vis major.* In the cases of insanity and *se defendendo,* the act of killing is excused because it is unjust to blame the actor who succumbs to the pressure of circumstances (either external or psychological). At the extreme point on the spectrum, there is no act of killing at all; for the pressure of circumstances is so great that the actor's self-control is totally negated.

---

abortion. *Cf.* the role of multiple murders in justifying capital punishment, §4. *supra.*

This chart is not presented as a discussion of any of the difficult issues bearing on partial and total psychiatric disturbance. These questions will receive due attention at the proper place. In the present context, it is more important to perceive the special quality of homicide as admitting of five degrees of culpability. The notion that there are degrees of culpability, and the dependence of these degrees either on interaction with the victim or on psychiatric criteria, is one of the major insights achieved in the long history of punishing homicide.

§5.1.4. The Outer and Inner Circles of Liability. In this section we shall endeavor to bring together a number of diverse claims we have made about the structure of homicide. In particular, we wish to state more precisely the relationships among the harm-oriented and act-oriented approaches to homicide and the practice of tainting.

In order to explicate these interconnections, let us consider the structure of homicide as two concentric circles. The outer circle represents the minimal criteria necessary for tainting someone who causes the death of another. The circle consists of three arcs: (1) an act, (2) causation, (3) the death of a human being. The inner circle encompasses all cases subject to punishment at common law, either for manslaughter or murder. The band of cases between the inner and outer circles represents all the instances in which the actor is tainted for causing death but not fairly subject to criminal liability.

Using these concentric circles, we can picture more precisely the diverse ways of thinking about homicide. At early common law and in Biblical law, meeting the criteria of the outer circle generated a minimal penalty—forfeiture of goods or flight to a city of refuge. That cases in the band between the two circles were punished, but not severely, testified to a reconciliation of the practice of tainting with the principles of justice. The practice of tainting, by itself, would have led to execution of all persons who caused the death of another. But if the axe blade slipped out of the helve and killed a bystander, and there was no negligence on the part of the woodcutter, it would have been obviously unjust to punish solely on the criteria of tainting.

The law sought a middle course between the imperative of expiation in killing and the imperative of doing justice. The middle course was found in subjecting these cases of blameless taint to a censure that spared the life of the slayer. Forfeiture of goods and banishment to a city of refuge were heavy burdens to bear, but as mitigated penalties, they bore witness to the ascendent influence of criteria for excusing those whose act of killing was neither intentional nor negligent.[39]

As the practice of tainting waned in the eighteenth and nineteenth centuries, the same structure of concentric circles continued to shape legal analysis. They provided the foundation for the harm-oriented analysis of liability. To paraphrase Blackstone's rule: All cases falling within the outer circle were murder unless they were excused, justified or mitigated. In other words, cases within the outer circle also fell by inference within the inner circle unless the inference was checked by a claim of excuse or justification or mitigation. The effect of an excuse was to keep the case in the band between the two circles. The effect of justification would be to knock the case out of the outer circle and to exempt the killing from possible taint. The effect of provocation was to shunt the inference from the outer to the inner circle to the special category of manslaughter. The idea underlying these claims was the same: if the facts fell within the outer circle, the currents of analysis drove the case toward classification as murder. The defendant bore the laboring oar to counteract these currents and to maneuver his case onto the banks of an excuse, justification or mitigating claim.

If we limit the inquiry to the claims of accident, mistake and provocation, we can use our concentric circles to explicate the transition from the harm-oriented to the act-oriented mode of legal analysis. The essence of the transition was to collapse the two circles

[39] The discussion in this section is admittedly ambiguous about excuses, such as duress, *se defendendo* and insanity, whose status was not called into question by the transition from the harm-oriented to the act-oriented analysis of liability. For a discussion of these excuses, whether they were recognized and remained excuses at common law, see §10.4 *infra*.

into one. Claims of accident or mistake would no longer check the inference from a prima facie case to a conclusion of liability; their converse became the elements of intentional and negligent killing in a new, consolidated circle of prima facie liability.

The concentric circles of liability still inform the analysis of homicide cases and criminal liability in general. Every time the courts employ the concept of an "affirmative defense" they think implicitly in the mode of concentric circles. The outer circle is the prima facie case; the function of the affirmative defense is to prevent the prima facie case from becoming conclusive—i.e., from falling within the inner circle. Though mistake and accident are no longer considered affirmative defenses, other claims often are—including provocation, self-defense and insanity. The implication of labelling an issue as an "affirmative defense" is to require the defendant to bear either the burden of persuasion or the burden of going forward on the issue. Later, when we turn to systematic reflections on the burden of persuasion, we shall find that the concept of the "affirmative defense," as we have explicated the idea here, is by no means essential to the criminal law.[40] Its rootedness in our thought stems, in part, from a way of thinking acquired in taking seriously the outer circle of liability—the criterion of an act causing death—as a prima facie standard of liability.

The second major influence of the outer circle of liability is that its three elements appear to be subject to more rigorous appellate scrutiny than jury-findings on the issue of intention, negligence, insanity and other elements of culpability. Though we have neither precise evidence nor self-conscious judicial pronouncements to support this proposition, we repeatedly encounter a willingness by appellate judges to reverse convictions if the elements of (1) acting, (2) causation, or (3) human death are not supported by the evidence produced at trial. On issues related to culpability, in contrast, there appears to be a strong inclination to defer to the jury's finding of fact. We shall see this general proposition borne out in the discussion of the ensuing section, though admittedly, the proposition is only anecdotally empirical.

[40] See §§7.1 to 7.3 *infra*.

§5.2. *The Outer Circle of Liability.*

There are a few issues of jurisprudential subtlety to compare with the questions of (1) human action, (2) causation, and (3) the onset of death. These are the arcs that circumscribe the outer circle of liability. They represent the minimal criteria for the practice of tainting at common law. The first two issues—action and causation—are of general concern to the law, yet significantly, neither question stands out as important in the patterns of subjective or of manifest criminality. A human act is required in these crimes as well, but absent a practice of tainting, a nonculpable act is never sufficient to justify a sanction.

Similarly, the issue of causation is implicit in some offenses such as receiving property by false pretenses and treason by giving aid and comfort to the enemy. But in none of these cases does the question of causation raise the conundrums that we encounter in the law of homicide. The jurisprudence of causation is the legacy of the law's persistent effort to determine when a death may be attributed to the conduct of a particular person.

§5.2.1. The Jurisprudence of Acting. The implicit rule both of Biblical and early English common law was that no one could be tainted for the occurrence of death without having acted so as to cause the death. In the Biblical context, the act had to be one that immediately caused death. It was not sufficient that one acted in the past to acquire an ox that subsequently gored a neighbor to death.[1] Nor was it sufficient that one's body was the instrument of death—as, if one accidentally fell upon the victim.[2] That there was no act causing death in these cases meant, in the Biblical scheme, there was no need for expiation. There was no duty to flee to the city of refuge.

Disputes about the concept of acting were critical to early

§5.2. [1] Exodus 21:28–29.

[2] S. Mendelsohn, The Criminal Jurisprudence of the Ancient Hebrews 60 (1906). *Cf.* N. Hurnard, The King's Pardon for Homicide 101 (1969) (noting that tree-climbers who fell on their victims were usually acquitted).

common-law cases marking out the relative spheres of forfeiture for excusable homicide and outright acquittal in the absence of an act. The recurrent sources of dispute were the running down cases and archery accidents in which the victim ran into the path of an arrow. In the running down cases, the driver typically lost control of his team and someone on the highway was killed. Acquittals were sometimes granted in these cases,[3] presumably on the theory that the horses in motion constituted a normal state of affairs and if by pure accident, they should break loose, there was no human agency in the killing. Yet in these situations, the law of deodands sometimes applied against the animals and the cart that caused death.[4] A good example of an archery accident that resulted in an acquittal was the case of William, son of Joyn de Barely, tried in 1279.[5] According to the jury's account of the accident, William saw a target and fired an arrow at it. While the arrow was in flight, the victim, Alice, ran into the path of the arrow and was struck. After an initial finding of death *per infortunium* and submission of the required petition for a pardon, the jury reconvened and acquitted William. Cases of this type raise problems both of causation and of human agency, and, admittedly, the two issues are not readily separable.

Whether the accent is placed on the issue of acting or on causation, the problem was one at the outer circle of liability. The extant materials on these early cases of the common law did not state explicitly that the problem is one of human agency.[6] In the statement of the issue that comes closest to the modern focus of human action, the inquiry turned on whether the death was attributable primarily to the act of the victim or the act of the defendant. In the

[3] See the case of William de Wilton, discussed in Hurnard, *supra* note 2, at 103.

[4] See the cases cited in *id.* at 101–03.

[5] *Id.* at 279.

[6] Nonetheless it would seem to be misleading to interpret these acquittals as expressing judgment about blame or negligence. This modern manner of thinking (see *id.* at 101–02; Green, *The Jury and the English Law of Homicide 1200–1600,* 74 Mich. L. Rev. 413, 445–47 (1976)), ignores the important conceptual distinction between acquittal for no homicide and a judgment or pardon for an excused homicide. My assumption is that common-law judges and jurors took this distinction seriously.

archery accidents, in particular, the death could be attributed to the act of the victim, and the defendant could be thus absolved. The assumption was that if one person was tainted by death, there was no need to spread the taint to another.

One recurrent hypothetical in the common-law texts was that of a victim *A* who impaled himself on the knife or pitchfork of *B*. Coke had reasoned that *A* was guilty of suicide, for he was the primary agent.[7] Hale took a more refined contextual view of the problem and reasoned that if *B* has retreated to the wall and is holding the knife, *A*'s running onto the knife is not suicide,[8] but a case either of *per infortunium* or *se defendendo*.[9] Hawkins reasoned simply that if the context is one of self-preservation, the killing should be treated as *se defendendo*.[10] The critical fact is that *B*, even if he is motionless, "exerts his strength in his own defense."[11] This is an important evolution, for it testifies to surmounting the image of motion as the criterion of action causing death. That the defender *B* was the acting party could be derived from the contextual motive of his holding the knife in place.

This is as far as the common-law commentators came in isolating the issue of human action. Of contemporary problems in the theory of action, such as punishment for addiction, we shall have more to say in the next chapter.[12]

§5.2.2. The Jurisprudence of Causing Death. A particular death can be attributed to the conduct of a particular person only if the conduct causes the death. As no one can be tortiously liable for a death that he has not caused, no one can be criminally tainted or blamed for a death beyond the causal sweep of his conduct.

Yet the requirement of causal connection makes more appar-

[7] 3 Coke 53–54.

[8] 1 Hale 413.

[9] *Id.* at 480: *per infortunium* if *A* "falls upon the knife of *B* without any thrust or stroke offered at him by *B*"; *se defendendo* if "some act" was "done by the party killing."

[10] 1 Hawkins 103.

[11] *Ibid.*

[12] See §6.4.2 *infra*.

ent sense in the field of torts than it does in the modern approach to criminal liability for death-producing acts. The harm must be attributable to the tortfeasor in order to justify requiring him to pay the loss. If the minimal requirement of the causation were abandoned, it would be hard to see why any particular defendant, rather than millions of other persons who have acted similarly in the past, should be required to pay for the particular loss to the particular victim.

The requirement of causation in homicide cases is problematic because, given modern notions of liability based on the culpability of acts, it is particularly difficult to explain why the occurrence of death matters. Suppose someone shoots at a patient lying in a bed; the bullet strikes the patient's heart. Yet a subsequent autopsy reveals that the patient had been dead for an hour when struck by the bullet. If we assume that the bullet would have been fatal, we cannot be puzzled by the clear rule of law: no liability for murder because the victim was already dead. Or suppose that *D* mortally wounds *V*, but while *V* is lying in the hospital receiving treatment, an epidemic of scarlet fever breaks out and kills several patients, including *V*.[13] Again the Anglo-American rule is that *D* should be liable at most for attempted murder; the scarlet fever rather than the otherwise fatal wound caused the death. The outcome is the same if, after the wounded *V* enters the hospital, he receives unusually reckless treatment that brings about his death.[14] Even if the victim might have died in any event, there is no liability for homicide—except, perhaps, by the physician who rendered the reckless treatment.

These are puzzling rules, for they make the actor's liability turn on fortuities that occur after the event for which the actor may be properly blamed, namely, the attempt to kill. The common-law rule was that the actor might be liable if death occurred at any time up to a year and a day after the mortal blow. Long after the

[13] Bush v. Commonwealth, 78 Ky. 268 (1880); *cf.* People v. Cook, 39 Mich. 236 (1878) (overdose of morphine in hospital).

[14] Rex v. Jordan, 40 Crim. App. 152 (1956) (hospital physicians administered drug to which the victim was known to be intolerant).

blow was inflicted, prosecutors must wait to see if liability for homicide accrues. If the victim dies within the legal period, liability may arise; if he dies one day later, or if he dies as a result of scarlet fever or reckless medical care, there is no liability. With everyone waiting to see whether the victim dies (and whether he might die by an unexpected intervening cause), the law of homicide comes to resemble the election of Harry Truman: nothing is certain until all the returns are in.

It would be plausible to define a law protecting life in terms that made the occurrence of death irrelevant. The critical issue would be an act endangering life. An attempt to kill, particularly if manifested unequivocally in the actor's behavior, would be treated the same as an actual killing. Conduct highly dangerous to human life would be treated as equivalent to reckless homicide. The rationale for eliminating the issues of causation and death would be that the purpose of the law should be to punish and to deter blameworthy assaults on the interest in life. The actual occurrence of death and its causal attribution are irrelevant to the sets of acts that should be deterred, and it is also irrelevant to the criteria rendering the accused blameworthy for his conduct. The man who shoots at an apparently alive but dead patient, is arguably no less blameworthy than the assassin who has the bad luck to shoot and kill a living patient.

This way of recasting the law of homicide may be seen as an application of the pattern of subjective criminality in place of the pattern rooted in the occurrence of harmful consequences. The proposal raises the broader issue whether the occurrence of harm appropriately bears on the just level of punishment. This general issue has generated what has probably been the deepest debate in the German theoretical literature of this century. We shall take up this debate in the next chapter and, contrary to the intimations of the present discussion, I shall argue in favor of considering the actual occurrence of harm as a relevant variable in gauging the just level of punishment.[15]

A. The Degree of Causal Contribution. One strategy for

[15] See §6.6.5 *infra*.

denying an apparent causal link between the defendant's behavior and the death is to claim that the death is simply too remote from the defendant's act. This is the implicit rationale in a wide range of deaths that never even receive prosecutorial scrutiny. If a contractor embarks on a large and dangerous project, say, building a bridge or an undersea tunnel, he might be able to calculate that three deaths would be actuarially certain, even if all safety precautions are taken. Despite his anticipating the deaths, he would not be held criminally accountable when they occur. Of course, his conduct might not meet the criteria of culpability that defined the inner circle of liability; yet even at the outer circle, his decision to build the bridge would fail to qualify as a cause of death. It is true that if he had not decided to build the bridge, the deaths would not have occurred. Thus his undertaking the project is a factor, but for which the deaths would not have resulted. Yet not every factor that meets the standard of "but for" causation is sufficient for the outer circle of liability. In Anglo-American law, the additional requirement is typically called the rule of "proximate cause." In German law, these cases of remote effects are resolved under the doctrine of *soziale Adequanz*,[16] which imposes limits on the norms of the criminal law. However the doctrinal issue is formulated, the intuitive judgment remains clear that the contractor is not causally tainted by the inevitable deaths occurring in a carefully executed construction project.

The more complicated cases of those actually litigated are those beset by multiple and concurrent causes of death. The problem is how much the defendant must contribute to the occurrence of death for his conduct to constitute a "cause." The question is put neatly in the controversial case of Stephenson v. State,[17] in which the accused kidnapped the victim and subjected her to prolonged sexual abuse, during which he bit her several times and inflicted other injuries; the day after the initial attack, the victim managed to acquire six tablets of poisonous bichloride of mercury and to swallow them in an apparent effort to commit suicide. Though she received medical care, she died about a month later.

[16] Jescheck 190–92.
[17] 205 Ind. 141, 179 N.E. 633 (1932).

The cause of death was a combination of many factors, including the poison and an infection that had developed in one of the bite wounds that the defendant had inflicted on her. There was some hesitation, which we shall take up below, about the defendant's liability for the effects of the poison. The inquiry thus fastened on the effects of the injuries the defendant inflicted on the victim. Could they provide a basis for holding that the defendant caused the death? The infection had healed at the time of death, yet the residual effect of the infection may have been one of the many causes of the victim's demise. Is it important that the bites and other injuries were inflicted as part of the defendant's sexual abuse of the deceased? Or should the analysis of causation proceed independently of the criteria of culpability? Though the jury in *Stephenson* might have interwoven the distinct questions of culpability and causation, the instructions on the law read simply that a person is guilty of homicide if he inflicts an injury that "contributes mediately or immediately to the death"[18] of the victim. Perhaps we could be more precise than merely to ask whether the defendant's act "contributes" to the death. Yet there are no theoretical guidelines to tell us what we should be precise about. So far as the requirement of causing death derives from the practice of tainting, how can we go about deciding, in principle, how much causal contribution would be necessary for a homicidal taint? If we had a gauge for weighing causal input in quantitative units, we would not know how many units to demand for liability.[19] There seems to be no choice but to leave the entire matter in the hands of the jury under the vague standard of "contribution."

These problems in assessing causation—liability for remote effects and the degree of involvement necessary for a causal tie—are two aspects of the same issue: How intensely must one be involved with evil in order to be tainted by it? In secular terms,

[18] *Id.* at 191; 179 N.E. at 650.

[19] *Cf.* the analogous problem of determining when the taint of an unconstitutional search and seizure dissipates and ceases to "contaminate" derivative evidence. Wong Son v. United States, 371 U.S. 471 (1963).

how closely must an actor be identified with harm to say that the harm is his doing?

The degree of involvement with the result is only one factor bearing on causal analysis. Subtle issues inhere in interweaving the defendant's contribution with the subsequent acts of the victim or of third parties.

B. The Victim Endangers His or Her Own Life. The *Stephenson* case was complicated by the victim's swallowing six tablets of mercury and thus accelerating her demise. The general issue raised by this attempted suicide was whether it was "voluntary." If the suicide was fully voluntary, the argument for the defendant would be that the cause of death was the suicide and not the sexual attack. In the view of many theorists,[20] the attribution of a harm cannot be traced past a voluntary, intentional act that brings it about.

Stated abstractly, the principle makes some sense: purely voluntary conduct is not caused by antecedent events. The problem is that in real life, the self-destructive conduct of a victim is never completely voluntary. If the defendant in *Stephenson* had not kidnapped and abused the victim, she would not have attempted to commit suicide. In a later case, the appellate courts had little trouble concluding that the suicide attempt is the natural outgrowth of the defendant's criminal acts.[21]

There are other cases that are admittedly more troublesome. Suppose the defendant either quarrels with his wife or beats her so as to cause her to flee from the family home in inclement weather. Death results from her spending the night outside. Convictions in this type of case are typically reversed.[22] For several reasons, the self-destructive act appears to be more the choice of the wife than the product of the defendant's acts. First, the response is less extreme than an intentional suicide: the most the wife does is take a risk of death by spending the night outdoors.

[20] See, most notably, H. Hart & A. Honoré, Causation in the Law 292 (1959).

[21] Jones v. State, 220 Ind. 384, 43 N.E.2d 1017 (1942) (defendant raped girl, who then jumped or fell into river and drowned).

[22] E.g., Hendrickson v. Commonwealth, 85 Ky. 281 (1887); State v. Preslar, 48 N.C. 417 (1856). See H. Hart & A. Honoré, *supra* note 20, at 293.

That the response is less extreme suggests that it is more within her control.[23] Secondly, the act is motivated by anger and spite as well as fear, and these other motives have springs independent of the defendant's provocative act. Indeed the causal issue may be in fact nominal in these cases; the more decisive consideration might be whether there is a duty to prevent self-destructive acts of an estranged spouse.

This was the way the issue was framed in a 1954 German case, in which a husband abandoned his wife under circumstances in which she might commit suicide. His conviction for negligent manslaughter was reversed; the issue was not causation, but whether his leaving her in a situation of potential distress was wrongful conduct. The court held that the risk of her suicide did not generate a duty to remain at home.[24]

As these factual variations become more subtle, it is important to distinguish between the issue of a criminal act at T_1 causing a self-destructive act at T_2 and the independent duty to intervene and prevent the harm at T_2. In the German case, the court held that there was no wrongful act to the wife at T_1 and implicitly no duty to prevent harm at T_2.[25] The problem is obviously different if at T_1 the defendant commits an assault or rape, and as a result the victim later commits suicide.

C. *An Intentional Intervening Act by a Third Person.* If victims of violent assaults do not voluntarily commit suicide, one might more plausibly maintain that a third-party assassin, coming on the scene after the victim is wounded, acts fully voluntarily and thus precludes attribution of the death to the first actor. Hart and Honoré maintain that "the free, deliberate and informed interven-

[23] Compare cases in which a threatened victim responds by jumping out of a window or a moving car; Whiteside v. State, 115 Tex. Crim. 274, 29 S.W.2d 399 (1930); Sanders v. Commonwealth, 244 Ky. 77, 50 S.W.2d 37 (1932); these extreme responses are readily perceived as involuntary and the resulting death is attributed to the defendant.

[24] Judgment of December 17, 1954, 7 BGHSt. 268.

[25] *Cf.* cases where a duty to prevent a spouse's suicide is affirmed, *supra* §4.5.4, at notes 80–82.

tion of a second person, not acting in concert with the first, and intending to bring about the harm . . . is normally held to relieve the first actor of criminal responsibility."[26] This principle may be conceptually appealing, but an examination of the Anglo-American criminal cases does not provide much support for this theory of "breaking the causal chain." The homicide cases cited by Hart and Honoré typically raise the problem of minor injuries by the first actor and a fatal intervention by the second.[27] It is difficult to infer from these cases that if the defendant inflicts a fatal wound, the victim is lying in the roadway bleeding, and a stranger then delivers the *coup de grace,* the first actor will be relieved of liability.

The German courts have explicitly rejected the principle that in homicide cases the voluntary intervention of a third party can insulate the original actor from liability for the ensuing death.[28] If the actor negligently delivers poison to a third party and the latter uses it intentionally to kill the victim, the actor is liable for negligent manslaughter.[29] Similarly, if the suspect abandons her daughter when there is a substantial risk that the daughter will kill the child she is expecting, the suspect will be liable for negligent manslaughter of the child.[30] In the 1954 case considered above, the abandoned wife killed not only herself but her child. Though the defendant's abandonment did not generate liability for the suicide, he did have a duty to minimize risk to the child and his conviction for negligent manslaughter of the child was affirmed.[31] All of these cases would be analyzed, in contemporary Anglo-American tort theory, as questions bearing on the "ambit of the risk." If the defendant's negligent risk included the likelihood that a third

[26] H. Hart & A. Honoré, *supra* note 20, at 292.

[27] People v. Elder, 100 Mich. 515, 59 N.W. 237 (1894) (defendant bartender struck victim after altercation; bystander then struck fatal blow); Wilson v. State, 24 S.W. 409 (Tex. Crim. App. 1893) (defendant struck victim; defendant's brother then inflicted fatal stabbing). *But cf.* Smith v. State, 50 Ark. 545, 8 S.W. 941 (1888).

[28] But note the effort to revive the doctrine under the rubric of *Regressverbot,* see Naucke, *Über das Regressverbot im Strafrecht,* 76 ZStW 409 (1964).

[29] Judgment of October 17, 1930, 64 RGSt. 370.

[30] See note 24 *supra.*

[31] *Ibid.*

party would act intentionally, the subsequent voluntary act is treated as the realization of the risk, rather than a "superceding cause."[32]

This is not to say there is no merit to the principle proposed by Hart and Honoré. Yet the best illustrations supporting the thesis are found in cases other than homicide. To take the authors' example, suppose that a smoker is extinguishing his cigarette in an ashtray and at that moment a bystander pours gasoline on the cigarette, thus inflaming the ashtray, the table, and the house.[33] It seems clear that the bystander is the one who caused the fire, not the smoker. The reasons are illuminating. It is true that the smoker's bearing the lighted cigarette is a necessary condition for the fire and thus it meets the "sine qua non" test for causation. Yet the smoking and extinction of lighted cigarettes is a routine event that creates the frame for the arsonist's act. The issue is not so much the "voluntariness" of the bystander's pouring gasoline on the cigarette, but the fact that the availability of lighted cigarettes (as well as the presence of oxygen in the air) is but a background condition for igniting the fire. When we return to the theme of causation in a later context, we shall see that this example is but an instance of Hart and Honoré's generally sound view of the relationship between abnormal events and causation.[34]

In the present context, the important point is that the availability of an injured victim is not a normal part of the frame in which a third party acts to kill. That the victim is injured or endangered by the defendant's conduct stands out from all other background features, and it is not flattened into a mere condition of the homicide by the third party's intentional intervention.

There is no easy solution to the problem of causation. The metaphysics of proximate cause, degrees of contribution and inter-

[32] See, e.g., Hergenrether v. East, 61 Cal. 2d 440, 393 P.2d 164, 39 Cal. Rptr. 4 (1964) (defendant left keys in truck on skid-row street; held liable for personal injuries caused by thief who stole the truck); Hines v. Garrett, 131 Va. 125, 108 S.E. 690 (1921) (plaintiff was raped after defendant railroad negligently went past her stop and left her off in apparently dangerous area).

[33] H. Hart & A. Honoré, *Causation in the Law*, 72 L.Q. Rev. 58, 79 (1956).

[34] See §8.2 *infra*.

vening causes will continue to affect even the most rational penal system. The reasons are several. First, the inquiry into causation is categorical. A death is attributable to someone or it is not. There is no room for a compromise verdict as there is in the assessment of culpability for criminal homicide. Secondly, the issue of causation, along with the elements of acting and the occurrence of death, goes to the foundation of liability. Whether a particular set of facts constitutes an adequate cause of death receives closer scrutiny on appeal than the question whether a particular set of facts constitutes malice. Appellate courts are more likely to reverse on the issue of causation than they are on the basis of inadequate proof of intent, malice, insanity, or the absence of provocation or self-defense. While the courts may often defer to juries on the latter issues bearing on culpability, the issue comprising the outer circle of liability demands special scrutiny.[35]

A third significant factor is that the courts are bound to render these appellate decisions in an all-or-nothing fashion without having a general theory to guide their assessment whether in close cases they should find for the defendant or the prosecution. As we have already stressed, the occurrence of death does not relate to any of the modern policies and principles that inform the theory of criminal responsibility. Rooted in the practice of tainting, the causal inquiry bears neither on the definition of conduct that should be deterred nor on the criteria for justly blaming someone who endangers human life. Even more significantly, there is no general trend of the law that the courts may fall back on in close cases. In the law of torts, by contrast, the long-range trend in favor of compensating victims might influence the outcome of close cases on the issue of causation. In criminal cases, there may be a long-range trend favoring the accused on the issue of culpability. Yet it is not clear whether this trend does or should properly shape the analysis of causation. The problem of causing third-party killings in felony-murder cases suggests a connection, for this is an area in which the law on the issue of culpability places its thumb on the

[35] Notice the special attention afforded the issue of causation in felony-murder cases where defendant's acts induce a third party to shoot the victim, *supra* §4.4.7, at notes 144–63.

state's side of the scale. In cases like *Washington,*[36] the courts revived the indispensability of a causal connection with death in order to curtail the sweep of the felony-murder rule. Where the criteria of culpability are not refined, the courts might properly devote more attention to the scrutiny of the causal connection required for homicide.

Perhaps the most difficult issue in the theory of causation is whether the issues of causation and culpability should be kept rigidly distinct or whether the presence of a particularly heinous motive should influence the analysis of causation. The shift from a harm-oriented to an act-oriented mode of analysis would tend to support the interweaving of criteria of causation with criteria of culpability; this interweaving might lead to the view, for example, that those who intentionally cause harm should be liable for more remote consequences than those who negligently cause harm. This seems to be the position today in the law of torts. While the rule of foreseeability limits tort liability for negligent risk-taking, it does not limit the extent of liability for intentional battery leading to remote consequences.[37]

Regardless of whether this interweaving of issues is proper in the law of torts, it seems dubious in assessing liability for homicide. Culpability bears on the just assessment of punishment, but it does not follow that a particularly culpable actor should be held liable for a result that would not be attributed to a non-responsible defendant. Suppose that *Stephenson* had been partially or fully insane at the time that he inflicted wounds on his kidnap victim. Should the degree of insanity influence the analysis whether the wounds contributed adequately to the victim's death? It is certainly clear that under the harm-oriented mode of analysis, causation and culpability are distinct issues. A causal nexus is required even before the defendant need be put to his proof that the killing was excused. Yet under the affirmative mode of analysis, the issue

[36] People v. Washington, 62 Cal. 2d 777, 402 P.2d 130, 44 Cal. Rptr. 442 (1965).

[37] Restatement of Torts §279, comment c; Restatement (Second) of Torts §870; Tate v. Canonica, 180 Cal. App. 2d 898, 5 Cal. Rptr. 28 (1960) (intentional infliction of emotional distress leading to suicide).

of culpability comes to the forefront and is more likely to become intermingled with the analysis of causation.

There is one other point about causing death that bears notice. The tie between the practice of tainting and the modern requirement of causation in homicide cases helps us understand why the law was so late in punishing the failure to prevent death. It was not until the mid-nineteenth century that Anglo-American courts began to convict persons of criminal homicide for failing to render aid and letting another person die.[38] These are cases, as we shall argue later in detail, where the actor is liable even though he has not caused the death of the victim.[39] Of course, a bystander may cause death in the trivial sense that "but for" his failure to act, the victim would not have died. But there is no causing of death in the sense implicit in the tradition of homicidal tainting. Because there is no causal link in this deeper sense, liability turns on whether there is a duty to intervene and save the person in distress. In analyzing the outer circle of liability—an act causing death—we have no occasion to advert to the issue of duty. Nor does the concept of duty appear in the analysis of culpability—at least as the four states of culpability are analyzed in the Model Penal Code.[40] There are some profound reasons why the issue of duty emerges when the problem is the failure to prevent death, and it is worth pausing to consider why the field of failing to intervene is so significantly different.

The law of homicide is built on the premise that everyone has a duty not to cause death. If an act causes death, then under the harm-oriented mode of analysis it is murder—unless justified, excused or mitigated. Because the duty is universal, it need not be alleged and proved. Yet there is no universal duty to prevent death from occurring; if there were, we should all be tainted by innumerable suicides and accidental deaths that occur in our community. We

[38] The first significant case was Regina v. Instan, [1893] 1 Q.B. 450 (defendant lived with her aunt and failed to care for her during illness).

[39] *Id.* at 454: "failure to discharge her legal duty . . . accelerated the death . . . if it did not actually cause it."

[40] MPC §2.02(2).

might not be criminally liable for these deaths unless we had a fair chance of preventing them, but at least the deaths would be attributable to us—in the sense that the common law regarded all those who caused death as tainted and subject to a forfeiture of goods. Prior to the nineteenth century, the common law did not regard those who failed to prevent death as even minimally responsible in this way. And if we are inclined to hold some people liable for failing to intervene, we must do so on the basis of a principle that is more discriminating than the universal imperative against causing death. To be more discriminating, we need to fasten our attention on a factor that was irrelevant in the common law, namely, the relationship between the victim and the party who could intervene. Liability in these cases, then, does not build on causing death, but on the failure to fulfill responsibilities implicit in particular relationships. The concept of "duty" is the vehicle by which we select those relationships that require people to intervene to prevent the death of others.

§5.2.3. The Jurisprudence of Life and Death. The question in the third arc of the outer circle of liability is infrequently litigated, for it is usually obvious when human death occurs. There is an important story to be told in tracing the evolution of homicide to cover all cases of causing death, whether of slave, foreigner, or kinsman. But the issue that will concern us here is of greater contemporary moment. Both the beginning of human life and its natural termination pose innumerable difficulties, and with the current controversies about abortion, termination of life-sustaining treatment and organ transplantation, they are of great importance.

The threshold question is whether we should seek a single concept of human life and natural death to cover the varied range of legal contexts in which the issue might arise. To take the issue of death first, one might well argue that the law should distinguish among the contexts in which it matters whether a person is regarded as dead. For example, a person might be deemed "dead" as a murder victim but not for purposes of removing the person's organs for transplantation. A comatose patient might be deemed "dead" for purposes of terminating therapy, but for no other purpose.[41] Despite the modern jurisprudential preference for breaking down concepts to fit the context in which they function,[42] the clear tendency today is to fashion a single standard of biological death. Most proposals focus on a variation of "brain death" as manifested by a flat electroencephalograph reading for a specific period of time.[43] For whatever reason, there is no serious consideration of the possibility that a person might be "dead" for one purpose but not another.

But not so with the beginning of life and the legal status of fetuses. For the purposes of recovering damages for prenatal injuries, a fetus of any age is considered an interest worthy of protection.[44] The law of abortion, with the imprimatur of the United States Supreme Court,[45] veers toward postponing the moment at which the fetus becomes a life protected by the law. What is true about therapeutic abortion, as we shall see, is not true about the malicious killing of the fetus. And if the fetus is protected against malicious killing under the law of homicide, it need not follow that the fetus is a person for the purposes of recovering in tort for wrongful death.[46] For each context of the law, we are apparently willing to settle for a different moment at which the fetus becomes a human being.

It is not even entirely clear whether we should use the term "person," "human being," or "live person" to state what it is to be one of us. The word "alive" is not apt, for the fetus is unquestionably alive from the moment of conception. What is at stake is not life, but the acquisition of a legal personality. This evaluative

[41] For a detailed discussion of the problem of terminating therapy, see §8.2.4.

[42] The concept of domicile was one of the first concepts to be so analyzed. See the seminal work of W. Cook, The Logical and Legal Basis for the Conflict of Laws 194–210 (1942).

[43] See Ad Hoc Committee of the Harvard Medical School, *A Definition of Irreversible Coma,* 205 J.A.M.A. 337 (1968).

[44] See e.g., Bonbrest v. Kotz, 65 F. Supp. 138 (D.D.C. 1946); Woods v. Lancet, 303 N.Y. 349, 102 N.E.2d 691 (1951); Prosser 336–38.

[45] Roe v. Wade, 410 U.S. 113 (1973).

[46] See Justus v. Atchison, 19 Cal. 3d 564, 565 P.2d 122, 139 Cal. Rptr. 97 (1977) (recovery denied).

dimension to the problem accounts for a different judgment of value in different contexts. But recognizing this fact only brings us back to the issue of death and makes us wonder why death—or the loss of human personality—is not treated as an evaluative rather than a biological issue.

Our immediate concern is the beginning of human status in the law of homicide. Two California cases bring us to the heart of the controversy. In People v. Chavez,[47] the defendant, without medical assistance, delivered her baby into a toilet bowl; without tying the umbilical cord, she wrapped the baby in newspaper and concealed it. The autopsy of the dead baby revealed that it had bled to death through the umbilical cord. The evidence strongly supported the inference that if the baby had received normal post-natal care, it would have lived. More recently, in the ambivalent mood generated by the movement to legalize abortion, the California Supreme Court had to decide whether willfully and maliciously killing a viable fetus, contrary to the will of the mother, constituted murder. In Keeler v. Supreme Court,[48] the defendant encountered his ex-wife, who was then pregnant by another man; becoming upset by her bearing another man's baby, the defendant assaulted her, shoved his knee into her abdomen, and declared that he was "going to stomp it out of [her]."[49] The fetus was born dead, with a skull fracture, which in the opinion of the expert witness "could have been the result"[50] of the defendant's assault.

In both cases, all the elements of criminal homicide were present, except for one: did the death of the fetus constitute the death of a human being? The court decided that in *Chavez,* the victim was a human being, and that therefore the defendant's act constituted criminal homicide. In *Keeler,* the judges came to the opposite conclusion: the maliciously killed fetus was not a human being. More important than these results is the methodology for trying to classify borderline cases within the ambit of criminal homicide. One approach would be to ask the instrumentalist question,

[47] 77 Cal. App. 2d 621, 176 P.2d 92 (1947).
[48] 2 Cal. 3d 619, 470 P.2d 617, 87 Cal. Rptr. 481 (1970).
[49] *Id.* at 623, 470 P.2d at 618; 87 Cal. Rptr. at 482.
[50] *Ibid.*

whether the defendant's behavior was of the sort that the law should discourage. If the judges had looked at the problem from this perspective, the courts presumably would have reached the opposite result of convicting Keeler and acquitting Chavez. The incident in *Chavez* was hardly one to trigger social concern. Mothers not caring for their newborn infants appears to be more a problem for social assistance than a proper concern of the criminal courts. Keeler's stamping the viable fetus to death comes much closer to the paradigmatic forms of wicked and dangerous conduct that the law sanctions with criminal punishment.

The difficulty with this instrumentalist approach is that it sidesteps the critical issue: the defendant had a right not to be convicted unless he had actually killed a human being. To make the concept of humanness subservient to the law's purposes is to define away the protection offered by the legal rule. It might accomplish more to punish people like Keeler for murder and to make medical and counselling service available to people like Chavez. But the rule of law precludes the instrumentalist adaptation of the concept of life. Whether the babies killed in these two cases constituted human beings has to be resolved by addressing the concept of humanness, not by inquiring about the good that will follow from one definition or its alternatives.

The beginning of human life might be defined by invoking a significant medical event, such as the cutting of the umbilical cord. Yet why should this event be more important than the emergence of the head from the birth canal or the baby's first cry? In approaching this problem of definition, the critical issue would seem to be maintaining the coherence of the moral imperative against killing. To link the crime to an arbitrary event would undercut the moral force of the imperative in these borderline cases. Rather than pick some single event, the California appellate court sensibly reasoned in *Chavez* that the fetus is a human being as "soon as the birth process begins."[51] Our perceptions of the fetus change when the process of birth begins, and therefore it is plausible that we should come under a stricter moral imperative to respect its life.

[51] 77 Cal. App. 2d at 624, 176 P.2d at 93.

Though this standard is not as precise as some particular medical event, it may represent the maximum precision possible under the circumstances.

The status of the viable fetus in *Keeler* was complicated by the movement to legalize abortion. Just a year before *Keeler*, in its 1969 decision in *Belous*,[52] the California Supreme Court held that penalizing abortion except where necessary to save the life and health of the mother was unconstitutional; the grounds were both that the statute was excessively vague and that it encroached upon the mother's alleged right of privacy in determining whether she would carry the fetus. This was one of several cases leading to the Supreme Court's holding in 1973 that the states could not prohibit abortions at all in the first trimester of pregnancy.[53]

As with many social movements, the drive to legitimate abortion represents a coalition of incompatible views. There are some proponents of abortion who deny that the unborn child is an interest worthy of any protection at all. Others acknowledge the interest of the fetus, but stress the superior rights of the mother. Among the latter group, some stress the tangible interests of the mother in physical and emotional health; others take the mother's autonomy over the reproductive process to be the critical issue. The complex alliance of opinion favoring abortion generates diverse sentiments about the problem in *Keeler*. Those who deny that the fetus is an independent legal interest would favor acquittal of the homicide charges and conviction at most of assault. At the opposite extreme, those who acknowledge the significance of the fetus but stress the superior autonomy of the mother over the birth process would regard Keeler's act as a double evil: both an assault upon the fetus as inchoate life and a violation of the mother's autonomy in controlling her reproductive system.

Faced with an issue of this moral complexity, the California Supreme Court fashioned a solution to the problem in *Keeler* by invoking the common-law doctrine that the fetus had to be

[52] People v. Belous, 71 Cal. 2d 954, 458 P.2d 194, 80 Cal. Rptr. 354 (1969), *cert. denied*, 397 U.S. 915 (1970).

[53] Roe v. Wade, 410 U.S. 113 (1973).

born alive in order to be the victim of homicide.[54] If the child was born alive and then died of prenatal injuries, the person who caused the injuries could be held guilty of homicide. The difficulty with this rule is that it admits of two distinct readings:

1. a substantive interpretation: only the death of a child born alive constitutes human death under the law.

2. an evidentiary interpretation: being born alive is conclusive proof that the fetus was alive at the time of the injury.

The first reading pointed to Keeler's acquittal, for the fetus was born dead. The second reading implied that at common law, he might have been guilty of criminal homicide. The critical issue would be whether the fetus was alive at the time of injury. Absent the proof of a live birth, other evidence might suffice to establish the same ultimate issue. The majority of the court took the substantive reading as authoritative; the dissent, the evidentiary interpretation.[55] The implication of the majority's holding was that Keeler was not guilty, but would have been, had he kicked less hard and the baby were born alive and then died. The resulting paradox is that homicide can be committed against a being not yet human; liability turns solely on whether the being is human when it dies.

The jurisprudential basis of Justice Mosk's opinion for the majority is worth underscoring. The guiding assumption of the opinion is that any expansion of California law beyond the common law of homicide would violate the accused's constitutional right of fair warning of the act punishable as a crime.[56] This is a good example of the special appellate scrutiny reserved for issues in the outer circle of liability. The judges have not displayed and would not display similar sensitivity to judicial innovations on the issues of malice and culpability. There was certainly no clear-cut rule of felony-murder when the state's statutes incorporated the common law of murder in 1850.[57] Yet, today, the word "murder" in §189 is

[54] See 3 Coke 50; 1 Hale 433.

[55] 2 Cal. 3d at 639, 470 P.2d at 630; 87 Cal. Rptr. at 494 (Justices Burke and Sullivan, dissenting).

[56] *Id.* at 633; 470 P.2d at 626; 87 Cal. Rptr. at 490.

[57] See §4.4.4 *supra.*

read to support the second-degree felony-murder rule.[58] Were the mandate of fair warning taken as seriously in felony-murder cases as it was in *Keeler,* the rule would soon founder on the barrier of *nulla poena sine lege.*

In the wake of the *Keeler* decision, the California legislature amended the statutory definition of homicide so as to encompass cases such as Keeler's malicious killing of a viable fetus.[59] While the previous definition of murder succinctly stated the law in a formula of twelve words, the new definition is a complex structure that seeks to protect the fetus under the law of murder without encroaching upon the Therapeutic Abortion Act.[60] The critical change is, in effect, that killing a fetus with malice aforethought is murder, subject to an exemption if the mother consents to the killing, or the killing is committed by a licensed physician in order to save the life of the mother.[61] It is certainly odd to lump together the crimes of feticide and of murder. The consent of a third party (the mother) is a good defense to the former; but not even the consent of the victim constitutes a defense to the latter. The principle of lesser evils provides a justification for the former, but it is not applicable to the latter.[62] Another oddity in the legislative scheme is that while the definition of murder is changed, the definition of manslaughter is not. This means that if in a case like *Keeler,* the defendant can invoke provocation or diminished capacity as a defense, his crime could not be mitigated to manslaughter and he should escape liability altogether.

A more critical issue in this new statutory protection of the fetus from malicious killing is whether the statute can be reconciled with the unclear constitutional teachings of Roe v. Wade.[63] If, according to that decision, abortion may not be prohibited in the first three months of pregnancy, does it follow that the malicious killing of the fetus during this early stage, contrary to the mother's

[58] *Ibid.*
[59] Cal. Stat. 1970, c. 1311, §1.
[60] Cal. Health & Safety Code §§25950 et seq.
[61] Cal. Penal Code §187(b)(2).
[62] See Regina v. Dudley & Stevens, 14 Q.B.D. 273 (1884). See §10.4.1 *infra.*
[63] 410 U.S. 113 (1973).

wishes, is also protected by the Constitution? There is admittedly some ambiguity whether the concept of a "fetus"—the word used in the statute—encompasses the embryo during the early stages of development. The inescapable constitutional problem, which has already triggered appellate litigation, is whether the malicious killing of the fetus after the first trimester, but prior to viability, is also protected under Roe v. Wade. This conundrum is not so easily resolved, for, as we have already noted, the legalization of abortion suffers from a radical ambivalence. If a legislature may not constitutionally identify non-viable fetuses as human lives, then the malicious killing of a twenty-week-old non-viable fetus could not constitutionally be treated as murder under the California statute. On the other hand, if the critical point is the autonomy of the mother over her reproductive system, then there is no reason why the criminal law should not support the mother's desire to carry an embryo or fetus from the very moment of conception.

§5.3. *From Desecration to a Pattern of Harmful Consequences.*

The way we have presented the theory of homicide, the crime stands unique in Western criminal law. To find another offense that combined the features of desecration, tainting and liability for negligence as well as liability for failing to prevent the desecration, we have to rely on our imagination. Suppose, for example, that casting dirt onto a holy site constituted a transcendent harm. We could imagine a practice of treating those who unwittingly brought dirt onto the site as tainted. Only those who negligently produced the harm would be blamed and punished; others, who acted unwittingly, would have to make expiation in some other way. One would also expect that those who witnessed the carrying in of dirt would be duty-bound to intervene and prevent the desecration.

Even this hypothetical offense fails to capture the subtlety of homicide; for, as we noted, one of the noteworthy historical marks of homicide is the offender's interaction with the victim. The resulting refinement of the criteria of culpability has vastly enriched the entire criminal law. No other offense shares this feature with the criminality of killing.

The reason that homicide stands alone in this pattern of liability is a consequence of its lying at the intersection of two strands of thought that interweave in the history of criminal law. The first strand is a traditional sentiment that the law may properly punish those who bring about harms of transcendent significance. The crimes so generated are sometimes called crimes against religion or morality, and include many offenses, such as profaning the Sabbath, which one would not ordinarily compare with homicide. The second strand derives from the secularization of homicide into a crime against the great worldly interest in human life. In this section, we shall attempt to extrapolate from homicide to a broader theory of liability. The agenda will be first to assess the problem of desecration in a secular society, and then to turn to a modern version of homicide as a crime of worldly harm.

§5.3.1. **Desecration in a Secular Society.** Implicit in the notion of "desecration" is the invasion of a sacred realm. Human life is commonly regarded as sacred and therefore homicide is properly thought of as a form of desecration. Yet it is difficult to find other examples of the criminal law's protection of the sacred from desecration.

Relying on the word "desecration" one might come to "flag desecration" as a possible, though unconventional analogue to homicide. Using the word "desecrate" is a curious way to refer to acts expressing contempt of the flag. However much patriots revere and respect the flag, one would think—or at least hope—that they do not regard it as sacred.[1] In fact, the law of flag desecration reflects none of the features that we regard as critical to the structure of homicide. There is no practice of tainting persons who in-

§5.3. [1] The analogous crime in German is defined simply as "casting contempt" (*Verunglimpfung*) on the flag; StGB §90a(2), as is the federal offense, 18 U.S.C. §7000. *Cf.* note 4 *infra*.

advertently "deface," "defile," or "trample" upon the flag.[2] All of these verbs of execution are read to require an intent to express contempt for the flag.[3] Accordingly, the crime is not committed negligently; nor is there authority suggesting that one could commit the offense by failing to intervene—say, by failing to pull the flag out of the mud. It is worth noting that the crime of flag desecration has encountered sustained constitutional attack in recent years, and it is unclear how much of the crime will survive the powerful arguments against the vagueness of its terms[4] and the tendency of prosecutions to interfere with speech protected under the First Amendment.[5]

In this search for other crimes of desecration, we must also consider the crimes "against nature": sodomy, intercourse with animals and other so-called unnatural sex acts. In referring to these acts as "unspeakable crimes" against nature, earlier commentators[6] must have had a conception of a transcendental natural order that was violated by homosexual acts and intercourse with animals. Yet the notion of natural order at work in these discussions is obviously not the same as the range of natural human instincts. Those

[2] People v. Myers, 23 Ill. App. 3d 1044, 321 N.E.2d 142 (1974) (defendant stood on flag momentarily; conviction rev'd on ground this was insufficient for trampling).

[3] Commonwealth v. Phipps, 21 Ches. Co. Rep. 108 (Pa. 1972) (rev'd); State v. Turner, 78 Wash. 2d 276, 474 P.2d 91 (1970) (rev'd). Affirmed convictions are found primarily in two types of cases: (1) use of the flag for commercial purposes; Halter v. Nebraska, 205 U.S. 34 (1907) (defendant used flag on label of beer can); and (2) verbal and physical abuse of flag and country, particularly in wartime, e.g., State v. Schlueter, 127 N.J.L. 496, 23 A.2d 249 (1941) (defendant claimed she was a Nazi and tore up flag); Johnson v. State, 204 Ark. 476, 163 S.W.2d 153 (1942) (defendant said flag was "just a rag"). *Cf.* State v. Saulino, 29 Ohio Misc. 25, 277 N.E.2d 580 (1971) (defendant painted flag on truck with Mickey Mouse in place of stars).

[4] Smith v. Goguen, 415 U.S. 566 (1974) (flag on seat of pants; charge that defendant "treated flag contemptuously" held unconstitutionally vague); Commonwealth v. Morgan, 331 A.2d 444 (Pa. 1975) (flag on seat of pants; rev'd; "casting contempt" clause held unconstitutionally vague; "defiling" limited to physical destruction).

[5] Street v. New York, 394 U.S. 576 (1969) (defendant burned and abused flag in protest meeting; conviction for mutilation rev'd; verbal abuse protected by First Amendment).

[6] 4 Blackstone 215 ("the very mention of [the crime] is a disgrace to human nature").

activities that are taboo and that do in fact run counter to human instincts need not be prohibited by the criminal law. The outstanding example is cannibalism, which, so far as I know, has not found explicit prohibition in any Western criminal code. People may be just as horrified at the thought of others eating human flesh as they are in contemplating acts of sodomy. Yet the law intervenes to condemn and punish activity only when humans are in fact tempted to engage in it.[7] Unspeakable acts that are truly contrary to nature do not invite the law's concern. Thus the "natural order" infringed by sodomy is not the revealed nature that we perceive, but a transcendent nature that renders some acts sacred and others "an abomination" in the sight of God.

Under this interpretation of "unnatural" sexual activity, there is a harm brought about by sodomy and buggery, but the harm is to a transcendental rather than a secular interest. The issue raised by these offenses is not whether the state should paternalistically protect people from acting immorally, but whether the state may use the criminal law to protect perceived transcendental interests. As John Stuart Mill argued influentially in *On Liberty*: "the only purpose for which power can be rightfully exercised over any member of a civilized community against his will, is to prevent harm to others."[8] This means that the purpose of the criminal law is to prevent secular harm, not transcendental harm. And secular harm always impinges concretely on the interests of particular individuals.

It is not so clear why the state should not be able to defend transcendental interests. Though Mill's thesis is readily defended as an argument against paternalism, there is nothing paternalistic about enjoining people from violating interests that the society takes to be sacred. Yet the clear tendency of the criminal law in the post-religious societies of the West is to abandon the sacred and concentrate on concrete harms to particular individuals. It is surely the case that in a heterogeneous society, rent by moral dissensus, there is likely to be more agreement whether homicide and larceny

[7] See S. Freud, Totemism and Taboo 123 (S. Strachey trans. 1913).
[8] J.S. Mill, On Liberty 22 (1859).

violate significant interests than whether sodomy and profaning the Sabbath tread upon transcendental interests.

If there is growing consensus that criminal sanctions should not be used to protect transcendental interests, the impact of this consensus takes distinct and contradictory forms. True, there is a widespread movement to decriminalize some sexual offenses, particularly private sexual behavior between consenting adults.[9] But there is an equally strong tendency to reinterpret other violations of the sacred in a new idiom of secular harm.

Instead of reasoning that profanation of the Sabbath is an offense against God, the Supreme Court argues that Sunday closing laws serve the secular interest of securing a day of quiet and rest.[10] Instead of taking the sacred seriously, the drafters of the Model Penal Code justify punishment for the "desecration of venerated objects" only if the actor knows that his act "will outrage the sensibilities of persons likely to observe or discover his action."[11] This technique for secularizing the offense shifts the locus of harm from the transcendent to the human interest in not being offended. The analogous technique in the field of sexual offenses is to limit either prosecution or formal liability to "open and notorious" acts that are likely to offend other people.[12] The notion that ordinary "sensibilities" warrant protection under the criminal law is widely and uncritically accepted.

Yet there are several good reasons for questioning whether the violation of "sensibilities" justifies treating conduct as criminal. First, if it is an exercise of speech that offends sensibilities, the

[9] See, e.g., MPC §213.2 ("deviate" sexual intercourse subject to liability on the same grounds as heterosexual rape); Cal. Penal Code §§286, 288a (Supp. 1976) (anal and oral intercourse subject to liability only if committed by force, in exploitation of a minor or in prison); StGB §175 (as amended 1973, homosexual acts subject to liability only if committed with a male under the age of 18).

[10] McGowan v. Maryland, 366 U.S. 420 (1961).

[11] MPC §250.9. This formula is repeated in the following newly drafted desecration statutes: Colo. Rev. Stat. §18-11-204 (but "intent to cast contempt or ridicule on flag" also sufficient); Del. Code tit. 11, §1331; Kan. Stat. §21–4114; Pa. Cons. Stat. Ann. tit. 18, §5509.

[12] See Ill. Ann. Stat. c. 38, §11–7 (condition for criminal adultery is that the "behavior is open and notorious").

First Amendment, as now interpreted, does not permit suppression.[13] Freedom of conduct does not receive the same constitutional protection as freedom of speech, but it is not so easy to explain why protecting sensibilities should justify suppression of the former, but not the latter. Further, we are not willing to protect all sensibilities against "offensive" conduct. If people in a particular locale are offended by interracial marriages, they may not prohibit the cohabitation of mixed couples.[14]

Miscegenation is an exception not only because the interests of married couples are strong, but because we take the reaction of those offended to be irrational. The implication is that only "rational" sensibilities warrant protection, which shifts the brunt of the inquiry to determining when sensibilities are rational. An apparently good reason for regarding sensibilities as rational is that they respond to what people once regarded as sacred, or at least worthy of veneration. They are the afterglow of a once resplendent transcendental value. This accounts for why few questions are raised about the rationality of being offended in cases of desecrated flags, bodies and tombstones.

Another curious feature about "sensibilities" as a protectible interest is that reference to the interest seems appropriate only in a few isolated contexts, such as desecration of venerated objects and unconventional sexual behavior. It would be odd to justify the prosecution of abortion on the ground that abortions offend the sensibilities of many people. Similarly, it would be unconvincing to argue that voluntary euthanasia warranted punishment simply because it was offensive. The debate about abortion turns on our perception of the fetus as human; the debate about voluntary euthanasia turns, in part, on our ongoing sense for the sacredness of human life. Though many people might be offended by the legalization of abortion or voluntary euthanasia, their sensibilities do not seem to warrant protection under the criminal law. One can only wonder, then, why sensibilities are worth considering in cases of flag desecration.

[13] Cohen v. California, 403 U.S. 15 (1971).
[14] Loving v. Virginia, 388 U.S. 1 (1967).

This discussion of desecration in a secular society confirms our initial judgment that homicide has no precise parallels in the criminal law. Yet it is desirable to broaden the pattern of liability represented by homicide. To do this, we should think of homicide as a crime against the wordly interest in human life. This view of homicide admittedly fails to explain attitudes toward consent to being killed, and it ignores the background of tainting in the jurisprudence of homicide. With these qualifications in mind, we can proceed to a view of homicide that admits of links with crimes of serious secular harm.

§5.3.2. A Pattern of Harmful Consequences. If we think of homicide as the invasion of the secular commodity of life, we can draw some important parallels among homicide, battery and the destruction of property. All of these offenses have the following points in common: (1) There is a concrete harm to a personal interest (death, bodily injury, destruction of property); (2) this harmful consequence might be brought about either by natural processes or by human conduct; (3) it is possible and plausible to punish both negligent infliction of the harmful consequence and the failure to intervene and prevent the harm's occurring. These features are sufficient to generate a general pattern of liability, which we shall call the pattern of harmful consequences. After clarifying the central notion of a harmful consequence, we shall turn to the illuminating contrasts between this third pattern of liability and the earlier elaborated patterns of manifest and subjective criminality.

The notion of a "harmful consequence" is used technically to circumscribe a range of offenses in which the harm might occur either naturally or by human design. Thus "harmful consequences" to persons and property are conceptually separable from human action.[15] Death occurs naturally or by human hand. But "dispossession" of an object occurs only if someone takes the object from the possession of another. Giving aid and comfort to the enemy requires

[15] This notion of harm is purposefully distinguished from the German concept of *Erfolg* (result), which is used as a basic unit of classification. *Erfolgsdelikte* (crimes entailing results) include larceny and "insulting behavior" as well as homicide. See Jescheck 196. The concept obscures important distinctions.

that someone do the giving. The promise of this concept of "harmful consequences" will become apparent in due course, but first we must defend the definition against a plausible objection.

One might well object that the distinction between, say, death and dispossession is merely terminological. One could define the harm in larceny as "loss" of an object, and recast the crime as "causing the loss of an object with intent to make the loss permanent." The loss of an object might occur naturally or by human design, and thus our redefinition of larceny shows that there is no essential difference between the harm in larceny and the harm in homicide. The problem is that this redefinition of larceny would overshoot the mark. It would collapse stealing and the destruction of property into one offense. It is hardly adventitious that all legal systems we have considered recognize the distinction between taking with intent to deprive, on the one hand, and destruction without taking, on the other. There is a point to singling out the inchoate offense, taking with intent to deprive permanently, and that point is lost in redescribing the offense as causing the loss of property.

It is often the case that when a crime requires a particular result, and that result presupposes human action, the implicit reason for so defining the required result is to elicit the suggestion of furthered, threatened harm. This is the case with "dispossession," "giving aid and comfort to the enemy" and "breaking and entering" as required elements for their respective offenses. In contrast, a harmful consequence, as we use that term, is always a completed, consummated harm. When we refer to death, destruction and disfiguring, we take the worst to be known.

The strategy in our definition of "harmful consequences" is to isolate a particular mode of legal reasoning. The inquiry proceeds from the consequence to the actor who brought it about. We shall refer to this mode of reasoning backwards from consequence to agent as "objective attribution."[16] It is not uncommon for Anglo-American courts to use the term attribution to refer to the issue of

[16] The term in German is *objective Zurechnung;* for a clarification of the difference between "objective" and "subjective" attribution, see §6.7.1 *infra*.

causation.[17] In fact, the criteria of attribution encompass not only causation, but other theories of personal accountability. Two of these alternative theories of attribution—the duty to prevent harm and complicity in the acts of another—are grouped together in Chapter Eight under the heading of "derivative liability."

The reason that we filter off injuries latent with human conduct is that these injuries do not pose the same difficulties of attribution. To know that a chattel has been "dispossessed" is to assume that someone else acquired possession of it. To know that an enemy agent has been "given aid and comfort" is to assume that a particular person rendered aid. In the pattern of harmful consequences, in contrast, it is an open question whether particular incidents of harm are attributable to human actors. The occurrence might be traceable to natural rather than human causes.

Our definition of harmful consequences enables us to formulate a theorem about the permissible range of recklessness and negligence as bases for liability. The theorem is that negligent and reckless risk-taking are an appropriate basis for liability in bringing about any harmful consequence also sanctioned as an intentional offense. Anglo-American courts have traditionally abstained from punishing negligent (or reckless) battery, arson, and destruction of property. But other legal systems do extend liability in these fields, and there may be good reason to do so.[18] The movement in tort law toward social insurance may require a different social mechanism for controlling excessive risk-taking. At least there appears to be no rational basis for limiting liability for culpably taking excessive risks of harm to the field of homicide.

The negative corollary of our theory is that risk-taking does not provide an appropriate basis for liability for crimes such as treason, attempts, larceny, burglary, and rape, that fall outside the pattern of harmful consequences. For the time being we shall take this limitation as a descriptive observation. Later, when we turn to the important distinction between mistakes and accident, we shall

[17] See the California cases on whether third-party killings constitute felony-murder, §4.4.7, at notes 161, 162 *supra*.

[18] See §5.1, note 30 *supra*.

probe the deeper connection between the concept of a harmful consequence and the availability of risk-taking as basis for liability.[19]

§5.3.3. **The Three Patterns of Liability.** To summarize our discussion of specific offenses, we shall review and contrast the three patterns of liability. The patterns of manifest criminality, of subjective criminality and of harmful consequences each focusses on a different aspect of criminal conduct. Manifest criminality starts with an examination of the criminal act, subjective criminality with the intent to violate a legal interest and the pattern of harmful consequences with the accrual of harm. Thus each of the patterns attaches to one of three prominent facts of crime—act, intent and harm. Yet it would be a mistake to think that these three patterns are different perspectives on the same phenomenon. The argumant of this book is that these are different species of criminal conduct and despite the nominal overlap of terms like "act" and "intent," the critical differences must be seen for what they are.

The pattern of *manifest* criminality takes a particular form of act to be essential to liability. The act must manifest the actor's criminal purpose and further it must, in the typical case, constitute an unnerving threat to the order of community life. Those who commit crimes in this pattern can be seen and caught in the act, and the use of defensive force to prevent the crime is a characteristic social response. The issue of intent is subsidiary to the manifest act, and the claim of not intending the crime functions as an excuse to the incriminating effect of appearances. The harm in this context is the impact of the manifestly criminal act on the peace and order of the community.

The pattern of *subjective* criminality takes the actor's intent to violate a protected interest as the core of criminal conduct. The function of the act in execution of the intent is to demonstrate that firmness of the actor's resolve and to provide one among many sources of evidence of the particular intent. The potential harm in this pattern is the threat to a protected legal interest.

The pattern of *harmful consequences* assumes a harmful event

[19] See ‘6.6.6 *infra*.

that is conceptually independent of human action. Liability is based on the objective attribution of this harm to a responsible person and the determination of culpability in bringing it about or failing to prevent it. Negligence and recklessness supplement intention as a basis for gauging culpability.

Having outlined these three patterns of liability and having traced them through a wide range of criminal offenses, we should try to be more precise about what we mean by a "pattern of liability." The idea has both descriptive and normative content. The patterns describe the criminal law as it evolved over time, and tensions between the patterns, particularly between manifest and subjective criminality, provide a medium for interpreting a number of doctrinal disputes. The patterns also have normative implications, for they each state a plausible and coherent theory for prohibiting and punishing conduct as criminal. The patterns are a guide to diverse modes of reasoning about existing offenses, and they generate plausible arguments for creating new offenses, such as the suggested extension of negligence in the pattern of harmful consequences.

The implication of there being at least three patterns of liability is that the criminal law must be grasped as a polycentric body of ideas. There is no single mode of thinking that accounts for all crimes. Not even the three patterns account for more than many of the major offenses.[20]

It is important to keep the polycentric nature of the criminal law in mind as we turn, in the second half of this book, to efforts to synthesize the entire criminal law in a theory of the general

[20] Prohibited sexual behavior (adultery, incest, statutory rape) poses examples of offenses that fall in the gaps left by the three patterns of liability. These sexual offenses do not meet the criteria of a "harmful consequence" because the illicit coupling obviously implies human action. The crimes arguably meet the criteria of manifest criminality; at least rape would appear so to qualify. But the evil in incest is not the unnerving of the community, but sexual contact itself. It does not matter whether the sexual contact occurs in private or in public. This explains an important difference between the Biblical license to kill the manifest thief, Exodus 22:2, and the license to kill the adulterous spouse and her lover, Deuteronomy 22:22. The former license obtained only so long as the thief manifested danger, but the latter continued in force even after the adulterous act was consummated.

part. There is much to be gained from developing the general part, for there are obviously some planes on which synthesis is possible. The danger in formulating general propositions about the criminal law is that one pattern of liability—often the pattern of harmful consequences—is taken as paradigmatic of the whole criminal law. Unnecessary disputes in the theory of the general part often arise because both sides refuse to recognize the polycentric nature of the criminal law. Even as we make our effort at synthesis, we shall repeatedly refer back to the three patterns of liability in dissolving false disputes and recalling the diversity often concealed by nominal unity.

Part Two

Rethinking the General Part

Chapter Six
The Quest for the General Part

§6.1. *The Need for Synthesis.*

The criminal law is rooted in a set of distinct offenses, each with its problems of definition and its set of defenses that counteract the implications of incriminating events. Yet the quest of Western legal theory for the last hundred years or so has been the cultivation of a general part of the criminal law. The general part goes beyond the particular offenses and even particular patterns of liability, such as we have articulated in the first five chapters of this book. The general part has as its object the study of issues that cut across all offenses and merit analysis in isolation from their specific applications.

The quest for a general part has much to commend it. If self-defense is an issue in assault as well as in homicide cases, then the contours of self-defense should be worked out in a general fashion, rather than assayed once in the context of one crime and again in the context of another. If the problems of mistake of fact, mistake of law, duress, necessity, and mental abnormality arise repeatedly across the field of criminal law, then these issues require detached reflection and a resolution that would encompass the problems of each specific application.

The theory of the general part is of great assistance in legislative drafting; the structure of a code gains in efficiency if recurrent issues are assayed in a single section. A related task of the general part is to define particular terms that are used in the definition of specific offenses. One of the more notable achievements of the Model Penal Code is the limitation of relevant states of culpability to four possibilities (purposely, knowingly, recklessly, and negligently causing harm) and the skillful definition of each in the introductory provisions of the code. The general part of a code may state general maxims of criminal justice, such as the highly influential §20 in the California Penal Code: "In every crime or public offense there must exist a union, or joint operation, of act and intent, or criminal negligence." Analogous provisions in the Model Penal Code declare broadly that no person is guilty "of an offense unless his liability is based on conduct which includes a voluntary act or the omission to perform an act of which he is physically capable."[1]

The propositions of the general part are both descriptive and normative. The descriptive function is to bring unity to the criminal law by finding universal features, such as the alleged universality of the "union of act and intent, or criminal negligence." The normative function builds on the descriptive theory by inferring from the latter certain propositions that are essential to a just criminal law. There may be different foundations for inferring the principled desirability of the act requirement from the factual observation that an act is characteristic of all offenses. One foundation for this inference would be simply a respect for history; if the cumulative experience of the criminal law is to insist upon a voluntary act, then why should we now depart from this practice? The difficulty with this approach is that it provides no basis for distinguishing adventitious historical encrustations from principles that warrant our respect.

A more persuasive, yet not completely satisfying, argument, is that particular features of the criminal law, such as a voluntary act

§6.1. [1] MPC §2.01(1).

and perhaps the union of act and intent, are conceptually connected to what we mean by the term "criminal law." Therefore, if we are going to identify our system of sanctions with the tradition of the criminal law, we are bound to carry forward certain essential features of the tradition. Of course, this argument says nothing about what we are bound to do if we break with historical practice and rename the criminal law a system of "social control." It seems that the history and the "nature" of the criminal law are both relevant, though neither can provide an adequate foundation for the normative aspirations of the general part. What is needed is a more general political or moral theory to support the normative claims that will invariably concern us in the remaining chapters of the book.[2]

The theoretical work on the general part, at least in the Anglo-American literature, is plagued by a great confusion of terminology. *Mens rea, actus reus,* culpability, criminal intent, objectivity, subjectivity, state of mind, justification, excuse—these are among the many terms that are used with great abandon and ambiguity. As a preliminary to further work on the theory of the general part, we must devote this chapter to a clarification of terms and to the introduction of a number of distinctions that will assist us, both in understanding the extant literature and in moving toward our own theory of the general part. These preliminary sections, then, are designed as a guide to the perplexed; the reader is encouraged to refer back repeatedly to this chapter as a guide to later work in the book.

§6.2. *Some Preliminary Distinctions.*

A number of distinct purposes coalesce in casting the language of the general part. One way to avoid the snares of ambiguity and

[2] Let there be no pretense that I have a "general political or moral theory," however much it might be needed. This book proceeds on the assumption that pending a general theory, normative work on the criminal law is possible and necessary.

confusion in the available idiom is to command the underlying distinctions that are important in debates about the general part. The following are some of the critical distinctions that can help us organize our thinking about the concepts we shall introduce later.

§6.2.1. Descriptive and Normative Uses of the Same Terms. One of the persistent tensions in legal terminology runs between the descriptive and normative uses of the same terms. Witness the struggle over the concept of malice. The term has a high moral content, and when it came into the law as the benchmark of murder, it was presumably used normatively and judgmentally. Yet Fitzjames Stephen and succeeding generations of English jurists have sought to reduce the concepts of malice to the specific mental states of intending and knowing. California judges, in contrast, have stressed the normative content of malice in a highly judgmental definition, employing terms like "base, anti-social purpose" and "wanton disregard for human life." For the English, malice is a question of fact: did the actor have a particular state of consciousness (intention or knowledge)? In California, malice is a value judgment about the actor's motives, attitudes and personal capacity.

If the English have tried to reduce the normative concept of malice to a state of fact, other commentators and courts seek to invest nominally descriptive terms with moral force. Though the terms "intent," "state of mind," and "mental state" appear to be descriptive, legislators and courts use these terms to refer to issues that require normative judgment. The proposed federal criminal code refers to negligence as a "state of mind," [1] even though inadvertent negligence requires, above all, a normative judgment that the actor should have known of the risk. Jury instructions in California use the term "mental state" to refer to the normatively charged issue of malice.[2] The California courts also use the nominally descriptive term "intent" as equivalent to a "criminal intent," and thus read the statutory required union of "act and in-

§6.2. [1] Proposed Federal Criminal Code §302(d).

[2] Caljic §8.11 (1976 Supp.); People v. Conley, 64 Cal. 2d 310, 411 P.2d 911, 49 Cal. Rptr. 815 (1966).

tent"[3] to imply that culpability in a normative sense (i.e., "criminal intent") is necessary for every conviction.[4] The implication in statutory rape cases is that the reasonable mistake about the age of the girl negates the actor's "criminal intent" or "moral culpability" and thus constitutes a complete defense.[5]

The confusion between normative and descriptive language is so pervasive in Anglo-American criminal law that it affects the entire language of discourse. There appear to be very few terms that are exempt from the ambiguity. The term "intent" may refer either to a state of intending (regardless of blame) or it may refer to an intent to act under circumstances (such as failing to inquire about the age of a sexual partner) that render an act properly subject to blame. The term "criminal intent" does not resolve the ambiguity, for a criminal intent may simply be the intent to do the act, which, according to the statutory definition, renders the act "criminal," i.e., punishable under the law. There may be nothing morally blameworthy in keeping a pair of brass knuckles as a conversation piece, yet that intent renders the act punishable[6] and, in this sense, is a criminal intent.

It is obvious that the very word "criminal" is affected by the same tension between descriptive and normative illocutionary force. When used normatively, "criminal" refers to the type of person who by virtue of his deeds deserves to be branded and punished as a criminal. When used descriptively, as in the phrase "criminal act" it may refer simply to any act that the legislature has declared to be "criminal." Thus the term "criminal intent" may mean the intent to act under circumstances that make it just to treat the actor as a criminal in the pejorative sense. This is what the California Supreme Court has in mind when it reasons that the

[3] People v. Hernandez, 61 Cal. 2d 529, 534, 393 P.2d 673, 676, 39 Cal. Rptr. 361, 364 (1964).

[4] *Cf.* the normative use of the term "general criminal intent" in Long v. State, 44 Del. 262, 65 A.2d 489 (1949) (reasonable mistake as to validity of prior divorce negates "general criminal intent" to commit bigamy); and the parallel use of "wrongful intent" in People v. Vogel, 46 Cal. 2d 798, 299 P.2d 850 (1956) (reasonable mistake as to prior divorce negates the required "wrongful intent").

[5] See note 3 *supra.*

[6] See People v. Ferguson, 129 Cal. App. 300, 18 P.2d 741 (1933).

requirement of a "criminal intent" implies that a person who enjoys intercourse with a girl underage is not guilty of statutory rape if he reasonably believes that she is overage;[7] if his mistake is free from culpability, he does not deserve to be treated as a criminal. But it is equally plausible to use the term "criminal intent" to refer to the intent or knowledge sufficient to commit a crime as defined by the legislature. The adjective "criminal" in this context simply means that the intent is sufficient to render the act punishable under the statute.

It would seem that the term "culpability" ordinarily has normative force, for in non-legal English, a person is culpable only if he is justly to blame for his conduct. It would follow that if conduct were excused by virtue of duress or insanity, the actor would not be culpable. Yet the Model Penal Code defines acting purposely and knowingly as "kinds of culpability." [8] Though the code is not explicit in its solecism, it would seem to follow that if a person purposely committed larceny while subject to duress, he would be acquitted; yet it would still be true that he acted culpably.

There is no term fraught with greater ambiguity than that venerable Latin phrase that haunts Anglo-American criminal law: *mens rea*. Glanville Williams defines *mens rea* to mean "the mental element necessary for the particular crime." [9] Of course, the term "mental element" may be employed either descriptively or normatively, yet in this context it seems clear that Williams means to refer to a factual state of affairs. Intent, used descriptively, is an example of a required "mental element." [10] In another passage, Williams argues that the issue of duress should not be seen as negating either intention or *mens rea*.[11] Thus he would conclude, in a fashion parallel to the Model Penal Code's use of "culpability,"

[7] See note 2 *supra*.

[8] MPC §2.02(2).

[9] Williams 31; *accord:* Sayre, *Mens Rea*, 45 Harv. L. Rev. 974, 1026 (1926); S. Stewart, A Modern View of the Criminal Law 46 (1969) ("an intention to achieve . . . the result forbidden by law"). Regina v. Tolson, 23 Q.B.D. 168, 184–93 (1889) (Stephen, J.).

[10] Williams 31 ("*mens rea* means intention or recklessness as to the elements constituting the *actus reus*").

[11] *Id.* at 389.

that someone who was acquitted on grounds of duress nonetheless acted with *mens rea*. However prestigious this line of analysis might be, the courts fortunately remain unimpressed. Engaged as they are in the processes of judgment and condemnation, the courts repeatedly stress the normative content of *mens rea*,[12] in the same manner as the California court brought out the normative element in "criminal intent."

This tension between descriptive and normative usage carries significance for the structuring of issues in the criminal law. Descriptive theorists, like Stephen,[13] Turner,[14] Williams[15] and others in the English tradition, are apt to see problems of insanity, duress and mistake as extrinsic to the analysis of *mens rea* and criminal intent. Normative theorists, in contrast, are able to integrate these "defensive" issues into their formulation of the minimum conditions for liability.[16] If *mens rea* raises a normative issue of just and appropriate blame, then there is no *mens rea* or "criminal intent" when the intentional commission of the offense is excused by reason of duress, insanity, or reasonable mistake about an attendant circumstance (e.g., the age of the girl in statutory rape).

Whether one thinks of *mens rea* (or any equivalent term, such as "culpability") descriptively or normatively bears great practical significance. First, as we shall see in Chapter Seven, the normative theory of culpability provides an important (though not essential) premise in the argument requiring the prosecution to disprove claims of duress, insanity and mistake by proof beyond a reasonable doubt.[17] Secondly, a commitment to a descriptive or normative theory of *mens rea* shapes one's attitude toward negligence as

[12] Regina v. Bourne, 36 Crim. App. Rep. 125 (1952); United States v. Currens, 290 F.2d 751, 753–74 (3d Cir. 1961) (insanity negates *mens rea*).

[13] Regina v. Tolson, 23 Q.B.D. 168, 184–93 (1889).

[14] 1 J. Turner, Russell on Crime 53 (12th ed. 1964); Turner, *The Mental Element in Crimes at Common Law*, 6 Camb. L.J. 31 (1936).

[15] See notes 9 & 10 *supra*.

[16] The normative view is developed in Packer 107--118 (referring to his thesis as "negative approach to the problems of *mens rea*" for it stresses the effect of excuses in negating *mens rea*); Kadish, *The Decline of Innocence*, 26 Camb. L.J. 273, 275–282 (1968); *cf.* P. Brett, An Inquiry Into Criminal Guilt 40 (1963).

[17] See §7.3 *infra*.

a ground of liability. Descriptive theorists are likely to view negligence as an aberrant basis of liability;[18] normative theorists are more inclined to view negligence as a proper ground for blaming an actor for making a mistake or causing an accident.[19]

One might be inclined to think that this tension between normative and descriptive usage could be eliminated simply by coining new terms that are patently either normative or descriptive. Yet we have seen that "intent" may be employed normatively, and "culpability" descriptively. The faith that new terminology would eliminate the problem of ambiguity ignores the underlying dynamic of the problem. The language of the general part suffers distortion and manipulation, because the contemporary state of criminal theory is ambivalent about the role of blame and condemnatory judgment in the criminal law. Descriptive theorists[20] seek to minimize the normative content of the criminal law in order to render it, in their view, precise and free from the passions of subjective moral judgment. On the other hand, normative theorists, like Packer and Kadish,[21] seek to keep the language of the criminal law close to the daily problems of assessment and blame that infuse the criminal process.

The energy fueling this systematic ambiguity comes from diverse sources. Some theorists may think that using moral terms in the law lacks rigor and destroys the neutrality of the legal system. Others may think that moral issues are relevant to legal liability, but that these issues ought to be suppressed in the statement of the law to the jury. Others may sincerely think that moral issues

[18] Turner was flatly opposed to negligence as a ground for punishing homicide. See Turner, *The Mental Element in Crimes at Common Law,* 6 Camb. L.J. 31, 44–48 (1936); Williams says that negligence is not a form of *mens rea* and that is a good thing, for it inhibits the punishment of negligent offenses. Williams 102–03. Hall is opposed to punishing negligence, Hall, *Negligent Behavior Should Be Excluded from Penal Liability,* 63 Colum. L. Rev. 632 (1963); this view may be partly informed by identifying *mens rea* with "actual distinctive states of mind," Hall 71; *but cf.* Hall 70–104 (stressing the normative dimension of *mens rea*).

[19] See the authorities discussed in Fletcher, *The Theory of Criminal Negligence: A Comparative Analysis,* 119 U. Pa. L. Rev. 401, 410–426 (1971).

[20] See notes 9, 13, 14 *supra.*

[21] See note 16 *supra.*

are either too subjective and personal for serious consideration in a social discipline like the law. These are some factors that may impel courts and theorists toward value-free rules and concepts; the reality of judgment, blame and punishment in the criminal process generates the contrary pressure and insures that the quest for a value-free science of law cannot succeed in the process as we know it.

In this book, we try to avoid these ambiguities by using terms in the way they are ordinarily understood by lay speakers. To describe an act as intentional is neither to approve nor disapprove it, but to say that an actor is "culpable" or "blameworthy" for his deed is unquestionably to blame him and disapprove of the act. We shall try to avoid using the artificial words of the law—*mens rea, actus reus,* and "mental state." All of these are ambiguous beyond repair and, fortunately, we can do quite well without them.

§6.2.2. Conceptual and Empirical Propositions. Another source of confusion in the terminology of the general part is the impact of propositions, the truth of which depends on gently twisting and distending key terms. Usually, these propositions are of the form: *X* is an essential feature of every criminal offense. Here is a list of terms that often appear in the place of the variable *X*:

1. Harm
2. Punishment
3. Culpability (in the normative sense)
4. Wrongdoing
5. A Human Act or Omission

Now the first question we have to ask about these propositions is whether they are conceptual or empirical. If they are conceptual, the argument is that in the nature of things, a criminal offense presupposes harm, punishment, culpability, wrongdoing and an act. If any one of these propositions were correct, it would be by virtue of the concept of crime; it would be implicit in the meaning of "crime" and "criminal offense" that it was subject to punishment or that it caused harm. On the other hand, if these propositions are empirical, the argument is not one of implicit meaning, but of relative evidence. The difference is not so much the source of the claim, for a conceptual proposition might take form as an extrapolation from the details of the criminal law. The difference between the two types of proposition lies in the way their proponents respond to counter-examples. Conceptual propositions should hold in all cases, and therefore counter-examples are particularly threatening. Empirical propositions need not assert that X is true, but merely that X is true in 80 percent or 85 percent of the cases. New evidence of cases where X does not hold simply requires a downward adjustment of the percentage.

Conceptual propositions have the virtue of expressing grand truths. They strike at the essence of the criminal law. Their disadvantage is vulnerability to counter-examples. This is particularly a problem in the present state of the criminal law, for virtually every aspect of the system has witnessed great upheaval in the last century and a half. This means that most assertions about the nature of crime are subject to empirical counter-examples. If the argument is that crime causes harm, what does one say about attempts and possession offenses? If the proposition is that crime presupposes a culpable act, what does one say about strict liability? If the more modest claim is that crime always requires at least an act, what does one say about the notorious case of Rex v. Larsonneur,[22] in which the accused was brought forcibly into England and then convicted of being an alien "found in the United Kingdom" without permission?

The appeal of conceptual propositions is so great that we repeatedly commit ourselves to them and then struggle with the inevitable counter-examples.[23] There are four prominent strategies for responding to counter-examples and it is worth studying how they work. Let us take the claim that causing harm is an essential aspect of criminal conduct. This proposition is of the form: C (Crime) only if *H* (Harm). The first proposed counter-example is the law of attempts. This is not so challenging for we can append "the threat of *H*" to "*H*" and say that is what we mean by "harm."

Still counter-examples are easy to find: impossible attempts

[22] 97 J.P. 206 (Crim. App. 1933).

[23] See Strahorn, *The Effect of Impossibility on Criminal Attempts*, 78 U. Pa. L. Rev. 962 (1930).

(shooting at a tree stump, putting sugar in the intended victim's coffee cup) and possession offenses (particularly the case of possessing brass knuckles as a family heirloom). Now four strategies come into focus:

1. We can deny that the counter-example is a case of crime.

2. We can push and pull on harm to make it fit the counter-example.

3. We can retreat even further and say that all we mean by our proposition is that typically or paradigmatically, crime presupposes harm.

4. The last resort is to claim that the counter-example is simply wrong. It is not the law and therefore one does not have to account for it.

The first strategy is common.[24] It is expressed in the courts' reasoning that possession offenses are "regulatory" in nature.[25] They are not real instances of crime, but appendages to the criminal law designed to provide a prophylactic against crime. This may well be true, but the move is open to the following serious objection. "Crime" has to be defined functionally as (at least) that set of acts punished in the criminal process under the criminal code. Otherwise, it could be argued, the concept of crime would have no empirical base. It follows, arguably, that "crime" is whatever the legislature says it is.

The second strategy would permit one to accept this functional definition of crime, but one would have to wrestle with the concept of harm in order to make the proposition stick.[26] The notion of harm could be diluted further: it is not necessarily the threat of harm in the particular case that matters, but whether the act is of

[24] A classic instance of the strategy is the defense of the proposition that punishment is inflicted only on the guilty. In response to the counter-example of an innocent person's being punished, Anthony Quinton argues that the suffering inflicted on the innocent is not "punishment"; Quinton, *On Punishment* in H. Acton, The Philosophy of Punishment 59 (1969).

[25] See People v. Lovato, 258 Cal. App. 2d 290, 65 Cal. Rptr. 638 (1968), discussed *supra* §3.4.1, note 21.

[26] This strategy is pursued in Hall 216–20; Robinson, *A Theory of Justification: Societal Harm as a Prerequisite for Criminal Liability*, 23 U.C.L.A.L. Rev. 266 (1975).

the *type* that threatens harm. If this is what "harm" means, perhaps we can hold to the view that crime presupposes "harm." But what does the notion of "type" mean? How do we know that putting sugar in coffee is of the same type as actually poisoning the victim? The notion of harm appears to be infinitely expandable. At a certain point we have to wonder whether our proposition is still subject to falsification. If we cannot imagine a crime that *would not* threaten harm, the proposition has become vacuous and, in the view of some, meaningless.[27]

The third strategy is another example of retreating in the face of a counter-example.[28] We give up the term "always" and fall back to the position that paradigmatically, crime presupposes harm. This still expresses a truth about the criminal law, or at least about the core of the criminal law. Counter-examples are but emanations of the penumbra; they do not upset truths about the core. This strategy is but a variation of the first. Instead of denying that possession offenses are crimes, we deny that they are "core cases" of crime. One advantage of this strategy over the first is that it sidesteps the positivist's argument that the legislature specifies what crime is. No one has the authority to determine, in advance, what the core of the criminal law is, and thus the concept falls to the imagination of the legal theorist. The problem is that the concept of the core is so vague that one is at a loss to prove or disprove that a particular crime lies at the core of the criminal law.

The fourth strategy, arguing that the counter-example is simply wrong, is obviously a move of a different order. Until now the analysis has been descriptive rather than normative. Yet inquiries about the law are invariably normative, and it is preferable to concede the role of theory either in generating an apology for the status quo[29] or in steering the law in a better direction. However,

[27] On the genesis of and problems implicit in this criterion of meaning, see Ashby, *Verifiability Principle*, 8 Encyclopedia of Philosophy 240–42 (1967).

[28] For a good example in another context, see Wasserstrom, *H. L. A. Hart and the Doctrines of "Mens Rea" and Criminal Responsibility*, 35 U. Chi. L. Rev. 92, 93--95 (1967) (defending Jerome Hall's view that criminal responsibility requires moral culpability as a paradigmatic claim).

[29] Note the apology for the felony-murder rule, *supra* §4.4.5.

as English scholars seek to suppress the normative content of malice and *mens rea,* legal theorists all over the world prefer to cast their theories as scientific rather than normative claims. Normative claims are more difficult to defend and therefore we are readily seduced by the supposed neutrality of descriptive and conceptual arguments.

Although the claim that all crime presupposes harm is, in my view, a weak conceptual argument, we will explore a number of other, more appealing conceptual claims that have overt normative significance. Some of these we will defend and others we shall attempt to debunk. The claim that the concept of crime presupposes a culpable act provides a defensible platform for attacking strict liability. On the other hand, the claim that negligence is an objective standard of liability is a conceptual argument that we shall seek to undermine.[30]

In the work we have before us, we should be mindful of the lesson to be learned in the distortions produced by the second strategy, by the effort to save conceptual propositions at the price of vacuous truth. In order to build a theory of criminal law, we should use concepts that we understand. There are in fact numerous distinctions among types of harm, and so these should be worked out before we seek to erect a proposition about harm in the criminal law. What is true about secular destruction (homicide, arson) might not be true about cases in which the "harm" consists in a legally prescribed result without destruction (the taking in larceny, the giving of aid and comfort to the enemy in treason).[31]

[30] See §6.8 *infra.*

[31] It is useful to distinguish, as in German theory, between the "result" (*Erfolg*) and "encroachment on a legally protected interest" (*Beeinträchtigung des geschützten Rechtsguts*), see Jescheck 198. If an offense requires a particular result (larceny as well as homicide, but not offenses of risk-creation), proof of the result is necessary for liability. The latter question of the protected legal interest and its encroachment is a jurisprudential issue, analyzed independently of the criteria for liability. *Cf.* the Soviet concept, "object of the offense," Kurs (GP 1970) at 111 (maintaining that every offense has an "object," i.e., it infringes on the "social relations of a socialist society"). Part of the problem in the analysis of "harm" is that it oscillates between these two concepts—the positive concept of "result" and the jurisprudential concept of "encroaching on a legal interest."

This is but one of many important distinctions that we can perceive if we analyze the concept of harm in isolation, rather than manipulate the concept to defend a proposition about the essence of crime.

§6.2.3. Analyzing Statutes and Explicating the Structure of the Criminal Law. Another source of difficulty in the quest for the general part arises from differing attitudes toward the legislative role in shaping the criminal law. Is the criminal law entirely a creature of enacted, positive law? Or does the criminal law consist of an accrued body of principles, with their own traditional content and implicit structure? The positivist view of the criminal law has been ascendant in Anglo-American thinking for the last several generations, and helps to account for a good deal of the theoretical indifference and even hostility to any view that would hold that the criminal law has its own inherent structure. In the German legal tradition, in contrast, the guiding assumption has always been that the criminal law has its own immanent structure—independent of legislative definition—and the task of theory is to explicate and refine the principles implicit in this structure. This differing emphasis on the extent to which criminal law is a creature of legislative will accounts for many discrepancies between the Anglo-American and the German approaches to the theory of the general part.

In the scheme of the Model Penal Code, for example, the critical concepts are two: the material elements of offenses and the "culpability state" required for each material element. Material elements include all issues bearing on liability, except purely procedural notions such as venue and the statute of limitations.[32] The important step in analyzing an offense is determining which culpability state—purposely, knowingly, recklessly, or negligently—is required for each material element. Once this required element of culpability is read from the applicable statute, one can determine, for example, whether a mistake must be non-negligent to exculpate the actor. With few exceptions,[33] the Model Penal Code fails to specify when particular kinds of mistake should excuse. It merely

[32] MPC §1.13(10).
[33] See MPC §213.6(1) (mistakes as to age of children).

provides a skeleton on which the legislature can more neatly pack its determinations of required states of culpability.

The apparatus generated by the Model Penal Code stands in contrast to the conceptual propositions worked out in the German quest for the immanent structure of criminal offenses. The purpose of German theory has not been to facilitate the analysis of legislative judgments, but to understand the criminal law as a received body of interrelated concepts and practices. The theme of German theory has been to develop what is called a *Verbrechenslehre*—a theory on the nature of criminal offenses abstracted from the particularities of legislation. The ideas and concepts spawned by this theoretical effort are often foreign to the Anglo-Saxon ear; some of them resist translation into English. Others, such as the notions of excuse and justification, bear a systemic significance far beyond that which they enjoy in Anglo-American theory.

Of course, we should not exaggerate the difference between the German and Anglo-American styles of theoretical work in the criminal law. The Model Penal Code takes some features of criminal conduct that ought to be beyond legislative reach.[34] German theory certainly does not ignore the role of the legislature in making the initial determination of prohibited acts. Yet there is a fundamental difference in attitude toward legislation in the two cultures that corroborates the point we have stressed about the orientation of theoretical work. The Model Penal Code is written as though the drafters were relatively free of the restraints of history. They could dispense with the concept of "intent" and define a new term, "purposely."[35] More significantly, they could take reformist stands on issues such as the felony-murder rule,[36] the scope of duress,[37] the nature of provocation,[38] and the availability of necessity as a justification.[39]

Whatever our preconceptions about the role of legislation in

[34] MPC §2.01(1) (voluntary act or omission); §2.02(1) (no absolute liability except for petty offenses, called violations).

[35] MPC §2.02(2)(a).

[36] MPC §210.2(1)(b) (analyzed as recklessness).

[37] MPC §2.09 (implicitly available in homicide cases).

[38] MPC §210.3 ("provocation" replaced by the more subjective doctrine of "extreme mental or emotional disturbance").

[39] MPC §3.02.

civil law jurisdictions, the fact is that the general part of the new 1975 German Criminal Code is little more than a restatement of ideas that had crystallized in the case law and scholarly literature. The function of penal legislation in the German style is not to slash through Gordian knots. These knots must come unravelled slowly, with painstaking care, first in the literature and then in the courts. The final stage of development is the anchoring of the new consensus in legislative language. German criminal legislation, particularly in the general part, does not create consensus; it follows it.[40]

This attitude toward legislation correlates readily with attitudes toward the nature of theoretical work in the general part. The basic question is whether the task of theory is to facilitate legislation or to understand the descriptive and normative principles that transcend the particulars of legislative action and judicial interpretation. Thinking of the criminal law as a body of principles yields a particular kind of theoretical inquiry and, at the same time, inhibits legislative efforts to shape the criminal law. In the more positivistic environment that prevails in Anglo-American jurisdictions, the criminal law has come to be relatively more dependent on the action of legislatures and courts. This inhibits scholarly inquiry into the nature of criminal law and encourages legislatures to remake the criminal law according to their will.

A theory of the structure of criminal law requires an apparatus significantly different from the notions that are used to parse and apply statutory provisions. In the ensuing sections, we shall begin to elucidate these structural notions by working our way through the basic concepts of the criminal law.

§6.3. *Punishment and Its Rationale.*

The best candidate for a conceptual proposition about the criminal law is that the infliction of "punishment" is sufficient to render a

[40] Two notable examples are mistake of law, StGB §17, see §9.4.1 *infra;* and necessity as a justification, StGB §34, see §10.2.2 *infra.*

legal process criminal in nature. In the United States, the labelling of a process as "criminal" triggers certain basic constitutional guarantees, such as the right to counsel and the right to a jury trial.[1] As a test for when processes are criminal, the Supreme Court unhesitatingly invokes the concept of "punishment" as the relevant criterion.[2] That a sanction is inflicted in the criminal courts for a violation of the criminal code is sufficient to classify the sanction as "punitive," but there are recurrent problems in assessing the punitive nature of other sanctions, such as administrative commitment, expatriation, deportation, fines for custom violations and the deprivation of social security benefits.[3] That the legislature has identified these sanctions as civil in nature does not control the constitutional issue, for if the sanction is "punitive," if it constitutes "punishment," then regardless of the legislative label, the process is criminal and the constitutional guarantees apply. If we wish to understand the criminal law, we must first understand its most prominent feature: the infliction of punishment.

§6.3.1. On What Punishment Is. The nature of punishment must be distinguished from its purpose or rationale. It is only when we have a case of punishment before us that we may begin to talk about whether the justification for the punishment is retribution, deterrence, or rehabilitation. The contemporary philosophical approach to this problem is to specify the features of those core cases that we ordinarily call "punishment" in English discourse. H. L. A. Hart has identified five features of "punishment" in the standard cases.[4] These are worth quoting in full:

> [1] Punishment must involve pain or other consequences normally considered unpleasant.
>
> [2] It must be for an offense against legal rules.

§6.3. [1] U.S. Const. amend. VI.

[2] Kennedy v. Mendoza-Martinez, 372 U.S. 144 (1963); Helvering v. Mitchell, 303 U.S. 391 (1938).

[3] See generally Comment, *The Concept of Punitive Legislation and the Sixth Amendment: A New Look at Kennedy v. Mendoza-Martinez,* 32 U. Chi. L. Rev. 290 (1965).

[4] Hart, *Prolegomenon to the Principles of Punishment* in H. L. A. Hart, Punishment and Responsibility 4–5 (1968).

[3] It must be of an actual or supposed offender[5] for his offense.

[4] It must be intentionally administered by human beings other than the offender.

[5] It must be imposed and administered by an authority constituted by a legal system against which the offense is committed.

These criteria help us eliminate some metaphoric applications of the notion of punishment. Suppose that a father kills his child in a drunken stupor. He confesses to the police, but the prosecutorial officials refuse to prosecute on the ground that the death of his son is already sufficient "punishment" for his wanton drinking. Though the first three of Hart's criteria would be satisfied, the latter two would not be. This is hardly a counter-example to Hart's theory, for saying that the father was punished by his own acts seems to be a metaphoric extension of the core concept.

On the other hand, the impeachment and conviction of President Nixon for "high crimes and misdemeanors"[6] would have satisfied all five criteria, yet it seems doubtful that we should consider impeachment a case of punishment. The reason that we balk intuitively at classifying impeachment as punishment probably is that removal of the president is constitutionally authorized to protect the public, not to inflict "unpleasant consequences" on the offending president.[7] Nonetheless, impeachment "involves" these consequences and thus Hart's first element is met.[8] The counter-example of impeachment could be accommodated by redrafting the

[5] Note that Hart admits the possibility of punishing the innocent. *Cf.* Quinton's contrary claim, *supra* §6.2, at note 24.

[6] U.S. Const. art. II, §4.

[7] Note that the presidential pardoning power has no effect on impeachment proceedings, U.S. Const. art. II, §2; also, by common assumption, impeachment does not constitute prior punishment under the double jeopardy clause, U.S. Const. amend. V. Neither of these features of impeachment would be tenable if it constituted criminal punishment.

[8] Another counter-example to Hart's thesis is the execution of the goring ox to avoid religious contamination of the community. See §5.1.1 at notes 11–15 *supra*. All of Hart's criteria are satisfied, yet we would hardly call execution for this purpose punishment. The criteria could be amended to require the offender (as well as the punishing authority) to be a human being. But is it true that only human beings can be "punished"? So far as we can teach intelligent animals to follow rules, it seems that we can punish them for violating the rules.

first element to read: "Punishment must be imposed for the sake of inflicting pain or other consequences normally considered unpleasant." It is not surprising that Hart himself preferred the notion of incidental pain and unpleasant consequences. Injecting a necessary motive to inflict pain would commit him, more than he would presumably wish,[9] to retribution as the general justifying aim of punishment.[10]

These same issues and doubts attend Hart's second necessary condition for punishment, namely, that the sanction be imposed for "an offense against legal rules." Is the notion of "offense" the same as that of crime? If so, then the concept of punishment will not be of much value as a test for the scope of the criminal process. Little would be gained by treading the circular path of defining the criminal law by appealing to the concept of punishment, and then defining punishment by reverting to the concept of crime.[11] Yet if an "offense against legal rules" is not equivalent to criminal conduct, what is it? It is obvious that not every violation of a legal rule entailing unpleasant consequences is a case of punishment (even if all the other conditions are met). Tort liability for negligence per se, based on the violation of a statutory norm, would meet this test. So would unfair labor practices, enjoined by the National Labor Relations Board. Yet we would have some difficulty identifying the tort judgment and the labor injunction as instances of punishment.[12]

It may be that Hart's test can help us understand the rudimen-

[9] Hart, *supra* note 4, at 12, 18.

[10] *Cf.* Baier, *Is Punishment Retributive?* in H. Acton, The Philosophy of Punishment 130 (1969), who stresses that punishment by its nature is retributive and that "the aim of [punishment] is to hurt all and only those guilty of an offense." *Id.* at 132. Baier's theory has the merit of explaining why impeachment is not punishment: the aim is not to hurt the president, but to remove him from office.

[11] See Wasserstrom, *Some Problems with Theories of Punishment,* in J. Cederblom & W. Blizek, Justice and Punishment 173, 176–77 (1977).

[12] There is a lot packed into the notion of punishment *for* an offense. Arguably, tort liability is not imposed *for* the violation, but in order to compensate the victim; the labor injunction, not *for* the past violation, but in order to prevent recurrence in the future. A careful analysis of punishment *for* an offense leads one to considerations of motive and the Baier thesis discussed in note 10 *supra.*

tary difference between civil commitment, compulsory militarv service, quarantine, on the one hand, and criminal punishment on the other. The former does not presuppose the violation of any legal rule; the latter does. Yet the truly difficult problems in determining the scope of the criminal law are left unresolved. We may share an intuitive sense that deportation, expatriation, tort damages, customs fines, and impeachment are not cases of criminal punishment, yet it is by no means easy to explain why. It is particularly difficult to explain why a prison term for the morally neutral act of possessing brass knuckles is a case of criminal punishment, but deportation for a morally heinous act is not.[13] It may be that in a legal context, we can do no better than associate the criminal process with certain characteristic sanctions, such as capital punishment, whipping, and punitive (rather than therapeutic) confinement. This association is, of course, historically determined. It is a far cry from a theory of punishment or of the criminal process.

The advent of imprisonment as a characteristic criminal sanction has added to the uncertainties that abound in the notion of punishment. While ceremonial execution and whipping were virtually always associated with the criminal process, the institution of coercive confinement has many uses. Custodial supervision is widely deployed in the treatment of the mentally ill and the rearing of the young, as well as in the punishment of the guilty. Whenever the state imposes coercive confinement, one can expect an uneasy sense that the confinement is in fact a form of punishment and therefore the decision to confine should be surrounded by the procedural protections required by the Sixth and Fourteenth Amendments.

Debates about whether legal processes that result in confinement are criminal in nature tend to fluctuate between two conflicting perspectives. According to one point of view, if the state's

[13] Fong Yue Ting v. United States, 149 U.S. 698 (1893). It may be that the motive of removing or separating the offender is sufficient for the sanction to be non-punitive. Compare the cases of impeachment, text, at note 6 *supra*, executing the goring ox, *supra* note 8, and deportation. A necessary condition of punishment may be the affirmation of the bond between the offender and the punishing authority; separation and removal rupture the bond and therefore cannot count as punishment. But what about disowning a child? Isn't that a form of punishment?

purpose is therapeutic, the confinement is non-punitive and its imposition is exempt from the procedural niceties of jury trials, the participation of counsel, and the confrontation of witnesses. This point of view prevailed for decades in providing insulation from constitutional scrutiny for the modern juvenile court, an institution that was thought not to punish, but to help juveniles in distress.

According to the conflicting point of view, the state's purpose—whether to help or to harm—is irrelevant; what counts is the impact of the sanction on the party who suffers it. In the leading case of *Gault,*[14] the Supreme Court took significant steps to expand the constitutionally required protections in state juvenile court proceedings. The concept of procedural due process was interpreted to require that juveniles enjoy the privilege against self-incrimination, that they receive the assistance of counsel, and that they be able to exercise the right to confront witnesses against them. The rationale for restructuring juvenile courts in the image of adult due process was that, however "euphemistic the title . . . ," a home for juveniles was "an institution of confinement in which the child is incarcerated for greater or lesser time."[15] Thus the perspective of the sanction's impact controlled over the insulating effect of a therapeutic purpose. The euphemisms of treatment and rehabilitation paled in contrast to the reality of incarceration.[16] Yet the court resisted the arguments of those who sought to equate the confinement and treatment of juveniles with the punishment of criminals. Though many elements of due process apply to juvenile courts, not all of the protections of the Sixth Amendment, particularly not the right to a jury trial,[17] fall within the constitutionally required procedures in juvenile cases.

The tension between the state's purpose and the objective im-

[14] In re Gault, 387 U.S. 1 (1967).

[15] *Id.* at 27.

[16] The same tension between motive and impact shapes the debate about the intrusions that constitute "searches" under the Fourth Amendment. *Compare* Plitko v. State, 11 Md. App. 35, 272 A.2d 669 (1971) (good-faith inventory search consistent with Fourth Amendment) *with* Mozzetti v. Superior Court, 4 Cal. 3d 699, 484 P.2d 84, 94 Cal. Rptr. 412 (1971) (impact of search prevails over motive, Fourth Amendment applicable).

[17] This reservation in *Gault* was affirmed in McKeiver v. Pennsylvania, 403 U.S. 528 (1971).

pact of the sanction pervades constitutional deliberations about the concept of punishment. Though a philosophical inquiry into the nature of punishment may distinguish cleanly between therapy and punishment, the same distinction does not necessarily control the constitutional debate. The pressure to extend the procedural guarantees of criminal trials has generated a subtle shift away from what the court regards as the euphemism of treatment, to the impact of confinement on the individual. Thus in the constitutional debate, the impact of coercive confinement leads to a potentially broader view of punishment than one would generate under a philosophical analysis that stresses the purpose for which the punishment is imposed.

§6.3.2. The Rationale of Punishment. The diverse rationalia of punishment fall into two groups that should be neatly distinguished. One group finds the justification of a criminal sanction in the predicted consequences of condemning the particular defendant as a criminal and depriving him of his liberty. Among these rationalia are general deterrence, which means that the good of punishing one criminal derives from the likelihood that others will thereby be influenced not to commit the same crime; special deterrence, which means that the punished offender will be deterred from future offenses after his release; rehabilitation or reform, which means that as a result of treatment during incarceration, the convicted offender will be cured of the impulse to engage in criminal activity. All of these predicted goods are highly speculative. The degree to which punishment achieves any of these ends is disputed, and in the particular case, it is almost impossible to predict the incremental value of punishing one more offender, or punishing a repeated offender, one more time. In contrast to these speculative goals, which turn on what will happen in the future, a fairly certain consequence of coercive confinement is that during the period of confinement, the offender will not pose a threat to persons outside the prison. We may refer to this consequence of punishment, which is achieved as well by civil commitment, simply as the value of isolation. All four of these goals are grouped under the general heading of "social protection" as the purpose of punishment.

In contrast to these consequentialist goals, the principle of retribution holds that punishment is just regardless of its consequences. Of course, desirable consequences may follow from punishment, but these incidental benefits do not enter into a retributive rationale. What makes punishment just, regardless of the social good that might follow, is that it is a fitting social response to the commission of the crime.

Both consequentialist and retributive rationalia of punishment bear serious flaws. The defect in the four consequentialist theories of social protection is that if they become the exclusive rationale for punishment, they focus attention on the good that will follow and ignore the desert of the particular suspect. As the National Socialists well knew in controlling inmates in slave labor camps, occasionally hanging an innocent person effectively deters disobedience by other inmates. As to dangerous suspects, the values of special deterrence and isolation may be realized regardless of whether the dangerous person has committed an offense. Judges in traffic courts are readily tempted by the philosophy that regardless of whether the particular suspect has committed the violation, a punitive fine will make him drive more carefully in the future. The goal of rehabilitation is particularly insidious because the coercive power of the state is cloaked by benevolent motives;[18] if the suspect is "sick" and in need of treatment, it seems totally irrelevant whether on a particular occasion he "happened" to commit a crime. Looking to the good that will follow from punishment distracts the attention of the judges from the past and, in particular, from the particular offense that the defendant has committed. Not only does the point of requiring an actual offense become unclear, but the appropriate length of imprisonment comes to depend more on the projected dangerousness of the offender (or on his need for treatment) than on the gravity of the offense triggering the conviction. Thus the goals of social protection tend to suppress

[18] My mind was first opened to this issue by reading *The Rehabilitative Ideal,* in F. Allen, The Borderland of Criminal Justice (1964). *Cf.* Morris, *Persons and Punishment,* in H. Morris, On Guilt and Innocence 31 (1976). The issues were kept alive by C. S. Lewis, *The Humanitarian Theory of Punishment,* 6 Res Judicatae 224 (1953).

two important principles of justice; first, that only the guilty should suffer conviction and punishment; and, secondly, that the extent of punishment should be proportionate to the crime committed.

These potential injustices are compounded by indeterminate sentencing, which trades on a mixture of benevolent rehabilitative motives and the social interest in maximizing the isolation of dangerous offenders. The anxieties suffered by inmates subject to the discretion of parole boards has awakened widespread sympathy for the dignity of inmates and induced a greater commitment to respect for their personal autonomy. This shift in attitude is due, in no small measure, to the highly effective way in which inmates have pressed their complaints upon the public, the courts, and the political process.[19] We are now inclined to see the rehabilitative idea of earlier decades not as a sincere effort to help, but as a systematic dehumanization of offenders. Disparities in sentencing for the same offense, which would not bother us if we believed in the virtues of individualized treatment, have now become a matter of national concern.[20] It may be that the rehabilitative ideal was too deeply and too naively held, for the failure to produce results has generated widespread cynicism in the United States, both about rehabilitation and indeterminate sentencing.

This disillusionment, and perhaps the natural ebb and flow of intellectual history, has rekindled interest in retributive theories of punishment.[21] Retribution simply means that punishment is justi-

[19] See e.g., In re Lynch, 8 Cal. 3d 410, 503 P.2d 921, 105 Cal. Rptr. 217 (1972) (potential life sentence for second offense of indecent exposure unconstitutional as cruel and unusual punishment); In re Rodriguez, 14 Cal. 3d 639, 537 P.2d 384, 122 Cal. Rptr. 552 (1975) (Adult Authority had a statutory duty to set a release date for sex offender serving an indeterminate, potentially life term; the time spent must be proportionate to the crime).

[20] See e.g., Report of the Twentieth-Century Fund, Fair and Certain Punishment (1976).

[21] For a sign of the times, note the emphasis on retributivism in the essays collected in J. Cederblom & W. Blizek, Justice and Punishment (1977); *cf.* the commentary on current trends in Wilson, *The Political Feasibility of Punishment*, *id.* at 107. See also A. von Hirsch, Doing Justice (1976); Armstrong, *The Retributivist Hits Back*, in H. Acton, *supra* note 9, at 138.

fied by virtue of its relationship to the offense that has been committed. It is obviously not to be identified with vengeance or revenge, any more than love is to be identified with lust. It is also distinguishable from the fashionable consequentialist argument that it is socially desirable to channel the hostile energies of society into the punishment of criminals; not to do so would supposedly risk the greater evil of private vendettas and blood feuds.[22] The critical feature of a retributive argument is that if it is sound, it justifies punishment as of the moment that the punishment is imposed. One need not wait to see whether the predicted good (deterrence, avoiding private vendettas) actually accrues. Of course, the word "retribution" is not in itself an argument for making criminals suffer. Nor in a secular society is it much of an argument to refer to the Biblical injunction of an "eye for an eye . . ."[23] One way to make out an argument for retributive punishment is to focus on the criminal act as the source of the offender's obligation to suffer punishment. Writing in the tradition of Kant and Hegel, Herbert Morris has developed the theory that the offender is duty-bound to suffer punishment, for his offense creates an imbalance of benefits and burdens in the society as a whole.[24] Those who obey the law incur burdens that offenders refuse to take upon themselves. To rectify this imbalance the offender must suffer an appropriate punishment. His refusal to conform generates the proverbial "debt" that must be paid. This argument makes some sense with regard to crimes that tempt many of us, such as illegal parking, or even cheating on our income tax. Yet it is less plausible to argue that we all suffer a burden in ab-

[22] This point is developed with admirable clarity in Gregg v. Georgia, 428 U.S. 153, 231 (1976) (Marshall, J., dissenting, arguing against a retributive rationale for the death penalty).

[23] Despite the *lex talionis,* it is a mistake to think that the Biblical conception of punishment was exclusively retributive; the execution of murderers served the highly instrumental purpose of "returning the blood of the homicide victim to God." See §4.1 at notes 1–3 *supra.*

[24] H. Morris, *supra* note 18, at 34–36. A distinct argument is that punishment expresses respect for the offender's choices as a person. *Id.* at 48–49. *Cf.* the argument that the punishment affirms the bond between the offender and the punishing authority, *supra* note 13.

staining from the core crimes of murder, rape, arson, robbery, and burglary.

Whether Morris' case for retributive punishment is correct or not, it provides a model of clarity for the analysis of just punishment. He grounds the duty to suffer punishment in the act of wrongdoing and its consequences, not merely in the offender's having wicked thoughts or even in his acting in a way properly subject to blame. This is an important point, for in many recent discussions, there is a tendency to assume that any consideration of moral culpability is tantamount to a retributive theory of punishment.[25] Of course, someone might be able to argue that acting out wicked thoughts in itself creates a duty to suffer punishment. Yet we should need some convincing arguments to explain why that duty is incurred.

The potential injustices of consequentialist arguments and the weakness of retributive theories have generated numerous efforts to combine these distinct rationalia in an eclectic justification for imposing sanctions in the name both of justice and of social protection.[26] One effort is typified by the Model Penal Code's taking it as a purpose of the code that conduct "without fault"[27] should be safeguarded from condemnation as criminal. Another provision speaks of protecting offenders against "excessive, disproportionate or arbitrary punishment,"[28] but there appears to be nothing in the code to prevent setting prison terms in particular cases with a view to social protection and rehabilitation.

H. L. A. Hart's mode of synthesis is the most convincing. Instead of speaking of a union of goals in each criminal case, Hart distinguishes rigorously between the justification of the entire institution of criminal punishment and the justification of punish-

[25] See §6.6, at note 30 *infra*.

[26] The effort at synthesis runs throughout the recent philosophical and legal literature. See, e.g., Packer 62–70; Rawls, *Two Concepts of Rules*, 64 Phil. Rev. 3 (1955).

[27] MPC §1.02(1)(c). It is curious that, so far as one can tell, the code neither defines "fault" nor mentions the concept again.

[28] MPC §1.02(2)(c).

ment in particular cases.[29] The general justifying aim of punishment as an institution may well be deterrence, but it does not follow that deterrence should inform the distribution of punishment in particular cases. The latter is a problem of justifying distribution of the burdens of the system, rather than the system itself.

The analogy that comes to mind is the distinction between justifying the income tax as a whole and justifying the imposition of burdens on particular taxpayers. The justification of the system as a whole is raising revenue for the government; the justification of burdens on particular taxpayers is (roughly) the taxpayer's relative ability to pay. It would obviously be improper to interweave these two levels of justification and justify the denial of claim for a charitable deduction on the ground of the claimant's relative ability to pay.[30] Similarly, if the justification for the criminal law as a whole is the isolation of dangerous offenders, it is improper to decide particular cases by appealing to the alleged offender's relative dangerousness.

Hart fails to develop a thesis about distributing the burden of punishment in particular cases. He does argue that only unjustified and unexcused offenses should be punished. But the emphasis is on the injustice of punishing someone who has not had a fair chance of avoiding liability, rather than on desert, wrongdoing or culpability as affirmative rationalia for distributing the burdens of the punitive system.

The ore of punishment is too rich to be sifted adequately in one light sweep. The problem of just punishment recurs in our discussion of the general part. It is of central importance in our working

[29] Hart, *supra* note 4. Hart might properly object to this characterization of his thesis, for he explicitly rejects "retribution" as the rationale for just distribution; *id.* at 12, 18. *But cf.* the later clarificatory remarks. *Id.* at 231-35. Hart's conclusions are the same as Packer's and Rawls', *supra* note 26, but the analysis is different.

[30] This analogy strikes me as more illuminating than Hart's example of private property. The model of taxation is also invoked to criticize indifference to the just distribution of accident costs, W. Blum & H. Kalven, Public Law Perspectives on a Private Law Problem: Auto Compensation Plans (1965).

out the distinction between wrongdoing and attribution[31] and in discussing the relationship between harm and wrongdoing.[32]

§6.4. *The Concept of Acting.*

The three patterns of criminality reflect subtly different perspectives on human action. In the pattern of manifest criminality, the significance of the criminal act is that it manifests criminality and unnerves the community's sense of security. In the pattern of subjective criminality, the notion of the relevant human act is broadened to include any gesture or motion that reveals that the criminal plan has passed from the realm of thought into the realm of execution. In the pattern of harmful consequences, the act functions as but a minimal condition for assessing personal accountability for the harmful consequence. Though there are these subtle differences, the requirement of an act is common to the major patterns of liability, and therefore the requirement of an act becomes a primary candidate for a universal principle of criminal liability.

As a descriptive proposition, the principle would be that acting is a pervasive feature of criminal liability. It appears in all three patterns of liability, and in the isolated offenses outside these patterns there are arguably no persuasive counter-examples. The more venturesome normative claim is that acting is a necessary condition for just punishment. The difficulty with both the descriptive and normative propositions is specifying what we mean by "an act." An act as opposed to what? Sometimes the concept of a human act is contrasted with an "omission"; sometimes with a status or condition; sometimes with "acting involuntarily" as in cases of hypnotism and sleepwalking. To clarify the proposition that criminal liability presupposes a human act, we need to

[31] See §6.6.1 *infra.*
[32] See §6.6.5 *infra.*

consider these contrasting situations in which "an act" is arguably absent.

§6.4.1. Acts and Omissions. One common way of stating the distinction between acts and omissions is that the former are active assertions, the latter, a form of passive abstention. Both "acts" and "omissions" can be brought under the general rubric of "conduct";[1] but the feeling persists that the distinction is fundamental. In the German literature, in particular, omissions are described as the "negation" of acts.[2] This sense for the difference between acts and omissions derives, it seems, from a long-standing practice of defining a human act as "a willed muscular contraction."[3] It follows that omissions are not acts, for though they might be willed, they do not consist in a "muscular contraction."

There are at least two good reasons for abandoning this way of thinking and speaking about "acts." First, it is tautological to define acts by appealing to the will. For how do we know whether the will is exercised without first knowing whether it is an act that we are seeking to explain? There is, to be sure, a difference between a person's raising her hand and her hand's rising, but if we are not sure what is happening, it merely restates the question to ask whether she "wills" the bodily movement. Further, even if this circularity were not a problem, it is not clear why focussing on the "will" would lead us to distinguish between bodily movements and motionless acting.[4] It is as much an act of will for the guards at Buckingham Palace to stand motionless as it is for tourists to stroll back and forth in front of them. Conscious non-motion is a greater assertion of personality than casual acting. One can only be

§6.4. [1] See MPC §1.13(5). Similarly, the German concepts of *Handlung* and *Unterlassung* are both instances of *menschlichen Verhaltens.* Welzel 31, 200.

[2] See Welzel 200; G. Radbruch, Der Handlungsbegriff in seiner Bedeutung für das Strafrechtssystem 140 (1904).

[3] Holmes 54; Radbruch, *supra* note 2, at 75, 98. Perkins 475 n.20; Restatement (Second) of Torts §2. For a critique of this account of acting, see H. Morris, Book Review, 13 Stan. L. Rev. 185 (1960).

[4] One line of thought in the German literature focusses on the "will," but recognizes that passivity is willed as much as is activity, E. Beling, Lehre vom Verbrechen 9 (1906); Baumann 193.

puzzled by the widespread belief that the distinction between motion and non-motion is of importance to the law.

If there is a special problem in punishing omissions, we can learn what it is only by examining the contexts in which lawyers conventionally talk about "omissions" or "failing to act." In fact, there is a radical cleavage between two forms of liability for "omissions." According to one type, the focus of liability is a breach of a statutory obligation to act—for example, for failure to render aid at the scene of an accident;[5] to report a crime;[6] to file an income tax return.[7] We shall call this the field of liability for "breach of a duty to act." The contrasting field is the imposition of liability for failing to intervene, when necessary, to prevent the occurrence of a serious harm such as death or the destruction of property. Borrowing the French idiom, we shall refer to this second type of liability as "commission by omission."[8]

There are both formal and substantive differences between the two fields of liability. The formal difference is that liability for "breach of duty" is based solely on a specially enacted statute instructing all persons in a particular situation to act in a particular way. Liability for "commission by omission" is based on the extension of a traditional offense, primarily homicide, but arguably arson, battery, rape and other serious offenses as well. The former raises no problem under the maxim *nulla poena sine lege;* the latter, based as it is on judicially recognized duties to intervene, is arguably unconstitutional.[9] The substantive difference is that liabil-

[5] This offense is widely recognized in Continental jurisdictions: See StGB §330c; Code Pénal §63; Ugol. kod. (RSFSR) §127(1). See generally Feldbrugge, *Good and Bad Samaritans: A Comparative Survey of Criminal Provisions Concerning Failure to Rescue*, 14 Am. J. Comp. L. 630 (1966).

[6] See StGB §138.

[7] 26 U.S.C. 7203. For other examples drawn from federal statutes, see Weinreb, *Comment on the Basis of Criminal Liability*, 1 Working Papers of the National Commission on Reform of Federal Criminal Law 105, 116 (1970).

[8] German and Soviet textbooks distinguish between these two categories of omissions as "pure" (*echte Unterlassungsdelikte*) and "impure" (*unechte Unterlassungsdelikte*), respectively. See, e.g., Jescheck 199; Kurs (GP 1970) at 152. This terminology is so confusing (why is one type more "pure" or "genuine" than the other?) that it is better to coin our own terms.

[9] See §8.4.2 *infra*.

ity for breach of a statutory duty does not presuppose the occurrence of harm. The failure to render aid at the scene of an accident may increase the risk of harm, but liability is complete the moment that the duty-bound actor flees the scene of the accident. That the victim survives without harm is irrelevant to the breach of the duty to act. In contrast, the death of the victim is essential for committing homicide by omission; the burning of a structure is essential for committing arson by omission; and bodily injury to the victim, for committing battery by omission. The gravamen of liability for "breach of duty" is the breach itself; for commission by omission, the occurence of a particular result.

The first part of Chapter Eight is devoted exclusively to the problem of imposing liability for "commission by omission." As we shall then argue in detail, the critical distinction between commission by act and commission by omission is not to be found in the contrast between bodily movement and standing still. The issue is imposing liability in the absence of the actor's causing the required result. Developing this argument requires that we first clarify the concept of "causation"—a concept that proves to be of pivotal importance in the theory of liability.[10]

At this juncture we shall limit our discussion to liability for breaching a statutory obligation and attempt to assess whether there is an important difference between breaching a duty by acting or by failing to act. The first possible difference is that with respect to some cases of breach of duty, it is difficult to determine precisely when the breach occurs. In the pattern of manifest criminality, it will be recalled, the moment of commission is readily discerned, for the criminal purpose must manifest itself in a heightened moment of danger to the community. If the statutory breach consists, for example, in the failure to report a crime, it is difficult to establish when, in principle, the failure is complete. The failure is a continuing state of affairs and there is no "natural" point of consummation. It is equally difficult to determine when the act occurs in the pattern of subjective criminality. There is no point in

[10] See §8.2 *infra.*

the continuous process of breaching the duty at which the actor's intent moves from the "realm of thought" to the "realm of action." Admittedly, in some cases of statutory breach, say, failing to render aid or to give one's name and address at the scene of an accident, it would be relatively easy to discern the moment of breach. Leaving the scene with knowledge of the situation would be strong evidence of an intent not to perform.

Another troublesome feature of breaching a statutory duty to act is that in many cases the actor is not likely to be aware of his or her duty of affirmative action. Witness Lambert v. California,[11] in which the United States Supreme Court reversed the conviction of a woman who violated a Los Angeles ordinance requiring all "convicted persons" to register with the police within five days of entering the city. The permissible term of "five days" solves the problem of determining when the offense is committed; there was no doubt that Ms. Lambert had breached her duty to register. The problem was not the breach, but the constitutionality of punishing someone who did not know of her duty to act. Ms. Lambert attempted to prove that she was unaware of the ordinance, but the trial court refused to hear the defense. The Supreme Court held that a conviction under these circumstances violated the due process requirement of "fair notice."

There are two reasons why the problem of "fair notice" is likely to be more acute in cases like *Lambert*, where the crime consists in the breach of a duty to act. First, statutory duties to act often (but not always) arise in the borderland of the criminal law; it is not surprising that one might breach one or several duties of this sort in total ignorance of the law. Secondly, there is nothing in the act of entering the city of Los Angeles that should have put Ms. Lambert "on notice" of her duty to register with the police. In many cases of affirmative conduct—driving a car, running a bar or a hotel, storing explosives—individuals can be fairly expected to apprise themselves of their statutory duties. But there was no similar "triggering mechanism" in the facts of *Lambert*.

[11] 355 U.S. 225 (1957).

This second point was decisive in the decision that Ms. Lambert's conviction violated due process. Though the majority stressed the status of the breach as "conduct that is wholly passive,"[12] the concept of omission was neither necessary nor sufficient to the finding that the actor did not have fair notice of the duty to act. If the duty is to give one's name and address at the scene of an automobile accident,[13] a recalcitrant driver could probably not raise a claim of ignorance as a satisfactory defense.[14] The reason is that involvement in an accident is sufficient, in common experience, to put people on notice of a duty to cooperate; a statutory penalty for failure to give one's name and address is more readily supportable than the conviction in *Lambert*. In contrast, the principles underlying *Lambert* should arguably apply in cases of affirmative conduct where the actor does not have adequate notice of the illegality of his conduct. If it were a misdemeanor "to possess a master key without a license," one wonders whether the mere acquisition of possession would be sufficient to put the actor on notice. The larger problem raised by *Lambert* is the excuse of mistake of law—an issue that is treated more adequately in Chapter Nine.[15] For now, we should note that the distinction between statutory breach by acting and failing to act may provide a perspective for assessing the injustice of disregarding mistake of law as an excuse, but it seems that the details of the particular statute are more important than conceptual distinctions between acts and omissions.

This review of two reasons for distinguishing between acts and omissions suggests that there might be good reasons for legislatures to tread carefully in enacting statutory duties to act and for courts to apply special criteria for assessing the culpability of breaching a statutory duty to act. But neither consideration sug-

[12] *Id.* at 228.

[13] Cal. Vehicle Code §20002(a)(1).

[14] In California v. Byers, 402 U.S. 424 (1971), the Supreme Court upheld a statute of this type, *supra* note 13, against the argument that the required act violated the Privilege Against Self-Incrimination. Note the analogy drawn to other required performances, such as filing income tax returns. *Id.* at 428.

[15] See §9.4 *infra*.

gests a categorical difference in principle between penalizing acts and penalizing omissions. We started this discussion with the question whether the principal requirement of a human act casts doubt on the justice of punishing the breach of statutory obligations. Our conclusion is qualified. Some problems remain[16] and we shall take these up in Chapter Eight when we turn to the distinct field of liability for commission by omission.

§6.4.2. Acts Contrasted with Conditions. The nineteenth-century definition[17] of "acting" expresses the intersection of two ideas: bodily movement and operation of the will. The absence of the first leads to the contrast between acts with omissions; the absence of the second leads to a host of other comparisons: an act as opposed to a reflex, a status, a condition, a disease. The ambiguity of these cases where the "will" is not operative is whether we should refer to them as "involuntary acts" or deny their being "acts." The issue runs much deeper than the proper choice of terms. We intuitively recoil at the notion of punishing disease or conditions, and we are likely to express our intuition by saying that criminal punishment presupposes an act. Yet what is there about the act that is important? Is it the factor of voluntary conduct or is there some other dimension of acting that—apart from the issue of voluntariness—makes punishing "non-acts" objectionable?

The problematic decision in Robinson v. California[18] invites us to consider this ambiguity. The State of California prosecuted Robinson under a statute that made it a crime both to use narcotics and to be "addicted to the use of narcotics";[19] the offense carried a maximum sentence of one year in jail. The state had to prove at trial only that the suspect was found "as an addict" within the jurisdiction and venue of the court. The United States Supreme Court held that while therapeutic confinement of addicts

[16] The primary problem is whether punishing "omissions" infringes on liberty more than punishing "acts." See §8.2.3 *infra*.

[17] See note 3 *supra*.

[18] 370 U.S. 660 (1962).

[19] Cal. Health & Safety Code §11721.

was acceptable, the state could not use the apparatus of the criminal law to identify and confine proven addicts. The condemnation and punishment implicit in the criminal conviction rendered the sanction against addiction "cruel and unusual punishment" in violation of the Eighth and Fourteenth Amendments. The majority opinion, written by Justice Stewart, wavered in its identification of the general class of problems typified by the status of "being an addict." Now the problem was that addiction was punishment for a "status";[20] now, as punishment for an "illness" or "disease."[21]

There may be something fundamentally wrong in punishing persons for the crime of being a leper or having a common cold. But precisely what is wrong with it? One explanation offered is that these "illnesses" may be contracted innocently or involuntarily. It is possible to become addicted in the course of medical treatment, or even in the womb, from the blood of a mother who is an addict. There is no suggestion that in *Robinson* the addiction was contracted involuntarily. But it might be so contracted in some other case, and that was supposedly sufficient to find that Robinson's conviction was unconstitutional.

Another explanation offered for the evil of branding addiction a crime is that the offense could be established without proving that the defendant had ever "touched any narcotic drug within the State or been guilty of any antisocial behavior there. . . ."[22] Implicit in the constitutional conclusion are two basically different views about why "acts" are essential to a proper criminal conviction. The first argument, which stresses the involuntary nature of the addiction, takes the relevant set of opposites to be "acts" and "involuntary acts." The second argument stresses the jurisdictional requirement of an act within the state—any act, even an "involuntary act." From the jurisdictional point of view, the relevant contrast is "acts" as opposed to "status" or "condition." The decision in *Robinson* was overdetermined in the sense

[20] 370 U.S. at 666.
[21] *Ibid.*
[22] *Ibid.*

that both of these arguments applied to the particular prosecution. The impact of the decision would turn, however, on which of these facets of the case would prevail in subsequent interpretations of the case.

The first argument in *Robinson* carried the ingredients for a powerful constitutional antidote to convicting a range of persons who could not avoid their criminal behavior. The likely candidates were chronic alcoholics and addicts, all of whom arguably committed criminal offenses "involuntarily." Whether intoxication and addiction should constitute excuses to criminal violations is properly reserved for our later discussion of excuses.[23] The problem that concerned the courts in the aftermath of *Robinson* was whether the constitutional requirement of an "act" meant "voluntary act" and necessitated the recognition of various excuses resembling addiction.

In the way that history would have it, this problem was resolved in a case that was particularly unattractive for elevating the requirement of a "voluntary act" to the level of a constitutional rule. In Powell v. Texas,[24] a suspect convicted of being drunk in public complained that his conviction violated the dictates of *Robinson;* the reasoning was that as a chronic alcoholic he suffered from a disease and that therefore his punishment was "in effect" punishment for a disease comparable to being an addict. Of course, it would have been impermissible to make the status of being an alcoholic a crime; the question was whether one could extend the principle to prevent commission of all crimes that were bound up with the pattern of behavior known as alcoholism. Four judges of the Supreme Court were willing to go that far;[25] in their view, the teaching of *Robinson* was that no one could be convicted for "being in a condition which he had no capacity to change or avoid."[26] Powell allegedly had a compulsion to drink, and when drunk, to appear in public. If this compulsion could be established

[23] See §10.4.5 *infra.*
[24] 392 U.S. 514 (1968).
[25] 392 U.S. at 554 (Justices Fortas, Douglas, Brennan, and Stewart, dissenting).
[26] *Id.* at 568.

as a matter of fact, Powell would be punished on criteria that were equivalent to the standard of "being an alcoholic." If the case had arisen after a more convincing trial on the issues of alcoholism and, in particular, of Powell's condition,[27] this dissenting position might have gained the fifth vote of Mr. Justice White and thus generated a constitutional precedent of revolutionary proportions. As it was, the defendant Powell had admitted on the stand that on the day of the trial he had only one drink and was able to stop;[28] there was obviously something suspect about the trial court's finding that Powell was a chronic alcoholic even though alcoholism was not admitted as an excuse.

To limit the impact of *Robinson,* the four-vote plurality, voting to affirm Powell's conviction, insisted on a distinction that the dissent (as well as Justice White in his concurrence) sought to suppress. It was the distinction between addiction (or alcoholism) as the name of a crime and the invocation of these conditions as a ground for excusing the crime by the same name. The defect in *Robinson* was that the statute punished addiction as crime, not that addiction generated a constitutionally mandated excuse. As Justice Marshall reasoned for the plurality in *Powell,* it would be undesirable to anchor the evolving criteria of culpability and excuses in constitutional cement. Yet *Robinson* still carried force as an injunction against making it a crime to be an addict, an alcoholic, mentally ill, or a leper. Thus the relevant set of contrasts for the four-vote plurality was not between "acts" and "involuntary acts," but between acts and the array of non-acts—illnesses, statuses or conditions—that might be used to define crimes.

Though the Court does not explicate a rationale for the constitutional impermissibility of punishing these conditions other than acts, a plausible rationale inheres in the repeated point in *Robinson,* reiterated in *Powell,* that there is something untoward about punishing someone without proving that "antisocial behavior" had taken place within the jurisdiction of the court. The status of

[27] Mr. Justice White concurred in affirming the conviction on the ground that there was no evidence of a compulsion to appear "in public." *Id.* at 550.

[28] *Id.* at 519.

being an addict is analyzable into two components: acts of using a narcotic and the propensity to continue using the drug. Thus the status of being an addict is comparable to being a thief. The latter status also requires that someone have stolen in the past and have the disposition to continue stealing. In both cases, the propensity to continue the activity is essential for the condition either of being an addict or the status of being a thief. It is obviously this propensity that might prompt a legislature to prohibit the respective status. Comparing being an addict with being a thief brings the problem into proper focus, without the distracting rhetoric about punishing illness and involuntarily contracting the disease in one's mother's womb. Let us turn, then, to what might be wrong with the legislature's making it a crime to be a thief, even a "common thief." If we conclude that punishing the status of being a thief would be improper on jurisdictional grounds, then we should have a relatively easy time concurring in the jurisdictional variation of the argument in *Robinson* and *Powell* that punishing addiction is impermissible.

The state has a legitimate interest in protecting property from thieves, yet it appears to violate the traditional conception of the criminal law to convict people on the basis of their criminal propensities. Though the state may intervene with administrative, non-punitive measures against kleptomaniacs, there are even some intriguing problems in this context that are worth considering. It seems that to justify even a non-punitive measure against the thief, the state would have to ground the thief's propensity to steal in a condition of mental or psychological abnormality. One of the unanalyzed problems in the field of civil commitment is the extent to which the state is bound to respect the principle that all citizens are presumptively self-actuating, responsible agents. Commitment on the basis of "sociological predictors" (e.g., race, experience, social trauma, etc.) would run afoul of this principle designed to respect the autonomy of all members of the community. We noticed earlier that in the field of possession offenses, the courts uphold this principle of respect for individual autonomy and therefore invalidate statutes prohibiting the possession of burglary tools that presume (or dispense with) an intent to use the tools.[29] To overcome the presumption of self-actuation in a case of civil commitment, the state must show that the actor is out of control. That is, the state must prove that the actor is in a condition "he is powerless to change." While punishing illness with criminal sanctions is impermissible, a condition of illness proves to be an essential condition for the use of administrative confinement. It is not dangerousness per se that justifies civil commitment, but dangerousness in someone who is insane, a sexual psychopath or a mentally abnormal kleptomaniac. Addiction qualifies as one of the states in which actors are thought to be out of control, and therefore we can readily understand the Supreme Court's approving commitment of addicts found within the state.

Several important propositions follow from this analysis of the relationship between illness and civil commitment. First, the duty of the state to respect human autonomy applies as an ideological postulate, both in the criminal law and in the field of civil commitment. Secondly, the presumption of self-actuation may be overcome by showing that the actor is psychologically incapable of controlling himself. Once this presumption is overcome, the state may proceed against dangerous persons by imposing civil commitment. But—and this is where *Robinson* gets its bite—a dangerous propensity, standing alone, cannot justify either civil commitment or criminal punishment. Neither punishing nor committing a psychologically normal thief is justifiable, however dangerous the supposed thief might be.

The critical reason for this conclusion is the political postulate that the state is bound to respect the autonomy and capacity for self-actuation of its citizens. Civil commitment of a normal person

[29] See §3.4 *supra*. *Cf.* People v. Satchell, 6 Cal. 3d 28, 489 P.2d 1361, 98 Cal. Rptr. 33 (1971), in which the court refused to regard a possession offense as "inherently dangerous" for the purpose of the felony-murder rule. The judgment that an ex-felon's possessing a sawed-off shotgun was "inherently dangerous" could only have been based on a prediction that the possessor would decide to use the gun. That prediction would have violated the imperative to respect the autonomy of all citizens.

violates this postulate, as does punishing a propensity to steal. With regard to punishment, it is no help to link the propensity with psychological abnormality, for that compounds the problem by imposing punishment against someone who is unable to control his behavior.

It might be objected that a thief is someone who has committed acts of thievery in the past. Why can the state not justify its punishment on the basis of those past acts? It can, and it often does, but the acts must be proven and they must occur within the jurisdiction and venue of the court. The common-law principle of jurisdiction is territorial. For courts in California to decree the punishment of past acts, the prosecution must prove that the acts occurred in California and indeed in the county in which venue is laid. The appeal of punishing an addict or a common thief is that the prosecution could establish these statuses on the basis of acts that occurred outside the jurisdiction. Someone might properly be labelled an addict or a thief, even if the status is inferred from acts that occurred in Nevada. This circumvention of the jurisdictional requirement is precisely what the Supreme Court would not allow. Thus we may understand the Court's repeated reference to the failure of the prosecution to prove that "antisocial behavior" had occurred in California.

Thus we may conclude that punishing a common thief reveals the same constitutional defect as punishing a narcotics addict. The critical point is not the involuntary status, but taking either the propensity or past acts outside the jurisdiction as the crime.[30] This is a plausible interpretation of *Robinson* that explains why the majority of the Court would declare the crime of being an addict unconstitutional, but would not extend the holding to cases of involuntary behavior. The vice of *Robinson* was that the state sought first to use the criminal sanction to further its interest in preventing anticipated and predictable acts of narcotics usage; and, secondly, that by defining the crime as addiction, it sought to circumvent the ordinary jurisdictional and venue requirements. Both of these vices flow from penalizing a status that might be inferred

[30] 370 U.S. at 679 (Harlan, J., concurring).

from events that occurred outside the jurisdiction. Though this interpretation is plausible, its weakness derives from its failure to capture that aspect of the case that supports the judgment that the punishment was "cruel and unusual." This dimension of the constitutional rationale is most convincing when Justice Stewart argues that "even one day in prison would be cruel and unusual punishment for the 'crime of having a common cold.' "[31] This rhetoric leads one invariably in the direction of the four dissenting judges in *Powell*, for what makes the punishment of the common cold bizarre is precisely its being acquired involuntarily. The case of the common cold differs significantly from punishing addiction and the status of being a thief, for the latter two conditions entail propensities to engage in antisocial behavior. It is this propensity that prompts the state to intervene. There is no comparable interest in punishing a common cold, and therefore the punishment appears particularly gratuitous and cruel.

§6.4.3. The Teleological Theory of Acting. It may not tell us much to define an act as bodily movement generated by the will,[32] but Anglo-American legal scholars have seen no reason to challenge this convenient formula. Not much turns on it in any event, for the only time that the question comes into play is when there is a discernible ground, such as sleepwalking[33] or hypnosis, for believing that a nominal act is not properly attributable to the agent and his doing. Thus all the practical legal problems turn not on the definition of an act, but on the specific grounds for treating bodily movement as natural phenomenon rather than as the assertion of a human agent.[34]

[31] *Id.* at 667.

[32] See note 3 *supra*.

[33] See Fain v. Commonwealth, 78 Ky. 183 (1879); Regina v. Charlson, [1955] 1 W.L.R. 317 (brain tumor).

[34] This is the line of reasoning that H. L. A. Hart used to advance his theory of acts as "defeasible ascriptions." Hart, *The Ascription of Responsibility and Rights*, in A. Flew, Logic and Language 145 (First Series 1968 ed.). The problem with this view is that it lacks a criterion for determining when a particular ground will defease the ascription of action. To find a criterion, one is led back to the variations of "the will." See MPC §2.01(2)(d) (a bodily movement is not an act if it "is not a product of the effort or determination of the actor").

This traditional definition of acting has generated a deep ideological rift in German legal theory. In the early 1930s, Professor Hans Welzel began to develop an alternative theory of "acting" that eventually became the cornerstone of an entire theory of criminal responsibility.[35] The essential point in Welzel's attack on the received notion of acting, which at that time corresponded to the standard Anglo-American definition, was that acting was teleological, goal-directed activity. Human acting could not be understood simply as bodily movements, triggered by the will, without perceiving the aim of the action. Human action, Welzel argued, was intrinsically purposive, not merely the external manifestation of an inner mechanism called the will. Welzel dubbed his theory the *"finale Handlungslehre,"* which is captured in English as: "the goal-directed theory of human action." We shall refer to Welzel's work simply as the "teleological theory."

A major stimulus to Welzel's creative effort was his aversion to a set of ideas that had gained ascendancy in German thought in the late nineteenth century. The ideas that Welzel reacted against are not hard for us to understand, for they are still prominent, and indeed of growing influence in Anglo-American culture. This dominant perspective stresses causal as opposed to intersubjective understanding as the medium for comprehending human events. Heavily influenced by the methodology of the natural sciences, we are inclined to feel that we understand phenomena by perceiving mechanistic connections between cause and effect. The perspective thus neglected is the interdependence of human subjects and modes of understanding that arise from human interaction.

A causal orientation issues often (though not necessarily) in a deterministic view of human conduct. If our only way of comprehending human conduct is to trace it back to its causes, we are inclined to think of all human acts as the product of circumstances.

[35] For the early papers, see Welzel, *Kausalität und Handlung,* 51 ZStW 703 (1930–31); Welzel, *Studien zum System des Strafrechts,* 58 ZStW 491 (1938); the best repository of the theory's development and fluctuation are the eleven editions of H. Welzel, Das Deutsche Strafrecht (1st ed. 1947; 11th ed. 1969). On the debates in the German literature, see the extensive bibliography in Schönke-Schröder-Lenckner §13, preliminary notes, at 111–12.

Determinism (the theory that all human action is compelled) is obviously incompatible with the theory of personal responsibility that underlies the criminal law. Thus the pursuit of causal understanding to its extreme conclusion invariably creates a crisis in the ideological foundations of punishment and criminal responsibility.

Welzel's target was the preoccupation with the causal mode of understanding in the criminal law. As a result, he referred to the opposing theory of human action, namely, that acts were products of the will, as the "causal theory" of acting.[36] He rejected any view that held that the will or a set of desires caused the external bodily movements identified as acting. His teleological conception of acting escaped the flaws of the causal perspective by holding that a human act could be comprehended only so far as the agent's goal was perceived. Action was not blind, he insisted, it was "seeing."[37] Of course, on the surface of things, it is not clear how an emphasis on teleology transcends the causal, mechanistic point of view. One could think of motives as the causes of actions.[38] Do not animals act teleologically in hunting their prey? In what sense, then, does the notion of pursuing a goal help us understand the concept of human action?

Though Welzel himself insisted that his theory was rooted in a conception of acting, most of his successors have tended to stress his contribution to related fields of criminal theory, such as the criteria for establishing wrongdoing[39]—a subject that will later engage us.[40] My own view is that if properly interpreted, Welzel's theory of acting represents a significant philosophical advance. Yet a few points must be made in this interpretation that Welzel himself might not necessarily accept as emendations of the theory.

First, we should sort out the different applications of the term "causal" in this area and be clear about the alternatives. Some people who advance the methodology of the natural sciences

[36] See G. Radbruch, *supra* note 3.

[37] Welzel 33.

[38] For a discussion of the problem, see Urmson, *Motives and Causes,* 26 Proc. Aristotelian Soc. 179 (1952), reprinted in A. White, The Philosophy of Action (1968).

[39] See Nowakowski, *Zu Welzels Lehre von der Fahrlässigkeit* 1958 JZ 335, 336.

[40] See §6.6.5 *infra.*

might be committed to a deterministic philosophy of human conduct, but this view cannot be attributed to Radbruch and others against whom Welzel mounted his attack. Alternatively, a "causal theory" of acting might refer to a mechanistic conception of the relationship between the will and the manifestation of the will; the will "produces" the act in the external world. Yet it would not foil Welzel's relentless attack to drop the notions of causation from the metaphysics of acting and willing. What seems to be of deeper concern is the methodology of perceiving human conduct as human. This can be done only if one de-emphasizes causation and stresses the perception of human acting as a form of intersubjective understanding. The difference between bodily movements and human acts is that when someone is acting we can perceive a purpose in what he or she is doing. What we perceive when we grasp that someone is acting is not a manifestation of the will, but the assertion of a particular purpose. The essence of Welzel's argument, and by and large it is correct, is that we do not perceive someone as acting unless we also perceive that the person is after something. Another way of making this point is that we always see particular acts, rather than some general phenomenon called acting. We see people breaking into houses, putting sugar in coffee, and loading revolvers. Of course we also perceive a range of human activity that is of no particular relevance to the criminal law—walking down the street, dancing, and driving automobiles. The notion of "purpose" might not be entirely appropriate in this latter set of cases, for the activity is often engaged in as an end in itself.[41] It should also be noted that this theory does not generate a distinction between animal action and human action. Both animals and humans can engage in purposive activity as well as play and other activities that are regarded as ends in themselves. In order to get at the distinction between animal action and human action, we should have to probe the independent notion of "deciding" to

[41] Welzel is fully aware of this point and sees no difficulty in regarding activity itself as the end of acting. Welzel 36--37.

engage in particular acts. Animals may purposively stalk their prey, but they do not decide to do so. This notion of deciding to act remains enigmatic. Unhappily, it seems to pull us back in the direction of considering the "will" as an essential element of human acting.

Welzel's theory could be restated, perhaps with profit, not as a theory of acting, but as a theory about the relationship of acting and intending. The proposition that an act cannot be understood apart from its purpose implies that an act should not be separated from the actor's intention. Intending a result is implicit in the nature of acting, at least in the array of cases of morally and socially significant conduct. Welzel objected strongly to the view that intending an act was to experience an inner state that was the mental replication of the external act.[42] Intending and acting are bound up together; the two dimensions of the same phenomenon should not be disassociated and treated separately in the analysis of criminal liability.

Welzel's theory of acting and intending coincides with other strains in modern philosophy. It dovetails with Wittgenstein's sustained attack against the mentalist bias in philosophical psychology. Intending, Wittgenstein argues, is not an inner experience, a mental state, an event of consciousness—or any of those other things that lawyers are wont to say.[43] Acting intentionally is a way of acting.[44] Perceiving that others are acting and intending is implicit in a way of life in which we are all reared. To learn the language of "intending" is to learn when the circumstances warrant saying that someone intended to hit another rather than to say that the contact was accidental or absent-minded. The most appealing aspect of Welzel's theory of acting is that it overcomes the

[42] Welzel 43 (criticizing Mezger's view that the actor's intention was but "mirror image" (*Spiegelbild*) of the act).

[43] L. Wittgenstein, Philosophical Investigations §580 ("An 'inner process' stands in need of outward criteria").

[44] *Ibid.* ("The intention with which one acts does not 'accompany' the action any more than the thought 'accompanies' speech").

false dichotomy between acting and intending that pervades theoretical work in the criminal law.

Though widely discussed in German-speaking countries, Italy, Japan, and Latin America, Welzel's theory has failed to gain the acceptance of the majority of those interested and well versed in the theory. The major stumbling block is that this persuasive theory of acting and intending works well in the field of intentional offenses, but encounters difficulty in other areas. An act directed to a particular result does not appear to be a universal condition of liability, for many crimes, particularly negligent offenses, are committed without intending the legally relevant result. What are we to say about the act involved in drunk driving, firing a revolver willy-nilly, filling a prescription without proper care? These are acts that create a substantial and unjustified risk of harm, yet are they teleological acts? In these cases, it is not the goal, but the manner of execution that creates the problem of criminal liability. Thus the temptation is to conclude that the only act relevant for the criminal law is the voluntary act (regardless of purpose) that generates risks to others. A healthy sense of economy in legal analysis resists introducing considerations that are irrelevant to liability, and therefore there is an ongoing uneasiness about a theory of acting that requires attention to the goal of conduct when the conduct is legally significant only because it creates excessive risks of harm.

It would be difficult to say that this problem in the field of negligence constitutes an argument against the philosophical merit of Welzel's theory. His theory of acting might be right as a philosophical proposition, but it may not be the best theory for maintaining the maxim of the criminal law that liability presupposes a human act. Unfortunately, theories that are correct philosophically may not always be the most useful for the analysis of problems in the criminal law. And what is useful for criminal lawyers may unhappily entail serious philosophical fallacies.

The general significance of the theory of human action in the criminal law derives from the assumption that "an act" is required for liability. Thus the debate about the nature of acting is in effect a debate about an element that everyone takes to be essential to criminal liability. These ramifications of the concept of acting are particularly acute in German theory, for not only liability but several components of liability presuppose a human act. This is notably true about the concept of wrongdoing, which we begin to explore in depth, beginning in §6.6. Thus further evaluation of Welzel's theory is deferred until we have occasion to study the relationship between acting and wrongdoing.

§6.5. *The Concept of Intention.*

A long tradition supports the analysis of intention *(dolus)* in abstraction from the particular offenses and particular patterns of liability. The centrality of intentionality in the analysis of criminal liability finds its warrant in a number of features of the criminal law. First, liability for acting intentionally, or intentionally bringing about a particular result, is characteristic of all three patterns of liability. Secondly, the analysis of intention is closely connected with the theory of mistake as a defense. If the intention required for a particular offense encompasses an element *X*, then the belief that *X* is not present (a mistake about *X*) will negate the required intention. If some general element is required in every case of intentionally committing an offense—for example, knowing that the act is wrongful—then a mistake about that element will provide a ground of exculpation in every case. Thirdly, as we noticed in the preceding section, the theory of intention is intimately connected with the development of Welzel's teleological theory of acting.[1]

The centrality of intention in defining criminal conduct generates the misleading phrases "criminal intent" and "wrongful intent" which are used normatively to refer to an intent under

§6.5. [1] The relationship between the second and third of these points generated one of the more interesting efforts to refute Welzel's thesis. See Engisch, *Der Unrechtstatbestand im Strafrecht* in Hundert Jahre deutsches Rechtsleben 401, 426–27 (E. von Caemmerer ed. 1960), discussed §6.6.5, at note 35 *infra*.

circumstances in which the actor's conduct as a whole is blameworthy.[2] In the discussion that follows, we shall leave aside these normative issues and seek to understand the notion of acting intentionally as a question of fact.

§6.5.1. **Intending and Desiring.** The central issue in the debate about the nature of intentionally committing an offense turns on the relationship between intending and desiring. In German[3] and Soviet law,[4] it is generally assumed that an actor intends a result only if he desires to bring about that result.[5] There is considerable support for an analogous account of intending in the common law.[6] Yet an influential analysis beginning with John Austin in the nineteenth century[7] holds that intending should be considered apart from the issue of desiring. It would follow that acting intentionally consists merely in "having" certain cognitive states, such as the foresight of consequences and the knowledge of what one is doing. The Model Penal Code offers a definition of acting "purposely" that minimizes the importance of the desires, wishes, or wants of the actor.[8] The critical facts in deciding whether someone purposely commits an offense are his "conscious object" and

[2] See §6.2.1 *supra*.

[3] According to the standard definition: *Vorsatz ist das Wissen und Wollen der Tatbestandsverwirklichung* (Intention is knowing and wanting the realization of the definition of the offense). Welzel 64; Jescheck 218.

[4] Ugol. kod. (RSFSR) §8 (intention requires foresight and desire as to socially dangerous consequences).

[5] The French have failed to refine their concept of intention. See generally Mercadel, *Recherches sur l'intention en droit pénal*, 1967 Revue de science criminelle 1.

[6] Holmes 53 ("the wish" for specified consequences is an essential aspect of intention); J. Salmond, Jurisprudence 393 (7th ed. 1924). *Cf.* Hall 108–17.

[7] 1 J. Austin, Lectures on Jurisprudence 433–34 (2d ed. 1861) ("intended consequences not always desired"). It is difficult to follow Glanville Williams on this issue. *Compare* G. Williams, The Mental Element in Crime 25 (1965) (desire not essential to the intent required for attempted crime), *with id.* at 53 (distinction between intent and recklessness is "desire" except that the "inevitable accompaniment of what is desired" is also intended).

[8] MPC §2.02(2)(a): "A person acts purposely with respect to a material element of an offense when:

(i) if the element involves the nature of his conduct or a result thereof, it is his conscious object to engage in conduct of that nature or to cause such a result; and

(ii) if the element involves the attendant circumstances, he is aware of the existence of such circumstances or he believes or hopes that they exist."

his "beliefs" about attendant circumstances. Yet the actor's "hope" that a particular circumstance obtains is sufficient to say that he acts purposely with regard to that element; this, as we shall see later, has curious implications.

There are two contexts in which we may wish to know whether intending a result presupposes that one desire that result. First, the relationship of desire to intention might matter in disputes about whether an intended act was voluntary. Secondly, desire and other attitudes might bear on the distinction between intentionally and recklessly bringing about a result. We shall take up the first point in this section, and then turn to the boundary between intention and recklessness.

Suppose a man suffering from a brain tumor picks up his son and throws him out of a window; medical evidence supports the conclusion that because of his brain tumor he had no "choice" at all in executing his act.[9] Did he intend to injure his son? It seems clear that in this case he had no desire to inflict injury. It is also clear in this case that he did not act voluntarily; indeed there is some doubt whether there was any "act" at all. Yet the man does not throw his son out of the window in a spasm or in a fit. He methodically opens the window, lifts up the boy, and throws him out. His "conscious object" was to throw the boy out of the window. These facts point in the direction of saying that he threw him out intentionally.[10] One reason it is so difficult to classify this case is that it diverges so much from our ordinary experience. None of us was taught the concept of intending—or indeed the concept of acting—with this type of case in mind.

The systemic significance of distinguishing between intention and desire is clear. If intention is "defined" restrictively, then the apparatus of analysis must include a distinct ground for solving cases of involuntary conduct. The need for this independent ground explains the added significance that Anglo-American theory gives to the requirement of a voluntary act. The Model Penal

[9] See Regina v. Charlson, [1955] 1 W.L.R. 317.

[10] But, as Paul Brest pointed out to me, it does not follow that he injured the boy intentionally.

Code contains a distinct provision denying liability in cases of involuntary acts which would obviously include conduct induced by a brain tumor.[11] There is no comparable provision in the new German penal code and none in the 1960 RSFSR Criminal Code. A broader concept of intention, one that included an element of desiring, might render a separate provision on voluntariness superfluous.[12] The requirement of "desire" could be interpreted to fulfill the task borne by the separate provision requiring a voluntary act.

It would be difficult to say that separating the issues of voluntariness (desire) and intention yields a powerful systemic advantage. Yet it might be argued that some clarity is achieved by breaking down the concept of intention and thus channelling attention to the difference between self-control and acting with a particular objective.

§6.5.2. **Intention and Recklessness.** The basic cleavage in the states of mind used in criminal legislation is between those that focus on the actor's goal (willfulness, intention, purposefulness) and those that focus on the risk that the actor creates in acting (recklessness and negligence). The difficult problem confronted in all legal systems is working out the precise boundary between these two clusters of mental states—or, more precisely, between these two ways of committing offenses.[13] Discussing diverse statutory schemes in one sweep is likely to be confusing, for the reformed American statutes now tend to recognize the middle category of "knowingly" committing an offense.[14] Continental statutes

[11] MPC §2.01(1): "A person is not guilty of an offense unless his liability is based on conduct which includes a voluntary act or the omission to perform an act of which he is physically capable."

MPC §2.01(2) lists paradigmatic instances of involuntary conduct and concludes with the comprehensive clause that all conduct is involuntary if it "is not a product of the effort or determination of the actor, either conscious or habitual." *Id.* §2.01(2)(d).

[12] *Cf.* Kurs (GP 1968) at 415--16 (stressing the concept of "desire" as a vehicle for exploring the actor's voluntariness). This analysis is apparently unnecessary in German theory, for the system takes the requirement of an act (*Handlung*) to be self-evident.

[13] This qualification is necessary to avoid labeling "negligence" as a mental state.

[14] MPC §2.02(2)(b): "A person acts knowingly with respect to a material element of an offense when:

have no comparable form. Therefore we shall begin the discussion by focussing on the classic distinction between *dolus* (intention) and *culpa* (negligence). Recklessness is a form of *culpa*—equivalent to what German scholars call "conscious negligence." The problem of distinguishing "intention" and "recklessness" arises because in both cases the actor is aware that his conduct might generate a specific result.

Two preliminary remarks are in order. First, there would be little dispute about distinguishing "intention" from "recklessness" if the former were not a term of art, encompassing many situations that we would not call "intentional" in ordinary language. If a parent gets up at night to shut the window and despite his efforts to be quiet, the noise wakes up a baby sleeping nearby, we would not say that the parent intentionally woke the baby—and most certainly he does not do it "on purpose." If a prisoner in an effort to escape blows up the prison wall with knowledge that guards are present and one of the latter dies in the explosion, we would not say that the prisoner intentionally killed the guard. Yet in legal systems across the Western world, the concept of "intention" is interpreted broadly to include these probable side-effects of intentional conduct. This willingness to sweep in probable side-effects is what generates the problem of demarcation relative to recklessness. If the side-effects are not very probable—say, there are no guards visible at the time of the explosion—the killing might well be considered reckless rather than intentional.

Our second preliminary remark is that this problem of demarcation arises only in some patterns of liability. Though legal systems may differ on this point, there is good reason to believe that in the patterns of manifest and subjective liability, the "intent" required is a genuine intent—as we understand that word in ordinary English. Take larceny as an example. It is hard to imagine "an intent permanently to deprive the owner of his property" unless

"(i) if the element involves the nature of his conduct or the attendant circumstances, he is aware that his conduct is of that nature or that such circumstances exist; and

"(ii) if the element involves a result of his conduct he is aware that it is practically certain that his conduct will cause such result."

that were the goal rather than a side-effect of the actor's conduct. All inchoate offenses arguably require a narrowly defined intent to consummate the ultimate offense. This is most clearly true about crimes defined as "assault with intent to rape or murder." It is also true about burglary and the intent to commit a felony after entry. It is also true about criminal attempts,[15] though some writers have reservations.[16] Legal systems typically employ some term to indicate that what is required in these cases is not simply an "intention" the way the term is ordinarily understood. Anglo-American lawyers are wont to refer to a "specific intent"[17]—in one of the many acceptations of that term.[18] The Model Penal Code's definition of "purposeful" commission covers these cases.[19] German lawyers distinguish between *Vorsatz* (intention) and *Absicht* (purpose or aim) and use the latter term to refer to the intent requirement in larceny, fraud and various forms of inchoate offenses.[20]

With these reservations, we are left with the question: when is there a problem of distinguishing "intention" from "recklessness"? The problematic cases arise in the pattern of harmful consequences. In the case of these offenses, a specific palpable result is a condition of the offense, and the question is whether if the actor takes a very high risk of bringing about that result, he can be held accountable as though he intended the result. If the statute proscribes only intentional commission of the offense, or if the intentional commission is punished more severely, this is a matter of practical importance.

There are two distinct foci in efforts to distinguish between bringing about a result intentionally and bringing it about reck-

[15] Thacker v. Commonwealth, 134 Va. 767, 114 S.E. 504 (1922).

[16] MPC §5.01, Comment at 29 (Tent. Draft No. 10, 1960); Williams, *supra* note 7, at 24–25. The German doctrine of *dolus eventualis* would support Williams' result. See text at notes 24–27 *infra*.

[17] J. Michael & H. Wechsler, Criminal Law and Its Administration 586 (1940); MPC §5.01, Comment at 27 (Tent. Draft No. 10, 1960).

[18] See §6.5.6 B *infra*.

[19] MPC §2.02(2)(a) *Cf.* Proposed Federal Criminal Code §302 (a) (defining "intention" narrowly to exclude side-effects).

[20] Jescheck 220, 238; *but cf.* Welzel 78 (noting that *Absicht* is used in different senses).

lessly. One approach is to stress the relative degree of risk that the result will occur; the other, to stress the actor's attitude toward the risk. Let us attempt to apply these diverse perspectives in two hypothetical situations:

A. The prison-break hypothetical: the prisoner blows up a wall in order to escape. A guard is either killed or injured. Is the prisoner liable for intentional homicide or battery?

B. The stewardess on a hijacked airplane renders a parachute defective in the expectation that the hijacker, a known and feared terrorist, might use the chute. He does and is either killed or injured.[21]

To assess whether the injury or death in these cases is to be regarded as intended, we can proceed simply by assessing the relative probability that the explosion would hit the guard or that the hijacker would use the chute. Most legal systems would treat the side-effect of an explosion, if sufficiently probable, as a case of directly "intending the result."[22] The parachute case is more subtle,[23] as is the case of a prison break where the risk of injuring a guard is low.

To analyze these cases comparatively, we have to bring into the open an important doctrinal difference between German and Soviet law, on the one hand, and Anglo-American (and possibly French)[24] law on the other. The former systems draw the distinction between intentional and negligent conduct by including *dolus eventualis* within the contours of intending a particular result. *Dolus eventualis* is defined as a particular subjective posture toward the result. The tests for this subjective posture vary; the possibilities

[21] This example comes from Williams, *supra* note 7, at 53.

[22] As to German law, see Jescheck 221; Soviet law, Kurs (GP 1968) at 415 (example of pushing someone into river, with knowledge that he can't swim); on the supposed common-law rule that "substantially certain" results are intended, see Perkins 747; LaFave & Scott 196; Restatement (Second) of Torts §8A.

[23] See §5.2.2 *supra* on the issue whether the intentional act by the hijacker would "break the causal chain."

[24] On the rejection of *dolus eventualis* as an element of intention in French law, see 1 Bouzat & Pinatel §178, at 265; Mercadel, *supra* note 5, at 29. The text is qualified because these writers fail to specify what they or the courts mean by *dol éventuel.*

include everything from being "indifferent" to the result,[25] to "being reconciled"[26] with the result as a possible cost of attaining one's goal.[27] The implication is that recklessness (or "conscious negligence" as it is called in German and Soviet law) requires an affirmative aversion to the harmful side-effect.[28]

If we apply the definitions of the Model Penal Code to the case of the defective parachute, the issue of killing "purposely" would turn on whether the stewardess' "conscious object" was to cause the death of the hijacker; killing "knowingly" would depend on whether she was "practically certain" he would use the chute and fall to his death. Given the appropriate interpretations of "conscious object" and "causing death" we might be able to find a purposeful or knowing killing under these definitions.[29] The standard of *dolus eventualis* would point more clearly to liability for intentional killing. Why does the stewardess render the parachute defective if she does not want the hijacker to use it? Thus her subjective emotional posture toward the killing would be controlling.

The difference between the standard of the Model Penal Code and *dolus eventualis* would emerge in a variation of the prison break case in which the killing of the guard was unlikely. If it is not the actor's conscious object to kill and if he is not "practically certain" that death will result, then the Code would not permit a finding of killing "purposely" or "knowingly." But the actor's subjective posture might be just as incriminating. He might be indifferent or "reconciled" to harming people in the blast, and thus even if he thought that the likelihood of personal injury was very low, he would act with *dolus eventualis.*

[25] Kurs (GP 1968) at 418.

[26] This is a liberal translation of the German phrase: *sich mit der Rechtsgutverletzung abfinden.* On this and other formulae for defining *dolus eventualis,* see Jescheck 222-24; Schönke-Schröder-Cramer §15, notes 68-79, at 200-03.

[27] The best way to state the distinction is to employ a contrafactual conditional. If the actor knew that the side effect was going to occur, would he act in the same way? If yes, then the actor is reconciled to the side effect. See A. Eser, Strafrecht I, at 54-55 (2d ed. 1976). Compare this contrafactual conditional with the theory of attempting, *supra* §3.3.4 *supra.*

[28] Schönke-Schröder-Cramer §15, note 70, at 201, rejecting the standard of probability.

[29] We leave aside the possibility of self-defense as a justification.

The doctrine of *dolus eventualis* has vast repercussions in German and Soviet theory. If a rapist puts his hand over his victim's mouth with indifference to her fate and she dies, the killing is intentional. This broad conception of "intentional" killing explains why these systems can dispense with a doctrine of felony-murder.[30] As to the intent required for attempted offenses, German law treats *dolus eventualis* as sufficient for liability.[31] This means that if a man shoots into a room full of people without the intent to injure anyone but indifferent to whether he does, he is guilty of at least attempted murder.[32]

So far as the Anglo-American conception of intention is concerned, there is no doctrine with the sweep of *dolus eventualis.* It is very unlikely that in a case of low probability of harm, an English or American court would find an intentional killing, arson or battery. The orientation of the system is toward actual risk and knowledge of risk, not the inner posture of the actor. This emphasis on external events yields the infelicitous dogma that a person's intent is to be judged by the "natural and probable consequences of his acts." But the same orientation avoids turning to the jury and asking whether in his heart, the actor "was reconciled" with the likelihood of death.

The comparative analysis of *dolus eventualis* is extremely subtle. That the concept is missing in the Anglo-American literature prompts us to look for surrogates, such as the felony-murder rule. We should also recall that in the common law, intentional killing is not the only basis for establishing the most egregious form of criminal homicide. A review of the Anglo-American law of murder reveals criteria of risk-taking, sufficient for murder, that closely resemble the criteria for *dolus eventualis.* For example, the Model Penal Code treats reckless killing, "manifesting extreme indifference to the value of human life," as equivalent to purposeful

[30] For the application of the felony-murder rule in this type of case, see Regina v. Beard, [1920] 2 A.C. 479 (H.L.).

[31] Jescheck 388; Rudolphi in SK §22, note 2, at 171.

[32] *Cf.* notes 15, 16 *supra.*

and knowing killing.[33] Thus the factor of "indifference to life" need not bear on the definition of "intention" if the functional outcome for the law of murder is the same.

The basic question is whether the actor's attitude alone can warrant classification at a higher level of culpability than would be supported by the risks he creates. Can the lust for death compensate for a low risk of harm? It is important that the Model Penal Code inserts the issue of "indifference" only to qualify the standard of recklessness.[34] Yet the German literature, in contrast, suggests that if the actor regards death "as possible" and he acts with *dolus eventualis,* the killing would be intentional even if the risk of death is not as great as that required for negligent homicide.[35] Thus if the risk were low in the parachute case, the stewardess might be prima facie accountable either for intentional homicide, or for no crime at all, but not negligent homicide. That negligent homicide is not "included" in intentional killing points to a structural difference between the two systems, but it is one that should be checked against a rigorous examination of all the German cases.[36]

The closest analogue in Anglo-American theory is the Model Penal Code's provision on "purposeful conduct" as to attendant circumstances. Take a case in which the actor sets fire to what appears to be an empty tent, yet she "hopes" that her enemy is then in the tent. Even if the risk that the tent was occupied was minimal and thus below the threshold of negligence, her "hoping" that it was occupied would be sufficient to classify the burning as

[33] MPC §210.2(1)(b). *Cf.* the California test for malice: act "done for a base, anti-social purpose, and with a wanton disregard for human life." Caljic §8.11 (Supp. 1976).

[34] Similarly, the California standard requires "a high probability of death." *Ibid.*

[35] One writer rejects the relevance of probability to *dolus eventualis* on the ground that the improbability of hitting a distant, but intended target does not preclude a finding that a successful hit was intentional. Schmidhäuser 436.

[36] For example, one of the leading cases posed a situation of strangulation leading to death. See Judgment of April 22, 1955, 7 BGHSt. 363; it is not surprising that this was treated as intentional killing. The problem would be to find a case where intending a result was affirmed on a low risk of the result as a side-effect.

arson of an occupied structure.[37] In fact, many of the leading cases on *dolus eventualis* pertain to "attendant circumstances" of conduct, such as whether the victim of a statutory rape is over the age of 14.[38] Thus some applications of *dolus eventualis* are compatible with doctrines of the Model Penal Code.

§6.5.3. **Intending and Omissions.** One of the assumptions of Anglo-American legal theory is that the same basic concepts of "intent" and "negligence" apply with equal rigor to cases both of affirmatively causing harm and failing to avert harm. German and Soviet legal theory rejects this assumption and recognizes that "intending" in a case of an omission is fundamentally different from intending in cases of affirmatively causing harm. The RSFSR Code elegantly captures this distinction. Intention in both cases of acts and omissions requires "foresight of the socially dangerous consequences"; in addition, intention in acting requires a "desire that the result occur"; intention in failing to act requires merely that the actor "consciously permit" the result to occur.[39]

There is something undeniably odd about saying that if a sunbather fails to rescue a drowning swimmer, she intends the swimmer to die. The reason for this oddity is that the failure of the sunbather to intervene does not "cause" or "bring about" the death. She merely "permits" it to occur. Of course, some people might say that permitting and causing are the same and they could rely on the "but for" theory of causation to prove their point: if the sunbather's intervention would have saved the swimmer, that is sufficient to say that non-intervention "caused" the death. A better treatment of this problem is reserved for Chapter Eight, in which we will consider liability for failing to prevent death. As this discussion suggests, an adequate treatment of the problem will require an effort to refute the "but for" theory of causation.

§6.5.4. **Intention in Ordinary Language.** A philosophical inquiry into the contours of a concept does not pursue a definition, but

[37] MPC §2.02(2)(a). *Cf. id.* §220.1(1)(a) (arson defined as starting a fire with the purpose of destroying "a building or occupied structure").

[38] See Judgment of November 27, 1952, 1953 NJW 152.

[39] Ugol. kod. (RSFSR) §8.

rather an account of a concept that is already implicitly defined in our language. A serious philosophical effort would draw attention to numerous distinctions that are suppressed in the effort to fashion a system for analyzing legal problems. First, it is by no means clear, as we assumed earlier, that the notions of desire and volition are interchangeable. Secondly, one should have to clarify the difference between a strong and a weak sense of desiring. A bank teller who opens a safe at gunpoint desires (in a weak sense) to save his life, but does not desire (in the strong sense) to turn over the money to the thief. There is a parallel distinction between strong and weak senses of the concept of voluntariness. Whether we say that the teller desires to open the safe, or opens it voluntarily, depends on whether we use these terms in their strong or weak sense.

Even more significantly, a philosophical analysis of English usage teaches us that these problematic terms (voluntariness, desire, intention) are not applicable in all contexts of human action. The notion of voluntariness, for example, gets its grip when there is some reason to think that conduct might not be voluntary. If a soldier is summoned for dangerous duty, we might wish to know whether he signed up voluntarily. Yet with regard to routine conduct, such as a driver's making a left-hand turn, we would not ordinarily ask whether he did so voluntarily. The question itself would be puzzling and prompt us to consider reasons why his turning might not have been voluntary (did someone force him to turn left?). It follows from this analysis of usage that many routine acts of daily life are not aptly described either as voluntary or as involuntary.

The same point holds in analyzing intention and desire. Absent unusual circumstances, it would be odd to inquire whether the driver intended to turn left or whether he had the desire to turn left. The question might make sense if the driver were looking for an address on the right, and we were puzzled about whether in turning left, he simply was confused about his right and left side, or whether perhaps he changed his mind and decided to give up looking for the address. Then we would want to know what his intention was.

It follows that acting intentionally is not necessarily the opposite of acting unintentionally. In the driver's case it would be odd to say that he turned left either intentionally or unintentionally. The same would be true of manifold activities of our daily lives—shutting the door, folding our arms, patting down our hair. In all of these cases the notions of voluntariness, intending, desiring are properly at work only if there is something special about the case that prompts our question. The great virtue of this philosophical analysis is that it brings these puzzling notions back to their natural habitat. The method of analyzing ordinary usage invites us to consider what these terms mean as they are used, not what they "mean" when wrenched out of context and defined for the purposes of legal analysis.

The method of philosophical clarification runs afoul of the prevailing method of legal analysis. The bias of the law is that every act of causing harm must be subject to classification as either voluntary or not, either desired or not, either intended or not. The engine of the law requires us to make a decision in every case, and therefore there is no room for a middle ground where the concept idles, where it is odd to describe the case one way or the other.

The need to force borderline cases into one category or the other often entails a serious philosophical error. As H. L. A. Hart demonstrated convincingly in the analysis of voluntariness,[40] the need to classify all cases in a scheme of two categories induces the search for the essence of these problematic features of human conduct. By grabbing hold of the essence of voluntariness or of intending, we have a standard that we can apply to all cases and thus solve the problems at the fringes. The essence seems always to be found in some internal event, some feature of consciousness, that is present in all cases of acting voluntarily and intentionally. Producing this essence is what Wittgenstein called "the conjurer's trick";[41] the fallacy of assuming that "something happens" inter-

[40] H. L. A. Hart, *The Ascription of Responsibility and Rights* in A. Flew, Logic and Language 145 (First Series 1968 ed.).

[41] L. Wittgenstein, Philosophical Investigations §308 (1953).

nally whenever one acts intentionally follows from assuming that because there is a word intention, it must name some particular thing. Thus legal theorists think of intention as a "mental state" or a "state of mind" that is present whenever one acts intentionally. The task of clarifying this reified essence is to find other essences, such as the essence of desire and voluntariness, and to inspect how these things fit into each other. It may be that the demands of systemic thinking in the law pull us into the search for these chimerical essences. If so, we should at least be mindful of the difference between an accurate philosophical account of voluntariness and intention and the way we customarily think in constructing the edifices of legal analysis.

§6.5.5. Intention and Motives. In this discussion of the nature of intention, we have avoided the murky field of distinguishing intentions from motives. That distinction has appealed to many writers, who have been wont to assert that motives are irrelevant in the law.[42] The merit of this generalization is the limited point that an actor's ultimate reason for acting may not bear on his liability. It does not matter whether he steals in order to buy Christmas presents for his children or to support his heroin habit. In some legal systems, it does not matter whether he kills out of jealousy or in order to prevent the decedent from testifying in a criminal trial. Of course, these considerations bear on sentencing and they may enter into the analysis of the requisite motives for murder under German and Soviet law.[43]

At one level, the claim that motives do not typically bear on criminal liability is a technical point about the way offenses are usually defined. But there is also a deeper point suggested by the claim that the actor's ultimate purposes do not bear on his or her culpability for criminal conduct. The deeper point will become clear when we refine the theory of just punishment in §6.6.

§6.5.6. A Glossary of Intents. To conclude our discussion of "intention" we offer here a glossary of the expressions in which

[42] Hall 99 (motives irrelevant to *mens rea*); 2 Stephen 111–12.
[43] §4.5.3 *supra*.

the word "intention" appears. Some of these terms have already received attention; others will come up in later chapters. The important point to note about these terms is their ambiguity. Virtually all of them do double and triple duty.

A. *Wrongful Intent, Criminal Intent.* These terms can mean either:[44]
   1. an intent that under the circumstances of the act renders the actor properly subject to blame, or
   2. the intent required for liability under a criminal statute.

B. *Specific Intent.* This term can mean any of the following:
   1. a well-defined, particular intent (e.g., an intent to deprive the owner permanently of his property),[45] or
   2. an intent to realize a particular objective (if the intent is specific in this sense, undesired side-effects are not included),[46] or
   3. an intent that affects the "species or degree"[47] of a crime and therefore may be negated by a claim of intoxication.[48]

C. *General Intent (dolus generalis).* This can mean any of the following:
   1. an intent simply to do the act that one does,[49] or
   2. a continuing intent that unites an unsuccessful attempt to kill with unintended killing in one complex sufficient for criminal homicide,[50] or

[44] §6.2.1 *supra.*

[45] This is apparently all the term means in Caljic §8.79 (1976 Supp.).

[46] *Cf.* the discussion of the intent required for a criminal attempt, *supra* notes 15, 16.

[47] Cal. Penal Code §22.

[48] See generally on the excuse of intoxication, §10.4.5 *infra.*

[49] Mercadel, *supra* note 5, at 20 (citing Garçon, who defined *dol général* as a "conscious and voluntary act to violate the law").

[50] This usage is common in German law, see Jescheck 234 (typical case: *D* strangles the victim with the intent to kill; believing the victim dead, *D* stages a suicide by hanging, which in fact produces death). *Cf.* Jackson v. Commonwealth, 100 Ky. 239, 38 S.W. 422 (1896), *rehearing denied,* 100 Ky. 268, 38 S.W. 1081 (1897) (*D* gave victim cocaine with intent to kill; later, believing her to be dead, he decapitated her. Conviction aff'd).

3. the opposite of a specific intent as defined in B(3), or
4. the same as *wrongful* and *criminal* intent in the sense of A(1).

D. *Ulterior Intent.* The unexecuted intent added to a consummated act, as in the offense of burglary: breaking and entering with the intent to commit a felony. The "intent to commit a felony" is ulterior.[51] It is a form of "specific intent" as defined in B(2) and typically qualifies as a "specific intent" under B(3).

E. *Conditional Intent.* This term has different meanings in German and in English.
1. In German, the term "conditional intent" (*bedingter Vorsatz*) is another way of referring to *dolus eventualis.*[52] It qualifies in German law as a form of intent.
2. In English, a "conditional intent" means an intent to commit the harm if a certain condition is not fulfilled;[53] for example, to kill one's lover if he or she does not return. With a few exceptions,[54] this type of "conditional intent" is treated as though it were a straightforward intent.

§6.6. *The Concepts of Wrongdoing and Attribution.*

The purpose of this chapter is not only to clarify the terminology of theoretical discourse in Anglo-American criminal law, but also to enrich the range of available concepts in English by introducing analogues to some of the fecund ideas elaborated in the German theoretical literature. The point of this comparative inquiry is not only

[51] See Smith & Hogan 257.

[52] See text at notes 25–31 *supra.*

[53] LaFave & Scott 200; MPC §2.02(6). The comparable term in German is *bedingter Handlungswille;* see Jescheck 225.

[54] See MPC §2.02, Comment at 129 (Tent. Draft No. 4, 1955).

to fathom the profundity of German criminal theory, but also to provide a reservoir of concepts for possible absorption in Anglo-American theory. In this section we shall explore the rich distinction between wrongdoing and the subjective attribution of a wrongful act (or event) to a particular person.[1]

The closest analogue to this distinction in Anglo-American theory is the well-established demarcation between the analysis of criminal acts and the question of responsibility for those acts. A non-responsible actor is someone who is not properly held accountable for his acts. He is guilty but insane; or guilty but because of his age, not subject to the jurisdiction of the criminal courts. Thus the distinction between the criminality or the wrongfulness of the act and the question of holding a particular person accountable for the act is not foreign to the Anglo-American frame of mind. We distinguish between characteristics of the act (wrongful, criminal) and characteristics of the actor (insane, infant). Indeed, the Model Penal Code builds on this distinction by defining insanity as a state of non-responsibility involving, in part, the absence of "substantial capacity to appreciate the wrongfulness"[2] of the criminal act. This definition would not be coherent unless the issue of responsibility were separable from the issue of wrongfulness; if non-responsible acts were not wrongful, it would not make sense to say that the insane actor did not appreciate the wrongfulness of his act.

The problems of sanity and responsibility are an example of the broader inquiry that, for want of a better term, we shall call the problem of subjective attribution or simply "attribution." The premises underlying the analysis of attribution are (1) that an act may be found to be wrongful without an analysis of attribution, and (2) no one may be properly punished for a wrongful act (an act of wrongdoing) unless the act is attributable to him. Another way to state the issue of attribution is that it raises the question

§6.6. [1] "Objective attribution" (*objective Zurechnung*) generally refers to problems of causation. See §6.7, at notes 2, 3 *infra;* unless otherwise indicated, the term "attribution" in the text means "subjective attribution."

[2] MPC §4.01(1) (alternative wording).

whether an individual may be justly held accountable for a particular act of wrongdoing.

The major difference between German and Anglo-American theory is that the German analysis of the distinction between wrongdoing and attribution goes far beyond the questions of insanity and infancy. Working out a sound distinction between the two categories of issue requires detailed theoretical attention to numerous borderline questions such as intention, negligence, duress, necessity, mistake of fact, and mistake of law. Each of these issues might arguably be classified as adhering to the category of wrongdoing or to the category of attribution. The primary focus of German theory in this century has been the attempt to elaborate a structure of liability for criminal acts by determining which issues are properly classified in one category or the other. This attempt at classification has served to illuminate not only the notions of wrongdoing and attribution, but also the nature of the specific legal issues that the theorists have sought to classify. Eventually we shall turn to some of the debates that have raged in the German literature, but first we have to attend to the theoretical foundations of extending the distinction between wrongdoing and attribution beyond the questions of insanity and infancy. As we shall see in due course, there are important practical implications to this entire endeavor.

There appear to be two important theoretical pillars for the distinction between wrongdoing and attribution. The first is the observation that there are two types of norms in the criminal law. The second is the conceptual relationship between punishment and wrongdoing.

§6.6.1. Wrongdoing and Norms. The basic norms of the criminal law prohibit particular acts or require that particular acts be performed. These norms may be stated in the form "thou shalt not do *X*" where "doing *X*" may stand for "killing," "stealing," "raping," and so forth. Or these norms may be stated in the form "thou shalt do *Y*" under particular circumstances where "doing *Y*" may stand for "filing an income tax form," "answering a question before a congressional committee," or "reporting a crime." These are what H. L. A. Hart has identified as the primary norms of a legal system.[3] They impose duties of compliance on individual citizens. The addressee of these norms is not the judge, but the citizen who seeks both to do his duty and to avoid jeopardy under the law.

There are a host of issues in the criminal law that cannot properly be stated in these primary norms of prohibition and command. For example, it makes little sense to integrate the issues of insanity, duress, or mistake into a set of directives to the citizenry. The point of recognizing insanity and duress as defenses is not that the norm is amended to read: "Thou shalt not kill unless thou art insane or under a threat of death." The point of recognizing reasonable mistake of fact as a defense in statutory rape cases is not that the norm is corrected to read: "Thou shalt not engage in intercourse with a girl under the age of 18 unless thou art reasonably mistaken about her age." If a defendant argued that he was not guilty of statutory rape because he had formulated a reasonable judgment that the girl was overage, his attitude would probably be taken to involve bad faith and a reckless disregard of the risk that the girl was under age.[4] The point of all these issues—insanity, duress, and mistake—is not that they generate exceptions to the norms prohibiting conduct, but rather that they provide excuses for violating the prohibitory norms.[5]

There are other issues that properly can be integrated into the prohibitory norm; for example, self-defense may be taken to modify the norm against killing to read (roughly): "Thou shalt not kill unless thine own life or limb is in great danger." The defense of self-defense implicitly creates a license to kill that modifies the norm against killing, but no one would argue that insanity or mistake generates a license to kill.

[3] H. L. A. Hart, The Concept of Law 78 (1961).

[4] See §6.6.6 *infra*.

[5] Hart has written about excuses in several contexts, see e.g., Hart, *Prolegomenon to the Principles of Punishment* in H. L. A. Hart, Punishment and Responsibility 1, 17-24 (1968), but he failed to integrate excuses into his theory of law. It would be a mistake to treat excuses as secondary rules conferring capacity, *cf.* Hart, *supra* note 3, at 28, 79, as though committing a crime were akin to making a contract. But one might, arguably, treat "excuses" as secondary rules conferring power on judges to abstain from punishment in particular cases.

This distinction between issues that modify the prohibitory norm and those that do not lies at the foundation of the distinction between wrongful conduct and attribution. Wrongful conduct may be defined as the violation of the prohibitory norm as modified by all defenses that create a privileged exception to the norm. The analysis of attribution turns our attention to a totally distinct set of norms, which do not provide directives for action, but which spell out the criteria for holding persons accountable for their deeds. The distinction as elaborated here corresponds to the more familiar distinction between justification and excuse. Justificatory claims, such as self-defense, negate wrongdoing; they represent the denial of a condition implicit in the prohibitory norm (i.e., unless your life or limb is in danger). Excuses, in contrast, do not negate wrongdoing. Rather they challenge the attribution of the wrongful act to the actor.

Several points on terminology are in order. First, we should be explicit about the distinction between wrongful conduct and wrongdoing. The former is a purely formal concept, defined by the incompatibility of the act with the norms of the legal system. The concept of wrongdoing is material or substantive. To say that the actor is a wrongdoer or that he has engaged in wrongdoing is to pass judgment on the intrinsic quality of his deed. Wrongfulness is a categorical attribute, but wrongdoing is a matter of degree. Murder and larceny are equally wrongful in the same way that both violate legal norms. But murder is a greater wrong—a graver case of wrongdoing—than larceny. Determining the degree of wrongdoing is obviously a subtle problem of moral judgment.

Every wrongful act is at least a nominal case of wrongdoing. Admittedly, the wrongdoing is muted in some offenses such as illegally possessing weapons and driving through a red light. As a moral category, however, wrongdoing is broader than the notion of wrongful conduct. Intentionally inflicting emotional distress is an instance of wrongdoing, but not a wrongful act under the criminal law.

We may speak of attributing either wrongful acts or wrongdoing to the actor, and in most contexts the ambiguity need not concern us. To say that the actor is accountable for wrongdoing is simply another way of saying that the wrongdoing is attributable to him or her. We shall use the term "culpability" in the normative sense to refer to accountability, but there is an important difference between the two concepts. The notions of attribution and accountability represent an independent dimension of liability. Acts can be wrongful, but the actor, not accountable; or the act justified and lawful, and the actor, accountable.[6] Culpability, in contrast, is limited to wrongful acts. A justified act is not wrongful, and the actor not culpable. Further, the degree of culpability is linked to the degree of wrongdoing. The personal culpability for murder is greater than for larceny. We could use the term "blameworthy" to refer to culpability, but some people may think of blaming a wrongdoer as the expression of a sentiment such as contempt or scorn. There is no passion of this sort implied in saying that an actor is accountable or culpable for a wrongful act.

The concepts of justification and excuse provide another perspective on the same set of concepts. A justification negates the wrongfulness of the act and denies the element of wrongdoing. An excuse negates the actor's accountability for the act. The implication of either a justification or an excuse is that the actor is not culpable, but the reasons are different. In the case of a justification, there is no wrongful act to render the actor culpable. In the case of an excuse, the act is wrongful, but the absence of personal accountability negates the actor's culpability. In the next several chapters, we shall concentrate on the affirmative concepts of wrongdoing and accountability. In Chapter Ten we explore the additional perspective provided by the theory of justification and excuse.

§6.6.2. Punishment and Wrongdoing. The distinction between wrongdoing and attribution (accountability, culpability) enables us to raise a critical set of issues in the rationale of punishment. The revival of retributivist theories of punishment has led many theorists to advocate that punishment ought to be imposed accord-

[6] See, e.g., the analysis of accountability for lawful risks in tort law, Fletcher, *Fairness and Utility in Tort Theory*, 85 Harv. L. Rev. 537, 551-56 (1972).

ing to desert. As it stands, that proposition is readily accepted. Difficulties arise when we try to determine the criteria that influence the extent or degree of an offender's desert. In particular, is desert a function solely of conduct on a particular occasion? Or might desert be influenced by a string of similar criminal convictions in the past? Assuming that prior convictions indicate that a violator is more dangerous, do they also justify a finding of greater desert for the last criminal act?

This issue has come to the fore recently in a thoughtful report by Andrew von Hirsch for the Committee for the Study of Incarceration.[7] von Hirsch's argument is that punishment ought to be inflicted according to desert and that a prior criminal record increases desert.[8] The critical steps in this inference are (1) desert is a function of culpability, (2) a criminal record increases culpability. Thus it seems that in the name of justice, we can serve society. We can lock up recidivists for longer terms and justify the isolation as a punishment fitting the crime.[9]

Though undoubtedly made in good faith, this argument carries particularly insidious implications both for the practice and theory of criminal law. The practical effects will be felt by repeat offenders. The theoretical problem derives from the claim that increased isolation is justified in the name of desert and retribution. If the argument were that recidivists were particularly dangerous and punishment ought to be inflicted in proportion to the offender's dangerousness, we could at least try to argue against the proposition on empirical grounds. There might be some data that one could use to argue that some recidivists are no more dangerous than comparable categories of persons never punished. But this is precisely the type of unethical, repressive use of governmental power that von Hirsch seeks to avoid.[10] Thus he appeals to

[7] A. von Hirsch, Doing Justice (1976).

[8] *Id.* at 84–88.

[9] Aggravated penalties for repeat offenders are now widespread in the United States, see e.g., Ariz. Rev. Stat. §§13--1649, 13--1650; Ark. Stat. Ann. §§43--2328 through 43--2330; Colo. Rev. Stat. §16--13--101; Del. Code Ann. tit. 11, §§4214, 4215; Me. Rev. Stat. §1742; Mich. Stat. Ann. §§21.1082, 21.1083; Tex. Penal Code §12.42; Wis. Stat. Ann. §939.62.

[10] A. von Hirsch, *supra* note 7, at 85.

justice and the concept of desert to justify increased terms for recidivists.[11] By grounding his claim in a theory of justice, he insulates his theory against empirical attack. No data can refute his theory. The thesis can be refuted only by showing that von Hirsch is wrong in his philosophical and conceptual analysis.

In order to develop a contrary thesis on the bearing of recidivism on desert we shall have to develop a general theory on the relevance of both wrongdoing and accountability to just punishment. Upon having the general thesis before us, we shall interpret von Hirsch's claim as a thesis about the additional wrong allegedly implicit in repeated offenses. Interpreted in this way, von Hirsch's view is plausible but, as I shall attempt to show, incompatible with other principles we take seriously. The purpose of this discussion is not so much to refute von Hirsch's thoughtful contribution, but to use his claim as a medium for working out important theoretical points.

A. The Components of Desert. We may take as common ground with von Hirsch that punishment ought to be inflicted according to the offender's desert in committing particular criminal offenses. The components of desert are wrongdoing (which von Hirsch calls "harm") and culpability. It is also common ground that a greater degree of wrongdoing justifies greater punishment.[12] The wrongdoing of homicide is greater than a possession offense and therefore a greater punishment is warranted. We can leave aside for a moment how we "know" that wrongdoing is greater in one crime than another. The importance of the violated or threatened social interest is important, as is the proximity or the degree of danger to that interest. The grading of wrongdoing is patently an evaluative and irreducibly political issue. For the purpose of the present discussion, however, we may assume that it is possible to reach consensus on a scale of relative wrongdoing.

Now what is the relationship between wrongdoing and a judgment of culpability based on holding the actor accountable? If the actor is fully accountable, he ought to be fully punished. Yet if

[11] Compare my own critique of recidivism as it bears on capital punishment, §4.6 *supra*.

[12] A. von Hirsch, *supra* note 7, at 79–80.

his culpability is partial, he ought to be punished less. Lesser culpability justifies a mitigated punishment. This is the common experience of our legal system, as expressed in the doctrines of provocation, diminished capacity, and even earlier in the reduced penalty provided in cases of homicide *se defendendo* and *per infortunium*.[13] The analytic model underlying this scheme is that accountability for an offense, say homicide, is complete when the actor acts voluntarily and intentionally causes death.

Thus the maximum level of punishment is set by the degree of wrongdoing; punishment is mitigated according as the actor's culpability is reduced. This distinction is critical in understanding our system of criminal law. The wrongdoing of homicide is causing human death; the dimension of wrongdoing is not affected by provocation[14] or diminished capacity. Yet the actor's culpability for the wrongdoing is reduced in these cases and therefore the punishment is properly mitigated. Thus we can understand the widely held view holding a culpable accomplice liable for murder even though the person perpetrating the killing is partially or totally excused. The wrongful act of killing remains constant and each participant in the crime is judged according to his or her personal culpability.[15]

Assuming for the moment that this analysis is correct, let us ask how prior convictions affect the offender's desert. It is hard to see how a string of prior burglary convictions could increase the wrongdoing of the current burglary charged in the indictment. Of course two counts of burglary might justify a greater punishment than one. Killing two persons is a greater wrong than killing one. But von Hirsch's proposal is not to relitigate prior criminal acts, presumably already prosecuted and punished, as though they were additional counts in the pending indictment. That would be patently unconstitutional as double jeopardy.

The critical premise in von Hirsch's thesis is not only that

[13] See the analysis of culpability as a matter of degree, §5.1.3 *supra*.

[14] This is not so obvious, particularly in view of the alleged rule that the victim must actually contribute to his death. This contribution might arguably affect the degree of wrongdoing. See §4.2.1, at notes 13–14 *supra*.

[15] These issues are taken up more fully in the study of complicity, §8.6 *infra*.

diminished culpability serves to reduce punishment, but also that increased culpability may justify increased punishment. Let us assume for the moment that prior convictions increase culpability: what can we make of the thesis that added culpability justifies a greater punishment for the same act of wrongdoing? The fact is that the thesis is foreign to our experience of crime and punishment. Suppose that one Sam snatches a quarter from a child playing on the street. Assuming the appropriate intent, and absent an excuse, we have no trouble classifying this case as petty larceny and it should be punished as petty larceny. Now let us add a particularly nasty motive that makes Sam as culpable as we can imagine. Sam has no need for the quarter, but he likes to pick on children. Suppose the child was a foreigner and that Sam hates foreigners. We could go on in this vein, but it is hard to see how these nasty motives would justify an additional penalty. If the actor commits larceny intentionally and voluntarily, his accountability and culpability are complete and there is no need to inquire further into his motives. This indeed is the merit to the partial truth of the common law that the law pays no heed to the actor's motive. Better stated, the law pays no heed to criteria that make a voluntary, intentional act arguably more culpable in some persons than in others.[16]

B. Defiance as Wrongdoing. If he is arguing against the weight of tradition, von Hirsch should have some good arguments to prove that increased personal culpability merits increased punishment. There is one substantive and one evidentiary claim.[17] The substantive claim is that: [18]

[16] But note that the German law of homicide considers motive an aggravating factor, §4.5.3 *supra*.

[17] The evidentiary claim is essentially that the more often the actor is punished, the more sure we can be that he is guilty. *Id.* at 85–86. This is, at best, an argument in favor of admitting prior convictions, despite their prejudicial impact, as evidence bearing on *modus operandi.* von Hirsch confuses "greater evidence of culpability" with "greater culpability." Even if there were no difference between evidence and substance, it is hard to see why prior convictions should matter. If lesser evidence might lead to a compromise verdict, it does not follow that "greater" evidence (more than proof beyond a reasonable doubt!) should lead to increased punishment.

[18] *Id.* at 85.

A repetition of the offense following . . . conviction may be regarded as more culpable, since [the actor] persisted in the behavior after having been forcefully censured for it through his prior punishment.

It is worth noting, initially, the contradictory ways in which repeated offenses may be mustered in arguments for and against the accused. In *Robinson* and *Powell,* repeated acts of addiction and public drunkenness tended to excuse the offender, for they hinted at a "condition he was powerless to change."[19] If we change our assumptions and postulate that the actor is totally self-actuating, then he is condemned by repeated instances of addiction and drunkenness. But what is it that warrants the postulate of total self-actuation? Might we not at least have some doubts about the extent to which repeated offenders are in control of themselves? I am willing to concede that absent a valid excuse, a second offense is voluntary and the actor is accountable and should be punished again. But von Hirsch wants more than that. He claims that the second offense is even more culpable, as though somehow it were more "voluntary" than the first offense.

The key to understanding von Hirsch's argument is the statement: the offender "*persisted* in the behavior." Think of a parent who punishes a teenager who has stayed out too late. The punishment is loss of allowance for a week. If the teenager "persists" in staying out too late, the parent might raise the punishment—after all, the parent seeks compliance with the rules of the house and it might be necessary to raise the punishment in order to achieve it. This example makes von Hirsch's argument at least prima facie plausible.

But let us think more about the case of the teenager. The implication of his "persisting" is not that the offense is more culpable the second time, but that there are signs of an additional wrong of defiance against the parental authority. Suppose that after the first offense, the teenager said, "I don't care how much you punish me. I am going to stay out as late as I want to." Should the parent now wait for the second offense in order to increase the

[19] See §6.4.2 *supra.*

punishment? Perhaps a few lawyers might. But most would feel justified in setting the first punishment at an even higher level.

Punishment for offenses within the family is different from punishment in a liberal society. The impulse to punish within the family derives primarily from the need to maintain both the authority of the parents and compliance with the family's rules. If a child persists or threatens to persist in violating the rules of the house, he implicitly undermines parental authority. This is the element of defiance or "rebellion" that constitutes the additional wrong in repeated violations of the rules. Parents interested in maintaining their authority naturally resist rebellion and use whatever measures are necessary to insure compliance with the family's rules. The reason for this is not simply parental greed for authority, but a recognition that there is no viable alternative in stable family life to the authority of the *particular* parents. If they lose the capacity to enforce rules, the alternatives are either chaos or the dissolution of the family.

This rebellion against authority is what, to my mind, underlies von Hirsch's argument that a second offense deserves greater punishment than the first. If the family were an appropriate model for civil society, he might be right. But (thank God) the family is not the model for liberal society. Would we have a society in which an offender would risk an additional term in jail if he said, "I will take my punishment, but then I will go back to shoplifting"? Perhaps contrite offenders are punished more leniently, but should proud offenders be punished more severely? Is it a personal wrong to the legislature, to the courts, or to law enforcement personnel for an offender either to threaten or to commit repeat offenses? In raising this issue, we come close, in my mind, to an important difference between a liberal society, based upon the rule of law, and one species of totalitarian society, based upon the cult of personal leadership. In a liberal society, based upon the rule of law, authority is not charismatic, but formal. Legislators, judges and law enforcement personnel occupy legally defined offices: they are not entitled to react to a "persistent" criminal as though their personal authority were challenged. In totalitarian societies based upon personal leadership, on the other hand, the leadership does exercise charismatic authority, and a rejection of society's rules counts as rejection of the leader's personal authority. In these latter societies, punishment in the family may be an apt model for punishment in civil society.

By working through this analogy with the family, we have attempted to show that von Hirsch's argument is not that recidivism renders the actor personally more culpable for the same act of wrongdoing, but rather that persistent violation expresses a rejection of established authority. This is an additional wrong that arguably raises the level of wrongdoing and justifies an increased penalty. Yet this view of authority and defiance clashes with the basic premises of a society based upon formally defined offices. In a society of free and responsible adults, organized to live by the rule of formal authority, the defiant offender is punished according to what he or she does, not according to the implied threat of further disobedience.

The contemporary pressure to consider prior convictions in setting the level of the offense and of punishment reflects a theory of social protection rather than a theory of deserved punishment. The rule of thumb is that recidivists are more dangerous and that society will be better served if the recidivists are isolated for longer terms. This view raises empirical and methodological issues in gauging the dangerousness of recidivists and it poses serious ethical issues in punishing a person more severely on the basis of past crimes already once punished. These are issues that must be confronted directly, with no illusions about the camouflage offered by the concepts of retribution and desert.

§6.6.3. On the Indispensability of Wrongdoing. Our critique of the thesis that recidivists should be punished more severely would hardly have been possible without a clear understanding of the distinction between wrongdoing and attribution (culpability). This distinction enables us to isolate the way particular factors bear on the justification of punishment and to sharpen our reasons for accepting or rejecting arguments of just punishment. Though this distinction is of critical importance to the criminal law, it is virtually ignored in Anglo-American and French jurisprudence.

Soviet theory treats it ambivalently.[20] The only systems that have developed the structure of wrongdoing and attribution are the German system[21] and those of the host of other countries that have received and applied German ideas (Japan, Italy, Latin-American jurisdictions). One wonders why there is this cleavage in the world and why important insights into the nature of the criminal law should remain confined to particular legal cultures.

The answer may be that only legal systems (such as the German system) that take retributive punishment seriously would be inclined to focus on the element of wrongdoing—that aspect of criminal conduct for which punishment is imposed. So far as punishment is oriented toward the future, namely, toward deterrence and rehabilitation, legal theorists are less likely to stress the element of wrongdoing. The more complicated reason for ignoring this critical concept is that the positivist bias of French, Soviet, English and American jurisprudence inhibits theoretical work on concepts that transcend legislative and judicial decisions. The concept of wrongdoing, as well as the concomitant distinction between wrongdoing and attribution, present the foremost examples of theoretical constructs that are implicit in the criminal law as an institution of blame and punishment. It is likely to be taken seriously only when theorists turn to the criminal law as a body of ideas and practices with a reality deeper than the positive prescriptions of courts and legislatures.

Common-law jurists recognize the distinction in cases of insanity, for there the theoretical point is buttressed by a procedural form: the verdict of not guilty by reason of insanity. To develop the theoretical distinction as richly as the German scholars have done, one has to go beyond these procedural forms and recognize the general idea of being not guilty for wrongful conduct—even though this general concept finds no precise procedural expression.

[20] See §6.7.4 *infra*.

[21] On the history of the distinction in German law, see Eser, *Justification and Excuse*, 24 Am. J. Comp. L. 621, 624-629 (1976).

To assert that wrongdoing is essential in every criminal offense is to build on two conceptual claims: first, that punishment is characteristic of the criminal process; and secondly, that it is in the nature of punishment that it is imposed only for a violation of norms directing people how to conform to the law. The violation of the norm establishes the element of wrongdoing. If the norms are morally neutral, as, for example, in the case of many possession offenses, it might be plausible to use the more neutral term "unlawful" behavior. Positivists are inclined to use the term "unlawful" in all cases of wrongdoing, for their jurisprudence holds that enacted legal rules are the exclusive source of relevant norms. Yet for our present purposes, the extent to which the "law" consists of positively enacted rules is not the central problem. The issue is whether wrongful behavior should be regarded as essential to the infliction of punishment in the criminal process.

It is important that we distinguish this issue from the nominally similar question posed in a system of criminal law that collapses the distinction between wrongdoing and attribution. Fitzjames Stephen defined an "unlawful act" of homicide so as to presuppose the culpability of killing intentionally, knowingly, or with culpable negligence.[22] In this system, which merges wrongdoing and culpability, there is nothing controversial about saying that criminal punishment presupposes an unlawful act. It seems indeed to follow from the maxim *nulla poena sine lege*. The more difficult version of the question takes hold only if the concept of wrongdoing is distinguished from culpability.

What should we say, for example, about strict liability in tort or in criminal law? Is this an instance of liability without wrongdoing or without culpability? Tort damages are sometimes thought of as a form of taxation on dangerous enterprises or imposed as a "cost of doing business." This view of the sanction is compatible with the notion of liability without wrongdoing; one need not do anything wrong to incur a tax or a business cost. Yet strict liability in the criminal law could not be imposed by analogous reasoning. Being sentenced to jail—or even being censured

[22] F. Stephen, Digest of the Criminal Law §222, at 143 (1877).

by the court—cannot be thought of as a tax or as a risk of running a pharmaceutical house. The fault that need not be proved in cases of strict liability is not the fault of wrongdoing, but the fault of culpability.[23] When strict liability is imposed on a corporate officer for introducing adulterated drugs into interstate commerce, the wrongful act is the distribution of the dangerous drugs.[24] What makes the liability "strict" is that the defendant's culpability need not be proven at trial.[25] It is presumed from the violation of the norm prohibiting the distribution of adulterated drugs.

The argument that wrongdoing is essential in criminal cases, even in cases of strict liability, is derived from the nature of criminal sanctions. Condemnatory sanctions are imposed for something worthy of condemnation; that which is condemned is the wrongful act. Thus there is a critical difference between arguing that wrongdoing is essential to criminal punishment and claiming that culpability ought to be considered in justly imposing punishment. The first is a conceptual claim; the second is an argument that the absence of culpability renders punishment unjust. The conceptual argument presupposes that the notion of punishment is sufficiently determined to permit inferences about the implications of "punishing" in a particular case.

If we assume that punishment presupposes wrongdoing, there are still some troublesome questions to confront. The first is whether wrongdoing, in turn, presupposes an external element; and the second is whether the occurrence of harm aggravates the level of wrongdoing. These issues are the foci of the ensuing two subsections.

§6.6.4. On the Externality of Wrongdoing. To summarize the results of our inquiry in the first five chapters of this book, we may say that the patterns of manifest criminality and of harmful consequences support the generalization that an external element of conduct is essential to wrongdoing. The pattern of subjective

[23] On the ambiguity of "fault" and its impact on tort theory, see Fletcher, *supra* note 6, at 556–60.

[24] See United States v. Dotterweich, 320 U.S. 277 (1943).

[25] In *Dotterweich* the court relegated the issue of culpability to the "good sense of prosecutors." *Id.* at 285.

criminality poses the range of counter-examples. Yet within the latter pattern, there is some ambiguity about whether an external element is present. It is true that in the subjective theory of larceny, of burglary, of attempts, and of treason, there is no required external element that incriminates the actor. But in the subjective theories of larceny, burglary, and treason, there is an objective condition to liability—namely, that the actor "take the property of another," that he "enter a dwelling house," or that he render "aid and comfort" to the enemy. The problematic residue is the field of attempts, particularly impossible attempts, typified by the famous hypothetical problem of putting sugar in someone's coffee with the intent to kill. In the whole range of non-incriminating attempts, it is difficult to discern an external element of wrongful behavior; for in these cases the violation of the legal norm cannot be established without first inquiring into the actor's intent.[26]

Our purpose here is not to rehearse the debate between the objective and subjective theories of attempts, but rather to set that debate in the context of the broader question about the necessity of an external element in wrongdoing. An array of arguments comes into play, but it is doubtful that any of them is totally convincing. As in the earlier discussion, we can appeal to the nature of punishment, and particularly to the premise that punishment is imposed for wrongdoing. From this premise we derive the distinction between wrongdoing and attribution. The rationale of this distinction is that punishment is imposed for something that is distinguishable from the personality of the actor. This distinction supports the view that the ground of punishment (that for which it is imposed) is something external that is attributed to the actor in assessing the actor's accountability for his wrongdoing. The final step in the argument is that this external element—that for which the actor is punished—should be manifested, externally, in a violation of an objective norm regulating human conduct.

When punishment is imposed in cases of impossible attempts, the ground of punishment seems to collapse in the analysis of at-

[26] In Nowakowski, *Zu Welzels Lehre von der Fahrlässigkeit* 1958 JZ 335, the author seriously considers whether impossible attempts should be treated as crimes without wrongdoing. *Id.* at 336.

tribution. The intent to harm constitutes both the violation of the norm and the basis of attribution. Yet this is not the only possible analysis. One could argue that punishment is imposed for acting out an intent to harm; the basis for holding the actor accountable for this acting out is that he decided to form the intent and he decided to act on it. The voluntary decision, preliminary to the intent and the acting out, becomes the basis of attribution. Thus it is possible to think of the intent itself as the wrongdoing, attributed to the actor on the basis of a decision.[27]

It seems that we shall need something more than the concept of punishment in order to support the claim that wrongdoing is by its nature external and that the intent to harm is insufficient to constitute wrongful conduct. Another line of thought builds on the observation that the criminal law is characteristically concerned about preventing external harms. Even crimes of desecration entail harm to transcendent interests. Crimes such as heresy and "lusting in one's heart" are thought properly reserved for ecclesiastical or divine judgment. From this historic feature of the criminal law, one might argue that the element of external wrongdoing should be present in every case of punishable conduct. Yet this inference is hardly ineluctable, for there is no reason why punishing subjective wrongdoing might not promote the protection of life, limb, property, and national security. In fact, the rationale for inchoate offenses is precisely that they do provide more effective protection of external interests than crimes that require an element of external wrongdoing.

Oddly, it seems easier to defend the principle of manifest criminality than it is to defend a principle that criminal conduct should be objectively discernible as a violation of a legal norm. That criminal conduct be manifestly criminal might be required on a number of theories. It could be argued that conduct should be regarded as criminal only when it is of the type that paradigmatically unnerves the community. This theory would at least enable us to specify what punishment was inflicted for: namely,

[27] For a discussion of some of these issues, see Morris, *Punishment for Thoughts*, in H. Morris, On Guilt and Innocence 1 (1976).

the rupturing of social bonds entailed by unnerving and disturbing conduct.

Alternatively, the requirement of manifestly criminal conduct might be defended on evidentiary grounds, as indeed it often is in contemporary jurisprudence. It is so difficult to discern the subjective state of intending, the risks of convicting the innocent are so great, that one should arguably insist on incriminating conduct as an essential element of the prosecution's case. The difficulty with this argument is that it is hard to make a rule of preferred evidence stick; the plane of equally probative evidence—e.g., confessions, admissions—is so slick that rules of evidentiary preference invariably begin to slide.

The principle of manifest criminality is defensible; but even when supplemented by the law of homicide and other crimes of causing palpable harm, it hardly accounts for the full array of contemporary crimes. To hold the conservative line of manifest criminality, the theorist must reject the pattern of subjective criminality as aberrational. Yet the more data that must be suppressed as irrelevant, the stronger the normative principle must be. At this stage of theoretical development, it is doubtful that we have a normative rationale for manifest criminality sufficiently powerful to resist the historical momentum toward crimes of subjective criminality.

§6.6.5. **Wrongdoing and Harm.** In the preceding discussion we developed the claim that wrongdoing is an essential element of criminal conduct, but we failed to establish that wrongdoing requires an external manifestation. Thus, all we can say about wrongful conduct is that it is a violation of a valid norm prohibiting or requiring specific conduct. This formal feature of wrongdoing does not help us much, for one of the primary stimuli for our interest in wrongdoing is that the severity of punishment should reflect the gravity of the wrong. Thus we need a technique for gauging degrees of wrongdoing and that requires that we go beyond the criteria that all wrongful acts have in common.

The place to search for a scale of wrongdoing is the range of legal interests that are either violated or threatened by wrongful acts. The relative importance of these interests, ranging from life to property to peace and quiet in the neighborhood, provides a basis for ranking wrongful acts. But assessing the threatened legal interest is only a beginning. Various offenses stand in varying degrees of proximity to the same legal interest. Possessing sawed-off shotguns and intentional killing both impinge on the interest in life, but the former more remotely, obviously, than the latter. The greater the threat to the protected interest, the greater the wrong; the more remote the act, the lesser the wrong. Thus evaluating wrongdoing requires both a ranking of legal interests and a technique for estimating degrees of proximity and remoteness from the violation of the interest.[28]

Crimes defined in the pattern of harmful consequences—homicide, battery, arson—represent a simplified version of this problem. All of these offenses require an actual violation of a legal interest as a condition of liability. Yet the nature of harmful consequences, as we have defined them, raises an additional complexity. The harmful result is conceptually independent of the offender's act. In this respect, crimes in the pattern of harmful consequences are distinguishable from crimes, such as larceny and burglary, in other patterns of liability. Burglary violates the legal interest in peaceable habitation, but the violation is conceptually dependent on the act of burglarizing. It is hard to imagine someone "breaking and entering" without violating the interest at stake. But one can easily imagine would-be offenders doing everything in their power to commit murder, arson, battery or false imprisonment without the harm's actually accruing. The bullet goes astray. The time bomb designed to ignite the house does not go off. The place of supposed confinement turns out to have another exit. In all these cases, the act is complete so far as the actor's effort matters; but the crime is not complete because the harm does not accrue.

The actual occurrence of harm in the pattern of harmful consequences raises a deep, unresolved issue in the theory of criminal

[28] The same criteria inform Holmes' test for determining when an act of preparation ripens into a criminal attempt. See §3.3.2, at note 27 *supra*.

liability. If the consequences accrue, the actor is guilty of a consummated offense; if not, he or she is guilty of, at most, an attempt. The consensus of Western legal thought is to punish attempts less severely than consummated offenses. Though this is a deeply entrenched practice, it has yet to receive an adequate explanation and theoretical justification. It is not enough to argue in the vein of the preceding paragraphs that attempts are more remote from the violation than the consummated offense. That argument is convincing where an *act,* such as possessing a sawed-off shotgun, proves to be relatively remote from the violation of the legal interest. Thus it would be plausible to argue that attempts at the early stages should be punished less severely than attempts in which the actor has done everything in his power to bring about the harm. But the act in this latter category of last-step attempts is the same as the act that produces the harmful consequence. The only difference is that a causal process beyond the actor's control sometimes generates harm, and sometimes not. The problem is explaining why this factor of chance, extrinsic to the wrongful act, should influence the gravity of the wrong and the level of punishment.

It is important to see that the problem arises in cases of negligent as well as intentional wrongdoing. If negligent risk-taking issues in death, the actor might be liable for manslaughter; but if nothing happens, the negligent risk-taker is not liable at all. If she were reckless in creating the risk, she might be liable in some jurisdictions for the newly framed offense of "reckless endangerment."[29] Again we confront the question why, if the risk-creating act is the same, the fortuitous accrual of harm should matter in the assessment of punishment.

There is important work on this problem in both the Anglo-American and German literature. Yet both bodies of thought, in my opinion, reveal shortcomings. The Anglo-American literature tends to identify the problem as a matter of relative culpability.[30] It

[29] MPC §211.2 (reckless risk of death or serious bodily injury punished as a misdemeanor). The provision has been widely adopted. See e.g., Colo. Rev. Stat. §18--3–208; Conn. Gen. Stat. §53a–64; Ga. Code §26–2910.

[30] H. L. A. Hart, Punishment and Responsibility 129 ("Here a retributive theory . . .

is easy to make the claim that the actor's culpability is the same regardless of the fortuitous occurrence of harm; no one can fairly be held accountable for the playing-out of chance. Yet this claim about accountability is beside the point. For if the dimension of wrongdoing is the same in a successful and unsuccessful attempt, the classical theory would require equal punishment for both; increased punishment for the successful attempt can be justified only if the wrong is greater.[31] Thus, the issue is properly stated as whether the act of wrongdoing is aggravated by the occurrence of a harmful consequence.

This statement of the issue is accepted as a matter of course in German theory, but the approach of German authors reveals other problems. The issue is stated broadly as whether wrongdoing is manifested in acts or in results. Three distinct positions have crystallized in the German debate:[32]

1. The objective theory holding that wrongdoing is solely a matter of external results.
2. The personal theory holding that only acts are relevant.
3. The social theory of wrongdoing, which includes both acts and results.

This scheme of the conflicting schools requires an immediate clarification. All parties to the debate concur that wrongdoing presupposes a human act or omission, but they disagree on the meaning of this requirement. The objective theory holds that only the external impact of human conduct determines the degree of wrongdoing; the implicit notion of acting requires merely a manifestation of the will. In contrast, the other two theories build on the teleological theory of acting,[33] which holds that in cases of intentional offenses, the notion of acting cannot be separated from

---

is in grave difficulty; for there seems to be no difference in wickedness . . ."). *But cf. id.* at 130–31 (stating and criticizing an alternative retributive theory holding: "if he has done the harm, he must pay for it, but if he has not done it, he should pay less"); Dworkin & Blumenfeld, *Punishment for Intentions,* 75 Mind 296 (1966).

[31] See §6.6.2 *supra.*

[32] For a good survey of the issues, see Krauss, *Erfolgsunwert und Handlungsunwert im Unrecht,* 76 ZStW 19 (1964).

[33] See §6.4.3 *supra.*

the actor's goal—that is, from his intention. Thus when the personal and social theories of wrongdoing stress the relevance of acting on wrongdoing, the operative difference between their views and the objectivist school is that the actor's criminal intention is essential to a finding of wrongdoing. In contrast, the objective theory implies that the denial of intention, particularly in cases of mistake, is properly raised as an excuse—a challenge to the attribution, rather than to the wrongfulness of the act.

The difference between the objective and the two alternative theories of wrongdoing is reflected as well in the evolution of Anglo-American doctrine. The objective theory corresponds to the result-oriented mode of analyzing liability for homicide. The outer circle of liability—a human act causing death—establishes the element of wrongdoing (or the prima facie case, in English terms) and the issues of mistake and accident go to the question whether the homicide is excusable. The personal and social theories correspond to the act-oriented mode of analysis. The issue of intentional killing adheres to the determination of wrongdoing, and the category of excuses is reserved for issues bearing on the voluntariness of the act (duress, necessity, insanity).[34] The debate among these conflicting schools is worth considering in some detail. After surveying the competing arguments, we shall explain why this impressive theoretical literature fails to solve our problem on the relationship between harmful consequences and just punishment.

A. Arguments for the Three German Theories. The objective theory is supported by an array of arguments, some better than others. One argument is that the purpose of the criminal law is to prevent external harm; wrongdoing should consist, therefore, in the causing of external harm. This claim is plausible, but it is a long way from saying that harm is relevant to saying that causing harm is conclusive on the degree of wrongdoing. The burden of the objective theory as opposed to the social theory is to maintain that causing harm is all that matters in establishing wrongdoing.

Another argument to support this view is that mistakes are always raised as excuses; if so, it follows that mistakes negate per-

[34] For a review of these modes of analyzing homicide, see §4.1 *supra*.

sonal accountability rather than wrongdoing.[35] Since mistakes and the actor's intention are reciprocal issues, it follows that the actor's intention does not bear on wrongdoing. The strength of this argument turns entirely on the assumption that mistakes always function as excuses. There is little reason to make this assumption and indeed in Chapter Nine, we attempt to show that mistakes function in diverse ways, sometimes as excuses, sometimes not.

Other arguments for the objective theory are more powerful. One could well argue that the essential meaning of wrongful conduct is that it represents a danger that need not and ought not be tolerated by others. If conduct is wrongful, it should be subject to police intervention and the private right of self-defense.[36] This is what it would mean to say that the conduct is incompatible with the norms of the legal system. If this is what "wrongfulness" means, then there is good reason to say that the issue is purely objective. Whether self-defense is permissible is determined solely by the objective impact of the act. Even if created by mistake or accident, a threat to the life or limb of another is properly resisted. This argument supports the view that an intent to harm is not necessary for wrongful conduct. But, we should add, this is true only in a subclass of cases. The argument based on what may permissibly be resisted applies only to unconsummated threats and risks. It does not extend to cases in which the harm has already occurred, for after the harm is done there is no longer an issue of permissible prevention. Thus, this argument does not bring us closer to resolving the quandary whether the accrual of harm justifies increased punishment relative to a last-step attempt.

Yet another argument for the objective theory builds on the logic of violating imperatives. The premise of the argument is that wrongful conduct consists in the violation of an imperative to ab-

[35] See Engisch, *Der Unrechtstatbestand im Strafrecht* in Hundert Jahre deutsches Rechtsleben 401 (E. von Caemmerer ed. 1960).

[36] See §10.5 *infra*. Followers of the personal theory respond to this argument by distinguishing sharply between the "wrongfulness" required to render an act criminal and the "wrongfulness" required to justify necessary defense. The latter is interpreted broadly, to include any threat to a legal interest protected under either private or criminal law. Welzel 85; Stratenwerth 136. *But cf.* the critique of this bifurcation of "wrongful conduct" in Baumann 309--10.

stain from or to engage in particular acts. The law requires motorists to stop at stop signs. Suppose that a motorist does not see the sign and drives through. It is clear that he has violated the law, and that his violation does not presuppose an intent or even negligence in driving past the sign. If wrongdoing is synonymous with violating a duty, then the motorist's act is wrongful and the objective theory seems to get a grip. One might also observe that in issuing imperatives, we say simply, "Do not blow smoke in my face." It would be odd if not ungrammatical to qualify the imperative by saying, "Do not blow smoke in my face intentionally." It follows, arguably, that the violation of the imperative is an objective fact, not a matter of intentional action. There is some merit to these claims, but again it is not clear that this defense of the objective theory extends to cases in which the objective element is causing a particular harmful consequence.

A good defense of the objective theory requires a return to the harm-oriented theory of homicide. If one sees an act causing death as an evil, then it follows that wrongdoing—at least in homicide cases—consists in causing harm. But, this is a limited defense. It applies to the analysis of homicide at only one stage of history. Even if we still adhered to the harm-oriented view of homicide, we should recall that causing death was treated as an evil by virtue of the taint implicit in taking human life. It is unlikely that we could extend the argument to other crimes, such as battery and arson, in the pattern of harmful consequences.

The arguments for the personal theory are twofold. One argument derives from the nature of acting, and the other, from the nature of legal norms. Welzel developed the personal theory of wrongdoing by working through the implications of the teleological theory of acting. Wrongdoing presupposes a human act; a human act presupposes a purpose and, therefore, wrongdoing presupposes a purpose, or more specifically, the intent required for commission of the offense. The teleological theory of acting is appealing, but this syllogism hardly supports the radical claim of the personal theory that harm is irrelevant to wrongdoing. In order to make that our claim, the personal theory must draw on a theory of legal norms.

The relevant theory of norms is that the rules of the criminal law are designed not simply to avoid external harm (as the objectivists claim) but also to guide human conduct. The claim is not that norms dictate or determine human conduct, but that they guide conduct in the sense that they provide autonomous agents with reasons for acting. The critical point is that norms "motivate" lawful human conduct.[37] Wrongful conduct consists therefore in improperly motivated violations of the norm. This last step in the inference is hardly entailed by the theory of norms, for the purpose of the norms need not determine the nature of wrongdoing. But the claim of the personal theory seems to be that if the law treats human agents as autonomous agents capable of proper motivation, the theory of wrongdoing should also incorporate criteria of improper motivation.

The rejection of harm as a relevant consideration follows from the view that the law speaks only to matters that are within human control. The occurrence of harmful consequences is fortuitous, beyond the scope of human control. Therefore, the occurrence falls outside the range of legal imperatives and should not bear on the analysis of wrongdoing. If the victim's death is a condition for prosecution of intentional or negligent homicide, the fact of death should be seen as an objective limitation on liability, rather than a factor justifying either liability or the level of punishment.

Each of the arguments for the personal theory of wrongdoing invites a response. The emphasis on the nature of acting generates the frequent criticism that Welzel's theory of acting does not account for wrongdoing in cases of excessive risk-taking;[38] the wrong in risk-taking does not consist in improper motivation, but in the failure to take proper precautions. Of this problem there will be more to say in the next subsection.

The response to the argument about the nature of legal norms

[37] The prevailing German term is *Bestimmungsnorm,* see Stratenwerth, *Handlungs- und Erfolgsunwert im Strafrecht,* 79 Schweizerische Zeitschrift für Strafrecht 233, 247–48 (1963); but the infelicitous connotation of this term is that the norm determines or dictates the actor's choice to conform his conduct to law.

[38] Jescheck 167-68; Nowakovski, *supra* note 26; E. A. Wolff, Der Handlungsbegriff in der Lehre vom Verbrechen 13-14 (1964).

is to challenge the assumption that the law consists exclusively of imperatives. It is equally plausible to argue that the law consists as well of norms that specify the way particular acts ought to be evaluated (*Bewertungsnormen*). As with norms bearing on the excusability of conduct, the addressee of the evaluation-norms is not the individual citizen, but the fact-finder at trial.[39] Though this claim about supplementary evaluation-norms does not imply any particular view about the weight to be attached to the occurrence of harm in the theory of wrongdoing, it does appear to be sufficiently flexible to accommodate the popular sentiment that harmful acts constitute a graver instance of wrongdoing than acts that merely threaten harm.

It is hard to see how the debate between these two schools could be resolved by claims about the nature of law. Depending on what we pack into our assumptions about the nature of law, we can derive either the personal theory or one of its alternatives.

The social theory of wrongdoing is a synthesis of the objective and personal theories. Some supporters of the theory may be relieved to find a compromise, but the argument for the theory, as developed by Maihofer,[40] rests on deeper philosophical considerations. Welzel claimed that his theory of acting was logically prior to the law and social convention.[41] Maihofer attacked this premise frontally and developed a sophisticated thesis on the social meaning of harmful acts. The death of the victim is not simply a result separable from the act of attempting to kill. It is part of the meaning of the act. We use verbs entailing harm—killing, burning, kicking—precisely because we think of these acts in a special way. It follows from these conventions of social life that we may properly distinguish between killing and killing *manqué* (attempting to kill) in assessing the proper response of the criminal law.

The social theory has much to commend it, but we invariably crave a theory based not only on language and social convention,

[39] In the case of excusing norms, the addressee is also the legal decision-maker rather than citizen. See §10.3.4 *infra*.

[40] Maihofer, *Der soziale Handlungsbegriff*, Festschrift für E. Schmidt 156 (1961). *Cf.* Jescheck 168-71; E. A. Wolff, *supra* note 38, at 29-39.

[41] Welzel, *Studien zum System des Strafrechts*, 58 ZStW 491 (1938); H. Welzel, Um die finale Handlungslehre 10 (1949).

but also on the justice and rationality of distinguishing between last-step attempts and consummated harm. The theory may elude us, but there are still a few arguments that we might profitably consider.

Before leaving the debate among the three theories of wrongdoing, we should note the importance of our earlier work on the three patterns of liability as a medium for interpreting the conflict among German theorists. The objective theory finds its strongest support in the law of homicide and particularly in the older view that causing death was a form of desecration. The objective theory also finds a foothold in the pattern of manifest criminality, for acts that manifestly threaten harm are properly resisted by private acts of self-defense; and that perspective, as we noted, provides one interpretation of the concept of wrongdoing. The personal theory, in contrast, finds its best support in the pattern of subjective criminality, particularly the subjective theory of larceny and of attempts. If there is no requirement of manifest criminality in these cases, there is no way of discerning a wrongful act without considering the actor's intent. It is no accident that in defending his theory, Welzel refers repeatedly to the law of larceny and of attempts.[42]

The flaw in the German debate, it seems to me, is the assumption that one theory of wrongdoing must account for all patterns of liability. The objectivists assumed that homicide was the paradigm of the entire criminal law; the personal theorists assumed that attempts and other crimes of subjective criminality were representative of the whole. There is no reason to accept the premise that only one theory of wrongdoing accounts for the entire criminal law. The personal theory may be the only acceptable explanation of wrongdoing in cases of impossible attempts, but it does not follow that the same theory carries over to the analysis of homicide. The objective theory is plausible in homicide, but it obviously cannot account for crimes in the pattern of subjective criminality.

B. The Evidentiary Value of Harm. It is often argued that the occurrence of harm fulfills an important evidentiary function. If the actor has succeeded in killing, he is more likely to have ac-

[42] *Id.* at 11–12.

tually intended the death. If a reckless driver causes harm, he is more likely to have been truly reckless. Whether this be empirically true or not, it hardly generates a principled argument for differential punishment. If we are unsure about whether the attemptor actually intended the death of her victim, we should not punish her at all. Nothing undermines the integrity of the criminal law more than the thesis that partially proven guilt is equivalent to a partial offense. If the degree of proof can be traded off against the degree of the offense, then we should abandon the pretense that the state must prove guilt beyond a reasonable doubt.[43]

Further, the evidentiary thesis for differential punishment fails to account for the depth of the cultural attachment to harm as a relevant factor in assessing wrongdoing. The vein runs too deep to be explained away as sediment left by the law of evidence.

C. Harm and Remorse. A totally different approach begins with the observation that persons who inadvertently cause harm feel greater remorse than those who have "close calls." If a reckless driver goes into a skid and collides with another car, he is likely to feel different from another driver, equally reckless, whose car merely slides into an embankment. If an assassin aims, shoots and hits her intended victim, she is likely to feel different about her act than she would if the bullet had gone astray. Feelings of guilt and remorse are appropriate where harm is done, but if all is the same after as before the act, there would be nothing to be remorseful about, and the actor's feelings of guilt would make us wonder why he wanted to suffer inappropriate anguish. Feelings of remorse and guilt are closely connected with causing harm, for these feelings are part of a broader pattern of human interaction. The notions of causing harm, injuring others, feeling guilt and making amends are all part of the patterns by which human relationships are disturbed and then restored. The notion of guilt cannot be lifted out of context and fitted to cases where there is merely a risk of harm, but no concrete impact on the lives of others.

The notions of guilt and remorse, as we have outlined them

[43] For another use of this argument, see the views of von Hirsch on punishing recidivists, at note 17 *supra*.

here, are sharply different from feelings of shame, which might be appropriate in cases where there is no harm. If I contemplate killing the Pope and never do anything about it, I might feel ashamed of myself, but it would be out of place to feel guilty about my intentions. Feelings of shame are triggered by the realization that one is not the kind of person one thought one was; feelings of guilt, by acts that rupture our relationships with other persons.[44]

Now why should these notes on guilt and shame be relevant to the theory of differential punishment for causing harm? It is true that those who cause harm would be more inclined to regard a more severe punishment as appropriate and just; those who fail to cause harm would be outraged if they were punished as though they had. But what is the link between this observation about human nature and the theory of just punishment? What we need is an additional premise that would read: "Punishment is just only if it is regarded as just by those who suffer it." The way to make sense of this premise is not to think of taking surveys among inmates, but to ask ourselves whether if we were punished the same for culpably causing harm and for having a "close call," we would regard ourselves as justly treated. My assumption is that we would not; and if not, we can hardly defend treating others in a way that we would not regard as acceptable.

There are admittedly some unresolved issues in this discussion. How do we distinguish between healthy and neurotic guilt? How do we know that the feeling of deserving greater punishment if one causes harm is not an expression of neurotic guilt?[45] Why is it that criminal punishment relates more to feelings of guilt than to feelings of shame? Is it that punishment is an institutionalized means of "making amends" for harm done? If these questions are not answered adequately in this book, there may be some consolation in their being, to my mind, the deepest issues of crime and punishment.

§6.6.6. Wrongdoing, Mistakes and Accidents. The concepts

[44] For some thoughtful comments about guilt and shame, see H. Morris, *supra* note 27, at 59-63.

[45] This problem was called to my attention by Alan Dershowitz.

of risk and risk-taking are now so ingrained in legal thought that we fail to realize both how recent the emergence of the concept is, and how central it is to the way we think about negligence. Though every family of languages has an indigenous root for "intention," the Latinate term "risk" has found its way into French (*risque*), German (*Risiko*), and Russian (*risk*). Like the terms "telephone," "television" and other discoveries of the industrial West, the term "risk" transcends linguistic boundaries.

The concept of risk enables us to think about the likelihood of harm in abstract terms. We can grasp the effect of conduct—the creation of the risk—apart from the conduct itself. And once the risk is separated from conduct, we can evaluate the risk and decide whether it is socially beneficial or harmful. We can apply the utilitarian calculus, assess the potential benefits and cost, each as affected by the probability of realization, and decide whether the risk is "reasonable" or "justified."

This process of reification leads us to think of risks as a type of harm. We can formulate imperatives in which the concept of risk fills the place typically reserved for specified harm. "Don't risk injury to your neighbor." "Don't take risks on the highway." While we found it odd to say, "Don't kill intentionally," there is nothing untoward about enjoining someone against creating an unreasonable risk of death. The injunction may be vague, but the syntax is right.[46]

This way of thinking about risks carries vast implications for the theory of negligence. If the risk itself is a form of harm, then even the objective theory of wrongdoing would take the creation of an excessive risk of death, bodily injury or destruction of property as a form of wrongdoing. The problem of holding the risk-creator accountable for the wrong is a distinct inquiry. The wrongful risk might be attributed to the actor on the ground that he knew of the risk (recklessness) or that he should have known of the risk (negligence). This bifurcation of negligence into the distinct questions of wrongdoing and attribution finds an echo in the Model Penal

[46] The reification of risk is shared by both "paradigms" of tort liability explicated in Fletcher, *Fairness and Utility in Tort Theory*, 85 Harv. L. Rev. 537 (1972).

Code's structuring of negligence and recklessness. The issue of wrongdoing is captured in the question whether the risk is "substantial and unjustified";[47] the issue of attribution, in the case of negligence, by the elaborate question whether [48]

> the actor's failure to perceive it, considering the nature and purpose of his conduct and the circumstances known to him, involves a gross deviation from the standard of care that a reasonable person would observe in the actor's situation.

This wordy test simply raises the question whether the actor can be fairly blamed for not knowing of the risk.

While there is considerable debate in the German literature about the bearing of intention on wrongdoing, there is little disagreement that the dimension of excessive risk adheres to the dimension of wrongdoing. Welzel's teleological theory of acting and the "personal" theory of wrongdoing point to the same result. But the bifurcation of negligence emerged in German theory even before Welzel's challenge to the analysis of intentional wrongdoing. Engisch advanced the theory in 1930,[49] even though he later argued against Welzel's views.[50] The major difference between the analysis of intention and the analysis of negligence is that the latter is not influenced by debates about the nature of human action. In fact, one of the persistent criticisms of the teleological theory of acting is that it fails to account for the non-teleological phenomenon of wrongful risk-creation.[51]

That there are two distinct dimensions of negligence helps us clarify two doctrinal paradoxes. The first paradox, which anticipates a theme that will later concern us in detail,[52] inheres in the analogy between the claims of lesser evils and of justified risk-taking. Both require a comparison of costs and benefits; and a justi-

[47] MPC §2.02(2)(c) and (d).

[48] MPC §2.02(2)(d).

[49] K. Engisch, Untersuchungen über Vorsatz und Fahrlässigkeit im Strafrecht 344–60 (1930).

[50] Engisch, *supra* note 35, at 426-27.

[51] See note 38 *supra*.

[52] See §7.4 *infra*.

fied act is one whose benefits outweigh its costs. The paradoxical difference between the two fields is that no one is liable for the consequences of a justified risk,[53] even without knowing of the risk's justifying benefits, while the justification of lesser evils is available only to those who know and rely on the act's justifying benefit. If both issues are resolved under a utilitarian calculus, why is knowledge irrelevant in one case and essential in the other? The answer is to be found in the earlier point that in cases of negligent risk-creation, the risk itself is perceived as the harm. If the risk is reasonable or justified, there is no harm—no objective basis for liability. Without harm there is no wrongful act and therefore no basis for holding the actor accountable for wrongdoing. The actor's state of mind cannot generate liability in the absence of a wrongful act. On the other hand, in cases of lesser evils, the harm consists in the intentional commission of the offense and the claim of lesser evils functions not to negate the harm, but to justify it. The claim that will concern us later is that relying on the justifying benefit—or a justificatory intent—is essential to a valid claim of justification.[54] Though I believe that this analysis is correct, it rekindles the embers of another paradox. If the excessive or unreasonable risk is the harm, why do we require the risk of death to materialize in actual death? This takes us back to the issue that we struggled with in the preceding subsection.

Yet another paradox arises from the converse case. As there is no liability for inadvertently running a justified risk, there is also no liability for consciously running a justified risk. The actor need neither believe nor hope that harm will not occur.[55] Yet, paradoxically, if he takes the risk of a mistake, say about the age of a girl he seduces, he must act in good faith.[56] He must actually believe that the girl is overage. Why is there this difference between risks of accidents and risks of making a mistake? The paradox is

[53] *But cf.* the Continental doctrine of *dolus eventualis, supra* §6.5.1, which permits a finding of intentional wrongdoing even if the risk is minimal.

[54] See §7.4 *infra.*

[55] But see note 53 *supra.*

[56] See Caljic §10.11 ("reasonably and in good faith believed that the female person was of the age of eighteen years . . .").

resolved if we keep in mind the distinction between wrongdoing and attribution. I will attempt to show that the risk of accident is a problem of wrongdoing, as to which good faith is irrelevant. The problem of mistake, in contrast, typically arises in the context of attribution or assessing whether the actor can be fairly blamed for a wrongful act. Accordingly, good faith properly comes into play in assessing the blameworthiness of engaging in wrongful conduct.

The place to begin is with a clarification of the distinction between accidents and mistakes. To paraphrase J. L. Austin's examples,[57] if I shoot at a tree stump and the bullet ricochets and hits a man standing nearby, my hitting him is an accident; but if I shoot at what I take to be a tree stump and it turns out to be a man, my hitting him is the consequence of a mistake. Accidents occur in the realm of causation. When expected forces go awry, the result is an accident. Mistakes occur in the realm of perception. As of the moment of shooting at the tree stump, the question whether an accident will occur is as yet undetermined. But as of the moment of acting, the mistake has either been made or not. A fatalistic culture knows no concept of accident, but mistakes are universally possible. It was no accident that Oedipus killed his father and slept with his mother, but it was a tragic mistake. These differences are embedded in our syntax. Accidents "occur" or "happen"; but mistakes do not just happen, they are "made."

This conceptual work helps us see why accidents bear on wrongdoing, but mistakes usually do not. The notions of accident, risk and chance interrelate as one set of ideas. Whether an accident is negligent depends on the risk the actor created. If the risk falls below the threshold of "substantial" or "unjustified," there is no socially harmful danger in creating the risk. If there is no social danger, there is no act of wrongdoing and therefore no basis for requiring the actor to act in good faith.[58]

[57] Austin, *A Plea for Excuses*, 57 Proc. Aristotelian Soc. 1 (1956–57), reprinted in H. Morris, Freedom and Responsibility 6 (1961).

[58] This discussion assumes that the social danger of acting controls the analysis of wrongdoing. This assumption is advanced most forcefully in Soviet legal theory, which takes "social dangerousness" to be the criterion of wrongdoing. See Kurs

Mistakes, even reasonable mistakes, do not negate the danger implicit in the defendant's conduct. Suppose a witness testifies falsely that she saw the defendant at the scene of the crime. The danger implicit in her false testimony is not negated by her mistake. Suppose a man has intercourse with a woman whom he mistakenly takes to have consented to the act; the danger of forcible intercourse is not minimized by the mistake, even if it is a reasonable mistake. That the danger of the act is not affected by a mistake suggests that the wrongdoing of a mistaken act is often the same as that of the intentional act. There may be other cases, particularly larceny, when a taking by mistake is likely to be discovered and corrected, and therefore the mistake does bear on the actual dangerousness of the act. Recalling the diverse patterns of liability, we would not claim that mistakes always fulfill any particular function in the structure of liability.

We can make some useful claims, however, about the relative pervasiveness of mistakes and accidents in the analysis of liability. Accidents are limited to crimes that require a causal link between the defendant's act and the occurrence of a harmful consequence. The notion of a harmful consequence, as we defined it earlier,[59] refers only to injuries that might occur either naturally or as the result of human action. The range of consequences does not include injuries that by definition presuppose human action—as do, for example, "dispossession" of a chattel or the "giving of aid and comfort to the enemy." Accidents occur by chance, without the contribution of human action. Thus accidents occur only relative to those injuries, such as death, bodily injury and the destruction of property, that might occur either naturally or by human design. It follows that the domain of accidents is limited to crimes in the pattern of harmful consequences.

The powerful corollary of this theorem is that accidents never occur in the patterns of manifest and subjective criminality. One

(GP 1968) at 460--61; Ugol. kod. (RSFSR) §7(2) (de minimis violations, which are not socially dangerous, do not constitute crimes); §13 ("social dangerousness" as the criterion for attacks that may be resisted by defensive force).

[59] See §5.3.2 *supra*.

can take a stranger's umbrella by mistake, but one cannot "take" it by accident. One can give "aid and comfort" to someone whom one does not suspect to be a spy, but one cannot "give" aid and comfort by accident. It might inadvertently help a spy if I accidentally kill the CIA agent on his tracks, but the accidental killing is not a form of "giving" aid and comfort. One can break into a neighbor's house by mistake, but accidentally falling through the window is not an act of "breaking and entering." The reason that the concept of "accident" does not fit these crimes in the patterns of subjective and manifest criminality is that there is no element of "chance" that intervenes between the defendant's act and the occurrence of the prescribed result. And the reason, in turn, for the absence of chance is that the prescribed result presupposes an element of human conduct. If there is no "taking" or "dispossession" without a human act, these results cannot materialize by chance. All of these inferences follow from the definition of harm in the pattern of harmful consequences and the absence of harm in this sense from the other patterns of liability.

In contrast to the limited domain of accidents, mistakes occur ubiquitously across the full range of criminal offenses. They arise in cases of homicide as well as larceny, rape as well as treason. The strategies for asserting mistakes will later receive detailed attention in Chapter Nine. For our present purposes, it is important to note that mistakes as well as accidents inform the analysis of negligence. The wrongdoing of negligence attaches to the risk created; the element of accident occurs in the realization of the risk. Yet the actor might be mistaken or ignorant about the gravity and cost of the risk. The exculpatory effect of the mistake is resolved in the inquiry whether the actor "should have known" of the risk. Probing what the actor "should have done" bears on his accountability or culpability in running the risk. This evaluative question forms the core of the process of attributing the wrongful risk to its creator and holding the latter accountable for it.

If mistakes bear on the attribution of negligent risks, they also raise a question of accountability in other cases of socially dangerous conduct. Recall the case of the mistaken witness. If negligent perjury is a crime, as it is under German law,[60] how do we order the issue of negligence—as a test of wrongdoing or of attribution? So far as social danger controls the assessment of wrongdoing, it is clear that false testimony is wrongful, whether or not the witness is negligent in believing what she does. Now it does not follow from this example that mistakes always bear on attribution rather than wrongdoing. Yet in those situations where it does, we have a basis for assessing the requirement that mistakes be made in good faith. Although the good-faith requirement is not necessary, as a matter either of policy or of logic, the bearing of the mistake on culpability invites the qualification that the actor not display indifference to the social danger of his conduct. To recall the analysis of reasonable risks and ensuing accidents, indifference should not incriminate the actor if the risk that he creates is socially beneficial. It is only indifference to socially harmful, wrongful conduct that undercuts a claim that the conduct should be excused.

However illuminating these distinctions might be, they have yet to take hold in Anglo-American legal thought. The Model Penal Code lumps together mistakes and accidents in its definition of reckless and negligent risk-taking.[61] Negligence as to the consent or age of a sexual partner is the same as negligently creating a risk of death. There is always economy in over-simplification, but in this case, the reduction of mistakes and accidents to a single mold obscures important differences. Yet these differences are likely to gain appreciation only in the matrix of a clearly understood difference between wrongdoing and attribution. Though it hints at this distinction in its definition of recklessness and negligence, the code displays no interest in its structural importance.[62]

The reductionist definition of negligence in the Model Penal Code raises an important question about the range of offenses that we should call "negligent." Is there a crime of negligent statutory

[60] StGB §163.

[61] MPC §2.02(2)(c) and (d) (disregarding a risk that a "material element exists" equivalent to disregarding the risk that it "will result").

[62] Compare the collapse of putative self-defense into actual self-defense, MPC §3.04, discussed *infra* in §10.1.2.

rape simply because negligence is sufficient to negate a claim of mistake as to the age of the girl? Or should the notion of negligence be limited to negligently causing harm in crimes such as homicide, arson, battery, and destruction of property? We implicitly adopted the latter view in our earlier assertion that crimes of negligence are limited to the pattern of harmful consequences.[63] Negligence outside this pattern affects the analysis of mistakes, but not of accidents. In view of the structural differences between accidents and mistakes, it is useful to limit the term "negligence" to the analysis of the former, which implies that only offenses in the pattern of harmful consequences are committed negligently. In the end, however, the use of the word "negligence" is not as important as understanding critical structural distinctions in the analysis of liability.

§6.7. *Tensions in the Theory of Attribution.*

The concept of attribution enables us to see precisely what is at stake in the recurrent references to guilt, culpability and blameworthiness in assessing criminal liability. These terms do not raise questions of the actor's general moral worth or even of his moral wickedness in a particular situation. They pinpoint the specific inquiry whether it is fair to hold the actor accountable for an act of legal wrongdoing. Someone might be accountable for a wrongful act, say, of possessing brass knuckles, without being the slightest bit immoral. Yet there is a relationship between moral assessment and the analysis of attribution, which will receive due attention when we turn to the theory of mistake.[1]

The question of wrongdoing is resolved under the set of primary legal norms, prohibiting or requiring particular acts, as supplemented by norms of justification, which provide a license to

[63] See §5.3 *supra.*

§6.7. [1] See §9.1.1 to §9.1.3 *infra.*

violate the primary norms. The question of attribution is resolved under an entirely distinct set of norms, which are directed not to the class of potential violators, but to the judges and jurors charged with the task of assessing whether individuals are liable for their wrongful acts. The attribution of wrongdoing to a particular actor turns always on whether it is fair to hold that individual accountable for the wrongful act. The grounds for denying attribution are called excuses. We shall devote a portion of Chapter Ten to particular grounds of excusing, such as duress, necessity, insanity and mistake. At the present juncture, however, it is important to establish the conceptual distinction between wrongdoing and attribution and to explore some source of resistance to the recognition of attribution as distinct inquiry in assessing liability.

As a preliminary point, we should distinguish two senses in which one might use the concept of attribution. "Objective attribution" is the term employed in the German literature to refer to the general process of holding individuals accountable for the occurrence of harm or the acts of other persons.[2] Causation in the pattern of harmful consequences is a standard of objective attribution.[3] Chapter Eight raises two fields of objective attribution—failure to avoid harm and complicity—that fall outside the standard of causation, properly understood. Objective attribution is a necessary condition for holding a person liable for a harmful event.

Subjective attribution, in contrast, presupposes an act of wrongdoing and raises the question whether a particular individual is accountable for the wrong. Our concern in this section is subjective rather than objective attribution, and we shall understand the term "attribution" in that sense.

§6.7.1. The Descriptive Theory of Attribution. The basic tension in the theory of attribution is whether the criteria for hold-

[2] See Rudolphi in SK, preliminary notes 57–81, at 21–33.

[3] Note the concern of the California Supreme Court whether a killing committed by the victim of a felony can be properly attributed to a felon threatening the victim, Taylor v. Superior Court, 3 Cal. 3d 578, 583, 477 P.2d 131, 133--34, 91 Cal. Rptr. 275, 277--78 (1970) (defendant's vicarious liability as an accomplice dependent on whether victim's killing robber was "attributable to the intentional acts of his [other] associates . . .").

ing an actor accountable for wrongdoing are descriptive or normative. The descriptive theory is reflected in the claim that there is some single feature of all criminal conduct—such as foresight of consequences—that serves to link the actor to the wrong and justify liability. The objective theory of wrongdoing implied a version of this theory, at least as to intentional offenses.[4] The claim was that the actor's awareness was the subjective medium for attributing the wrongful act to the actor. Thus the German Code of 1871, §59, provided in its first paragraph:

> If in committing a criminal act the actor does not know of the circumstances included in the "definition" of the offense, then these circumstances are not attributable to the actor.

According to this provision, a mistake as to an element of the "definition"[5] negates not only the actor's knowledge and intention, but the attribution of the definition to the actor. The assumption is that an individual can be held accountable for the objective elements of the offense only if those elements are attributed to him. The metaphor that comes to mind is that of knowledge as a beam of light, projecting the external elements of wrongdoing onto the screen of the actor's consciousness and personality.

In our discussion of the objective theory of wrongdoing, we noted the argument that mistakes function as excuses, denying the attribution of wrongdoing. This is not true about all mistakes, and in Chapter Nine we shall show how subtle the theory of mistake can be. Yet from the proposition that mistakes sometimes function as excuses, we can hardly infer a theory of attribution free of all normative judgment. There are two major stumbling blocks to a value-free theory of attribution. The first is the problem of negli-

[4] This view was called the psychological theory of culpability (*psychologischer Schuldbegriff*), for it held that culpability—the test of attribution—consisted in a particular psychic or mental relation between the actor and the result. See F. von Liszt, Lehrbuch des deutschen Strafrechts 135–36 (10th ed. 1900).

[5] The term "definition," corresponding to the German term *Tatbestand*, is clarified in §7.4.1 *infra*. The "definition" is the set of incriminating elements of the offense that bear on wrongdoing, but it does not include criteria of justification or excuse.

gence; and the second, the problem of excuses based on overwhelming pressure or mental illness.

In the preceding section we developed a view of negligence that now serves to illuminate the problem of attribution. The wrongdoing of negligence consists in taking an excessive ("substantial and unjustified") risk of harm; attribution of the wrongdoing turns on whether the actor "should have known" of the risk. Or as the former German §59 provides in its second paragraph: if negligence is the basis of liability, then ignorance as to elements of the definition precludes attribution "only if the ignorance itself is free from fault." There is no plausible way of denying the normative dimension of these issues.[6] And thus there are only two ways of responding to the challenge posed by negligence. Either one recognizes that normative judgment is a proper basis for holding a negligent actor accountable for excessive risks or one seeks to eliminate negligence as proper ground of attribution and accountability.[7]

The theory of excuses other than mistakes provides an additional stumbling block to a value-free theory of attribution. In assessing claims of duress, for example, one cannot avoid the question whether the actor should have yielded to the external pressure. This is patently a normative issue. Yet there are various ways to maintain the illusion that claims of excuses turn on factual questions. First, one can hinge the excuse to a standard of "voluntary" conduct or the hypothetical conduct of a "reasonable person under the circumstances." It is false but plausible to argue that voluntariness is a descriptive rather than a normative standard. One might maintain, further, that the "reasonable person" represents a standard of conventionally acceptable behavior. And what is conventionally acceptable in the society is a question of fact, not of value.

With regard to the issue of insanity, there are two distinct

[6] But apparently Soviet scholars are still trying to do so. See §6.7.4 *infra*.

[7] With regard to treating culpable ignorance as a basis of attribution, see §§6.8.2 and 9.2.3 *infra*.

strategies for suppressing the normative dimension of attribution. One technique, which still prevails in the orthodox German literature, is to treat insanity as a medical question, resolved solely on the basis of expert testimony.[8] The other strategy, found notably in earlier Anglo-American thought, is to treat the insane as a class apart, subject to administrative control but not under the jurisdiction of the criminal courts. We shall take up this latter way of thinking about the insane when we turn to resistance to the concept of attribution in Anglo-American legal thought.

With this survey of the problems implicit in a descriptive theory of attribution, we should turn to the alternative, normative theory for assessing the accountability of individuals for their wrongful acts.

§6.7.2. The Normative Theory of Attribution. In the German theoretical developments of this century, two central ideas provided each other with reciprocal support. These are, first, the personal theory that claims intention as a feature of wrongdoing and, secondly, the claim that attribution or culpability is essentially a normative question. The latter theory holds that the process of attribution requires a judgment about whether the accused can be fairly held accountable for his wrongful act. The question of fair accountability is expressed in assaying whether the accused can be fairly blamed for his wrongdoing. The support of this theory is bound up with the structural position of intention in the analysis of liability. So long as intention was an aspect of attribution, theorists were easily distracted by the factual quality of assessing whether the external facts of wrongdoing were reflected in the actor's intention. By elevating the question of intention to the analysis of wrongdoing, the theory of attribution is, as it were, emptied of its factual content. Thus the soil of attribution became more hospitable to the growth of a theory of liability grounded in the normative judgment of personal accountability.

Though the personal theory of wrongdoing contributed in this way to the ascendancy of the normative theory of attribution, the

[8] See §10.4.4 B *infra.*

latter is in fact of older vintage,[9] and today even opponents of the personal theory subscribe to the normative analysis of accountability.[10] In the latter version of the theory, both the actor's intent and the normative assessment of the intent comprise the complex of judgments required for assessing accountability for wrongdoing.

If we leave aside the issue of intention, the primary normative question in assessing accountability is whether the actor could fairly have been expected to avoid committing the wrongful act. This single recurrent question unites the issues of ignorance as to excessive risk-taking, duress, insanity and mistake of law. Though the details of these issues must await our study of excuses in Chapter Ten, we can readily anticipate objections to a normative theory of attribution. The primary threat of a normative element in the law is that it undermines the positivist dream of a simple, well-defined set of rules for controlling judges and juries in their deliberations. To introduce the ultimate question of personal accountability into the law subverts the illusion of precision and liberates judges and juries to engage in moral assessment of the offender. This is a powerful source of resistance to the normative theory of attribution.

§6.7.3. **Responsibility and Attribution.** One strategy for suppressing the normative dimension of assessing attribution is to displace many of the problems of normative judgment into questions of status and capacity. This is the technique implicit in the tendency of Anglo-American theory to cultivate the concept of "responsibility" as the repository for questions that German theorists would regard as problems of attribution. Like the notion of attribution, the concept of responsibility focusses on the actor rather than on the act. Yet the difference is that the term does not function to assess whether an actor is accountable for a particular wrongful act, but whether he is "responsible" for his acts generally. The terms "responsible" and "non-responsible" are at-

[9] The seminal works were R. Frank, *Über den Aufbau des Schuldbegriffs* (1907) and Goldschmidt, *Der Notstand, ein Schuldproblem,* 1913 Österreichische Zeitschrift für Strafrecht 129, 224.

[10] See, e.g., Baumann 377--380; Schönke-Schröder-Lenckner §13, preliminary notes 113–15, at 144–45.

tributes of the actor's general condition, not of the particular way in which the act is committed. The primary instance of non-responsibility is insanity, yet the concept conventionally includes involuntary intoxication, immaturity, or infancy; and it might even be extended in discussions of negligence to include the actor's lack of capacity to perceive the risk.

Packing the problems of attribution into the concept of responsibility suppresses the normative question of accountability. The concept of responsibility invites the claim that the criminal law is applicable only to normal and responsible persons.[11] Lunatics and infants are subject to a realm of administrative regulation, as they were under the King's charge at common law. In this truncated criminal law, applicable by definition only to persons capable of acting culpably, it is easy to suppose that judgments of personal accountability play no part in particular cases.

Whether we focus on the issue of attribution or responsibility turns primarily on our theory of legal norms. To whom are legal prohibitions addressed? To all persons or only to those who violate them culpably? The answer has to be the former. It would be absurd to suggest that an involuntarily intoxicated person was not bound by the prohibition against homicide. If lunatics were once thought not to be subject to the criminal law, that view was buttressed by the belief that lunatics, like infants, were an easily discerned class of people. Now that we no longer believe that insanity is easily and conclusively determined, it is untenable to claim that the insane are subject to a different legal realm. That an insane person is excused for one act does not mean he is excused for all acts. Thus the focal point of inquiry must be the particular act and its attribution, not the general condition of the accused.[12]

§6.7.4. Guilt Without Attribution. Distinct legal systems are never alike in all respects, but comparative analysis often reveals significant similarities in national systems whose rhetoric and political ideology differ radically. A careful look at attitudes toward

[11] See, e.g., Turner, *The Mental Element in Crimes at Common Law*, 6 Camb. L.J. 31 (1936); Hall 436 n.85 ("an insane person is not bound by duties of the penal law").

[12] For further analysis of this tension in the concept of insanity, see §10.4.4 A.

attribution in recent Soviet legal theory and in Anglo-American thought reveals greater similarity than one would expect. Both systems have sought to cultivate a theory of criminal liability without a concept of attribution. A study of the Soviet effort to cultivate a theory of "guilt without attribution" is particularly illuminating; not only does it shed light on the political foundations of legal theory, but it may help us understand parallel movements in Anglo-American thought.

The years 1950–1955 have come to be known in the Soviet Union as the years of the great debate about the concepts of guilt and culpability. The debate was highly charged with political overtones; reading it today, one is impressed by the extent to which such fundamental differences could be aired publicly in the Soviet literature. Looking back on this debate in 1960, Professor Nikiforov commented that the struggle about the nature of guilt was so fierce that it was in fact "a war ending in victory for both sides, though [it was] fought in violation of all the rules of warfare and though both sides remained from beginning to end in their initial positions."[13]

The background to this debate consists of two important cultural forces. The first was the intellectual influence of German criminal theory, and in particular, the normative theory of attribution that had received ample clarification in the German literature by the late 1940s. Whatever the political relationship between Germany and the Soviet Union, German legal theories have always carried prestige in Russian intellectual circles. The debate was sparked with publication of Professor Utevsky's book "Guilt in Soviet Criminal Law,"[14] which together with other works published in the early 1950s, urged that Soviet theory adopt the normative theory of culpability and attribution.[15]

In this case, adaptation was not easy. The normative theory of

[13] Nikiforov, *Basic Principles of Criminal Legislation of the USSR and the Republics* in An Important Stage in the Development of Soviet Law 28, 34 (1960) [in Russian].

[14] B. Utevsky, Guilt in Soviet Criminal Law (1950) [in Russian].

[15] The opening salvos of the debate were fired at a colloquium of the Institute of Law in the Academy of Sciences; the colloquium centered on Utevsky's book as well as publications by Mankovsky and Sergeeva. The discussion, in all its fury, is reported at 1951(1) SGP 70.

guilt ran into frontal conflict with the growing emphasis on Socialist legality in the criminal process. With the abolition of punishment by analogy in 1958,[16] the thrust of Soviet legal theory had been to strengthen the rule of law in Soviet society. In Soviet terms, the rule of law implies the law of rules. The problem was whether the normative theory of attribution was compatible with governing the legal process by precisely defined rules that eliminated individualization and judicial discretion. The underlying fear was that the normative theory of guilt required discretionary evaluative decisions by trial judges and that this discretionary component violated the goal of regularity in the criminal process.[17]

In specific doctrinal terms, the debate revolved around two questions. The first was whether the concept of guilt could be analyzed into two components. The first component would consist of the forms of guilt or what the Model Penal Code calls the "kinds of culpability": namely, intention and negligence. The second component would consist of a general concept of culpability, which captured the essential features of these distinct forms. If there is an essential element to intent and negligence, it might be either descriptive or normative in form. From the Soviet point of view, the minimal claim is that the essential element of culpability is some descriptive element, such as a "mental state" or "psychic relationship between the actor and the deed." The bolder claim is the recognition that intentional and negligent conduct are merely necessary conditions for the normative judgment that conduct in violation of the law is properly subject to blame and punishment.

The nominalist's position in this debate held that the concept of guilt referred to the requirement either of intention or of negligence, depending on the particular statutory requirement.[18] The position runs parallel to the view advanced by Stephen, Sayre, and the Model Penal Code, all of which hold that there is no general concept of *mens rea* or culpability, but merely an array of diverse

[16] Basic Principles of Criminal Legislation §3.

[17] These fears were expressed by Piontovsky, Kaminskaya and Menshagin at the 1951 colloquium. See note 15 *supra*. See also Piontovsky, Foundations of Criminal Accountability, 1959(11) SGP 48, 54.

[18] *Ibid.*

mentes reae or "kinds of culpability."[19] In a modest retreat from this position, many writers were willing to concede that there is a general concept of culpability, but that this general concept is but the minimal common denominator, a "psychic relationship between the actor and his deed."[20]

The bolder view, argued eloquently by Utevsky, was not only that there was an essential element of culpability, but that this element had to be conceptualized as a distinct normative judgment about the blameworthiness of intentional or negligent conduct.[21] When the notion of culpability is thus abstracted from intentional and negligent conduct, it becomes a rudimentary theory of attribution. The next step in the conceptual evolution would be to see that insanity and other excuses negate this normative notion of culpability.

The distinct but related field of battle was a heated dispute about the foundation of criminal liability. The drive to strengthen Socialist legality brought into prominence the concept of the *sostav*, which is defined roughly as the "set of statutorily defined elements that rendered conduct socially dangerous and punishable under the law."[22] The notion of the *sostav* is similar to the "material elements of the offense" that we find at the foundation of the Model Penal Code.[23] The *sostav* was the critical weapon in the arsenal of those who fought under the banner of "strengthening Socialist legality." They resisted the normative concept of guilt as a "subjective" judgmental element that went beyond the rules composing the *sostav*. The rallying cry for this camp became: No liability in the absence of a *sostav*.[24] Thus fulfilling the *sostav* and not guilt or any other concept should provide the rationale for imposing liability in the Socialist system.[25]

[19] Regina v. Tolson, 23 Q.B.D. 168, 184–93 (1889) (Stephen, J.); Sayre, *Mens Rea*, 45 Harv. L. Rev. 974, 974-75 (1932); MPC §2.02(2). *But cf.* Hall 103.

[20] Kurs (GP 1968) at 404.

[21] Utevsky, *supra* note 14.

[22] Kurs (GP 1968) at 243–44; Alekseev, Smirnov & Shargorodsky, The Basis of Criminal Responsibility Under Soviet Law, 1961(2) Pravovedenie 73, 76 [in Russian].

[23] MPC §1.13(10).

[24] See Alekseev et al., *supra* note 22, at 74--75; Piontovsky, *supra* note 17, at 55.

[25] It is worth noting that there is no connection between the *sostav* and the Ger-

The opposing camp, led with great acumen by Professor Utevsky, concurred in the general principle of strengthening Socialist legality. No one was in favor of returning to punishment by analogy. Yet their view was that the *sostav* could not coherently provide the foundation for criminal liability under Soviet law. As Utevsky argued brilliantly in 1961,[26] there were two prominent instances of liability in the absence of a *sostav*. The first was liability for attempts, particularly in the early stages of preparation in which there were no overt signs of conformity with a statutorily defined offense. The second was the general field of accessorial liability: accomplices could be held accountable for the conduct of another, even though the accomplice's conduct did not satisfy a rule defining a particular offense.

If the *sostav* was not the foundation of liability, then the foundation had to be found, Utevsky argued, in the concept of guilt or culpability. In fact, the language of the 1960 Code lends support for his position. Section 3 of the 1960 RSFSR Criminal Code, bearing the heading "The Foundation of Criminal Liability," provides:[27]

> Only those persons are subject to criminal liability and punishment who are guilty (*vinovnoe*) of committing a criminal offense, that is, of engaging, intentionally or negligently, in socially dangerous conduct prohibited by the Code, . . .

This apparently straightforward provision conceals an ambiguity, which Utevsky could turn to his advantage.[28] The structure of the provision renders the following descriptions equivalent:

1. being guilty of committing a criminal offense;
2. engaging, intentionally or negligently, in socially dangerous conduct, prohibited by the code.

---

man concept of *Tatbestand* or "definition," discussed in §7.4.1 *infra*. The *sostav* covers all issues bearing on liability; the latter is limited to the prima facie case of wrongdoing. A claim of justification negates the *sostav*, but not the elements of the "definition."

[26] Utevsky, New Methods for Combating Crime and Some Questions of Criminal Accountability, 1961(1) Provovedenie 63 [in Russian].

[27] The Basic Principles of Criminal Legislation §3 contains the same provision.

[28] Utevsky, *supra* note 26, at 64–66.

Now there are at least two interpretations of "engaging" in prohibited conduct. This formula could define either the concept of an offense or the notion of being guilty of an offense. Utevsky chose the former interpretation, which implies that the notion of "guilt" is extrinsic and separable from "engaging, intentionally or negligently, in socially dangerous conduct." It follows that the foundation of liability consists not only of the elements listed in the explanatory phrase (intention or negligence, socially dangerous conduct, prohibition by the code), but, in addition, of doing all these things with "guilt." This ingenious exegesis revives Utevsky's theory of "guilt" or "culpability" as an independent dimension for assessing liability.[29]

The two debates, one about the nature of guilt and the other about the universality of the *sostav,* are intimately connected. Those who bank on the notion of the *sostav* as the fundamental concept of Soviet criminal theory hold to the indivisibility of the concept of guilt; they reject the notion of a normative concept of culpability that can be separated from the *sostav* and expressed as a judgment about the fairness of convicting in a particular case.[30] Those who agree with Utevsky that culpability or guilt is the foundation of liability must, by virtue of their position, take the view that intention and negligence are merely instances of a broader question of culpability that provides a link between the commission of the offense and the determination of individual responsibility.

The debate between the two camps goes beyond doctrinal maneuvers to encompass what the various protagonists regard as important values in the criminal process. Those stressing legality, the centrality of the *sostav,* and the view that culpability is nothing more than a psychic state, tend to argue that any other position would lead to excessive discretion and "chaos," in the courts of first instance.[31] The response, articulated forcefully in Utevsky's

[29] Utevsky makes two other solid points against the *sostav* as the foundation of liability: (1) neither Ugol. kod. (RSFSR) §3 nor any other provision of the code mentions the term *sostav,* and (2) the courts sometimes affirm the violation of the *sostav,* but nonetheless acquit. *Ibid.*

[30] See Alekseev et al., *supra* note 22.

[31] *Id.* at 85.

1961 article, is that the fixation on the *sostav* leads to insensitivity to the suspect's personal situation and the value of individualizing responsibility.[32] In the end, the debate seems to respond to the tension in all legal systems between the values of order and regularity on the one hand, and the value of individualized justice, on the other. Despite flickering resistance, the dominant view favors order and regularity in the judicial bureaucracy. The official definition of guilt or culpability, now articulated in the leading texts, is that guilt is nothing more than (1) a "mental" or "psychic state"[33] or (2) intentional and negligent conduct.[34] There is no distinct normative inquiry in the criminal process about whether the criminal act may be properly attributed to the individual suspect.

This dominant position in Soviet theory corresponds to many of the common teachings of Anglo-American commentators. There is no distinct theory of attribution, whether normative or of any other sort. Among those who share the rejection of the normative theory of culpability, there is admittedly a dispute about whether there is a descriptive essence to *mens rea*. The dominant view seems to be that there are only *mentes reae*—only specifically prohibited mental states—and no essential feature of *mens rea* common to all offenses.[35]

There is no reason to exaggerate this analogy between Soviet and Anglo-American legal theory. Yet when we turn to the theory of excuses, the converse side of the problem of attribution, we shall find again that the analogy between the two systems has some weight. The ideology that the two systems share is obviously legal rather than political. Both have a strong commitment to positivist jurisprudence, which takes the law to consist entirely in officially enacted rules. The positivist mentality resists notions like wrongdoing and attribution, which are rooted in the structure of liability rather than commands of the legislature. Yet all legal systems are in constant evolution, and the contemporary aversion to

[32] Utevsky, *supra* note 26, at 68–69.

[33] Kurs (GP 1968) at 404.

[34] Kurs (GP 1970) at 260.

[35] See note 19 *supra*. But *cf.* Turner, *supra* note 11, who argues that "foresight of consequences" is the essence of *mens rea*. Turner's synthesis was simplified by banishing negligence from the criminal law.

the theory of attribution, in both Soviet and Anglo-American jurisprudence, may be a transient phenomenon.

§6.8. *Objectivity and Subjectivity in Criminal Theory.*

One of the recurrent problems in the formation of theoretical claims about criminal liability is the limited stock of concepts and the haphazard use of the same portmanteau terms that unfold in different directions for a variety of different theoretical tasks. We have already noted the ways in which the concepts of act, intent and harm are employed without attention to the subtleties of contextual change. Yet no set of terms enjoys as much confusion as the notions of objectivity and subjectivity in the theory of liability. The question is repeatedly put, whether a standard, say of negligence or provocation, is objective or subjective. The question is perfectly appropriate, yet what is surprising is the way it is so readily answered. Leading writers, such as Glanville Williams, Herbert Packer and Jerome Hall, are quick to reply that negligent homicide is punished on the basis of an objective or external standard.[1] The implication is that this feature renders negligence a suspect basis of liability; unlike cases of "subjective fault" negligence is akin to strict liability. In other contexts "objective" and "subjective" are cast about as though they were dice with only one face of meaning. In fact they have several faces, and any discussion that fails to acknowledge this diversity of meaning proves to be loaded in favor of unarticulated and undefended theories of liability.

Before we turn to an explication of these distinct meanings of objectivity and subjectivity, we should note the high stakes that are implicitly wagered in claims about the objectivity of standards of liability. Any time a standard, say of negligence, is identified as

§6.8. [1] Williams 102; Packer, *Mens Rea and the Supreme Court*, 1962 Sup. Ct. Rev. 107, 144; Hall 120.

"objective" the implication is that the standard could not serve as a proper ground for blaming the particular individual to whom the standard is applied. Objective standards are identified as "social" rather than individual standards. If fault is found according to an objective standard, the implication is that the fault is "social" rather than individual. It follows that some injustice to the individual is inherent in the criminal law, for, as Holmes argued, the law "undoubtedly treat[s] the individual as the means to an end, and use[s] him as a tool to increase the general welfare at his own expense."[2] Thus if the criminal law must be justified on this ground, there is nothing particularly disturbing about standards of strict liability, the felony-murder rule, and other devices that might be insensitive to the actual desert of the offender. All of these devices are like objective standards of liability, for they "sacrifice the individual to the general good."[3] It follows from this account of the criminal law that the only sound rationale for punishment is social protection, not the distribution of punishment according to individual culpability.

Thus, what begins as a semantic dispute about the nature of objectivity and subjectivity in the criminal law carries us to the deepest questions about the rationale of punishment, the possibility of respecting the offender as an end rather than a means, and the prospect of reconciling the demands of social protection with justice to the individual accused.

In the discussion that follows, we shall seek to expose the fallacy in Holmes' utilitarian theory of criminal punishment. It does not follow that the law could not be recast to conform with Holmes' theory of social protection as the rationale of punishment. Indeed the rise in strict liability since the writing of *The Common Law* provides partial confirmation of Holmes' utilitarian theory of law.[4] Yet Holmes proposed his theory as an account of the common law as it had evolved up until the late nineteenth century, not as a reformist program to convert the law into an instrument that

[2] Holmes 46–47.

[3] *Id.* at 48.

[4] For a utilitarian theory of criminal sanctions relying on the rise of strict liability, see B. Wootton, Crime and the Criminal Law 47–51 (1963).

"sacrificed individuals to the general good." Thus the critical question is whether Holmes' theory of law is supported by the data available to him.

If we can establish that injustice to the individual is not inherent in the use of so-called objective standards, then we can isolate the normative question whether some injustice is warranted in view of overriding social goals. The aim is to assay these normative issues more clearly, without the beclouding effect of the Holmesian argument that objectivity and injustice flow from the nature of law and legal rules.

Our conceptual work on the distinction between objective and subjective standards will eventually take us back to the theme of the preceding sections, namely, the distinction between wrongdoing and attribution. The point that will emerge is that confusion about the objective nature of legal standards in the Anglo-American tradition is bound up with the failure to recognize and to cultivate the distinction between wrongdoing, on the one hand, and attribution and accountability on the other.

§6.8.1. **Utility and Objective Standards.** At least four different ideas interweave in the contrast expressed by the terms "objective" and "subjective." Note the following contrasts:

1. "Objective" standards are "standards of general application."[5] "Subjective" standards by implication take "account of the infinite varieties of temperment, intellect and education which make the internal character of a given act so different."[6]

2. "Objective standards" are external; they apply regardless of whether the actor thinks he is doing the right thing; "subjective" standards focus on the actor's state of mind.

3. The question of wrongdoing is an objective standard, for it focusses on the act in abstraction from the actor; the issue of attribution is subjective in the sense that it focusses on the actor's personal accountability for wrongdoing.

4. Standards are objective if they are factual; subjective, if they require a value judgment.

[5] Holmes 108.
[6] *Ibid.*

The first two contrasts between "objective" and "subjective" liability find their genesis in Holmes' influential work and therefore we shall focus on these two in refuting Holmes' thesis that objective standards entail a utilitarian theory of law. Both of the first two contrasts are designed to establish that objective standards in the law are logically inescapable. The way Holmes sets up the contrast, he is unquestionably right. Standards must possess some generality; a standard hewn to the unique attributes of each person would be no standard at all.

Holmes supposed that general standards made no "attempt to see men as God sees them."[7] It is hard to know what Holmes had in mind in drawing this distinction between divine and human judgment. An omniscient God may know everything about us, but it does not follow that God passes judgment by using a standard individually cut to the person to be judged. All judgment, whether divine or human, requires the application of standards; censure and condemnation are incoherent unless the censured behavior falls short of a standard. Thus, as used in Holmes' first contrast, the term "objective" is redundant. All standards are, to varying degrees, general. And there is nothing in the process of judging or the application of standards that supports a utilitarian theory of law.

Holmes' case for a utilitarian theory of law finds critical support in the second dichotomy between objective or external standards and those that are rooted in the actor's state of mind. As indicated by Holmes' opinion in the leading case of Commonwealth v. Pierce,[8] the alternative precluded by an objective standard would be one that took the defendant's own view of his conduct as controlling. In *Pierce,* the defendant, who was practicing publicly as a physician, had caused the death of a patient by applying kerosene-soaked flannels to her skin. Concluding that the standard of liability was "external," Justice Holmes wrote that the question was whether the treatment would have been "reckless in a man of [reasonable] prudence."[9] In the context of the case, however, it is

[7] *Ibid.*
[8] 138 Mass. 165 (1884).
[9] *Id.* at 176.

clear that all Holmes was concerned about was whether the defendant's view of the treatment would constitute a good defense. The point of saying that the standard was "external" was to stress that good faith was not a defense and that the defendant might be guilty even though he thought he was doing the prudent thing.

The analogous question in cases of provocation, duress and other excuses would be whether the defendant's view of the pressures on him should control the assessment of his behavior. Is it sufficient to reduce murder to manslaughter that the defendant merely says that he felt provoked? Or is it sufficient to excuse perjury that the witness says that she feared that if she told the truth, the defendant in the case would kill her? Obviously not. No one has ever contended that adequate provocation is identical with "feeling provoked" or the defense of duress with "feeling coerced." The subjective state of feeling provoked or coerced is a necessary condition for the exculpatory claim, but it is hardly sufficient. The additional element required is whether on all the facts, the party yielding to the feelings of provocation or coercion can be properly blamed for not resisting the external pressure. One way to express this inquiry into the blameworthiness of the conduct is to say that the standard of judgment is objective or external.

There is no incompatibility between "external" standards and personal culpability in running an excessive risk or yielding to external pressure. In the way Holmes and his followers think of these matters, however, there is a basic dichotomy between external standards and those that focus on the "personal guilt" of the offender. Packer distinguishes, for example, between subjective fault and objective fault. Knowledge is an example of the former, presumably because knowledge is a subjective state. A judgment that the actor should have known of an excessive risk is an instance of "objective fault."[10] It is objective because the standard is "external"; for Packer, this means that negligence is not a form of *mens rea*. These views, expressed in one of the important books of the 1960s, reveal how close our thinking still is to Holmes' theory

[10] Packer 128.

that personal culpability was equivalent to "the condition of a man's heart or conscience."[11]

The thesis that knowing and intentional acts are authentic instances of culpable conduct, but negligence is anomalous as an external standard, conceals a confusion between "being culpable" and "feeling culpable." That one act with a sense of guilt—with knowledge that one is doing wrong—is neither necessary nor sufficient for culpability. The state of the actor's mind or conscience is a factual claim. Guilt, fault and culpability are normative judgments, based on an evaluation of the actor's conduct and state of mind. To reason from a premise about the actor's intent to a conclusion about his fault, culpability or blameworthiness, we need this additional premise:

> If someone is acting wrongfully and he believes that he is doing wrong, then he is culpable for what he is doing.

Though this proposition is generally true, it is defeased by the full range of excusing conditions, including duress, necessity and insanity. What the actor thinks or believes hardly entails culpability in violating the law. If the act is beyond her control—if her "will is overborne"—subjective awareness of wrongdoing is hardly sufficient for fairly blaming the actor. The only way to rescue the concepts of "guilt" and "fault" from the implications of excuses is to retreat into a purely descriptive theory of culpability. A descriptive theory, however, yields the paradoxical result that someone might be "guilty" of the offense, but nonetheless acquitted by virtue of a valid excuse.

Once the normative dimension of culpability comes into focus, the difference between intentional and negligent wrongdoing no longer appears critical. Judging both forms of acting as culpable requires normative assessment in the light of possible excusing conditions. There may be some clear cases of intentional killing, where the normative question is easily resolved. But, there are also cases of negligent risk-taking where it is equally clear that the actor should have been more attentive to the risk. There might be

[11] Holmes 50.

more controversy about inadvertent risk-creation than there is about most cases of intentional wrongdoing, but this difference of degree should not obscure the commonality of normative judgment as the foundation for judgments of personal accountability.

Holmes' implicit strategy is to adopt the psychological or descriptive theory of guilt by equating the latter with the "condition of a man's heart or conscience."[12] With this theory as his target, Holmes then rejects the requirement of guilt and blameworthiness in particular cases. There is no doubt that the psychological theory of guilt ought to be rejected, but Holmes' mistake consists in not considering alternative theories for properly holding individuals accountable for their wrongdoing. If he had considered these alternatives, he might have tempered his commitment to the calculus of utility as the only rational account of the criminal law.

The argument of this book is precisely that there is an alternative mode for assessing individual culpability and accountability for wrongdoing. That alternative mode is expressed in the claim that the analysis of liability consists of both an objective and a subjective dimension. The objective dimension focusses on the act and, in some cases, on the harm that the actor causes. The subjective dimension focusses on the actor and the question whether the particular actor is accountable for the act of wrongdoing. The assessment of attribution and accountability obviously requires the application of standards to the particular situation of the actor. As worked out more elaborately in the theory of excuses, the standard has a variety of forms, but it always recurs to the same normative question: could the actor have been fairly expected to avoid the act of wrongdoing? Did he or she have fair opportunity to perceive the risk, to avoid the mistake, to resist the external pressure, or to counteract the effects of mental illness? This is the critical question that renders the assessment of liability just. And when sanctions are justly imposed, there is no need to assume, as does Holmes, that the determination of liability sacrifices innocent individuals.

This critique of Holmes is not designed to depict the criminal law as a system that is oblivious to the utilitarian value of pre-

[12] *Ibid.*

venting harm. The critical distinction, as Rawls, Hart and others have reminded us, is the difference between the system of punishment as a whole and the determination of liability in individual cases.[13] The system of enacting rules and punishing those accountable for violating them serves the interests of the community. If it did not, we would seriously have to consider alternatives. But from this systemic value, it hardly follows that "justice to the individual is rightly outweighed by the larger interests on the other side of the scales."[14] In the shadow left by Holmes' utilitarian theory on Anglo-American criminal justice, this distinction between the system and the individual case remains unperceived and unappreciated.

§6.8.2. Justice and Attribution. If the law ignored the question of attribution, namely, the question whether individuals were properly held accountable for their wrongful acts, the criminal law undoubtedly would generate some unjust decisions. If it were true that the only relevant norms of the legal system were those of wrongdoing, injustice would be inescapable in cases in which individuals could not but violate the law. The insane would be punished like the sane; those who acted under duress would be punished like those who acted freely. If this were the English common law, one might indeed need a utilitarian theory in order to make sense of the systematic indifference to the accountability of individual defendants. Yet this is not the law and it never has been the law of any civilized society. Even Holmes qualified his broad claims to recognize excuses in cases in which "a man has a distinct defect of such a nature that all can recognize it as making certain precautions impossible."[15] Thus in the analysis of negligence, the range of excuses should include blindness, infancy, and insanity. Though Holmes did not discuss the point, these excuses should not be interpreted as exceptions to the general standards of liability. There are not two standards: one for the sane and the other for the insane. Rather these questions of excusing violations of

[13] See §6.3.2 *supra*.
[14] Holmes 48.
[15] *Id* at 109.

the standards have to be seen as a supplementary set of norms that permit a judgment about whether a violation of the prohibitory norm should be attributed to the particular offender.

Despite these tentative probings, Anglo-American legal theory fails to cultivate the distinction between the objective dimension of wrongdoing and the subjective dimension of attribution. The assumption is that if excessive risk-taking is an objective standard, then negligence must be an objective and not a subjective issue. There is no serious consideration of combining objective and subjective criteria in a more complex theory of liability. But there is nothing in the nature of the law that precludes a two-tiered process of legal analysis. The question of wrongdoing is governed by "standards of general application." The question of attribution might properly be analyzed with a full consideration of individual differences and capacities.

The opposition to the distinction between wrongdoing and attribution springs from many jurisprudential sources. It thrives on the positivistic theory that the law consists of nothing but legislative commands or, in the terms that we have used, in directives that govern conduct. There is no room in this theory of law for norms that govern the just attribution of wrongdoing to particular individuals.

The bias against the distinction between wrongdoing and attribution also thrives on an empiricist view of the law, which identifies the law with the set of discrete decisions rendered by officials of the system. In Holmes' own influential definition: The law is "what the courts will do in fact." [16] There is an important link between this view of the law and the failure of *The Common Law* to recognize the distinction between wrongdoing and attribution. To appreciate the concept of wrongdoing, one must have a sense of the reality of legal constructs that goes beyond "what the courts do in fact." Wrongdoing that is excused and therefore not attributed to the defendant does not generate a conviction. It no longer entails a for-

[16] Holmes, *The Path of the Law*, 10 Harv. L. Rev. 457, 460–61 (1896) ("The prophecies of what the courts will do in fact, and nothing more pretentious, are what I mean by the law").

feiture of goods. Apart from the case of insanity, with its special verdict, there is no functional difference between a finding that the defendant's act was wrongful, but excused, and finding it was not wrongful at all. An empiricist bias is likely to make one hostile to distinctions that lack concrete procedural manifestations. A wrong that is not punished is like a right that is not enforced. Lawyers with an empiricist bent are uneasy about both.

The resistance to individualized or subjective standards of attribution derives from ostensibly different philosophical premises. Even if the distinction between wrongdoing and attribution were properly acknowledged in the Anglo-American tradition, there would be some difficulty comprehending how the process of attribution could take full account of individual differences. One source of resistance to individualized standards of judgment is the fear that if the process of judgment is individualized, the standard of judgment would collapse. This is a recurrent feature of the discussions about the characteristics of the defendant on trial that are to be considered in defining the reasonable person. If the defendant's head injury or impotence is considered in assessing the likely behavior of a reasonable person, then why not consider his irascibility, greed, jealousy or even his wickedness as a person? If the reasonable person were defined to be just like the defendant in every respect, he would arguably do exactly what the defendant did under the circumstances. Thus the standard of judgment collapses into a description of the particular defendant.

This argument finds nourishment in two features of Anglo-American jurisprudence. The first is the unresolved anxiety about sociological and psychological determinism that leads many people to believe *tout comprendre, c'est tout pardonner.* If we know everything about the defendant, we will invariably excuse him. Therefore if we make the standard of judgment too particular we shall have to excuse or mitigate the crime.

Closely related is the failure to attend closely to the types of character traits that properly subject wrongdoers to judgments of blame. The obvious difference between the irascible man and the impotent man is that, absent a documentable psychological impediment, we properly expect people to control their anger as we expect them to control greed and jealousy. Therefore persons who are irascible, greedy or given to jealousy hardly warrant preferential treatment in the assessment of their conduct. These are character traits for which people are properly held accountable, not excused. Yet no one is to be blamed for impotence, and therefore it is a feature of the defendant that must be considered in assessing whether he was adequately provoked by taunting or teasing related to his impotence. These comments do not purport to be an exhaustive analysis of the vices for which we are held accountable as contrasted with the impediments that mitigate and excuse our wrongdoing. I wish to point out merely that the subject of attribution cannot properly be considered if one ignores the subject of moral accountability. Yet the subject is generally ignored in the Anglo-American literature, and that is one of the factors leading to confused sentiments about the impossibility of individualized judgments of attribution.

A further source of resistance to individualized standards in the law is the sensible point that the law must classify cases roughly; people are either liable or not, and therefore there is no way to recognize "the infinite variety of temperament, intellect and education which make the internal character of a given act so different in different men."[17] It is true that in practical terms there is a limit to the capacities of the legal system to recognize grades and degrees of culpability.

The law functions by setting a minimum threshold of accountability as a condition for attributing wrongdoing. It is obviously easier for some to comply with the law than for others. For those who can avoid wrongdoing more easily and yet engage in criminal or tortious behavior, the minimum threshold of liability is readily met and easily surpassed. For others, the minimum level of accountability may be barely satisfied. So long as people are excused who fall below the minimal criteria for attributing wrongdoing, there is no reason to believe that ignoring individual differences generates injustice.

[17] Holmes 108.

Chapter Seven
The Structure of Wrongdoing

§7.1. *Introduction.*

Chapter Six might well be read as an extended essay with one point in mind; to establish that there is at least one structural principle immanent in the criminal law, the distinction between wrongdoing and attribution. In this chapter our inquiry turns to the inner structure of wrongdoing. We shall attempt to show that wrongdoing consists of two dimensions, one that we shall call the "definition of the offense" and another that we familiarly call "justification." A wrongful act is one that satisfies the definition of the offense and that is unjustified.

We shall approach this substantive distinction by working initially with its procedural precursors. For centuries, lawyers on the Continent spoke of the distinction between the inculpatory case and the exculpatory case; lawyers in the common-law tradition referred, and still refer to the prima facie case and affirmative defenses. This distinction comes to bear in determining a range of procedural burdens: the burden to plead in the indictment, the burden of going forward with the evidence, and, most importantly, the burden of persuasion.

This attempt to allocate the burden of persuasion in criminal cases generated considerable sensitivity to the distinction between the incriminating allegations of the prima facie case and the exculpatory claims of justification and excuse. The felt distinction between these categories of issues provides a procedural analogue to the substantive distinction between the definition of an offense and a justification for violating the norm underlying the definition. The twist of history is that this important distinction was lost in the movement toward the prosecution's bearing the risk of residual doubt on all substantive issues. Though this movement is sound, the implication is that the substantive distinction between definition and justification no longer finds expression in procedural forms.

The agenda of this chapter consists of three distinct inquiries. First, we shall explore the effort in eighteenth- and nineteenth-century Western courts to allocate the burden of persuasion in criminal cases. Secondly, we shall examine and explicate the movement toward abolishing this process of allocation and requiring the state to disprove all allegations bearing on the culpability of the accused. Finally, we shall return to the distinction between definition and justification and demonstrate its importance in assaying a number of critical issues in substantive criminal theory.

§7.2. *The Problem of the Burden of Persuasion.*

Contemporary practices in allocating the burden-of-persuasion can be described only as a jumble of idiosyncracies and ad hoc judgments. If we take a broad comparative view, we find that on some issues, such as self-defense,[1] duress,[2] and insanity,[3] there is a divi-

§7.2. [1] For the rule that the defendant must prove self-defense by a preponderance of the evidence, see Commonwealth v. Carbonetto, 455 Pa. 93, 314 A.2d 304 (1974); Wilson v. State, 261 Md. 551, 276 A.2d 214 (1971); Pompe, *La preuve en procédure pénale,* 1961 Revue de science criminelle 269, 282–83; 1 Bouzat & Pinatel §293, at 365; 2 *id.*, §1183, at 1129 n.1; Merle & Vitu 442. For authority that the prosecution

sion of authority in the common-law world and a corresponding taking of sides by European jurists. On other matters such as the claim of authorization to engage in regulated economic activity, the common-law courts tend to impose the burden of persuasion on the defendant.[4] At the opposite pole, Continental courts assign matters of authorization and license to the prosecution's charge.[5] Some jurisdictions, such as the Federal Republic of Germany, almost universally give the defendant the benefit of the doubt in issues bearing on liability;[6] other jurisdictions, particularly some states in the United States, still require the defendant to bear the burden of persuasion on dozens of issues bearing on wrongdoing as well as culpability.[7]

---

must bear the risk of residual doubt, see Commonwealth v. Rodriguez, Mass. Adv. Sh. 1864, 352 N.E.2d 203 (1976) (relying on *Mullaney*); State v. Hankerson, 288 N.C. 632, 220 S.E.2d 575 (1975) (relying on *Mullaney*); Regina v. Lobell, [1957] 1 All E.R. 734 (Crim. App.); Judgment of November 13, 1885, 7 Rechtsprechung 664; W. Stree, In Dubio Pro Reo 19–21 (1962).

[2] *Compare* Roy v. Commonwealth, 500 S.W.2d 921 (Ky. 1973) (burden of proof on defense) *with* Moore v. State, 137 Ga. App. 735, 224 S.E.2d 856 (1976) (burden on prosecution to disprove duress beyond a reasonable doubt). *Cf.* Lynch v. Director of Public Prosecutions, [1975]. 1 All E.R. 913, 91 (H.L.) (opinion of Lord Morris assuming the burden of disproving duress on the prosecution).

[3] On the breakdown of jurisdictions in the United States, see Commonwealth v. Kostka, Mass. Adv. Sh. 1608, 1624 nn.8–9, 350 N.E.2d 444, 453 nn.8–9 (1976); *cf.* 2 Bouzat & Pinatel §1183, at 1129 n.1 (expressing disapproval of a decision that ambiguously suggests the burden should be on the prosecution).

[4] E.g., Regina v. Oliver, [1943] 2 All E.R. 800 (Crim. App.) (defendant required to prove that he was licensed to sell sugar as a wholesaler); People v. Boo Doo Hong, 122 Cal. 606, 55 P. 402 (1898) (license to practice medicine); Rossi v. United States, 289 U.S. 89 (1933) (posting bond to operate a still).

[5] Though there are numerous provisions regulating the practice of the professions and use of titles, e.g., StGB §§132 & 132a, there is no suggestion, so far as I can tell, of a possible shift in the burden of persuasion.

[6] Jescheck 114; W. Stree, *supra* note 1, at 19–22. Exceptions include (1) amnesty provisions, which are regarded as extraordinary intervention in the criminal process, Judgment of April 22, 1921, 56 RGSt. 49, endorsed in Schwartz, *Das Grundgesetz in strafrechtlicher Praxis*, 1950 NJW 124, 125; (2) the defense of truth in libel cases, StGB §186.

[7] The N.Y. Penal Law, enacted in 1965, includes the following prominent provisions imposing the burden of persuasion on the defendant: §40.00 (duress); §40.05 (entrapment); §40.10 (renunciation of an attempt); §125.25(1)(a) (provocation as mitigating factor); §125.25(1)(b) (causing suicide as mitigating factor); §125.25(3) (defense to felony-murder rule).

If this haphazard pattern did not reveal the poverty of contemporary theory on the burden of persuasion, we need only examine two recent decisions by the United States Supreme Court. In 1975 the Supreme Court held that it was unconstitutional for a state to require a criminal defendant to prove provocation in a homicide case;[8] but in 1977 the Supreme Court upheld a state statute requiring the defendant to prove "extreme emotional disturbance" in order to mitigate a charge of murder to manslaughter.[9] The latter issue is the successor to provocation in the Model Penal Code[10] and the legislative revisions that have followed the code.[11] The two cases appeared to be indistinguishable, but five Justices on the Court managed to find a distinction. In *Mullaney,* the 1975 case, the issue of provocation was invoked to negate the prosecutorial allegation of malice, but in *Patterson,* the 1977 case, the state statute defined murder simply as an intentional killing; extreme emotional disturbance constituted an "affirmative defense" because it did not negate any specific element of the prosecution's case.[12] Thus the Supreme Court held that demands of due process were finely honed. If a state adopts the common-law view that an intentional killing is a species of killing with malice, it may not require the defendant to prove provocation; if the state concludes that the concept of malice is redundant and eliminates the term from its definition of murder as intentional killing, then it has the option of requiring the defendant to prove either provocation or extreme emotional disturbance. These two decisions cannot be explained by a change in the personnel of the Court or by one or two Justices' changing their vote. Four Justices who voted to reverse in *Mullaney* found the wedge between formally negating and not negating malice wide enough to accommodate a constitutional distinction. This flight into formal reasoning betrays a radical un-

[8] Mullaney v. Wilbur, 421 U.S. 684 (1975).

[9] Patterson v. New York, 432 U.S. 197 (1977).

[10] MPC §210.3(1)(b).

[11] E.g., Hawaii Penal Code §702(2); Ky. Rev. Stat. §507.020(a).

[12] N.Y. Penal Law §125.25(1)(a). The section refers to the defense as "affirmative defense," but this does not appear to be critical to the Court's reasoning in *Patterson.*

certainty, almost an anxiety, in approaching the problem as a matter of principle.

The contemporary confusion reflects the transition from an older consensus toward an uncertain future. The place to begin, then, is with the more uniform pattern that prevailed in nineteenth-century efforts to distinguish the prima facie case from affirmative defenses. French, German and common-law courts once found it relatively easy to distinguish between these two categories. The consensus was that the defense had to prove self-defense, insanity and other issues that we still call "affirmative defenses."[13] Our first task is to explore how this system worked and probe its ideological underpinnings.

§7.2.1. The Private Law Style. To understand the nineteenth-century perspective on the burden of persuasion, we have to turn to a study of the structure that lawyers of the time perceived as immanent in criminal disputes. At the midpoint of the century, the run of Western courts and scholars spoke of the burden of persuasion in criminal cases in an idiom borrowed from private litigation. They conceived of the criminal process as a dispute divisible into an inculpatory case resting on the prosecutor, and an exculpatory case resting on the accused.[14] To understand how this system worked, and to provide a background for movements toward greater protection of the accused in this century, we should turn to a study of the ideas underlying allocation of the

[13] E. Bonnier, Traité des preuves 22 (5th ed. 1888); A. von Feuerbach, Lehrbuch des peinlichen Rechts §86, §90 (insanity), §568 (self-defense) (11th ed. 1832); F. Wharton, Criminal Evidence 252–69 (9th ed. 1884); H. Kelley, Criminal Law and Practice 131 (1876); some nineteenth-century German writers and American judges perceived a distinction between self-defense and insanity; the latter, they said, was inconsistent with the defendant's criminal intent; thus one could expect the prosecution to establish the defendant's sanity beyond a reasonable doubt. J. Glaser, Lehre vom Beweis 90–93 (1883); 2 H. Zachariae, Handbuch des deutschen Strafprocesses 416–17 (1868); Hopps v. People, 31 Ill. 385 (1863); People v. Garbutt; 17 Mich. 9 (1868); State v. Bartlett, 43 N.H. 244 (1861).

[14] A. von Feuerbach, *supra* note 13, §568 and §570; H. Zachariae, *supra* note 13, at 416–17; Bonnier, *supra* note 13, at 22. For additional details, see Fletcher, *Two Kinds of Legal Rules: A Comparative Study of Burden-of-Persuasion Practices in Criminal Cases*, 77 Yale L.J. 880, 899–901 (1968).

burden of persuasion in private disputes and an examination of the way these ideas once influenced the criminal process.

The formal basis for allocation of the burden of persuasion in private litigation is the seemingly logical guideline expressed in the prestigious Latin phrase: *ei incumbit probatio qui dicit; non qui negat.*[15] The burden of proving a fact rests on the party who asserts it, not on the party who denies it. A corollary maxim provides a straightforward rationale for imposing the burden of persuasion on the defendant: *reus excipiendo fit actor.*[16] Matters of exception are to be proved by the defendant.

Underlying these maxims is the assumption that legal issues follow a well-defined logical structure. Expressed in the maxims from two different perspectives, the structural pattern is one of rule to exception. Relying upon a rule, a party comes forth as the proponent of the issue, and accordingly he must bear the burden of persuasion. In response to the asserted rule, the opposing party may do one of two things: he may challenge the facts rendering the rule applicable, or he may go outside the rule and argue that despite the rule's factual applicability, an additional consideration avoids the rule's legal impact. Thus, if a plaintiff asserts that a debt is due and unpaid, the defendant may either challenge the existence of the debt or he may argue that despite the debt he is not liable—say, by reason of the statute of limitations. On the former move, the defendant retains the posture of challenging the factual applicability of the rule requiring debtors to pay their debts; as an opponent to the rule, he benefits from the plaintiff's bearing the burden of persuasion. On the alternative move, the defendant interposes an exception, namely, the statute of limitations, to the rule of liability for one's debts. By bringing forth a reason for not applying the rule, he assumes the mantle of the proponent. By the logic of the Latin maxims, he must then persuade the trier-of-fact of the facts supporting this exception.

This logical scheme for relating issues as rules and exceptions confronts an immediate difficulty: how does one know whether a specific issue is part of the rule or an exception to the rule? If the

[15] The maxim is traceable to Paul, Lib. LXIX, Ad Edictum; Justinian, Digest 22.3.2.

[16] Ulpian, Lib. IV, Ad Edictum; Justinian, Digest 44.1.1.

rule on the statute of limitations were to read, "debtors must pay all debts enforceable under the statute of limitations," the defendant who asserted the applicability of the statute would be merely denying one fact necessary for applying the rule; by denying that the claim was "enforceable under the statute," he would have the posture of an opponent to the rule's factual applicability and would enjoy the better position on the burden of persuasion. By changing the wording of the rule, one can translate the statute of limitations from an exception into a premise for applying the rule. To overcome this difficulty, one must have recourse to an authoritative formulation of the applicable legal rule. Only if the formulation of a rule is given, can one specify whether an issue is an exception to the rule, rather than a premise for the rule's application.

The individuality of legal systems is expressed in their quest for authoritative formulations of the rules of liability. Civilian judges, working with law codified at its core, express the spirit of their system by relying on applicable code provisions to formulate issues. German scholars, for example, have worked out an elaborate scheme for determining whether, according to the code, an issue is an element of the rule or an exception to it.[17] In contrast, common-law jurists have sought to classify issues by interweaving the task of allocating the burden of persuasion at trial with the task of allocating the burden of pleading prior to trial.[18] The structured common-law system of pleading, with its rigid paths, was admirably suited to distinguishing rules from exceptions, denials from avoidance. To raise an issue in defense, the defendant had to choose either a plea in denial (general denial or specific traverse) or one of confession and avoidance. On the former plea, he was the opponent on the facts; on the latter, he appeared as the proponent of a new issue—an exception to the rule advanced by the plaintiff. To administer this system of defensive tracks, the

[17] For details on this point, see Fletcher, *supra* note 14, at 896.

[18] Nineteenth-century writers uncritically accepted the principle that the burden of persuasion should depend on the burden of pleading. T. Starkie, Evidence 534 (9th ed. 1869); J. Stephen, Digest of the Law of Evidence, Art. 93, at 152 (4th ed. 1877); contemporary writers find little value in the interweaving of the two burdens; the policy problems, they submit, are merely shifted from one area to another. F. James & G. Hazard, Civil Procedure 249–51 (2d ed. 1977); C. Clark, Code Pleading 610 (2d ed. 1947).

common-law courts were required to classify defensive issues as factual challenges or as exceptions to rules. Thus they had a basis for applying the Latin maxim that the proponent of an issue must prove it. As German scholars found an arbiter of burden-of-persuasion decisions in the syntax of their civil code, common-law jurists found parallel answers by gearing the burden of persuasion to decisions on the relative scope of the defensive pleas.

Decisions on pleading at common law may often have been made with an eye to the implications for the burden of persuasion, but this was not always the case. The system occasionally produced pleading rules at odds with the judiciary's preferences on the burden of persuasion. The notable example is the issue of payment in an action on a note. The allegation of non-payment is required in the complaint; otherwise, it is said, the complaint would lack a well-defined theory of recovery.[19] Having reached this conclusion, the common-law judiciary balked at the implication: that the creditor would have to prove non-payment. To avoid this result and others, the courts developed a number of ad hoc devices to check the influence of pleading rules on the burden of persuasion. To spare the creditor his burden, the courts argued the unfairness and inconvenience of expecting a party to prove a negative proposition;[20] admittedly, it is easier for the debtor to provide proof of payment—a single incident—than for the creditor to exhaust a wide variety of circumstances under which the defendant might have made payment. But the persuasiveness of the argument that one cannot prove a negative proposition is unpredictable: it does not alleviate the plaintiff's burden to prove non-consent in a battery case;[21] nor does it excuse the obligee from proving non-performance in other contract actions.[22] Another argument used to adjust the burden of persuasion is that the facts are "particularly within the knowledge" of one of the parties.[23]

[19] See Alden, *The Defense of Payment under Code Procedure,* 19 Yale L.J. 647 (1910).

[20] Edmonds v. Edmonds, 1 Ala. 401, 402 (1840); 2 B. Jones, Evidence 882–83 (2d ed. J. Henderson 1926).

[21] Dicenzo v. Berg, 340 Pa. 305, 16 A.2d 15 (1940).

[22] 9 J. Wigmore, Evidence §2486, at 274 (3d ed. 1940).

[23] *Id.* at 275; C. McCormick, Evidence 787 (2d ed. 1972).

These arguments constitute the battery of policy arguments that some scholars might advance as the sound approach to allocating the burden of persuasion. Yet these arguments prevail so haphazardly that sophisticated common-law scholars despair of finding a coherent theory to explain the system's burden-of-persuasion practices.[24]

The quest for the underlying structure of rules and exceptions falters for want of authoritative statements of legal rules. The quest for a set of policies to explain, on grounds of procedural fairness, why one party rather than another should bear the risk of nonpersuasion, has yet to generate more than a restatement of the practices of the courts.

The failure to produce guidelines for properly allocating the burden of persuasion encourages a functional perspective, which holds that rules on the burden of persuasion are a set of second-order substantive rules that regulate the interests of competing classes of litigations. There is no doubt that rules of burden of persuasion modify the rules of liability. If the defendant in a tort action must prove the plaintiff's contributory negligence, he loses much of the tactical value promised by the defense. If the debtor must prove an alleged payment, he is that much at a disadvantage. Thus the burden of persuasion proves to be a low-visibility tool for furthering the interests of tort victims, creditors and other classes of favored litigants. In many cases, the risks of litigation may be allocated with a view to the policy of softening some rules or hardening others. Yet in most factual disputes, the calls of legislative policy are weak and of many voices. To allocate the burden on borderline issues such as consent in battery prosecutions, the courts are naturally attracted to a neutral arbiter like the Latin maxim that the proponent of the issue must prove it.

This discussion of the burden-of-persuasion practices in private disputes has helped us to isolate three types of argument that influence the outcome of disputes on the burden of persuasion. The primary argument is that the issues of the law relate to each

[24] See F. James & G. Hazard, *supra* note 18, at 249; 9 J. Wigmore, Evidence §2486, at 278 (3d ed. 1940).

other in a structural pattern of rules and exceptions. The second argument is that particular principles of procedural fairness provide a surrogate for the identification of rules and exceptions; among these arguments are the claims that no one should have to prove a negative proposition and a party should have to prove issues when the evidence lies particularly within his knowledge or control. A third argument is that the burden of persuasion should be adjusted in order to modify substantive rules and to adjust the interests of particular classes of litigants. All of these arguments came to play major roles in nineteenth- and twentieth-century cases of the proper allocation of the burden of persuasion in criminal cases.

§7.2.2. **The Private Law Style in Criminal Litigation.** In contrast to the cacophony of conflicting practices today, nineteenth-century courts tended to concur that particular issues made up the prosecutor's inculpatory case and other "defensive" issues were to be proven by the defense. The Prussian Criminal Ordinance of 1805 even laid down the general rule: "One having the proof of the act against him is subject to the statutory punishment unless he proves that under the circumstances the act was not an offense." [25] This general principle was supported by Feuerbach,[26] Mittermaier,[27] and Bonnier [28] on the Continent; and by Foster [29] and Blackstone [30] in England.[31]

Continental courts readily came to the conclusion that the burden was on the defendant to prove self-defense and insanity.[32] In

[25] Prussian Criminal Ordinance §367, discussed in Küssner, *Über Beweislast und Präsumtionen im preussischen Strafverfahren,* 3 GA 32 (1855). The roots of this ordinance are in the Constitutio Criminalis Carolina of 1532, which also required the accused to prove defensive issues (e.g., §141 self-defense). A. Schötensach, Der Strafprozess der Carolina 78–81 (1904).

[26] A. von Feuerbach, *supra* note 13, §568, at 372, and §570, at 373.

[27] 2 C. Mittermaier, Das Deutsche Strafverfahren 365 (4th ed. 1845–46) (but note the author's doubts about the traditional distinctions).

[28] Bonnier, *supra* note 13, at 22.

[29] Foster 255.

[30] 4 Blackstone 201.

[31] For additional details on this nineteenth-century view, see Fletcher, *supra* note 14, at 899–902.

[32] See note 13 *supra.*

another situation suggestive of contemporary precedents in the United States, the Prussian High Court held that the defendant in a statutory rape case had to prove that he was mistaken about the age of his sexual partner.[33] The English commentaries and case law of the eighteenth and nineteenth centuries lack systematic thinking about the burden of persuasion. Yet in two types of criminal cases, there crystallized ample authority for the principle that the defendant bore the burden on exculpatory issues or on matters of exception to the definition of the offense.

The foremost of these two fields was the law of homicide, which, as we have already noted,[34] reflected a long-standing commitment to the principle that any act causing death was sufficient to inculpate the defendant. Matters of justification, excuse and mitigation were thought of as defenses. They functioned to exculpate the defendant from the incriminating impact of "the fact of killing being first proved."[35] Yet it did not follow from this harm-oriented mode of analysis that the defendant should bear the burden of persuasion on the issue. That inference was left to the work of Foster and Blackstone in the mid-eighteenth century. According to Foster, the prisoner had "satisfactorily" to prove circumstances of "accident, necessity and infirmity."[36] In Blackstone's influential formulation, the defense's case included "circumstances of justification, excuse and alleviation."[37] Yet the important point to realize about Foster's and Blackstone's formulation of this rule is that they both proceeded on the assumption that the facts in dispute were to be specified in a special verdict by the jury; the legal significance of these facts was to be assessed by the court.

The significance of this procedural difference is illustrated by the litigation in The King v. Oneby,[38] the single precedent cited by

[33] Judgment of November 4, 1853, [1854] Justiz-Ministerial-Blatt für die Preussische Gesetzgebung 5. The High Court reached the same conclusion on the defense of mistake of fact to a charge of assisting an illegal immigrant. Judgment of November 30, 1853, 2 GA 255 (1854).

[34] See §4.1 *supra.*

[35] The phrase is from Foster 255.

[36] *Ibid.*

[37] 4 Blackstone 201.

[38] 92 Eng. Rep. 465 (K.B. 1727).

Foster and Blackstone as support for their theory of the burden of proof. *Oneby's* case came before the judges of the King's Bench on a special verdict stipulating that the defendant had killed a man in a fight over a game of cards. The facts stipulated in the verdict did not admit of the construction that Oneby killed under provocation. Nor did the verdict, specifying as it did that the defendant and his victim were alone when the stabbing occurred, support the conclusion that Oneby killed maliciously, i.e., unprovoked by a sudden quarrel. That the verdict was silent on the issue worked to the defendant's detriment; the judges found him guilty of murder. Their rationale was straightforward: "[i]f *A* kills *B* and no sudden quarrel appears, it is murder; for it lies on the party indicted to prove the sudden quarrel."[39]

Buttressed by this case and Foster's prior analysis, Blackstone's reading of the law became the rationale for requiring the defendant satisfactorily to prove matters of self-defense,[40] duress,[41] insanity,[42] and provocation.[43] It was not until 1935, in the renowned *Woolmington* case,[44] that the English courts considered the rule afresh; and in that case the prosecution asserted the applicability of Blackstone's rule to the defense of accident in a homicide case—a defense on which no defendant in a major Western court of modern times had borne the burden of persuasion. Rejecting this extreme application of Blackstone's analysis, the House of Lords in its *Woolmington* decision took the first step toward a new policy of protecting criminal defendants in cases of doubt on "exculpatory" issues.[45]

The leading American precedent proved to be Commonwealth

[39] 92 Eng. Rep. at 473.

[40] Regina v. Smith, 173 Eng. Rep. 441 (N.P. 1837).

[41] M'Growther's Case, 168 Eng. Rep. 8 (1746).

[42] M'Naghten's Case, 8 Eng. Rep. 718 (H.L. 1843); Regina v. Stokes, 175 Eng. Rep. 514 (1848).

[43] See Commonwealth v. York, discussed at note 46 *infra*.

[44] Woolmington v. Director of Public Prosecutions, [1935] A.C. 462.

[45] The House of Lords extended the *Woolmington* rule in Mancini v. Director of Public Prosecutions, [1942] A.C. 1 (provocation) and Chan Kau v. The Queen, [1955] A.C. 206 (self-defense).

v. York,[46] in which Chief Justice Shaw, writing for Massachusetts' highest court, upheld instructions to the jury requiring that the defendant prove the "defense" of provocation by a preponderance of the evidence. The incorporation of Blackstone's rule in *York* influenced subsequent decisions around the country,[47] but there were many courts, particularly in the West, that rejected *York* from the outset and relied on the presumption of innocence to give the defendant the benefit of the doubt on all substantive issues.[48]

What was overlooked in the development from *Oneby* to *York* was the critical difference between cases tried on a special verdict on the facts and cases of a general verdict on the defendant's guilt. In a proceeding on a special verdict, the judges are required to reach a decision despite gaps in the factual determination. When there is no specification either that the killing was with or without provocation, there is need for a rule-of-decision to determine whether the defendant should receive the benefit of the jury's failure to make a finding. To supply this stop-gap rule, Foster reasoned that as to defensive claims, the matters "must appear in evidence before he [the defendant] can avail himself of them."[49] As Chief Justice Shaw said in *York:* a fact alleged and not proved is equivalent to one "not existing."[50] It would have to be that way on a special verdict. For if the verdict stands for a finding of fact, rather than a judgment of guilt, a reasonable doubt as to provocation would hardly be sufficient to assert in the verdict that there was provocation and heat of passion.[51]

The shift from the procedure of a special verdict on the facts

[46] 50 Mass. (9 Met.) 93 (1845).

[47] See cases cited Fletcher, *supra* note 14, at 903 nn.77–79.

[48] See cases cited §7.3, note 7 *infra*.

[49] Foster 255.

[50] 50 Mass. (9 Met.) at 113.

[51] This analysis is not sufficient to prove that silence in the special verdict in *Oneby's* case should accrue to the detriment of the accused. The additional premise was that malice was treated as implied or presumed unless there was some reason to think that there was proof of no malice. This was an implication of the harm-oriented mode of analysis, see §4.1 *supra*, and the assumption that the prosecution did not have to establish malice at trial, see Mackalley's Case, 77 Eng. Rep. 828 (1611).

to a general verdict of guilt brought out an ambiguity in the "burden of proof" that remained camouflaged in cases like *Oneby*. As is well known today, the phrase "burden of proof" may refer either to the burden of persuasion (the risk that the jury will regard the issue neither as proven nor as disproven) or to the burden of going forward (the burden of producing "some evidence" in order to receive an instruction on the issue).[52] The two prongs of the phrase refer to two different aspects of jury instructions. The burden of persuasion is expressed in the wording of the instructions; and the burden of going forward, in the decision whether to give the jury any instructions on the issue at all.[53] It is significant that the judges of the King's Bench in *Oneby's* case had no need to distinguish between the two senses of the term "burden of proof," for their task in that case was neither to rule on the content of instructions nor to decide whether instructions ought to have been given. They had merely to render the appropriate legal characterization of the facts stipulated in the special verdict.

The general verdict permits courts to distinguish between the burden of going forward and the burden of persuasion. It enables courts to interpret the language of *Oneby's* case ("It lies on the party indicted to prove the sudden quarrel") to refer merely to the burden of raising a triable issue of fact. Yet in his opinion in *York*, Chief Justice Shaw failed, for several reasons, to consider this alternative view of the burden of proof. In the mid-nineteenth century there was little, if any, sensitivity to the ambiguity;[54] and, more importantly, Shaw's perception of the problem was impeded by his conflating the judge's role in cases of special verdicts, where the distinction between the two burdens is insignificant,

[52] Contemporary usage stems from Thayer, *The Burden of Proof*, 4 Harv. L. Rev. 45 (1890).

[53] As an analogue to the common-law decision whether to grant a jury instruction on an issue, the civilian judge must decide whether to discuss an issue in his written evaluation of the evidence. A deficient opinion is a ground for reversal. Code de procédure pénale §593; St PO §338 (7).

[54] The Massachusetts court had acknowledged the distinction between the "weight of the evidence" and the burden of proof. E.g., Powers v. Russell, 30 Mass. (13 Pick.) 69 (1832). See generally Reaugh, *Presumptions and the Burden of Proof*, 36 Ill. L. Rev. 703, 706–13 (1942).

with the jury's role in cases of general verdicts, where the distinction is critical. His language evidences his confusion:[55]

> Proof beyond reasonable doubt is necessary to establish a fact against the accused; but preponderating proof—proof sufficient to satisfy the jury of the fact—is sufficient to establish a fact in his favor. But it must go to this extent; otherwise, there is nothing on which the jury can found their belief, and warrant them in considering the fact proved. It is not sufficient, therefore, to raise a doubt, even though it be a reasonable doubt of the fact of extenuation, simply because it is no *proof* of the fact. *And here, again, we think the point may be illustrated by considering how the case would stand on a special verdict.*

It is clear that Blackstone's rule on the burden of proof could transcend the context of the special verdict and become a rule on the risk of non-persuasion in cases on a general verdict. The reason for this remarkable adaptation is that distinguishing between the burdens of the prosecution and of the defense seemed like an intuitively plausible way to structure criminal litigation. That intuitive plausibility was nourished by the assimilation of the criminal process to the model set by private litigation. It seemed natural, in criminal as well as in private disputes, that certain issues should be alleged and proved by one party; and certain issues alleged and proved by the opposing party. Transcending this way of looking at the criminal dispute required an insight into the nature of the process and of criminal guilt that nineteenth-century judges did not command. In the next section, we shall see how, in the context of regular reliance on the general verdict, a new understanding of the nature of criminal guilt led to a radically different approach to the burden of persuasion in criminal cases.

Before turning to this process of reform, we should note a second context of the common law of crimes, in which thinking about the burden of persuasion reflected the influence of arguments drawn from private litigation. This general type of case is one in which a statute regulates a particular activity and provides that it is permissible in certain situations. The leading English case is

[55] 50 Mass. (9 Met.) at 116–17 (emphasis added).

The King v. Turner,[56] which came before the King's Bench in 1816 on Turner's claim that he had been improperly convicted of possessing game in violation of the Statute of 5 Anne. His argument was that for any number of reasons set forth in the statute, his possession of game might have been lawful and that the conviction was defective because the prosecution had failed to prove that these exculpatory conditions were absent. A clever argument it was, but Lord Ellenborough would have none of it. With the concurrence of the other judges, he held that the prosecution did not have to submit evidence to prove the absence of what he called "exceptions" to liability; on these issues, he reasoned, the defendant bore "the burden of proof." This was the rule in private cases, Lord Ellenborough conceded, and "there was no reason why the rule should not be applied to informations as well as actions."[57]

The decision in *Turner's* case is interesting for a number of reasons. First, it bespeaks the judicial tendency to regard the tasks of allocating the burden of persuasion as identical in criminal and in private cases. Secondly, it provides another example of the willingness of common-law judges to conflate the burden of going forward with the risk of non-persuasion. It might not be sensible procedurally to expect the prosecutor to introduce evidence on the absence of all the statutory grounds for permissibly possessing pheasants and hares. Yet acknowledging the prosecutor's problems of proof does not compel the conclusion that the defendant must bear the burden of persuasion on the issue; these difficulties properly justify only a demand that the defendant go forward on the issue. Once the defendant has raised a triable issue under one of the statutory exceptions, one might reasonably expect the prosecutor to bear the risk that in the end the jury would tender reasonable doubts on the issue.

This reading of the *Turner* decision is plausible, but it hardly meshes with the case's reception in practice. The common law regarded *Turner*, as it did *Oneby*, as a welcome affirmation of the

[56] 105 Eng. Rep. 1026 (K.B. 1816).
[57] 105 Eng. Rep. at 1028.

propriety of treating criminal defenses like private law defenses. The *Turner* case has generated a rare showing of solidarity among common-law jurisdictions. On an array of statutory offenses, ranging from the unlawful possession of narcotics to the unlawful practice of medicine, common-law courts demand that the defendant persuade the trier of fact of his license or authorization to engage in the regulated activity.[58]

In justifying the defendant's duty to persuade the trier of fact of statutory exceptions, common-law judges proceed as though the problem were one at private law. They use the idiom of rules and exceptions; they think in the categories prescribed by the Latin maxim *reus excipiendo fit actor.* They interweave rules of pleading with rules on the burden of persuasion.[59] Thus, if the prosecution need not negate the statutory exception in the indictment, as is often the case in liquor and narcotic violations,[60] that is sufficient to prompt a ruling that the defendant must bear the burden of persuasion on the issue.[61] But if the prosecution must negate the exception in the indictment, as is the case in the prosecutions for the unlawful practice of medicine, the courts invoke the kinds of arguments that are used to intercept the usual inference from the duty to plead in private cases. As the private defendant must prove the defense of payment, the criminal defendant must prove that he has a license to practice medicine.[62] In both settings the courts argue that the facts are within the defendant's knowledge,

[58] See, e.g., State v. Crowell, 25 Me. 171 (1845) (selling brandy without a license); Reed v. United States, 210 A. 2d 845 (D.C. Ct. App. 1965) (possession of narcotics without a prescription); *But cf.* Johnson v. Wright, 509 F.2d 828 (5th Cir. 1975), *cert. denied,* 423 U.S. 1014 (1976) (burden on state to show possession of firearm was unlicensed).

[59] In Regina v. Oliver, [1943] 2 All E.R. 800, the defendant had to prove that he was licensed to sell sugar as a wholesaler; the rationale was, in part, that the prosecution did not have to allege the absence of a license.

[60] See, e.g., Harrison Anti-Narcotics Act of Dec. 17, 1914, c. 1, 38 Stat. 785; Uniform Narcotic Act §18.

[61] Reed v. United States, 210 A.2d 845 (D.C. Ct. App. 1965) (narcotics); United States v. Holmes, 187 F.2d 222 (7th Cir. 1951) (narcotics).

[62] People v. Boo Doo Hong, 122 Cal. 606, 55 P. 402 (1898); *cf.* Commonwealth v. Bitzer, 163 Pa. Super. 386, 62 A.2d 108 (1948) (license to render service as a public utility).

or the prosecution need not prove a negative, or convenience demands that the defendant persuade on the issue. Of course, these arguments prevail in criminal cases as sporadically and unpredictably as they do in private cases. But that the courts deploy them in criminal as well as in private cases demonstrates that the judges regard the problem in both settings as the same.

§7.3. *The Revolt Against the Private Law Style.*

The critical assumption underlying the structuring of issues into an inculpatory case and a set of defenses is that there is no single all-encompassing issue that is both necessary and sufficient to establish criminal liability. This is indeed the case in tort litigation. The principle that he who faultfully causes harm is liable hardly states a sufficient condition for liability, for it requires supplementation by the defenses of assumption of risk and contributory negligence. The rule that he who contracts an obligation and fails to perform is liable is hardly sufficient, for it calls for amplification by rules pertaining to the impossibility of performance. The rules of private law naturally lend themselves to a division into the plaintiff's case and the defendant's possibilities of confession and avoidance. The reason is that there is no single idea or concept that lies at the foundation of liability in tort or contract.

§7.3.1. **The Emergence of a Normative Theory of Guilt.** The revolt against the private law style in criminal law derived from the rediscovery of an old idea: the criminal law should punish only the guilty. If the "guilty" were those who could fairly be blamed for wrongdoing, then the principle of punishing the guilty, and only the guilty, could generate a unifying perspective on criminal liability. This new perspective required that the concept of "guilt" or "culpability" be understood normatively. If "guilt" were synonymous with "being found liable under the law," then it would be analytically true that the state punishes only the guilty. If "guilt" and "culpability" refer simply to the mental state required for conviction, then the "culpable" are sometimes excused and exempt from liability;[1] in cases in which conduct is culpable but excused, the concept of culpability hardly furnishes a rationale for conviction. For this new view of the criminal law to take hold, the notion of "guilt" had to become synonymous with "culpability" or "blameworthiness" for wrongdoing. It was only then that the finding of culpability could function as a rationale for punishment.

It is not surprising, then, that the refinement of the normative theory of culpability[2] coincided in German legal history with the progressive shifting of the risk of residual doubt to the prosecution. If all substantive issues, both inculpatory and exculpatory, were threads in the fabric of guilt, then the differences among them appeared less significant. The distinction between whether harm had been done and whether the harm was justified by a claim of self-defense no longer appeared to be an adequate basis for allocating the burden of persuasion. Proceeding from the premise that the prosecutor had to prove the defendant's guilt, late nineteenth-century German courts readily came to the position that the prosecution had to disprove properly raised claims of self-defense and insanity.[3]

In Anglo-American law, the thrusting of blameworthiness to center of the criminal process coincided with the refinement of the presumption of innocence. Relating the presumption of innocence to the process of proof and conviction was a relatively new development. The doctrine appears in some early nineteenth-century civil disputes,[4] but it was apparently not until mid-century

§7.3. [1] This is the implication of the Model Penal Code's concept of culpability. Someone might be excused on grounds of duress, MPC §2.09, and yet have a culpable mental state under §2.02(2).

[2] See §6.7.2, at note 9 *supra*.

[3] Two important cases were the Judgments of November 13, 1885, 7 Rechtsprechung 664; and of October 23, 1890, 21 RGSt. 131. In the first case, the court endorsed the view of the trial judge that both participants in a brawl should be acquitted on the ground of self-defense if it appeared possible that either might have started it. In the second case, the court affirmed an acquittal on the ground of insanity. According to the opinion of the trial judge, there was a "probability" of insanity. Apparently, the prosecution thought that this was not enough for an acquittal; the court held that a "possibility" of insanity was sufficient to acquit.

[4] See Williams v. East India Co., 102 Eng. Rep. 571 (K.B. 1802) (defendant failed to

that judges[5] and commentators[6] began to use the presumption of innocence as a rationale for the prosecutor's burden of persuasion. The unresolved question was what it meant to be "innocent." Is an insane wrongdoer innocent? Is someone who kills accidentally innocent? Reflection on the issue leads us to the conclusion that everyone who is not fairly to blame for wrongdoing is innocent and ought to be protected by the presumption of innocence. The early cases rejecting the defensive burden of persuasion rely explicitly on the presumption of innocence.[7] By the end of the century the new view of the criminal process crystallized in the Supreme Court's opinion in Davis v. United States:[8]

> The plea of not guilty is unlike a special plea in a civil action which, admitting the case averred, seeks to establish substantive grounds of defense by a preponderance of evidence. It is not in confession and avoidance, for it is a plea that controverts the existence of every fact essential to constitute the crime charged. Upon that plea the accused may stand, shielded by the presumption of his innocence, until it appears that he is guilty; and his guilt cannot in the very nature of things be regarded as proved, if the jury entertain a reasonable doubt from all the evidence whether he was legally capable of committing crime.

In this single paragraph we find all the critical points in the revolt against the private law style of thinking about the burden of persuasion: (1) The plea of not guilty brings into issue all matters bearing on guilt; (2) guilt is negated by insanity and other substantive issues bearing on liability; and (3) the presumption of innocence provides the rationale for requiring the prosecution to

---

warn plaintiff that he was transporting a combustible item on plaintiff's ship; presumption of innocence invoked to require plaintiff to prove the issue).

[5] See Patterson v. State, 21 Ala. 571 (1852); State v. Tibbetts, 35 Me. 81 (1852).

[6] 1 S. Greenleaf, A Treatise on the Law of Evidence §29 (2d ed. 1844) (the first edition, published in 1842, discussed the presumption of innocence (at 39) without relating it to the degree of proof required in criminal cases). J. Stephen, A Digest of the Law of Evidence, art. 94 (1876), 1 P. Taylor, Treatise on the Law of Evidence 133 (1887).

[7] Maher v. People, 10 Mich. 212, 218 (1862); State v. McCluer, 5 Nev. 110, 113 (1869); *cf.* Trumble v. Territory, 3 Wyo. 280, 21 P. 1081 (1889); State v. Wingo, 66 Mo. 181 (1877).

[8] 160 U.S. 469, 485–86 (1895).

disprove guilt beyond a reasonable doubt. On the basis of this reasoning, the Court held that the prosecution must bear the risk of residual doubt on insanity. *Davis* became the leading case in the movement in the federal courts to require the prosecution to bear the risk of residual doubt not only on insanity, but on all substantive issues bearing on liability.[9]

The clear-headed reasoning of the Court in *Davis* provides the counterweight to Chief Justice Shaw's opinion in *York.* It reflects full appreciation for the general verdict of not guilty in contrast to the procedure of interpreting a special verdict. Yet the general verdict, by itself, would have changed nothing unless the judges also perceived the centrality of normative guilt in the criminal process. By linking the notion of normative guilt with the presumption of innocence, the Court could conclude that reasonable doubt on any substantive issue should be sufficient for an acquittal.

One year prior to the decision in *Davis,* the German Supreme Court resolved a tort suit for battery and made the same basic claim about the difference between private law and criminal law.[10] The defendant had struck the plaintiff with his staff and the question was whether the blow was justified as self-defense. In a tort action for battery, the trial judge found for the defendant on the ground that "it appeared probable" that the defendant's striking the plaintiff was warranted as a defensive act. If that was the state of the evidence, the Supreme Court countered, the claim of self-defense should have been rejected; that it appeared "probable" was insufficient to satisfy the defendant's burden of persuasion. The mistake of the trial judge had been to reason that if the defendant in a criminal case should get the benefit of the doubt in cases of self-defense, the same should be true of defendants in tort disputes.

For our purposes, the important facet of this decision is the Court's explanation of why criminal cases differ so significantly from tort disputes that a different approach to the burden of per-

[9] Frank v. United States, 42 F.2d 623 (9th Cir. 1930) (self-defense); Johnson v. United States, 291 F.2d 150 (8th Cir. 1961) (coercion).

[10] Judgment of May 8, 1894, 33 RGZ 352.

suasion should apply. In the Court's view, the structural posture of a claim of self-defense was radically different in the two processes. In a tort action, the claim of self-defense was not "merely a denial of the plaintiff's case" but the "setting up of a new matter." Thus it fell to the tort defendant to prove his affirmative claim to the complete satisfaction of the trier-of-fact. Yet how can it be the case that the same issue of self-defense sometimes appears as a denial and sometimes as an affirmative proposition? The answer is that the concept of guilt functions in criminal cases in a way it does not function in tort disputes. As the German Supreme Court stressed in this tort dispute:[11]

> [C]riminal sanctions should be used only against the guilty, a principle with which it would be inconsistent for a judge to hold a defendant guilty of intentional battery, even though it appeared probable *or possible* that the act was required by self-defense.

The same claim could not be made for the tort dispute, for the notion of guilt does not function in private litigation in the way it does in criminal cases. Even if personal fault is important in tort disputes, the notion of fault in torts does not range beyond the issues of a prima facie case. The defendant's fault is not necessarily negated or "denied" by defensive claims such as consent, assumption of risk and self-defense. The principle that guilt or culpability in the criminal process encompasses all issues bearing on liability derives from the even more basic postulate that criminal punishment should be levied only against the guilty. There is no comparable principle inhibiting the imposition of tort liability.

It may be an accident of history, but nonetheless intriguing, that in the same period at the end of the nineteenth century both German law and Anglo-American law extricated the criminal process from the style of thought rooted in private litigation. From a comparative point of view, this parallel development indicates that the momentum for reform transcended procedural systems as well as particular national policies. Continental writers often explain

[11] *Id.* at 353 (emphasis added).

the residual influence of private law thinking in the common law as the reflection of the adversary process.[12] It may be that the adversary process itself manifests a continuing association of criminal and private disputes. But our study has shown that there is no correlation between patterns in allocating the burden of persuasion and a commitment either to an adversary or an inquisitorial system of trial. The Prussian Criminal Ordinance of 1805 contained several provisions imposing the burden of persuasion on the accused and yet the burdens were borne in an essentially inquisitorial trial.[13] The evolution in German law did not occur against the backdrop of significant procedural changes. Also, other Continental courts, particularly those in France, have not kept pace with the evolution in Germany, and this disparity cannot be explained by divergent emphasis on adversarial as opposed to inquisitorial trials.

The critical factor in the development of a theory of the burden of persuasion unique to the criminal process is the perception of guilt as the central, all-encompassing condition of criminal liability. Whether this perception crystallizes in a particular legal system depends on many factors other than procedural forms. It depends most, it would seem, on the degree of self-consciousness about criminal punishment as a sanction different in nature from the imposition of civil liability. The notion of guilt is likely to take on its full judgmental richness only when theorists perceive the need to justify criminal punishment by appealing to the transpositive principle that only those guilty of wrongdoing should suffer criminal sanctions.

Though the movement to reform the burden of persuasion suggests that this moral insight took hold in Anglo-American law as well as in late nineteenth-century German theory, that judgment would be premature. In fact, the posture of English and American law toward guilt as a moral precondition of just punishment is

[12] A. Geyer, Lehrbuch des Strafprozessrechts 710–11 (1880); G. Vidal & J. Magnol, Cours de droit criminel et de science pénitentiaire 1035 n.2 (9th ed. 1949).

[13] See Küssner, *Über Beweislast und Präsumtionen im preussischen Strafverfahren,* 3 GA 32–34 (1855).

highly ambivalent. The movement to extricate the allocation of the burden of persuasion in criminal cases from the influence of private law issued in reform in some courts and not in others. In many jurisdictions, the burden on self-defense and provocation was cast on the prosecution,[14] but the burden on insanity and other issues remained on the defense.[15] In addition, other areas of the development indicate an aversion to take the requirement of normative guilt seriously. At about the time the process of reform in the burden of persuasion began, other Anglo-American courts began to recognize strict liability offenses in cases ranging from selling adulterated foodstuffs[16] to bigamy and statutory rape.[17] In view of these conflicting currents in the common law, it would be difficult to interpret the movement to reform burden-of-persuasion practices as an onrush of sensitivity to the nature of guilt and the criminal sanction. The personality of Anglo-American law is so conflicted that one can hardly expect a consistent transformation in one generation of decisions.

§7.3.2. **The Borderland of Culpability.** The proposition that crystallized in the German cases, in *Davis* and in other nineteenth-century cases[18] is that the state should bear the residual doubt on all issues bearing on the culpability and moral innocence of the accused. The challenge posed by this proposition was working out the contours of culpability. What did it mean for an issue to bear on the substantive rationale for punishment? It is clear that duress, self-defense, mistake and accident bore on culpability; and

[14] See cases and materials cited §7.2, at note 1 *supra*.

[15] This was notably the case in Great Britain and in California. *Woolmington* was extended to self-defense in Regina v. Smith, 173 Eng. Rep. 441 (1837), but the English courts still expect the accused to persuade on the issue of insanity. Regina v. Smith, 6 Crim. App. 19 (1910). Similarly in California, the courts extended the rule of reasonable doubt to self-defense, People v. Toledo, 85 Cal. App. 2d 577, 193 P.2d 953 (1948), but not to insanity, People v. Wolff, 61 Cal. 2d 795, 394 P.2d 959, 40 Cal. Rptr. 271 (1964).

[16] See generally Sayre, *Public Welfare Offenses*, 33 Colum. L. Rev. 55 (1933); MPC §2.05, Comment at 141--45 (Tent. Draft No. 4, 1955).

[17] E.g., State v. Goonan, 89 N.H. 528, 3 A.2d 105 (1938) (bigamy); State v. Duncan, 82 Mont. 170, 266 P. 400 (1928) (statutory rape).

[18] See note 7 *supra*.

equally clear that the statute of limitations and objections to the admissibility of evidence did not. But between these well-marked fields there was and still is a borderland of contested issues. We shall examine three of these issues, both because they are instructive of problems in allocating the burden of persuasion, but more importantly, because they capture characteristic difficulties of refining the substantive concept of culpability.

A. Insanity. With respect to ordering questions within the concept of culpability, insanity is both the easiest and the most recalcitrant of issues. The criteria of insanity sound unmistakably in the idiom of blameworthiness. The issue is whether the accused is responsible, whether he knew that his act was wrong, whether a mental disease or defect prevented him from conforming his conduct to law.[19] Taking this language to be controlling on the nature of the defense, several nineteenth-century courts readily concluded even prior to *Davis* that the prosecution must bear the risk of residual doubt on the defendant's sanity.[20]

But roughly half the jurisdictions in the United States still require the defendant to bear the burden of persuasion on the issue of insanity.[21] It is not that these jurisdictions explicitly challenge the principle that the state must prove *mens rea* or culpability beyond a reasonable doubt. The technique is rather to conceptualize the claim of insanity as extrinsic to a more narrowly construed notion of *mens rea*.[22] At the outset of our study of the general part, we noted the systematic ambiguity of the terms "mens rea," "culpability," "criminal intent" and "mental component" of the crime.[23] These terms may refer either to the facts of intention, knowledge

[19] For a discussion of the problems in defining insanity, see §10.4.4 *infra*.

[20] People v. Garbutt, 17 Mich. 9 (1868); Hopps v. People, 31 Ill. 385 (1863).

[21] For an up-to-date survey for jurisdictions in the United States, see Commonwealth v. Kostka, Mass. Adv. Sh. 1608, 1624 nn.8–9; 350 N.E.2d 444, 453 nn.8–9 (1976) (28 jurisdictions require prosecution to disprove insanity beyond a reasonable doubt; 23 require defendant to prove insanity by a preponderance of the evidence).

[22] For a textbook example of this style of reasoning, see the concurring opinion by Justice Rehnquist and Chief Justice Burger in Mullaney v. Wilbur, 421 U.S. 684 (1975).

[23] See §6.2.1 *supra*.

or recklessness or they may refer to a normative quality of acting intentionally, knowingly, recklessly or negligently under particular circumstances. In this context we see that the ambiguity is capable of generating divergent postures on the structural relationships of insanity and other excuses of persuasion. The normative theory of culpability supports the view that excuses, such as duress and insanity, negate culpability and thus function, structurally, as denials rather than as claims of confession and avoidance.[24] In contrast, the descriptive theory of culpability and *mens rea* as "mental states" buttress the opposing view that excuses are "new matter" proposed by the defendant in an effort to escape punishment for his "crime."[25] The latter style of thought takes us back to private law style in criminal cases. The proponents of a limited descriptive theory of culpability never explain how shifting the burden of proof on insanity is reconcilable with the presumption of innocence.

Noting the way the conceptual scheme influences our analysis is but the beginning of the inquiry. Why is it that some people are led to use a normative conception of culpability and others fall back on a descriptive theory that equates culpability with intent or knowledge? In the particular case of insanity, the failure to see that the issue negates culpability may derive from institutional considerations. The common observation is that the claim of insanity does not separate those subject to sanctions from those who may remain free. It functions rather to determine whether the social response to the defendant's conduct (condition) is to be imprisonment or hospitalization.[26] A jury finding of sanity leads to penal confinement; and the jury's accepting the defense leads to therapeutic confinement. Thus as Packer argued, the verdict of not guilty by reason of insanity is "a direction to punish but not to punish criminally."[27] This view of the defense is buttressed by

[24] See note 20 *supra.*

[25] See Mullaney v. Wilbur, 421 U.S. 684, 706 (1975) (concurring opinion) (". . . a defendant who sought to establish . . . insanity, and thereby escape any punishment whatever for a heinous crime, should bear the laboring oar on such an issue").

[26] See A. Goldstein, The Insanity Defense 144–45 (1967); J. Katz & J. Goldstein, *Abolish the Insanity Defense—Why Not?* 72 Yale L.J. 853, 867–68 (1963); 4 Blackstone 25 (identifying the rule of commitment as one of "our antient law").

[27] Packer 134.

special procedures for litigating insanity apart from the determination of "guilt" and "innocence."[28]

If this interpretation were correct, the verdict on sanity or insanity would schizophrenically combine incompatible issues in one decision. But the responsibility and blameworthiness of the accused are one issue; and the justification of civil commitment, another. The more sensible approach is to separate these questions and address each at the proper juncture, the first by assessing sanity at the time of the deed; the second, by assessing dangerousness to self and others at the time of trial. There is growing evidence that the separation of these issues is constitutionally required.[29] When the issues are properly separated, the claim of insanity comes back into focus. When disengaged from the process of civil commitment, the finding of insanity speaks unequivocally to the propriety of blaming the accused for his wrongful act. The implication of perceiving insanity in this way is to concur with the Supreme Court in *Davis* that the prosecution should bear the risk of residual doubt on the issue.

B. Entrapment. The claim of entrapment as a bar to liability is virtually unique to the criminal jurisprudence of the United States.[30] The claim applies to cases in which a law enforcement official induces someone to commit an offense who would otherwise not be "predisposed" to commit the offense.[31] The theory of the

[28] See Louisell & Hazard, *Insanity as a Defense: The Bifurcated Trial,* 49 Calif. L. Rev. 805, 805–06 (1961); Comment, *Due Process and Bifurcated Trials: A Double-Edged Sword,* 66 Nw. U.L. Rev. 327 (1971).

[29] Specht v. Patterson, 386 U.S. 605 (1967) (holding that a supplementary hearing is required under the Colorado Sex Offenders Act); Bolton v. Harris, 395 F.2d 642 (D.C. Cir. 1968) (holding that there is no constitutionally relevant distinction between ordinary civil commitment and commitment after a verdict of not guilty by reason of insanity).

[30] On tentative efforts to adopt the defense in England, Canada and other Commonwealth countries, see Heydon, *The Problems of Entrapment,* 32 Camb. L.J. 268, 278 (1973).

[31] On the various versions of the defense, and particularly on the distinction between the federal test which focusses on the predisposition of the accused and MPC §2.13 which focusses on whether a hypothetical person would have committed the offense, see Park, *The Entrapment Controversy,* 60 Minn. L. Rev. 163 (1976).

defense is buffetted by conflicting interpretations. One interpretation proceeds on the assumption that if an individual is seduced into committing an offense, he should not be held accountable for it. As the Supreme Court reasoned in the case establishing the doctrine, if the police "implant in the mind of an innocent person the disposition to commit an offense,"[32] the offender cannot properly be found guilty. On this theory, the defense of entrapment is as closely associated with normative culpability as is the claim of duress. In one case the actor is seduced by the wiles of a duplicitous police officer; in the other he is coerced by the threats of an overbearing will.

Critics of this view assimilate the defense to the various devices for controlling improper police behavior, such as the rule excluding unconstitutionally seized evidence.[33] The defense of entrapment is not available to those tempted by private parties to commit crimes; therefore, the critics argue, the purpose of the defense is clearly not to exculpate those led astray by the prompting of others.[34] Besides, one might add, it is one thing to excuse men and women coerced by threats of violence and quite another to excuse those who merely succumb to temptation. Indeed, succumbing to temptation is a paradigm case of blameworthy conduct. If one excuses a woman who succumbs to an offer of prostitution, one would also excuse officials who are seduced by attractive bribes. Thus, entrapment may not be an excuse at all; properly construed, it may be a device designed solely to discipline police behavior. This view finds its most vigorous expression in the Model Penal Code, which, in commentary, labels the defense "a complaint by the accused against the state for employing a certain kind of unsavory enforcement."[35]

[32] Sorrells v. United States, 287 U.S. 435, 442 (1932).

[33] See Carbajal-Portillo v. United States, 396 F.2d 944 (9th Cir. 1968); Donnelly, *Judicial Control of Informants, Spies, Stool Pigeons, and Agent Provocateurs*, 60 Yale L.J. 1091, 1111 (1951); Comment, *Due Process of Law and the Entrapment Defense*, 1964 U. Ill. L.F. 821; Note, *Entrapment: An Analysis of Disagreement*, 45 B.U.L. Rev. 542 (1965); MPC §2.10, Comment (Tent. Draft No. 9, 1959).

[34] For an effective response to this argument, see Park, *supra* note 31, at 240–43.

[35] MPC §2.10, Comment at 21 (Tent. Draft No. 9, 1959).

The response to this argument is to challenge the analogy between entrapment and the rules excluding unconstitutionally seized evidence. The effect of entrapment is not merely to exclude one item of evidence, but to bar the prosecution altogether. Further, the exclusionary rules are designed to enforce rights independently recognized under the Fourth and Fifth Amendments. In a typical case of a police officer's persuading a suspect to sell narcotics, however, there is no independent constitutional standard specifying how far the police may go.[36] To generate a standard of decision, proponents of this regulatory view of entrapment must fall back on general criteria of due process, which may amount to no more than vague uneasiness about unseemly deception by the police.

Thus the theory of entrapment is torn by conflicting interpretations, one of which relates the issue to culpability and another, which denies the relationship. There is no single theory of the defense that can explain both (1) the exclusion of entrapment by private parties and (2) the limitation to suspects not "predisposed" to commit the offense.[37] These implications of this conflict for allocation of the burden of persuasion are fairly straightforward. If entrapment is thought of primarily as a form of seduction, the claim constitutes a denial of culpability, and it follows that the burden of residual doubt on the issue should be borne by the prosecution. This is the prevailing view in the federal courts.[38] If, on the other hand, in the language of the Model Penal Code, the defense is "a complaint by the accused against the state for employing a certain kind of unsavory enforcement,"[39] it is plausible to expect the defendant to bear the burden on the issue. If the accused is the plaintiff on the "complaint" of entrapment, then general principles require that he support his claim by at

[36] This argument is developed in United States v. Russell, 411 U.S. 423, 430 (1973).

[37] The Supreme Court recently affirmed the exception in cases of a predisposition to commit the crime, Hampton v. United States, 425 U.S. 484 (1976).

[38] E.g., United States v. Watson, 489 F.2d 504, 509–10 (3d Cir. 1973); United States v. Groessel, 440 F.2d 602, 606 (5th Cir. 1971), *cert. denied*, 403 U.S. 933 (1971). See generally Park, *supra* note 31, at 262–67.

[39] MPC §2.10, Comment at 21 (Tent. Draft No. 9, 1959).

least a preponderance of the evidence. This is indeed the position of the Model Penal Code[40] and several states on the issue.[41]

C. Culpability and the Abandonment of Attempts. As another illustration of the borderland of culpability, we may recall the dispute about the proper rationale for the defense's voluntary abandonment of attempted, but unconsummated offenses.[42] One view of the defense is that the actor is culpable for the attempt, but the legal system waives its prerogative to punish in order to encourage other would-be offenders to desist at the last moment. The alternate view is that abandonment indicates that the actor's intent was never sufficiently firm to render him culpable for an attempt. Either interpretation suffices to explain why we acquit in cases of voluntary abandonment. Yet on the first view, the defense is extrinsic to the determination of the defendant's personal culpability; on the alternative view, the renunciation serves to negate the allegation of culpability. The German Supreme Court's deciding in the late 1950s that the rationale of the defense was its negating culpability[43] removed any doubts about whether the prosecution should bear the risk of doubt on the issue.[44]

The proper interpretation of abandonment as a defense raises a subtle jurisprudential problem. In the context of insanity we could argue from the contours and the language of the defense that insanity was an excuse for wrongdoing. This analysis was less compelling in the case of entrapment, for the features of the defense point in conflicting directions.

With respect to abandonment, however, the structural position of the issue turns not on the contours of the claim, but on its offi-

[40] MPC §2.13(2).

[41] E.g., People v. Stanley, 68 Mich. App. 559, 243 N.W.2d 684 (1976); State v. Taylor, 260 Iowa 634, 144 N.W.2d 289 (1966); People v. Walters, 264 Cal. App. 2d 834, 70 Cal. Rptr. 766 (1968).

[42] See generally §3.3.8 *supra.*

[43] Judgment of February 28, 1956, 9 BGHSt. 48.

[44] The nineteenth-century rule was that the defendant had to establish the defense of abandonment, J. Glaser, Lehre vom Beweis 94–95 (1883), but in its Judgment of February 19, 1963, 18 BGHSt. 274, 276, the Supreme Court commented that it was "self-evident" that the accused should receive the benefit of the doubt in cases of abandonment.

cial rationale. One theory places the issue outside the scope of culpability; the other brings it back within. How do we decide what the "true" rationale is? The only way to proceed, it seems, is to engage in the kind of reflection and debate that led German theorists to the conclusion that the issue properly bears on culpability. It might be tempting to resolve the debate with an eye to impact on the burden of persuasion. But if one devises the rationale with a view to its procedural benefits, one can hardly invoke that rationale to justify those effects. Thus the burden is on the theorist to reflect on the nature of the defense—on the assumption that it has a single nature.[45] The search for a rationale reduces to a choice between theories rooted in principles of just punishment and instrumentalist theories, such as the claim that the purpose of the defense is to induce attemptors to turn back. With regard to the specific issue of abandonment, our earlier investigation[46] supports the conclusion that the defense is rooted in the general theory of culpability for attempts, not in a policy of encouraging would-be criminals to change their minds.

§7.3.3. **Politics and Policies in Allocating the Burden of Persuasion.** Requiring the defendant to bear "the laboring oar" on an exculpatory issue often functions as a low-visibility device for qualifying defenses begrudgingly granted to the defendant. This is often the attitude manifested in the early stages of judicial or legislative recognition of an exculpatory claim. For example, the Model Penal Code recognizes a new defense of mistake of law in specified instances of relying on ostensibly competent but mistaken legal advice.[47] If an actor is excusably ignorant of the norm governing his conduct, he can hardly be blamed for happening to violate it; the defense undoubtedly negates the actor's culpability. Nevertheless the Model Penal Code requires a defendant to prove a claim of mistake of law by a preponderance of the evidence.[48] The commentary to the code offers no justification for this qualification

[45] For an exposition and defense of this mode of legal thought, see R. Dworkin, Taking Rights Seriously 102–04 (1977).

[46] See §3.3.8 *supra.*

[47] MPC §2.04(3). For an analysis of this defense, see §9.4 *infra.*

[48] MPC §2.04(4).

of the defense. Yet the legislative instinct for compromise often results in qualified action. And the compromise seems harmless. Adding a new defense means that the defendant has tactical advantages that he did not have before. It would seem that the legislature should have the prerogative of granting the defendant "half a loaf" by coupling the new defense with an unfavorable position on the burden of persuasion.

The same political pattern may be observed in other advances made by legislatures and courts to render the law more sensitive to the question of individual accountability.[49] The New York legislature modified the felony-murder rules to exempt cases in which the felon is in no way accountable for the homicide.[50] But the legislature qualified the reform by requiring the defense to bear the burden of persuasion on the issue.[51]

The High Court for the British Zone in Germany recognized a special defense on behalf of physicians who committed euthanasia during the Third Reich; the defendant physicians claimed that they feared that if they did not participate, others would do so, with an even greater toll in innocent lives.[52] Though the Court concluded that the physicians were blameworthy for the deaths, they recognized a special defense extrinsic to question of blameworthiness. But, the Court hastened to add, the burden would be on the defense to prove that their conduct resulted in a net savings

[49] See, e.g., the transition in the California case law on newly recognized claims of reasonable mistake. In People v. Vogel, 46 Cal. 2d 798, 299 P.2d 850 (1956), the court held that the defendant in a bigamy prosecution has the burden of proving a reasonable mistake as to the divorce of his first wife. In People v. Hernandez, 61 Cal. 2d 529, 393 P.2d 673, 39 Cal. Rptr. 361 (1964), the court held that as to reasonable mistake of age in a statutory rape case, the prosecution must bear the risk of reasonable doubt.

[50] N.Y. Penal Law §125.25(3).

[51] *Ibid.* (". . . it is an affirmative defense that . . ."); §25(2) (defining "affirmative defense" to mean that the defendant bears the burden of persuasion by a preponderance of the evidence).

[52] Judgment of March 5, 1949, 1 Entscheidungen des Obersten Gerichtshofes für die Britische Zone 321; Judgment of July 23, 1949, 2 *id.* 117. These cases are discussed in §10.4.6 *infra*.

of life. By defining the issue as extrinsic to culpability, the Court had the option of qualifying the defense by shifting the burden of persuasion.[53]

This technique of law reform is understandable. The new defense is controversial, it is often vague, many people fear that it might be abused. It seems like a sound compromise to condition the defense on the defendant's bearing the burden of persuasion. If courts and legislatures could not qualify their reforms, they might prefer to retain nominally unjust laws and rely on prosecutorial discretion to guard against abuses in practice.

But there is some doubt whether this practice of political compromise can be defended in principle. The issue is not whether the legislature is constitutionally empowered to withhold either half a loaf or the full loaf. The problem is whether it is right to withhold either. But to make a convincing case that qualifying issues bearing on culpability is wrong in principle, one should have to defend two propositions. The first is that the legislature and the courts should recognize the full range of excuses bearing on culpability. If the legislature does not render the law just, then the burden is on the courts to do so. It requires some argument to show that the courts have this flexibility to refine the criteria of excuses. This argument is taken up later as an aspect of the general thesis that the legislative control over the criminal law should be limited to the definition of offenses, and not encompass criteria of justification and excuse.[54]

The second proposition is that questions of substance should be kept distinct from questions of proof. This distinction is by no means commonly accepted in Anglo-American law. There is frequent confusion, for example, whether the requirement that an exculpatory mistake be reasonable is a rule of substance (reason-

[53] The classification of the special exemption as a question extrinsic to culpability has received strong criticism. See Welzel, *Zum Notstandsproblem*, 63 ZStW 47 (1951); Schmidt, Comment, 1949 SJZ 559; Welzel, Comment, 1949 MDR 373, but neither of these commentators recognizes the significance of the Court's doctrinal move as the necessary first step in a decision to shift the burden of persuasion.

[54] See §7.5.2 *infra*.

ableness means being "free from fault") or a rule of evidence (the mistake will be considered only if supported by reasonable grounds).[55] This interweaving of substance and evidence yields an easy apology for shifting the burden of persuasion to the defendant. If the legislature and the courts can hedge defensive claims by adding substantive limitations, such as the rule that mistake be reasonable, there is no reason why they should not employ evidentiary burdens as an equivalent form of hedging. There is no functional difference, one might argue, between a state's employing the *M'Naghten* test on insanity and requiring the prosecution to bear the risk of reasonable doubt and adopting a more liberal test with the burden of persuasion on the defendant. It may be that some defendants are disadvantaged by one approach and others by the other. But there is no way, in principle, to say that a liberal rule of substance, with a stringent rule of evidence, is better or worse than a stringent rule of substance, coupled with a rule of evidence more favorable to the accused.[56]

The only response to this sophisticated move is to insist that substantive rules be assessed on their own terms. The issue is not whether they are good or bad for the prosecution or the defense, but whether the rules are supportable as a matter of principle. We later consider, for example, the problem of distinguishing between cases where any mistake has an exculpatory effect on those in which the mistake must be free from fault.[57] It is critical that one regard that determination as amenable to principled analysis. For if the determination is based solely on a preference for the prosecution or the accused in a particular context, then indeed rules of substance do function like the burden of persuasion.

The attempt to show that it is wrong in principle to use the burden of persuasion to qualify claims bearing on culpability takes us to a troublesome methodological issue in criminal theory. We cannot plausibly argue that hedging defenses with evidentiary

[55] See §9.2.3 *infra*.

[56] *Cf.* Park, *supra* note 31, at 263 (pointing out that the Second Circuit's shifting the burden of persuasion on entrapment to the defendant is offset by a more liberal definition of the defense).

[57] See §9.2 *infra*.

rules is wrong unless we can also maintain that hedging the same issue with substantive limitations is also improper and unjust. The Model Penal Code's shifting the burden of persuasion on mistake of law as a defense is not subject to criticism unless the Code's truncated version of the excuse is also subject to rational criticism. Yet there is no straightforward argument to prove that the substantive issues bearing on wrongdoing and culpability are subject to principled analysis. This entire book seeks to come to grips with that problem.

But if we assume that the substantive law is subject to principled analysis, then we can see the importance of stating the relevant criteria forthrightly, without the confusion and implicit compromise entailed by shifting the burden of persuasion. If the criteria of liability are refined and regarded as just, we then confront the question whether it is proper to single out some issues and require the defendant to bear the burden of persuasion. Why should the defendant get the benefit of the doubt on the issue of intent, but not on the questions of self-defense or insanity? This is the fundamental, recurrent question. It was stated clearly in Davis v. United States, and it is asserted by everyone who invokes the presumption of innocence in the criminal process.

§7.3.4. The Burden of Persuasion as a Constitutional Issue. For a brief period of time, it appeared that the Supreme Court was prepared to elevate the principle of Davis v. United States to constitutional status. Building on its earlier decision in *Winship,*[58] the Court held in *Mullaney* that due process requires the prosecution in a murder case to prove malice and disprove all inconsistent claims, such as provocation, beyond a reasonable doubt.[59] Justice Powell's opinion for the Court repeatedly stresses the relationship between provocation and "the degree of culpability attaching to criminal homicide."[60] There was no dissent, but only a concurring

[58] In re Winship, 397 U.S. 358 (1970) (holding unconstitutional a juvenile court statute that permitted prosecution to establish liability by a "preponderance of the evidence").

[59] Mullaney v. Wilbur, 421 U.S. 684 (1975).

[60] *Id.* at 696; *cf. id.* at 702 (absence of provocation is a "fact so critical to criminal culpability").

opinion of two Justices, which reserved the issue of insanity for separate consideration.[61] The majority seemed to stand squarely behind the principle that if an issue bears on culpability, due process requires the prosecution to bear the risk of residual doubt on the issue.

In the Court's about-face, two years later in *Patterson,*[62] five Justices explicitly disavowed the relevance of culpability to the constitutionality of shifting the burden of persuasion.[63] *Mullaney* was reinterpreted to require merely that the state "prove every ingredient in an offense beyond a reasonable doubt."[64] Whether an issue is an ingredient of an offense depends on whether the legislature says that it is, either explicitly or implicitly in its drafting of the offense. Thus, so far as principles "implicit in ordered liberty" set limits on allocating the burden of persuasion, those principles go no further than requiring state legislatures to identify issues that they wish to regard as "affirmative defenses."

It would be a mistake to read *Patterson* as anything but a de facto overruling of *Mullaney*. With slightly less agony, the Court repeated its former foray and retreat from applying the due process clause to substantive criminal law. In *Robinson,*[65] the Court set forth boldly to question the definition of offenses based on a status or condition that the actor was powerless to control, only to retreat definitively in *Powell,*[66] a brief six years later. Admittedly, the problems posed by *Robinson* and *Mullaney* are different, but the same concerns about unduly interfering with state substantive criminal law motivated the retreat both in *Powell* and *Patterson*. In the brief interval between the two cases on the burden of persuasion, the Court became cognizant of problems that apparently it had not perceived when it set forth to tilt again with the substantive criminal law.

[61] *Id.* at 204.
[62] Patterson v. New York, 432 U.S. 197 (1977).
[63] *Id.* at 214.
[64] *Id.* at 215.
[65] Robinson v. California, 370 U.S. 660 (1962). For an analysis of the case, see §6.4.2 *supra.*
[66] Powell v. Texas, 392 U.S. 514 (1968).

The first problem was the vast array of state statutes shifting the burden of persuasion that were called into question by the broad principle articulated in *Mullaney*.[67] The second was the problem of inhibiting law reform with statutes that recognized new defenses qualified with the kind of evidentiary qualification we discussed in the preceding section.[68] Unless the Court was prepared to determine when a state could constitutionally withhold new defenses, it seemed implausible to restrict the option of state legislatures to tamper with the burden of persuasion as a technique of political compromise.

Patterson should be read as a decision based on principles of federalism and respect for the independent evolution of state systems of criminal law. It would be great misfortune if the case were read to endorse, in principle, the states' requiring defendants to bear the burden of persuasion on so-called affirmative defenses. The Court never says that it approves of the compromise adopted by the New York legislature, yet the majority does approve of a decentralized system of criminal law, with each state free to struggle with the problem of compromise and principle in working out rules on the burden of persuasion.

My own view is that *Mullaney* was a hasty intervention in a complex body of law that is under revision and reconsideration. Though the decision was right in disapproving Maine's decision to shift the burden on provocation, it does not follow that every principle of justice must be anchored in the due process clause. In this respect, the retreat in *Patterson* is not a setback, but a recognition that the Supreme Court cannot undertake to specify the principles that should bind the states in the ongoing process of law reform. The aim of criminal theory should not be the working out of principles for

[67] 432 U.S. at 207 (referring to 25 affirmative defenses in the New York statute, each requiring the defendant to bear the burden of persuasion).

[68] Even the dissent by Justices Powell, Brennan and Marshall was forced to concede that the state may shift the burden of persuasion on so-called "new ameliorative defenses." *Id.* at 229–30. *But cf.* Underwood, *The Thumb on the Scales of Justice: Burdens of Persuasion in Criminal Cases*, 86 Yale L.J. 1299 (1977), in which the author, writing after *Patterson*, argues that if a state recognizes a defensive issue, the prosecution must bear the risk of residual doubt on the issue.

the Supreme Court to enact as the mandate to the Constitution, but to refine the criteria of just punishment as an intermediate body of theory. There is room in our system of justice for a set of principles below the Constitution, but higher than the rules of positive law. If it is right to gauge punishment according to wrongdoing but not to increase punishment on the basis of culpability, that principle should speak to legislators and judges by virtue of its intrinsic merit. If it is right not to distinguish among issues bearing on culpability in allocating the burden of persuasion, a consensus on that principle should emerge and eventually shape the decisions of state legislatures and courts.

The task of rethinking the criminal law requires constant criticism and debate. To incorporate transient results in the Constitution is both to confess the failure of an intermediate body of theory and to stunt the process of debate and development.

§7.4. *The Structure of Wrongdoing.*

In our study of trends in allocating the burden of persuasion, we found that the concept of culpability in a normative sense was the linchpin of the newly machined rule casting the burden on more and more issues to the prosecution. These results on the burden of persuasion might be justified regardless of the internal structural relation of issues bearing on culpability. All the issues might be regarded as unidimensional "elements of the offense" under the Model Penal Code,[1] or they might be related to each other in the three-tiered structure of German law that we shall explicate in this section. In either event, the all-encompassing notion of culpability provides the necessary common denominator for calculating who should bear the burden of persuasion on a particular issue. This common denominator is expressed in the consistent practice of the

§7.4. [1] MPC §1.13(9).

German courts, in the evolution of the case law in England and the United States, and recently, in the constitutional vision of Mullaney v. Wilbur.

In this section we turn away from the common denominator of culpability and direct our attention to the factors that define the internal structure of liability for crime. We take as our starting point the distinction between wrongdoing and attribution that we worked out in Chapter Six. That distinction has received more refined elaboration in German theory than in other legal systems, but we noted that it is implicit as well in doctrines of the common law. The notion of attribution is simply an affirmative description of the finding that wrongful conduct is unexcused and, in this sense, culpable.

With this shared distinction as our background, we turn now to an important distinction within the concept of wrongdoing that is acknowledged even less in the literature and the precedents of Anglo-American law. Unfortunately, we lack the terminology in English to delineate the inculpatory and exculpatory dimensions of wrongful conduct. The exculpatory dimension is captured in the English term "justification":[2] yet we lack a term corresponding to the German *Tatbestand*[3] and Spanish *Tipo*[4] that expresses the inculpatory facet of criminal conduct. The term "elements of the offense" fulfilled that function at an earlier stage, when the prosecution bore the burden of persuasion on the "elements of the offense";[5] and the defense, on all matters of mitigation, excuse and justification.[6] Yet with the evolution toward prosecutorial burdens across the board, the meaning of "elements of the offense" has expanded to encompass all necessary and sufficient conditions of liability, including the absence of justifying and excusing conditions.[7] The term "prima facie" case does refer

[2] On the distinction between justification and excuse, see §10.1 *infra*.

[3] The critical work in the crystallization of the German concept was E. Beling, Die Lehre vom Verbrechen (1906).

[4] See 3 L. Jiménez de Asúa, Tratado de Derecho Penal 743–98 (3d ed. 1965).

[5] See Quillen v. State, 49 Del. 114, 110 A.2d 445 (1955) (absence of self-defense not an "element of the crime").

[6] See §7.2 *supra*.

[7] MPC §1.13(9); Leonard v. People, 149 Colo. 360, 369 P.2d 54 (1962).

to the inculpatory elements of wrongful conduct, yet the connotation of the "prima facie" case is evidentiary, and the point that we wish to make is that there is an important structural and substantive difference between the inculpatory and exculpatory dimensions of wrongdoing. The irony of history is that in the nineteenth century it was easier to render the distinction in English; expressed in decisions allocating the burden of persuasion, the distinction had a concrete procedural reality.

To fill this gap in our language, we shall propose the term "definition" to refer to the inculpatory dimension of wrongdoing. The definition of homicide is killing another human being with malice aforethought. The modern definition of larceny is taking movable property from the possession of another with the intent permanently to deprive the owner of his property.

It is important to underscore what these definitions exclude and what they include. They *exclude* questions of justification and excuse. The issue of justification comprises the second component in the theory of wrongdoing; the issue of excuse raises the distinct issue of attribution. In the examples of homicide and larceny, the stated definition *includes* the element of intent, and in the instance of homicide, the excessive risk-taking that would constitute malice. This way of stating the definition represents an implicit stand in the dispute among the three theories of wrongdoing.[8] By including the element of intention in the definition of the offense, we reject the contrary claim of the objective theory of wrongdoing.

Adding the term "definition" to our discourse helps us express the distinction between the mental elements of liability and the concept of culpability in the normative sense. The mental elements of the offense, such as intention and knowledge, are subjective components of the definition; the concept of culpability arises in connection with the distinct inquiry into the attribution of wrongful conduct.

Though the distinction between definition and justification has yet to be articulated in Anglo-American law, we shall attempt

[8] See §6.6.5 *supra.*

to show that the distinction is of considerable theoretical power. There are at least four areas of legal dispute where recognizing the distinction could have concrete consequences. First, it is of critical importance in deciding when external facts, standing alone, should have an exculpatory effect. Secondly, it might bear on the analysis of permissible vagueness in legal norms. Thirdly, it might bear on the allocation of power between the legislature and judiciary in the continuing development of the criminal law. And fourthly, it might be of importance in analyzing the exculpatory effect of mistakes. The latter subject is reserved for Chapter Nine, when we turn systematically to the subject of mistake.

In this chapter we shall assay the first three problems—external facts, vagueness and legislative competence—with a view to vindicating the importance of the distinction between definition and justification. We shall appeal initially to the plausibility of the distinction in explaining our intuitive judgments. To deepen the account, we shall turn to a theory of norms and invoke this theory to support our proposed structure for analyzing criminal liability.

§7.4.1. **Definition and Justification.** Let us consider a variety of situations in which a suspect engages in perfectly legal conduct but with a wicked intent:

1. *Y* marries a second time in the belief that he is still married. In fact, his wife has procured a valid ex parte divorce in another jurisdiction.

2. *C* writes a letter to suspect *B*, inviting *B* to use *C*'s car whenever *B* wishes. Before receiving the letter, *B* takes *C*'s car with the intent to steal it.

3. A physician *P* is about to inject air into the suspect *X*'s veins with the intent to kill him. Ignorant of *P*'s intentions, *X* decides to use this opportunity to assault him. As the needle is poised, *X* grabs the physician and begins to choke him.

In all three of these cases there is a critical fact, which, if known and acted upon by the actor, would unquestionably preclude liability. In the first case, it would be the prior divorce; in the second, the victim's consent; and the third, the physician's wrongful aggression. The more difficult problem is whether in these cases, where the actor is unaware of the exculpating fact, he should still be acquitted. His act is objectively right, but subjectively wrong. It is the converse of the problem to be treated in the theory of mistake, where the conduct is objectively wrong, but subjectively right.

This is not the first time in this book that we confront the problem of doing the right deed for the wrong reason. It arises in one fashion in the theory of impossible attempts.[9] In the three hypothetical cases above, there might well be liability for attempted bigamy, attempted larceny and attempted battery. Yet the problem that engages us at this stage is whether the actor should be liable for the consummated offense of bigamy, larceny or battery.

Our initial intuitive response to the three hypothetical cases is likely to be the following. In the first case, the actor is not guilty of bigamy, no matter how wicked his intent; in the third example he is guilty of battery, even though the physician is attacking him. And in the second case, we might not be sure whether consent should be a defense when the actor is unaware of it. These intuitions seem to be sound. Yet how do we account for them? Why is there no liability in the battery case? Why are we in doubt about larceny in a case of uncommunicated consent?

If we are concerned about accounting for our intuitions in these cases, the distinction between definition and justification serves us well. So far as an element constitutes part of the inculpatory dimension of wrongdoing, it must be objectively satisifed in order to convict. Its absense is sufficient to justify an acquittal even though the actor is mistaken and thinks he is committing a crime. Analogous examples are easy to find. A would-be killer is not guilty of murder, regardless of his intent, if he shoots at and hits a dead body. The common-law rule, still nominally in force in many states, was that no one could be guilty of raping his own wife.[10] If the victim of a rape was the wife of the

[9] See 3.3.3 *supra*.

[10] 1 Hale 629; Cal. Penal Code §261. The rule appears to discriminate against married women and is therefore not easily reconciled with the equal protection clause of the Fourteenth Amendment.

suspect, he would not be guilty even if he thought he was raping another woman. The elements "killing a human being" and "raping a woman not one's wife" are components of the inculpatory case,[11] of the definition, and therefore the conventional rule is that the absence of these objective elements precludes conviction regardless of the actor's intent.

In contrast, the question of self-defense appears to be a paradigmatic instance of a justificatory claim. It is not the absence of self-defense that inculpates someone for an intentional killing or battery. Rather it is the presence of self-defense that provides a good reason for violating the norm against killing and assaulting other human beings. The consensus of Western legal systems is that actors may avail themselves of justifications only if they act with a justificatory intent.[12] Thus the patient who does not know that he is being attacked cannot avail himself of the claim of justification.[13]

The problem with consent in cases of larceny is that it is difficult to determine whether non-consent is an element of the definition or consent is a claim that justifies the taking. On the former view, we would treat non-consent as analogous to the requirement in bigamy cases that the actor be married at the time of the second putative marriage; in both situations, the absence of the objective prerequisite of the offense would lead to an acquittal. On the other hand, if we perceive consent to be analogous to self-

[11] An alternative interpretation of the exclusion of married women from rape laws is that the criminal law prefers not to meddle in intra-family sexual disputes. *Cf.* StGB §247, which provides that theft and embezzlement within the family are subject to prosecution only if the victim files a complaint. This jurisdictional interpretation of the rape law would imply that the victim's status (married to suspect) was extrinsic to the issue of wrongdoing and therefore neither an issue of definition nor of justification.

[12] MPC §3.02 ("the actor believes"); Schönke-Schröder-Lenckner §32, preliminary note 14, at 394; Jescheck 245–46; Stratenwerth 148–50; there is no opposing sentiment expressed in the Soviet or French literature, nor is the question directly discussed. See generally Kurs (GP 1970) at 342–401; Kurs (GP 1968) at 460–535; 1 Bouzat & Pinatel §§279–300, at 358–73. But *cf.* the Austrian position *infra* note 24.

[13] For a well-developed argument contrary to this view, see Robinson, *A Theory of Justification: Societal Harm as a Prerequisite for Criminal Liability,* 23 U.C.L.A.L. Rev. 266 (1975).

defense, namely, as a good reason for violating the norm, we should be inclined to require that the would-be thief know of the consent before he could rely on it as an exculpatory claim.[14]

Before we begin to lean one way or the other in the analysis, we should attempt to understand more about the definitional and justificatory dimensions of wrongdoing. We should remind ourselves that all we have done so far is describe our intuitive judgments that certain objective elements are necessary for conviction (e.g., a valid prior marriage in bigamy, a live victim in homicide), while other objective elements provide a defense only if the actor is aware of them (e.g., being subject to a wrongful attack). We have yet to give an account of why these intuitive judgments might be sound. Why should it be the case that elements of the inculpatory case need be objectively present? Why is it not sufficient that the actor believe they are present? To take the other side of the distinction, why should a person have to know that he is being attacked in order to avail himself of the defense? Why is it not sufficient that he is in fact attacked?

Considering first the contours of the definition, we must confess that the requirement of specified objective elements is not easy to explain. The problem takes us back to the analysis of *Topolewski*,[15] the pattern of manifest criminality,[16] and the objective theory of attempts.[17] In all of these contexts we encountered a conflict between the objective dimension of criminal conduct and the use of the criminal law to isolate and confine dangerous persons. So far as the latter purpose is dominant, the objective dimensions of criminal conduct come to appear implausible, and even arbitrary. The only way to make sense of objective requirements is to see them as aspects of a particular theory of criminality. The paradigmatic cases of manifest criminality generate objective elements

[14] The status of consent is also disputed in German law, which distinguishes between *Einverständnis* (negating the definition) and *Einwilligung* (a justification). See Jescheck 275–83; Stratenwerth 124–29; see generally P. Noll, *Übergesetzliche Rechtfertigungsgründe im besonderen die Einwilligung des Verletzten* (1955).

[15] See §2.1.3 *supra*.

[16] See §3.8 *supra*.

[17] See §3.3.2 *supra*.

in the definition of crimes, for it is only by virtue of these objective elements that conduct can be manifestly and observably criminal. Yet not all objective elements meet the test of manifest criminality. It would be difficult, for example, to regard a marriage ceremony as manifestly criminal and socially unnerving simply because one of the participants happened, technically, to be still married.[18]

The more plausible defense of objective requirements is the proposition already tentatively defended, that the element of wrongdoing must contain an external element. The external element is necessary to explain the phenomenon of punishment. According to the traditional view of punishment, the sanction is inflicted for the doing of harm, the taking of excessive risks or some other observable objective interference in the external world.[19]

In contrast to this view, an instrumentalist conception of punishment would convert objective requirements into a seemingly arbitrary relic of the past. If the purpose of each criminal prosecution is to determine whether the suspect is dangerous, then it makes no sense at all to acquit people like Topolewski and our hypothetical actors who engage in legal conduct with a criminal purpose.[20]

Turning to the other face of the distinction, we have yet to account for the rule that in cases of alleged justification, the actor must at least be cognizant of the justificatory circumstances. There might be a stronger and weaker version of the rule; the stronger version would require that the actor be motivated exclusively by the justificatory criteria; the weaker version, that he merely be aware of them.[21] In any event, the objective fact that the actor is

[18] If the observer knew of the prior valid marriage, the second ceremony would be manifestly criminal; for remarks on this recurrent problem in the theory of manifest criminality, see §2.2.1 *supra*.

[19] See Robinson, *supra* note 13, at 266–69; Hall 219–22, Morris, *Persons and Punishment* in H. Morris, On Guilt and Innocence 33 (1976) (stressing the concrete "interference" with the interests of others as a characteristic element of criminal conduct).

[20] For a thoughtful instrumentalist approach to the problem of harm, see Schulhofer, *Harm and Punishment: A Critique of Emphasis on the Results of Conduct in the Criminal Law*, 122 U. Pa. L. Rev. 1497 (1974).

[21] Another variation would arise in cases of necessity as a justification, StGB

being attacked by his intended victim would not by itself generate a defense of self-defense.

This requirement of a justificatory intent is by no means self-evident. The argument against the requirement is that the objective facts of justification negate the moral or social harm represented by the defendant's conduct; if there is no harm, there should be no criminal liability.[22] There is no reason for a social response, no ground for punishing the suspect. It would follow that if the state does intervene, the sanction is in the nature of a preventive rather than a punitive measure.

Some European cases support this purely objective theory of justification. In a nineteenth-century German case, some forestry agents entered the defendant's house to look for deer that her son had hunted and killed illegally.[23] The defendant forcibly resisted the search. She was charged with "facilitating" her son's illegal shooting of deer. Yet it turned out that the agents did not have authority to enter the house. Though the defendant did not know of the defect in their authority, her resisting their entry was held to be justified. Her motives were irrelevant. One could easily imagine analogous cases in the United States, particularly in the execution of unconstitutional searches and seizures. If physical resistance were justified solely on objective criteria, the argument would have to be that resisting illegal official conduct is a social good, regardless of the actor's reasons in doing so.

In a recent Austrian decision,[24] the judges again reached the conclusion that objective criteria may be sufficient to justify conduct. The context was a prosecution for abortion in which it turned out that unbeknownst to the physician, there were good medical and legal grounds for justifying the abortion. The implica-

---

§34, where it is sometimes held that the actor must "conscientiously" weigh the competing interests before he decides to violate the prohibitory norm. See text §10.2, at note 16 *infra*.

[22] See Robinson, *supra* note 13, at 266–69.

[23] Judgment of Nov. 10, 1882, 4 Rechtsprechung des Reichsgerichts in Strafsachen 804.

[24] Judgment of Oct. 29, 1959, 30 Entscheidungen des Österreichischen Obersten Gerichtshofes 308.

tion of this, as well as of the older German decision, is that the absence of justification functions as an element of the definition. The element is negated by the presence of a justification. Thus there is no significant difference between the question whether the fetus is alive at the time of the abortion and the question whether the abortion lacks a justification. In either case, the absence of the objective circumstance would preclude liability for the offense. The only difference is that in one case the required circumstance is positive (that the fetus be alive) and in the other it is negative (that the abortion be unjustifiable).[25]

Collapsing the distinction between definition and justification eliminates the distinction between conduct that is perfectly legal and conduct that nominally violates a norm but is justified by the assertion of a superior interest or right. It treats killing a human being in self-defense on a par with hunting and killing a coyote. It suggests that a physician's pounding a patient's chest is of the same order as pounding a nail. Perhaps distinctions of this importance should be recognized in the law, but if so, we should expect to find reasons for the distinction more compelling than its intuitive appeal.

The warrant for the distinction between definition and justification has to be found in a more general theory of inculpation and exculpation in the structure of criminal liability. We shall attempt to clarify the distinction by probing the nature of prohibitory norms and privileges. This clarification of the theory will not only buttress our analysis of requiring knowledge as to some external elements and not others; it will lead us to consider the relevance of the distinction between definition and justification to two other problems in the analysis of criminal liability: (1) the problem of

[25] The theory that claims of justification are negative elements of the definition finds substantial support in the German literature. See, e.g., Engisch, *Der Unrechtstatbestand im Strafrecht*, 1 Hundert Jahre Deutsches Rechtsleben 401 (E. von Caemmerer ed. 1960); Kaufmann, *Tatbestandseinschränkung und Rechtfertigung*, 1955 JZ 37. The primary impact of the theory is that mistakes about justificatory claims are treated like mistakes about the definition. For independent reasons, Soviet theorists refuse to treat claims negating wrongdoing and social danger as extrinsic to the definition (*sostav*). See Kurs (GP 1968) 462–63. *Cf.* §6.7.4 *supra*.

permissible vagueness and (2) the allocation of authority to legislatures and courts in developing the criteria of liability.

§7.4.2. **On Norms and Privileges.** We should begin by asking why particular forms of conduct are incriminating. Why is it that killing, stealing and harmful aggression are usually chastised as wrongdoing? Of course, there may be justified instances of aggressive and violent behavior, but these are cases in which the inculpatory dimension is overridden by criteria of exculpation. To account for the phenomenon of blame and censure, let us think of inculpatory conduct as the violation of a prohibitory norm. For examples we need only think of the basic commandments of Western society. Thou shalt not kill, thou shalt not steal—these are the basic prohibitions on which there is consensus even in morally relativistic, post-religious societies. Yet these simple imperatives that we invoke in blaming others point merely to paradigmatic instances of wrongdoing. In order to make out a complete case of responsible wrongdoing, whether in law or in moral discourse, the simple imperatives must be supplemented in exceptional cases. The supplementary criteria are grounds of justification and excuse.

We may now explicate the definition of an offense more rigorously as the violation of a prohibitory norm. Features of this violation are, first, that the violating conduct incriminates the actor in a given society at a given time; and further, that the violation is typically sufficient to regard the act as wrongful and to hold the violator personally accountable for his wrongdoing. Explicating the concept of definition in this fashion helps us understand why the absence of relevant objective circumstances precludes the finding of a violation. The norm refers to particular objective circumstances: do not kill a human being, do not take the property of another, do not be married to two people at once. If these objective elements are absent in fact, though the actor thinks they are present, there is no violation of the prohibitory norm. In this respect, norms are like promises. One could hardly maintain that an obligor violates a contractual promise merely by thinking that his acts constitute a violation; similarly, it should be clear that a wicked person does not violate a prohibitory norm merely by believing that he does.

Before taking the next step in the argument, we should be clear about the ground covered. What is the ontological status of these norms that are violated by incriminating conduct? Where do we find them? The answer is that we posit these norms as a way of providing an account of why certain forms of conduct are incriminating. In some cases, such as killing and stealing, we have additional cultural evidence for the existence of prohibitory norms. Yet the root social fact is the practice of blaming others for their conduct. Without that social practice, we could not speak of incriminating conduct; and without the latter, we could not posit prohibitory norms.

If the violation of a legal norm, like the breach of a promise, has an objective dimension, the next question is whether claims of justification turn solely on objective criteria. If so, the fact of killing an aggressor would be sufficient to justify homicide even if the actor did not know of the aggression. The fetus' threatening the welfare of the mother would be sufficient to justify an abortion, even if the operating physician did not know of the condition. In analyzing this problem we should keep in mind that a justification is interposed to challenge the wrongfulness of conduct satisfying the definition of the offense.[26] Thus the precise problem is whether objective facts (e.g., the fact of the victim's aggression) are sufficient to negate the allegation of wrongfulness in precisely the same way that objective facts (e.g., the victim's being dead before the shots were fired) are sufficient to preclude a violation of the prohibitory norm. As we discuss the problem in this chapter, we pose the equivalent, but transposed question: are objective facts sufficient to make out a claim of justification? Or need the actor know of the facts that justify his conduct?

We can make some headway on this issue by seeing that grounds of justification represent licenses or permissions to violate the prohibitory norm.[27] A justification is not a conflicting norm

[26] For preliminary notes on wrongdoing and wrongfulness, §6.6.1 *supra.*

[27] The analogous term in German is *Erlaubnissatz.* See, e.g., Jescheck 240–41; Stratenwerth 67–68. I am indebted to Professor Jaime Malamud of Buenos Aires for convincing me of the centrality of the idea of permission in the notion of justification.

imposing a countervailing duty to act. There is no breach of duty in giving way to an aggressor.[28] One is permitted to kill or injure another in self-defense, but never legally required to do so.[29] This permissive aspect of justified conduct is captured in the term "privilege," which is commonly used as a synonym for "justification." [30] Thus the apt way to describe the structural relationship between prohibitory norms and privileges is that one has a duty to obey a prohibitory norm and a privilege to violate it when justificatory circumstances are present.

This analysis, incidentally, conforms to Hohfeld's explication of basic legal relationships.[31] The correlative of the duty to obey the norm is the right of others to demand compliance; the correlative of the privilege to violate the norm is the "no-right" of others to prevent the violation.

Now the question is whether explicating claims of justification as privileges helps us support the conclusion that knowledge of the justificatory circumstances is necessary to say that the violator has exercised his privilege. There are three arguments on behalf of the view that it does. First, preliminarily, what is true about violating norms (namely, that objective facts are sufficient to bar conviction) does not necessarily carry over to the distinct field of privileges. Secondly, and more to the point, a conceptual analysis of "exercising a privilege" supports the view that the act of "exercising" or "acting under" a privilege presupposes knowledge of the justifying circumstances. To derive this conclusion, we need only inquire what we mean when we say that someone has "acted in" self-defense or has "exercised a privilege" generated by the imminent risk of danger to others. What we mean in these cases, I

[28] The possibility of duty to fight aggressors is considered in the Soviet literature, but the duty is rejected. Kurs (GP 1968) 467–68; Kurs (GP 1970) 349–50.

[29] Governmental officials might, of course, be subject to a duty to use force. On the difference between governmental and private privileges, see §10.1 *infra*. Note that Blackstone identified justifiable homicide with what the law required. 4 Blackstone 178 (example of an executioner carrying out a death warrant).

[30] This synonymity is expressed in MPC §3.11(1), which uses the term "privilege" to refer to the grounds of justification regulated in Article 3.

[31] See generally W. Hohfeld, Fundamental Legal Conceptions 162–63 (1923).

take it, is that the actor adverts to the relevant circumstances in acting. If he is ignorant of the impending aggression or the risk to others, he may act so to benefit himself or others, but it is not correct to say that he has "exercised" his privilege. Of course, one might dispute this analysis by questioning whether so much should turn on the word "exercise." Yet the concept of privilege carries with it a set of linkages in our language. And one of these is that what we do with privileges is exercise them. We do not "obey" or "comply" with them as we do with norms.[32] We "exercise" them, and this notion has built into it the requirement that we know of the circumstances that permit us to justify our conduct.

If this conceptual argument is unsatisfying, it is because it does not account for our language's crystallizing as it has. We should seek an independent rationale for the same conclusion that goes beyond our linguistic habits and explains why the language has taken its present form. Thus we are led to a third argument for the requirement of justificatory intent.

This last argument builds on the assumption that claims of justification represent exceptions to prohibitory norms. As exceptions, these claims should be available only to those who merit special treatment. Injecting the element of merit makes the actor's intent relevant, for objective circumstances alone cannot establish the special merit of someone who treads upon the protected interests of another. For someone who violates a norm to deserve exceptional treatment, he or she must at least know of the circumstances supporting the claim of an exception.

The virtue of this argument is that it provides an account for the requirement of justificatory intent without calling into question the sufficiency of objective circumstances in precluding a finding that the actor violated the prohibitory norm. In assessing the latter question, there is no issue of special treatment, no problem of the actor's merit. The question whether one violates a norm and satisfies the definition of an offense presupposes the finding

[32] It is fair to say that one may unwittingly "comply" with an order or with a law, but one does not unwittingly "exercise" a privilege.

of particular public facts. That these facts are absent tells us nothing about the actor's merit or desert, but rather has the effect of undercutting the authority of the state to inquire further about the actor's potential liability.

§7.4.3. On Distinguishing Between Norms and Exceptions. The foregoing exposition basks in the clarity of a few simple cases. Yet the distinction between definition and justification is not always as simple as it is in homicide cases. In a whole range of offenses, it is not so easy to discern whether a particular issue is an element of justification or whether its reciprocal is an element of the definition. Let us look at some of these borderline cases:

1. Is the issue of necessity (lesser evils) in abortion cases a claim of justification or is non-necessity an element of the definition? How does the relevant norm read? Is it: Do not commit abortions? Or is it: Do not commit unnecessary abortions?

2. Is consent always a matter of justification, or is nonconsent an element of the definition of rape or larceny? How does the norm against stealing read? Do not take the goods of another? Or is it rather: Do not take the goods of another without consent?

It would be a mistake to think that we could resolve these borderline issues by any abstract, logical test. The interpretation of abortion, of larceny and rape springs from the concrete realities of our social and moral life. In particular, we cannot begin to classify necessity and consent as elements of the prohibitory norm or of justification without gauging contemporary attitudes toward abortion, taking goods and fornication. It is not so long ago that abortion was paradigmatically wrong and justified only in the exceptional situation of an imminent threat to the life of the mother. There might be a society in which touching or moving the object of another was just as suspect as interfering with the person of another. The question is whether in our society, in the here and now, these forms of conduct are identifiable as typically wrongful. Without turning to our own sensibilities, we cannot begin to distinguish between the prohibitory norm and claims of justification.

To make the point clear, let us consider a case where we would readily concur that a particular issue belongs to the definition of the offense. Take the offense of reckless driving. Logically, one could claim that the norm was directed against all driving. In exceptional cases, safe (or non-reckless) driving would justify a violation of the norm. In this mode of thinking, a case of safe driving would be treated as a justified violation of the norm; if recklessness were an element of the definition, non-reckless or safe driving would not violate the norm. Under both versions, reckless driving would be treated as an unjustified or wrongful violation of the norm. Despite this functional equivalence, it is clear how the distinction between definition and justification should apply in this case. In our society, under normal circumstances, it would be incoherent to prohibit driving altogether. No one would know what to make of the norm. The only morally coherent norm would be one that prohibited reckless driving. It follows that "recklessly" is an element of the definition. The implication is that if driving is objectively below the threshold of recklessness, it is immaterial whether the driver thinks that he is driving recklessly. The objective fact is sufficient to preclude liability.

The minimal demand on the definition of an offense is that it reflect a morally coherent norm in a given society at a given time. It is only when the definition corresponds to a norm of this social force that satisfying the definition inculpates the actor. There is nothing inculpatory about driving. Nor is anything incriminating or inculpatory in carrying an object. Adding the element that the object belongs to another makes the act more incriminating; including the element of the owner's nonconsent brings us closer to a prima facie case of wrongdoing.[33]

Changing social mores can undercut the moral bite of a norm that was once coherent and forceful. A good example is the norm against abortion, which was once as clear and categorical as the norm against killing. When the necessity of an abortion to save the life of the mother was initially recognized as a defense, there was

[33] The definition of larceny presumably includes "the intent permanently to deprive the owner of his property." See §2.4 *supra*. Acting with this intent would have to be included in the prohibitory norm.

doubt that the function of the necessity was to justify the violation of the norm. Yet as consensus on abortion began to disintegrate, an imperative against abortions began to appear to many people as grossly overdrawn. To regain the moral bite of the original norm, the element of non-necessity needed then to be included in the prohibitory norm. This may be one of the factors contributing to the decision of the Austrian Supreme Court in 1959 that a physician did not commit punishable abortion even though he did not know that the fetus' position endangered the life of the mother.[34] If the norm is defined to prohibit only unnecessary abortions, the objective fact that the mother's life was in danger should have been sufficient to bar liability.

This discussion of reckless driving and abortion illustrates the general methodology for distinguishing between the prohibitory norm and the countervailing criteria of privilege. The norm must contain a sufficient number of elements to state a coherent moral imperative. This is another way of saying that the norm must be so defined that its violation is incriminating. The questions of moral force and of the incriminating effect of conduct are resolved under the mores of the relevant society at the time of the deed.

Unfortunately, this methodology may be insufficiently precise to resolve cases in the borderland between definition and justification. The issue of consent in larceny is particularly difficult to classify. We find it hard to determine whether taking and using another's property is sufficiently incriminating to constitute an incriminating event. Should the element of non-consent be added to seal the inculpatory effect? Need we consider the intent permanently to deprive as an aspect of prohibitory norm? If not, how do we justify our assuming that this intent is a required element of the definition? There is no doubt that we have a method that works for a broad range of cases. But we should not claim too much for an analysis that rests upon suggestive questions such as whether a norm carries a coherent moral imperative and whether conduct is incriminating. These are questions of degree and, unhappily, we live in a legal world that does not permit us to recog-

[34] See note 24 *supra*.

nize degrees, but rather requires us to slice the spectrum into opposing categories.

§7.5. *Due Process and Fair Warning.*

There is a tendency in common-law jurisdictions to think of the legislature as supreme in all questions bearing on criminal liability. The maxim *nulla poena sine lege* is held to apply both to the recognition of new claims of excuse and justification as well as the levying of newly defined prohibitions.[1] The official view is that judges should tamper neither with the categories of exculpation nor with the categories of inculpation. The impact of this dogma on the development of excusing conditions is not particularly severe, for courts often recognize unlegislated excuses by treating them as claims denying the required culpability.[2] Yet justificatory claims do not negate the conventional elements of the prosecutor's case. There are precedents in which courts treat claims of justification as negating a legislated element of "unlawfulness." [3] But in contrast to German theory, the common-law courts do not recognize legal "wrongfulness" as an immanent dimension of every crime. As a result, the common-law courts have had particular difficulty recognizing the justification of necessity or lesser evils. The

§7.5. [1] See Keeler v. Superior Court, 2 Cal. 3d 619, 470 P.2d 617, 87 Cal. Rptr. 481 (1970), where the court implied in passing that the criteria of justification and excuse were subject to legislative control to the same extent as the question whether a fetus was a "human being" for purposes of homicide. *Id.* at 632, 470 P.2d at 624–25, 87 Cal. Rptr. at 488–89. See to the same effect the opinion by Lord Kilbrandon in Lynch v. Director of Public Prosecutions, [1975] 1 All E.R. 913, 942 (H.L.).

[2] E.g., Rex v. Steane, [1947] 1 K.B. 997 (excuse of duress held to negate the required intent "to assist the enemy"); Hopps v. People, 31 Ill. 385, 394 (1863) (insanity viewed as a denial of "criminal intention"); People v. Hernandez, 61 Cal. 2d 529, 393 P.2d 673, 39 Cal. Rptr. 361 (1964) (reasonable mistake as to age negates the required "criminal intent").

[3] Rex v. Bourne, [1938] 3 All E.R. 615 (Cent. Crim. Ct.) (abortion to preserve health of mother not "unlawful").

defense percolates through discussions of constitutional, natural and contractual rights,[4] but no court, so far as I know, has ever recognized the issue in broad and principled language. The reason is that the common-law courts are accustomed to deferring to legislative authority over the contours of criminal liability.[5]

This is a dogma that we should reconsider. Is there any reason why legislative authority should extend to questions of justification and excuse as well as the definition of offenses? Having explicated these structural components of liability we can now attend to a new set of questions. We should concede that the maxim *nulla poena sine lege* applies to the definition, but should it preclude the judicial recognition of new claims of excuse and justification? It is generally conceded that the law should provide fair warning of conduct that might be punished. One aspect of the principle of fair warning is that criminal statutes must be well defined. If they are too imprecise and require people to guess at their meaning, they will be declared void for excessive vagueness.[6] The question that troubles us is whether the issue of vagueness should affect the recognition of issues extrinsic to the definition. The defense of necessity or lesser evils is vague. Does it follow that all offenses subject to the justification of necessity are excessively vague? Relying on the distinction between definition and justification, we shall attempt to rethink the question whether the principles of legislative control and specificity apply to all issues bearing on liability. The structure of the argument requires that we turn first to the problems of specificity and vagueness.

§7.5.1. The Problem of Vagueness. Not all justificatory claims are vague. Consent, superior orders—these are as precise as any prohibitory norm. Yet the claims of self-defense and necessity

[4] See §10.2.3 *infra*.

[5] Yet, ironically, even in recent decades, the courts have expanded liability for common-law misdemeanors, e.g., Shaw v. Director of Public Prosecutions, [1962] A.C. 220 (H.L. 1961) (conspiracy to corrupt public morals); Commonwealth v. Mochan, 177 Pa. Super. 454, 110 A.2d 788 (1955) (obscene phone calls).

[6] E.g., Papachristou v. City of Jacksonville, 405 U.S. 156 (1972) (vagrancy ordinance unconstitutionally vague); International Harvester Co. v. Kentucky, 234 U.S. 216 (1914) (price and trade regulation unconstitutional).

are unavoidably open-textured. One never knows precisely when deadly force may be used and when it may not. In the context of lesser evils, it is always a matter of judgment whether one of two competing interests should be deemed superior. The problem is whether this degree of vagueness is more readily tolerated in the framework of privilege than at the level of the prohibitory norm.

The question was posed in an intriguing California decision, which held the California abortion statute unconstitutionally vague.[7] The statute prohibited unnecessary abortions, and necessity was defined by reference to saving the mother's life and health. The court held that balancing the fetus' value against the mother's health required physicians to guess, at their peril. There was no way to determine when an abortion was free from the risk of criminal sanctions. This decision seems plausible in the context of abortion, but it carries far-reaching implications for all offenses subject to the defense of lesser evils. Larceny is subject to justification if the taking is necessary to avoid a greater evil.[8] This standard is just as vague in larceny cases as it is in the context of abortion. Yet we could not seriously propose that the crime of larceny is unconstitutionally vague. The only way, it seems, to avoid that inference from the California decision would be to invoke the distinction between definition and justification. The argument would be that the norm against abortion is directed solely to non-necessary abortions. The norm against stealing, in contrast, still enjoys moral force as simple moral imperative; unlike abortion, it need not be restricted to unnecessary action in order to state a plausible moral precept. The significant fact about abortion, or "termination of pregnancy" in the modern euphemism, is that it has become acceptable in so many different situations that the prohibitory norm must contain a reference to non-necessary intervention. Larceny, in contrast, is still wrongful in the routine run of cases, and only in exceptional situations might a claim of lesser evils come into play.

[7] People v. Belous, 71 Cal. 2d 954, 458 P.2d 194, 80 Cal. Rptr. 354 (1969), *cert. denied*, 397 U.S. 915 (1970).

[8] This is true, at least, in those states that have adopted a provision modelled after MPC §3.02. See §10.2.3 *infra*.

The distinction between abortion and larceny illustrates why the problem of vagueness is more troublesome at the level of the definition. The breakdown of a simple norm against abortion has coincided with a multiplication of the situations in which abortions are regarded as acceptable—eugenic abortions, abortions after a criminal rape, as well as abortions to preserve the interests of the mother. The problem of deciding whether an abortion is permissible is now a daily fact of medical practice. In the case of larceny, however, the phenomenon of justification is still exceptional. Whatever vagueness adheres in the claim of necessity affects our judgment solely in situations where criteria of necessity warrant a privileged violation of the norm. Yet it is not clear what should follow from this distinction between routine and exceptional problems of interpreting vague rule. A number of arguments could be advanced.

First, it might be said that vagueness at the level of a privilege is not problematic, for it arises only infrequently. Vagueness in routine cases is more troublesome because it happens more often. That is certainly true, but the argument is reminiscent of claims about shifting the burden of persuasion on newly created defenses. If the legislature chooses to regulate a field, it must meet the criteria of sound legislation. If the defect of vagueness in claims of justification is curable, then it is up to the legislature to remedy the defect. At a more fundamental level, we should question whether claims of justification should be seen as special exemptions bestowed upon the defendant. There is a contrary school supporting the claim that self-defense is a natural right. Numerous cases treat the claim of lesser evils under the natural right to shelter one's children or the constitutional right to protect one's property. If claims of justification have this status in the minds of many, one should hardly be cavalier about whether the issues should be treated as special exemptions.

If there is a convincing argument for exempting exculpatory claims from the vice of vagueness, it would have to be that the principle of fair warning applies only to paradigmatic instances of wrongdoing. The cases covered by the definition of the offenses arguably represent the range of problems that people think about in ordering their daily affairs. Cases of justification and excuse typically arise *in extremis,* where actors have little time to contemplate the legality of their conduct.[9] There is something to this point, yet there are cases in which people obviously do advert to the contours of privileges in deciding what to do. Is it not important to a homeowner to know whether the privilege of necessary force permits the killing of a burglar who threatens no personal harm? Is it not important to a school teacher to know the circumstances and the procedures for using corporal punishment, if it is permitted at all? The more we explore the problem of fair warning in the field of justification, the more we see how complicated the issue is.[10]

§7.5.2. Legislative Control over the Refinement of the Criminal Law. One implication of limiting the principle *nulla poena sine lege* to the definition of new offenses is that we could then more readily justify the judicial creation of new justificatory claims. As we shall see in Chapter Ten, the German courts have few inhibitions about developing "extra-statutory" claims of privilege. This freedom of the courts to refine the criteria of liability derives not only from limiting the maxim *nulla poena sine lege* to the definition of new offenses, but from a transcendent conception of legally wrongful conduct. This conception of wrongful conduct, which is taken to be a necessary dimension of every offense, permits the courts to engage in bold innovations that permit the violation of legislative prohibitions.

These judicial innovations admittedly work more clearly to the benefit of defendants than does vagueness in detailing the grounds for justification. The effect of a judicially created privilege is to restrict the scope of punishable conduct rather than expand it. Yet the judicial recognition of new grounds of justification raises some

[9] This would not be true for the claim of consent. But consent, as we have seen, is a borderline problem in many respects.

[10] The problem seemed to me less subtle in my earlier paper; Fletcher, *The Right Deed for the Wrong Reason: A Reply to Mr. Robinson,* 23 U.C.L.A.L. Rev., 293, 312–16 (1975).

difficult, unresolved problems. If, for example, the courts should boldly declare that lesser evils constitutes a defense, do they then lose the prerogative of reversing themselves and abolishing the claim? After all, abolishing justification generates a new class of punishable behavior and therefore the judicial action arguably runs afoul of the maxim *nulla poena sine lege.*

This problem is posed today in the German system. For reasons we shall explore later,[11] the German law reform of 1975 failed to recognize the limitation of reasonable force as an outer boundary to the privilege of necessary defense in halting minor forms of aggression.[12] According to a strict interpretation of the new code, there is no inhibition against using even deadly force, when necessary, to prevent thieves from escaping. Yet considerable judicial authority supports the view that even when it is necessary, deadly force is impermissible to prevent petty harms.[13] The problem with the judiciary's restricting the defense in this way is that it generates a class of punishable acts that, according to the legislative language, should be exempt from punishment. The only way to defend this innovation by the courts is to treat the scope of privileges as radically distinct from the scope of the definition. The courts may arguably tamper with the former, but not the latter. One must confess to being less than fully persuaded by the force of the distinction in this context.

To review the arguments of the second half of this chapter, we asserted initially that the distinction between definition and justification was critical to understanding why objective facts were sometimes sufficient to preclude a conviction. We explicated this view by developing the theoretical difference between norms and privileges. We then sought to apply these distinctions in assessing vagueness as a vice and determining the proper allocation of authority between the legislature and the courts. As to these latter claims, we found the distinction between definition and justification suggestive but, at the same time, problematic.

[11] See §10.5 *infra.*

[12] StGB §32.

[13] The theory supporting this limitation is developed *infra* in §10.5, at notes 72–76 *infra.*

§7.6. *The Structure of Offenses: A Review.*

The movement to disengage the theory of criminal law from the structure of private litigation thrust the normative issue of culpability center stage in the drama of criminal trials. The overriding significance of culpability has the effect of (1) generating a sense for the functional equivalence of all issues bearing on substantive criminal liability, and (2) of requiring the state to bear the risk of non-persuasion on all of these substantive issues. Yet there is great merit in digging beneath this superficial symmetry in order to explicate the structural relationships of issues that relate in different ways to the ultimate question of culpability. The virtue of explicating this structure is that we can generate a set of categories for assessing questions such as the requirement of justificatory intent and the relative role of the legislature and the judiciary in developing the substantive criminal law. Though conceptual clarification does not entail any set of answers, it does help us frame important questions. The discourse of Anglo-American law would be greatly enriched if we could adhere to the structure that we have elicited from the range of issues bearing on culpability. For the sake of review, we shall restate that structure, and mention some of the principles and questions associated with each dimension of liability. This review will consolidate the results of our inquiry to this point and provide an introduction to the following three chapters.

§7.6.1. **The Definition of the Offense.** This is the set of objective and subjective elements that constitute the incriminating case against the accused. The contours of the definition are set by the prohibitory norm. The prohibitory norm, in turn, must be cast so as to state a morally coherent imperative in the particular society. Definitions are always overly broad, for they enjoin theft, homicide and battery in categorical terms. The definition must be read, together with the exceptions represented by claims of justification and excuse, in order to arrive at the conduct that is actually subject to punishment.

The definition consists of objective and subjective elements. If any one of the objective elements is absent, there is no possibility of establishing the offense; and the prosecution fails. There is some dispute about whether the violation of a prohibitory norm always requires subjective as well as objective elements. For the sake of simplicity, we shall adhere to the view that the question of intent is a subjective element of the definition in larceny, homicide, attempts and analogous offenses. This subjective element of the definition raises a question of fact about the actor's mental state. It corresponds to the dominant view in the common law about the meaning of *mens rea* and the Model Penal Code's criteria for "kinds of culpability." In cases of negligent and reckless conduct, the definition includes the element of excessive risk-taking. This element might be defined as an "unreasonable risk" or a "substantial and unjustified risk." The element of awareness of the risk in cases of recklessness would also adhere to the definition. The prohibitory norms in these cases are directed against running excessive risks of harm to protected legal interests.

The minimal demand of the maxim *nulla poena sine lege* is that the legislature, and only the legislature, be charged with the authority of enacting definitions of crime. The principle of fair warning requires that the legislature define the prohibitory norms of the society. The demands of legislative specificity are stricter in the category of definition than in the analysis of justification and excuse. Yet there are some claims of justification on which people do rely in planning their conduct, and those too should be subject to the constitutional requirement of specificity.

§7.6.2. **Wrongdoing and Justification.** The violation of the prohibitory norm does not entail liability unless it is wrongful. In the typical case, the violation of the definition is wrongful. Yet in extraordinary cases, the conduct might be justified by appeal to a conflicting norm permitting the violation. The paradigmatic instances of justification are lesser evils, self-defense and acting in the name of the law to effect an arrest or prevent an escape from custody. Claims of justification always require a union of objective elements and a subjective intent. The nature of a justification is that the actor has good and sufficient reasons for violating the norm constituting the definition. Justified conduct in violation of the definition is not wrongful, but neither is it perfectly legal, as is conduct that falls outside the scope of the definition. This type of harmful conduct might, for example, support tort liability for the harm done.

The authority of the judiciary over contours of wrongful conduct is in dispute. A legal system in which there is a strong sense for overriding principles of law might vest the judiciary with the authority to determine when conduct violating legislative norms is wrongful, in which case the judiciary would be empowered to recognize new claims of justification. A strongly positivist legal system would recognize the exclusive authority of the legislature to determine when conduct is justified. In a positivistic climate, the terms "wrongdoing" and "wrongful conduct" are likely to merge with the concept of unlawfulness, with the legislature in full control over what constitutes the law. The topic of justification, and particularly the contours of particular claims of justification, are explored further in §§10.2 and 10.5.

§7.6.3. Culpability, Attribution and Excuses. The distinction between wrongdoing and attribution, which we elaborated in Chapter Six, corresponds to the distinction between justification and excuse. Claims of justification negate the dimension of wrongdoing; claims of excuse negate the element of attribution or culpability. The underlying theory of excusability is that it is unfair to hold the particular suspect accountable for his wrongful act. The diverse grounds of excuse, which we shall explore in Chapters Nine and Ten, include insanity, duress and various forms of mistake. In cases of negligence and recklessness, the issue of attribution is whether the particular individual can be fairly held accountable for running an excessive risk of harm. A claim of justification is a privileged violation of the prohibitory norm. The functional impact of a justification is to modify the norm by carving out a limited field where the conduct is not wrongful. Valid claims of excuse do not modify the prohibitory norm. Excused conduct is still wrongful: the norm against the conduct remains intact. To recognize an excuse is to judge that the particular suspect cannot be fairly held liable for the violation.

The judgment of attribution is patently normative. In the typical case, however, the normative judgment follows readily from the commission of wrongful conduct. It is only in the unusual case that a valid excuse intrudes to preclude liability. Because the issue poses an ongoing judicial obligation to evaluate individual accountability for wrongdoing, there is a tendency in positivistic legal systems to eliminate the category of excuses and to collapse the questions both of excuse and justification into the definition of the offense. This tendency is most pronounced in Anglo-American and Soviet law; we return to this topic in Chapter Ten when we turn to the particular grounds for excusing wrongful conduct. We shall note then that there is in this context, as well as in the theory of justification, an ongoing tension between legislative and the judicial control over the refinement of the criminal law.

Though we use the notions of culpability, attribution and excusability as though they were coextensive, we should note some important differences among them. The term "attribution" is technical, and therefore we can let it stand for what we will. We choose to employ the term to refer to the judgment that a particular individual may fairly be held accountable for his wrongdoing in violation of a legislative prohibition. The notion of excusing is the precise reciprocal of attribution; it is the judgment that the individual cannot be fairly held accountable. Both of these ideas are broader than the concepts of culpability or blameworthiness as they might be understood in ordinary English. In the core cases of violent aggressive criminality, unexcused wrongdoings may be blameworthy in a moral sense. But there are many instances where the wrongful act consists merely in the violation of a legislated norm; a good example would be norms prohibiting the possession of drugs, weapons or tools used in counterfeiting or burglary. Though this conduct is technically wrongful, it could be difficult to regard the attribution of this wrongful conduct as culpable in a moral sense. If the term "culpability" is distended to cover these cases of *malum prohibitum,* the term loses its moral force and becomes a term of art comparable to attribution.

The concept of attribution (non-excusability) may also apply to systems of liability where claims of justification are irrelevant, and therefore the notion of wrongdoing does not apply in the ordinary sense. One might construct a plausible system of tort liability based solely on inexcusably causing harm; the claim of lesser evils would be irrelevant to the duty to render compensation.[1] This is indeed the apt way to describe so-called strict liability in the law of torts. Liability is imposed for justified risk-taking that results in harm, yet the risk-taking must be attributable to the particular individual or enterprise that the plaintiff seeks to hold accountable. The notion of culpability or fault is out of place in this context, yet the theories of excuse and attribution still function to generate defenses to liability.[2]

The virtue of our conceptual apparatus, as we shall discover in the remaining chapters, is that we may now probe a variety of issues more deeply than has been possible in the ambiguous discourse of the common law. In the next two chapters we shall apply the apparatus in systematic study of three recurrent themes of the general part: the problem of punishing omissions, the theory of complicity and the theory of mistake.

§7.6. [1] For a theory of this sort, see the paradigm of reciprocity in Fletcher, *Fairness and Utility in Tort Theory*, 85 Harv. L. Rev. 537, 543--56 (1972). There are some mistakes in this theory, but it is still sufficiently plausible to serve as an example.

[2] *Id.* at 551–56.

Chapter Eight
The Theory of Derivative Liability

§8.1. *The Concepts of Direct and of Derivative Liability.*

The standard cases of criminal liability are those in which an individual violates a prohibitory norm, with neither justification nor excuse. He may act in concert with others, but his conduct is assessed on its own terms. The crime perpetrated might take a variety of forms. It might be an act of causing harm, such as homicide, or an inchoate offense, such as conspiracy or possession of contraband. It might be an affirmative act or a failure to act, as in the failure to file an income tax form or the failure to answer a question before a congressional hearing. The standard form of perpetration is readily adapted to all of these variations in the form of criminal conduct.

There are two species of criminal liability that fall outside the standard cases of perpetration. The first is failing to intervene to prevent a harm that the law seeks to prevent. Someone fails to render aid to a stricken party and the latter dies. Depending on the circumstances and the relationship between the parties, the party who fails to intervene might be liable for criminal homicide. This form of liability is often called "commission by omission." The other problematic field is accessorial liability for criminal acts committed by others. In the idiom of the common law, "aiders and abettors" can be held liable for the wrongful act[1] committed by the perpetrator. In this chapter, we shall propose a novel perspective for analyzing these two special forms of liability. The claim is that these two branches of liability not only lie outside the core cases of perpetration, but that they share a number of important features. Note the following:

1. In both cases of failing to intervene and of accessorial liability, the actor is punished for a violation of the same prohibitory norm that covers standard cases of perpetration. There is no crime of "letting someone die" or "being an accessory." The basic prohibitory norm is supplemented by special doctrines to cover failing to intervene (commission by omission) and accessorial liability.

2. Both fields are marked by a problematic causal link between the conduct of the accused and the harm (or wrongful act) for which he is held accountable. The party who fails to intervene and rescue someone in distress "causes" death in the sense that there is no liability if the intervention would not have saved the life of the victim. Yet the failure to intervene does not cause death in the same sense that shooting or strangling the victim does. Failing to intervene does not "taint" the passive party in the sense already explored.[2] Similarly, the accessory "causes" the wrongful act of the perpetrator in the sense that he renders concrete assistance by supplying the weapon or giving counsel and advice to the perpetrator. Yet aiding the crime of a responsible, self-actuating perpetrator does not "cause," "control," or "determine" the latter's conduct. The accessory contributes to the crime, but the execution is not his doing.

3. The concept of intentionally committing an offense does not fit readily in either category. The physician who fails to stop at a highway accident can hardly be said to "intend" the death of a vic-

§8.1. [1] There is a problem in describing an act for which the accessory may be held accountable as "wrongful" or "punishable." For the conflicting theories on this point, see §8.5.2 *infra.*

[2] See §5.1.1. *supra.*

tim by driving on. Similarly, the manager of an answering service who knowingly provides aid to a ring of call girls may intend to facilitate prostitution, but it would be odd to say that in providing the service, he "intends" to commit an act of prostitution. These difficulties in applying the concept of intent are closely related, as we shall see, to the problematic causal link discussed above.

These latter two points about causation and intent are admittedly debatable. The view that I shall urge demands careful argument. In this preliminary sketch of the theory, I rely simply on the intuitive oddity of referring to "causing" harm and "intentionally" committing a crime in cases of commission by omission and accessorial liability.

The experimental thesis of this chapter is that both forms of liability—commission by omission and accessorial liability—can be grouped under the single heading of "derivative liability." "Derivative" liability is contrasted with "direct" liability in the standard cases of perpetration. Liability is derivative in the *formal* sense that in neither field—failing to avert harm or aiding the crime of another—is the defendant's conduct sufficient in itself to constitute a violation of the norm under which he is punished. Supplementary doctrines permit the courts to extend liability to cases that the legislature has not identified as criminal in enacting specific norms such as those against homicide, arson and larceny.

Liability is derivative in the *substantive* sense suggested by the problematic causal link between the actor and the independent process for which he is held accountable. In cases of failing to avert harm, this independent process is the natural flow of events. If a parent refuses to call a doctor to aid a sick child and the child lives, there is no liability; if the child dies, the parent might well be liable for manslaughter. Whether the child lives or dies is obviously not subject to the control of the parent in the same way as the parent's own conduct is subject to his or her minute direction.

Similarly, in cases of complicity in the crimes of another, the imposition of liability depends upon whether the principal carries out the planned crime. If the accessory counsels the principal or provides him with the tools of the crime, and the principal never carries out the plan, there is no accessorial liability. It might be objected that if this is the substantive sense of derivative liability, then homicide and all kindred offenses are derivative: there is no liability unless the death or analogous harm actually ensues. This objection obscures the important difference between the core sense of causing harm and the problematic sense of causation in failing to prevent harm and aiding a perpetrator. This critical distinction will admittedly not become clear until we devote due attention to the concept of causation.[3]

The primary value of the proposed concept of derivative liability is that it enables us to formulate several propositions that otherwise remain obscure. In working our way through the details of the law, we shall find that fields of commission by omission and accessorial liability share two architectonic concerns. The first is whether particular factual situations should be treated as cases of direct or of derivative liability. This recurrent concern derives from the strategic value of classifying a case as an instance of derivative liability. While intentionally causing death is prima facie wrongful and punishable, letting someone die by failing to intervene is punishable only if there is a special duty to intervene. There is an obvious advantage in arguing, for example, that turning off a mechanical respirator in anticipation of the patient's death is a case of derivative rather than direct liability; under the particular facts of the case, there might not be a duty to continue aid to the patient. In the field of accessorial liability, the advantage of being treated as derivatively rather than directly liable depends on the particular legal system. In many systems, but not in Anglo-American law, accessories are punished less severely than perpetrators. Yet even those systems that do not officially punish accessories less severely may reach the same result under a system of discretionary sentencing. If American courts are to return to a system of prescribed sentences for specified offenses, it would be good to consider whether the substantive law of liability should prescribe a lower level of punishment for accessories. What judges now do as a matter of discretion may someday have to be spelled out in the substantive law.

[3] See §§8.2.1 through 8.2.3 *infra*.

The second feature common to both fields is the setting of minimum criteria for derivative liability. In the field of commission by omission, the threshold is defined by the imposition of particular duties to intervene and prevent harm. In the arena of accessorial liability, the issue is when one must desist from interacting with persons who one knows are about to commit crimes. Must a gas station attendant refuse, at the risk of liability as an accessory, to sell gas to someone who says that he is on his way to commit arson? In both fields, the working out of these minimal criteria raises subtle issues in the conflict between liberty and social protection.

§8.2. *Derivative Liability for Omissions.*

The field of liability for "omissions" encompasses not only cases of commission by omission, but also liability for the breach of a specific statutory duty to act. This latter category, which we discussed in Chapter Six, represents cases of direct rather than derivative liability. These instances of failure to act are typified by the breach of a duty to submit a tax return, to answer a material question before a congressional committee, or to give one's name and address at the scene of an accident. Provided that the defendant has a fair notice of his obligation, there is nothing suspect about these statutorily imposed duties to act. Therefore, these cases of statutory breach represent instances of direct liability no different in structure from liability for prohibited affirmative conduct.

In the context of this chapter, we should restate the way in which these statutory violations are distinguishable, formally and substantively, from cases of derivative liability for failure to avert harm. Formally, the breach of a statutory duty, say the filing of an income tax return, is a case of direct liability, for the actor is held accountable under the statute generating the duty to act. Cases of derivative liability, in contrast, represent extensions of offenses that are typically committed by affirmative conduct. In a substantive sense, liability for failure to report taxable income is direct rather than derivative, for the offense is complete at the moment of breach. Derivative liability, in contrast, is based on some independent process of events over which the defendant has minimal control, and therefore liability is not subject to determination until these events run their course.[1]

Logically, liability could be derivative in one sense but not the other. For example, one might think that liability might be at least formally direct if the legislature specified all the cases in which there was a duty to intervene and prevent death. It would not be sufficient, however, for the legislature to decree in general terms that the failure to fulfill a duty to prevent death would support a charge of criminal homicide.[2] It would still be incumbent on the courts to work out these duties in specific cases, and the general legislative rule would hardly avoid any of the objections that one might have to judicial development of the substantive rules of liability.

The field of derivative liability for omissions must be carefully staked out on two fronts. At the one frontier, the field must be distinguished from direct liability for omissions, as we have sought to do in the preceding paragraphs. At the other frontier, the field must be marked off from cases of direct liability for negligently causing harm. Many cases of negligent manslaughter might be interpreted as omissions constituting the breach of a duty. A driver fails to turn on his lights. A railroad switchman fails to keep a lookout. A surgeon fails to remove a sponge from the patient at the end of an operation. As a result of all these "failings" a significant harm occurs. The omission of proper care could be seen as analogous to the failure of a parent to render aid to a sick child, but this analogy would be highly misleading. These negligent fail-

§8.2. [1] The distinction between these two types of omission is commonplace in Continental legal thought, see A. Kaufmann, Die Dogmatik der Unterlassungsdelikte (1959); 1 Bouzat & Pinatel §§113–117, at 183–93; Kurs (GP 1970) at 151–52, but it is rarely stressed in the Anglo-American literature, except by authors with a Continental background. For a discussion of the distinction, see Kirchheimer, *Criminal Omissions,* 55 Harv. L. Rev. 615 (1942).

[2] See, e.g., MPC §2.01(3)(b) (no liability for commission by omission without a "duty . . . imposed by law"). StGB §13, discussed in §8.4.2, at note 12 *infra.*

ures are embedded in larger activities. In these particular cases, the negligent breach of duty converts the driving, the railroad crossing, and the medical operation into unexpected hazards. The negligently managed activity creates a substantial and unjustified risk of harm. If the harm materializes, the cause appears to be the negligent activity as a whole rather than the isolated failure to exercise due care. In these cases, therefore, it is more fitting to describe the relevant duty as a duty of care in managing an activity rather than a duty to intervene and prevent harm.

There are undoubtedly cases in which it is difficult to decide whether the omission occurs within a larger activity that causes harm or whether it constitutes an isolated failure to intervene. A parent's failing to feed a child or failing to provide adequate protection in the winter might be treated as part of the larger enterprise of caring for children. Failing to keep a dangerous dog locked up might be seen as part of the larger enterprise of maintaining the dog. If the case is seen as one of negligent affirmative activity, the general duty not to injure others would be prima facie sufficient for liability. If the case is seen as a problem of omission, the issue of duty can be a stumbling block in establishing liability. Thus there is great practical significance to the subtle classification of a case as negligent risk-taking or as the failure to intervene to prevent harm.

Two related considerations provide some assistance in working out this critical distinction. First, one should ask whether the duty is owed to someone who is already in a situation of distress. If a sick child is in need, the failure to render aid is a case of failing to intervene rather than negligent parenting. It is less plausible to say that a nighttime motorist two blocks away is already in a situation of distress if she should soon encounter an oncoming car without lights. Accordingly, the failure of the oncoming driver to turn on his lights is a case of negligent motoring, not a failure to intervene to prevent the collision. Secondly, it is helpful to inquire whether the duty to be imposed is directed to a specific person or whether it is owed to the public as a whole—or at least to a large number of people in the vicinity. The duty to intervene is typically owed to a specific person in distress; the duty to exercise care is owed to a large number of unidentified potential victims. These considerations help us understand why, as a practical matter, negligent manslaughter is recognized in the context of activities that are dangerous to begin with and deadly when mismanaged—driving, handling guns, and using drugs.[3] The duty in these cases is not owed to a specific person in distress but to the public as a whole, and therefore liability is appropriately considered direct liability for negligently causing death, rather than derivative liability for failing to avert harm.

To summarize our demarcation of the problem, derivative liability for failing to avert harm must be distinguished both from (1) direct liability for breach of a universal statutory duty, and (2) breach of a general duty of care in cases of negligently causing death. The underlying rationale for this demarcation is that derivative liability presupposes four elements: (1) a harm that is to be attributed to the actor, (2) an independent human or natural process that is the primary cause of the harm, (3) the actor's ability to prevent the harm and his failure to do so, (4) a duty to intervene and prevent the harm. Direct liability for breach of a statutory duty falls outside the scope of the inquiry, for, contrary to the first requirement, the analysis of liability does not require the attribution of harm to the actor.[4] Negligently causing death by breaching a general duty of care fails to qualify under the second requirement, for the primary cause of the harm is the negligent conduct itself and not an independent human or natural process.

These claims about causation may strike some readers as puzzling. Too much may seem to turn on the nebulous concept of causation. Therefore we should pause to consider the impact of diverse theories of causation on the theory of derivative liability.

§8.2.1. Causation and Derivative Liability. The prevailing

[3] See §4.3.1 *supra.*

[4] Jescheck 458–59; Schmidhäuser 657; *but cf.* Hall 199, who claims that harm is relevant as to both types of omission. That may be true, but only commission by omission requires actual harm as a condition of liability, *cf.* Welzel 203, agreeing in effect with Hall that there is no substantive (material) difference between the two types of omission.

theory of causation in the criminal law, both in Germany[5] and the United States,[6] is the expansive test: an event *X* causes an event *Y* if, but for *X*, *Y* would not have occurred. This test, conventionally known as the *sine qua non* or "but for" test, treats all necessary conditions for a particular harm as "causal." The implication is that a failure to intervene and prevent a suicide causes death in the same sense as strangling the victim to death. A doctor's failing to aid a stranger in need causes death in the same sense that injecting air into a patient's veins causes death. If the implications of the "but for" test are followed through, there is no important difference between the causal role of acts and of omissions. It follows as well that for every crime there are an infinite number of causes. The fact that no one killed *B* the day before *A*'s assault is as much a "cause" of death as *A*'s actually killing *B*.

There is no doubt that the "but for" test captures an important truth about causation; if *B*'s death would have occurred regardless of *A*'s act, then we cannot say that *A* caused the death. We apply this rule of thumb in cases of failing to avert death as well as affirmative acts leading to death. If the swimmer would have drowned, no matter what measures the lifeguard might have taken, we cannot say that the lifeguard's ignoring the plea contributed to the death. The lifeguard should not be held accountable for the death unless he could have prevented it.

The confusion in the orthodox view is that a necessary feature of causation (namely, satisfaction of the "but for" test) is taken to be a sufficient condition of causation. The effects of conflating the necessary and sufficient conditions for causation reverberate throughout the criminal law. The noteworthy implications are:

1. There is no difference between necessary conditions and causes.

[5] Schönke-Schröder-Lenckner §13, preliminary note 73, at 132; Rudolphi in SK §1, preliminary note 39, at 15; Jescheck 208–210. For a thoughtful critique of the "but for" test in German law, see Naucke, *Über das Regressverbot im Strafrecht*, 76 ZStW 409 (1964).

[6] MPC §2.03(1)(a); LaFave & Scott 249; there is considerable awareness about a defect in the "but for" test that is not of immediate concern to us, namely, the case in which two sufficient causes concur, rendering neither necessary (e.g., two fatal shots fired simultaneously). See *id.* at 249–50; Hall 268–70; Perkins 699–700.

2. Because the causal link is limitless, some new concept must be devised to eliminate far-flung effects from the range of liability. Common lawyers speak about proximate cause; German lawyers have developed the theory of *soziale Adequanz* as a way of reaching many of the same results. Both of these techniques shift the problem of far-flung effects from the theory of causation to the domain either of policy (proximate cause) or the interpretation of the applicable legal norms *(soziale Adequanz).*

3. The concept of causation does not express a noteworthy difference between acts and omissions; if the failure to prevent harm satisfies the "but for" test, it is causal in the same sense that any acts leading to harm are causal.[7]

For the purposes of our present inquiry, the third implication is devastating. If there were no important causal differences between acts and omissions, we could not even begin to develop a theory of derivative liability. That theory, as we noted above, presupposes that the party who fails to avert a significant harm is held liable even though he is not the primary "cause" of that harm. This distinction between primary and lesser causes is untenable under the "but for" theory. The progress of this chapter depends on our making an adequate case against this orthodox theory that treats all necessary conditions, all acts and omissions, as equivalent causes.

Our aim is to develop a theory of causation that will give adequate expression to the difference between acts resulting in consequences such as human death and omissions that fail to prevent these consequences. The implicit agenda of the argument is to shift our focus away from the analysis of human conduct in isolation and toward an analysis of conduct as it affects the external world. The former perspective is "atomistic" in the sense that it

[7] Some German writers have sought to avoid this implication by amending the "but for" test to eliminate possible intervening factors. See Welzel 44 (example: *A* and *B* each hand *C* a stick to beat *X*; *C* uses *A*'s stick; that *C* did not use *B*'s stick is not a causal factor). This view was apparently developed in G. Spendel, Die Kausalitätsformel der Bedingungstheorie für die Handlungsdelikte 38 (1948), cited at Welzel 44. *Cf.* Jescheck 468 (denying the causal effect of omissions).

takes human acts or omissions as isolated events to be analyzed apart from their effects on other persons and their interests.

Atomistic theories come in a naive and a more sophisticated form. The naive theory follows from the definition of acts as "willed bodily movement." Omissions are the negation of acts and therefore should be defined as the absence of bodily movement—or pure passivity.[8] Although this definition of "acting" is still current, it is hard to find anyone today who seriously argues that omissions should be defined as the "absence of movement."[9]

The more sophisticated atomistic theory is that omissions are defined by the absence of the specific act which, if carried out, would satisfy the actor's legal obligations.[10] Accordingly, one does not forbear from action in general; one forbears from a specific action required under the circumstances. The argument is that, unlike "acting," "omitting" is a transitive verb. For the term to apply, one must "omit" something—and that something is the act required by the applicable social, moral, or legal rule.[11]

The sophisticated theory reduces to the observation that some norms prohibit conduct and others require conduct. Omissions are the violation of norms that require conduct. That is true, but the claim is no more profound than saying that "acts" are the violation of norms that prohibit conduct. What the sophisticated theory fails to do is give an account of why liability for failing to act is so problematic in all Western legal systems. Why are there so few norms requiring conduct? Is there an important difference between norms that simply require an act and those that require intervention and the prevention of particular harmful results? These are some of the questions we hope to answer by developing a "relational" theory of human conduct—one that focusses on acts as they affect other human beings and their interests.

[8] See §6.4.1 *supra*.

[9] The issue is not often discussed in the Anglo-American literature, but see Perkins 591–92.

[10] This thesis is well developed in the German literature; the leading work is A. Kaufmann, *supra* note 1; see also Welzel 200–02; Stratenwerth 61.

[11] See A. Kaufmann, *supra* note 1, at 25 (noting that this argument was first developed by von Liszt).

A relational theory of human conduct stresses interaction among individuals and the role of action in affecting others. While the emphasis in atomistic theories is on expressing one's will in movement and in choices, the relational theory brings into relief the way in which our conduct changes our relationships with other persons. The damage we do to others is a critical aspect of our acting in a community of vulnerable persons. A relational theory of acting means that the consequences of our acts must be seen as an integrated aspect of our acting relative to others. The occurrence of death is inseparable from the act of killing; the destruction of a dwelling is essential to an act of arson. Of course, there are some acts, such as speeding on the highway, that do not entail consequences. But in the range of criminal acts that generate harmful consequences, the consequences and the assertion of the will are an integrated whole. This view of acting, it is worth noting, has a precursor in the "social" theory of action, as developed by Maihofer and other German writers.[12]

In order to develop a relational theory of acting, we are impelled to reject the "but for" theory of causation and develop a view of causation that permits us to attribute consequences to particular actors. The proof that the "but for" theory is inadequate to this task of causal attribution is readily found in the new American literature on the economic analysis of legal problems. The literature is dominated by a causal nihilism that equates the position of the person who breathes polluted air with the factory that pollutes the air or, to take another favorite, the position of the farmers whose crops are burned with the railroad emitting the fire-inducing sparks.[13] Both parties (polluter and breather, railroad and farmer) are necessary for the occurrence of the harm and therefore there is no way to determine who "causes" what. If the victim chose to breathe elsewhere or to move her crops, there would be no harm; therefore her staying where she is (her omission) is as much

[12] See §6.6.5, at note 40 *supra*.

[13] See Coase, *The Problem of Social Cost*, 3 J. Law & Econ. 1 (1960); R. Posner, Economic Analysis of Law 34–39 (2d ed. 1977).

a cause of harm as the active emitting of pollutants and sparks. The proponents of this view concede that their argument is limited to an "economic" analysis of legal problems. But in fact their causal nihilism is a direct implication of the "but for" theory of causation. It is true that "but for" the continuing presence of the victim, there would be no harm. The logical extension of the "but for" theory invariably generates scepticism about who is intruding against whom.

What I will attempt to show is that "intrusion" or "interference" is essential to a relational theory of acting. And the way to develop this theory is to consider theories of causation that permit us to say the polluter intrudes against the party gasping for clean air or that the railroad intrudes against the farmer seeking to nurture his crops.[14]

The course of the argument will take us first to a "common sense" theory of causation, as developed primarily by H. L. A. Hart and A. Honoré.[15] Upon exploring the concept of causation in the abstract, we shall find that the inquiry is advanced by turning to concrete causal verbs, such as killing, assassinating and executing. The aim of the inquiry is to defend the critical difference between killing and letting die, between assassinating and letting someone be assassinated. The "but for" theory of causation collapses this critical distinction and therefore we must look elsewhere for an account for the basic relationships of causing harm that are rooted in our language.

§8.2.2. An Alternative to "But For" Causation. The essential claim of the "but for" theory is that all necessary conditions for an event should count as "causes" of that event. While we may accept this principle as one requirement of causation, we shall argue that the concept demands more. The argument for that additional ele-

[14] It is significant that reactions against the economic approach to tort law implicitly reject the equivalence of all necessary conditions. See Epstein, *A Theory of Strict Liability*, 2 J. Leg. Stud. 151, 166–71 (1973) (relying on everyday examples of aggression); Fletcher, *Fairness and Utility in Tort Theory*, 85 Harv. L. Rev. 537, 543–51 (1972) (non-reciprocity of risk presupposes a concept of intrusion).

[15] H. Hart & A. Honoré, Causation in the Law (1959).

ment of causation builds on two claims. The first is historical, and the second, conceptual and linguistic. The historical claim builds on earlier discussions of the practice of tainting in the law of homicide.[16] An essential condition of the taint and of the resulting forfeiture of goods was that the defendant's act caused the death. It is important that in the entire early history of homicide there is no discussion of tainting in cases of failure to prevent death. Liability for omissions emerged in the nineteenth century, only after the practice of tainting and forfeiture came into eclipse.[17] This is powerful evidence that the common law functioned with a different theory of causation. The practice of tainting, with the resulting forfeiture of goods, would not have been possible if all persons who might have prevented death were tainted. Tainting arose from entanglement with evil, from getting blood on one's hands, from personal contact with the occurrence of death. It did not arise simply from indifference to the fate of others. If there is anything that is basic in the morality underlying all Western approaches to homicide, it is that strangling a victim is fundamentally different from looking the other way when a stranger is drowning.

The conceptual argument against the "but for" test starts with the elementary question: what is a theory of causation about? It is possible that we have a term of art in mind, in which case we are entitled to stipulate any definition we wish. The price of a free-ranging stipulation is that we lose contact with reality. If we wish to build a system of criminal law on the basis of a concept that exists in the world, then we must attend to the way the concept functions in our daily lives. This means that we must examine our reasons for making causal inquiries and pay close attention to the way we ordinarily speak about "causing" harm.

One important feature of causal inquiries is that we do not ordinarily inquire about the cause of normal or continuing states of affairs. We speak about the cause of death, but not about the cause

[16] See §5.1.1 *supra*.

[17] One of the earliest common-law cases is Regina v. Instan, [1893] 1 Q.B. 450, upholding a conviction for manslaughter. Lord Coleridge conceded that defendant's failing to aid her aged aunt "did not actually cause" the death. *Id.* at 454.

of life. Why not? Death at a particular moment is unplanned and unexpected and therefore we wish to know why it happens. But a healthy person's remaining alive does not stimulate our interest in explaining the world around us. Things would be different, of course, if we expected someone to die in an airplane crash and she survived. Then we might appropriately ask: how did she survive? To what does she owe her added days of life? (Note that we still have some difficulty framing our question with the word "cause.") This difference between life and death demonstrates that causal inquiries are not always appropriate. When inappropriate causal questions are raised, as if someone should ask you the cause of your being alive today or the cause of the water still being in the ocean, we are likely to wonder.

It would be difficult to give a complete account of when causal inquiries are appropriate, but one obvious category is precisely the range of accidents, unexpected events, and untoward acts that preoccupy the law. We probably find it odd to ask: What caused him to wear clothes to the office? But we would never find it odd to inquire: What caused the crash? Why did he breach his contract? What prompted her to kill her child? Any death, any unexpected destruction of property, any injury to a human being—these are the stuff of causal inquiries.

If we see that "results" that lend themselves to "causal" questions are a special class of events, we should not be surprised to learn that causes, too, are different from ordinary and routine events. Every cause must satisfy the "but for" criteria and be a necessary condition of the events occurring. Apart from that minimal qualification, "causes" are like the "effects" that they explain. Among all the necessary conditions for a particular event, the "causes" are those conditions that make the difference under the circumstances. They are the abnormal and unexpected factors that stand out from the background and help to explain the particular result. There are some factors that might be causal in one situation and not in another. For example, we would not say that the presence of oxygen in the air was the cause of a forest fire (even though "but for" the oxygen the fire would not have occurred). Yet there might be situations, such as in laboratory experiments, in which the presence of oxygen was unexpected and therefore it would be properly discerned as a causal factor.

Now it is entirely possible that an omission might be either an event that we wish to explain (why was she absent from class?) or the abnormal and unexpected factor that constitutes a causal explanation. If we wish to know why the plant died, the best explanation might be the owner's failure to water it. If we wish to know why the baby died, the best explanation might be that its mother purposefully starved it to death. Yet if an old woman succumbs to pneumonia in New Jersey, it would be bizarre to explain the death by saying that a particular physician in Florida did not attend her when she was sick. Of course, the "but for" test would have us believe that the physician's failure to come from Florida was "a cause" of death (assuming the pneumonia was curable), as was the failure of every other doctor to treat her a "cause" of death. By identifying every necessary condition as "a cause," the orthodox "but for" test frustrates our effort to explain the death. The best explanation of the old lady's death might be simply that she died of natural causes.

It is important to underscore the concession in the preceding paragraph that some failures to act might cause death (e.g., failure to feed a child).[18] The important difference between the "but for" test and the ordinary person's notion of causation is this: the former theory takes all failures to act as causal if intervening would have prevented the harm. The latter theory distinguishes between omissions that are merely necessary conditions and specific failures that stand out as the unexpected abnormal factors explaining the untoward event.

This emphasis on the normal and the expected injects criteria of convention into the perception of causation. If smoke alarms in

[18] My views have little in common with a third conception of causation that denies the causal potential of all omissions. This third argument is that omissions have no material force and thus cannot affect the world. This view is seriously entertained in the Soviet literature, Kurs (GP 1970) at 197–98 (discussing authors on both sides of the issue) and probably accounts for the opposition of some German writers to omissions causing harm. See Jescheck 468 (citing the maxim "ex nihilo nihil fit").

the home are highly unusual, we could hardly explain the death of children in a home fire by saying that the family did not have a smoke alarm (we might as well explain the death by saying the fire department failed to have a station next door). Yet if every other house in the city has an alarm, we might well explain the death of children by pointing to the absence of an alarm that could have saved their lives. The rule of convention means that what was not a cause yesterday might become a cause tomorrow. And what was formerly a cause might cease to be more than a necessary condition. Indeed, this is the way we are inclined to think about literacy in relationship to success in the world; literacy might previously have been sufficient to assure success, now it is at most a necessary condition. This degree of fluidity and uncertainty in the concept of causation makes one wonder whether this commonsense concept of causation is well suited to function as a basic building block in a theory of criminal liability.

In the next section, I will suggest that the concept of causation can be given a more secure footing by focussing on specific causal verbs, such as "killing," "starving," "strangling," "poisoning," and the like. But first it is important that we complete our critique of the orthodox "but for" theory that inhibits our efforts to distinguish between liability for caused and uncaused death.

The most damaging evidence against the "but for" theory of causation is that even its proponents do not consistently use the standard they espouse. A case in point is the Model Penal Code. In §2.03, the Code commits itself to the orthodox rule that

> (1) Conduct is the cause of a result when:
>
> (a) It is an antecedent but for which the result in question would not have occurred. . . .[19]

The term "conduct" is defined earlier as an "action or omission,"[20]

[19] The remaining provisions of MPC §2.03 do not bear on the discussion. §2.03 (1)(b) refers to additional "causal requirements imposed by . . . the law defining the offense." The only example offered in the commentary is the "year-and-a-day" rule restricting liability for homicide, see MPC §2.03, Comment at 132–33 (Tent. Draft No. 4, 1955). The rest of §2.03 takes up the criteria for "proximate cause" and thus does not bear on whether an omission is a cause-in-fact.

[20] MPC §1.13(5).

and therefore it is clear that §2.03(1)(a) encompasses all failures to act but for which "the result in question would not have occurred."

The inconsistencies arise from the drafter's using the term "cause" in the definition of specific offenses. "Criminal homicide" is committed by anyone who "causes the death of another human being" with one of four culpable states of mind.[21] If taken seriously, this definition would imply that anyone who knowingly abstained from aiding someone in distress would, if death ensued, be guilty of murder. It might be thought that the definition of "knowing" conduct would come to the rescue, but that definition also turns on the concept of causation. Applying §2.02(2)(b) in this context, we learn that "a person acts knowingly with respect to [the element of death] . . . if he is aware that it is practically certain that his conduct will cause [death]." It follows that if a stranger is practically certain that his failing to rescue a drowning child will result in death, he "knowingly causes" death and is guilty of murder.

Though there might be some who would welcome this sweeping extension of the law, the drafters of the Model Penal Code clearly did not intend to conflate the common-law difference between acts and omissions. Section 2.01(3)(b) restates the traditional rule that liability for commission of an offense by omission turns on whether a "duty to perform the omitted act is . . . imposed by law." The requirement of a duty to act would be superfluous if we read the definition of murder together with the definition of "causing."

This tension between the rule of "but for" causation and the definition of particular offenses recurs throughout the Code. Section 220.2 makes it a felony to "cause a catastrophe by explosion, fire, . . . [etc.] by any means of causing widespread injury or damage. . . ." If this provision were read together with the definition of causation, it would follow that anyone who consciously fails to report a fire (where the report would prevent widespread damage)

[21] MPC §210.1(1).

would be guilty of a felony. One would hope that this is not what the drafters had in mind.

The pervasive confusion in the Model Penal Code is easy to explain. The drafters felt called upon to define the word "cause" and therefore they fell back on the orthodox theory of "but for" causation. However, when they use the word "cause" in defining specific crimes, they revert to the English language and thus think and speak about "causing" as do the rest of us in our daily lives. In defining murder as "knowingly causing death" they did not mean to obliterate the distinction between strangling a victim and letting her die of an overdose of morphine. The intended meaning is obvious. It is only the failure to reflect upon the implications of "but for" causation that produces the confusion.[22]

§8.2.3. **Verbs of Interference and Causation.** The causal confusion of the Model Penal Code illustrates a deeper point. It is possible to adhere to the "but for" theory of causation as a purely jurisprudential matter; but if one does, one should avoid using the word "cause" in drafting specific legal rules and definitions. Jurisprudential theories will not affect the criminal law if the false theories are never put to the test. The Model Penal Code and its progeny aside, Western statutes and commentators have consistently defined homicide by relying on the verb "to kill" rather than on the concept of causation.[23] Thus in the analysis of homi-

[22] This confusion is repeated in several state statutes that have followed the Model Penal Code. See, e.g. Hawaii Penal Code §214 ("but for" standard of causation); §701 (murder committed by one who "intentionally or knowingly causes the death of another person"); Tex. Penal Code §6.04(a) ("but for" standard of causation); §19.02(a)(1) (murder committed by one who "intentionally or knowingly causes the death of an individual").

[23] Cal. Penal Code §187 ("unlawful killing"); StGB §212 ("*wer einen Menschen tötet*"); Ugol. kod. (RSFSR) §102 (crime labelled "intentional killing"); *but cf.* Code Pénal §295 (*meurtre* defined simply as *l'homicide commis volontairement*); some newer statutes have adopted the "but for" test of causation, but avoid the word "cause" in the provisions on homicide, see Pa. Cons. Stat. tit. 18, §303(a) ("but for" causation); §2502(a) (murder of the first degree defined as "intentional killing"); other statutes define criminal homicide as "causing death" but do not seek to define causation. See Proposed Federal Criminal Code §1601(a) (murder); Can. Rev. Stat. C–34, §212(a)(i) (murder committed by one who "causes death" and "means" to do so).

cide, the language of definition insulates the practical solution of legal problems from the inadequacies of the "but for" theory of causation.

This is not to say that legislative prohibitions never employ the word "cause." Yet the context of usage often is the specification of an added penalty in the event that a completed offense issues in a greater harm than that intended.[24] For example, §226 of the German Code provides that if "an assault and battery causes death," the minimum punishment should be three years imprisonment. This provision does not admit of confusion between acts and omissions, but rather presuppose a prohibited affirmative act as a condition for the aggravated offense.

Construing the term "causation" in §226 of the German Code generated the leading precedent in German law favoring the "but for" theory of causation.[25] An examination of this case, however, indicates that the holding has little bearing on the analysis of causal effects of omissions. The defendant slapped the victim in the face and the victim unexpectedly died. The defense was that the death was unforeseeable.[26] The court rejected the relevance of foreseeability on the ground that the terms of §226 did not require culpability relative to the occurrence of death. This is a very limited holding, and its premise on the relevance of culpability is hardly compatible with the basic principles of German law. Nonetheless, the case is generally taken to stand for the adoption of the "but for" test in German criminal jurisprudence.[27]

There is much to be learned from putting aside the language of "causation" and focussing instead on the verbs that are typically used in defining criminal homicide. The foremost verbs of homicide are "killing" and "slaying"; the means include "strangling," "stabbing," "poisoning," "starving," "shooting," "drown-

[24] For a survey of other examples in English legislation, see H. Hart & A. Honoré, *supra* note 15, at 328.

[25] Judgment of September 28, 1951, 1 BGHSt. 332.

[26] *Cf.* State v. Frazier, 339 Mo. 966, 98 S.W.2d 707 (1936) (victim of assault was a hemophiliac and bled to death; liable for manslaughter).

[27] See note 5 *supra*.

ing," and, of course, various manners of execution: "stoning," "burning," "gassing," "hanging," "decapitating," and "drawing and quartering." The common thread of all these ways of killing is that they are all distinguishable from cases of letting die. Standing by and letting someone drown is not the same as "drowning"; letting someone be killed by stoning is not the same as "stoning." The act of "creating," "taking," or "running" a risk is plainly distinguishable from "tolerating" a risk. That these distinctions are so deeply embedded in our language implies that they are also rooted in our moral consciousness. The difference between killing and letting die, between creating a risk and tolerating a risk, is one of the principles that sets the framework for assessing moral responsibility.

There is certainly no correlation between activity or motion, on the one hand, and the use of affirmative verbs of killing, on the other. A parent might starve a child to death by refusing to feed it. A water company might poison the public by systematically omitting to purify the water. These "motionless" activities are appropriately described by an affirmative verb of killing.

If we leave aside the case of parents who refuse to feed children, the recurrent legal problems of failing to prevent death do not lend themselves to description with affirmative verbs. A physician refuses to treat a patient. A niece fails to care for her aging aunt. A man fails to call a physician after his mistress takes an overdose of morphine. None of these cases would normally be described as "killing." Nor is there a specific verb that might apply to the omission of the physician, the niece, or the neglectful lover. These are cases of "letting die." And all cases of letting die are of a piece. To paraphrase the opening lines of *Anna Karenina:* every person who kills, does so in a different manner, but all those who "let die" do so in the same way.

This critical distinction between affirmative acts of killing and the passivity of letting die enables us to restate the difference between direct and derivative liability for the occurrence of death. Direct liability for death is based on an act of killing; derivative liability is based on an act of letting die. As we have seen, one can kill by standing still; and as we shall see later, one can "let die" by moving one's body. The issue is not motion, but the particular link that exists between the act and the occurrence of death.

This analysis runs parallel to our theory of causation. The refutation of the "but for" thesis is based on the close connection between "causing death" and acts of killing, rather than letting die. This equation is implicit in the Model Penal Code's relying on "causing death" as the critical verb in the definition of homicide. Yet in view of the relative ambiguity of causation, we should not insist on a precise correlation between causing death, on the one hand, and affirmative verbs of killing, on the other. There might be some cases of "letting die" that could arguably be described as causing death.[28] If this conflict should arise, we should prefer to rely on the more specific verbs that appear, traditionally, in the definition of criminal homicide.

The point that we have yet to assay is why, as a matter of moral principle, the law should distinguish so sharply between killing and letting die. Why is the former always prima facie forbidden and the latter subject to the additional scrutiny whether there is a duty to prevent death? This is the deeper moral issue to which we now turn.

§8.2.4. Liberty, Interference and Allocation. The most common argument for distinguishing between acts and omissions in moral and legal theory is that penalizing omissions raises a more acute problem of circumscribing liberty than does punishing affirmative acts. This way of stating the problem is but an invitation to clarify why punishing omissions raises an issue of liberty. Whenever the law prohibits or requires conduct, the liberty of the individual is affected. What is so special about requiring someone to prevent death? It would be odd to argue that passivity, per se, warrants a preferred position in our moral and legal life. It is a far greater tyranny for the state to prohibit innocuous acts, such as going out after dark, than to require bystanders to render aid at the scene of an accident.

[28] This point was called to my attention by Philippa Foot.

If we take John Rawls' theory of liberty as a guide, we are led to the view that the critical issue is interference with the rights of others, rather than the virtues of passivity. Rawls takes as the first principle of justice that every person is entitled to a maximum amount of liberty compatible with a like liberty for all.[29] It follows that what may be permissibly restricted is conduct that interferes with the liberty of others. Religious freedom may not be restricted, but religious persecution may be. The former does not interfere with the religious freedom of others, but the latter does. The concept of "interference" is essential to the Rawlsian scheme; without it, there would be no way to distinguish between conduct that could be enjoined in the name of liberty and that which justice requires us to tolerate as a form of liberty.[30]

The concept of "interference" must be distinguished rigorously from the failure to "allocate" goods and services.[31] The former encroaches upon the liberty of others, the latter does not. Killing is an obvious instance of interfering with the rights of others; letting someone die is a failure to allocate goods and services. The failure to allocate does not compromise the liberty of anyone; it is compatible with the maximum amount of liberty enjoyed by all. Indeed the act of allocation creates disparities of goods and services that require a particularized justification. The justification is typically that the person receiving the allocation is "in need" or "in distress." Yet having one's needs satisfied is not, at least not in Rawls' scheme, an issue of liberty.[32] This is not to say that

[29] J. Rawls, A Theory of Justice 60, 195–257 (1971).

[30] Note the critique of Rawls' theory in Grey, Book Review, 25 Stan. L. Rev. 286 (1973). Grey's tactic is to invoke the causal skepticism characteristic of economic thought, and to argue that the right to live in a society "free from the discomfort produced by the practice of religions . . . one regards as blasphemous . . ." is as much entitled to protection as the freedom of religious belief. *Id.* at 312–13.

[31] See generally T. Eckhoff, Justice 3–10 (1974).

[32] The distribution of goods other than liberty is governed by Rawls' second principle of justice: "Social and economic inequalities are to be arranged so that they are both (a) reasonably expected to be to everyone's benefit and (b) attached to positions and offices open to all." J. Rawls, *supra* note 29, at 60. But note that the issue of concrete human "need" raised here could not be assayed in the original position, where individual attributes are not known to the participants.

there is no question of justice in failing to satisfy the needs of another, but the analysis of injustice requires attention to the concrete context of failing to aid.

The notion of "interference" underlying Rawls' first principle of justice supports the radical distinction in Western jurisprudence between causing harm and letting harm occur. Causing serious harm by killing, assaulting, destroying the property of another, is always prima facie forbidden.[33] Letting harm occur is punished only if there is a personal duty to render assistance. The explication and clarification of these special duties will later engage us in detail.

The distinction between killing and letting die finds its warrant not only in the rationale for prohibition, but in the assessment of culpability in determining who should be liable either for killing or letting die. If we look at all the people who cause a particular death as potential candidates for liability, we can rely upon aspects of their causal contribution to narrow the field to those who are culpable and appropriately held liable. On the other hand, when many people have stood by and let someone die, either we have too many candidates for liability or we have none at all.

A helpless old woman succumbs to starvation. Many people know of her condition and do nothing; the postman, her hired nurse, her daughter, the bill collector, the telephone operator—each of them allows her to die. Could we say, on analogy to causing death, that permitting the death to occur should serve as the criterion for selecting these people as candidates for liability? If we say that they are all prima facie liable, then the burden falls on the criteria of justification and excuse to decide which of them, if any, should be liable for wrongful death or criminal homicide. The problem is whether the criteria of justification and excuse are sufficiently sensitive to resolve the question of liability. What kinds of questions should we ask in assessing whether the failure to render aid was justified or free from culpability? Did each voluntarily

[33] Note that Rawls' critic, Nozick, also accepts the concept of "intrusion" as a basic starting point for moral theory. R. Nozick, Anarchy, State and Utopia 71–73 (1974) (discussing "boundary crossings").

omit to render aid? Did any of them face a particular hazard in doing so? Were any of them in a particularly favorable position to avert the risk of death? If these are the questions we must ask in assessing culpability and affixing liability, we are at a loss to discriminate among the candidates for liability. Each acted voluntarily and with knowledge of the peril; none faced personal hazards in offering assistance; and their capacities to avert the risk were equal. If we collapse the distinction between interference and allocation, between killing and letting die, we would be at a loss to determine which of those persons who were prima facie liable should be punished under the law.

In cases of killing or of creating risks of death, we have a subtle set of techniques for distinguishing between culpable and non-culpable homicide. Each causal agent is chargeable with a different risk that death would occur. The risks differ in degree and scope. Some bear a more remote relationship to the harm; others seem reasonable in light of the circumstances. These differences in the posture of each causal agent toward the risk of death enable us to assess their individual culpability with some sensitivity.

In contrast, the group of people who tolerate a risk of death cannot be charged with a particular degree of contribution in the death that occurs. One could speak of the relative likelihoood that each might avert the death by rendering assistance. Yet it is hard to see how we would assess forgoing an opportunity to prevent death. How do we compare the costs and benefits of failing to allocate aid? Is it reasonable or unreasonable for a father to let his sixteen-year-old son participate in drag races on the city streets? He promotes no end of his own by failing to intervene. His reasons are those of indifference and fear of involvement—the same reasons that prompted 38 people in New York City passively to witness the murder of Kitty Genovese. Reasons of this kind do not lend themselves to a calculus of reasonableness.[34] How does one weigh a person's fear of involvement against the occurrence of harm? And without a calculus of reasonableness, one can hardly

[34] *But cf.* Epstein, *supra* note 14, at 190, who assumes the contrary.

expect to discern whether the risk is permissible and whether the actor is culpable for letting it occur.

The implications of this analysis are that the notion of duty in cases of letting harm occur fulfills two important functions. Not only does it provide a surrogate for the causal link, but the affirmation of the duty provides a basis for assessing culpability. The breach of the duty to allocate assistance is sufficient to attribute the harm to the actor. And the knowing breach of the duty is also sufficient to establish a prima facie case of culpability. There is no single concept in the analysis of affirmatively causing harm that bears the weight we place on the concept of duty in cases of failing to intervene and prevent harm.[35]

§8.2.5. **The Quinlan Case.** An arena for testing our general theory of direct and derivative liabilty is the topical and troublesome problem of interrupting treatment to terminal patients. Consider the case of a dying, comatose patient sustained by an artifical respirator. The physicians wish to turn off the respirator, but they are fearful that doing so in expectation of the patient's death might be interpreted as intentional killing, thus making them both criminally and tortiously liable. This recurrent situation in modern medicine received international attention in the prolonged litigation about the care to be rendered to Karen Quinlan. Her parents desired that the respirator be discontinued. Yet the attending physicians refused to do so until the New Jersey Supreme Court held that the constitutional right of privacy entailed the permissibility of shutting off the machine.[36] To the surprise of many, the shrivelled and comatose Karen continued to breathe without the aid of the respirator. One year later she was still alive. What is intriguing for our purposes is whether the case may be resolved within the framework of the distinction between killing and letting die. In my view it can, and even the supposed constitutional right to die must be adapted to account for this fundamental distinction in the structure of the criminal law. From the permissibility of shutting off the respirator, it could hardly be inferred that a patient had a

[35] On the criteria for establishing duties of intervention, see §8.3 *infra.*

[36] In re Quinlan, 70 N.J. 10, 355 A.2d 647 (1976).

constitutional right to die by having a physician inject air into her veins.[37]

The situation in the *Quinlan* case is so provocative because it poses a direct conflict between the traditional doctrine of acts and omissions and the analysis of killing and letting die that we have proposed. There is no doubt that shutting off the respirator constitutes a "muscular contraction" resulting from the operation of the will. According to the nineteenth-century view of acting, this willed muscular contraction would be sufficient to render the event an act rather than an omission. If we add the "but for" theory of causation, the shutting off of the machine and the subsequent death of the patient would constitute an act causing death. Further, the act causing death would be intentional and it would be difficult to escape liability for murder.

There is something unquestionably bizarre about equating this medical decision with a gunman's killing in cold blood. One might try to lift this burden from medical practice by considering the doctor's beneficent motives in shutting off the respirator. Even though these motives would not constitute a complete excuse under the law today, someone might argue that they should. The difficulty is that recognizing the motive of euthanasia as either an excuse or a justification would legitimate cases of overtly terminating the lives of persons who either desire to die or whose lives are deemed unworthy. Voluntary euthanasia raises serious institutional problems in determining when someone has rationally consented to being killed. Involuntary euthanasia carries obvious risks of abuse. Both voluntary and involuntary euthanasia have become more questionable in light of the practice of transplanting organs from newly dead bodies. If there ever was a neutral decision about whether a terminal patient ought to die, the matter is now torn by conflicting interests.

The advantage of working with the distinction between killing and letting die is that we can preserve the inhibition against euthanasia at the same time that we loosen the supposed duty to

[37] The court acknowledges this critical distinction at several places. *Id.* at 52, 54; 355 A.2d at 670, 671.

keep terminal, comatose patients on the respirator. The question is whether we can make a plausible case that shutting off the respirator is merely a case of letting or permitting death to occur. If so, the critical question in analyzing liability would be whether in light of the particular relationship, the physicians were duty-bound to keep Karen on the respirator. Shifting from the track of direct to derivative liability does not necessarily lead to a different legal outcome. But by introducing the issue of duty and stepping outside the norm against killing, we relax the pinions of the strict prohibition against terminating the lives of innocent persons.

To put the *Quinlan* case in proper perspective, consider the possible liability if the physician failed to put Karen on the respirator in the first place. This would be a case of failing to allocate a medical resource, rather than overtly killing the patient. Unless there were a duty to use the respirator, there would be no liability for the omission. It does not follow that all cases of withholding medical aid would be analyzed simply as a failure to allocate assistance. If the physician withheld an expected blood transfusion after an operation, the act of withholding would surely be a cause of death. In a situation like the *Quinlan* case, it might be appropriate to analyze the initial decision not to use the respirator as a failure to allocate aid, rather than an interference with the interests of the patient. This conclusion would be buttressed, first, by the fact that the patient was on the verge of death, with a minimal chance of recovery; and secondly, by the effect of the particular therapy—the artificial respirator—in postponing death by sustaining respiration, rather than providing a therapeutic benefit leading either to recovery or to the enjoyment of conscious life. Under these facts, the decision to use the respirator should be seen as an extraordinary intervention that prolongs life and thus permits the possibility of therapeutic treatment.

Does putting the patient on the respirator irreversibly change the situation so that the withdrawal of support is equivalent to an act of killing (if the patient dies)? Or can the withdrawal be identified, *nunc pro tunc,* with an initial decision not to intervene at all?

My claim is that in the limited set of cases, where the patient is on the verge of death and cure is unlikely, the decision to withdraw the respirator is equivalent to not employing it in the first place. It is a failure to continue the application of a particular therapy and thus properly subject to scrutiny under the discriminating filter of duty rather than under the categorical norm against killing.

As intuitive support for this claim consider the analogous case of a physician, dining at leisure at a restaurant, who goes to the aid of a stranger at the next table who suddenly collapses with an apparent heart attack. The physician applies cardiopulmonary resuscitation in an effort to keep the stricken man alive, but then, concluding that the patient is lost, he gives up and shortly thereafter, the stricken man dies. Even if continued resuscitation would have kept the patient alive for several minutes, it would be odd to say that the physician killed him by abandoning his effort. The cause of death is patently the heart attack, not the failure to continue the effort at resuscitation. In this situation, letting the patient die falls into the same category of analysis as an initial failure to intervene. If there is liability, it must be established by analysis of the physician's duty under the circumstances.

The shift from cardiopulmonary resuscitation to an artificial respirator would not seem to change the basic situation. It is true that the cost to the laboring physician is greater if he is personally applying aid rather than if he employed the machine. Yet our reason for treating the interruption of resuscitation as equivalent to an initial failure to aid was not the burden on the physician, but rather the extraordinary nature of the intervention and the minimal likelihood that continued intervention would save the patient.

The more difficult question is whether the intervention by a third person would be treated the same as the physician's decision to terminate therapy to the dependent patient. If the decision by the physician (or anyone acting under him) is subject to analysis as a failure to avert harm, does it follow that Karen Quinlan's parents' surreptitiously shutting off the respirator would be treated in the same way? My own view is that there is a critical difference between the physician's decision and unauthorized intervention by a third party. The decision to allocate aid, where there is no duty to do so, creates a special relationship with the dependent person. The physician acting beyond his duty may reverse his decision to aid. But it does not follow that a third person can intervene and deprive the beneficiary of the benefits of that aid. There is a critical moral difference between an American's terminating his own charitable annuity to a poor child in Greece and the Greek government's interfering and seizing the funds. This analysis presupposes, of course, that neither the physician nor the charitable American is duty-bound to render aid in the first place.

All we have concluded in this discussion is that the physician's turning off the respirator in the *Quinlan* case is a case, potentially, of letting die, rather than killing. Whether there is legal liability for letting a terminal patient die depends on the scope of the physician's duty to the patient. This is a matter that we shall take up presently.

It is worth reflecting on the methodology that leads us to the conclusion that shutting off the respirator (coupled with an ensuing death) is a case of letting die, rather than killing. The guiding question is whether in ordinary English we would describe the process as "killing" or "letting die." Our intuitive sense of usage pulls us toward the description, "letting die."

Now some people might object to relying upon our intuitions or on our sense for English usage in working out important legal distinctions. After all, our intuitions are often fuzzy, and usage, idiosyncratic. That may be true, but it is not clear that we have any choice. Even if we rely on a constitutional canon like the right of privacy, we still have to struggle with the range and details of application. In the end, if we wish to preserve the distinction between euthanasia and terminating therapy, we have to return to our intuitions about killing and letting die. The hope is that in a community of theorists thinking and discussing these problems, we could minimize the personal idiosyncrasies in a consensus about the distinctions that are critical in our system of criminal law.

§8.3. *Derivative Liability: The Criteria of Duty.*

As we have stressed, the distinction between direct and derivative liability is expressed in the requirement of establishing a special duty in order to extend a prohibitory norm to cases of failing to avert harm. As we turn now to the analysis of specific duties and their rationalia, we should keep in mind two questions: the first is determining that there is a duty and the second is pinpointing the scope of the duty. Even if it is established that a particular relationship requires intervention to avert harm, there are limits to the duty of intervention and the assessment of these limits requires separate consideration.

The general theoretical basis for recognizing a duty to avert harm is that in the context of the relationship and under the particular circumstances, the failure to avert harm is as egregious a wrong as causing the particular harm. The impulse to recognize these duties, then, is fundamentally an impulse toward moral consistency in the criminal law.[1] After canvassing the particular grounds for recognizing duties, we shall return to this general rationale and see if we can specify more concretely why we recognize derivative liability. Our discussion will be organized around the sources of duty mentioned in the German and Anglo-American cases and commentary.[2]

§8.3.1. The Personal Relationship Between the Defendant and a Dependent Person. The most widely recognized duties to

§8.3. [1] See the remarks by Lord Coleridge in Regina v. Instan, [1893] 1 Q.B. 450, 454 (the failure to punish the niece who let her aunt die "would be a slur upon and a discredit to the administration of justice in this country"), and the views of Hans-Heinrich Jescheck in the deliberations leading to StGB §13, 2 Niederschriften über die Sitzungen der Grossen Strafrechtskommission 276 (not punishing egregious cases of letting die would be unjust).

[2] French courts and commentators maintain that, in principle, there is no liability for commission by omission. 1 Bouzat & Pinatel §113, at 183–84. The slack is taken up by Code Pénal §63, which penalizes the failure to render aid in an emergency. The Soviet literature recognizes liability for commission by omission, but does not devote much attention to the field. See Kurs (GP 1970) at 152; Kurs (GP 1968) at 328.

prevent harm are those that arise in the context of familial relationships. The typical cases in Anglo-American law are those in which a parent neglects to care for a child[3] or a husband or wife refuses to summon medical aid for a stricken spouse.[4] The cases that have come up on appeal in Anglo-American courts have all been the simple situations in which one party falls ill and the other does nothing or does too little to avert the risk of death. The resulting prosecution and conviction appears almost always to be for manslaughter rather than murder. The reasons for recognizing these duties are a composite of the relationship of interdependency in family life and a sense for the required loyalty that derives from blood relationships. Further, as we noted earlier, the core case of a mother's starving (failing to feed) her child is readily analyzed as a case of direct liability for causing death.

German cases recognize the duty to intervene and avert death in more complicated situations, such as in a case in which a wife came upon her husband committing suicide and did nothing to prevent it.[5] Even though neither suicide nor attempted suicide was punishable, the wife was obligated to avert the death of her husband. In another case, a younger son learned of a plot within his family to poison their aged and troublesome father. Though he did nothing to aid in the plot, he neither called the police nor advised the old man of the danger. He was held accountable on a theory of derivative liability for failing to prevent death.[6] This latter case illustrates the fluidity of the line between commission by omission and accessorial liability.

[3] See Stehr v. State, 92 Neb. 755, 139 N.W. 676 (1913) (father convicted for allowing child to freeze to death); People v. Chavez, 77 Cal. App. 2d 621, 176 P.2d 97 (1947) (mother failed to care for newborn infant). *Cf.* Regina v. Bubb, 4 Cox Crim. Cas. 457 (1850) (defendant had undertaken to care for child and failed to do so).

[4] Territory v. Manton, 19 P. 387 (Mont. 1888) (defendant failed to care for drunken wife exposed to inclement weather); State v. Mally, 139 Mont. 599, 366 P.2d 868 (1961) (defendant failed to provide medical aid for his wife); *but cf.* the older case, Rex v. Smith, 172 Eng. Rep. 203 (1825) (no liability for letting idiot brother starve to death).

[5] Judgment of February 12, 1952, 2 BGHSt. 150.

[6] Judgment of November 29, 1963, 19 BGHSt. 167.

The more troublesome cases in this field are those in which there is one but not both of the elements: interdependence in daily life and a close familial tie. If husband and wife are living apart, are they obligated to respond to calls of the other in distress? How about parents and children living apart? Are in-laws living under the same roof obligated to aid each other? How about the reciprocal obligations of two unrelated roommates? The variations of these cases are infinite. In some cases, as between parent and child, it would seem that the tie of blood should be strong enough to generate a legal duty to preserve life. In other situations, the duty should have to spring from the facts of communal living and prolonged interdependence.[7]

The leading case in Anglo-American law denying the duty to avert death is People v. Beardsley,[8] in which the defendant was initially convicted of manslaughter for failing to take adequate steps to aid a woman with whom he spent a weekend in an adulterous fling. At the end of the weekend, when both of them were intoxicated, the woman swallowed several grains of morphine and passed out. The defendant ensconced her in a neighbor's apartment, but neither he, the neighbor, nor another young man involved in the incident, took further steps to aid her. The conviction was reversed on the ground that there was no duty to take further measures on behalf of the stricken woman.

It would be a mistake to read this case as holding that duties to aid should be limited in the common law to marital or legitimate relationships. The point that the court stressed in justifying the reversal was that there was an element of risk in the weekend assignation and that the victim, who had "ample experience in such affairs,"[9] undertook those risks with her eyes open. The affair

[7] The factual variations are great. Does a son-in-law have a duty to aid his mother-in-law? The Supreme Court intimated that there was a duty in its Judgment of May 15, 1959, 13 BGHSt. 162 (defendant let his mother-in-law commit suicide; reversed on other grounds); the commentators say "no"; Schönke-Schröder-Stree §13, note 18, at 160; Rudolphi in SK §13, note 49, at 99.

[8] 150 Mich. 206, 113 N.W. 1128 (1907).

[9] *Id.* at 214; 113 N.W. at 1131.

had not gone far enough to establish the degree of interdependence that would support a legal duty to do more than the defendant did. If the parties had lived together for a long period, there might well be reciprocal duties of care. That the affair was adulterous is not a significant fact and not one that the court—even in 1907—regarded as critical. According to a general principle of German law, if two people, regardless of sex, go on a drinking spree, neither has an obligation to aid the other when he or she becomes intoxicated.[10] The venture has risks built into it, which the parties voluntarily undertake. As applied to *Beardsley,* this principle would seem to lead to the same conclusion of no criminal liability. It was true in *Beardsley,* though it might not always be the case after weekend sprees, that the defendant himself was intoxicated and hardly in a position to think clearly about what should be done to help a friend in distress. Though the common-law courts are loath to recognize intoxication directly as an excuse, the denial of a duty in the case of temporary binges provides an indirect means of excusing the surviving party.[11]

§8.3.2. **A Community of Shared Risks.** The foregoing analysis suggests that with the exception of drinking sprees, the binding together of people to confront common risks entails reciprocal duties of aid. The common cases would be seamen going to sea, mountaineers joined in a single party, astronauts in a single space ship—these would be fairly clear cases of joint enterprises entailing reciprocal duties. It would not follow, however, that a mountaineer would be duty-bound to everyone on the mountain who might get into a dangerous situation. The range of interdependent duty is limited to those who by jointly undertaking the venture, implicitly commit themselves to each other.[12]

§8.3.3. **Contract and Undertaking.** It is commonly said that

[10] Schönke-Schröder-Stree §13, note 41, at 167; Rudolphi in SK §13, note 57, at 101.

[11] *But cf.* Territory v. Manton, 19 P. 387 (Mont. 1888) (*D* held liable for letting his drunken wife freeze to death even though he too was drunk).

[12] The borderline case is whether sharing common living quarters is sufficient to generate reciprocal duties of care. See Deering, *Strafrechtliche Garantenpflicht aus homosexueller Lebensgemeinschaft?* 1972 MDR 664.

duties to avert death can arise from contract.[13] This seems to be an oversimplification, for in those cases in which there is a contractual duty, there is an independent ground for recognizing a duty of care—namely, an undertaking to care for someone in a dependent position. An illustrative case in Anglo-American law is *Instan*,[14] in which a niece took up residence with her aged aunt and undertook to care for her. Apparently, she ignored her commitments and the aunt died. The finding of manslaughter for failure to avert death brought together a number of criteria, including the blood relationship, their living in the same house, a contract to care for the aunt, and the undertaking to do so. Of all these components, the contract would seem to be important only as evidence of a commitment to the undertaking. If the niece had undertaken to care for the aunt as an act of charity and then acted similarly in negligent disregard of her duty to the dependent patient, it would hardly be helpful to get entangled in the intricacies of consideration and contractual validity. Because in most cases of contractual obligation there is also an undertaking to render aid, there is no particular harm in speaking, redundantly, of contract as a relevant source of duty. In the cases of caring for patients, for example, there always seems to be both an aborted process of care as well as a breached contract.

Let us consider a hypothetical case to illustrate the point that an executory contract, standing alone, cannot generate a duty to avert danger. Suppose that two parents contract with a baby sitter to take care of their child from 8:00 P.M. to midnight on a particular night. When the baby sitter fails to show at 8:00 P.M., the parents leave for the theater. At 8:30 P.M., with the baby sitter still not there, a fire breaks out and the child perishes in the flames. There is no doubt that the baby sitter is liable for breach of her contract of employment, without ever having taken up her duty to care

[13] LaFave & Scott 185; Perkins 595–96; Jones v. United States, 308 F.2d 307 (D.C. Cir. 1962) (rev'd for failure to make adequate factual finding to support duty to care for child) Kurs (GP 1970) at 152 (duties assumed on the basis of contract or occupational role); the older German literature also refers to a contract as a source of duty. See Schönke-Schröder-Stree §13, note 8, at 158.

[14] Regina v. Instan, [1893] 1 Q.B. 450.

for the child; yet it would seem bizarre to hold her liable for criminal homicide. The parents obviously bear great responsibility for leaving before the sitter showed up. On the other hand, if the sitter came and undertook to care for the child for the evening and then proceeded to go out drinking shortly before the fire broke out, the sitter would be liable for breach of her duty, regardless of whether there was a valid supporting contract. The critical factor in these baby-sitting hypotheticals appears to be the actual undertaking to care for the child, not the background of contract.

A recent German case illustrates how closely interwoven the theories of contract and of undertaking can be in practice.[15] A tenant had contracted with her landlord to sand the ice-covered sidewalk in front of the apartment house in which she lived. This she failed to do and as a result a pedestrian slipped and was injured. The tenant was charged with negligent battery.[16] The rationale for the charge was that the landlord was bound by a local ordinance to sand the sidewalks, he contracted with his tenants that they, in turn, should fulfill his duty; the defendant, when her turn had come up, had breached her duty. On this rationale for the charge, the pedestrian was a third-party beneficiary of the contract between the tenant and her landlord. On the assumption that a contract could generate a duty sufficient for derivative criminal liability, the trial court convicted the defendant.

The appellate court explicitly rejected the contract as a relevant source of duty and cited a long list of authorities to demonstrate that the literature had long concurred in the same view. The rationale for this unequivocal stand is one that should appeal to lawyers in the common-law tradition. The policies of criminal and of contract law are radically different. Therefore, there is no reason to gauge criminal liability by the rules of contractual duty. There is, however, an undeniable jurisprudential temptation to simplify the analysis of criminal liability by linking it to some other body of

[15] Judgment of the High State Court (*Oberlandesgericht*) in Celle, May 4, 1961, 1961 NJW 1939.

[16] StGB §230.

law, particularly in view of the difficulty of elaborating the grounds for duties in cases of derivative liability. Though it rejected the trial court's rationale, the appellate court affirmed the conviction. The true ground for the conviction was that the tenant had undertaken to take care of the sidewalk on the days that the responsibility fell to her. It is not clear what the minimal criteria for the undertaking were, except that she moved into the apartment house and signed the lease, including the clause concerning the sidewalk. The court drew the convincing analogy between the tenant in this situation and a physician on call for a particular evening. Presumably, if a physician made himself available to the community and then failed to answer an emergency call, he would be liable for the consequences. Yet it is important to note that if the defendant had merely signed the lease but never moved into the apartment, the court would probably not have found an "undertaking" to care, in turn, for the sidewalk.

The theory of undertaking is one of the least refined headings for establishing duties to avert harm. The hypothetical cases that nag Anglo-American students of the law are those of motorists, who, being under no duty to aid accident victims, stop their cars and commence to render minor forms of aid to a roadside victim. If a motorist throws a blanket over the accident victim, is he obligated to do more? Does he have to stay with the injured party until he is out of danger? When does the undertaking take hold and what is the scope of the resulting duty? The problem seems to be theoretically intractable. Perhaps it is a good sign that there are few cases in the field. The humanitarian instincts of those who stop to render aid are usually sufficiently sound to guide them through the situation. The most we can elicit as legal guidelines to the problem are, first, that the parties stopping to render aid should not, under any circumstances, leave the injured party worse off than he was before. The mere act of stopping may entail some duties, for other motorists might pass by on the assumption that the victim is being attended to. Yet the scope of the Good Samaritan's duty is ineluctably murky (it does not help much to say that he should act reasonably). In view of the vagueness both in the ground and the scope of duties incurred by undertaking to render aid, one should have doubts whether this field of human interaction is properly included in a theory of derivative liability for homicide.

§8.3.4. The Defendant's Creating the Danger. In the typical case of derivative liability for failing to avert harm, the defendant comes on the scene after the potential victim has fallen into jeopardy. The problem is whether he, as an outsider to the dangerous situation, must intervene and rescue the party in distress. Yet in other cases that seem more difficult, the defendant himself is the one who creates the danger to the potential victim. This can happen in a variety of ways. The suspect assaults the victim and leaves him lying, disabled, in the street. Or he, without fault on his part, runs down a pedestrian and leaves him there, bleeding. In another variation, he rapes a girl and she, distraught, falls into a stream and drowns as he looks on with satisfaction.

The preliminary distinction required in the analysis of these cases is whether the defendant is criminally culpable for causing the original state of distress. If he is, there is considerable support for a duty to prevent complications of the original crime. Yet it is difficult in this field to filter out the cases that stand squarely for a duty to prevent death. Many of them lend themselves to analysis as homicide by affirmatively causing death. For example, if the defendant assaults a victim and leaves him in the roadway to be run over by oncoming traffic, and indeed the victim is run over, this is a straightforward case of manslaughter or murder.[17] That another automobile actually causes death does not undermine the defendant's responsibility.[18] Although there might not have been an initial intent to kill, the intent to inflict grievous bodily harm is sufficient for murder in England and in many American jurisdictions. The rape case, in which the victim throws herself into the water and the defendant fails to rescue her, is even more straightforward; for here the felony-murder rule would point to a conclusion of murder in the first degree.[19]

[17] People v. Fowler, 178 Cal. 657, 174 P. 892 (1918) (conviction for murder, aff'd).

[18] See §5.2.2 *supra*.

[19] See Jones v. State, 220 Ind. 384, 43 N.E. 2d 1017 (1942) (analyzed as a case of duty to save drowning rape victim).

At the other end of the spectrum are those cases in which the defendant justifiably inflicts injury in self-defense and then leaves the victim to die. The consensus in German and American law is that there is no liability for the death resulting from a justified blow.[20] This conclusion requires qualification, for even if the injury is justified, there may be an independent ground for recognizing a duty to avert the death of the injured aggressor. The aggressor might be the parent or the spouse of the defendant, or he might be someone dependent on medical or psychiatric care from the defendant. Once the aggressor is disabled and the defendant is no longer in danger, these other sources of duty should control and require affirmative intervention to save the injured party. Secondly, this is one of several contexts in which it is important to distinguish between actual self-defense and putative self-defense (i.e., the defendant mistakenly believes that he is under attack). Though Anglo-American jurisprudence lumps these two categories together under the privilege of self-defense, the better view (which we shall explore later)[21] is that putative self-defense is merely excused, not justified.[22] Therefore, if the defendant injures an innocent person in the mistaken, though reasonable, assumption that the victim was threatening the defendant's life, the defendant should not be able to leave him there to die as though he were an actual aggressor.[23]

The difficult middle range of cases are those in which the defendant causes the distress to the person in need of aid and yet does so without either wrongdoing or culpability on his part. This

[20] King v. Commonwealth, 285 Ky. 654, 148 S.W.2d 1044 (1941) (fatal blow inflicted in justified defense of *D*'s father); Judgment of July 29, 1970, 23 BGHSt. 327 (injury inflicted in legitimate self-defense).

[21] See §10.1.2 *infra*.

[22] Even if the victim is an actual aggressor, the prevailing rule appears dubious. The analogy between warfare and necessary self-defense, see §10.5.3 *infra*, redounds in this context to the benefit of the injured aggressor. Is not a victorious army required to aid enemy troops injured in the field? Why should less be demanded of a defender who successfully rebuffs an attack? The opposing view might find support in the origins of defensive force as a private act of punishment, see §1.3.1 *supra*.

[23] For German texts sympathetic to these doubts, see, e.g., Baumann 257–58; J. Welp, Vorangegangenes Tun als Grundlage einer Handlungsäquivalenz der Unterlassung 205 (1968).

is a contested field in both German and American law, particularly in the domain of road accidents. The German Supreme Court recently held that there was no derivative liability for homicide in a case in which a motorist non-negligently injured a bicycle rider, stopped his car, but then continued driving.[24] Though the motorist was criminally liable for the minor offense of failing to render aid at the scene of an accident, his minor offense was insufficient to hold him liable, derivatively, for homicide. In a legal system such as the Anglo-American system, which lacks a general duty of first aid in cases of emergency, there may be more pressure in these highway incidents to deploy derivative liability for homicide. Yet sentiment in the United States still seems appropriately restrained about treating these unfortunate incidents as cases of criminal homicide. There are so many complex psychological factors that influence people not to stop on the highway that the stigma of manslaughter is likely to exceed the crime. If there are ongoing concerns about alienation and caring for others in modern society, it would be preferable to follow the European pattern and enact the general offense of failing to render first aid in an emergency.[25]

§8.3.5. **Statutory Duties.** Anglo-American commentators and judges often list statutes as a source of a duty to avert criminal harm.[26] What they have in mind is not a statutory holding that in a particular situation, one person is obligated to save the life of another. Rather the claim is that legislatively imposed duties, which are breached regardless of ensuing harm, can suffice to establish liability for failing to avert a consequential harm. A parallel logical leap affects the use of contractual duties to justify derivative liability for homicide or battery. If a resident is obligated either by statute or contract to clean the sidewalks in front of his house, the breach of his duty can render him liable for negligent battery or even negligent homicide.

There is a fallacy that lurks in this logic that is best revealed

[24] Judgment of July 19, 1973, 25 BGHSt. 218.

[25] StGB §330c; Code Pénal §63. *But cf.* the dangers of recognizing a statutory duty to aid, text at note 32 *infra*.

[26] LaFave & Scott 184–85; Jones v. United States, 308 F.2d 307 (D.C. Cir. 1962) (dictum). This is also the former German view. See note 13 *supra*.

in the context of a specific case. In People v. Nelson,[27] the defendant violated New York's multiple dwelling law by failing to install sprinklers and fire escapes in his apartment house. A fire broke out and several persons died who arguably would have survived the fire if there had been adequate means of egress. The defendant was convicted solely on the ground that he owned the apartment and had violated the safety ordinance. The conviction was affirmed on appeal, with the issue of culpable negligence being treated as irrelevant.

This is a good example of formal liability.[28] The defendant is held accountable solely because death ensues from his unlawful act. This was the ground for a vigorous dissent,[29] and there appears to be little doubt that the decision is at odds with the trend toward anchoring convictions for manslaughter in the proof of culpable negligence. Yet for our present purposes, what concerns us is the implicit rationale that a duty to install fire escapes suffices to establish a duty to avert death.[30]

If a rose is a rose is a rose, it does not follow that a duty is a duty is a duty. A statutory duty to take particular safety measures may carry a light penalty to stimulate compliance. In contrast, the duty to avert death is based on the moral assumption that in the particular situation, the failure to avert death is equivalent to killing. In German theory, violating a specific legislative duty to act does not automatically generate liability for ensuing harm. If a motorist fails to render aid to a roadside victim, he is guilty of a minor criminal offense; if the victim dies, it does not follow that the

[27] 309 N.Y. 231, 128 N.E.2d 391 (1955).

[28] See §4.4.2 *supra*.

[29] 309 N.Y. at 236, 128 N.E.2d at 394 (Van Voorhis, J., and Friessel, J., dissenting).

[30] Note that the opinions themselves do not frame the problem as one of failing to intervene to prevent death. Indeed the case could be stated as negligently operating an apartment house. See the analysis in §8.2.1 *supra*. *Cf.* Commonwealth v. Welansky, 316 Mass. 383, 55 N.E.2d 902 (1944) (failure to provide proper fire exits interpreted as reckless risk-creation). In the German literature, this problem is conceptualized as liability for risks emanating from houses, cars, machines, and animals under the actor's supervision and responsibility *(Sachherrschaft)*. See Schönke-Schröder-Stree §13, notes 43–50, at 167–69; Rudolphi in SK, notes 27–31, at 92–94.

motorist is guilty of criminal homicide.[31] One can only be puzzled by the failure of common-law theorists to recognize this profound difference between the two types of duty. Earlier we suggested that enacting a general duty to rescue in emergencies would deflect prosecutions away from homicide to the minor offense of failing to rescue.[32] Yet we should not ignore the opposite risk that the statutory duty to rescue would be interpreted as a sufficient basis for derivative liability for homicide.

§8.3.6. **Duties To Control Third Persons.** A body of case law has arisen to cover situations in which one party fails to prevent another from committing a crime. A husband stands by and watches another man rape his wife. The husband will be held guilty for rape, yet it seems preferable to consider these cases as an aspect of accessorial liability. The problem of failing to intervene in the crime is an aspect of the broader field of determining who is accessorially liable for the wrongdoing of another.[33]

§8.3.7. **The Scope of Duties To Avert Harm.** Once it is established that there is a duty to prevent harm, the breach of which will render a person derivatively liable, the focus of inquiry shifts to the scope of the duty. It is clear that there is no duty categorically to inhibit a particular result, regardless of the cost and effort to the defendant. What then are the criteria for determining how far one must go to save someone in distress?

Though contractual duties are not a sufficient basis for establishing duties to avert harm, the understanding between the parties might be enough to mark the outer boundaries of the duty. To return to the example of the baby sitter considered above, suppose that the sitter agrees to stay on until midnight. She leaves when the parents fail to return at that time, and a half hour later, the fatal fire breaks out. This situation poses a close question of potential liability. If the understanding that she is permitted to leave at midnight is not sufficient to insulate her from criminal liability, we should have to develop sophisticated criteria for determining

[31] See note 24 *supra.*
[32] See text at note 25 *supra.*
[33] See §8.5.2 *infra.*

when her reasons for leaving excused the breach of her duty to care for the children. Presumably it would be sufficient if she had a conflicting obligation at midnight, or should it matter what that obligation was (another job? a date? her parents' or spouse's wanting her to be at home?). On the other hand, if to avoid these complications we treated the parties' understanding as controlling, what would be the sitter's options if the parents called at 11:30 P.M. and reported that they had had an automobile accident and would not be home for another two hours? Does the sitter still have an absolute right to leave at midnight? Perhaps the way to resolve these conflicting cases is to treat the understanding as controlling, subject only to a situation of necessity that imposes a duty on the sitter analogous to the duty of the owner of the property to tolerate invasions and use of his property in a state of emergency.[34]

We noted a German case in which a spouse was held derivatively liable for failing to prevent her husband from committing suicide.[35] Yet suppose an elderly couple, fearful of hospitals, agreed (in writing, if need be) that if either should fall sick, the other would not call for medical assistance. Should this agreement be interpreted as a suicide pact that would render the survivor criminally liable? One should think not. Yet the outcome might depend on whether the particular illness that materialized was readily susceptible to medical care.

It is tempting, generally, to resolve the scope of a physician's duty by appealing to the understanding of the physician and the patient or, in lieu of an actual understanding, to a supposed agreement inferable from customary practice.[36] Actual agreements to limit terminal therapy should be respected, but the far more typical case is like that of Karen Quinlan, in which the patient does not anticipate the problem of her own terminal care and at the moment of decision is unable to express a preference, not to mention

[34] See BGB §904, discussed in §10.2.1 *infra*.

[35] See note 5 *supra*.

[36] At least I succumbed to this temptation in my earlier paper, *Prolonging Life*, 42 Wash. L. Rev. 999, 1015–16 (1967).

a well-considered preference. The notions of consent and agreement are so prestigious as legal rhetoric that courts are likely to invoke a fictitious notion of third-party consent in allowing the next of kin to represent the patient's interest. This, unfortunately, is one of the several bases for the New Jersey Supreme Court's decision in the *Quinlan* case.[37]

The notion of implicit agreement, inferable from community practice, is even more dangerous because in difficult cases, such as the use of the respirator, medical practice is likely to be in flux. One of the serious impediments to permitting discontinuance of the respirator in the *Quinlan* case was the expert testimony at trial that "removal from the respirator would not conform to medical practices, standards and traditions."[38] If that is so, it would be difficult to argue that customs of the community generated an implicit limit to the physicians' duty to maintain Karen on the respirator.

In the final analysis of these cases of the physician's responsibility to terminal patients, it proves difficult to advance the inquiry beyond the distinction long recognized in moral thought: the physician is bound to take ordinary measures to save a patient, but he is not bound to take extraordinary measures. The difficulty, of course, is fathoming the distinction between the ordinary and the extraordinary. If penicillin and insulin were once novel and extraordinary drugs, they are not today. Yet if convention is controlling in what is extraordinary and what is not, we find ourselves again grappling with diverse and conflicting community practices. The distinction between ordinary and extraordinary care emerges as one of the convergent grounds of decision in *Quinlan*. The court's account is simply this:[39]

> The use of the same respirator or like support could be considered "ordinary" in the context of the possibly curable patient but "extraordinary" in the context of the forced sustaining by cardiac respiratory processes of an irreversibly doomed patient.

[37] In re Quinlan, 70 N.J. 10, 355 A.2d 647 (1976).
[38] *Id.* at 25, 355 A.2d at 655.
[39] *Id.* at 48, 355 A.2d at 668.

This theory has the merit of going beyond community practices in linking the physician's duty to the objective likelihood of the patient's recovery. In this painfully difficult clash between our respect for life and realistic limits on our ability to cure the sick, there may be no more intelligent way of setting a limit to the physician's duty of care.[40]

§8.4. *Derivative Liability for Omissions: Some Doubts.*

Derivative liability for failing to avert death is a well-established institution in the common law as well as in German and Soviet law. Yet it is not a necessary feature of modern legal systems. The French refuse to recognize the institution.[1] And it is one about which we ought to have more doubts than we do.

There are three types of objection we might raise to the institution. The first is a conceptual and theoretical challenge. The second is a serious claim that the entire practice violates the constitutional maxim *nulla poena sine lege.* And the third is a point about necessary accommodations in a legal system that persists in punishing failures to avert death. Raising these objections should lead us to reflect more about why the institution is so steadfastly maintained in many modern legal cultures.

§8.4.1. **Conceptual Problems.** There is no problem in thinking of someone intentionally or knowingly violating a statutory duty. That would be the case if it was the person's purpose in acting, not to perform his duty to answer a question or to file a tax return by a particular date. One could even speak of the actor's negligently violating his duty—a description that would be appropriate if he was ignorant or mistaken about the circumstances con-

[40] The test adopted in StGB §13 is whether "the failure to act is [morally] equivalent to bringing about the result by affirmative conduct." For comments on this and alternative tests in German law, see Fletcher, *Criminal Omissions: Some Perspectives,* 24 Am. J. Comp. L. 703, 716 (1976).

§8.4. [1] See §8.3, note 2, *supra.*

stituting the breach, and his ignorance or mistake was easily avoidable. If he failed, say, to advise himself of the date, his failure to file a required return might readily be seen as a negligent breach. This analysis is merely an application of general principles already elaborated.

Yet when we turn to the case of failing to avert harm, our concepts of intention and negligence no longer appear to be at home. If a nurse sits idly by and knowingly lets her patient die, can we say that the nurse intends the death of the patient? Does it matter whether the nurse fervently wishes the death of her patient? Regardless of the nurse's mental attitude, there is something odd about saying that in not rendering care she "intends" the death of her patient. If two people are fighting and a bystander wishes that one of them would win and the other lose, it could hardly be said that by failing to intervene, the bystander "intends" the favored party to win. It is even more inappropriate to say that by standing by and failing to intervene, he "carries out" or "executes" his intentions. The most we can say in these cases is that the nurse or the bystander wants or wishes death to occur. But wanting something to happen is not the same thing as intending it to happen. The distinction between wanting and intending is that the latter is executed in an intervention causing harm. This is explicitly recognized in the Model Penal Code's definition of acting purposely and knowingly: a person acts purposely with regard to a result only if it is his "conscious object . . . to cause such a result"; and knowingly with regard to the result only if he is "aware that it is practically certain that his conduct will cause such a result."[2] As we have already noted, the typical failure to render aid does not constitute a primary cause of harm. This explains, I believe, the intuitive oddity of "intending" a particular result by failing to intervene. By contrast, there is nothing linguistically amiss in "intentionally" or "negligently" breaching a duty where the duty consists in acting a particular way, rather than in averting an im-

[2] My assumption is that in this section, the drafters composed in English, not in the special language of "but for" causation. See §8.2.2 *supra*.

pending harm. The language of breaching duties is different from the language of responsibility for particular occurrences of harm.[3]

Similarly, we confront difficulties in applying the notion of negligence to cases of failing to avert harm. The modern notion of negligence encompasses cases both of culpable ignorance and culpable accidents. Earlier we pointed out how important it was to recognize these two categories of negligence.[4] The distinction reemerges in this context. Let us consider, first, what it would mean to be liable for a culpable accident in failing to intervene to prevent harm. What does it mean to fail, by accident, to avert harm? If that locution is coherent at all, it suggests trying to rescue someone but failing, by accident, to reach him. The good-faith but abortive effort is hardly our problem. When we think about the party who chooses not to intervene, we find it hard to understand what an "accident" would mean in his letting the harm occur. And if the notion of accident cannot get a foothold, we could hardly ask whether the accident is sufficiently culpable to warrant liability for negligence.

One could speak about culpable ignorance in failing to take note of someone else's distress. But in the litigated cases of failing to intervene and avert death, the actor knows of the need to intervene; at least there appear to be no cases disregarding an alleged mistake as to the need to intervene. Nonetheless, these knowing failures to prevent harm are treated as negligent manslaughter. The oddity is that the factual situations do not lend themselves to description either as culpable accidents or a culpable ignorance of the danger.

The reason for this conceptual anomaly is that, apart from the problems of ignorance and mistake, the notion of negligence expresses an assessment of affirmative risk-creation. Failing to intervene does not create a risk that lends itself to the usual comparison of costs and benefits. The notions of risk-creation and

[3] For slightly different arguments supporting a distinct theory of "intention" in cases of omissions, see A. Kaufmann, Die Dogmatik der Unterlassungsdelikte 73--81 (1959).

[4] See §6.6.6 *supra.*

risk-taking run parallel to the concept of causation. In those situations in which the failure to intervene does not cause harm, neither does it create risks of harm.

One might appropriately wonder why lawyers are not particularly disturbed by these conceptual oddities. Two reasons present themselves. First, the prevailing theory of causation permits us to speak, counterintuitively, of every necessary condition for harm as a cause of that harm. The failure to intervene in one person's killing another is as necessary a condition of the victim's death as the assassin's pulling the trigger. If the causal effect of omissions can be thus equated with the causal effect of acts, the distortion of "intention" to cover both cases is a minor extension of the confusion. Secondly, the literature and cases of the common law persistently identify the breach of duty with the responsibility for the occurrence of harm. This is the confusion that supports the reliance on contractual and statutory duties in generalizing about derivative liability for omissions. There is method in mixing up these two types of duty. For our notions of intent and negligence do apply to the breach of contractual and statutory duties. Therefore, with a slight twist and a gentle shove, they can leap the categorical divide and apply as well in cases of derivative liability.

These conceptual oddities of extending the notions of intention and negligence to the cases of failing to avert harm hardly constitute a reason for abrogating liability in the whole field. They do help us understand the structural difference between causing harm and failing to avert it. And they provide an additional argument for distinguishing between statutory duties, which are breached regardless of the ensuing harm, and judicially imposed derivative liability for failing to avert a serious harm.

§8.4.2. Constitutional Arguments. The more serious critique of derivative liability is that the entire institution runs afoul of the maxim *nulla poena sine lege*. By imposing duties to avert death, judges in effect create new crimes. They punish conduct that was not declared, by statute, to be punishable at the time of commission. This is precisely the type of judicial activity that is precluded as a constitutional matter in West Germany[5] and in the United

[5] Grundgesetz (Basic Law) §103 II.

States. Although the maxim *nulla poena* is not mentioned in the United States Constitution, the legislative duty to provide fair warning of punishable conduct is a recognized element of due process.[6] Creating a whole new common-law offense would be patently unconstitutional. It is not clear why creating a pocket of derivative liability is not also unconstitutional.[7]

There are at least two arguments that can be mounted against this constitutional critique. The first is that the judicial recognition of duties to avert harm is based on interpretation of the law rather than judicial legislation. In this respect, the argument continues, the problem of working out duties to render aid is indistinguishable from the interpretation of other vague standards such as negligence. The parry to this thrust is to pause and ask: what precisely is being "interpreted" when judges recognize duties to avert death? There is no general legislative standard that advises us when there ought to be a duty and when not. If anything is being interpreted, it is the norm against homicide as a whole. The process of interpretation leads us to treat certain cases of failing to avert harm as morally equivalent to causing harm. Yet if this is the process of interpretation, it represents a paradigmatic instance of punishment by analogy. The rationale for creating common-law crimes by analogy to existing legislation is that certain forms of conduct, overlooked by the legislature, are just as bad as those penalized in the criminal code; therefore it is up to the courts to achieve consistency in the criminal law by sweeping in these overlooked offenses. One would be hard pressed, indeed, to distinguish derivative liability for failing to avert harm from the suspect practice of punishment by analogy.

The second response to the constitutional challenge would be

[6] Lambert v. California 355 U.S. 225 (1957); Keeler v. Superior Court, 2 Cal. 3d 619, 470 P.2d 617, 87 Cal. Rptr. 481 (1970).

[7] Note the contradiction in the Model Penal Code. §1.05(1) lays down the rule of *nulla poena sine lege:* "No conduct constitutes an offense unless it is a crime or violation under this Code or another statute of this State." *But* §2.01(3)(b) provides that liability for commission by omission applies if "a duty to perform the omitted act is otherwise imposed by law." The commentary says: "It should of course suffice, as the courts now hold, that the duty arises under some branch of the civil law." MPC §2.01, Comment at 123 (Tent. Draft No. 4, 1955).

to stress that all those who refuse to render aid to others in distress engage in immoral and wrongful behavior. The courts only punish a sub-set of those cases that might be regarded as immoral failures to help a fellow citizen in trouble.[8] The problem thus is not the penalty incurred by those punished, but justifying the element of grace to those not punished. If someone ends up on the criminal side of the line, he has no reason to complain: he could have avoided criminal liability by avoiding all wrongful failures to rescue others. This is a specific application of the more general argument: the wrongdoer must take his chances. It is akin to the argument, which we shall take up later,[9] that a wrongdoer should run the risk that his victim will turn out to be different from what he reasonably expects. The wrongdoer (or wrongful omitter) must run the risk that the courts will punish his failure to render aid. This principle proves to be one of the pervasive maxims of Anglo-American criminal law, and it obviously has an impact on other legal systems as well. Yet the principle that the wrongdoer has no rights is not so much a response to the constitutional critique of derivative liability as it is an alternative constitutional order. It is an order in which fair warning of punishment is not important, for everyone knows or should know when he is acting (or omitting) wrongfully.

In the debates and hearings leading to the new German criminal code, the constitutional problem of punishing the failure to avert harm became a focal point of dispute.[10] After some initial efforts to suppress the issue, the consensus emerged that the new code would have to include a provision that would bring derivative liability in from the cold. Yet the fear was that the factual variations were so complex that they would not lend themselves to the discipline of black-letter rules. What emerged was §13 of the 1975 Code, which (roughly translated) prescribes:

> (1) Whoever fails to avoid the occurrence of a result that conforms to

[8] This argument is advanced in Maurach GP 597.

[9] See §9.3.3 *infra*.

[10] See generally Fletcher, *Criminal Omissions: Some Perspectives*, 24 Am. J. Comp. L. 703, 707–09 (1976).

the definition of the offense, is punishable under this code if principles of Right require him to make sure that the result does not occur and if the failure to act is [morally] equivalent to committing the offense,[11] by affirmative conduct.

(2) The penalty may be mitigated according to §49(1).[12]

Several points about this provision are worth noting. First, the language does not purport to specify the grounds for imposing derivative liability, and therefore the constitutional problem is hardly resolved. Nonetheless, the general principle specified in the statute goes further than the comparable rule in the Model Penal Code, which tells us only what we already know: "Liability . . . may not be based on an omission unless . . . a duty to perform the omitted act is . . . imposed by law."[13] Secondly, the German provision brings into focus a criterion of determing when the law should recognize duties to avert harm. The criterion is the principle of equivalence between causing harm and failing to avert harm. This may not be a precise standard, but at least it specifies the framework of debate. It is preferable to assuming that the duties to avert harm are already embodied in the law and need only to be recognized as the need arises.

§8.4.3. Accommodations. If there is to be derivative liability for failure to avert harm, one might expect an indulgent posture of the courts toward the problem of mistake of law. Defects in the standard of fair warning might be corrected by acquitting those excusably ignorant of their legal duty to render aid. The difficulty with this argument is again the point that derivative liability attaches only to those who are, in fact, engaged in morally disapproved failures to aid their fellow human beings. It would be difficult to contend that their mistakes about their legal duties render them free from censure.

The irony is that in the cases of statutorily defined duties to act, where there is no judicial problem, one is more likely to en-

[11] The term here is *Verwirklichung des gesetzlichen Tatbestandes,* which means, literally: "the realization of the definition of the offense."

[12] For a translation and discussion of StGB §49(1), see §8.6, at note 2 *infra.*

[13] MPC §2.01(3).

counter innocent mistakes of law. A good example is Lambert v. California,[14] in which the defendant was punished under a Los Angeles ordinance making it a misdemeanor for "convicted persons" to remain in Los Angeles more than five days without registering with the police department. The defendant had no knowledge of a duty to register and there was "no probability of such knowledge."[15] This excusable lack of knowledge was sufficient, in the opinion of the Supreme Court, to render the conviction unconstitutional.

The precedent in *Lambert* appears to be distinguishable from the problem of mistake of law in cases of failing to avert harm. The important point in Ms. Lambert's situation is that there was nothing that should have alerted her to the legal consequences of remaining within Los Angeles. As a result, the state's obligation to provide notice to the potential offender loomed more prominently. But if someone is in distress, there is an event that "alerts the doer to the consequences"[16] of failing to render aid. Whether there is a plausible excuse based on mistake of law depends on whether the actor has been alerted in this way.[17] In cases of statutory omissions, there is not likely to be an event that puts the actor on notice; in cases of derivative liability, there is always an event—the potential victim's distress—that alerts the actor to the need to do something. Thus there are two related reasons why the excuse of mistake of law is not likely to be a suitable lever for keeping derivative liability within constitutional bounds. Not only is derivative liability imposed on those who breach a moral duty, and who therefore have difficulty arguing that their failure to rescue was blameless, but further, derivative liability appears to be imposed only on those who are put on notice of an emergency and the need to intervene.

This discussion brings into focus the true problem of judicial definitions of duty in cases of derivative liability. The problem is

[14] 355 U.S. 225 (1957).
[15] *Id. at 227.*
[16] *Id.* at 228.
[17] See generally §9.4 *infra.*

not so much fair warning, as it was in the *Lambert* case. Rather the issue is one of separation of powers. Is it permissible within the constitutional scheme for courts to extend the contours of criminal offenses, even if there is fair warning to those held liable? Restrictions on the role of the judiciary find their warrant in the separation of powers as well as arguments of fairness to the accused. This is the case with regard to bills of attainder and ex post facto laws.[18] There should be similar sensitivity to constitutional limitations on the judicial role in the field of derivative liability.

§8.4.4. Why Punish the Failure To Avert Harm? In view of the conceptual anomalies and the constitutional infirmities of punishing the failure to avert harm, one appropriately wonders why we do it. As a category of "criminals," people who fail to avert harm are hardly dangerous to society. Bank robbers, rapists, hired assassins, muggers — they are dangerous because they take the initiative in causing harm. They plan crimes and carry them out. Yet people who fail to avert harm exercise no initiative. They get caught in a situation in which they falter. Someone needs help and they cannot bring themselves to render it. Yet how often is that likely to happen in the life of the ordinary person? Perhaps in the case of lifeguards, police officers and ship captains, there might be recurrent incidents of failing to rescue dependent people. These are particularly easy cases to domesticate in a legislative rule, for the duty to avert harm is implicit in the professional role. Yet it is a rare incident indeed when someone is confronted with the need to rescue a member of the family or an accident victim. The rationale for penalizing this range of human failures would seem to be rooted in considerations other than protection of the public.

The ground for punishment in these cases appears to be outrage at the refusal to render aid to another person in distress. Modern society almost covets its sense of being disturbed at the disintegrating ties of community. It is simply shocking that someone would see an accident victim and fail to render aid. It is "mor-

[18] See Comment, *The Bounds of Legislative Specification: A Suggested Approach to the Bill of Attainder Clause,* 72 Yale L.J. 330 (1962); United States v. Brown, 381 U.S. 437 (1965).

ally self-evident" that some cases of failing to avert harm should be treated as homicidal. As the Indian Law Commissioners viewed the extreme cases:[19]

> It will hardly be disputed that a gaoler who voluntarily caused the death of a prisoner by omitting to supply that prisoner with food, or a nurse who voluntarily causes the death of an infant entrusted to her care by omitting to take it out of a tub of water into which it has fallen, ought to be treated as guilty of murder.

The analogous argument in German law is the principle of moral equivalence between failing to prevent harm and causing harm.

There is nothing wrong with fuelling the criminal law with all this moral energy. Yet one appropriately wishes that, at least in Anglo-American law, there was as much attention paid to other moral principles. We all too often ignore the principle of proportionality of punishment,[20] and the principle that only the morally culpable should suffer criminal punishment.[21] And yet we develop new pockets of liability on the basis of moral outrage. It would be preferable, in my view, to channel our moral sensitivities into the theory of justification and excuse, and to avoid passion in fields that verge on the unconstitutional extension of criminal punishment.

§8.5. *Perpetrators and Accessories: Derivative Liability for Human Conduct.*

The the is of this chapter is that two seemingly diverse fields of liability can be brought under the single heading of "derivative liability." Liability for failing to avert harm bears a critical resem-

[19] As reproduced in J. Michael & H. Wechsler, Criminal Law and Its Administration 120, 121 (1940).

[20] See the analysis and critique of cases on mistake in §9.3 *infra*.

[21] See §6.7.2 *supra*.

blance to aiding and abetting another in the commission of a criminal act. In both cases there is a primary process generating harm and the actor is held accountable by virtue of his position relative to that process. His position might be that of someone who fails to intervene to prevent a natural process, or it might be that of someone who lends aid to the criminal plan of another. Bringing these seemingly diverse problems into a common matrix of derivative liability generates insights concealed by conventional habits of classification. It helps us see, for example, that the problem of liability for failing to avert harm has little to do with the distinct field of direct liability for a statutory breach. It will help us see as well that in many cases for aiding and abetting, setting the minimal threshold of liability is remarkably akin to the problem of recognizing duties of intervention.

At the outset of the chapter, we noted three perspectives uniting the field of failing to prevent harm with accessorial liability. These points bear repeating, with special attention to their applicability in extending liability to accessories:

A. *The Formal Basis of Liability.* As the special part of contemporary criminal codes does not specify when a party failing to intervene is liable for commission by omission, the definition of particular offenses does not tell us when accessories are liable for aiding and abetting the offense. The constitutional problem raised above has less of a grip, however, for modern codes do typically lay down general provisions specifying the criteria for accessorial liability.[1]

B. *Causation.* The issue in this context is not primarily the weakness of the "but for" theory of causation, but the general issue of "causing" independent human conduct. The aider and abettor contributes either advice or material aid, but he does not "cause" the primary perpetrator to commit the offense.

C. *Intent.* The accessory has the intent to aid and to facilitate the offense, but it is anomalous to say that in carrying out this intent, he "intentionally commits" the offense.

§8.5. [1] StGB 1871, §§47–49; StGB §§25–31; Code Pénal §60; Ugol. kod. (RSFSR) §17; Cal. Penal Code §31; MPC §2.06; Proposed Federal Criminal Code §401(a).

§8.5. *The Theory of Derivative Liability*

As the preliminary issue in the first half of this chapter was distinguishing between the direct violation of norms and derivative liability, we confront an analogous issue in the field of accessorial liability. Perpetrators or principals are those who are directly liable for the violation of a norm; accessories are those who are derivatively liable. The important premise that will guide our discussion is that liability as an accessory presupposes that some other person is the perpetrator of the crime. Whether the perpetrator must be convicted before the accomplice is tried is a procedural problem that should not distract us from the substantive issue. The principle is that there is neither a criminal act nor accessorial liability without a primary perpetrator of the offense.

It is important to see that this proposition about accessorial liability holds true even in those Anglo-American jurisdictions that have abolished the common-law classifications of principals and accessories before the fact. For example, the California Penal Code holds that all persons "concerned in the commission of a crime . . . [including those who] aid and abet in its commission . . ."[2] are to be held as principals. The assumption implicit in this language is that there be an offense committed by someone. The same assumption informs the Model Penal Code's definition of "accomplices."[3] Whenever it is assumed that someone other than the defendant "commits the offense," then the liability imposed on the defendant is derivative.

The comparative analysis in this context is more difficult than in the field of omissions, for legal systems divide essentially into two camps on the subject of complicity. There are those, like the German and Soviet systems, that recognize the principle of mitigating punishment for accessories, and those, like the French and Anglo-American systems, that do not officially recognize a mitigation of punishment for lesser participation. One says "officially" for it is still possible in these latter systems that punishment is mitigated informally, in the exercise of prosecutorial and judicial

[2] Cal. Penal Code §31.

[3] MPC §2.06(3) ("accomplices of another person in the commission of an offense . . .").

discretion. It is obvious, however, that those systems that openly hold that accessories warrant lesser punishment ascribe greater importance to the field of accessorial liability.[4]

In view of the difficulties of comparative analysis, it is urgent that we be clear in our use of terms: we propose to use the following terms as indicated:

1. A *perpetrator* is someone whose liability can be established independently of all other parties. The common-law term is "principal," but it is preferable to avoid confusion with the doctrines of principal and agent in private law. The perpetrator's liability is direct and not derivative of someone else's committing the offense.

2. *Accessories* are all those who are held derivatively liable for another's committing the offense. The category includes *instigators* as well as *aiders-and-abettors.*

3. An *accomplice* is any partner in crime—a co-perpetrator or an accessory. The subject of complicity covers all issues bearing on liability as a perpetrator or an accessory.

The agenda before us is to outline three categories of perpetrators and two categories of accessories. These five ways of participating in criminal activity are clearly expressed in German legal theory and recognized, with varying degrees of explicitness, in other legal systems, including Anglo-American law. Once these five categories are clearly before us, we shall explore the reasons for distinguishing between perpetration and accessorial liability. This will give us an occasion to assess the desirability of current legal practice in Anglo-American jurisdictions.

§8.5.1. Direct Liability for Perpetration. The model of perpetration is a single actor, carrying out the crime by himself. The

[4] This may account for the extraordinary disinterest in complicity in the English-speaking world. The German literature is voluminous. The bibliography in Schönke-Schröder-Cramer at 323–24 contains approximately 100 books and articles, about twice as many as listed on insanity. The only articles of note in English appear to be Sayre, *Criminal Responsibility for Acts of Another,* 43 Harv. L. Rev. 689 (1930); and Perkins, *Parties to Crime,* 89 U. Pa. L. Rev. 581 (1941). There are useful chapters in Williams 346--423 and LaFave & Scott 495--522, but the subject is ignored in Hall and in Packer. The Model Penal Code failed even to provide a commentary to its proposal. Would that the field were better charted!

concept of perpetration relies upon this model even when others are involved in instigating or aiding the perpetration of the offense. Most legal systems make some effort to define this primary category of perpetration. The Model Penal Code says simply that an actor is "guilty of an offense if it is committed by his own conduct."[5] The new German code stresses that the perpetrator must "commit the criminal act himself."[6] The RSFSR Code adds the provision that the perpetrator must "directly" commit the offense.[7] It would seem that there is little difficulty in determining the category of perpetration but this appearance of simplicity dissolves if we refine the notion of "committing" the criminal act to include a subjective disposition to regard the crime "as one's own." As we shall see,[8] German courts have on occasion held that persons acting on the instructions of others lack this subjective commitment and therefore are merely accomplices in the crime perpetrated by the person issuing the instructions.

As a supplement to this primary category, most legal systems assume that two or more persons might be "co-perpetrators." Think of the person who holds the victim while his cohort carries out a rape or assault. These cases are problematic because the conduct of the person holding the victim does not, by itself, meet the definition of rape or assault. In a more complicated variation, the conduct of neither person, by itself, satisfies the objective elements of the definition. In a common-law case of obtaining property by false pretenses, one person might deceive the victim and another might receive transfer of title. The first is responsible for the false pretense; the second, for the receipt of the goods. Neither alone perpetrates the entire offense. Yet they act together in the joint execution of a common plan. The critical element in German law is that the parties act in concert (*gemeinschaftlich*) in executing the plan.[9] It is important to note that a conspiracy to commit a crime

[5] MPC §2.06(1).
[6] StGB §25(1).
[7] Ugol. kod. (RSFSR) §17(3).
[8] See the *Staschchynsky* case discussed in §8.7.1 *infra*.
[9] StGB §25(2).

does not entail joint perpetration,[10] for some of the conspirators may well be passive in the actual execution of the particular criminal act.

A third form of perpetration, which we shall call "perpetration-by-means," is a more subtle institution, for it encompasses persons who are not actively engaged in the carrying out of the criminal act. Paradigmatic instances are using a child or an insane person to implement a criminal plan of which the latter is totally unaware. Suppose *A* gives a child *B* an innocuous-looking poison to put in the intended victim's food. If the child carries out the request, the perpetrator is *A*, not *B*. The assumption is that *B's* act is merely the means by which *A* perpetrates the offense. But regarding a human being as a "means" or an "instrument" is at best a metaphor, and the problem that recurs in this field is why *A* is not an accessory in *B*'s act of poisoning the victim. If culpability and liability were a necessary condition for identifying *B* as the perpetrator, then one would have a simple explanation for why the law does not so treat *B*. Yet the rule in many legal systems is that the person who carries out the act might be classified as a perpetrator even if he is not liable for the offense.[11] Thus one needs a refined theory to explain why *A* is a perpetrator-by-means rather than an accessory in *B*'s non-punishable perpetration of the poisoning.

Virtually all legal systems, it should be noted, recognize the institution of perpetration-by-means. The Model Penal Code provides that an actor is guilty of an offense if, with the requisite state of mind, he "causes an innocent or irresponsible person to engage in the [proscribed] conduct."[12] The German code says simply that the perpetrator is anyone who commits the offense himself or "through another."[13] Other legal systems recognize the doctrine as implicit in the concept of perpetration.[14] This doctrinal

[10] See §8.7.2 *infra*.
[11] See §8.7.3 *infra*.
[12] MPC §2.06(2)(a).
[13] StGB §25(1).
[14] Kurs (GP 1968) at 613.

sketch of the types of perpetrator leaves numerous difficult questions to be assessed. We shall encounter these problems presently when we address ourselves to specific questions about the distinctions implicit in the categories of perpetration and accessorial liability.

§8.5.2. Two Categories of Accessories. There are two ways in which an actor can be derivatively liable for the crime of a perpetrator. He can aid or abet the criminal act, in which event he occupies a subsidiary status in the criminal enterprise, or he can instigate or solicit the criminal act, which renders his status closer to that of a full partner in the crime. German and Soviet law explicitly recognize this distinction between two types of accessories; French and Anglo-American law treat them both as accessories in the broad sense.

The category of aiding-and-abetting confronts problems of limitation on two fronts. On the one hand, the problem is distinguishing between aiding-and-abetting and conduct that is wholly exempt from criminal liability. This lower frontier is staked out by specifying the kind of contribution the actor must make to the perpetrator's criminal plan. Most statutory schemes rely simply on the concept of "aid" to specify the minimal contribution necessary to make a person an aider-and-abettor.[15] Of course, the aid must be rendered with a view to facilitating the perpetrator's offense. The RSFSR Code specifically outlines the relevant forms of aid as "advice, instructions, supplying the means, eliminating obstacles, and promising in advance to conceal the crime, its instrumentalities, traces, or fruits."[16] Most cases at the lower frontier of accessorial liability are unproblematic, but there is one set of problems that will later invite consideration. This is the set of cases in which a person engaged in a regular course of business sells or supplies an article to someone, knowing that the recipient is planning to commit a crime. The supplier knowingly contributes to the crime, but the question is whether

[15] StGB §27(1) (*Hilfe*); *cf.* StGB 1871, §49(1) (*Hilfe durch Rat oder Tat*); Cal. Penal Code §31 ("aiding-and-abetting," "advising," or "encouraging"); MPC §2.06(3)(a)(ii) (aiding or attempting to aid).

[16] Ugol. kod. (RSFSR) §17(6).

he must deviate from the ordinary course of commercial life in order to hinder his customer's criminal plan.[17]

At the upper frontier, the problem in the theory of accessorial liability is distinguishing the accessory's subsidiary contribution from the three ways of perpetrating the offense. Thus there are three and sometimes four boundaries that must be worked out: the accessory must be distinguished from the primary or direct perpetrator, from the co-perpetrator, from the perpetrator-by-means; and in those systems that distinguish between instigators and aiders-and-abettors, these two forms of accessorial liability must also be marked out.

There is one other point about accessorial liability that is worth noting at this preliminary stage. By definition, an accessory's liability is derivative of that of the perpetrator. The problematic issues are, first, whether the perpetrator must actually be guilty of the offense and, secondly, whether, in addition, the perpetrator must be convicted before the accessory can be indicted. To take the latter procedural issue first, the common law underwent a long period of reaction against its initial rule requiring conviction of the perpetrator prior to the levying of derivative liability on the accessory. By the time of Blackstone, this rule had been relaxed so that the indictment against the accessory was sound if the principal had received a pardon, or had claimed benefit of clergy.[18] Parliament abolished this procedural impediment altogether in 1826,[19] and soon thereafter in the United States, criminal codes commonly displayed provisions stating that accessories may be prosecuted without regard to the trial and conviction of the perpetrator.[20]

Eliminating this procedural impediment brings into focus the more difficult issue whether, in principle, the accessory may be liable even though the perpetrator is not guilty of the offense. One theory of accessorial liability, which we shall label the "broad"

[17] See §8.8.2 *infra*.

[18] 4 Blackstone 323–24. *Cf.* 2 Stephen 235--36.

[19] 7 Geo. IV, c. 64, §9 (1826).

[20] E.g., Cal. Penal Code §§31, 971, 972; Mass. Ann. Laws c. 274, §3.

theory, would require merely that the perpetrator wrongfully violate the law. Even if the perpetrator's wrongful act is excusable, his accessory might nonetheless be liable for culpably furthering a wrongful act. Thus if *A*, who is insane, intimidates *B* to assault *X*, and *C* assists the two of them by handing *B* a club, *A* and *B* would both be excused on the grounds, respectively, of insanity and duress. Yet their conduct would be wrongful. Under the "broad" theory of accessorial liability, *C* could be accessory and liable on the basis of his own unexcused participation in the wrongful assault.

In contrast, a "narrow" theory of accessorial liability would require that the perpetrator be liable for the wrongful act. The "narrow" theory would be endorsed by those who think of complicity as a matter of imputing the liability of one person to another. On this view, which collapses the distinction between vicarious and accessorial liability, the accessory cannot be liable unless the perpetrator is liable: absent a punishable offense by the perpetrator, there is no basis for holding the accessory accountable. One might be led to the view that the perpetrator must be culpable by a theory of vicarious liability; all the ingredients of liability must be found in the acts of the perpetrator and these, in turn, are imputed to the accessory.

As a matter of principle, the "broad" theory has much to commend it. The argument is that while wrongfulness is a feature of acts considered abstractly, culpability is always personal. The accessory should not be liable unless he personally is culpable for the crime of the perpetrator. There is no justification for fictitiously "imputing" the culpability of the perpetrator to the accessory. The next step in the argument is that in a prosecution against the accessory, it is the latter's culpability that is relevant; the perpetrator's culpability is incidental. Once the theory of imputed culpability is rejected, there seems to be little warrant for requiring the perpetrator to be culpable.

Requiring that the perpetrator act wrongfully is a different matter; for if the accessory is liable on a theory of derivative and subsidiary liability, the acts of the perpetrator must objectively constitute a violation of applicable legal norms. If the perpetrator's conduct is justified, there is no act-in-chief for which the accessory may properly be held accountable. The critical point is that excusing the perpetrator does not have the effect of undercutting the wrongfulness of the violation, but justifying his conduct does. A justified violation is compatible with legal norms and therefore not an apt basis for accessorial liability.

This "broad" view of accessorial liability received legislative regulation in the German law of torts before it emerged as a doctrine of criminal liability. In contrast to the Anglo-American theory of the employer's vicarious liability for the torts of the employee, the German Civil Code of 1900 adopted the principle that the employer must be personally negligent in the selection and supervision of his employees.[21] Yet to hold the German employer liable, the injured party need prove only that the employee wrongfully caused the injury. The difference between common-law respondeat superior and the German Civil Code is illustrated in the following diagram:

Respondeat Superior
(the "narrow" theory)

	Employer	*Employee*
Wrongful Act	–	X
Culpability	–	X

German Civil Code §831
(the "broad" theory)

	Employer	*Employee*
Wrongful Act	–	X
Culpability	X	–

Though the "broad" theory of accessorial liability was recognized in German tort law at the turn of the century, it was not officially received in the criminal law until 1943. Though a Nationalist Socialist decree of that year changed the law,[22] the doctrine

[21] BGB §831.
[22] Ordinance of May 29, 1943, 1 RGBl. 341.

does not appear to bear the marks of totalitarian criminal theory. The "broad" theory has long been recognized in France,[23] and one might even argue that there is implicit support for it in the common-law cases that hold that an actor may be complicitous in the conduct of a perpetrator that is excused by reason of insanity, entrapment, duress, or mistake.[24] The ambiguity in these cases, however, is whether the actor is accountable on a theory of accessorial liability or by virtue of his being a perpetrator-by-means. When we take up this topic in detail, we shall find there are good reasons in principle for a legal system's recognizing both the "broad" theory of perpetration and the doctrine of perpetration-by-means.

§8.5.3. A Special Category of Instigation. The German[25] and Soviet[26] systems distinguish between instigation of an offense, on the one hand, and aiding-and-abetting, on the other. The instigator is an accessory rather than a perpetrator. The party who carries out the solicited crime is the perpetrator. The liability of an instigator, like that of an aider-and-abettor, is derivative of the perpetrator's wrongful act. This means that if the perpetrator never goes so far as to attempt the solicited act, the instigator is not liable.[27]

The more difficult question is not why the instigator should be distinguished from the perpetrator, but why the instigator should be distinguished from the aider-and-abettor. Neither French law nor the Anglo-American common law recognizes the distinction. There is no difference in these systems between someone who procures or commands the act, and someone who assists the act by supplying counsel or the means for committing the of-

[23] 1 Bouzat & Pinatel §777, at 752–53.

[24] United States v. Azadian, 436 F.2d 81 (9th Cir. 1971) (perpetrator of bribe acquitted on grounds of entrapment; accessory convicted); Regina v. Cogan & Leak, [1975] 3 W.L.R. 316 (Crim. App.) (perpetrator's conviction for rape reversed on grounds of mistake; accessory then held as a perpetrator-by-means); State v. Haines, 51 La. Ann. 731, 25 So. 372 (1899) (dictum to the effect that accessory could be held for rape of his wife if he coerced the perpetrator).

[25] *Compare* StGB §26 (*Anstiftung*) *with* §27(1) (*Beihilfe*).

[26] *Compare* Ugol. kod. (RSFSR) §17(5) (instigators) *with* §17(6) (aiders-and-abettors).

[27] *But cf.* direct liability for solicitation, regardless of whether the solicited crime is executed. StGB §30; MPC §5.02.

fense. The reason for this differentiation in one family of systems, but not the other, is straightforward. German and Soviet law recognize a higher level of punishment for instigators as compared with aiders-and-abettors; French and Anglo-American law do not. Indeed, one of the arguments in the French literature for punishing accomplices and perpetrators alike is that some accomplices are instigators, and at least this group of accomplices warrants the same punishment as full perpetrators.[28]

Differential punishment is one of the guiding levers behind the whole apparatus of criminal roles, and therefore we shall take up the subject below when we seek to explain why these five categories of liability might commend themselves to a legal system that seeks to reduce the play of discretion in the sentencing process.

§8.5.4. Neighboring Concepts of Complicity. The preceding five categories are advanced as a matrix for analyzing the basic problems of complicity. To vindicate this choice of terms, we should pause in this section to explain the relevance of competing concepts and assess how they relate to the delineated categories of perpetration and accessorial liability.

A. Accessories After the Fact. The common law employed a set of categories closely related to those outlined above. The basic distinctions were among principals in the first degree, principals in the second degree, accessories before the fact, and accessories after the fact. The first three terms conform respectively to (1) primary perpetration and perpetration-by-means, (2) co-perpetration, and (3) complicity by instigation as well as by aiding-and-abetting.

The one common-law category that we have not included in our scheme is the accessory after the fact. This type of accessory does not contribute to the commission of the crime, but rather to the felon's efforts to avoid detection. According to the rule, the offense is committed by anyone who knows of the felony and "receives, relieves, comforts or assists" the felon.[29]

One form of criminal activity that invited punishment under

[28] 1 Bouzat & Pinatel §797, at 770–71.
[29] 4 Blackstone 37; 1 Hale 618–22.

this doctrine of assistance after the fact was the act of receiving stolen property. As late as the early twentieth century, the French punished *recel* (receipt of stolen property) as a crime derivative of the underlying felony of theft.[30] The Anglo-American development was different. Hale had concluded that the knowing receipt of stolen property did not render the receiver a felonious accessory after the fact. To be guilty of felony, and not merely of a trespass, the accessory had to receive and harbor the thief, not merely receive the goods.[31] Parliament thereafter intervened with a statute that deemed the receiver to be an accessory after the fact.[32] In a series of developments in the nineteenth century, the offense of receiving evolved toward its present status as an independent felony.[33]

The development of receiving stolen goods as an independent crime betokens the general fate of liability for being an "accessory after the fact." Harboring a criminal and facilitating escape are independent wrongs, injuring the social interest in law enforcement rather than compounding the wrongs represented by the antecedent felony. As perjury is a crime independent of the crime whose prosecution might be defeated by perjurious testimony, harboring a felon or covering up a crime is an independent assault on the administration of justice. The category of "accessories after the fact" is being rapidly replaced in the United States, as well as in other jurisdictions, by specially legislated offenses of obstructing justice.[34] Thus the problem of assistance after the deed is of little further relevance in our study of the complicity and derivative liability.

B. Conspiracy. The crime of conspiracy must be sharply dis-

[30] The law was changed by the law of May 22, 1915. See 1 Bouzat & Pinatel §808, at 779.

[31] 1 Hale 618.

[32] 3 & 4 Wm. & M., c. 9, §4 (1692).

[33] See J. Hall, Theft, Law and Society 55–58 (2d ed. 1952).

[34] MPC §242.3 (hindering apprehension or prosecution); §242.4 (aiding consummation); §242.5 (compounding by receiving proceeds of the crime). *Cf.* StGB §257 (helping offender secure benefits of crime); §258 (hindering prosecution); §138 (failure to report specified offenses); Ugol. kod. (RSFSR) §§88^{1}, 190 (failure to report specified offenses); §§88^{2}, 189 (concealing specified offenses); the separation of obstructing justice from the concept of accessorial liability is a recent accomplishment of Soviet legal theory. See Kurs (GP 1968) at 634–38.

tinguished from the categories of complicity. Conspiracy is a distinct offense, consummated upon entering into the agreement to commit the offense.[35] Yet this single crime fills a number of diverse functions that are satisfied by other doctrinal devices in Continental legal systems. By functioning as an additional count in indictments against those who jointly commit offenses, it provides a means for aggravating punishment for group perpetration. More significantly, membership in a conspiracy generates a standard for holding each conspirator complicitous in the crimes of fellow conspirators. The only restriction on this test of complicity is that the crime be committed in furtherance of the conspiracy's felonious objective. The important point about this connection between conspiracy and complicity is that conspiratorial membership functions not as a category of accessorial liability but as a test for what it means to be a co-perpetrator. Whether this test is a sound one shall concern us in due course.[36]

C. Vicarious Liability. Another concept that must be sharply set off from the theory of complicity is "vicarious liability." This form of liability relates to complicity as strict liability relates to the principle of culpability. That liability is "vicarious" simply expresses the conclusion that the defendant will be held liable for the acts of another. It is not a rationale for holding the defendant liable.

The term "vicarious liability" appears to be used prominently (1) either in cases of strict liability of an employer for the criminal acts of his employee,[37] or (2) in cases that were formerly regarded as problems under the felony-murder rule.[38] The difference between older applications of the felony-murder rule and the principle of vicarious liability is illustrated by the case in which one of

[35] See §3.6.1 *supra.*

[36] See §8.7.2 *infra.*

[37] Commonwealth v. Koczwara, 397 Pa. 575, 155 A.2d 825 (1959) (defendant held liable for employee's sale of liquor to a minor, but subject only to fine, not imprisonment).

[38] Taylor v. Superior Court, 3 Cal. 3d 578, 477 P.2d 131, 91 Cal. Rptr. 175 (1970) ("if petitioner were an accomplice to the robbery, he would be vicariously responsible for any killing attributable to the intentional acts of his associates . . .").

the co-conspirators kills himself, or induces a third party to kill him, in the course of the felony. An expansive use of the felony-murder rule would lead to liability on the ground that each conspirator was accountable for the occurrence of death in the course of the felony. The principle of vicarious liability, now employed in the California felony-murder cases, requires that the person actually causing the death be liable for murder.[39] If the person causing the death is the victim himself, and if criminal homicide is defined as the unlawful killing of another (not just any) human being, then the victim is not liable for his own demise, and there is no crime to be imputed to the other members of the conspiracy.

The doctrine of vicarious liability presumably originates in the common-law rule of respondeat superior; the employer is vicariously liable for the torts committed by his servant in the course of his employment. The rule requires that the servant actually commit a tort; wrongfully causing harm will not suffice. Thus the law of the master's tort liability supplies the key ideas in the criminal law doctrine of vicarious liability: (1) there must be a punishable crime by the perpetrator; (2) there must be a particular kind of relationship between the perpetrator and the party to be held liable (i.e., employment, a criminal conspiracy); and (3) the criminal act must be committed in furtherance of or in the scope of that relationship.

From a comparative perspective, it is striking that ideas rooted in the law of torts should have influenced both German and American criminal law. The German law of accessorial liability in wrongful (but not culpable) conduct is first expressed as a rule of the civil code, regulating the tort liability of employers.[40] The common rule of vicarious liability originates in the totally distinct theory that the torts of the employee may be imputed to the employer regardless of the latter's personal fault.

That there is this common pattern of development is not meant to suggest that vicarious liability is just as plausible as the system of accessorial liability based upon the accessory's personal fault. Indeed it is difficult to take vicarious liability seriously as a

[39] People v. Antick, 15 Cal. 3d 79, 539 P.2d 243, 123 Cal. Rptr. 475 (1975).
[40] See §8.5.2 *supra*.

doctrine of the criminal law. Tort scholars have been puzzled for decades to explain the tort rule in employer liability cases.[41] If economic policies may be invoked to explain the rule, these hardly apply to the question of justly holding an individual liable in the criminal law. If vicarious liability is to be explained on the ground of metaphysical identity of principal and agent (*Qui facit per alium facit per se*), one should hope that the principle of individual responsibility would prevail in the criminal law. The most that can be said for vicarious liability is that it might function as a conclusory label that is applied only when there is a plausible but unexplicated ground of accessorial liability in the facts of the case.

Thus we have explained, let us hope, why our inquiry may proceed without considering the doctrines of accessoryship after the fact, conspiracy and vicarious liability as categories of complicity. The former is properly regarded as a separate crime of obstructing justice; the latter two doctrines are but approximations for determining when there is ground for holding someone as a co-perpetrator or an accessory. At the proper place, we shall see how the availability of conspiratorial and vicarious liability has inhibited the refinement of the common-law criteria of complicity.

§8.6. *The Rationale for Differentiated Participation in Criminal Plans.*

The question we have postponed too long is why the law should take note of the five ways in which one may participate in a criminal act. Why should it matter whether one is a perpetrator or an accomplice and, even more discriminatingly, whether one is a perpetrator, instigator, accessory or perpetrator-by-means? As the Model Penal Code bears witness, a legal system can survive without cultivating these distinctions. Aiding another person to com-

[41] See Steffen, *The Independent Contractor and the Good Life,* 2 U. Chi. L. Rev. 501 (1935).

mit a crime renders one an accomplice, and being an accomplice is simply one way of "being guilty of an offense." This way of approaching the problem of what the code calls "liability for conduct of another" is but a technique for rounding out the definition of particular offenses. Every offense has built into it a penumbral orbit of liability for those who aid others in committing the offense.

Under the Model Penal Code, nothing appears to turn on whether a participant in a crime is classified as a perpetrator or an accessory. The critical difference among legal systems is whether various grades of complicity are punished differentially.[1] German and Soviet legal theories are both committed to the proposition that accessories should not be punished as severely as perpetrators. According to the current German code, the punishment for an accessory is reduced according to the following statutory scheme:[2]

1. Instead of life imprisonment, the punishment is imprisonment for not less than three years.
2. In cases of prescribed terms of imprisonment, the maximum term may be reduced to three-fourths of the prescribed maximum. The same reduction applies to monetary penalties.
3. The minimum term of imprisonment is mitigated as follows:
   A. from a minimum of ten or five years to a minimum of two years.
   B. from a minimum of three or two years to a minimum of six months.
   C. from a minimum of one year to a minimum of three months.
   D. In other cases the statutory minimum is retained.

Instead of prescribing an elaborate scheme for mitigation of the accessory's punishment, the Soviet codes prescribe merely that the "degree and character of each participant's contribution to the crime must be assessed by the court in determining the sentence."[3]

§8.6 [1] Note Blackstone's reasons for English law's recognizing the distinctions among principals and accessories. 4 Blackstone 39–40. If we disregard accessories after the fact and procedural distinctions, these reasons have little remaining force.

[2] StGB §49(1).

[3] Ugol. kod. (RSFSR) §17(7).

In contrast to these systems of mitigation, Anglo-American and French law are committed to the principle that accessories and perpetrators should be punished alike.[4] This fundamental cleavage in the approach to punishing accessories determines both the relevant categories of complicity and their survival in modern legal theory.[5]

In view of this principle of uniform punishment, one wonders why the French and Anglo-American systems ever recognized the distinctions among perpetrators, joint perpetrators and accomplices. The reason in both systems appears to have been an initial commitment to the theory of derivative liability. The accessory could be punished only if the perpetrator was guilty. The alternative to this view, as we noted in the case of the Model Penal Code, is to treat "aiding-and-abetting" someone else's conduct as a form of direct liability, based upon a broadened definition of the relevant offense.

The important question is whether, in principle, accessories should be punished less severely than perpetrators and accessories. For if they should, then we incur the burden of carefully distinguishing between accessories and the other four types of participants. To make out an argument that the punishments should differ, we should recall our earlier work on the relevance of wrongdoing and culpability to the measure of punishment.

The claim we developed in Chapter Six is that punishment should be inflicted in proportion both to wrongdoing and culpability.[6] Increased wrongdoing justifies an aggravated penalty, while aggravated culpability does not. The difficulty in applying these principles in cases of accessorial liability is determining

[4] Code Pénal §59; *cf. id.* §302 (special mitigation for mothers who kill newly born infants, not applicable to co-perpetrators or accessories). MPC §2.06 (all accomplices are "guilty" as though they were perpetrators).

[5] But note that the distinction between perpetrators and accessories emerges in some curious places. The current state of English law is that duress is available as an excuse for aiding and abetting a homicide as a "principal in the second degree." Lynch v. Director of Public Prosecutions, [1975] 1 All E.R. 913 (H.L.), but not for committing murder as a "principal in the first degree," Abbott v. Queen, [1976] 3 W.L.R. 462 (P.C.).

[6] See §6.6.2 *supra*.

whose wrongdoing and whose culpability should influence the level of punishment. If we adopt the "broad" theory of accessorial liability, we can settle at least the latter point: each party to the crime should be punished according to his or her personal culpability. The issue of wrongdoing is more subtle. The wrongdoing of the perpetrator sets the maximum permissible punishment, but according to some theories of accessorial liability, the wrongdoing of the accessory is less than that of the perpetrator, and therefore the accessory's punishment should generally be mitigated. Let us take a closer look at these claims.

§8.6.1. **Punishing the Accessory for the Perpetrator's Wrong.** Suppose that *A* assists *B* in committing homicide. *B* invokes the defense of diminished capacity and is convicted of manslaughter. May *A* be convicted of murder if he is fully accountable for his act? According to the classical theory of punishment, the answer depends on whether the claim of diminished capacity reduces the level of the perpetrator's wrongdoing or merely her culpability. The more plausible view is that diminished capacity affects the perpetrator's culpability, and therefore the perpetrator's invoking the defense does affect the potential liability of the accessory for murder. On the other hand, consider the following case that might arise under the German statutory provision covering killing on request.[7] A terminal cancer patient *V* requests her physician *P* to give her a fatal overdose of morphine; *P* agrees and asks nurse *N* to prepare the overdose. *N* does so, knowing that the overdose will kill the patient but without knowing of *V*'s request. If the physician is liable at most for "killing on request," is the nurse to be treated the same way? Or is the nurse, who did not know of the request, liable for intentional homicide? Again, the answer turns on whether the patient's request mitigates the wrongfulness of the killing or merely the physician's personal culpability. It is plausible to argue, as do many German writers, that the patient's request mitigates the wrongfulness of the killing and therefore the nurse, regardless of his state of mind, should be held to no higher

[7] StGB §216. See §4.5.4. A *supra.*

offense.[8] The difference between diminished capacity and the patient's request is that the former pertains exclusively to the person of the actor; the request of the patient, in contrast, qualifies the killing as one that is partially justified.

The more difficult problems arise with regard to the circumstances that aggravate an intentional killing. Suppose that the perpetrator intentionally tortures the victim to death. The accessory intends to aid in the killing and knows, as well, of the perpetrator's plan to torture the victim. The factor of torture would make the perpetrator liable for murder under German law and first-degree murder under the California statute. But what of the accessory's liability? Is she liable for murder-by-torture or just for an intentional killing? Why should the accessory be liable for murder-by-torture if she did not actually carry out the torture? There appear to be two possibilities and neither is entirely satisfactory.

1. Suppose that torture aggravates the level of the perpetrator's wrongdoing: the argument that it does would be that torture aggravates the heinousness of the killing. In view of the accessory's accountability for the perpetrator's wrongdoing, it would follow that the accessory was liable for murder-by-torture. This solution might be desirable, but it would entail difficulties in the reciprocal case in which the perpetrator intends merely to kill the victim swiftly and painlessly and the accessory devises a way to make the killing torturous. If torture bears on wrongdoing and not on culpability, then the accessory's personal motives would not aggravate the offense.

2. Suppose that torture bears on the culpability of the actor, not the level of wrongdoing. That would permit a conviction in the case immediately above, of the accessory who, unbeknownst to the perpetrator, engineers a torturous death. But treating torture as a factor bearing on culpability and thus as a basis for aggravating the offense would violate the principle that culpability should serve to decrease, but not increase, the level of punishment.

[8] Schönke-Schröder-Eser §216, note 16, at 1281; G. Arzt, Delikte gegen die Person 60 (1977).

This intricate ratiocination has the greatest practical bearing in working out the law of capital murder in the United States. Suppose that the accessory aids a perpetrator who kills "for pecuniary gain."[9] The perpetrator may be accountable for this aggravating circumstance, but is the accessory? Conversely, suppose the accessory acts "for pecuniary gain," but the perpetrator does not. Can the accessory alone be held for capital murder? These are unsolved problems of great moment. So far as we are concerned about the justice of punishment, we have no choice but to continue our search for a method to determine the bearing of particular circumstances on culpability, wrongdoing and the just level of punishment.

§8.6.2. The Rationale for Categorically Mitigating the Accessory's Punishment. Although the preceding discussion indicates that there are some situations in which the accessory may be punished more severely than the perpetrator, the classical principles of just punishment generate two arguments for categorically mitigating the accessory's punishment. The mere fact that an actor is an accessory, particularly an aider-and-abettor, should arguably either (1) mitigate the wrongdoing of the accessory's act, or (2) mitigate the culpability of the accessory's act. The former argument focusses on the objective contribution of the accessory to the consummation of the crime; the latter argument, on the accessory's subjective posture of subservience relative to the perpetrator.

Both objective and subjective arguments are prominent in the voluminous German literature, although the question posed in these materials is not whether accessories should be punished less, but rather whether a particular actor should be classified as an accessory, with mitigated punishment as a possible side-effect. With the principle of mitigation anchored in the 1871 Code,[10] the theoretical writing has focussed on the statutory distinctions among aiders-and-abettors, instigators and various forms of perpetrators.

The objective theories, oriented toward mitigated wrongdoing,

[9] This ground is common among the statutory aggravating factors for capital murder. See §4.6 *supra*.

[10] StGB 1871, §49(2) (accessories to be punished according to the criteria applicable to criminal attempts).

have appeared in two forms. A formal version of the theory holds that all actors whose conduct does not satisfy the definition of the offense are accessories.[11] This approach would obviously expand the category of accessories to include a co-perpetrator who holds the victim while his partner commits assault or rape. It would also eliminate the category of perpetration-by-means, for the latter does not himself act to fulfill the elements of the definition. An alternative objective theory stresses the degree of the accessory's causal contribution to the offense.[12] Intuitively, it seems that the person who supplies the murder weapons contributes less than the person who pulls the trigger. Yet the causal contribution of both is necessary, and it is virtually impossible to quantify the degree of causal contribution. As a result, this objectivist approach has failed to generate workable criteria for discerning whether, say, a confederate who keeps a lookout for the police is an accessory or a co-perpetrator.

The subjectivist approach, which the courts have favored since the late nineteenth century, holds the critical question to be whether the actor takes the act "to be his own" or the "act of another."[13] If the former, the actor is a perpetrator; if the latter, he is an accessory. It would seem that this highly subjective criterion would also be unworkable in practice, for how could the trier of fact determine the attitude of the suspect at the time of the deed? Yet this test has proved to have extraordinary staying power in German jurisprudence.

An intermediate theory, which has gained considerable support in the literature, takes the criterion of perpetration to be hegemony and control over the execution of the criminal act. An accessory is defined negatively as someone who does not have the requisite hegemony and control. This theory, known as the *Tatherrschaftslehre*,[14] dovetails well with the argument made in the be-

[11] For a review of the theory, see Jescheck 492; C. Roxin, Täterschaft und Tatherrschaft 34–38 (3d ed. 1975).

[12] See Jescheck 492; Roxin, *supra* note 11, at 38–41.

[13] The first major case was the Judgment of January 7, 1881, 3 RGSt. 181.

[14] The leading work is C. Roxin, *supra* note 11.

ginning of this chapter that accessorial liability is based on a problematic causal link between accessorial acting and the perpetrator's consummation of the offense. The causal link is problematic precisely because the perpetrator, and not the accessory, maintains control over execution of the crime. The accessory cannot cause that over which he does not have control.

There is considerable evidence that this German theory of "hegemony-over-the-act" lies embedded in the common-law conception of a "principal." To explain this hypothesis, let "*F*" stand for the actor-up-front, actually carrying out the deed; and "*R*" for the actor-in-the-rear, who remains behind the scenes. Now the interesting point about the concept of the principal is that in criminal law, *F* is the principal and *R* the accessory; but in the private law of agency, *R* is always the principal, and *F* the agent. In one case, the principal is the actor-on-stage; in the other, he is the actor-behind-the-scenes.

This reversal of roles is readily explained by the hypothesis that the "principal" is always the dominant party in the transaction. In criminal schemes, the principal is the actor-on-stage, who makes the final determination whether to commit the discrete criminal act. In an ongoing commercial relationship between principal and agent, master and servant, the principal remains behind the scenes and directs the activity of the agent. These considerations are still reflected in the law of agency, for if *F* enjoys sufficient autonomy, he is no longer an agent, but an independent contractor. The tort liability of the independent contractor is not imputed to the principal, for, as the doctrine goes, the semiautonomous independent contractor does not act as an extension of the principal's will.

This comparison of principals in criminal and in private law yields some important implications: First, it confirms the analogy between the German theory of *Tatherrschaft* (hegemony-over-the-act) and the common-law concept of a principal. And further, it generates a critique of vicarious criminal liability in Anglo-American criminal law. Vicarious liability represents an extension into criminal law of the private legal theory of the principal's dominance over the agent acting on his behalf. This conception of dominance, and the ensuing liability of the principals for the act of the agent, might make sense in the commercial world, but when transported to the field of criminal law, it flouts the reality of the autonomous action by the actor executing the criminal act.[15]

§8.7. *Specific Problems of Demarcation.*

To probe the problems of distinguishing clearly among the five categories of criminal participation, we turn now to a series of recurrent and difficult questions at the boundaries among the categories.

§8.7.1. **Is the Person Who Culpably Executes the Deed Always a Perpetrator?** One would think that the person on the scene—the man or woman who pulls the trigger—would always be treated as a perpetrator rather than as an accessory. Yet the subjective theory of perpetration and complicity admits of the opposite result. In a leading case decided in 1962,[1] the German Supreme Court applied the subjective theory to the case of one Stashchynsky, an agent of the KGB, who performed two political assassinations in West Germany. Even though the defendant executed the killing with his own hands, the Court held that he was to be regarded as an accessory of the KGB rather than as a perpetrator. The rationale was that Stashchynsky did not perform the killings "as his own acts, but as the instrument or assistant in the act of another."[2] The specific facts that supported this view of the case were that (1) the KGB had ordered the killings and prescribed the exact manner, time and place of execution, (2) the defendant feared that if he did not comply, he himself would be executed as a traitor, and (3) the defendant had no personal interest in the deed, e.g.,

[15] *Cf.* the problem of distinguishing between accessories and perpetrators-by-means, discussed in §8.7.3 *infra*.

§8.7. [1] Judgment of October 19, 1962, 18 BGHSt. 87.

[2] *Id.* at 95.

he was neither promised nor given compensation for the assassinations. Yet these facts were not sufficient to undercut the defendant's culpability for the killings. He was guilty of murder, but only as an accessory.

The problem in assessing this decision is determining the relevance of subjective considerations, particularly the question whether Stashchynsky regarded the killing "as his own act" or the "act of another." One could well understand the impact of subjective considerations so far as they bore on the actor's culpability and therefore justified treating him as an accessory and mitigating his punishment. Stashchynsky's fear of reprisal was a factor of this sort, for if sufficiently acute, this fear would have generated a good claim of duress as an excuse. Thus this fear supports the claim that he is less than fully culpable for carrying out the assassinations. In contrast, it is not so clear that his thinking of himself in a subservient position to the KGB undermines his culpability. And why should it matter whether he received a monetary award for the killings? Would he then have been less subservient? The court stresses that the actor's "personal weakness" was a guiding factor in classifying his conduct as accessorial; a stronger person, who could stand up to the ideology of the Soviet regime, would be more readily held accountable as a perpetrator. This sounds like the language of excusing conditions. Yet one is puzzled by the suggestion that regarding oneself as subservient to another is in the nature of an excuse, even a partial excuse.[3]

The *Stashchynsky* case represents one of the many unsatisfying results generated by the subjective theory of complicity. An assassin is converted into an accessory because, in the Court's view, he did not think of the act as his own. Not only does this criterion express an undue faith in the fact-finding powers of the Court, but it is highly questionable to gear mitigation of punishment to the way the actor conceives of his act. If neither of two conspirators

[3] An earlier example of the same reasoning is the so-called "bathtub" case, Judgment of February 19, 1940, 74 RGSt. 84. The mother of a newborn infant asked her sister to drown the child. The sister did so and was convicted of homicide as a perpetrator. Her conviction was reversed on the ground that because she merely wished to further the mother's act, she was only an accessory.

regarded the act as his own, neither would be liable as a perpetrator. If, in addition, the self-conceived accessory was mistaken about whether another person was participating as a perpetrator, there might not be a perpetrator, and derivative liability for the accessory would be precluded. These unacceptable consequences have led the academic community almost unanimously to reject the subjective theory [4] and turn to theories that would regard the person who culpably carries out the crime accountable as a perpetrator.[5]

This latter view prevailed in the 1975 legislative reform; the new code provides that a participant in a crime will be punished "as a perpetrator if he commits the criminal act himself or through another."[6] It is hard to avoid the conclusion that Stashchynsky "committed the act himself." Thus the famous case on the complicity of a KGB agent survives only as historical testimony to the legal imagination.

§8.7.2. When Is a Conspirator a Co-perpetrator? The central question in any system of complicity is distinguishing between co-perpetrators and accessories. The former are punished as full perpetrators, regardless of the liability of anyone else; in many systems, the latter are punished less severely and their liability is derivative of a wrongful act by a perpetrator. The subjective and objective, as well as the "hegemony" theories all seek a rational point of demarcation between acting as a co-perpetrator and acting as an accessory.

In this section we shall focus on a specific issue that arises at the boundary between perpetration and accessoryship. The question is whether a conspirator, one who agrees to the commission of the crime, is to be treated as a perpetrator of crimes committed in furtherance of the conspiracy. It is well established in American law that membership in a conspiracy serves as a criterion for liability as a co-perpetrator of substantive crimes committed by other

[4] C. Roxin, Täterschaft und Tatherrschaft 54–55, 105 n.52 (3d ed. 1975); Jescheck 494; Welzel 109–10; Stratenwerth 217. Herzberg, *Grundfälle zur Lehre von Täterschaft und Teilnahme,* 1974 JS 236.

[5] StGB §25.

[6] The theory of "hegemony over the act" is, to my mind, the most persuasive of these alternatives. See generally C. Roxin, *supra* note 4.

conspirators. Under the stringent *Pinkerton* rule, even an incarcerated conspirator may be held accountable for crimes committed by conspirators still at large.[7] The effect of this doctrine is to eliminate the distinction between accessories and perpetrators in consensual criminal ventures. Rendering aid to an existing conspiracy may make one a party to the group, but never as an accessory, only as a full member of the conspiracy. The logic is that contribution betokens an agreement; an agreement implies a conspiracy; and a conspiracy entails liability as a perpetrator. If Anglo-American law were ever to admit of a more refined classification of actors as accessories and perpetrators, the system would have to abandon the doctrine of conspiratorial complicity, which effectively prevents treating a member of a conspiracy as an accessory rather than a perpetrator.

The official position of German law is that mere membership in a conspiracy is insufficient to classify a conspirator as a co-perpetrator in the crimes of other conspirators. Both the old code and the new specify that only those participants are co-perpetrators who "jointly" execute the criminal act.[8] Merely agreeing that one member of the group should commit the crime is not enough to constitute "joint" execution.[9]

Though the two systems might generate different results in some cases, there are some German decisions that resonate with the excesses one might expect to find under the American doctrines of vicarious liability and felony-murder. Consider the following case decided by the German Supreme Court in 1958.[10] Three robbers, *P*, *M*, and *T*, armed themselves and agreed to shoot

[7] Pinkerton v. United States, 328 U.S. 640 (1946). Proposed Federal Criminal Code §401(b). *But cf.* MPC §§2.06, 5.03 (no recognition of conspiratorial complicity). For a discussion of the abuse of the *Pinkerton* rule, particularly in far-flung conspiracies, see Johnson, *The Unnecessary Crime of Conspiracy,* 61 Calif. L. Rev. 1137, 1146–50 (1973).

[8] StGB 1871, §47; StGB §25(2).

[9] Judgment of June 21, 1955, 8 BGHSt. 70, 73 (conspiracy to smuggle insufficient to make each conspirator a perpetrator; decision based on the "subjective" theory of perpetration).

[10] Judgment of January 23, 1958, 11 BGHSt. 268.

anyone who threatened to apprehend them. As they were running from the scene of the robbery, *M* looked over his shoulder and saw someone pursuing them. He shot at the figure, allegedly with the "intent" to kill. The pursuing person, who was injured but not killed, turned out to be the co-conspirator *P*. All three robbers, including the injured *P*, were charged and convicted of attempted murder.

There were problems even in justifying the conviction against *M*, the robber who fired the shot. After all, he intended to shoot a pursuer, perhaps a police officer, but certainly not a confederate in the robbery. The Court held that this mistake was insufficient to prevent his liability for attempted murder. The more difficult hurdle, of course, was justifying the conviction of *P*, the injured victim, for what was in effect his own attempted murder. German law concurs with contemporary American law in defining murder as the killing of "another"; in what sense was *P* a co-perpetrator in the attempted killing of "another"? The Supreme Court relied on a two-step inference in order to extend liability to *P*, and both steps reveal a highly subjective conception of criminality. The first step was to define *M*'s act according to *M*'s perception of what he was doing; thus the act was not shooting at *P*, but shooting at a pursuer. This brought the act within the agreement of the parties, but the question remained whether *M*'s shooting at the "pursuer" was "jointly" executed; this requirement, it will be recalled, must be fulfilled in order to classify a co-conspirator as a co-perpetrator. Here too the Court adopted a subjective interpretation of joint execution. Three factors are cited to support the conclusion that the victim was a co-perpetrator of his own injury: (1) *P* participated in the agreement which strengthened the resolve of the others to shoot pursuers; (2) *P*'s participation in the robbery indicated that he regarded that shooting of pursuers as "his own act"; and (3) *P* shared in the hegemony over the act of shooting, in the sense that he could have called out to his confederates not to shoot. These doctrinal ploys, particularly the second and third points, are a trifle fanciful. Their use by the Supreme Court reveals the danger of linking a subjective theory of attempting with a subjective theory of complicity. The results are of the extreme sort that one might have thought possible only under rules of vicarious liability.[11]

There is much in the reasoning of this German decision that reminds us of arguments favoring the liability of conspirators as co-perpetrators. Each robber strengthens the will of the others;[12] each could frustrate the crime and does not. For all these similarities, the rule of the German case hews tightly to the limits specified in the agreement between the parties.[13] The black-letter rule in the American cases is that the liability of conspirators and other accomplices may extend to crimes beyond the scope of the agreement, so long as they are in "furtherance of the common design."[14] The proposed federal criminal code requires that it be "reasonably foreseeable that the conduct would be performed in furtherance of the conspiracy."[15] If this test were applied to the facts of the German case, it would not have been important whether the robbers had agreed to shoot pursuers. If *P* had known (or even had reason to know) that *M* was armed, the outcome would have been the same; for then it would have been "reason-

[11] For a critique of the decision, see Spendel, *Zur Kritik der subjektiven Versuchs- und Teilnahmetheorie*, 1969 JS 314.

[12] Compare the rationale for conspiracy as an inchoate offense in MPC §5.03, Comment at 97 (Tent. Draft No. 10, 1960) ("Sharing lends fortitude to purpose").

[13] See Judgment of November 9, 1933, 67 RGSt. 343 (*D* gave *X* a revolver to commit larceny by force. *X* used the gun in an attempt to intimidate *V* to turn over her money. Held, *D* guilty of aiding an attempted aggravated larceny, but he did not intend to aid a crime of "intimidation," StGB §255, and therefore not liable as an accessory to *X*'s attempted "intimidation").

[14] LaFave & Scott 515–17.

[15] Proposed Federal Criminal Code §401(b)(3). *Cf.* Kan. Stat. Ann. §21-3205(2) (liability for unintended offense if "reasonably foreseeable . . . as a probable consequence of committing or attempting to commit the crime intended"); Minn. Stat. Ann. §609.05 (same language as Kansas). So far as these rules are designed to reflect the common law, they appear to go far beyond the decided cases. If we leave aside cases decided under the misdemeanor-manslaughter and felony-murder rules, the only example of the general rule is an assault committed in the course of a larceny, robbery or burglary. See People v. Lushenko, 170 Cal. App. 2d 772, 339 P.2d 956 (1959) (*D* held liable for assault commited by accomplice in robbery). Other cases deny liability. See, e.g., State v. Lucas, 55 Iowa 321, 7 N.W. 583 (1880) (no conspiratorial liability for theft beyond scope of planned robbery); United States v. Peoni, 100 F.2d 401 (2d Cir. 1938) (though *D* liable for passing counterfeit bills to *X*, not liable for consequences of *X*'s passing bills to *Y*).

ably foreseeable" that *M* would shoot a pursuer in their flight from the scene of the crime.

As a historical matter, this far-reaching liability derives, presumably, from the influence of the law of agency on the theory of criminal accountability. As the master is vicariously liable for his servants' torts committed within the "scope of employment," the conspirator is vicariously liable for all crimes committed by his partners in their roles as conspirators. The nexus of liability proves to be neither the agreement nor actual support, but rather the status of being a conspirator. This status is like that of an employer who hires persons to work on his behalf. Vicarious liability based on actual control might make some sense in the field of torts, but it is patently absurd to think of conspirators controlling each other's acts. This is another instance in which Anglo-American tort law reflects greater sensitivity to individual justice than does the criminal law.[16] The tort defendant has the option of arguing that his control over the servant was so restricted that the latter should be treated as an independent contractor, thus potentially exempting the tort defendant from liability. Not even this limited egress is open to the conspirator charged under the *Pinkerton* rule of conspiratorial complicity.

The influence of other heavy-handed doctrines, such as the felony-murder and misdemeanor-manslaughter rules, makes it difficult to assess the operative significance of extending the liability of co-perpetrators to all "reasonably foreseeable" acts of the other perpetrators. If *X* procures *Y* to perform an illegal abortion on *V*, and the latter dies in the operation, the homicide obviously exceeds the scope of the agreement between *X* and *Y*. A rule of formal liability for criminal homicide would make *X* and *Y* liable even without proof that *Y* performed the operation negligently.[17] If there were no formal rule of liability, the conspiracy between *X* and *Y* might be sufficient to make *X* liable for *Y*'s criminally negligent killing. Thus in cases where parties in the role of *X* are held liable for criminal homicide, it is difficult to determine whether

[16] See §4.4.8 *supra*.

[17] See Regina v. Creamer, [1965] 3 All E.R. 257 (Crim. App.).

the operative rule is one on the scope of complicity or the effect of a formal rule of liability.

As a theoretical matter, the basic problem in the Anglo-American law of complicity springs from ambivalence about whether criminal law is similar to or different from the private law of agency. Our language—our referring to the actor executing the deed as the principal—indicates that we regard persons who commit crimes as autonomous and hegemonous over their acts. Yet our doctrines of vicarious liability and liability beyond the scope of the agreement suggest that sometimes we regard the actor-behind-the-scenes as the dominant figure. It may be that the former model appeals to us in cases of isolated criminal acts; and the latter, in cases of organized crime. But if the theory of criminal liability is to become more refined, we must confront this ambivalence and begin to think about why conspirators are held liable for crimes that they do not perpetrate.

§8.7.3. **Accessories and Perpetrators-by-Means.** Ambivalence about who is in control over the execution of a criminal plan is most acute in cases at the intersection of doctrines of accessorial liability and of perpetration-by-means. To return to our earlier terminology, let "*F*" stand for the actor-up-front, executing the deed; and "*R*" for the actor-in-the-rear, who remains behind the scenes. The range of cases we will consider are those in which *F* is not liable for a criminal act, and the question is whether there is some basis for holding *R* liable, either as an accessory in *F*'s wrongful act or as a perpetrator acting through an innocent agent. There are three important variations of the problem. *F*'s conduct might be wrongful but excused, it might be justified, or it might be legal in the sense that it does not violate the definition of any offense.

A. F's conduct is wrongful but excused. If *F* commits the crime while he is insane, under duress or acting under an excusable mistake, his conduct is still wrongful and the "broad" theory of accessorial liability would support treating *R*, who aided in the deed, as an accessory. There are a few cases of this type in Anglo-American law,[18] but little evidence of a theory of accessorial liabil-

[18] United States v. Azadian, 436 F.2d 81 (9th Cir. 1971) (perpetrator of crime of bribing acquitted on ground of entrapment; accessory convicted); State v. Haines,

ity;[19] the consistent approach is to treat *R* as a perpetrator-by-means acting through his agent *F*. A good example is the recent decision in Regina v. Cogan and Leak,[20] in which Leak allegedly intimidated his wife to have intercourse with Cogan. Leak remained in the room and observed Cogan lie with his wife, who sobbed during the intercourse but did not otherwise resist. Cogan was convicted of rape, and Leak was an aider-and-abettor. On appeal, Cogan's conviction was quashed on the ground that under the newly announced *Morgan* rule (which we take up later),[21] his belief that the woman had consented was a complete defense. The problem was whether Leak's conviction as an aider-and-abettor would have to fall with Cogan's conviction as a principal.

If the appeal had been heard under German law, the critical issue would have been whether Cogan's act was wrongful despite his mistake. The English Court of Appeal gives the impression that it regarded the act as wrongful, for it stresses that Mrs. Leak had been raped even though Cogan was not accountable for it.[22] The argument on the other side would be that the mistake as to consent negates the required intent and that intent is included as an element of wrongful intercourse. A more careful consideration of the effect of a mistake as to consent must await the systematic discussion in Chapter Nine.[23]

Rather than rely on a theory of accessorial liability in a wrongful act, the English court reasoned that in fact Leak was the perpetrator, and Cogan merely his "means to procure a criminal purpose."[24] The premise of the court's opinion is that whenever

---

51 La. Ann. 731, 25 So. 372 (1899) (dictum recognizing possibility of liability of husband if he coerces third party to rape his wife).

[19] In *Azadian, supra* note 18, the court found it necessary to explain entrapment as a defense unrelated to the perpetrator's "criminal intent," 436 F.2d at 82–83. This qualification would not be necessary under the "broad" theory of complicity. As an excuse, entrapment does not negate the wrongfulness of the act. See §7.3.2 B *infra*.

[20] [1975] 3 W.L.R. 316 (Crim. App.).

[21] See §9.2.2 *infra*.

[22] [1975] 3 W.L.R. at 319.

[23] See §9.2.2 and §9.2.3 *infra*.

[24] [1975] 3 W.L.R. at 318.

accessorial liability is inapplicable, the theory of perpetration-by-means is available to fill the gap. Even if Leak's contribution was barely sufficient to meet the threshold of accessorial contribution, the acquittal of Cogan would be sufficient to treat Leak as a perpetrator.

A German court might also have concluded that Leak was the perpetrator-by-means, but a necessary condition for this finding would be that Leak was the dominant party in carrying out the sexual penetration of his wife. His standing by and watching the act would presumably not be sufficient. In the German idiom, he would have had to have "hegemony" over the act. Cogan would have to function as the actual instrument of his will. Though the English court says that this was the case, the opinion fails to cite facts to show that Leak dominated Cogan in the carrying out of the rape.[25]

There is some Anglo-American authority for the proposition that the party not actually acting must dominate his "instrument" in order to qualify as a perpetrator-by-means. We reasoned earlier that domination and control are implicit in the concept of a principal, particularly as used in the law of agency. In one leading criminal case, the court commented in dictum that a husband can "rape" his own wife through an intermediary, but only if he forces the "unwilling" instrument "by threats and violence, against his will and consent, to have sexual intercourse with the wife. . . ."[26] The Model Penal Code requires that the perpetrator-by-means "cause an innocent or irresponsible person to engage in [the prohibited] conduct."[27] If we take this requirement of "causing" to mean something more than "aiding" (which in the language of the code is what accomplices do),[28] then we have a standard much like the German criterion of "hegemony."

[25] It is not clear whether Leak induced and exploited Cogan's alleged mistake as to Mrs. Leak's consent. If so, there would be a good basis under German law for regarding Leak as the dominant party. Jescheck 506.

[26] State v. Haines, 51 La. Ann. 731, 732, 25 So. 372, 373 (1899).

[27] MPC §2.06(2)(a).

[28] MPC §2.06(3)(a)(ii).

A demanding requirement of causation as a condition for perpetration-by-means fits our original thesis of derivative accessorial liability. What makes the liability of accessories different from that of perpetrators is precisely the weaker causal link. Accessories contribute to the result, but they are not in the control of the process leading to consummation of the crime. They "aid" in the "commission of the offense" but they neither "commit" the offense nor determine its commission.

In the case against Cogan and Leak, the appellate court might have felt that justice required affirmance of Leak's conviction and therefore his reclassification as a perpetrator-by-means. This seemed to be the only option because the theory of accessorial liability remains undeveloped. More precisely, it is the notion of "committing an offense" that has yet to receive the required clarification. If Mrs. Leak was "raped" by Cogan's penetration, as the court maintains, then, in this sense, Cogan committed the offense. His act was wrongful, but excused. If the "broad" theory of accessorial liability would take hold in Anglo-American theory, one could properly hold a subsidiary party as an accessory. This would have the advantage of reserving the notion of perpetration-by-means to cases in which the party behind the scenes in fact dominates and controls an "innocent or irresponsible agent."

B. F's conduct is justified and therefore not wrongful. The theory of complicity becomes more complicated if *F* acts in self-defense or under another valid justification. The problem is whether *R*, who aids *F's* act, can be held either as an accessory or a perpetrator-by-means. Suppose that *X* attacks *F* and *F* responds in knowing self-defense. *R* comes upon the scene, and thinking that *F* has started the fight, *R* hands *F* a club, the better to finish off his opponent. *R* acts with the intent to injure and believes that the act is wrongful. The question is whether *R's* intent is sufficient to hold him accountable for the consequences of *F's* justified act of self-defense.

This hypothetical problem is important in understanding the foundation of accessorial liability and indeed criminal accountability in general. One of the few premises that guide our thinking about liability is that criminality presupposes a wrongful act.[29] Accessorial liability is a special case, for it is not the actor's wrongful act that is controlling, but the wrongdoing of the perpetrator. In the case of self-defense posed above, the perpetrator does not act wrongfully and therefore there is no wrong objectively to attribute to the accessory *R*.

It is tempting to conclude that *R* cannot be liable under any theory of perpetration or complicity. This is the view urged by the Pennsylvania Supreme Court in *Redline*,[30] a case of alleged third-party felony-murder. In response to an armed robbery, a police officer shot at the two fleeing robbers and killed one of them; the survivor was charged with murdering his confederate. Assuming that the issue was accessorial liability, the court reasoned that[31]

> the homicide was justifiable and, obviously, could not be availed of, on any rational legal theory, to support a charge of murder. How can anyone, no matter how much of an outlaw he may be, have a criminal charge lodged against him for the consequences of the lawful conduct of another person? The mere statement of the question carries with it its own answer.

For the Pennsylvania Supreme Court, it was self-evident that there should be no accessorial liability for a justified act of self-defense. The justified act of killing was like the running of a reasonable and justified risk. As the actor's intention cannot make him accountable for the harm resulting from a reasonable risk,[32] his intention cannot make him accountable for the harm resulting from a justified act of self-defense.

All of this seems reasonable, but the argument failed to impress either the commentators or the courts in other jurisdictions, particularly in California.[33] Consider this counter-example devised

[29] See §6.6.3 *supra*.
[30] Commonwealth v. Redline, 391 Pa. 486, 137 A.2d 472 (1958).
[31] *Id.* at 509; 137 A.2d at 483.
[32] See §6.6.6 *supra*.
[33] The most troubling point was the Pennsylvania court's claim that the killing of an innocent bystander was merely excused and not justified and therefore an appropriate basis for accessorial liability. 391 Pa. at 509; 137 A.2d at 483. This dis-

by Kadish and Paulsen to show that it is intuitively plausible to hold one person accountable for the justified acts of another:[34]

> Suppose two felons are holed up in a house and engaged in a gun battle with surrounding police. One felon tells the other to run for it out the back door where the coast is clear. He does this because he wants the other felon dead and he knows the police have the back door well-covered. As the other felon dashes out, gun in hand, he is shot by police.

Kadish and Paulsen suggest, quite properly, that under these facts the surviving felon should be held accountable for the justified killing by the police. We might agree, but it is important to probe the persuasiveness of this hypothetical case. The critical factor is that the deceiving felon not only dominates, but orchestrates the events leading to the death of his confederate. This is a paradigmatic case of hegemony over the act of an unsuspecting instrument. The surviving felon is held not on a theory of derivative liability, but of perpetration-by-means.

It would be difficult to reason from this hypothetical case to the conclusion of liability under the facts of *Redline*, for there the police officer came upon the scene of the robbery and began shooting. It would be difficult to maintain that the surviving felon had caused and dominated the acts of the police officer in the sense required for liability as a perpetrator-by-means. In a trivial sense, the surviving felon "caused" the death, for if the two of them had not committed the robbery, the officer presumably would not have shot the confederate. But something more than "but for" causation is necessary to establish the required dominance over the acts of a third party.

Rejecting the implicit emphasis in *Redline* on accessorial liabil-

---

tinction prompted Justice Traynor to quip that liability thus "turn[s] upon the marksmanship of citizens and policemen." People v. Washington, 62 Cal. 2d 777, 780; 402 P.2d 130, 132, 44 Cal. Rptr. 442, 444 (1965). *Cf.* LaFave & Scott 552 n.41 ("There may be a semantic difference between the two words ["excusable" and "justifiable"] but on principle there should be no difference in consequence").

[34] S. Kadish & M. Paulsen, Criminal Law and Its Processes 294 note (3d ed. 1975).

ity, the California Supreme Court approached the problem of third-party killings of co-felons exclusively on a theory of perpetration-by-means. Thus Justice Traynor stressed in *Washington* that the surviving felon must "commit" the homicide himself.[35] This means that he must do something to induce the third party to shoot. The succeeding cases have struggled with the question whether the suspect must "initiate a gun battle" or merely make threatening gestures with a gun.[36] The detailed analysis in the cases implicitly accepts the assumption that the surviving felon must exercise a requisite degree of control over the third-party shooting to be liable as a perpetrator-by-means.

C. *F's act is formally legal.* The doctrine of perpetration-by-means extends not only to justified acts, but to acts that are formally legal in the sense that they do not violate the "definition" of any offense. An illuminating case came to the German courts in the early 1950s on the basis of events that transpired under the National Socialists.[37] The defendant had falsely accused her son-in-law of sabotage in order to have him arrested by the secret police. The son was arrested, confined for more than a week and then acquitted of the charge. The defendant was thereafter prosecuted and convicted of intentional false imprisonment.[38] The Supreme Court affirmed her conviction on the theory that she exploited the secret police and thus committed the offense as a perpetrator-by-means. Even if it is assumed that the police had adequate grounds to detain the suspect, the legality of the detention would not shield the suspect from liability.

As a general matter, the fraudulent use of the legal process to impose harm on another entails liability for intentionally bringing about the particular result. This doctrine found early expression in the English common law under the heading *in fraudem legis.* Taking the goods of another under a fraudulently acquired writ of ejectment generated liability for larceny.[39]

[35] People v. Washington, 62 Cal. 2d 777, 781, 402 P.2d 130, 133, 44 Cal. Rptr. 442, 445 (1965).

[36] See §4.4.7 *supra.*

[37] Judgment of June 10, 1952, 3 BGHSt. 4.

[38] StGB §239.

[39] See Farre's Case, 84 Eng. Rep. 1074 (1665).

We might be able to accept the doctrine of perpetration-by-means in these cases of fraudulently exploiting the apparatus of the law. But a recent case in the United States requires us to think about imposing limits on the principle that *R* can be liable for the legal acts of *F*. Suppose that the act of *F* consists in the assertion of a constitutional right such as the privilege against self-incrimination. Cole v. United States[40] holds that if *R* induces *F* to claim the privilege to protect both himself and *R*, the latter can be guilty of "corruptly influencing a witness" and obstructing "the due administration of justice."[41] Part of the problem with this conviction is the vague definition of the offense. That problem aside, we should have some doubts about liability for inducing the assertion of a constitutional right. In the other cases of exploiting *F's* legal or justified behavior, *R* manages to bring about an undeniable harm to a specific victim (death, confinement, loss of property). It is far more tenuous to argue that the consequences of asserting a constitutional right constitute a social harm for which the actor-behind-the-scenes should be held accountable. It would be unthinkable (one would hope) to fit the definition of an offense to a case of inducing a homeowner to refuse to allow the police to search his home without a warrant. It is equally dubious to regard convincing another to assert rights under the Fifth Amendment as a basis for criminal liability.

§8.7.4. The Special Status of Instigators. As we have already noted, German and Soviet law distinguish between two categories of accessories. Those who merely aid and abet the perpetrator receive the benefit of a possible mitigation of punishment: those who merely instigate or solicit the offense are derivatively liable for the perpetrator's crime but they do not receive the benefit of mitigation. Anglo-American and French law include both forms of participation under one broad category of accessorial liability and do not formally recognize mitigation for instigators or aiders-and-abettors.[42]

The category of instigation requires demarcation relative both

[40] 329 F.2d 437 (9th Cir. 1964), *cert. denied.* 377 U.S. 954 (1964).
[41] 18 U.S.C. §1503.
[42] See §8.5.3 *supra.*

to other accessories and to perpetrators-by-means. The lines of demarcation are subtle. Advising or counselling renders one an accessory; but ordering or soliciting renders one an instigator. The KGB in the *Stashchynsky* case was an instigator, as was Leak, presumably, in his inducing Cogan to rape Mrs. Leak. The German code tells us merely that the instigator must "determine" (*bestimmen*) the conduct of the perpetrator.[43] What this means is that the instigator must induce the perpetrator's decision to act.[44] If the perpetrator resolves on his own to commit the crime and comes to the suspect for advice and counsel, the latter is at most an accessory.

Instigation is distinguished in two respects from perpetration-by-means. First, the party carrying out the deed is himself a responsible perpetrator;[45] secondly, the instigator induces the decision to act, but he does not exercise hegemony over the execution of the deed. These differences came to the fore recently in an English case in which the defendant had solicited two men to beat up her husband.[46] The two fell upon the husband and inflicted a minor laceration on his scalp, enough to constitute "a wounding" under the Offenses Against the Person Act. The two men were convicted of the misdemeanor of "unlawfully and maliciously wounding" another person.[47] The defendant was charged and convicted of the felony of "unlawful and malicious wounding" with "the intent . . . to do some grievous bodily harm."[48]

The dispute on appeal centered on the theory of complicity. Should the defendant be treated as an accessory to the misdemeanor perpetrated by the two men? Or should she be viewed as

[43] StGB §26. *Cf.* StGB 1871, §48 (listing the following specific means of instigation: material reward or promises, threats, misuse of influence or authority, intentionally inducing or encouraging a mistake). *Cf.* Ugol. kod. (RSFSR) §17 (defining an instigator as one who "inclines" another to a criminal act).

[44] Schönke-Schröder-Cramer §26, note 4, at 361.

[45] According to StGB §26, the instigated or solicited party must commit the offense "wrongfully and intentionally." If the primary actor is excused, the perpetrator is still derivatively liable.

[46] Regina v. Richards, [1973] 3 W.L.R. 888 (Crim. App.).

[47] 24 & 25 Vict. c. 100, §18 (1861).

[48] *Id.* §20.

a perpetrator-by-means of the felony, the two men merely being her instrument for inflicting the wounding? If the former, the felony conviction could not stand; if the latter, the conviction was proper. Counsel for the Crown argued effectively that the law requires the culpability of each accomplice to be assessed independently and if so, there was nothing illogical about holding the defendant liable for the felony. The appellate court apparently assumed that if the defendant was to be liable for the felony, it would have to be as a perpetrator-by-means, and then proceeded to offer sound arguments why she should be treated as instigator and accessory to the misdemeanor rather than as a perpetrator of the felony. "One offense and one offense only"[49] was committed, and that was the wounding committed by the two men, without the intent to inflict grievous bodily harm. The reason there was no distinct offense in execution of the defendant's intent was that "the acts were perpetrated at some distance from where the defendant was."[50] She was not in control of the incident and therefore the acts of the men could not be regarded as the means for her committing a felony. Thus the only available theory was accessorial liability as an instigator, which implied that she was liable for no more than the misdemeanor. This is presumably the result that a German court would have reached on the same facts.

This case suggests a germ of common logic in the analysis of derivative liability in Continental and Anglo-American legal theory. Though there are many differences, there may be agreement on two critical premises: (1) An aggravating intent, such as the intent to inflict grievous bodily harm, cannot generate a higher level of liability for an accessory. This is an application of the principle that the accessory's culpability may mitigate liability but not increase liability. (2) The institution of perpetration-by-means applies only to actors who exercise control over their agents in the execution of the deed. This commonality of assumptions, though imperfectly expressed, suggests that the categories of our analysis have an intuitive appeal that transcends the positive law of particular legal systems.

[49] [1973] 3 W.L.R. at 892.
[50] *Ibid.*

§8.8. *Minimal Criteria for Accessorial Liability.*

The structure of our exposition of complicity corresponds to the outline followed in the discussion of commission by omission. The approach is, first, to work out the distinction between direct and derivative liability and, secondly, to focus on the minimal criteria for accessorial liability. As the second question requires us to analyze the criteria for duties to intervene and prevent harm, we are now led to work out the minimal threshold for accessorial liability. How much does someone have to contribute to the crime of another in order to be accountable as an accessory? The problem arises in the following three distinct contexts:

§8.8.1. **Parties to Conspiracies.** In Anglo-American law the minimal criteria for accessorial liability are often assessed under the nominally distinct question of membership in a conspiracy. In the typical case, the defendant knows of illegal activity by a group of persons and nonetheless provides a service with knowledge that the service will facilitate the illegal activity. He might sell sugar to illegal distillers, provide an answering service for a group of prostitutes or sell gas to someone who says he is driving around looking for a woman to rape. The question in these cases is whether the supplier becomes a party to the conspiracy and thus complicitous under the *Pinkerton* rule in crimes committed by co-conspirators.[1] Because the doctrine of conspiratorial complicity collapses the distinction between accessories and perpetrators, the effect of finding membership in the conspiracy is to make the defendant a co-perpetrator of substantive offenses committed in furtherance of the conspiracy.

The criteria used by the courts to resolve this problem of conspiratorial membership correspond almost exactly to the subjective theory of perpetration in German law.[2] In the leading case of *Falcone,*[3] the Court of Appeals for the Second Circuit held that a sugar

§8.8. [1] See §8.7.1, at note 7, *supra.*

[2] See the discussion of the *Stashchynsky* case, §8.7.1 *supra.*

[3] United States v. Falcone, 109 F.2d 579 (2d. Cir. 1940), *affirmed,* 311 U.S. 215 (1940).

retailer did not become a member of a conspiracy to distill illegal spirits merely because he knowingly aided the illegal activity by selling sugar to the conspirators. As Learned Hand wrote: "He must in some sense promote their venture himself, make it his own, have a stake in the outcome."[4] This latter phrase—"stake in the outcome"—has become the catchword of discussions of suppliers' entailing liability as conspirators. Falcone's conviction was reversed, but shortly thereafter the Supreme Court provided us with an example of a supplier's having a stake in the outcome. In *Direct Sales,*[5] the defendant, licensed to sell morphine sulphate, sold large quantities of the drug to persons using it illegally. The excessive quantities and the defendant's practice of stimulating purchases were sufficient to meet the *Falcone* test of a "stake in the outcome." The formal test used by the Supreme Court, however, was that these facts established the defendant's "intent to further" the buyers' illegal activity.[6]

The recurrent emphasis in these cases, and even in cases that nominally reject the criterion of a "stake in the outcome,"[7] is whether the supplier is subjectively identified with the illegal objective. He must regard the illegal acts as "his own."[8] He becomes identified with the act if, as in *Direct Sales,* his financial interests become interwoven with those of the conspirators. In searching for empirical manifestation of subjective identification, the German courts also seized upon the actor's "having an interest" as an evidentiary test of perpetration.[9] It is worth recalling, however, that in the German context, the subjective test of regarding the act "as one's own" functions to distinguish perpetration from accesso-

[4] 109 F.2d at 580.

[5] Direct Sales v. United States, 319 U.S. 703 (1943).

[6] *Id.* at 715.

[7] Backun v. United States, 112 F.2d 635 (4th Cir. 1940) (defendant sold stolen property to Zucker who transported the goods in interstate commerce; defendant held guilty as an accessory).

[8] *Id.* at 638; "the felony committed by Zucker flowed from the will of Backun as well as from his own will."

[9] See Judgment of June 25, 1954, 6 BGHSt. 226, 229 (defendant convicted as coperpetrator of rape for holding victim down during the act; the court reasoned that "the defendant's interest in the act was an index of his treating the act as his own. . . .").

rial liability. In *Falcone, Direct Sales* and related cases, the issue is whether the defendant satisfies the minimal threshold of liability, not whether his liability is that of an accessory or a perpetrator.

The resort to a subjective test in these cases is virtually inescapable. The alternative would be to try to measure the degree of the defendant's causal contribution to the illegal scheme. That is particularly difficult to do where the defendant is engaged in a business, and the sale or service is rendered in the ordinary course of business. If Falcone did not sell sugar to the distillers, they could have bought it elsewhere. If the defendant does not make his answering service available to women he knows are "call girls," the prostitutes can easily go to his competitor.[10] There is a sense in which providing sugar or the answering service contributes or facilitates the criminal act, but there is another sense in which they are purely incidental. The receipt of these services is part of the background of props against which the illegal drama is played.

From the standpoint of the supplier, the problem of refusing services to known criminals closely resembles the problem of intervening to prevent impending natural harm.[11] The grocery store, the gas station, the physician, the answering service all provide routine services. Does the business-person have a duty to make an exception just because he or she knows that the purchaser is engaged in illegal activity? That question of duty corresponds to the problem of the motorist who must decide whether to stop his car and render aid to an accident victim. The assumption underlying both fields is that people are entitled to carry on their lives without deviating every time doing so might help a person in distress or hamper the execution of a criminal plan.

There are important differences, however, between the two fields of derivative liability. First, the person who intervenes to rescue another in distress has the capacity to avert the harm; the

[10] People v. Lauria, 251 Cal. App. 2d 471, 59 Cal. Rptr. 628 (1967) (defendant furnished answering service to ring of call girls and knew of their illegal activity; conviction rev'd on the ground that crime was a misdemeanor and there was inadequate proof that defendant had a "special interest" in the call-girl conspiracy).

[11] See generally §8.3 *supra*.

supplier who denies his goods or services to known conspirators cannot avert the crime, for if the supplies are readily available, the conspirators can go elsewhere. Secondly, this unexercised potential to avert harm is the only causal link between the defendant's omission and the natural occurrence of the harm; but supplying sugar, the answering service, or hypodermic needles to heroin addicts, all contribute at least minimally to the commission of the offense. Thirdly, the imposition of a duty to intervene is never resolved by inquiring whether the bystander "identifies" with the occurrence of harm; but the duty to desist from supplying service may arise from subjective identification with the illegal plan.

§8.8.2. **Minimal Facilitation.** The inquiry into the threshold of liability takes on different contours where the technique is not to rely on conspiratorial complicity, but directly on the criterion of "aiding" the criminal act of another. This approach implicitly acknowledges that accessorial liability has a lower threshold of liability than perpetration.

It is common ground that the accessory must intend, by giving aid, to further or facilitate the plan of the perpetrator.[12] The question is whether there is any minimum degree of aid necessary for liability. The problem resembles the analysis of criminal attempts, where it is also assumed that the actor must have a particular intent, and the controversy centers on the type of act necessary for liability. The German Supreme Court decided at an early date that the minimal threshold of acting was low indeed. In an 1882 case, the defendant had given a compatriot a key that supposedly would fit a cellar door and thus enable the compatriot to steal wine from the cellar.[13] It turned out that the key didn't work and the compatriot had to break into the cellar to commit the crime. Though the intended aid did not materialize, the defendant was guilty as an accessory to the theft. In a case decided a year later, the defendant's friend announced to him that he intended to pummel a third person.[14] The defendant lent his friend a smock to

[12] MPC §2.06(3)(a); LaFave & Scott 505–07 (noting some distinctions in the definition of the required intent).

[13] Judgment of April 20, 1882, 6 RGSt. 169.

[14] Judgment of May 10, 1883, 8 RGSt. 267.

wear during the beating so that the friend would not dirty his clothes. This minimal aid was sufficient to hold the defendant as an accessory. In both of these cases, the critical point was that the defendant's intended aid had strengthened the perpetrator's resolve. One reason the court did not take the objective element of aid more seriously is that it was already committed to the subjective theory of attempts.[15] If the objective dimension of attempting was not important, the judges reasoned, the objective threshold of aid should not become a stumbling block in prosecuting accessories who intend to aid in the perpetration of crime.

It is obviously possible to render aid even though the perpetrator does not know it. The recurrent case is one in which the accessory, unbeknownst to the perpetrator, intervenes to prevent someone from stifling the anticipated crime.[16] Removing the potential obstacle facilitates the crime, even though the perpetrator is not strengthened in his resolve.

One recurrent pattern of case, both in German and American law, is that of a suspected accessory present at the scene of a crime who knows that a crime is about to be committed but does nothing to prevent it. So far as the issue is facilitation, the cases tend to assume that a bystander must act so as to strengthen the resolve of the perpetrator. His conduct can have this effect if he agreed prior to the crime to assist the perpetrator; then his presence at the scene of the crime is in itself effective encouragement.[17] Or, if there is no prior agreement, he can encourage the perpetrator at the scene by words or gestures of encouragement.[18] The difficult problem is whether intended encouragement at the scene of the crime must actually have a psychological effect on the perpetrator. If the perpetrator does not know of the intended encouragement, can the

[15] See §3.3.5 *supra*.

[16] State ex rel. Attorney General v. Tally, 102 Ala. 25, 15 So. 722 (1894) (on impeachment proceedings, judge charged with aiding and abetting homicide; he sent telegram to prevent aid from reaching victim).

[17] Hicks v. United States, 150 U.S. 442 (1893).

[18] For a particularly low level of required encouragement, see State v. Parker, 282 Minn. 343, 355, 164 N.W.2d 633, 641 (1969) ("defendant's presence [at the robbery] and acts helped to make all crimes possible").

would-be accessory still be liable on a theory of attempted aid? This problem is different from the case in which the accessory removes a potential obstacle to the crime, for that constitutes objective aid regardless of the perpetrator's knowledge.

The Model Penal Code declares that "attempted aid" is sufficient for liability as an accomplice.[19] This extension of the traditional notion of accessorial liability has found acceptance in a large number of new state statutes.[20] Even though the problem is not likely to arise often, the principle of liability for "attempting to aid" is worth pursuing. This unusual extension might lead us to appreciate the theoretical foundation for accessorial liability.

It is not difficult to reconstruct the reasoning that led to the Model Penal Code's recommendation. The premise is that actually aiding the perpetrator is a harmful consequence of the "accessory's" act. If we adopt the principle of subjective criminality and the personal theory of wrongdoing,[21] we are led to dispense with harmful consequences as a condition of liability. As the Code endorses liability for all impossible attempts[22] and "reckless endangerment,"[23] there is no reason why it should not dispense with the element of harm in cases of aiding-and-abetting. After all, whether the aid is actually rendered is fortuitous; the actor is equally culpable and his dangerousness is equally great if the perpetrator never receives the aid.

The implication of this line of reasoning is that if a would-be aider-and-abettor shouts encouragement or otherwise attempts to aid an assassin, the effort to aid renders the actor guilty of the perpetrator's offense. She is as guilty as though she had killed the victim! This result is internally inconsistent with other principles of the Code. It is not difficult to show that the would-be aider-and-abettor of homicide is not guilty of an attempted homicide. And yet, paradoxically, she is as guilty of homicide as though she were

[19] MPC §2.06(3)(a)(ii).

[20] E.g., Hawaii Penal Code §222(1)(b); Pa. Cons. Stat. Ann. tit. 18, §306(c)(1)(ii); Tex. Penal Code §7.02(2).

[21] See §6.6.5 *supra*.

[22] MPC §5.01(1)(a).

[23] MPC §211.2.

a perpetrator, without the benefit of mitigation available to those who merely attempt but do not actually kill.

There are two reasons why attempted aiding and abetting falls below the threshold of an attempted crime. First, if we are considering the case of the bystander who shouts encouragement to an assassin who does not hear her, it would be far-fetched to argue that shouting aid constitutes a "substantial step" toward the commission of the offense. It seems clear that shouting aid falls below the degree of proximity to consummation reflected in the six categories to which the Code seeks to *extend* liability for a criminal attempt.

Secondly, the would-be aider-and-abettor need not have the intent required for a criminal attempt. The required subjective state for aiding and abetting is the purpose of "promoting or facilitating the crime";[24] attempted murder requires a "purpose of causing" death.[25] It might be possible for someone whose purpose is to promote a homicide committed by another also to have the intent to cause death, but this need not be the case. Promoting and facilitating an event are not the same as causing it. If the perpetrator is very likely to kill, regardless of whether he receives aid, the accessory's minimal contribution does not meet the minimal test of "but for" causation, and a fortiori it fails to meet the more demanding criteria of the "common-sense" view of causation. That one can contribute to a result without causing it lies at the foundation of accessorial liability.[26]

That the would-be accessory might not be liable for an attempt, and yet is subject to a greater punishment, is one of the anomalies that follow from taking the principle of subjective liability to its logical extreme. That the accessory actually contributes to the commission of the crime is part of what it means to be an accessory. There is no social wrong in acting to aid the crime of another, unless the aid actually furthers the criminal objective or

[24] MPC §2.06(3)(a).

[25] MPC §5.01(1)(b).

[26] See Schönke-Schröder-Cramer §27, note 8, at 365 ("the accessory's aid must facilitate the perpetrator's act but it need not itself cause it")

strengthens the resolve of the perpetrator. Even though the personal theory of wrongdoing in the German literature dispenses with the significance of harm in assessing wrongdoing, not even avid proponents of this theory propose liability for attempted aiding-and-abetting.

In this context, the distinction between aiding and instigating an offense takes on critical significance. German law[27] concurs with the Model Penal Code[28] that instigation and even attempted instigation should each constitute an offense in its own right. There is no systemic contradiction in imposing direct liability for instigation, even though the instigated party never consummates the planned offense. The instigator, it will be recalled, induces the perpetrator's decision to act. As contrasted with merely aiding an existing criminal plan, instigation arguably satisfies the "but for" criteria of causation. If the perpetrator were not instigated, the chances are much less that he would commit the offense on his own. Thus instigating an offense comes closer to causing the harmful consequence. And the act of instigation comes closer to the standard of a criminal attempt.

Carving out instigation or solicitation as an inchoate offense is no more questionable than defining possession as an offense that is completed regardless of the ensuing consequences. In both cases, however, it is necessary to posit an ulterior intent to bring about the offense in chief.[29]

In this chapter we have explored the ways in which liability for commission by omission resembles the theory of complicity. The points of intersection between these seemingly disparate fields warrant our treating them both as aspects of "derivative liability." The problematic role of causation, the contrast between direct and derivative liability in the two contexts, the task of setting minimal criteria of duty and of complicity—all of these points bear

[27] StGB §26 (instigation), §30(1) (attempted instigation).

[28] MPC §5.02(1) (solicitation), §5.02(2) (uncommunicated solicitation punishable).

[29] See §3.4 *supra*.

out the analogy between the two fields. We should recall, however, that our purpose in proposing the theory of derivative liability is heuristic. The analogy brings out important similarities, but the virtues of this new perspective should not conceal the important points of difference between liability as a perpetrator for failing to avert a criminal harm and liability as an accomplice in the criminal act perpetrated by another.

Chapter Nine
The Theory of Mistake

§9.1. *Introduction.*

The most difficult problems in criminal theory are generated by dissonance between reality and belief, between the objective facts and the actor's subjective impression of the facts. In Chapter Seven we explored the implications of the facts being innocent, but the actor's beliefs being criminal. Now we turn to the vast set of problems connected with the facts being incriminating, but the actor's beliefs, innocent. This is the general problem of mistake and ignorance about conduct that nominally violates a legal prohibition. If the actor knows of the circumstances in these cases, he surely would be liable for his conduct; but if he does not know, we confront the general theoretical question about the extent to which his ignorance provides an excuse for his legal violation.

Our discussion will begin by categorizing the various types of mistakes that might arise in criminal proceedings; we shall then consider three postures toward mistakes and their implications, and finally we shall assess strategies and arguments both for acknowledging the exculpatory effect of mistakes and for denying that effect.

§9.1.1. What Mistakes Are About. The literature of the common law, along with that of other legal systems, has long tended to divide mistakes into two categories: mistakes of fact and mistakes of law. Our hope will be to show that this form of classification is insensitive to the wide variety of mistakes that can arise in criminal cases. As we shall see in the following schema of mistakes, questions of fact and law arise, recede and interweave at every turn. The structural position of the mistake proves to be as significant as whether the mistake is one of law or fact. Here, then, is a sampling of mistakes, organized according to structural categories of liability:

A. *Mistakes about elements of the definition.*
This category encompasses a wide variety of mistakes. Let us assume for the time being that the objective elements, about which the actor is mistaken, adhere to the definition of the offense rather than to claims of justification and excuse.
1. A mistaken belief that what one is shooting at is a bear when in fact it is a fellow hunter.
2. A mistaken belief that one's sexual partner is overage when in fact she is not.
3. A mistaken judgment about whether particular conduct falls within a known offense. In a case like *Middleton,* one might believe, mistakenly, that the failure to return excess funds to the bank teller is exempt from all forms of criminal punishment.
4. A mistaken belief that conduct of a particular type—say, private homosexual conduct between consenting adults—has been legalized in the particular jurisdiction.

B. *Mistakes related to justificatory claims.*
5. A mistaken belief that one is being attacked by an aggressor. One responds in putative self-defense.

6. A mistaken belief that deadly force is permissible, if necessary, to apprehend a petty thief.
7. A mistaken belief that, as a teacher, one has the right to use corporal punishment as a disciplinary measure.

C. *Mistakes about excusing conditions.*

8. A mistaken belief that unless one commits perjury, one will be killed by the defendant under prosecution.
9. A mistaken belief that the excuse of duress encompasses homicide as well as lesser offenses.
10. A mistaken belief that the jurisdiction recognizes the excuse of necessity as well as duress. The actor relies on this belief in escaping from prison in order to avoid a homosexual rape.

D. *Mistakes in cases of negligent risk-taking.*

11. A mistaken belief that conduct will decrease rather than increase the risks, say, of a railroad collision. Having misread the timetable, a switchman switches the track so as to put the trains on a collision course.
12. A mistaken belief about the relative costs and benefits of a particular course of conduct. A nightclub owner mistakenly concludes that the safety benefits of additional fire escapes are more than offset by the financial cost and their aesthetic disadvantages.
13. A mistaken belief that only risks to persons, and not to property, constitute punishable negligence.

E. *Mistakes about elements extrinsic to culpability.*

14. Defendant acts in ignorance of an element that subjects him to the jurisdiction of a particular state or of the federal courts. E.g., defendant takes a stolen car to a neighboring city without realizing that he is crossing the state line and thus subjecting himself to federal prosecution.

Twelve of these fourteen categories derive from applying a refined version of the distinction between fact and law in each of these four structural categories. The refinement recognizes that some mistakes are based on misperceptions of the world (cases 1, 5, 8, and 11); and others on a false belief about the enactment or abolition of a legal norm (cases 4, 7, 10 and 13). The middle category raises questions both of fact and of law: the mistake goes to the application of an existing legal norm to a particular set of facts (cases 3, 6, 9 and 12). So far as one works with merely two categories—fact and law—this middle range of cases is forced into one inapt category or the other.

More important even than this refinement of mistakes of fact and law into three categories instead of two is the recognition that the object of the mistake might influence the analysis of liability. The claim is that it should matter whether the mistake is about an element of the definition, a claim of justification, a claim of excuse or the creation of risk. These four categories intersect with the three types of mistakes and generate twelve of the fourteen problematic cases. The point of this chapter is to show that each of these categories raises special problems of analysis.

One preliminary point on terminology. We adhere in this chapter to the earlier distinction crafted between mistakes and accidents.[1] Our concern is with the former, not the latter, but we interpret the concept of "mistake" to include cases of ignorance. In many of the cases posed, the actor may have no thoughts whatsoever about the age of his sexual partner (case 1) or the risk implicit in his conduct (case 11). In these situations inadvertence and ignorance are treated as though they were mistakes about the relevant circumstance. In some situations, an affirmative belief is necessary to make out an exculpatory claim; this is particularly true about mistakes pertaining to the circumstances of justification and excuse. The putative defender in case 5 must believe that he is being attacked in order even to have an arguable defense, and therefore ignorance cannot be treated as equivalent to a mistake. In other contexts, however, ignorance can function like a mistake: in case 4, ignorance of the legal norm might excuse the actor as

§9.1 [1] See §6.6.6 *supra*.

readily as the mistaken belief that the legislature had abrogated the prohibitory norm. In the event that the context is ambiguous, we shall indicate whether ignorance and inadvertence can be assimilated to our analysis of mistakes.

§9.1.2. **Outcomes in the Analysis of Mistakes.** The fourteen problematic cases have to be mapped onto three possible legal outcomes. If the mistake is made in good faith, then: (1) the mistake might bar liability altogether; (2) the mistake might bar liability only if the making of the mistake (or the inadvertence) is itself free from culpability; or (3) the mistake might have no effect at all on the outcome of the case.

A. Mistakes Negating Intent. The first outcome derives from an analysis of the intent required for liability. If the intent required for homicide is the intent to kill a human being, then a mistake as to whether one is shooting at a human being precludes a finding of intentional homicide. If the intent required for larceny is the intent to deprive the owner of his property, then the belief that one is taking one's own book or umbrella precludes an intent to deprive the owner (for the taker thinks he is the owner). The logic of this argument is simple. The required intent is "the intent to do *A*"; if the actor believes that not-*A* is the case, then he cannot have the "intent to do *A*." It follows from the logic of this argument that any mistake—reasonable or unreasonable—precludes a finding of the required intent. The use of this strategy presupposes, of course, a determination of the intent required for the offense.

It is important to note that the impact of a successful use of this strategy depends on whether the offense is subject to prosecution on the basis of negligence. Larceny, for example, is subject to prosecution only for intentional commission. Thus if a mistake bears on the intent required for larceny, it categorically prevents conviction regardless of whether the mistake is reasonable or unreasonable. But if, as in the case of homicide, the offense can be committed negligently, then we can fall back on an alternative strategy as a basis for convicting of the less serious negligent offense. This alternative is treated in the ensuing subsection.

B. Mistakes Negating Culpability. The second outcome—

that the actor benefits only from faultless or reasonable mistakes[2]—might surface in one of three doctrinal forms. First, if the prosecution is for an offense that can be committed negligently, then the mistake is of no avail if it is negligently made. Thus if shooting the fellow hunter in case 1 is prosecuted as negligent homicide, the actor's mistake becomes the basis for the charge of negligence. Any mistake will preclude a conviction for intentional homicide but only a non-negligent (reasonable, faultless) mistake will exculpate the actor from the charge of negligent manslaughter.

Alternatively, the mistake might have to meet the criteria of reasonableness in any case in which it pertains to an element extrinsic to the required intent. In our hypothetical case 2, for example, a court might plausibly require that for the accused statutory rapist to be acquitted, his mistake about the age of the girl must be reasonable. The argument for this outcome is that the mistake is an excuse negating the actor's culpability rather than a mental element of the definition. The definition is satisfied and the act is wrongful, but the mistake negates the actor's accountability for the wrongful act. But so far as the rationale for exculpation is that it is not fair to hold the actor accountable, the rationale is bounded by the requirement that the actor have made reasonable efforts to avoid the mistake. The denial of culpability fails if the mistake itself is culpable.

The difference between these two variations on requiring mistakes to be free from fault is that in the former instance, the defendant is convicted of the lesser, negligent offense; in the latter cases, the rejection of the mistake leads to conviction of the intentional offense. The effect in these latter cases is to treat an unreasonable mistake as though it were equivalent to knowledge of that element of the offense. It is obvious that someone who makes

[2] Some writers have been concerned about the supposed gap between the objective standard of reasonableness and the subjective standard of culpability. See Keedy, *Ignorance and Mistake in the Criminal Law,* 22 Harv. L. Rev. 75, 85 n.5 (1908). In §6.8 *supra,* I argued that negligence was compatible with personal fault; that is the sense in which we use the terms "unreasonable" and "negligent" in the text.

a good-faith, but unreasonable mistake about the age of a sexual partner is not as culpable as someone who means to seduce a young girl, and yet the law lumps the two together. The difference can reassert itself in discretionary sentencing, but one would think it preferable for the criteria of liability more accurately to reflect the gravity of each offense. Of this problem and its possible solutions, there will be more to say later.[3]

The third context in which the requirement of reasonableness asserts itself is in mistaken claims of justificatory facts, particularly the mistaken claim that defensive force is necessary to avert an apparently aggressive attack. This merging of apparent or putative self-defensive force with actual self-defense poses a paradox in the theory of justification and excuse, which is better reserved for the next chapter.[4] Our present concern is with the requirement that the belief in the justificatory facts be reasonable. The common-law texts routinely required that these mistakes, so far as they had exculpatory effect at all, derive from deceptive appearances.[5] But the Model Penal Code took the novel stand that any good-faith belief in justificatory facts would support an acquittal,[6] unless the offense was subject to prosecution for negligent commission.[7] This means that an unreasonable belief in the necessity of defensive force would constitute a complete defense to battery, but if death should ensue, the unreasonable mistake would provide a basis for a manslaughter conviction. The compromise verdict in homicide cases may be sound, but it is odd to recognize a complete defense in cases of unreasonable mistake simply because there is no intermediate offense of negligent commission. The effect is to treat an unreasonable mistake about justificatory facts the same as one might treat an unreasonable mistake about whether the goods one took were one's

[3] See §9.4 *infra.*

[4] See §10.1.2 *infra.*

[5] 1 Hawkins 110; 1 East 274–75.

[6] MPC §3.02 (lesser evils), §3.04 (defense of self), §3.05 (defense of others), §3.06 (defense of property), §3.07(1) (arrest), §3.07(5) (preventing suicide), §3.08(2) (maintaining classroom discipline).

[7] MPC §3.09(2).

own or the thing one shot at was a human being.[8] It may be that the Code's generous treatment of unreasonable mistakes in cases where the offense is not subject to negligent commission reflects skepticism about whether one can ever be culpable for making a mistake. Whatever the reason, the Code's approach has not gained a following in state legislatures revising their criminal codes. The standard practice in the newly reformed codes is to require forthrightly that mistakes about justificatory facts be reasonable in order to have an exculpatory effect.[9]

The first two strategies for recognizing mistakes are readily summed up as alternative forms of logical negation. If the mistake negates the required intent, then any good-faith mistake will suffice; if it merely negates the actor's culpability, then the mistake must be reasonable—that is, the making of the mistake must be free from culpability. Of course, we have yet to determine when one strategy should apply and when the other; the search for a theory to map some mistakes onto one solution and some, onto the other, is the primary concern of this chapter. A residual task remains in explaining exactly what we mean by the "culpability" of remaining ignorant or making a mistake. To be clear, we should note that with reference to mistakes, the terms "unreasonable," "culpable" and "negligent" are used interchangeably.

C. Irrelevant Mistakes. The third possible outcome is that the mistake, even if reasonable, should have no exculpatory effect at all. This outcome is most readily defended where the mistake does not bear on the actor's culpability. Thus in case 14, the mistake about crossing the state line pertains to a jurisdictional pre-

[8] That is, the mistake with regard to justificatory facts is treated as equivalent to a mistake about an element of the definition. There is, in fact, considerable support for this view in German law. See §9.4, note 47 *infra*.

[9] Hawaii Penal Code §300(1), §304; Ill. Ann. Stat. c. 38, §7–1; Pa. Cons. Stat. Ann. tit 18, §501, §505; Texas Penal Code §9.31; Wis. Stat. Ann. §939.48(1). But note that with regard to the specific problem of negligent mistakes in cases of homicide, the MPC's proposed mitigation to manslaughter has gained considerable support. See Ill. Ann. Stat. c. 38, §9–2(b) (unreasonable mistake as to justificatory facts classified as possible manslaughter); *cf.* Texas Penal Code §2503(b); LaFave & Scott 583–86.

requisite, not to an element bearing on culpability for transporting stolen cars. But the category of irrelevant mistakes goes far beyond this simple case. The maxim that mistakes of law do not excuse specifies a category of irrelevant mistakes even though a mistake about the legality of one's conduct bears on whether one can be fairly blamed for violating the law.

Mistakes are sometimes genuinely irrelevant to a just determination of liability and sometimes, as in many cases of mistake of law, they are deemed irrelevant for practical or utilitarian reasons. We shall refer to the latter cases, where mistakes are ignored even though they bear on culpability, as instances of strict liability.

The agenda is first to explore a variety of arguments for recognizing the exculpatory effect of mistakes, either because they negate the required intent or because they negate culpability. We turn then to the range of considerations that justify treating mistakes as irrelevant, and in conclusion we probe more deeply in the special problem of mistake of law.

§9.2. *Arguments Favoring the Exculpatory Effect of Mistakes.*

The major focus of our investigation—why mistakes must sometimes be reasonable and sometimes not—is readily resolved if the mistake negates the intent required for the offense. If we are given an authoritatively defined intent and a mistake negates that intent, then the outcome is straightforward. This is what we shall call a "formal" approach to the problem, for it presupposes an unquestioned starting point—the authoritatively defined intent. The alternative, substantive approach to the problem, seeks to get behind the stipulated intent and assess how the intent ought to be defined; the pursuit of that definition, of course, is equivalent to asking which mistakes ought categorically to preclude conviction.

§9.2.1. Mistakes Negating the Required Intent. The pursuit of an authoritative definition of intent is reminiscent of the analogous pursuit for the authoritative rules of liability necessary in a formal system for allocating the burden of persuasion.[1] In the search for the required intent, as in allocating the burden of persuasion, the temptation is to rely heavily on statutory form.[2] This formal methodology underlies the recognition of the mistake in People v. Weiss.[3] The defendant was charged in New York with kidnapping a suspect in the famous Lindbergh case; he argued that he believed, in good faith, that he had legal authority, which he allegedly derived from a special deputy in New Jersey, to arrest and detain the suspect. In fact he was not authorized, and the trial court excluded from evidence all testimony tending to show the defendant's good-faith mistake. The New York Court of Appeals reversed the conviction for kidnapping on the basis of a close exegesis of the statute. The crime was defined as "wilfully seiz[ing] . . . another, with intent to cause him, without authority of law, to be . . . confined or imprisoned within this state."[4] The question was whether the phrase "without authority of law" was a necessary element of the required intent. If it was, it followed that the defendant's mistaken belief in his authority, however unreasonable, would imply that he did not have the required intent to act without authority of law. According to the New York Court of Appeals, this was the correct reading of the statute. Apparently, it was critical that the words "without authority of law" appeared in the statute after the word "intent"; if the components had been transposed, so that the statute read, "seizing another, without authority of law, with the intent to detain him . . . ," the mistake would not have negated the required intent and would not have barred the conviction.

This kind of formalistic reading of statutes might have enabled the court to muddle through the case at hand, but one can-

§9.2. [1] See §§7.2 and 7.3.4 *supra*.

[2] See, e.g., Patterson v. New York, 432 U.S. 197 (1977) (critical fact was that the New York version of provocation did not formally negate malice or any other element of the prima facie case).

[3] 276 N.Y. 384, 12 N.E.2d 514 (1938).

[4] *Id.* at 386, 12 N.E.2d at 514 (emphasis omitted).

not be particularly impressed by a decision holding that anyone who believes that he has legal authority to arrest someone else is exempt from liability for kidnapping and false imprisonment. The way in which the components, "intent" and "without authority of law," happen to fall within the statute hardly warrants the inference that the legislature crafted the statute to produce an acquittal in cases of unreasonable as well as reasonable mistake.

There are other cases in which it seems to make more sense to treat every good-faith mistake as a complete bar to liability. In Morissette v. United States,[5] the defendant was convicted of violating a federal theft statute[6] for taking bomb casings from governmental land. His defense was that he believed the casings were abandoned. The trial court convicted on the ground that the statute merely required an intent to take the casings from federal land.[7] Given this construction of the required intent, the trial court correctly found that the defendant's mistake did not negate the intent required for the offense.

The Supreme Court unanimously reversed the conviction. Justice Jackson's opinion for the Court reasons ambiguously that Congress did not intend to dispense with the requirement of "criminal intent"[8] or a "mental element"[9] in its legislative adaptation of common-law larceny. If these terms are read descriptively,[10] it would be hard to detect a disagreement with the trial court, for the conviction was rooted in the "mental element" of intentionally taking the casings from government land. This seems to be an instance, however, in which these ambiguous terms are employed with normative force. For the required intent to be "criminal," it had to include an objective that would properly render the defendant subject to blame as a "criminal." Morissette was hardly to blame for the taking of the bomb casings in the apparently reasonable belief that they were abandoned.

[5] 342 U.S. 246 (1952).
[6] 18 U.S.C. §641.
[7] 342 U.S. at 249.
[8] *Id.* at 273.
[9] *Id.* at 264.
[10] On the systematic ambiguity in the use of these terms, see §6.2.1 *supra.*

The opinion did not address itself to the question whether an unreasonable mistake would also preclude a conviction under the federal statute. However, if the point of Justice Jackson's argument was that the federal statute implicitly incorporated the intent required for common-law larceny, then it would follow that even an unreasonable mistake would be sufficient for acquittal.[11] Larceny requires an intent permanently to deprive the owner of his property, and the crime is negated by a claim of right, "however puerile or mistaken" the claim may be.[12] Morissette acted under claim of right to take abandoned casings as junk and this in itself was sufficient, according to the case law, to preclude conviction for larceny. Under an alternative analysis, Morissette's belief that the casings were abandoned meant that he thought the property was without an owner; thus he could not have had the intent to deprive the owner, the government, of its property. If we assume that the court read the statute to incorporate the common-law crime, then any mistake made in good faith would negate the intent required for conviction. There was no need to establish that the mistake was reasonable or free from fault, only to convince the jury that the mistake in fact was made.

The question that should concern us is why, from the point of view of whether mistakes must be free from fault, *Morissette* seems to be so much more convincing than *Weiss*. Both cases suggest that any good-faith mistake as to the element in question (authority of law, ownership of the casings) negates the intent required for conviction. But *Weiss* seems to go too far in generating an excuse for persons who hastily and negligently assume they have the authority to arrest and detain other persons. If unreasonable mistakes about relevant elements preclude a conviction for larceny, the sweep of the exemption appears more plausible.

We can account for this felt difference between the cases by invoking the distinction between elements of the definition and elements of justification. The contemporary German approach to

[11] The term "criminal intent" can be used to require a reasonable mistake; see People v. Hernandez, 61 Cal. 2d 529, 393 P.2d 673, 39 Cal. Rptr. 361 (1964).

[12] See §2.4.3 *supra*.

defining the scope of the required intent is to begin with an analysis of the definition. The required intent attaches to every element of the definition,[13] but not necessarily to elements of justification.[14] The issue in *Weiss* was patently a matter of justification; having the legal authority to arrest someone is a good reason for violating the norm against kidnapping and forcible detention. In *Morissette,* the mistake went to an element of the definition; that is, to the norm against permanently taking the property of another. The implication of Morissette's mistake is that he did not intentionally violate that norm. Thus if we say that the required intent extends to every element of the definition, any mistake about the ownership of property, even one that is hasty and negligent, should preclude a conviction for larceny. Yet it does not follow that a mistake about an element of justification, as in *Weiss,* would enjoy the same status as a bar to liability, particularly in cases in which the mistake was made negligently.

The claim, therefore, is that the required intent ought to encompass the elements of the definition. The definition, in turn, is determined by finding the minimal set of criteria that, in the given society, conveys a morally significant prohibition. The assumption is that persons should be subject to criminal liability (for intentional crimes) only if they intentionally violate a morally coherent and significant prohibitory norm.[15] As we learned in studying the personal and social theories of wrongdoing, there are good reasons for regarding the actor's intent as an element bearing on wrongdoing, and specifically on the definition of the offense.[16] Thus the effect of a mistake as to one of the elements of the definition is not to excuse a wrongful act, but to negate the violation of a prohibitory norm. If one takes a neighbor's book under the belief that it is one's own, the taking does not satisfy the threshold specified in the definition of the offense.

[13] StGB §16, sentence 1 ("Whoever commits an act without being cognizant of an element of the definition does not act intentionally"). *Cf.* StGB 1871, §59.

[14] The treatment of mistakes as to justificatory facts is controversial. *Compare* the authorities cited *supra* §9.1, notes 8–9, *with* Welzel 168–69 and authorities cited.

[15] See §7.4.1 *supra.*

[16] See §6.6.5 *supra.*

Mistakes as to justificatory elements, however, do not affect either the violation of the norm or the wrongful nature of acting in ignorance. If an actor believes that he is being attacked and responds with force, his injurying the putative aggressor is a wrongful but excused battery.[17] The putative aggressor can avail himself of justified force in response, and the others who aid the putative defender (but not knowing of his mistake) can be held liable as accessories in the perpetrator's wrongful act.[18] If a mistaken claim of justification functions as an excuse, then one can expect it to meet the standard applied to other excusing conditions—namely, that it actually excuse the actor from blame. As the claim of duress must satisfy normative criteria,[19] so must the claim of mistake as an excuse satisfy normative criteria—namely, the requirement of reasonableness—in order effectively to excuse the wrongful act.

Given the difficulty and controversy intrinsic to this field of problems, we would be naive to think we had a definitive, unassailable solution to the enduring problem of determining when mistakes must be reasonable in order to have an exculpatory effect. The thesis is tentative, and to aid those who might wish to carry the effort further, we should restate the critical premises for recognizing that some mistakes have a categorical exculpatory effect. The premises are these:

1. The definition of an offense is the violation of a prohibitory norm.[20]
2. The prohibitory norm identifies the minimal set of objective circumstances necessary, in the given cultural context, to state a coherent moral or social imperative.[21]
3. There is no violation of a prohibitory norm unless the actor

[17] As we noted earlier, §9.1, at note 4, Anglo-American law confuses the issue of putative self-defense, which is an excuse, with actual self-defense, which is a justification. For a discussion of the antinomies in this confusion, see §10.1.2 *infra*.

[18] See §8.7.3 *supra*.

[19] See §10.4.2 *infra*. As to the normative criteria bearing on provocation, see §4.2.1 *supra*.

[20] See §7.4.1 *supra*.

[21] *Ibid.*

acts intentionally or knowingly with respect to the elements of the definition (the prohibitory norm).[22]

It follows from premises 1 and 3 that the definition includes the required intent. Accordingly, it follows that any mistake as to an element of the definition itself precludes a finding that the definition is satisfied (i.e., the mistake negates the intent, and the intent is a subjective component of the definition). A mistake as to one of these elements therefore has the same effect in barring liability for an intentional offense as the absence of one of the objective elements. A mistake with respect to ownership of property negates the intent required for larceny, and therefore has the same impact on liability as the objective circumstances of the chattel's not being covered by the law of larceny. Of course, if the offense is one that can be committed negligently, then the mistake only bars conviction for the intentional offense.

The premises supporting the alternative track requiring that mistakes be reasonable are the following:

4. Relevant mistakes about elements extrinsic to the definition are excuses.[23]
5. Elements of justification are extrinsic to the definition.[24]
6. Excuses are not valid unless they negate the actor's culpability.[25]
7. A mistake does not negate culpability unless the making of the mistake was blameless.[26]

We can generate arguments for these seven propositions. Indeed much of this book has been devoted to developing the apparatus that enables us to state these propositions and to confer upon them some initial plausibility. The discussion of wrongdoing buttresses the third proposition, but also reveals how controversial

[22] This follows from the social and personal theories of wrongdoing. See §6.6.5 *supra*.

[23] Obviously there are some mistakes about elements extrinsic to the definition that have no exculpatory effect. See §9.3 *infra*.

[24] This is an outcome of the extended discussion in §7.4 *supra*.

[25] If this is true, it is analytically true, i.e., implicit in the nature of excusing. See §10.3 *infra*.

[26] The argument for this proposition is found in §9.2.3 *infra*.

it is. The analysis of the right deed for the wrong reason supports the fifth proposition, but the argument, it will be recalled, is painstaking and far from conclusive. The most we can claim for this set of seven propositions is that they chart a systematic approach to the problem of determining when mistakes must be qualified by the requirement of reasonableness. They are but a beginning, awaiting refinement and perhaps refutation in the work of others. The virtue of the system, if it is sound, is that it provides a technique for going beyond a purely formal search for an authoritatively defined intent. It is little credit to the legal craft to invest its faith in the fortuities of legislative drafting. We are impelled to go beyond a formal theory of mistake and to cultivate a substantive, systematic theory on the relevance of particular kinds of mistakes.

We began with one question and are now left with another. The initial question was: When should we impose the requirement of reasonableness? Our system of seven premises leaves us with another quandary: How do we know when an issue functions as an element of the definition, and when is it a justification? There are admittedly paradigmatic cases: ownership of property is an element of the definition; defense of self and others are claims of justification. But there are borderline cases. To press our admittedly fragile theory, we shall try to apply it in one of these borderline situations: consent in cases of rape.

§9.2.2. The Borderland of Definition and Justification. As the issue of consent troubled us in assessing the requirement of a justificatory intent,[27] analogous quandaries arise in working out the proposition that the required intent ought to encompass all elements of the definition. The question that we shall consider is the function of consent in rape cases. Is non-consent an element of the definition? Or does consent function as a justification for fornication? In probing this specific problem we shall try to assess whether the concepts of definition and justification provide useful guidelines in prescribing when any mistake will suffice for acquittal and when the mistake must be reasonable.

[27] See §7.4.3 *supra.*

The issue recently came to the fore in a *cause célèbre* decided by the House of Lords. In a bizzare set of facts in Regina v. Morgan,[28] the Lords upheld a conviction for rape but also concluded that any mistake, even an unreasonable mistake as to the victim's consent in rape cases, would preclude liability. In the particular case, the four defendants had overpowered the victim and had forcible intercourse with her. Yet they had allegedly been told by the victim's husband that she would dissemble resistance presumably to gain some perverse satisfaction in being "forced" to submit. The trial judge instructed the jury that not only did the defendants have to "really believe" that the victim consented, but that the belief had to be reasonable. On appeal from their conviction, the defendants argued that any belief in the victim's consent undercut their intent to rape and therefore precluded liability. A majority of the judges concluded that this legal point about the intent required for rape was correct but that on the facts, the trial judge's instructions were not prejudicial and therefore the conviction should be affirmed.

The conclusion of the judges in *Morgan* has caused a furor in England and in Commonwealth countries.[29] Critics have called the *Morgan* decision a "rapist's charter," for it stands for the proposition that anyone can commit rape and get away with it if he can convince a jury that he believed in good faith that the woman consented. Of course, all of this furor ignores the serious problem of actually convincing twelve men and women that the actor actually believed the victim consented. If it is true, as the House of Lords maintains, that the jury would not have believed the defendants in *Morgan*, there are not many cases in which they would be duped by a meretricious defendant.[30]

The more important question is whether, assuming that the jury can do its job, a good-faith mistake as to consent ought to

[28] [1975] 2 W.L.R. 923.

[29] See Curley, *Excusing Rape*, 5 J. Phil. & Pub. Aff. 325 (1976). *But cf.* the defense of *Morgan* in Cross, *Centenary Reflections on Prince's Case*, 91 L.Q. Rev. 540 (1975).

[30] *But cf.* Regina v. Cogan & Leak, [1975] 3 W.L.R. 316 (Crim. App.) (on facts similar to *Morgan*, conviction of Cogan reversed on ground that jury found he believed wife had consented, but without reasonable grounds).

constitute a denial of the intent required for rape. The House of Lords had to assay this question as a matter of principle, for there was no English case that dealt explicitly with the question. Dictum in an Australian opinion favored the requirement of reasonableness as a limitation on the mistake.[31] But this dictum is arguably interpreted as a procedural qualification. More on this point later.[32]

Not only was there little wisdom to be found in the precedents on rape, but the two leading English cases on the exculpatory effect of mistakes appeared to be readily distinguishable. In *Tolson*,[33] decided as a Crown Case Reserved in 1889, the judges concluded that a reasonable mistake as to the death of one's first spouse should constitute an excuse for bigamy. In Sweet v. Parsley,[34] the House of Lords concluded that a reasonable mistake as to whether tenants were using cannabis constituted an excuse to the statutory offense of "permitting" premises to be used in violation of the Dangerous Drug Act. These cases are distinguishable from *Morgan* in two important respects. First, neither *Tolson* nor *Sweet* directly assayed the question whether any mistake, or only a reasonable mistake, should constitute an excuse. In *Tolson,* the trial judge, Fitzjames Stephen, refused to admit the defendant's belief in the death of her husband as a defense to the statutory violation. It did not matter whether her belief was reasonable or unreasonable. In *Sweet,* the defendant similarly was convicted without any opportunity to excuse the violation by proving a reasonable mistake as to the critical facts. Thus on appeal in both cases, the question was whether a reasonable mistake would be recognized as an excuse or whether the mistake would be totally irrelevant. In both cases, the mistake happened to be patently reasonable, and therefore in reversing the convictions on appeal, the judges had no reason to go further and consider the excusing effect of an unreasonable mistake. In neither opinion is there any defense of the limitation of reasonableness as compared with the

[31] Regina v. Sperotta and Salvietti, 71 State Reports (N.S.W.) 334 (1970). *But cf.* other Australian cases cited at [1975] 3 W.L.R. at 934.

[32] See §9.2.3, at notes 49–51 *infra.*

[33] Regina v. Tolson, 23 Q.B.D. 168 (1889).

[34] [1969] 2 W.L.R. 470.

more extreme case raised in *Morgan* that any mistake as to consent should preclude conviction for rape.

A second point of distinction is that both *Tolson* and *Sweet* raise questions of excusing statutory violations. Both bigamy and the regulation of dangerous drugs had found precise statutory regulation. But as of 1975, the English courts were still prosecuting rape essentially as a common-law offense. It is true that the Sexual Offenses Act of 1956 prescribed that "it is a felony for a man to rape a woman,"[35] but that is all the Act tells us about the nature of rape. Now this difference between an offense defined by statute and one defined in the common law may not be all that important, yet it weighed heavily in the deliberations in *Morgan*. That the actors in *Tolson* and *Sweet* had violated the statute contributed to the tendency to treat the problem as one of excusing a palpable wrong—the wrong of violating the statute. Focussing on the mistake as a problem of excuse leads invariably to the requirement that the mistake should excuse only if it is free from fault. Lord Simon favored an analogous view of forcible intercourse—as a wrong that had to be excused.[36] Yet the majority of the judges were disinclined to view rape in this way. They were led instead to resolve the problem by construing the intent required for rape as the intent to have intercourse against the woman's will.

What is interesting for our purposes is the methodology invoked to define this interpretation of the required intent. There was no authoritative guide in the case law or the applicable statutes. To defend his conclusion, Lord Cross fell back on the meaning of "rape" in ordinary language. If the ordinary person on the Clapham bus believed the defendants, would he say that they had committed rape? Lord Cross argues that the average man would reply, "No."[37] In contrast, Lord Cross reasons, the ordinary man would say that someone who married, with a spouse still alive, does commit bigamy regardless of his good faith; thus Lord Cross was able to distinguish *Tolson* as a case in which a wrong had to

[35] *Cf.* the current definition in Sexual Offences (Amendment) Act 1976, c. 82, §1.
[36] [1975] 2 W.L.R. at 940–41.
[37] *Id.* at 926.

be excused on reasonable grounds. Assuming that Lord Cross is right about what the ordinary person would say,[38] we should question whether this methodology is appropriate for the law. It is true that the law's notion of rape originates in common speech, but should the contours of rape be controlled forever by what the ordinary person would say? The argument is reminiscent of the earlier thesis that a shared image of thievery guided the development of common-law larceny.[39] But there is a critical difference. The shared image of the thief informed the manifest act as a threshold requirement of larceny. There were numerous technicalities of larceny that were hardly subject to decision by asking the common man about the nature of stealing. No one cared whether the common farmer thought that taking a dog or real estate deeds (objects not subject to larceny) rendered the taker a punishable thief. Yet Lord Cross would have us resolve difficult problems in the law of rape by asking the man on the crosstown bus: Did Morgan commit rape? In the early seventeenth century, Sir Edward Coke argued against King James that the law was a craft based upon "artificial reason," not upon the "natural reason" available to every man. We may not wish to go so far as Coke in limiting the methods of the law to a trained elite, but it seems equally in error to go to the opposite extreme, suggested by Lord Cross, and decide difficult cases simply on the basis of what the ordinary man would call rape.

Closer to the mark, Lord Hailsham proceeds by determining what is the "prohibited act" in cases of rape.[40] His assumption is that the required intent must extend to all elements of the prohibited act. This sounds very much like the methodology we pro-

[38] There seems to be a subtle difference between the question "Was she raped?" and "Did he rape her?" We are more inclined to answer "yes" to the former than to the latter. *Cf.* Regina v. Cogan & Leak, [1975] 3 W.L.R. 316, 319 (Crim. App.) (on similar facts, the court says: "one fact is clear—the wife had been raped"). In *Cogan & Leak,* the court affirmed a conviction against the husband standing by as the perpetrator of the rape by means of the innocently mistaken third party who had intercourse with the wife. Thus a bystander can be a rapist! What would the commuter on the bus say about that?

[39] See §2.2 *supra.*

[40] [1975] 2 W.L.R. at 932–33.

posed above, namely, that we determine which elements adhere to the definition of the offense and require intent as to all those elements. Yet it turns out that all Lord Hailsham means by the prohibited act is the set of elements bearing on liability, without attending to the distinction between inculpatory and exculpatory elements, definition and justification. He concludes that non-consent is an element of the prohibited act, and to prove that, he cites a string of common-law texts to support his conclusion that "the prohibited act in rape is non-consensual sexual intercourse."[41] The consent of the female undoubtedly bears on liability. The question is whether the requirement of intent extends to all the elements of the textbook rule, including the factor of consent.

If Lord Hailsham applied his method to homicide, he would generate some embarrassing results. The comparable black-letter statement on murder is that murder is the "unlawful killing of a human being with malice aforethought." The claim of self-defense negates both the element of malice and of unlawfulness; and therefore if malice and unlawfulness enjoy the same status as non-consent in rape cases, it follows that the absence of a valid claim of self-defense is part of the "prohibited act" in the idiom of Lord Hailsham. Thus it would follow that any mistake about the need for the defense of force would render the act totally innocent and exempt from liability. It is difficult to say that Lord Hailsham's reliance on textbook statements of the law constitutes a method appropriate to the task, for it fails to draw distinctions that we take to be necessary.

There are some cases in which any mistake is sufficient to preclude liability, others in which the mistake prevails only if free from fault. An adequate method would help us classify cases into these two groups. Yet both Lord Cross' reliance on ordinary language and Lord Hailsham's reliance on textbook definitions prove to be little more than tools for rationalizing the result in this case, and it is not even clear that the rationalization favors the right result.

Before we turn to our own methodology for resolving the

[41] *Id.* at 937.

problem in *Morgan,* we should note that as a historical matter, the decision in this case was probably more a reaction to past infelicitous decisions, than a result either of natural reason or of the artificial reason of lawyers. The decision in the back of the judges' minds was the notorious case of Director of Public Prosecutions v. Smith[42] in 1960, in which the Lords upheld a conviction for capital murder on jury instructions equating "willful murder of a police officer" with whether a "reasonable man [would] have contemplated that grievous bodily harm was likely to result to that officer. . . ."[43] These instructions were wrong on several counts, and it was an unfortunate turn in English jurisprudence that the Lords upheld the conviction. Yet the reaction to the case is even more unfortunate. Going to the opposite extreme, English judges and commentators are inclined now to think that any reliance on the projected behavior of a reasonable person injects "objective" liability into the criminal law and is therefore unjust.[44] It follows, as far as many English jurists are concerned, that requiring mistakes to be reasonable and free from culpability is to impose some sort of strict liability regardless of culpability.

Lost in this reaction to *Smith* is the difference between interpreting the meaning of intentional killing (which was the problem in *Smith*) and determining which elements bearing on liability ought to be included in the conduct that must be intentional. It is obviously wrong to determine whether the actor had an intention by asking what a reasonable person would have intended. But it hardly follows that the range of the required intent must include every element bearing on liability. Nor does it follow that the reliance on the standard of reasonableness implies a form of "objective liability." The long-range evil of *Smith* may not be the original sin, but excessive repentance in avoiding criteria of reasonableness.

If we attempt now to apply our thesis to the problem in *Morgan,* how should we proceed? If we can determine the elements of

[42] [1961] A.C. 290 (1960) (H.L.). Lord Hailsham refers to the case as one "full of warnings for us all," [1975] 2 W.L.R. at 933.

[43] [1961] A.C. at 323.

[44] Note Rupert Cross' reference to the "subjectivist bug" that has infected English criminal jurisprudence. Cross, *supra* note 29, at 551.

the definition, then the claim is that the required intent encompasses these and only these elements. But how do we determine whether non-consent is part of the definition of rape? The definition, it will be recalled, is the minimal set of elements necessary to incriminate the actor. Consider the following scale of elements arranged in order of ascending incrimination:

1. touching
2. sexual contact
3. forcible sexual contact
4. non-consensual, forcible sexual contact.

It is difficult to argue that touching per se is incriminating. In some societies, all forms of human contact might be regarded as trespassing on the domain of another, but we regularly accept a gentle hand on the shoulder as both the price and the benefit of group living. Sexual contact is obviously different. Intimate touching of the genitals is hardly routine; the touching requires a good reason. The reason, or the justification, might be the consent of the person touched or it might be the necessity of performing an operation in an emergency situation. This seems to me to be sufficient to regard the definition of rape as sexual penetration, with consent functioning as a ground for regarding the sexual act as a shared expression of love rather than as an invasion of bodily integrity.

The case in *Morgan* is even clearer, for the penetration was forcible. It is conceivable that a woman would enjoy being taken by force and that her consent would justify the forcible penetration. But it would be implausible to treat non-consent as well as force as necessary conditions for rendering the sexual act suspect. There seems to be little doubt that under the circumstances of *Morgan*, the consent of the woman should have functioned as a justification. And if that is the case, it is wrong to regard the intent required for rape as encompassing a belief in non-consent. If the perpetrators were mistaken about the supposed justification for forcible intercourse, their wrongful act might well be excused. But if the focus is on excusing their conduct, it is appropriate to require—in this case as in *Tolson* and *Sweet*—that their mistake be free from fault. If they were personally culpable in believing Morgan's lies about his wife, they could hardly claim their acts were blameless and therefore properly excused.

One might be tempted to think that the actual decision in *Morgan,* holding that any mistake about consent bars liability, expresses the mores of the new sexual morality. The stigma of fornication has softened; therefore one should have to show more in order to make out a case that sexual acts are socially unacceptable. It seems to follow that what makes rape wrong is non-consent, and therefore non-consent should be included in the definition of the offense.

This argument is seductive, but when stripped of a few ambiguities, it is much less attractive. First, it is wrong to think of rape as an aggravated species of fornication. Consent was irrelevant to the sin of unchaste intercourse and therefore, non-consent does not aggravate the fornication. Indeed, there is some Biblical evidence that forcible intercourse did not leave the taint of fornication on the woman.[45] Thus, it was better for the woman to be raped than to consent to fornication. So far as the sin of fornication required voluntary participation, rape and fornication are antithetical wrongs. And thus changing attitudes toward chastity hardly diminish the evil of rape.

Indeed one can well argue the opposite view. The more seriously one takes the sexual autonomy of adult men and women, the more incriminating an act of forcible intercourse of the type prosecuted in *Morgan.*[46] Further, if consensual sexual acts are socially acceptable, it does not follow that non-consent is a necessary component of the definition and therefore encompassed in the required intent. Arresting a suspect on the basis of probable cause is socially acceptable, but the element of probable cause is still a justification for the police intrusion. If the combination of two elements renders conduct acceptable, it is still often the case that one component standing alone is sufficient to incriminate the actor.

[45] Deuteronomy 22:23–27.

[46] Admittedly, the element of force is incriminating because it is an evidentiary index of non-consent.

Nonetheless, there are some doubts that we ought to concede about classifying consent as a justification for sexual contact. First, if we take self-defense and lesser evils as the paradigmatic claims of justification, then a justification functions as an exception to a prohibitory norm; consent to sexual contact, however, is the normal case rather than the exception. Secondly, claims of justification usually represent good reasons for inflicting harm. In contrast, consent dissolves the harm and converts the act into one of mutual benefit. Though these points give us doubts, it still seems preferable to treat consent to sexual contact as ground for exculpating incriminating conduct.

§9.2.3. Requiring That Exculpatory Mistakes Be Reasonable. There are recurrent references in Anglo-American textbooks and cases to the requirement that mistakes be reasonable.[47] Yet this requirement is stated simply as a doctrinal conclusion without any general theoretical work on whether the analysis of mistakes should be embedded, with other excuses, in the general theory of culpability. It is not even clear that the requirement of a "reasonable" mistake expresses a concern about culpability. For example, in the field of putative self-defense and other imagined circumstances of justified conduct, it is generally assumed that the mistake must be reasonable.[48] We could interpret this requirement as a concern about whether the actor's mistake is free from fault. But the doctrine could also be read as a theory about the justifying effect of appearances. If the circumstances warrant a reasonable belief, the actor is entitled to rely upon appearances, whatever the facts may actually be.[49]

There is a related argument that often enters into discussion about why mistakes must be reasonable. The substantive standard of reasonable mistake blends readily into an evidentiary standard for mistakes based on reasonable grounds. Thus one finds recurrent appeal to the evidentiary rule that in order for the issue of

[47] Perkins 940; Hall 366–67; *but cf.* Williams 201–06.

[48] See §9.1, notes 5, 9 *supra.*

[49] This interpretation of common-law doctrine is more charitable than the critique of confusing putative self-defense with actual self-defense in §10.1.2 *infra.*

mistake to be sent to the jury, the accused must show that the mistake was based on reasonable grounds.[50] Lord Simon relies on this argument in *Morgan* to support his view that the mistake as to the victim's consent must be reasonable.[51] It may be true, as a matter of practice, that only mistakes rendered believable by the circumstances of the case will in fact generate an acquittal. But there may always be unusual cases where the mistake might be free from fault even though there are insufficient objective criteria to say that reasonable grounds make the mistake plausible. This might be the case if the actor is partially intoxicated or of diminished psychological capacity. Or in a variation of *Morissette,* the actor might not be able to read English and understand the posted warnings against taking the bomb casings. There might be insufficient objective criteria in these cases to say that any reasonable person would have made the mistake. Yet because of his personal situation, the actor might be free from culpability in making the mistake. The evidentiary standard of "reasonable grounds" would preclude considering the mistake, even though the mistaken party was not fairly to blame under the circumstances.

In other situations, the courts refer to the requirement of a reasonable mistake with a view to the general issue of culpability and excuse,[52] but even then the analysis is often oblique. It seems preferable to package the issue of excusable mistake under some other doctrinal rubric. This is often done by taking the require-

[50] See United States v. Short, 4 U.S.C.M.A. 437, 16 C.M.R. 11 (1954). The defendant was charged with assault with intent to rape. The defense's claim was mistake as to consent. The law officer refused instructions requiring acquittal for any good-faith mistake as to consent. In upholding the ensuing conviction, the appellate court argued that only a reasonable mistake as to consent would excuse the defendant. The reasoning interweaves a requirement of reasonableness in the instructions to the jury with the claim that "it is axiomatic that, before a failure to instruct on a defense may be alleged as grounds for error, the evidence must show that the defense was reasonably raised." *Id.* at 444, 16 C.M.R. at 18.

[51] [1975] 2 W.L.R. at 942.

[52] For cases recognizing that, in principle, an exculpatory mistake should be free from fault, see, e.g., Gordon v. State, 52 Ala. 308 (1875) (as to offense of illegal voting, court held mistake would be of no effect if defendant voted recklessly or negligently); Mulreed v. State, 107 Ind. 62 (1886) (only reasonable belief in maturity of minor would excuse illegal sale of liquor).

ment of intent to mean "wrongful" or "criminal intent" and thus treating the mistake (but only if it is free from fault) as a negation of the required intent. In People v. Vogel,[53] the California Supreme Court concluded that a reasonable mistake of fact about a prior divorce negated the actor's "wrongful intent" to commit bigamy; a few years later in a statutory rape case, the same court concluded that a resonable mistake as to the age of the girl negated the required "criminal intent."[54] Adding the modifiers "wrongful" and "criminal" converts the issue of intention, which would be negated by any mistake, into the conceptual equivalent of culpability, which can be negated only by a reasonable, non-negligent mistake. The reason for retaining the language of intent is that it forges a nominal link to a provision in the California criminal code which requires that in every offense there be "a joint operation of act and intent."[55] Thus on the surface, the structure of the argument appears to be the same as the conventional reliance on mistakes to negate an authoritatively defined criminal intent.[56]

An apology for this doctrinal indirectness is that common-law courts are reluctant to reveal to the jury the extent to which a conviction rests on a moral assessment of the actor's wrongful conduct. But this view of the jury's incapacity to resolve normative issues seems also to infect the scholarly literature. Commentators are generally reluctant to confront normative issues in assessing excusing conditions, and particularly in the field of mistake. The problematic theory of mistake in Anglo-American law resembles the treatment of provocation in homicide cases, where the courts and commentators have similarly shied away from the criteria of moral responsibility underlying the claim of provocation.[57]

As a step toward overcoming these inhibitions about moral discourse, we should try to state precisely how individuals can be fairly blamed for making mistakes or for remaining inadvertent to

[53] 46 Cal. 2d 798, 299 P.2d 850 (1956).

[54] People v. Hernandez, 61 Cal. 2d 529, 393 P.2d 673, 39 Cal. Rptr. 361 (1964).

[55] Cal. Penal Code §20.

[56] *Cf.* Long v. State, 44 Del. 262, 65 A.2d 489 (1949) (reasonable, good-faith mistake negated "general criminal intent").

[57] See §4.2.1 *supra.*

the risks implicit in their conduct. The inquiry encompasses not only mistakes in the narrow sense, but the culpability of inadvertent negligence. It also provides a basis for our later assessment of mistakes of law and the just resolution of this troublesome field.

Let us begin by noting the arguments against the culpability of good-faith mistakes and inadvertent risk-taking. First, it might be argued that rewards are inappropriate for inadvertently bestowing benefits and, therefore, blame is inappropriate for inadvertently causing harm. If I go for a walk and my neighbor's lost dog follows me home and thus returns to its master, I hardly deserve credit for causing the dog to return. What is true for rewarding others ought arguably to be true for blaming others. If this is so, then it follows that individuals who inadvertently do the wrong thing should not be blamed. Secondly, it might be argued that all desert—whether credit or blame—presupposes a voluntary choice to do good or evil. If the actor is inadvertent, there is no choice and therefore no appropriate ground for blaming.

In response to the first argument, the reply is simply that rewarding and punishing are not symmetrical. Rewards are bestowed for supererogatory acts—acts going beyond one's obligations. Punishment is inflicted for breaching obligations to other members of society. One cannot receive credit for a supererogatory act without choosing to do it, but if the issue is one of fulfilling or violating one's obligations, the analysis might be different. If a stranger returns a lost book to the library, the borrower's duty to return the book is fulfilled. If a duty may be fulfilled without the responsible party's choosing to fulfill it, a duty may also be breached without choosing the breach. If a borrower fails to repay a debt when it is due, he breaches a duty; if a driver inadvertently violates the rules of the road, he breaches a duty to drive according to the law. The breach is an objective phenomenon. The problem posed by the culpability of inadvertence is not whether the breach occurs, but whether the inadvertent party can fairly be held accountable for it.

Now it is not clear why someone would insist that there is no accountability for a breach of duty unless the actor chooses the breach. Jerome Hall argues that the breach is not "voluntary" unless it is consciously chosen.[58] But this cannot be right. Voluntariness is not synonymous with choice. An act or failure to act is voluntary only if the actor could have done otherwise under the circumstances. An intentional act is voluntary if the actor could have abstained. A mistake is voluntary if the actor could have avoided the mistake. Inadvertent risk-taking is voluntary if, under the circumstances, the actor could have realized the risks implicit in his conduct. It is true that the conscious and intentional actor realizes at every moment that he might desist, whereas the mistaken or inadvertent actor does not repeatedly forego the opportunity of correcting himself. This might explain why intentional wrongdoing is regarded as more culpable than negligent wrongdoing, but it does not follow that blaming inadvertent risk-taking is never permissible.

There are two habits of mind that support the cleavage between the blameworthiness of intentional wrongdoing and the supposed blamelessness of inadvertently causing harm. The first is thinking of human conduct in isolation from the surrounding circumstances that influence and sometimes control our actions. And the second is the descriptive theory of attribution, which holds that wrongdoing is attributed to individuals on the basis of knowledge and conscious choice.[59] These two habits of mind nourish each other. If intentional wrongdoing is abstracted from the surrounding circumstances, it is tempting to think that attribution and accountability are simply a matter of affirming the actor's intent. One ignores the excusing influence of circumstances and thus filters off the evaluative judgment implicit in excusing. One forgets the important point we derived from the history of homicide.[60] Culpability is not a matter of intending or not intending, but a question of degree. And the degree of culpability is gauged by the actor's interaction with his victim and the relative dependence or independence from the surrounding environment. The isolation of

[58] Hall, *Negligent Behavior Should Be Excluded From Penal Liability,* 63 Colum. L. Rev. 632, 635–36 (1963).

[59] See §6.7.1 *supra.*

[60] See §5.1.3 *supra.*

conduct from the surrounding circumstances makes it more difficult to comprehend the culpability of inadvertence. What makes inadvertent conduct culpable is the failure to respond to circumstances that ordinarily trigger our sensibilities. If someone begins driving at night and forgets to turn on his lights, he is culpable for failing to respond to an implicit contextual signal. If a druggist fills a prescription and fails to notice that she is using a poison instead of the proper chemical, she is culpable for not being more attentive under circumstances in which she knows she ought to be careful. On the other hand, there is no culpability for ignorance where the circumstances fail to put the actor on notice of the relevant risk. Ms. Lambert's entering the city of Los Angeles was insufficient to trigger concern about whether she should report to the police department.[61] The standard of circumstances putting someone "on notice" requires close attention to the facts of the case and the actor's personal capacities. Even more significantly, the process of judgment also requires sensitivity to how much attentiveness we may fairly demand of one other.[62]

The perspective that supports the culpability of inadvertence and of mistakes is the normative theory of attribution that we developed earlier.[63] The normative theory of attribution takes the interaction of the actor with his surroundings to lie at the core of assessing personal culpability. Culpability for intentional wrongdoing turns on the degree of self-actuation, independent of surrounding influences. Culpability for inadvertence turns on the actor's failure to respond to circumstances that signal danger. As the descriptive theory of culpability relates symbiotically to a conception of conduct abstracted from surrounding circumstances, the normative theory of culpability thrives on emphasizing conduct in context. Assessing culpability is not a matter of appealing to moral rules of thumb, but of refining one's sensitivity to the complexity of facts that permit us either to blame or to excuse harmful

[61] Lambert v. California, 355 U.S. 225 (1957).

[62] For further exploration of this theme, see Fletcher, *The Theory of Criminal Negligence: A Comparative Analysis,* 119 U. Pa. L. Rev. 401, 423–26 (1971).

[63] See §6.7.2 *supra.*

conduct. In the case of intentional conduct, our sensitivities are directed to the influences of external pressures; in cases of inadvertence and mistake, the problem is evaluating the circumstances that might have alerted the actor to the danger implicit in his conduct.

§9.3. *Strategies for Disregarding Mistakes.*

The strategies for disregarding mistakes fall into two categories. One line of argument is that the mistake bears on a fact required for conviction but which does not relate to the actor's wrongdoing or culpability. A good example would be a mistake about whether the crime was carried out in California or Nevada. Even if the same conduct is punished under the laws of both jurisdictions, the California courts would take the case only if the act was performed or the harm was felt in California. Jurisdictional facts bear on whether a particular court will hear the case, but they do not bear on the justification for punishing the particular act as criminal. If the actor's wrongdoing remains constant regardless of the jurisdiction, then a mistake about a jurisdictional fact does not raise an issue of accountability for wrongdoing. And if the mistake does not bear on the actor's accountability for wrongdoing, then there is no reason for regarding even a reasonable mistake as an excuse from liability.

A second, and distinct, strategy for disregarding mistakes is to argue that even though the mistake bears on the actor's culpability, practical considerations require a conviction despite the actor's excuse. Liability despite a good excuse is "strict" in the sense that the criteria of liability deviate from the principles of just punishment. Because strict liability raises problems of individual justice, its application is subject to repeated scrutiny.

§9.3.1. Mistakes Extrinsic to Wrongdoing and Culpability. One can imagine other mistakes that are as handily ignored as the mistakes about the place of the crime. The actor might think that as an employee of a foreign embassy, he was a diplomat and therefore enjoyed diplomatic immunity for his crimes. Diplomatic immunity does not negate the wrongfulness of committing larceny or even of illegal parking; one could hardly maintain that a mistake about immunity should exempt someone from punishment.

A more difficult example is the exemption still recognized in the law of rape for cases of forcible intercourse against a wife.[1] Let us suppose that the suspect thought that his intended victim was his wife, when in fact she was not. Should we say in this case that the fact of coverture bears on the wrong that the defendant has committed? Or is this exemption to be considered as analogous to diplomatic immunity or the jurisdiction of the court? The theory of this exemption may originally have been that the wife's body was given over to the sexual command of her husband, and therefore there was no wrong in the husband's forcing her to comply. If the exemption were to survive today, it would have to be reinterpreted as a provision designed to respect the autonomy of the family from the sanctions of the criminal law. According to the former theory, the mistake would bear on the actor's culpability; according to the latter, it would not.

The German Code contains an analogous provision that prescribes a special procedural impediment to theft offenses committed within the family.[2] These offenses are subject to prosecution only if the victim files a complaint. The special fact whether the victim is a member of the family is regarded as a factor extrinsic to the actor's wrongdoing, and therefore a mistake about the ownership of the goods (say that they were owned by someone in the family) is irrelevant to the application of the provision.[3] This analysis might provide a convincing analogy for the treatment of mistakes about whether the victim of the rape was a spouse.

Another problem area is the set of special facts that are necessary to establish federal jurisdiction in the United States. These

§9.3. [1] See Cal. Penal Code §261.

[2] StGB §247. *Cf.* Code Pénal §380 (exempting specified familial thefts from penal but not civil liability).

[3] Schönke-Schröder-Stree, note 13, at 1442.

facts typically bear on whether the offense is committed in interstate commerce, whether it is committed on federal property, or whether the offense is committed against federal personnel. The element of interstate commerce is generally thought to be jurisdictional and therefore a mistake, say, about whether stolen bonds have been shipped in interstate commerce, is generally thought to be irrelevant.[4]

Mistakes about whether the victim assaulted a federal officer are more complicated. The status of the victim could easily be thought of as a factor aggravating the actor's wrongdoing. This problem recently came before the Supreme Court in United States v. Feola.[5] The defendants conspired to assault some persons who, unbeknownst to them, were federal undercover agents. The preliminary question, prior to the analysis of the conspiracy charge, was whether the intended offense, namely, assaulting a federal officer, was affected by the conspirator's ignorance of the officer's identity. Justices Stewart and Douglas argued that there was no doubt that the offense was in the nature of an aggravated assault; therefore, a mistake about the aggravating circumstances should be relevant in assessing the actor's culpability.[6] Yet the majority of the Court, in an opinion written by Mr. Justice Blackmun, reasoned that the "federal element" was jurisdictional, analogous to the requirement that stolen bonds be shipped in interstate commerce.[7] The argument for this conclusion appears to be that Congress intended to protect federal police functions and that this goal would be compromised by permitting mistakes to undercut the actor's culpability.[8] The thrust of this argument is not that the status of the officer is extrinsic to the question of culpability, but that other "policy" values require that considerations bearing on culpability

[4] United States v. Crimmins, 123 F.2d 271 (2d Cir. 1941) (jurisdictional mistake said to be irrelevant on substantive charge, but relevant on charge of conspiracy to receive bonds shipped in interstate commerce).

[5] 420 U.S. 671 (1975).

[6] *Id.* at 696.

[7] *Id.* at 672.

[8] Note that the court seeks to overcome the cleavage between jurisdictional and substantive issues. *Id.* at 676 n.9. See §9.4 *infra.*

be disregarded. This argumentative strategy, as well as others in the opinion, is better reserved for our discussion of strict liability.

The assumption underlying this analysis of the relevance of mistakes is that if factor *X* aggravates the actor's wrongdoing, then a mistake about *X* undermines the actor's accountability for the wrongful act. An alternative way of thinking fuses the issues of wrongdoing and liability and thus generates an argument for admitting mistakes bearing on jurisdictional and related issues. Suppose that an embassy employee relies upon seemingly competent legal advice in concluding that he was entitled to diplomatic immunity. This mistake is arguably entitled to as much weight as any other reasonable mistake about the legality of conduct. If the "law" encompasses every issue that bears on the outcome of legal disputes, then all mistakes about the conditions of liability might arguably be entitled to recognition. The problem with this argument is that it presupposes a specific theory for recognizing the exculpatory effect of mistakes of law. The unresolved question is whether a convincing theory about mistakes of law is possible without recognizing the distinction between wrongdoing and accountability. This matter will engage us in due course.[9]

§9.3.2. **Arguments for Strict Liability: Special Governmental Purposes.** We define strict liability to mean liability imposed for an act or omission in violation of the law, without considering at trial whether the defendant may exculpate himself by proving a mistake or accident bearing on the wrongfulness of his violation. The assumption is that there is a relevant mistake or accident that the court might consider and does not. It is important to distinguish among categories of strict liability and the diverse arguments made for disregarding relevant claims of mistake and accident.

One prominent category of strict liability is the modern set of offenses designed to protect the public from impure food and drugs. The offense is typically committed merely by supplying harmful drugs or foodstuffs. The only additional element is that

[9] See §9.4 *infra*.

the defendant stand in some causally responsible relationship to the marketing of the goods. Liability is strict, for the defendant is not able to exculpate himself at trial by showing that he was excusably ignorant of the impurities in the marketed goods, and that he could not fairly have been expected to prevent the incident from occurring.

In the absence of appropriate criteria in the definition of the offense, it is almost impossible to determine which members of a corporate enterprise are liable for releasing adulterated goods. Is it just the general manager? The personnel in charge of quality control? The shipping clerk? Why not hold the board of directors and even the stockholders liable? If these lines are to be drawn in any coherent fashion, we obviously need a firm theoretical ground for dispensing with the excuse of ignorance. It is only by having a theory of liability that we can decide who of the many potential, non-culpable figures in the commercial enterprise ought to be held accountable.[10]

There are two independent theories supporting this form of strict liability and it is important to keep them distinct. One theory is that the offense is merely a civil offense, and the fine is imposed regardless of culpability, proven or presumed, in order to stimulate more careful behavior in the future. It would follow from this view that the matter should be taken out of the criminal courts altogether and treated as an administrative matter, analogous to the imposition of penalties for the late submission of income tax returns.[11] Imprisonment would be ruled out; the maximum penalty would be a fine.[12]

The alternative theory of strict liability is that it is not strict at

[10] This problem of circumscribing the range of liability is a major theme of the dissenting opinion by Justices Murphy, Roberts, Reed and Rutledge in United States v. Dotterweich, 320 U.S. 277, 285, 287–293 (1943).

[11] Sayre, *Public Welfare Offenses,* 33 Colum. L. Rev. 55 (1933); Ginossar, *The Autonomy of Corrective Law,* 9 Israel L. Rev. 24 (1974).

[12] See Commonwealth v. Koczwara, 397 Pa. 575, 155 A.2d 825 (1959) (sentence of imprisonment deprived defendant of due process, where defendant was held vicariously liable for employee's illegally selling a drink to minor; fine held permissible). *Cf.* Sayre, *supra* note 11, at 79.

all, merely that the element of culpability need not be proven at trial.[13] The occurrence of the objective event, namely, marketing impure drugs or food, raises a presumption of culpable neglect by the supervisory personnel. In an unusual case, where the presumption does not seem to hold as to a particular party, we have to trust prosecutors to make a prudent discretionary decision.

The latter theory seems to fashion the judgments of at least the United States Supreme Court. The leading case is *Dotterweich,* in which the general manager of a drug company was held liable for his company's "introducing into interstate commerce" mislabelled bottles of cascara and digitalis in violation of the Pure Food and Drug Act. The act itself was silent both on (1) who in the company should be held liable for "introducing" the goods into interstate commerce, and (2) the relevance of ignorance and mistake to liability. The Court of Appeals construed the act so as not to apply to Dotterweich, the general manager;[14] but the Supreme Court reversed and held, five votes to four, that the offense was committed by all those who have a "responsible share in the furtherance of the transaction which the statute outlaws."[15] The limitation of liability to the class of those with a "responsible share" in the harmful event comes close to a standard of culpability, for a "responsible" relationship implies a duty and a capacity to prevent impurities in the drugs supplied by the company. The failure to perform this duty permits an inference of culpability. There is no way to be more specific about the class of people subject to liability; for as Justice Frankfurter wrote:[16]

> In such matters the good sense of prosecutors, the wise guidance of trial judges, and the ultimate judgment of juries must be trusted. Our system of criminal justice necessarily depends on "conscience and circumspection in prosecuting officers . . ."

[13] Wasserstrom, *Strict Liability in the Criminal Law,* 12 Stan. L. Rev. 731, 743–44 (1960).

[14] United States v. Buffalo Pharmacal Co., Inc., 131 F.2d 500 (2d Cir. 1942).

[15] United States v. Dotterweich, 320 U.S. 277, 284 (1943).

[16] *Id.* at 285.

This is an important and revealing admission. Justice Frankfurter concedes that in the final analysis the criminal law cannot generate definitive criteria about who is liable and who is not. The problem of imprecise standards is mitigated by the sound discretion of prosecuting officers. Thus the more difficult problems of assessing liability may be ignored, for in the end we have to trust in the personnel that administer the system. No one could doubt that in any body of criminal law there would be some play in the human joints of the system. Yet the whole problem is how much play we should allow. Referring to the indispensability of personal discretion in the administration of the law hardly proves that in a particular instance, the degree of discretion is either desirable or necessary. Yet Justice Frankfurter's concession demonstrates that the rationale underlying strict liability is indeed a theory of presumed culpability; the presumption need not be tested at trial, for the pretrial authorities resolve the issue of culpability in exercising "conscience and circumspection."

Though the penalty in *Dotterweich* was a fine of $1,500 and sixty days probation, the rationale of the Supreme Court's opinion could support imprisonment as well as monetary penalties. The factor of "sixty days probation" is sufficient to undercut the suggestion that the penalty was merely a civil penalty. Further, the Court's opinion in *Dotterweich* builds on an earlier case, which had approved an indictment for selling opium without requiring an allegation that the defendant knew the substance to be opium.[17] A conviction and violation of this section of the Narcotic Act carried a maximum prison term of five years.[18]

The connection between culpability and the standard of "responsible relationship" used in *Dotterweich* has become more refined in the subsequent case law. The problem came before the Supreme Court again in United States v. Park,[19] in which the critical problem was the vagueness of the instructions on the issue of "responsible relationship" to the condition constituting the stat-

[17] United States v. Balint, 258 U.S. 250 (1922).
[18] Act of December 17, 1914, §9, 38 Stat. 785.
[19] 421 U.S. 658 (1975).

utory violation. The events triggering the prosecution were the maintenance of rat-infested warehouses in which the Acme Corporation stored food that was shipped in interstate commerce. The government brought charges both against Acme and against Park, who was the company's chief executive officer. Acme pleaded guilty on all counts, but Park fought the charges on the grounds that other people in the corporate structure were responsible for sanitation. The case was sent to the jury on general instructions that required merely a finding that the defendant held a "position of authority and responsibility in the situation out of which the charges arose."[20] The resulting conviction failed to withstand appeal. What is intriguing about the opinion for reversal is the language invoked by the Court of Appeals to express its judgment that due process favored "fairness and justice over ease of enforcement."[21] Instead of focussing on the concepts of culpability and blameworthiness, the courts stressed the danger that the jury instructions might have generated a conviction without a finding of "wrongful action"[22] or "personal wrongdoing."[23] This choice of terms reminds us of the argument made earlier that the requirement of wrongdoing is in fact more fundamental than the requirement of culpability.[24] It is difficult to discern, however, whether the court self-consciously opted for the language of wrongdoing in defining the minimal requirements of due process.

Though the Supreme Court reinstated the conviction,[25] the opinion for the Court, written by Justice Burger, attempts to reconcile conviction of the corporate executive officer with principles of justice and culpability. Gone is the emphasis on *Dotterweich* and earlier cases on "balancing relative hardships"[26] and favoring the "innocent public" over the "innocent defendant."[27] Al-

[20] *Id.* at 665 n.9.
[21] United States v. Park, 499 F.2d 839, 842 (4th Cir. 1974).
[22] *Ibid.*
[23] *Ibid.*
[24] See §6.6.3 *supra.*
[25] United States v. Park, 421 U.S. 658 (1975).
[26] 320 U.S. at 285.
[27] *Cf.* United States v. Balint, 258 U.S. 250, 254 (1922).

though the Court repeats this utilitarian rationale for strict liability in recounting the opinion in *Dotterweich*,[28] it does not invoke the perspective of balancing hardships in justifying the reinstatement of Park's conviction. Rather, the Court focusses on the inference of blameworthiness from the defendant's having a "responsible relationship" to the condition violating the Pure Food and Drug Act.[29] A strictly utilitarian rationale for punishment would, depending on the circumstances, favor punishing in a case in which the violation was unavoidable, for punishment even in this extreme case of moral innocence might deter violations in the future.[30] Implicitly rejecting a utilitarian rationale, the Court stresses the admissibility of an excuse in cases in which the defendant was "powerless to prevent or correct the violation."[31]

This discussion leaves us with the conclusion that the Supreme Court has backed away from a theory of strict liability in cases arising under the Food and Drug Act, particularly where the problem is simultaneously one of determining which person should be liable and what the criteria of liability should be.[32] In another line of cases, however, *Dotterweich* is invoked to dispense with mistakes about violations of even more serious criminal statutes. In United States v. Freed,[33] the defendant was indicted for possessing an unregistered hand grenade. The indictment was dismissed for failure to allege that the defendant knew that the grenade was unregistered. The Court reinstated the indictment on the ground that there was no need to allege knowledge as to the element of non-registration. One difference between this case and the pattern represented by *Dotterweich* and *Park* is that the focus of the prosecution is limited to the particular person possessing the

[28] 421 U.S. at 667–70.

[29] *Id.* at 673 ("a 'responsible share' in a violation of the Act imports some measure of blameworthiness").

[30] For a critique of the utilitarian theory of excuses, see §10.3.5 *infra*.

[31] 421 U.S. at 673.

[32] It is of some interest that *Park* was announced the same day as Mullaney v. Wilbur, 421 U.S. 684 (1975), a decision that, if read expansively, stands for the view that due process requires proof of all issues bearing on culpability. *But cf.* Patterson v. New York, *infra* note 37.

[33] 401 U.S. 601 (1971).

grenades. There was no need to define the range of corporate personnel liable for corporate activities.

The opinion in *Freed* is written as though a reasonable mistake about whether the grenade was registered was totally irrelevant. Yet this would be a hasty interpretation. As in the earlier case of *Balint,*[34] the only point at issue was the framing of the indictment and the prosecutor's burden to go forward on the issue. Nothing is said about the case in which the defense raised a plausible claim that he believed the grenade was registered (suppose that an apparently authorized official gave him an invalid certification of registration). Justice Douglas commented for the Court: "One would hardly be surprised to learn that possession of hand grenades is not an innocent act."[35] This may be true, but all that follows from this observation is that registration is a justificatory claim to be raised by the defense.[36] That explains why the matter need not be alleged in the indictment.

The doctrine of strict liability is a dangerous instrumentality that should be handled with the utmost care; one can only feel great regret that it is employed as a makeweight in cases like *Freed* where it is unnecessary to support the judgment and where it does not in fact express the judges' better intuitions of justice. It may be that after the decision in *Park,* the Court will have to be more careful in citing *Dotterweich* and in speaking of the "interests of public safety" as a rationale for disregarding mistakes bearing on the culpability of the accused. Though in the standard case of possessing a hand grenade, the defendant might be culpable, there are exceptional situations in which a reasonable mistake would negate the inference of culpability. If, according to *Park,* the defendant should be able to put into issue whether he was powerless to prevent the illegal rat infestation, a defendant in a case like *Freed* should be able to raise the claim that his mistake about registration of the hand grenade was unavoidable and thus blameless.[37]

[34] United States v. Balint, 258 U.S. 250 (1922).

[35] 401 U.S. at 609.

[36] *Cf.* §9.2.1 *supra.*

[37] Prior to Patterson v. New York, 432 U.S. 197 (1977), one could have argued,

§9.3.3. Arguments for Strict Liability: The Wrongdoer Runs the Risk. In the line of cases represented by *Dotterweich,* the argument for strict liability is either: (1) that the offense is civil in nature and no proof of culpability is needed; (2) that the offense is criminal but the occurrence of the result generates a convincing presumption of culpability; or (3) the second argument, coupled with implicit reliance on pre-trial administrative decisions to determine when the inference of culpability is warranted. These three arguments must be kept to one side as we turn to a distinct theory for disregarding claims of mistake. This fourth strategy is grounded in the principle that wrongdoers take the risk of their conduct turning out worse than they expected. If a man makes a malicious assault on another, and the victim turns out to be a police officer, the wrongdoer should be held accountable for the aggravated offense of assaulting a police officer. This moralistic argument bears close examination, for it continues to wield vast influence in cases ranging from statutory rape to felony-murder. Even the Supreme Court called upon the argument recently in *Feola,* arguing that the defendants knew "from the very outset that [their] planned course of conduct [was] wrongful."[38] If the victim turns out to be a federal officer, the Court reasoned, "the offender takes his victim as he finds him."[39]

The leading case exemplifying this strategy for disregarding mistakes is Regina v. Prince,[40] decided as a Crown Case Reserved in 1875. Prince had nominally violated the Offenses Against the Person Act by taking a girl under the age of 16 out of the possession and against the will of her father.[41] His claim for acquittal was that he believed, on reasonable grounds, that the girl was overage. The

further, that because the mistake as to registration bears on culpability, the prosecution must disprove a properly raised claim of mistake beyond a reasonable doubt, Mullaney v. Wilber, *supra* note 29. After *Patterson,* however, it would be constitutionally defensible to treat registration as an affirmative defense, with the burden of persuasion on the defendant. See §7.3.4 *supra.*

[38] United States v. Feola, 420 U.S. 671, 685 (1975).

[39] *Ibid.*

[40] L.R. 2 Cr. Cas. Res. 154 (1875).

[41] 24 & 25 Vict. c. 100, §55.

jury found that the girl looked the age of 18, and that she had told him that she was 18 years old, and that Prince reasonably believed she was 18. The question reserved for the judges was whether Prince's good faith and reasonable belief excused his violation of the statute.

Of all the judges, only Brett, J., favored acquittal; his grounds were that "a mistake of fact, on reasonable grounds, to the extent that if the facts were as believed the acts of the prisoner would make him guilty of no criminal offense at all, is an excuse. . . ."[42] The other judges opted for variations of the argument that a wrongdoer must take his chances about whether the girl is underage in fact. The opinion particularly worthy of analysis is that by Baron Bramwell, joined by seven other judges; for Bramwell, it was sufficient for conviction: first, that Prince committed a wrongful act, and, secondly, that the consequences of committing a wrongful act should be strict liability as to aggravating circumstances, such as the actual age of the girl.

The first prong of this argument has troubled many people, for the act that was wrongful in Bramwell's theory was itself subject to neither criminal nor tort liability. This did not matter, for as the Baron puts it:[43]

> [W]hat I say is wrong, is the taking of a female of such tender years that she is properly called a *girl,* can be said to be in another's possession, and in that other's care and charge.

Thus Bramwell seeks to distinguish between the core evil of taking a girl out of the possession of her father and legislative approximation of the core evil. The specific age of 16 functions analogously to setting the threshold of nighttime in burglary cases at 6:00 P.M. If the crime is committed at 6:05 P.M., the actor's belief that it was a half hour earlier could plausibly be disregarded. The burglary occurs at "night," even though the actor believes that the time was earlier than the technical threshold of nighttime. The essential evil

[42] L.R. 2 Cr. Cas. Res. at 170.
[43] *Id.* at 175.

of nighttime burglaries is that they be committed in the dark, not that they fall after the arbitrary cutoff time of 6:00 P.M. Of course, if the burglary occurred before 6:00 P.M., there would be no liability, for the technical definition of night provides an objective condition of liability. The setting of an objective threshold of "night" may be useful in defining the formal elements of the crime, but it does not follow that mistakes about the time, even reasonable mistakes, should undercut liability.

The thrust of Bramwell's argument is that the girl's age in years relates to whether she is a girl in the same way the threshold of 6:00 P.M. relates to the concept of night. Both are fixed points for limiting liability. If the break-in occurs before 6:00 P.M. or if the girl is of age, the objective facts preclude liability. But if the objective prerequisites of liability are satisfied, we confront an entirely different question is assessing whether mistakes about these prerequisites should negate the actor's culpability. On other issues, Bramwell was receptive to the claim of mistake as a bar to liability. He specifically mentions mistakes about (1) the father's consent, and (2) whether the girl was then in the possession or under the charge of someone else. He implies further that a mistake about whether the girl was a "girl" would be treated the same; if the defendant believed that she was a mature woman, there would be no intentional wrongdoing. But the reasonable belief that she was 18 was insufficient to negate the intent to take a "girl" from the possession of her father.[44]

We might be sympathetic to this first stage of Bramwell's analysis, for it runs parallel to our own efforts to determine the minimal elements that constitute the prohibitory norm for a given offense. Bramwell's argument is simply that the prohibitory norm is defined by the imperative against taking girls of tender years from the possession of their fathers.[45] The specific age of 16 years is

[44] *Ibid.*

[45] The theory of wrongdoing implicit in Bramwell's opinion conforms to the objective theory, which takes the "forbidden act," apart from the intent, as the "wrong." See §6.6.5 *supra*. Intent is treated as an aspect of *mens rea* rather than the wrongful act. L.R. 2 Cr. Cas. Res. at 175.

not part of the prohibition. Yet the second step in the argument should give us pause. Why does it follow from intentionally committing a wrongful act that one should be held accountable for circumstances that turn out worse than one reasonably expects? Is it that wrongdoers have no standing to complain about what happens to them? If a trespass to land triggers a fuse causing an explosion and death to a bystander, not even Bramwell would go to the extreme of holding the trespassor liable for the murder.

There were some special facts in *Prince* that limit the doctrine that the wrongdoer takes the risk of unexpected consequences. First, the wrongful act was directed against the victims of the criminal offense, namely, the girl and her father. Secondly, the impact of the mistake as to the age of the girl is ambiguous. It is not clear, according to Bramwell's theory, whether Prince would have been more culpable if he had known that the girl was underage. If the age of the girl is analogous to the definition of nighttime in burglary prosecutions, then it appears to be more like a jurisdictional consideration than an element bearing on wrongdoing. On the other hand, Bramwell does support his conclusion with the example of someone who assaults a person who turns out to be a police officer.[46] The fact that the victim is a police officer aggravates the assault, and thus it appears clear that Bramwell is committed to the theory that the wrongdoer as to a particular victim assumes the risk that the crime, as to that victim, will turn out to be an aggravated degree of the wrong actually committed.

The important point to underscore in Bramwell's analysis is that he simplified his task by considering only two alternatives: either the actor's mistake was a total defense or it was no defense at all. He ignores the middle position argued by Brett, J., and later advanced by Stephen, J., in *Tolson*[47] that a reasonable mistake as to a material element would excuse the violation of the statute. Bramwell is led to his oversimplified version of the problem by a misconception of *mens rea*. He reasons that *mens rea* must be equivalent to the notion of believing, knowing, or intending—in other

[46] *Id.* at 176.

[47] Regina v. Tolson, 23 Q.B.D. 168 (1889).

words, of having a "mental state" relative to the elements of the crime. He had no appreciation of the critical distinction between the subjective elements of the definition and the dimension of excuses. Once caught in this confusion, one is invariably led to the Hobson's choice between giving full weight to the mistake about the girl's age and giving it no weight at all.

Bramwell's opinion captures one of the more tempting and, in the view of many, one of the more insidious arguments in criminal law. The general claim is that wrongdoers deserve what they get; or, to put it more precisely, they must assume the risk that things will turn out worse than they expected. This strategy wields a particularly strong influence in statutory rape cases where the recurrent question is whether the defendant should have known that the girl was over the age of consent.[48] The act of fornication renders the actor a wrongdoer and, as a result, he cannot avail himself of an unavoidable and blameless mistake as to the girl's age. The injustice of this practice comes in degrees. If fornication is punished in the jurisdiction and statutory rape is an aggravated offense, then the injustice consists in holding the defendant to the aggravated offense, however blameless his mistake might be. If fornication is not punished, then a greater injustice attaches to relying upon legal conduct in labelling the defendant as a wrongdoer who must act at his peril.

The Model Penal Code recommended reform and recognition of a reasonable mistake as a defense—except as to offenses requiring the female to be under ten years of age.[49] The California Supreme Court boldly recognized the claim of reasonable mistake in *Hernandez,*[50] but this precedent has been systematically rejected in other

[48] One of the articulate and leading older cases was People v. Ratz, 115 Cal. 132, 46 P. 915 (1896), overruled in *Hernandez, infra* note 50. For recent applications of the same doctrine, see, e.g., State v. Silva, 53 Hawaii 232, 491 P.2d 1216 (1971); Anderson v. State, 384 P.2d 669 (Alaska 1963); State v. Moore, 105 N.J. Super. 567, 253 A.2d 579 (1969). See generally Annot., 8 A.L.R. 3d 1100, 1102–03.

[49] MPC §213.6(1).

[50] People v. Hernandez, 61 Cal. 2d 529, 393 P.2d 673, 39 Cal. Rptr. 361 (1964). *Cf.* Caljic §10.11 (burden on state to disprove claim of reasonable mistake beyond a reasonable doubt).

state courts.[51] The courts seem no longer to reason about the issue. The claims of the defense are rejected with a ritualistic allusion to protecting young females and defendants' acting at their peril. This is an area where legislative reform appears to be the only likely path for ameliorating the influence of *Prince* in the field of statutory rape. A number of states have legislatively adopted the recommendation of the Model Penal Code,[52] and one can hope that these legislative changes signal an emergent pattern.[53]

In another field illustrating the same principle, a defendant named White was accused of the unusual crime of abandoning his wife while she was pregnant.[54] He admitted the abandonment but claimed that he did not know she was pregnant. The jury convicted him on instructions holding that his ignorance of her condition was irrelevant. In affirming the conviction, the appellate court defended the theory that "a husband abandoning his wife is guilty of wrongdoing . . . a violation of his civil duty [and therefore] he does so at his peril. . . ."[55] For the sake of contrast, we should note that this theory that wrongdoers act at their peril does not apply in cases of bigamy. The person marrying under a reasonable mistake whether the first spouse is still alive is hardly a conscious wrong-

[51] See recent cases cited note 48 *supra*. On the vicissitudes of the defense in England, see Cross, *Centenary Reflections on Prince's Case,* 91 L.Q. Rev. 540, 548–49 (1975).

[52] Ill. Ann. Stat. c. 38, §11-4(b); Ind. Stat. Ann. §35-42-4-3(e) (Supp. 1977); Wash. Rev. Code Ann. §9.79.160(2). *But cf.* statutes explicitly rejecting the relevance of mistakes as to age. Fla. Stat. Ann. §794.021; La. Rev. Stat. §14:80.

[53] My theory as outlined in §9.2.1 *supra* would lead to the more radical result of recognizing every mistake about the age of the girl as a denial of the required intent. It seems clear that the factor of age is necessary to state the minimal set of incriminating criteria. German law recognizes this more radical effect of mistakes about age. See Schönke-Schröder-Lenckner §176, note 21, at 1130. If the seduction is not intentional, the defendant is acquitted. This generous recognition of mistakes with regard to age needs qualification in two respects. First, the German concept of intent includes *dolus eventualis,* which means that indifference to the age of the girl would be sufficient to say that the seduction was intentional. See §6.4.2 *supra*. Further, even if the defendant is acquitted of statutory rape, he might be convicted of "insulting" the girl's honor under StGB §185. See §9.4, at note 60 *infra*.

[54] White v. State, 44 Ohio App. 331, 185 N.E. 64 (1933).

[55] *Id.* at 334, 185 N.E. at 65.

doer. Positing wrongdoing in abducting a young girl, committing fornication or abandoning a wife presupposes that the actor could be fairly blamed for at least this lower order of intentional wrongdoing. In cases of unwitting bigamy, there is no comparable intentional act for which the bigamist can be blamed. Whatever some cynics might think, the act of getting married is hardly an instance of intentional wrongdoing.

The doctrine exemplified by *Prince* and its progeny would not be so insidious if it were limited in its impact to cases of statutory rape and other infrequently prosecuted offenses. Yet its impact reaches far beyond the wrongdoing of fornication and other sexual peccadilloes. The doctrine that the wrongdoer must bear the risk of unexpected consequences provides one of the major ideological supports for the doctrines of felony-murder and misdemeanor-manslaughter. According to these formal rules of liability, as they are explicated at length in Chapter Four,[56] the commission of a crime provides the foundation for imputing liability for a death that occurs in the course of the crime. If the underlying offense is a misdemeanor, then liability for the resulting death is classified as manslaughter; if the underlying offense is a felony, the resulting death generates liability for murder. Though there are other rationalia for these harsh doctrines, the most influential prop is probably the doctrine that a criminal has no moral ground to object to liability for the deadly consequences of his wrongdoing.

The flaw in treating cases of accidental homicide as murder or manslaughter, as well as the flaw in the statutory rape cases, is that these instances of strict liability ignore the principles of just and proportional punishment. Punishment should be gauged according to the gravity of the actor's wrongdoing; and the actor should be punished for the full measure of an objective wrong only so far as he is accountable for the wrong.[57] It might be objectively wrong to seduce a young girl, but the actor is fairly punished for this wrong only if he can fairly be held accountable for the turn of events. And if he could not fairly have been expected

[56] See §§4.4.2, 4.4.4, and 4.4.7 *supra*.
[57] See §6.6.2 *supra*.

to know of the girl's age, he cannot be held accountable for that feature of the case. If a robber non-negligently drops a gun, which discharges and kills a bystander, the robber is accountable for armed robbery, but not for the resulting accidental death. Punishing according to the degree of the objective wrong, regardless of the actor's accountability for the wrong, is to mock the classical principles of just punishment. It is one thing to deviate from principles of just punishment in the name of social utility, and quite another, to punish according to a truncated and distorted theory of moral retribution.

The injustice of *Prince* and its aggravation in statutory rape[58] and formal rules of homicidal liability may well derive from an inadequate comprehension of culpability in cases of mistake and accident. As the concept of negligence has become more refined, the formal rule of liability for deaths in the course of unlawful acts has receded. The misdemeanor-manslaughter rule has given way to the standard of gross and sometimes of ordinary negligence.[59] The felony-murder has either been abolished or more tightly drawn.[60] There are some signs of legislative reform in the field of statutory rape.[61] The time may come when the courts will be able to resist striking out at a wrongdoer who causes more harm than that for which he can be fairly held accountable.

§9.3.4. Arguments for Strict Liability: Mistakes of Law. The maxim that ignorance of the law is no excuse is so well entrenched in many legal systems that one is not likely to think of this form of mistake as a factor bearing on culpability. As a result, the practice of disregarding mistakes of law, when they do negate culpability, may not initially appear to be a form of strict liability. The question is put nicely in cases like *Hopkins*,[62] in which the court held a

[58] It's worth recalling that one view of Bramwell's theory in *Prince* is that the age of the girl is but an objective condition of liability comparable to the rule that a nighttime burglary occurs after 6:00 P.M. See text at p. 725 *supra*. The statutory rape cases do not lend themselves to this analogy.

[59] See §4.4.2 *supra*.

[60] See §4.4.5 *supra*.

[61] See note 52 *supra*.

[62] See Hopkins v. State, 193 Md. 489, 69 A.2d 456 (1950).

clergyman liable for the statutory offense of posting signs soliciting marriage, even though he had been advised by the state attorney general that the particular signs did not violate the statute. There is no denying that in a case of this sort, the court imposes liability regardless of the actor's culpability in violating the statute. Of course, to make this point we have to use the term "culpability" in the normative sense, meaning fairly subject to blame for violating the statute. If the term "culpability" simply meant "having the intent required for violation of the statute," there is no doubt that Hopkins acted culpably. Yet, reducing culpability to a question of intent does not eliminate the problem whether it is just to convict someone who acts in reliance on apparently competent legal advice. We start with the assumption that a just conviction presupposes that the actor had a fair chance of avoiding his act of wrongdoing or his violation of a statute. It is difficult to say that Hopkins had that chance when he did everything in his power to determine whether posting the sign was legal in the jurisdiction. Not even Bramwell's theory in *Prince* can support the conviction, for there is no underlying wrongdoing in posting a sign soliciting marriages. There is no coherent reason for saying that the actor must run the risk that a judge would disagree with the attorney general.

Various efforts have been made to defend the principle that even a reasonable mistake of law should not constitute an excuse for wrongdoing. In the early stages of the criminal law, when the range of offenses was limited to aggression against particular victims and other obvious moral wrongs, it was more plausible to assume that everyone knew the law. If someone did not realize that rape or homicide was wrong, one might properly expect a proof of mental illness in order to make out a believable claim. It is not surprising that the *M'Naghten* test of insanity is linked to the question whether, because of a mental disease or defect, the actor did not realize that the particular act was wrong.[63]

The tight moral consensus that once supported the criminal

[63] M'Naghten's Case, 8 Eng. Rep. 718 (1843). See §10.4.4 *infra*, for further details on the *M'Naghten* test.

law has obviously disappeared. This has happened as a result both of the vast expansion of the criminal law into regulatory offenses and the disintegration of the Judeo-Christian moral consensus. In a pluralistic society, saddled with criminal sanctions affecting every area of life, one cannot expect that everyone know what is criminal and what is not. The problem is compounded in some fields, such as abortion and obscenity, by constantly changing standards of permissible conduct. The "obscenity" that could send Ralph Ginzburg to jail for five years[64] is now readily exhibited at adult theaters around the United States. Assuming that everyone who violates the law does so in disregard and disrespect of the law is obviously outdated. Maintaining that policy today verges on blindness to the problem of individual justice.

Oliver Wendell Holmes confronted the problem directly and found a harmonic consistency between disregarding mistakes of law and his favorite chord: "to admit the excuse at all would be to encourage ignorance . . . and justice to the individual is rightly outweighed by the larger interests on the other side of the scales."[65] This utilitarian rationale for the traditional rule is hardly convincing to those who try to assess whether, in a particular case, the interests of society outweigh the interests of the individual. Surely, Holmes would not favor sacrificing the individual, however innocent, for the sake of the general good, however minimal. Therefore in a particular case, we have to assess whether or not the scales weigh more heavily on one side or on the other. If we wish to embark on this task of adjudication, how do we decide, and how should lawyers demonstrate, that one side of the scale outweighs the other? The problem with pursuing the general good is that the results of one instance of applying the criminal sanction are so speculative as to be chimerical. The problem with punishing a morally innocent person is that if one is willing to do that at all, the harm entailed is likely to appear either minimal or infinite: either because one does not perceive the evil of punishing the in-

[64] Ginzburg v. United States, 383 U.S. 463 (1966).
[65] Holmes 48.

nocent, or because one does perceive the evil and regards it as so great as not to be worth any transient benefits. In either event, Holmes' proposal bears witness to his own famous aphorism about legal method: "General propositions do not decide concrete cases."[66] The utilitarian calculus is too commodious a crucible for resolving concrete problems of mistakes of law.

Another rationale for disregarding mistakes of law is Jerome Hall's theory that there is a fundamental logical contradiction between deferring to the suspect's view of the law and the theory of legality. This argument merits consideration, for it illustrates the confusion engendered by a failure to recognize the distinction between wrongdoing and culpability. Hall's argument on mistake of law is best stated in his own words:[67]

> If that plea [mistake of law] were valid, the consequence would be: whenever a defendant in a criminal case thought the law was thus and so, he is to be treated as though the law were thus and so, *i.e., the law actually is thus and so.* But such a doctrine would contradict the essential requisites of a legal system. . . .

The fallacy in this line of reasoning consists in shifting the meaning of the word "law" as we move from the premise to the conclusion. In the phrase, "whenever a defendant thought the law was thus and so," the word "law" refers to the norms about which the defendant might be mistaken. In the conclusion, "the law actually is thus and so," the word "law" no longer refers to a norm or a rule about which the defendant is mistaken, but to an empirical concept of law equivalent to whether the court actually acquits in the particular case. These two concepts of law have little to do with each other. The norms of the law provide reasons for acting and reasons for convicting those who transgress the law. The empirical set of decisions—"what the courts do in fact"—does not provide a reason for convicting or acquitting anyone. The practice of the courts does not justify itself.

[66] Lochner v. New York, 198 U.S. 45, 76 (1905) (dissenting opinion).
[67] Hall 382–83. (Emphasis in original.)

The norms of the law do not change when a jury finds that a particular suspect could not have been expected to know, say, that posting a particular sign violated the law against soliciting marriages. If the suspect violates the rule in reasonable reliance on advice of the attorney general, the conduct may be subject to an excuse, but it does not follow that the court has engrafted an exception onto the norm. The proof of that proposition is that if the suspect, acquitted on grounds of mistake, left the courthouse and posted exactly the same sign, he would obviously be guilty. Recognizing a mistake of law as an excuse does not alter the norm any more than recognizing insanity as an excuse alters the prohibition against the conduct in question.

The more general flaw in Jerome Hall's system of criminal law is the failure to recognize the profound significance of distinguishing between wrongdoing and accountability or culpability. Recognizing a claim of justification does in fact acknowledge an exception to the norm; but recognizing an excuse means merely that in the particular case, the actor cannot be fairly held accountable for his wrongdoing. Mistake of law is an excuse that leaves the norm intact. Its effect is merely to deny the attribution of the wrongdoing to the particular suspect.

If there were any doubts about this, we need only ask how the norms of the criminal law would read if a mistake of law precluded a finding that the norm was violated. Norms are designed to guide and influence conduct. The norm itself cannot include a condition about what should happen in the event that the norm was violated involuntarily or by mistake. If it is unlawful to possess brass knuckles, the norm could not be read to say: Thou shalt not possess brass knuckles unless thou art reasonably mistaken about whether it is legal to do so. Nor does it say: Thou shalt not do *X* unless thou art insane or under duress or involuntarily intoxicated. The norm only includes those elements about which the actor should make a decision in seeking to conform his conduct to the law. It is not up to the actor to decide whether he is insane, whether the duress of another is sufficient to excuse a violation, or whether he is reasonably mistaken about the legality of his conduct. It is impossible to give an account of excuses by referring to the content of the norm and the question whether the norm is violated. The question of excusing arises after it is established that the norm is violated. The grounds for excusing are extrinsic to the norm and reserved for assessment by the trier of fact.

These two arguments rejecting mistake of laws—one associated with Holmes and the other with Hall—correspond to the two themes that run through this section on disregarding mistakes. One general strategy for suppressing mistakes is utilitarian: It is socially beneficial to eliminate the possibility of acquittal on some claims of mistake. The other strategy is moral or conceptual: There is some reason in the nature of the things why the mistake ought to be irrelevant. Bramwell's theory in *Prince* is a moral argument for requiring the wrongdoer to act at his peril; Hall's argument is a claim of supposed conceptual necessity. The response to both of these latter arguments is to expose the weakness of their premises; if the refutation is effective, we are led to see the injustice of punishing regardless of accountability for wrongdoing (Bramwell), and the fallacy of arguing that recognizing mistakes of law violates the nature of a legal system (Hall).

Utilitarian arguments raise broader questions of moral philosophy and, therefore, they resist refutation by laying bare their premises. There is nothing hidden in Holmes' argument. "Public policy," he tells us, "sacrifices the individual to the common good."[68] An assault on this explicit and coherent premise requires far more than the feeble claim that it is unjust to sacrifice the individual to the common good. Unjust it may be, but one needs to ground the imperative to do justice in a set of values at least as compelling as the value of furthering the social good. The most compelling argument offered to date is the Kantian thesis that the categorical imperative requires us to respect persons as ends in themselves, and we violate this imperative when we punish a person solely to further interests of other persons. The skeptic might wonder how the practice of punishing criminals can escape the

[68] Holmes 48.

charge of using persons as means to the end of deterrence and social order. The answer to this objection takes us back to the classical theory of punishment. If punishment is based on accountability for wrongdoing, then the punishing agency does not act in disregard for the wrongdoer's autonomy. On the contrary, the imposition of punishment—as contrasted with civil commitment—expresses respect for the wrongdoer's autonomy and his capacity to avoid liability under the law.[69]

§9.4. *Domesticating Mistakes of Law.*

Of all the fields of mistake, there is none more problematic than mistakes about the legality of conduct. Though there is a tradition against recognizing these mistakes, a number of decisions reflect sensitivity to the dangers of punishing an unwitting violation. In *Weiss,* a mistake about legal authority was sufficient to negate the intent required by the statutory definition.[1] In *Morissette,* a mistake about ownership of the bomb casings negated the intent required for common-law larceny.[2] In *Vogel,* a reasonable mistake about the validity of a prior divorce excused the defendant's entering into a bigamous marriage.[3] In all of these cases, mistakes either about legal norms or about factual issues with legal components were sufficient to prevent conviction. Yet the issue in these cases is never directly assayed as a mistake of law. The question is always framed as a matter of discerning whether the mistake negates the required intent or whether the statute defining the offense supports recognition of the mistake as an excuse.

These cases reflect what we might call a formal approach to the problem. The mistake is recognized so far as formal legal mate-

[69] *Cf.* §6.8 *supra.*

§9.4 [1] People v. Weiss, 276 N.Y. 284, 112 N.E.2d 514 (1938).

[2] Morissette v. United States, 342 U.S. 246 (1952).

[3] People v. Vogel, 46 Cal. 2d 798, 299 P.2d 850 (1956).

rials (an authoritatively defined intent, a statute) provide a basis for rationalizing the exculpatory effect of the mistake. The tension in legal theory is whether to adhere to this formal method of rationalization or to transcend the particular, rationalized cases in the quest of principled solution to the problem. Both the German and American systems have struggled to frame the issue as a matter of principle. The development in the German literature has admittedly been longer, more painstaking and more deeply considered. But events are moving fast in the United States. Numerous state statutes have adopted variations of the Model Penal Code recommendation[4] to recognize a limited claim of mistake of law.[5] The Court of Appeals in the District of Columbia recently grappled with the issue in reversing the conviction of two Watergate defendants who thought their break-in was legally authorized.[6] A comparative analysis could well generate useful lessons for both systems.

§9.4.1. **The German Experience.** The subject of mistake of law has served as one of the important foci of the German literature of criminal theory. The impulse for investing extraordinary energy in the subject is not its practical significance, but rather the shared faith that a civilized legal system should be able to articulate a just resolution of the problem. If we need a comparative perspective on this type of inquiry, we should think of the attention devoted to certain procedural issues in the United States. It may be the case that *Miranda* warnings actually make a difference in some few cases, but the debate about extending the Fifth Amendment to the station house raised deeper questions about how we, as Americans, perceive our system of justice and how we perceive ourselves. Debates about substantive criminal theory play a comparable part in the German conception of a just legal system.

[4] MPC §2.04(3).

[5] Hawaii Penal Code §220; Ill. Ann. Stat. c. 38, §4-8(b); Tex. Penal Code §8.03. The literature in English has long evidenced a serious effort to carve out a fair excuse of mistake of law. See Perkins 936–38; Williams 291–293; Keedy, *Ignorance and Mistake in Criminal Law*, 22 Harv. L. Rev. 75 (1908).

[6] United States v. Barker, 546 F.2d 940 (D.C. Cir. 1976). For discussion of this case, see text at notes 65–72 *infra*.

The early stages of the German development reveal many of the doctrinal gambits that we now witness in American law. A late nineteenth-century case provides an intriguing parallel to the style of statutory exegesis that led to a reversal in People v. Weiss. The defendant, a licensed hunter, shot another man's dog on a hunting preserve; apparently the owner had been walking the dog on the preserve and the dog left the footpath in order to sniff a tree.[7] The charge against the defendant was the wrongful and malicious destruction of property.[8] The defendant claimed on his behalf that he thought that he was entitled to shoot any stray dog wandering on the property, particularly if the dog left the public footpath. This claim of privilege was totally unfounded in the law, but the Supreme Court ingeniously interpreted the statutory language in order to justify an acquittal on grounds of mistake.

The Court's options were limited; for as of 1889, there were two rules governing the issue of mistake: first, mistakes as to the definition provided a complete excuse as to intentional offenses,[9] and, secondly, mistakes of law were totally irrelevant.[10] The only way to generate an excuse for the zealous hunter was to interpret his mistaken claim of privilege as a mistake about the definition of the offense. As it happened, the word "wrongfully" appeared in the statutory language defining the defense of wrongfully destroying property. If the element of wrongfulness adhered to the definition, the following line of argument was available: (1) the alleged justification negated the element of wrongfulness; (2) if the conduct were actually justified, the definition would not be satisfied; and therefore (3) a mistaken claim of justification would be a mistake about the definition and a bar to conviction for intentional commission of the offense. The whole argument turns on the initial premise that wrongfulness is an element of the definition; the

[7] Judgment of March 26, 1889, 19 RGSt. 209.

[8] StGB 1871, §303, carried forward in StGB §303. (Whoever wrongfully destroys or damages the chattel of another will be punished by up to two years in prison.)

[9] StGB 1871, §59. *Cf.* StGB §16.

[10] Judgment of September 25, 1880, 2 RGSt. 268, 269 ("A mistake with respect to punishability is irrelevant"). See Arzt, *Ignorance or Mistake of Law*, 24 Am. J. Comp. Law 646, 647 (1976).

alternative view would be that even though the statutory language refers to the "wrongful destruction of property," the word "wrongful" refers to the independent dimension of justification, rather than to an element of the definition.[11] It would follow from this alternative theory that the elements of justification would be distinguishable from the definition, and a mistaken belief in a justificatory claim would, at the time, have been irrelevant.

Caught in the vise of these conflicting extremes, the German Supreme Court was in a situation much like that of the New York Court of Appeals in *Weiss*. Either it had to recognize a complete excuse, regardless of the reasonableness of the mistake, or it had to treat the mistake as one of law and disregard it altogether.[12] The Court chose to recognize every claim of honest belief in the right to destroy property as a complete defense, as the Court in *Weiss* recognized a defense in every case of a good-faith mistake about legal authority to seize and detain another. The style of the opinion also resembles *Weiss*. The judges rely upon the statutory language in order to support their conclusion that wrongfulness was an element of the definition. Thus, like their counterparts in New York, the judges seized upon what might have been the fortuities of legislative drafting as a way of resolving a particular case without confronting the broader theoretical issue.

In an attempt to formulate an approach to the broader question, scholars and courts at the turn of the century began to work with the distinction between mistakes about norms of the criminal law and mistakes about non-criminal legal issues. The latter question is typified by the question in bigamy or adultery prosecutions, whether the divorce of a prior spouse is legally effective. If the divorce is not legally valid, the actor's mistake about his freedom to remarry (or to engage in sexual relations) is not a mistake about the criminal norm, but about a mixed question, partly of fact and partly of private law. These mixed questions of law and

[11] This alternative was accepted in the critical 1952 decision, discussed at notes 31–44 *infra*.

[12] The option of convicting for negligent commission of the offense was precluded because negligent commission is punishable only if the statute so provides, StGB §15 (codifying the principle), and StGB §303 was and is silent on the issue.

fact were treated as mistakes about the definition of the offense.[13] The problem of mistakes in criminal cases about prior divorces, which has generated so much litigation in the United States, could well be resolved by following this early German distinction between mistakes extrinsic and mistakes intrinsic to the criminal law. There may be a sensible policy in enforcing a duty on everyone to be informed about the prohibitions and commands of the criminal law, but it hardly makes sense to make people guess, at their peril, about the vicissitudes of divorce law.[14]

However sensible this approach might have been as a first step, it eventually broke down under the weight of casuistic arguments. The distinction between mistakes intrinsic and extrinsic to the criminal law eventually became too fragile to support extended litigation.[15] A good example of shaving the distinction to the point of internal collapse may be found in a prosecution in 1901 against a man who, after divorcing his wife, had an affair with the wife's daughter by a prior marriage.[16] Both the man and the young woman were charged with incest, and the question was whether the divorce terminated the relationship that made the affair incestuous. The criminal code defines incestuous relationships to include those of "marital affinity." There is no doubt that there was such a relationship while the male defendant was married to the female defendant's mother. The question is whether that relationship continued after a valid divorce. The court held that it did, but then it had to decide whether the defendant's mistake on this point was a mistake about the criminal law or about private law.

[13] For examples of mistakes identified as extrinsic to the criminal law, see e.g., Judgment of March 3, 1884, 10 RGSt. 234 (defendants illegally killed a badger; conviction reversed in view of the possible mistake whether the animal was a badger and, further, whether it was a protected species); Judgment of October 23, 1908, 42 RGSt. 26 (mistake regarding German citizenship excused failure to report to military duty).

[14] This distinction between mistakes intrinsic and those extrinsic to the criminal law is advocated in Perkins 938.

[15] The judicial distinctions were never warmly supported in the literature; see A. Schönke, Strafgesetzbuch §59, at 179 (2d ed. 1944). For a caustic critique, see 2 K. Binding, Die Normen und Ihre Übertretung 327--400 (1918).

[16] Judgment of November 8, 1901, 34 RGSt. 418.

The defendants argued convincingly that the mistake was one about private law, for a provision of the civil code prescribes that "relationships of marital affinity continue even after the supporting marriage is dissolved."[17] Yet the Supreme Court held that its conclusion about the nature of marital affinity was not dependent on the civil code, and therefore the mistake was an inexcusable mistake about criminal norms. The rationale for this result was that the defendant's having lived with the girl as a stepparent should have induced a moral inhibition against subsequent cohabitation; and therefore the mistake was properly regarded as one about the import of the criminal norm against incest. This reasoning is not implausible, but it became apparent in cases of this sort that the distinction between mistakes of criminal law and mistakes of private law was not as workable and dependable as many had thought.

In a distinct category of case, the special treatment of mistakes extrinsic to the criminal code led to a beneficial line of development. The First World War brought an explosion of regulations governing the economy and the distribution of goods. It was clear to everyone that knowledge of the special penal regulations could not be demanded with the same rigor as applied to the morally intuitive rules undergirding the criminal code. Therefore, a special ordinance, enacted in 1917, acknowledged that a non-culpable mistake about the applicability of one of these regulatory rules would constitute a valid defense.[18] The Supreme Court recognized this standard of mistake of law, for example, in a prosecution for violating an ordinance regulating the distribution of coal.[19] This special treatment accorded to cases of *mala prohibita* reveals the double-edged effect of classifying an offense as criminal only by virtue of its statutory prohibition. On the one hand, if the criminality of conduct derives solely from statutory prohibition, courts and judges are more sympathetic to claims of mistake of law; on

[17] BGB §1590(2).

[18] Law of January 18, 1917, [1917] RGBl. 58.

[19] See Judgment of May 11, 1922, 56 RGSt. 337 (acquittal on the basis of insufficient publication of the ordinance reversed; the excuse of non-negligent mistake would be relevant on retrial).

the other hand, the conception of offenses as "public welfare offenses" led to a widespread sentiment in Anglo-American jurisdictions that conviction for one of these offenses carried little stigma, and therefore, there was no great evil in treating them as occasions for liability.[20]

The doctrinal moves exemplified in the cases of the "zealous hunter" and the "loving stepfather" are suggestive of gambits recently explored in many countries seeking to domesticate mistake of law as an excuse.[21] What makes the German debate unique is that in the early decades of this century, the discussion shifted from particularistic doctrinal moves to the broad issue of principle: Why should the court recognize a claim of mistake of law? How does the mistake relate to the analysis of definition, wrongdoing and culpability? What is the connection between normative and descriptive theories of culpability and conflicting theories for recognizing mistakes about the legality of conduct? The sustained effort to confront these questions is one of the major reasons that the German theoretical work of the last half-century has achieved international stature.

One factor refining the theoretical work was the emergence of two major schools of thought on the issue. Each school had its adherents and its arguments. Each stimulated the other to hone its claims. The one school started from the assumption that "awareness of wrongdoing" was an essential condition of intentional conduct. In effect, the premise was a universalization of the position expressed in the case of the zealous hunter, namely, that the wrongfulness or illegality of the conduct was an element of the definition. In the German literature, this theory was called the "theory of intention" for it presupposed that no one should be punished for an intentional commission of an offense unless the violation of the law was also deliberate.[22] A corollary of the theory

[20] See §9.3, at note 11 *supra*.

[21] *Cf.* Stefani & Levasseur 314 (discussing validity of distinction between mistakes extrinsic and intrinsic to the criminal law); 1 Bouzat & Pinatel §184, at 272 (same).

[22] Prior to the enactment of the new German code, the leading advocate of this theory was Jürgen Baumann. See J. Baumann, Strafrecht: Allgemeiner Teil 408–11

was that if a mistake of law was negligent, the actor could be punished for the negligent commission of the offense—provided the code encompassed negligence as a form of liability. The closest analogue to this doctrine in Anglo-American law is the interpretation often given to the word "willful" in statutorily defined offenses.[23]

The "theory of intention" gained support from an analogy with the principle, found as well in tests of insanity, that an insane actor does not know that he is doing the wrong thing. The High State Court in Kiel urged this analogy in 1946, when it reviewed the question whether a mistake about the applicability of an economic regulation excused the actor's violation.[24] The premise of the argument was that an insane actor did not act intentionally because he did not (and could not) know that he was doing the wrong thing. It followed, arguably, that anyone who did not know he was doing wrong should be exempt from punishment. The questionable leap in the Court's reasoning was that what was true in cases of an inability to perceive the wrongful nature of conduct should hold as well with regard to all mistakes about wrongdoing. This logical leap ignores the significance of the actor's capacity to act otherwise.

The conflicting school of thought started on the assumption that the problem of mistake of law should be treated as an aspect of the more general issue of normatively assessing the actor's wrongful conduct. Its primary loyalty in the theoretical pantheon was to the normative theory of culpability, which distinguishes rigorously between acting intentionally and acting culpably.[25] The implications of embedding the problem of mistake of law in the analysis of culpability are, first, that there is no conceptual difficulty in finding that the actor committed the offense intentionally

(4th ed. 1966); for an early expression of the theory, see 2 K. Binding, *supra* note 15, at 791 (intent presupposes "a decision to reject the statutory norm"). For a decision embodying this theory, see Judgment of the High State Court (*Oberlandesgericht*) in Kiel, April 13, 1946, 1946 Deutsche Rechts-Zeitschrift 126.

[23] United States v. Murdock, 290 U.S. 389 (1933) (good faith negated "willful failure" to supply information to revenue agent).

[24] See note 22 *supra*.

[25] Hans Welzel was one of the early and consistent partisans of this theory. See Welzel 164–76; Welzel, *Schuld und Bewusstsein der Rechtswidrigkeit*, 5 MDR 65 (1951).

even though he is ignorant of the wrongful nature of his conduct; and, secondly, that not all mistakes should excuse wrongful conduct, but rather only those that are free from fault. The standard for assessing whether the mistake is free from culpability is whether it is "unavoidable" or "invincible." The issue is not whether it is, strictly speaking, "unavoidable" in a physical sense. Unless the applicable law is kept secret or its interpretation is not subject to intelligent prediction, there are always some steps that the actor can take to find out whether his conduct conforms with the norms of the system. The issue of "unavoidability" resolves into a normative assessment about whether under the circumstances and in light of his personal capacities, the defendant could have been expected to be more careful before undertaking an act that turned out to be illegal. There might be cases in which the actor is totally oblivious of his wrongdoing, as in the case of a German reared in Yugoslavia who committed incest with his stepdaughter; in Yugoslavia, the affair would not have been punished as incest, and therefore the court regarded this mistake as "unavoidable."[26] In other cases, the mistake may be "unavoidable" in the sense that the defendant took all plausible measures to find out whether his conduct was legal.[27]

The major difference between these colliding schools of thought is not how the courts should treat unavoidable, non-culpable mistakes, for under both theories these mistakes would generate a complete bar to conviction. The theories diverge in their treatment of culpable, avoidable mistakes of law. The "theory of intention" treated "conscious" wrongdoing as an element of the intention; thus the theory was committed to the view that mis-

[26] Judgment of December 6, 1956, 10 BGHSt. 35. An interesting sidelight of the case is that the court explicitly rejects the argument that a wrongdoer acts at his peril, discussed in §9.3.3 *supra*. *Id.* at 39.

[27] In its Resolution of January 27, 1966, 21 BGHSt. 18, the Supreme Court defined a mistake as unavoidable (unüberwindlich) when "the actor in light of the circumstances of the case, his personality, his station in life and professional role, could not, even with the degree of conscientious thought that could be expected of him, perceive the wrong he was committing." *Id.* at 20.

takes of law negated intent, and therefore were functionally equivalent to mistakes about the factual elements of the definition. It followed that a negligent mistake of law could be punished only if the crime was one that, according to the code, could be committed negligently. This implied that outside the field of homicide, battery, arson, and perjury, any mistake about the legality of conduct would lead to a complete acquittal. That is a consequence that would give anyone pause. And thus some of the proponents of this theory supported new legislation, to fill the gap, either with additional crimes of negligence[28] or with a general crime of negligence toward legal obligations.[29]

The major practical appeal of the theory of culpability is that it provided a more satisfactory solution to cases in which the actor's ignorance or mistake is due to his culpable failure to apprehend the wrongful nature of his conduct. According to the "theory of culpability," these mistakes do not excuse the wrongful conduct, but they may provide a ground for mitigating punishment.[30] Thus to summarize the practical disparity between the two theories, the "theory of intention" held that a negligent mistake of law could entail liability only if the code prescribed liability for negligent perpetration of the offense; the "theory of culpability," that negligent mistakes did not preclude liability but could at most affect the gravity of the punishment.

The clash between these two schools of thought came to a head in 1952, when the full bench of the Supreme Court was convened to consider the question whether consciousness of wrongdoing was an essential element of the crime of extortion.[31] The case arose out of a lawyer's threatening a client that he would withdraw from her case mid-stream unless she paid an increased fee. According to the statutory definition,[32] the crime of extortion is committed only by "wrongful" threats inducing another person

[28] Schröder, *Die Irrtumsrechtsprechung des BGH,* 65 ZStW 178, 209 (1953).
[29] See the discussion of the Gürtner draft, 2 BGHSt. at 207.
[30] See StGB §17, sentence 2.
[31] Resolution of March 18, 1952, 2 BGHSt. 194.
[32] StGB §240.

to act. The lawyer's defense was obviously that he did not realize that threatening to withdraw from the case was a "wrongful" threat.

The statutory language admitted of the type of solution that we noticed earlier in the case of the zealous hunter.[33] If the court had treated "wrongfulness" as an element of the definition, any mistake about whether the threat was wrongful would have been a good defense. Yet the Court eschewed manipulation of the statutory language and turned instead, in a breathtakingly clear opinion, to the general problem of mistake of law in the German legal system.

Before taking up the conflicting theories of "intention" and of "culpability," the opinion reviews the history of the case law in the Supreme Court prior to the war and concludes that the doctrines employed in these cases were but arbitrary, formal devices that permitted the punishment of some innocent defendants.[34] What was needed was a fresh, principled reconsideration of the entire subject. To provide the foundation for this reconsideration, the Court posited two premises that should be of interest to lawyers in the common-law tradition. The first premise was that the nature of the criminal process required that mistakes of law, in some form, be considered as an excuse. The argument for this conclusion is that criminal punishment presupposes a finding of blameworthiness (guilt, culpability), which in turn requires a judgment that the actor had a fair chance of avoiding liability.[35] This opportunity does not exist if the actor violates the law as a result of unavoidable ignorance. At the same time, the Court recognized that members of a civilized community bear the burden not only of conforming their behavior to law, but of finding out what their legal obligations are.

The second premise was that the Code of 1871 had not exhaustively regulated the criteria of excuses, and therefore it was fitting and proper for the Supreme Court to develop and define a

[33] See text at note 7 *supra*
[34] 2 BGHSt. at 200–03.
[35] *Id.* at 200–01.

general excuse of mistake of law.[36] This commitment to judicial activism may come as a surprise to many common lawyers who think of Continental law as confined to the contours of statutes and codes. The fact is that in its scope and sophistication, in the self-confidence of judicial role conveyed, this opinion by the German Supreme Court has no equal in the Anglo-American precedents on substantive criminal law.[37]

There are two reasons for this confident assertion of judicial power. First, the Court could draw on the refined debate that had already taken place in the literature. Secondly, the support in German theory for the distinction between the definition of an offense and the criteria of excuses meant that the judges felt unrestrained by the principle *nulla poena sine lege* in refining the criteria of excusability. The judges' duty of deference to the legislature was limited to the definition of extortion. There was no reason to defer to the legislature where the issue at stake was the justice of punishing in a particular case of violating the legislative norm.[38]

Unmoored from the restraints of legislation and precedent, the judicial craft was put to the test. Carefully weighing the conflicting theories represented in the literature, the judges found three reasons for committing themselves to the "theory of culpability." First, as indicated earlier, the sentiment was that all citizens bear a duty to attend to their legal obligations, which implied that in many cases, mistakes about the law were in themselves culpable. The "theory of intention" implied that unless the code specifically provided for the negligent perpetration of the offense, any mistake, even a culpable mistake, would act as a bar to conviction. This implication of the opposing theory struck the judges as untenable. To supply an analogy on their behalf, it would be like recognizing all claims of submitting to duress as complete excuses, regardless of whether in the particular case the actor's feeling coerced was an undue response to the threat. Secondly, in order to fill this ob-

[36] *Id.* at 204.

[37] On the other hand, it would be hard to find German precedents on procedural issues with the breadth and power of decisions like Gideon v. Wainwright, 372 U.S. 335 (1963), and Miranda v. Arizona, 384 U.S. 436 (1966).

[38] See §7.5.2 *supra.*

vious gap in the law, the "theory of intention" required a corrective, such as that of a new crime to punish negligence-of-law.[39] The theory of this new offense would resemble the provision of the German code making it an offense to commit a crime, any crime, while intoxicated;[40] the proposed corrective to the theory of "intention" would make it an offense to commit a crime while ignorant of one's legal obligations. Though the Supreme Court did not invoke the argument, the most telling point against this proposal is the obvious distinction between intoxication and ignorance of the law. It may be true that the culpability of committing a crime while intoxicated is a function of the general risk apparent at the time of imbibing. Yet the culpability of a wrongful act committed in ignorance is a function of that particular act, and the defendant's failure to consider whether his particular course of conduct was illegal. There is no activity that entails a general risk of acting illegally in ignorance in the same way that excessive drinking entails the general risk of criminal conduct.

A third substantial objection to the "theory of intention" is that it does not provide a satisfactory solution to the problem of morally committed violators, of whom there have been and continue to be many in twentieth-century German society. The class of morally committed violators includes not only civil disobedients, but revolutionaries, terrorists, and others who pit themselves against the established social order. The threshold issue in analyzing whether these actors are "aware of their wrongdoing" is whether the notion of wrongdoing is interpreted in a normative or purely positivistic sense. The problem is akin to the debate about the meaning of the *M'Naghten* test for insanity: does "knowing that the act is wrong" mean grasping and appreciating the moral point behind the prohibition, or does it mean simply that the actor must realize that the legislature has prohibited the act in question?[41] The assumption of the German judges was that "awareness of wrongdoing" meant more than realizing that other people re-

[39] 2 BGHSt. at 207.
[40] StGB §330a.
[41] See A. Goldstein, The Insanity Defense 51--53 (1967).

garded the act as wrong; no one could be blamed unless he violated his own internalized sense of right and wrong. It would follow that civil disobedients and revolutionaries would fall outside the scope of the criminal law.[42] By interpreting the opposing theory in this way, the Court, as it were, "drove it into a corner" in which it appeared indefensible; no theory of criminal law can tolerate the wholesale acquittal of revolutionary criminals. This *reductio ad absurdum* redounds to the benefit of the "theory of culpability," which treats morally committed violators as culpable on the somewhat fictitious ground that they should realize that their dissident values are wrong and society's, right.[43]

In the final analysis, the Court's opting for the "theory of culpability" was based on a combination of principled criteria and a realistic sense of how far the criminal law could go in accommodating a pure theory of moral blameworthiness. As we shall see when we turn to the theory of excuses, this tension and accommodation are inherent in adapting a system of blame and punishment to the undeniable needs of social protection. The important point to note about the German Court's resolution is that it did not appeal directly to utilitarian criteria of social protection, but rather sought an accommodation within an alternative theory of blame and culpability.

This path-breaking decision in 1952 established the framework for subsequent litigation about the types of mistake that would be regarded as denials of the definition and those that would be treated in the assessment of culpability. Though there are many points still debated, the formula that originated in the "theory of culpability" is now anchored in the new criminal code. Section 17 reads:

If in the commission of the [criminal] act, the actor fails to perceive that he is doing wrong[44] and if he could not have avoided this mistake, the ac-

[42] *But cf.* J. Baumann, *supra* note 22, at 408–09, defending the "intention theory" against this charge.

[43] 2 BGHSt. at 208–09.

[44] It would be more convenient to use the expression, "the wrongfulness of act," but this translation is truer to the German phrase "*Unrecht zu tun.*" StGB §17.

tor lacks culpability. If he could have avoided the mistake, his punishment may be mitigated in accordance with §49(1).

The process generating this well-honed principle is worth recalling, for it illustrates the style of law reform in Germany. The process began with a debate in the literature; one of the contending theories of the scholars won adherence in the case law, primarily in the landmark decision of 1952. Several decades later the successful experience of the courts was solidified in a new statutory rule. The same process of reform may be noted in the other fields, particularly the claim of necessity as a justification[45] and liability for commission by omission.[46]

The new code has hardly solved all the problems in the field. To see some of the refinements generated by the literature and case law, let us recall the six mistakes about claims of justifications and excuse from our introductory typology. The mistake might be:

B) as to justifications,
   5. that one is being attacked by an aggressor.
   6. that deadly force is permissible to stop a petty thief.
   7. that as a teacher, one is privileged to use corporal punishment as a disciplinary measure.

C) as to excuses,
   8. that unless one commits perjury, one will be killed by the defendant in the case.
   9. that the excuse of duress encompasses homicide as well as lesser offenses.
   10. that the jurisdiction recognizes the excuse of necessity as well as of duress.

These cases are symmetrical in the mode of their genesis. The two categories of excuse and justification intersect with three ways in which one might be mistaken—about the facts, about the legal status of facts, and about the status of a legal norm. The solutions, however, are far from symmetrical. The consensus of German theory is that cases 6 and 7 would be covered by §17 of the new code,

[45] StGB §34. See §10.2.2 *infra.*
[46] StGB §13. See §8.4.2 *supra.*

which means that if the mistake were free from fault, the actor would be excused and acquitted.[47] In cases 9 and 10, however, the mistakes are treated as irrelevant, however reasonable they might be.[48] There are at least two reasons for this limitation. First, these mistakes do not negate the actor's choice to commit a wrongful act. Secondly, the range of excuses recognized in a particular system is a delicate political issue; if mistakes could expand the range of excusing conditions, the courts and legislatures would lose control over the scope of acceptable excuses.

More difficult problems are posed by cases 5 and 8. With respect to both, there is a general recognition that unavoidable or blameless mistakes should excuse the defendant. The question is whether these mistakes should be treated by analogy to mistakes about elements of the definition or by analogy to mistakes about legal norms.

As to case 5, mistakes about justificatory facts, there is considerable authority supporting the same outcome as applied to mistakes about the definition.[49] One of the leading cases supporting this view came to the German Supreme Court in 1952.[50] Several defendants who worked as supervisory personnel in a children's home were charged with aggravated battery for mistreating the children. They claimed that their often brutal handling of the children was justified as an exercise of their disciplinary privilege. The Court recognized that, in principle, the defendants standing *in loco parentis* had a disciplinary privilege, but that the defendants had used excessive punishment in some of the alleged incidents. The question was whether the excess was due to misapprehension of the privilege or whether it was due to a mistaken understanding of the factual incidents triggering the disciplinary punishment. So far as it was the former, the mistake related to the legal prohibition; so far as it was the latter, it bore on the definition of the offense. It was important in the context of the case that the charge

[47] Jescheck 347.
[48] *Id.* at 381.
[49] *Id.* at 348–49; Schönke-Schröder-Cramer §16, note 13, at 244.
[50] Judgment of June 6, 1952, 3 BGHSt. 105.

was battery, for even if many mistakes were treated as challenges to the definition rather than to culpability, negligent mistakes could still support a charge of negligent battery.

It does not follow from this decision that mistaken claims about other justificatory facts need be treated in the same way. In fact, there is considerable uncertainty about which justifications should be governed by the principle of this 1952 decision on disciplinary privilege and which should be treated as mistakes of law, even if the mistake relates to the factual conditions for claiming the justification. It is not adventitious that the courts are more indulgent toward mistaken claims of those grounds of justification, such as self-defense and disciplinary privilege, that tend to be invoked in prosecutions for homicide and personal injury—crimes that admit of negligent as well as intentional perpetration. On the specific issue of consent, as posed in *Morgan* or other variations of the problem, there is little direct authority in the German materials.[51]

With regard to case 8, mistaken belief in excusing facts, the subjective experience of pressure is just as great, whether the danger is real or imaginary. Thus mistake must be taken into account in some manner. From the range of conflicting theories,[52] the new code opted for the standard governing mistakes about legal norms (even though this is not a mistake about a legal norm).[53] Thus the mistake must be unavoidable in order that the actor's conduct be assessed as though the threat and the danger were real.

Before we turn to a comparative study of recent developments in the United States, we should note some qualifications about the current state of German law. First, one of the pretensions of the German theoretical revolution was that a superior conceptual apparatus had supplanted the timeworn terminology of mistakes of fact and mistakes of law. As expressed in parallel provisions of the new code,[54] the superior terminology is based on the distinction

[51] See Jescheck 350–51.
[52] See the summary in Jescheck 382--83.
[53] StGB §35(2).
[54] StGB §§16, 17.

between the mistakes about the definition, on the one hand, and all other mistakes on the other. The latter are called *Verbotsirrtümer* or, mistakes about the prohibited nature of the deed. Any resurgence of the old distinction between fact and law is a source of embarrassment. Yet in decisions such as the 1952 case on disciplinary privilege, the organizing principle is obviously the line between facts and norms.

Another area in which the distinction between fact and law is still operative is the field of mistakes about whether a particular factual situation falls under the definition of the offense. For example, it is a crime in Germany for a lawyer to counsel both sides of the same "legal dispute."[55] In one case, a lawyer defended the injuring party in an automobile accident against a criminal charge, and then took up the insurance claim of the victim in a civil proceeding. He claimed that these were different legal matters, not the "same dispute." Though he was wrong in this assessment, it seemed that his mistake went to the definition of the offense and because the crime did not admit of negligent perpetration, his mistake should have precluded liability. Not so, reasoned the Supreme Court, his mistake was a *Verbotsirrtum* (a mistake about the legal prohibition), and therefore it had to be gauged by the criteria of avoidability.[56] The rationale for this less favorable classification was that the mistake related to the legal assessment of the facts, not to what the facts were. Though the Revolution may have banished the old categories of fact and law, the *ancien régime* obviously reigns from the grave.[57]

Another qualification should be added to insure a proper perspective on the German system. Though the rule that all mistakes about the definition bar liability appears to be highly solicitous of the defendant's interests, there are some important adjustments in practice. For example, in the field of mistakes about the girl's age in statutory rape cases, which has caused so much difficulty in

[55] StGB §356.

[56] Judgment of March 24, 1955, 7 BGHSt. 261.

[57] For notes on additional cases and comments on general trends, see Arzt, *supra* note 10.

Anglo-American law, the courts have found a way around the protective features of the law of mistake. Though any mistake about whether the girl is underage will prevent a conviction for statutory rape,[58] there is another offense that readily applies to these cases. It happens to be a serious crime in Germany to offend someone else's dignity, either by word or deed.[59] Intercourse with a girl under the age of 14 (the age of consent) can be treated as an insult to her dignity; it is irrelevant whether she feels offended or whether the defendant is mistaken about her age. Yet ignorance or a mistake about the girl's age can qualify as *Verbotsirrtum* and provide an excuse if, of course, the mistake is "unavoidable."[60]

Another feature of German law that makes the system less protective than it seems at first blush, is the institution of prosecutorial appeal. If the trier of fact finds that the defendant was mistaken about an element of the definition or that a mistake about the norm was unavoidable, the prosecution can appeal the decision. This option obviously does not exist in Anglo-American law, and therefore in the single trial in which the defendant is in jeopardy, the rules governing the exculpatory effect of mistakes might understandably be more favorable to the prosecution. It is a close question of strategy whether a defendant should prefer a single threat of conviction under less favorable substantive rules or whether more attractive substantive rules are worth the risk of an appeal and retrial. This analysis reveals how complicated it is to form any judgments about whether the features of one legal system, including both substantive and procedural rules, are more attractive than those of another.

Yet these qualifications are not meant to undercut the signifi-

[58] Schönke-Schröder-Lenckner §176, note 21, at 1130.

[59] StGB §185 (*Beleidigung*, translated approximately as "insult").

[60] Judgment of October 28, 1955, 8 BGHSt. 357 (the girl was of age but slightly simple-minded; the *Verbotsirrtum* turned on defendant's belief that the girl could responsibly surrender her honor); Judgment of the High State Court (*Oberlandesgericht*) in Bavaria, January 30, 1963, 17 MDR 33 (1963). (Defendant was unaware that the girl was underage and therefore was acquitted of statutory rape, StGB §176, but was convicted of "insulting" the minor under §185; reversed, for failure of the trial judge to consider defendant's *Verbotsirrtum* relative to the girl's capacity meaningfully to consent.)

cance of the German system's having refined a general principle of excuse in cases of mistakes about whether conduct is prohibited. The development of this defense testifies to a concern for justice to the individual, and to the principle of convicting only in cases of a fair opportunity to avoid liability. As significantly, the refinement of this issue reflects on the merit of structuring the issues bearing on liability and comprehending the critical difference between wrongdoing and attribution, between violating a rule and determining whether the defendant can be fairly held accountable for the violation.

§9.4.2. **The American Instrumentalist Rationale.** There is considerable movement in the United States toward recognizing a limited defense of mistake of law.[61] But the technique for fashioning the defense bears little resemblance to the arguments found in the German literature and case law. Instead of starting from the concept of culpability and reasoning toward the criteria for excusing a wrongful act, the American materials begin by identifying the types of mistaken, official legal advice that, if reasonably relied upon, can generate an acceptable defense. In the Model Penal Code proposal[62] and in the states adopting variations of the same proposal,[63] the types of legal advice are tightly circumscribed. The source relied upon must be an "official statement of the law, afterward determined to be invalid or erroneous."[64] This excludes reliance on advice by counsel and unofficial advice from law enforcement personnel. Excluded also is total ignorance of the law, however reasonable it might be; for ignorance does not derive from reliance on a misleading official statement.

One could interpret these restrictions on the defense as an approximation of the broader issue of culpability, but there is nothing in the drafting of the statutory provisions that indicates a felt connection between reliance on an official statement of the law and the issue of accountability in violating the law. An alternative

[61] See note 5 *supra*.
[62] MPC §2.04(3).
[63] See statutes cited note 5 *supra*.
[64] MPC §2.04(3)(b).

instrumentalist rationale is suggested by Chief Judge Wilkey in the recent reversal of the convictions of Barker and Martinez, two of the Watergate defendants.[65] Wilkey reasons that although the general rejection of mistake of law is sound, "in certain situations there is an overriding societal interest in having individuals rely on the authoritative pronouncements of officials whose decisions we wish to see respected."[66] Thus the focus shifts from discerning the requirements of individual justice to the benefits that accrue to the public if reliance on official pronouncements confers immunity from criminal prosecution.

The problem under this instrumentalist approach is deciding which officials are those "whose decisions we wish to see respected." In the case against Barker and Martinez, for conspiracy to violate the civil rights of Dr. Fielding, the claim for the defense was that these two had relied on the advice of E. Howard Hunt that breaking into Dr. Fielding's office was authorized by the President's staff. The defendants knew that Hunt was connected with the White House; therefore they might reasonably have relied on the supposed legality of a clandestine entry in the name of national security. A good deal of the opinion favoring reversal stresses the subtlety of the legal question whether in fact the executive could order wiretapping or a search without a warrant. But what is missing is any sustained attention to the question whether E. Howard Hunt represented the type of person or public office "whose decisions we wish to see respected." The opinion discusses the desirability of inculating confidence in the orders of police officers,[67] but never explains why it is desirable for citizens to rely upon the advice of White House staffers that burglaries are permissible undercover operations.

Judge Merhige concurs in the reversal, but narrows the rationale to conform to the criteria of the Model Penal Code. There is no sense in which E. Howard Hunt's pronouncements about war-

[65] United States v. Barker, 546 F.2d 940 (D.C. Cir. 1976).
[66] *Id.* at 947.
[67] *Id.* at 948.

rantless searches and national security expressed an "official statement of the law." Therefore Judge Merhige felt constrained to link Hunt with John Ehrlichman, then Assistant to the President for Domestic Affairs.[68] Attributing the orders to a higher executive officer apparently made Hunt's statements more "official" and brought them within the ambit of the Model Penal Code. And further: "The Executive Branch . . . is vested with substantive responsibilities in the field of national security, and decisions of its officials on the extent of their legal authority deserve some deference from [the] public."[69]

The curious twist that becomes evident in this decision is that mistake of law is not considered an excuse bearing on culpability, but a variation on the justification of superior orders. What counts is not the blameworthiness of the violator, but the status of the person who told him to commit the violation. Unlawful military orders generate a good defense "provided the defendant does not know [the order] to be unlawful."[70] What the soldier does not know cannot hurt him: he has no duty to inquire about the lawfulness of the order. This is apparently the way the Court of Appeals thought about the "'footsoldiers' of the Watergate affair."[71] Chief Judge Wilkey draws the analogy between these footsoldiers and citizens ordered by a police officer to assist in making an arrest.[72] This way of looking at the problem ignores the special reason for being indulgent toward the soldier or citizen faced with the choice between a sanction for disobeying an order on the one hand, and executing an unlawful order, on the other. While

[68] *Id.* at 957.
[69] *Ibid.*
[70] MPC §2.10.
[71] 546 F.2d at 943.
[72] *Id.* at 948. Note that under MPC §3.07(4), cited *id.* at 948 n. 25, a citizen "summoned by a police officer to assist in effecting an arrest" is not liable for unlawful arrest unless he "believes the arrest is unlawful." The treatment of mistake and the duty to inquire are the same as for military orders, MPC §2.10. But Judge Wilkey concedes that a "citizen is under a legal obligation to respond to a proper summons and is in no position to second-guess the officer." *Id.* at 948. Apparently, Judge Wilkey thought of the Watergate "footsoldiers" as a parallel case.

the soldier cannot walk away from this conflict, Barker and Martinez could easily have abstained from the whole affair. They were under no conflict calling for our compassion.[73] To think of them as soldiers or citizens subject to official orders, as the Court suggests, is to miss the essential features of the situation.

[73] *Cf.* United States v. Ehrlichman, 546 F.2d 910 (1976), *cert. denied,* 431 U.S. 933 (1977). The prosecution and conviction of Ehrlichman were based on the same facts and the same charge. But Ehrlichman could not point to a higher-up who gave him an order, *id.* at 925--26. Though he might believe in the legality of the break-in as reasonably as did Barker and Martinez, there was no excuse.

Chapter Ten
The Theory of Justification and Excuse

§10.1. *Tensions in the Theory of Justification.*

The notions of justification and excuse have, by now, become familiar figures in our structured analysis of criminal liability. Claims of justification concede that the definition of the offense is satisfied, but challenge whether the act is wrongful; claims of excuse concede that the act is wrongful, but seek to avoid the attribution of the act to the actor. A justification speaks to the rightness of the act; an excuse, to whether the actor is accountable for a concededly wrongful act. For all this apparent simplicity, the notions of justification and excuse lend themselves to considerably more refinement. In this concluding chapter we shall undertake to refine these basic components of our system and, in the process, discuss several specific claims of justification and excuse.

§10.1.1. The Interactional Effects of Justificatory Claims. The questions of excusing and assessing accountability arise only in the institutional context of deciding whether someone can fairly be held accountable for a wrongful act. In a system of spontaneous justice, such as the early practice of executing nighttime thieves,[1] there is no place for a system of excuses. Susceptibility to private punishment turns solely on the incriminating effect of appearances. The excuses of mistake, accident, necessity and insanity begin to develop only as the process of condemnation of punishment moves from the scene of the deed to the reflective deliberations of the courtroom.[2]

The implications of this point are important. Whether a wrongful actor is excused does not affect the rights of other persons to resist or to assist the wrongful actor. But claims of justification do. In exploring why this is so, we shall discover the way in which claims of justification function in creating and negating the rights of persons in a situation of conflict.

Consider first the right of the victim to resist an aggressive act. Suppose a starving woman enters a grocery store and starts to take a loaf of bread.[3] When the shopkeeper moves to stop her, she explains that she and her baby have not had food in several days; they have no money and she must take the bread. Does the shopkeeper have the right to resist her taking the loaf? The general understanding, according to the Model Penal Code[4] as well as German, French, and Soviet law,[5] is that the privilege to defend property or personal interests depends upon whether the aggression is wrongful or unlawful. If the attempt to take the loaf of bread is merely excused and not justified, the attempted theft is wrongful and the storekeeper may use at least reasonable force to resist the intrusion. On the other hand, if the intrusion is justified, the property owner must tolerate the taking of the bread. This point was recognized in a leading case in the law of torts, in

§10.1. [1] See §2.2. *supra.*

[2] Of course, excuses are also important in the informal process of blaming and condemning an evil deed. The more general point is that excuses are directed to anyone who seeks to pass judgment on a wrongful act.

[3] This hypothetical case is inspired by the Judgment of the Court of Appeals in Amiens, France, April 22, 1898, [1899] Recueil Sirey II.1.

[4] MPC §§3.04 and 3.05.

[5] StGB §32(2); Merle & Vitu 437; Ugol. kod. (RSFSR) §13; Kurs (GP 1970) at 356 (sufficient that the attack be objectively socially dangerous).

which a ship captain attempted to take shelter from a storm by mooring his ship at a stranger's wharf.[6] The wharf owner's employee prevented them from docking, as a result of which the ship crashed onto the beach. The wharf owner was liable in damages, for the employee's resistance was unjustified. The reason was that the desire to take refuge from the storm was itself justified on the principle of lesser evils; therefore, the wharf owner was required to submit to the intrusion. If in contrast, the intrusion was merely excused, say, on grounds of mistake or insanity, the wharf owner presumably would not have been required to submit. It is worth noting that even when required to tolerate someone else's justifiable intrusion, the owner may collect damages for the loss incurred by the intrusion.[7] If the shopkeeper were required to tolerate the taking of bread from his store, he would have a valid claim under the law of torts for compensation.

It is not transparent why the right to resist should turn on whether the intrusion is justified or excused. Perhaps both should be resisted, perhaps neither. It is easier to see why justified conduct should *not* be resisted. The determination that the conduct is justified presupposes a judgment about the superior social interest in the conflict. If the superior social interest is represented by the party seeking to moor his ship or the woman attempting to take a loaf of bread, it is also in the social interest to suppress resistance. On the other hand, if the act of taking the bread is merely excused, the woman may not be to blame, but nor is the shopkeeper to blame for her personal condition. It is not clear why the law should require one innocent party to defer to another. If the shopkeeper would not have a duty to give her a loaf of bread, there is no apparent reason why he should let her take it.[8]

Consider the effect of a justification on the rights of third parties to assist the justified actor or to act in his or her place. Claims of justification lend themselves to universalization. That the doing

[6] Ploof v. Putnam, 81 Vt. 471, 71 A. 188 (1908). *Cf.* BGB §904, discussed in §10.2, at notes 11–12 *infra*.

[7] Vincent v. Lake Erie Trans. Co., 109 Minn. 456, 124 N.W. 221 (1910). *Cf.* BGB §904 (sentence 2).

[8] Compare the duty to aid other persons in distress, §8.3 *supra*.

is objectively right (or at least not wrongful) means that anyone is licensed to do it. The only requirement is that the act be performed for the justificatory purpose, namely, to feed the starving mother and child.[9] Excuses, in contrast, are always personal to the actor; one person's compulsion carries no implications about whether third parties will be excused if they act on behalf of the endangered defendant. Thus, if the starving mother's stealing the loaf of bread is justified, a third person should be able to steal the bread for the sake of saving the mother and her child from starvation. If, however, the desperate act of theft is merely excused, no one else would be able to assert that excuse. If other people do assist her in wrongfully overcoming the resistance of the shopkeeper, they would be presumably guilty as accomplices in the theft.[10] Their accessorial liability would not be undercut by the mother's personal excuse.

A valid justification, then, affects a matrix of legal relationships. The victim has no right to resist, and other persons acquire a right to assist—apart from one exception that need not detain us.[11] Excuses, in contrast, do not affect legal relationships with other persons; the excuse is a claim to be raised only relative to the external authority that seeks to hold the actor accountable for the wrongful deed.

§10.1.2. The Problem of Putative Justification. If all these claims seem intuitively plausible, the reader should reserve judgment. The fact is that Anglo-American criminal law has never recognized these fundamental distinctions. The common law[12] and now the Model Penal Code[13] and its progeny[14] interweave criteria of justification and excuse in cases in which the defending actor reasonably, but mistakenly believes that he is being attacked.

[9] See §7.4.2 *supra.*

[10] See §8.7.3 *supra.*

[11] The exception is the case in which the person behind the scenes exploits a justifying set of facts in order to inflict harm on another. *Ibid.*

[12] See 1 Hawkins 110.

[13] MPC §3.04. *Cf.* other sections of the code, listed in §9.1, at note 6 *supra,* which evidence the same merger of justification with putative justification.

[14] See, e.g., Del. Code Ann. tit. 11, §464(a); Hawaii Penal Code §304.

These situations, which we shall call putative self-defense, are regularly called cases of justification.[15] Assimilating a putative justification to an actual justification undermines the matrix of legal relationships affected by a claim of justification.

To show that this is so, let us take a hypothetical case and attempt to analyze it under the rules of the Model Penal Code. Suppose that a shopkeeper has repeatedly suffered burglaries and on the night of our case, a group of men attempt to break into his store. He fights them by firing several shots into the sky, but the group re-forms and presses the attack. A policeman comes on the scene and in an effort to resolve the difficulty he begins to approach the store. The shopkeeper takes him to be one of the burglars and fires at him as well as the others.[16]

Let us suppose, further, that the shopkeeper shoots merely to injure and that this degree of force is within the permissible range of permissible force under the circumstances. Now the next step in the analysis: The policeman is pinned down by the shopkeeper's gunfire. He realizes that the shopkeeper has mistaken him for one of the robbers. But in the din he cannot call out to the shopkeeper. What should he do? If he does not fire back, he may well be injured or killed. If he does fire and injure the shopkeeper, will he be criminally liable?

The Model Penal Code tells us that the privilege of defending oneself arises when "the actor believes that such force is immediately necessary for the purpose of protecting himself against the use of unlawful force. . . ."[17] Analogous language defines the privilege to use force in the defense of one's property and habitation.[18] Under the circumstances of the case, the actor clearly believes that such force is necessary to ward off the imagined attack by the policeman.

The question is whether the imagined attack is "unlawful" or

[15] LaFave & Scott 391; Perkins 994 (using the term "privilege").

[16] The case is inspired by Courvoisier v. Raymond, 23 Colo. 113, 47 P. 284 (1896).

[17] MPC §3.04. *Cf.* §3.09(2), which requires that the mistake be reasonable for the defendant to be acquitted.

[18] MPC §3.06.

believed to be "unlawful." In a later section of the Code, we are given a prolix definition of "unlawful force" which can, however, be reduced to a simple point: force is unlawful if it constitutes a tort or crime or would constitute a tort or crime but for a particular kind of defense.[19] We are not told precisely what kind of defense is compatible with the use of forces being "unlawful," but we are instructed that this peculiar kind of defense is not a "privilege" and, further, we are given examples of defenses that do not negate the unlawfulness of the force: "absence of intent, negligence or mental capacity; duress, youth or diplomatic status."[20] It is clear what the drafters had in mind but which they expressed so indirectly. The kinds of defenses that do not negate unlawfulness are excuses and claims extrinsic to culpability. It turns out that the Code's concept of unlawful force coincides precisely with the notion of "wrongful conduct" as we have used that term in this book.

The policeman is not exercising unlawful force. He is not exercising any force at all. But the section on defensive force says merely that the actor must believe that "such force is immediately necessary for the purpose of protecting himself against the use of unlawful force."[21] The syntax of this clause is admittedly ambiguous. One could read the code to say that either (1) the defendant must believe in the necessity to respond to that which is in fact unlawful force, or, more generously, (2) the defendant may exercise the privilege if there is no attack, but he believes there is. If the first alternative is correct, then there would be no defense at all available in cases of putative self-defense. If we wish to recognize a defense on behalf of the shopkeeper, we must opt for the alternative. As the Model Penal Code is structured, recognizing the defense confers a privilege on the shopkeeper to use reasonable force to thwart the imaginary attack by the officer.

Now what is the legal situation of the policeman under fire? Must he submit to the shopkeeper's defensive force? If he returns

[19] MPC §3.11(1).
[20] *Ibid.*
[21] MPC §3.04.

the fire and injures the shopkeeper, would he be guilty of criminal battery? If we are going to search for a rationale to acquit the officer, we should first consult our intuitions about whether the officer ought to be acquitted. The conflict is one between two innocent parties, and therefore we should have no difficulty concluding that in an exchange of fire between the officer and the shopkeeper, neither should be liable for hitting and injuring the other.

Could we justify the officer's response on the ground of self-defense? Does he believe that the response is necessary to avert unlawful force? If we apply the definitions of the code, we must unfortunately conclude that the officer's response does not qualify as a case of self-defense. First, the shopkeeper's force is not unlawful under the criteria of the code. He has a privilege to use force and the definition of "unlawful force" says explicitly that unlawful force is not privileged.[22] Further, we cannot say that the officer believes that force is unlawful, for he knows that the shopkeeper takes him, the officer, to be an aggressor and therefore he is aware of the factual presuppositions for saying that the force is priviledged and lawful. The conclusion is (almost)[23] ineluctable. If we follow the theory of the Model Penal Code, the officer cannot invoke a privilege to justify a forcible defense.

Might the officer have an excuse for using force to save his life? Though the Model Penal Code does not recognize an excuse of necessity, we shall later consider the German version of the excuse,[24] which, generally speaking, would accrue to anyone whose aggressive conduct was necessitated by self-preservation.[25] The difficulty of recognizing the excuse in the face of the shopkeeper's justification is the point we made earlier: justified conduct represents the superior social interest and therefore ought to prevail. Suppose an officer comes to arrest a suspect and, though the arrest is legal, the suspect resists; the officer counters with force. If the use of force escalates and the suspect injures the officer to avoid

[22] MPC §3.11(1).
[23] See the text at note 31 *infra*.
[24] StGB §35.
[25] See §10.4.3 *infra*.

being taken into custody, would we say that the injury might be excusable on grounds of personal necessity? Surely not. The valid arrest justifies the use of force and if the force is justified, the party subject to it must submit. Similarly, if the shopkeeper's use of force is lawful, then the officer must submit to the risk of death.

We are led to conclude that if the shopkeeper's use of force is justified, then a response by the endangered officer would neither be justified nor excused.[26] If the logic of the Model Penal Code leads to this counter-intuitive result, then there is something fundamentally wrong in the premises of the Code. The flaw is the assimilation of putative self-defense to actual self-defense.[27]

German and Soviet legal theory both separate the problem of putative self-defense from actual self-defense.[28] The former is a problem of mistake and it must be treated along the lines suggested in the preceding chapter. It is only actual force that justifies a defensive response. It follows from the distinction that the shopkeeper's responding to an imaginary attack is a wrongful but excusable use of force. If the assault upon the police officer is wrongful, then of course, his defensive parry is a case of justified self-defense. Thus in an exchange of gunfire, each would be acquitted for injuring the other: the shopkeeper, on grounds of excuse; the officer, on grounds of self-defense.

The structure of German theory, and particularly the distinction between putative and actual self-defense, generates better results than the Model Penal Code, which, as we have seen, fails to provide a rationale for acquitting the officer if he should injure the shopkeeper. But perhaps we are too hasty in concluding that the Model Penal Code is inadequate to the case. We might say that the shopkeeper is justified in firing at the officer, but that nonetheless the officer might regard his firing at him as "unlawful force." It

[26] If the officer were reasonably mistaken about the facts, then he might have an excuse.

[27] Note that in Courvoisier v. Raymond, 23 Colo. 113, 47 P. 284 (1896), the court distinguishes between justifiable self-defense and excusable cases of putative self-defense. *Id.* at 119–20, 47 P. at 287.

[28] Schönke-Schröder-Lenckner §32, note 65, at 446; Kurs (GP 1970) at 364–65; Kurs (GP 1974) at 187. The distinction is also discussed in the more sophisticated French literature. See Merle & Vitu 435 (distinguishing between apparent self-defense and putative self-defense).

might be privileged relative to the shopkeeper, but not relative to the officer who is innocent of unlawful aggression. It would follow that both sides were justified in their use of force. Another solution, though not provided in the Code, is that both sides are merely excused, the shopkeeper on grounds of mistake[29] and the officer on grounds of personal necessity.

It would strike most Continental theorists as contradictory to say that both sides to the conflict were justified in their use of force. It is in the nature of justification, they would say, that if two people are locked in a conflict, only one person can be justified.[30] Indeed, this point was assumed in our earlier discussion of the way in which a justification affects the rights of others. If a justification is merely personal, as an excuse is personal, then a valid justification would not affect the rights of the victim or of third parties.

It is difficult to know how much time to spend on this subjective and personalized theory of justification. So far as I know, no one in the English-speaking world has defended the thesis in the literature.[31] But it would not surprise me if many people were drawn to it. After all, it is one, and perhaps the only way to defend the blending of putative self-defense into actual self-defense. It is a view that finds some support in a number of features of our legal system. First, the distinction between justification and excuse has never received the kind of attention in Anglo-American law that it has in the German legal tradition. The theory of self-defense itself oscillates between a rationale of excuse and of justification. Indeed this is the reason we reserve our discussion of self-defense until we have canvassed both the theories of justification and of

[29] The implication of both sides being excused is that there would be no general right of intervention by third parties on either side. The German theory of necessity would permit intervention by close relatives on the side of the police officer. StBG §35. If the officer were justified, anyone could intervene on his behalf. StGB §34. It is not intuitively clear which view is preferable.

[30] But it would not be contradictory to say that neither side acted wrongfully. Some German writers reject this middle ground between lawful (rightful) and wrongful conduct. See Maurach GP at 292. Compare the discussion of inconsistent duties, §10.4.6 *infra*.

[31] But see Merle & Vitu 437 (*"L'attaque est juste par rapport à l'agresseur, elle ne l'est pas par rapport à la victime"*).

excuse.[32] If this is the case, then it is not surprising that putative self-defense—a theory of excuse—remains within the bounds of the composite defense regulated in the Model Penal Code. Another explanation for assimilation is the recognition that justification includes a subjective element—namely, the justificatory intent.[33] It is not a major leap from this recognition to treating mere belief in the necessity of self-defense as sufficient for the justification. That the belief must be reasonable is an untroubling qualification. The fallacy in this reasoning is assuming that self-defense must be either objective or subjective, not both. The contrary view, which holds that self-defense affects the rights of victims and third parties, calls for an objective dimension of wrongful aggression as well as a subjective dimension of justificatory intent.

There may be a deeper explanation for the common law's thriving despite its failure to distinguish between putative and actual self-defense. The merging of the two categories responds to some basic tenets in positivist jurisprudence. The focus of a positivist legal system is on deciding cases that come to the attention of the police and the courts. This emphasis on deciding the ultimate question of punishability suppresses the importance of justificatory claims in affecting the rights of persons who interact with the party using force. When we say that a claim of justification (but not of excuse) affects the rights of the victim and of third parties, we do not mean solely that their cases will be decided in a particular way. These rights generate good reasons for assisting or resisting the aggressive party in the context of conflict. They are rights that the courts should recognize, but their initial importance is in the principles by which people guide their conduct in daily life.[34]

Another principle related to positivist jurisprudence is worth mentioning. If our problematic case of the shopkeeper and the po-

[32] See §10.5 *supra.*

[33] See §7.4.2 *supra.*

[34] Simply stated, positivism holds that all law is enacted law; therefore, the focus of positivist theory is on the behavior of enacting agencies, the legislature and the courts. But note that in H. L. A. Hart's more sophisticated version of the theory there is ample recognition of the role of rules in the daily interaction of making and rejecting claims of right. H. Hart, The Concept of Law 87–88 (1961)

lice officer should ever arise, the positivist might argue, the solution would simply be for the public prosecutor to exercise his discretion and not prosecute. The last resort of the positivist is to confess the incompleteness of the rules that govern us. There comes a point at which the law must give way to administrative discretion.[35] If there is any single point that distinguishes the approach of this book from that of positivist jurisprudence, it is the unwillingness to retreat to prosecutorial discretion as a surrogate for the principled solution of human conflict.[36] When the solution comes as easily as the distinction between putative and actual self-defense, the resort to discretion is hardly tempting.

§**10.1.3. Is There a Single Theory of Justification?** The range of issues that we might call claims of justification includes consent, lesser evils, self-defense, defense of others, defense of property and habitation, self-help in recapturing chattels, the use of force in effecting arrests and executing legal judgments, as well as superior orders. Given the variety of justificatory claims, one is hard pressed to reduce the entire field to expressions of a single underlying theory of justification. Nonetheless, German theorists have repeatedly tried to find the single strand that would tie together these diverse claims. Earlier theorists argued that the underlying principle was that the violation of prohibitory norms was justified whenever the conduct was the "appropriate means to a proper end."[37] The modern claim is that all justificatory arguments can be reduced to a balancing of competing interests and a judgment in favor of the superior interest.[38] Though the latter argument is more precise and offers a more significant account than the vague theory relating appropriate means to proper ends, even the theory of interest-balancing fails to take into account important values that shape the theory of justification.[39] Of these additional values, we

[35] See *id.* at 132–33 (discussing judicial discretion).

[36] On the way in which discretion transforms a system of excuses into a system of grace, see §10.3.3. *infra.*

[37] See Graf zu Dohna, Die Rechtswidrigkeit 48 (1905).

[38] See generally Schönke-Schröder-Lenckner §32, preliminary note 6, at 391.

[39] See Eser, *Justification and Excuse,* 24 Am. J. Comp. L. 621, 629–31 (1976).

should take special note of the concept of autonomy and the significance of acting in the name of the government.

A. The Value of Autonomy. The principle that individuals are free and responsible agents informs the analysis of consent, and a version of autonomy shapes one theory of self-defense.[40] Once accepted, the value of autonomy does not lend itself to being offset by competing social interests. So far as the rationale of consent is that individuals should be free to waive their rights, this capacity of waiver is not a contingent value, subject to repeated balancing against the opposing array of interests.

There is some evidence that at the fringes, however, the principles of autonomy gives way to competing social values. The prevailing view in Western legal systems is that the individual has the right to take his own life or to torture himself,[41] but he does not have the right to authorize others to do the killing or to perform a sado-masochistic beating.[42] That there is a personal right to suffer in these cases indicates that the rationale for limiting personal autonomy is not a paternalistic governmental posture toward the victim's injuring himself. If the issue were paternalism, the government should employ sanctions as well against suicide and other forms of self-destruction.

A more convincing account of the distinction between self-injury and consenting to injury by others derives from the danger of implicating other persons in dangerous forms of conduct. The individual who kills or mutilates himself might affect the well-being of family and friends, but this result depends upon the actor's relationships with other people. In contrast, the self-destructive individual who induces another person to kill or to mutilate him implicates the latter in the violation of a significant social taboo. The person carrying out the killing or the mutilation crosses the threshold into a realm of conduct that, the second time, might be more easily carried out. And the second time, it might not be particularly significant whether the victim consents or not. Similarly,

[40] See §10.5 *infra.*
[41] See §4.5.4 A *supra.*
[42] *Ibid.*

if someone is encouraged to inflict a sado-masochistic beating on a consenting victim, the experience of inflicting the beating might loosen the actor's inhibitions against sadism in general. Of course, the criminogenic implications of participating in violence are an empirical issue. Yet assessing these criminogenic implications requires a subtle balancing of interests. The victim's interests in having others aid him in his suicide or in experiencing a masochistic beating must be weighed against the social dangers of introducing others to forms of conduct that the law seeks categorically to discourage.

An analogous conflict between personal autonomy and competing social interests is played out in one of the theories of self-defense that we take up in the last section of this chapter. Now it might be argued that if there is a balancing of interests at the fringes of these justificatory claims, it follows that an implicit balancing undergirds every case in which the claim of consent or self-defense is accepted. That the claim is accepted arguably implies it is not a case in which there is overweening social interest in its favor. Though this point has some merit, it ignores the thrust toward absolutism in the principle of autonomy in the fields both of consent and of self-defense. It would be plausible to reject all competing interests, and many radical individualists do. This commitment to the dignity of the individual is betrayed by reducing the value of autonomy to one interest among many in the calculus of utility.

B. Acting in the Name of the Government. Claims of justification divide themselves into those that are essentially private, and those that are exercised in the name of the government or the community as a whole. The former list includes lesser evils, necessary defense, consent and self-help. The governmental claims legitimate intrusions against personal and property interests in making an arrest, carrying out a search, effectuating a court order or carrying out a military order.

That the violation of personal and property rights is executed in the name of the government brings into focus procedural considerations that, generally, are beside the point in the assertion of private claims of justification. A police officer cannot justify an arrest or the search of a private dwelling simply on the ground that the particular invasion of individual interests was the lesser evil under the circumstances. The requirement of a valid warrant is not so easily sidestepped, either in German[43] or in American law.[44] The police officer cannot simply balance the competing interests and then decide to proceed on his own. Both systems of law allocate the competence to weigh the competing interests to judicial officers. It is only in the face of a special risk of escape or the destruction of evidence that the police are entitled to assert their own judgment about the necessity of immediate intervention.[45]

On the other hand, the satisfaction of the procedural prerequisites for governmental intrusions carries a legitimating effect that transcends the balancing of interests in particular cases. If an American magistrate has determined that there is probable cause to support the search of a private home, the search under a well-drawn warrant is justified—even if it should later turn out that the judgment of probable cause was improperly made. Though there is some controversy in the American case law about the circumstances when a complainant may "go behind the warrant" to challenge the magistrate's judgment, the overwhelming emphasis in constitutional litigation is on the form of the police complaint submitted in the ex parte warrant proceeding.[46] If the form of the allegations is correct and the police do not exceed the scope of a prop-

[43] StPO §98 (preference for judicial orders to seize evidence and instrumentalities of crime); §114 (judicial order to take a suspect into custody).

[44] Johnson v. United States, 333 U.S. 10 (1948) (stressing of supremacy of warrant requirement in Fourth Amendment); Camara v. San Francisco, 387 U.S. 523 (1967) (administrative searches require a warrant). This proposition was once subject to fewer exceptions than it is today, Carroll v. United States, 267 U.S. 132 (1925); *Cf.* United States v. Robinson, 414 U.S. 218 (1973) (search incident to arrest in all cases); Chambers v. Maroney, 399 U.S. 42 (1970) (search of impounded car permissible without a warrant). *Cf.* StPO §127 (permissibility of temporary detention without a warrant).

[45] E.g., Schmerber v. California, 384 U.S. 757 (1966) (blood test without a warrant); Terry v. Ohio, 392 U.S. 1 (1968) (stop-and-frisk permissible without a warrant).

[46] E.g., Spinelli v. United States, 393 U.S. 410 (1969); Aguilar v. Texas, 378 U.S. 108 (1964).

erly drawn warrant, there is little that the affected party can do to challenge the legitimacy of the intrusion.

From a comparative point of view there is an intriguing diversity of sentiment about which category of justificatory claims, the governmental or the private, should be taken as paradigmatic of the theory of justification as a whole. In the history of the common law, the notion of justified homicide was always closely associated with governmental conduct. In Blackstone's *Commentaries,* for example, the discussion of justifiable homicide begins with the official execution of condemned criminals and then turns to the official use of force in capturing criminals, preventing escapes, and suppressing riots.[47] As a supplement to this discussion, Blackstone introduces the notion of justifiable force by private parties to prevent murder, robbery, and nocturnal housebreaking.[48]

In contrast to Blackstone's finding the core cases of justification in governmental action, the modern European view takes the claims of private justification to be paradigmatic of the entire field of justified violations. The central claims of justification under this approach are the principles of necessity or lesser evils and necessary defense, including defense of others and defense of property. Thus in the German Codes of 1871[49] and 1975[50] as well as the RSFSR Code of 1960,[51] one finds refined treatment of these issues in the general part, with little or no attention to the range of governmental privileges. In German and Soviet textbooks, the theory of justification is expounded in the framework of lesser evils and necessary defense, with only supplementary mention of other claims of justification. Though the Model Penal Code contains a detailed provision on the "execution of public duty,"[52] the Code brings the issue of lesser evils and necessary defense into focus as

[47] 4 Blackstone 179.
[48] *Id.* at 179–80.
[49] StGB 1871, §53 (necessary defense).
[50] StGB §§32–35.
[51] Ugol. kod. (RSFSR) §§13, 14.
[52] MPC §3.03.

the primary grounds of justification. Thus the orientations of German and American legislation may well be converging on the centrality of private claims of justification.

A study of all justificatory claims would go beyond the scope of this book, and here we shall concentrate on the primary justificatory claims of lesser evils and self-defense. The claim of necessity or lesser evils is particularly important, for its emphasis on balancing competing interests may be the source of the widespread belief that all justificatory claims may simply be a variation of this core defense. Whether self-defense is in fact but a modification of lesser evils is reserved for the concluding section of this chapter. One of the tensions in the theory of self-defense is whether the claim functions as an excuse or a justification. Therefore our study of self-defense must await our analysis of excuses.

§10.2. *The Theory of Lesser Evils.*

In the course of a century, the claim of justification by choosing the lesser evil[1] has undergone a remarkable expansion. So far as can be determined, none of the major nineteenth-century Western criminal codes contained a general provision entitling persons to violate a prohibitory norm whenever an imminent risk threatened an even greater harm. It has since become standard for revised criminal codes to recognize the claim. This is true not only in the Soviet Union,[2] but in West Germany[3] and the United States.[4]

The general outlines of the defense tend to be the same. First,

§10.2. [1] The defense could also be called the claim of the "greater good." But there is an important point implicit in it called "lesser evils" instead. That it is the lesser evil reminds us that the prohibitory norm is violated and this is important in accounting for the requirement of a justificatory intent. See §7.4.2 *supra*.

[2] Ugol. kod. (RSFSR) §14.

[3] StGB §34.

[4] MPC §3.02. For states adopting variations of this provision, see notes 52–60 *infra*.

the violation of the prohibitory norm must be undertaken to save an interest greater than the harm entailed in the violation. For the sake of convenience, we shall refer to these competing factors as the harm avoided and the harm anticipated. The harm in both cases is computed by considering both the total harm that might eventuate and the probability that it will occur. This computation generates a present expected value both as to the harm avoided and the harm anticipated in violating the norm. The conduct is justified only if the present value of the harm avoided is greater than the present value of the harm anticipated. This means simply that no act is justified unless its benefit exceeds its cost.

Secondly, the violation of the norm must be the cheapest means available for avoiding the threatened harm. Even if the harm avoided is the greater interest, the violation will not be justified if there is an alternative reasonable means for avoiding the threatened harm. Finally, the conduct is justified only if it is undertaken to avoid an imminent and impending danger of harm. Though the Model Penal Code overlooks this requirement, both Germany and the Soviet Union recognize the limitation,[5] and American courts have adopted it as well.[6] Later we shall assess the jurisprudential significance of integrating the requirement of an imminent risk into the claim of lesser evils as a justification.[7]

The remarkable fact about Western legal systems converging in the basic outlines of this theory of justification is that there are at least two distinct philosophical foundations for the claim. The German system came to recognize the claim of lesser evils by way of judicial recognition of transcendental norms in the legal system. Lawyers in the Anglo-American tradition have argued for the same theory as an offshoot of positivistic and utilitarian theories of law. The point of the ensuing discussion is to trace how these divergent traditions have converged on a single defense with comparable contours.

§10.2.1. Lesser Evils in the German Tradition: The Statu-

[5] StGB §34; Ugol. kod. (RSFSR) §14.
[6] See notes 68–69 *infra*.
[7] See §10.2.4 *infra*.

tory Background. The German Code of 1871 was silent on the issue of justification by choosing the lesser evil. The Code contained a provision on necessity, but the details of the legislated rule reveal that the drafters had in mind a theory of excuse rather than justification.[8] First, the provision applies only when the imminent danger is a threat to the life or limb of the actor or a family dependent. Secondly, there is no requirement that the necessitated act be undertaken to preserve a higher interest; this means that there is no required balancing between the harm avoided and the harm anticipated in violating the norm. In 1871 legal draftsmen had apparently not reached the point of self-consciously identifying particular claims either as matters of excuse or of justification.[9] Therefore the interpretation of this provision on necessity remained subject to debate.

By the turn of the century, when the German Civil Code was drafted and enacted, the structure of defensive issues reflected greater sophistication and self-consciousness. The Civil Code identifies two claims of necessity treated explicitly as matters of justification. These are worth careful notice, for they apply in criminal as well as in civil cases, and they provide the background for the emergence of the general theory of justification in furthering the greater interest. Here are the two provisions, translated in full:

§228. Whoever destroys or damages the object of another in order to avert an imminent risk to himself or another, does not act wrongfully, i.e., he acts justifiably, if the damage or destruction is necessary to avert the risk and the harm anticipated is not disproportionate to the risk (the harm avoided). If the actor faultfully brought about the risk, he is liable for damages.

§904. The owner of an object is not entitled to prohibit intrusion [on his rights of ownership] if the intrusion is necessary to avert an imminent risk and the harm avoided is disproportionately large relative to the harm that accrues to the owner of the object. The owner of the object can claim damages for the harm that he suffers.

[8] StGB 1871, §54.

[9] The style was simply to specify that if the defense applies, "there is no punishable act" (*eine strafbare Handlung ist nicht vorhanden*). StGB 1871, §51 (insanity); §52 (duress); §53 (necessary defense); §54 (necessity).

The structural distinction between these two provisions is that under §228 of the Civil Code, the actor claiming necessity is in a defensive posture relative to the risk emanating from the object itself. This situation is exemplified by the facts in Cross v. State,[10] in which a rancher shot and killed marauding moose in order to prevent them from destroying his crops. Under §904 of the German Civil Code, the actor claiming necessity is in an aggressive posture and, though the intrusion is designed to avert a risk of harm, the risk does not emanate from the object damaged or destroyed. This situation is illustrated by two leading tort cases, Ploof v. Putnam[11] and Vincent v. Lake Erie Trans. Co.[12] In the former case, a ship captain sought to take refuge from a storm by mooring his ship to another's dock. The dock owner refused to permit the mooring and the ship was destroyed in the storm. The court held that the dock owner was obligated to tolerate the intrusion under the circumstances and therefore was liable for the damage to the ship. The *Vincent* case supplements this principle by holding that if the dock owner does tolerate the intrusion and suffers damage to the dock, he can collect damages from the ship owner taking refuge from the storm. Both of these rules are incorporated in the German Civil Code §904.[13]

Several additional points about these two provisions are worth noting. First, the issue of compensation in tort is neatly separated from the question whether the conduct is justified. In neither case does the duty of compensation imply that the conduct is unjustified and wrongful. Under §228, the duty of compensation arises only if the actor faultfully brings about the imminent danger.[14] Under §904, the duty of compensation applies in every case of aggres-

[10] Cross v. State, 370 P.2d 371 (Wyo. 1962).

[11] 81 Vt. 471, 71 A. 188 (1908).

[12] 109 Minn. 456, 124 N.W. 221 (1910).

[13] Note that the applicability of BGB §904, at least in criminal cases, depends on the intrusion's being compatible with basic social norms. See Jescheck 265–66, rejecting §904 as justification for seizure of a stranger's raincoat in order to save one's own suede coat in an unexpected rainstorm.

[14] The rationale for liability is arguably not forfeiture of the justification, but creation of the initial risk that leads to the necessitated conduct. See Soergel-Siebert, Bürgerliches Gesetzbuch §228, note 18, at 779 (1959).

sive necessity, where the actor intrudes upon the interests of another and damages an object that is not the source but the risk. Another interesting point is that neither provision is based squarely on the principle that the actor is entitled to further the greater interest and only the greater interest. Under §228, where the risk emanates from the damaged object, the harm anticipated in nullifying the threat may exceed the harm avoided. The only requirement is that the harm anticipated not "be disproportionate" to the harm avoided. That is, the act is justified even if its cost exceeds its benefit (but not by too much).

The converse rule of disproportionality applies in §904; when the actor intrudes upon an object that is not the source of the danger, the owner is required to suffer the intrusion only when the actor seeks to avoid a harm that is substantially greater than the harm to the owner who is required to tolerate the intrusion. This was indeed the case in Vincent v. Lake Erie Trans. Co., where the saving of the ship and its cargo was pitted against minor damage to the wharf. Yet in the *Vincent* case and in the commentary generated by the decision, the rule of justification appears to be a straightforward balancing of interests.

It is not entirely clear why the balancing should be tipped in favor of destroying objects that are the source of the risk, and against destroying objects that are not the source of the risk. It might be the case that the owner of an animal or machine that endangers others is more likely to be at fault than the owner of an object that is not the source of the risk. Yet there appear to be other notions at work as well. The endangering object appears to be treated, anthropomorphically, as an aggressive agent intruding upon the actor's autonomy. As self-defense against wrongful aggression justifies inflicting a greater cost than the resulting benefit, so "defensive necessity" against intruding objects permits a similarly skewed balancing of interests. One cannot but feel that adjusting the scales in this way puts too much emphasis on whether the injuring object happens to be in motion, rather than on the criteria of responsibility.

Though both of these provisions from the civil code are designed to protect the whole range of human interests, they serve only to justify intrusions against property interests. Thus their structure is the converse of the excuse provided by §54 of the 1871 Criminal Code. The coverage of these provisions is worth charting:

	defense available	
	to protect	*to intrude against*
StGB §54	life and limb of actor and dependents	all interests
BGB §228, 904	all interests	property

These were the only justificatory provisions recognized in the early twentieth century. There was no defense available when the limitations of both provisions applied. This was the case whenever the particular act invaded an interest other than property for the sake of neither life nor limb of the actor nor his dependent. The recurrent problem in the early decades of the century was abortion to save the life of the mother. The injury to the fetus was not an injury to property and therefore fell outside the justificatory provisions of the civil code. The danger to the mother could not excuse an abortion by a physician unrelated to the mother, for the provisions and excuse applied only to risk to the actor and his family. Thus it was in abortion cases that the German courts faced the greatest pressure to expand the range of justificatory claims.

§10.2.2. The Emergence of Extra-Statutory Necessity. The decisive case broadening the range of justificatory grounds came to the German Supreme Court in 1927.[15] A German physician ordered an abortion after he diagnosed a serious risk of suicide if the distraught mother were required to carry an apparently illegitimate child to term. The case had been tried twice, and both times the trial courts had acquitted the physician as well as the mother. Yet the German system does not permit nullification of the law at

[15] Judgment of March 11, 1927, 61 RGSt. 242.

the trial level, for the prosecutor is empowered to appeal an acquittal. In the second round, the prosecutor only appealed the acquittal against the physician who had authorized the abortion.

It was fairly clear that under the statutory law of the time, the physician was guilty. The relevant provision of the code, §218(3), proscribed "the killing of the fetus." There was no reference to an exemption or possibility of justification in cases of danger to the life of the mother, nor was there any modifying word in the statutory proscription, such as "maliciously" or "unlawfully," that might have lent itself to interpretation on behalf of the defendant. He killed the fetus and there was no recognized claim of justification or excuse. By the letter of the statutory law, he was patently guilty.

The narrow point of this dramatic decision was the recognition of a new theory of justification: the abortion would be justified if, after conscientious weighing of the competing interests, the doctor properly concluded that the interests of the mother outweighed those of the fetus.[16] The deeper significance of the holding lies in the jurisprudential assumptions that enabled the Court to move the law in a new direction. To grasp these assumptions, we have to pause and add a few words about the German theory of law.

Like other Continental European legal systems, German law recognizes the distinction between enacted laws (*Gesetze*) and a notion of transcendent, unenacted law (*Recht*). The former laws are binding by virtue of formal criteria; the latter by virtue of intrinsic rightness. The analogous distinction in English is between common law and common right. Though there is evidence that we used the term "right" in this normative legal sense in the seventeenth century,[17] the term has withered and died in the positivistic climate of Anglo-American jurisprudence. The notion of *Recht* differs from extra-legal concepts, such as morality and justice; for *Recht* is the law itself. It is law both in a descriptive and a pre-

[16] The requirement of "conscientious weighing" became explicit in the Judgment of April 20, 1928, 62 RGSt. 137, 138 (the issue was importing illegal goods into the Ruhr district).

[17] See Dr. Bonham's Case, 77 Eng. Rep. 638 (1610).

scriptive sense. It describes the ultimate principles of a particular legal system and prescribes their acceptance as binding rules.

In the context of the criminal law, the important implication of the concept of *Recht* is the derivative, normative conception of wrongfulness. As the term "law" yields the negative "unlawfulness," the concept of *Recht* generates an analogous negation of law. This state of being in violation of higher principles of law is captured in the term *Rechtswidrigkeit,* a term that is pivotal in modern German legal theory. This is the notion that spawned our own theory of wrongfulness as an essential feature of criminal conduct. We chose the term "wrongful" instead of "unlawful" or "illegal" in order to capture the normative dimension of conduct contrary to right principles of law.

The nature and indispensability of "wrongful" conduct in criminal prosecutions provided the pillars for the German Court's erecting a new theory of extra-statutory justification. The foundation for this edifice going beyond the written law is the claim in the 1927 abortion case: "The concept of an offense requires both that the alleged conduct conform to the definition of the offense and that it be wrongful (*rechtswidrig*)."[18] The best argument for this critical premise is that the nature of criminal conduct lies in its incompatibility with the norms of legality. Similar claims have already been advanced in suggesting the logical connection between wrongful conduct and punishment. In contrast, the notion of compensation for injury does not presuppose wrongful conduct. Both the German Civil Code as well as the common-law precedents distinguish the question whether harmful conduct is justified (not wrongful) from the issue whether the party causing harm must compensate the victim.

Given the indispensability of wrongful conduct in the immanent structure of criminal offenses, the judges in the abortion case posed the next question: Is the legislative judgment in recognizing particular grounds of justification conclusive on the issue of wrongfulness? It is at this juncture that the transcendent nature of *Recht* and its derivative concepts becomes critical. The court con-

[18] 61 RGSt. at 247.

cluded that legislative judgment is not conclusive on whether conduct is rightful or wrongful, for these notions transcend the realm of enacted written law. Thus the judges themselves are in a position to determine whether the conduct conforming to the statutory definition of an offense is wrongful and therefore subject to liability. The outcome of the analysis is an invitation to judicial refinement of the criteria of justification. By interpreting the concepts of criminality and of law, the court put itself in a position to override the legislative judgment about what forms of conduct are wrongful. If a legislature rejects or overlooks a particular justification, such as the claim of lesser evils, nothing stands in the way of the court's adopting the defense as a negation of the required element of wrongful conduct. This is precisely the conclusion of the German Supreme Court in 1927.

The brunt of the opinion in the case is devoted to considering the form that the new justification should take. The debate in the literature of the time was between two general theories of justification—one based on the rationale of pursuing the appropriate means to a proper end; and the other, based on balancing conflicting interests. The opinion concludes that the principle of balancing interests is the more precise formula and therefore adopts it. The only disadvantage of the standard of interest-balancing is that it implies that intentionally killing innocent persons is justifiable whenever necessary to save an even greater number of innocent people. This is an instance of justification that might appeal to utilitarians, but few theorists with Kantian leanings are likely to accept the principle that innocent life may be sacrificed to serve a more valuable end.

There are many sensitive moralists who maintain that abortion is a case of directly taking innocent life and therefore should not be subject to justification by countervailing interests. The only way to avoid this conclusion is to argue that the fetus is a lesser interest than a person already born or at least less significant than the mother whose life or health might be endangered. The view underlying this claim is that the value represented by the fetus increases as the pregnancy nears term. A viable fetus in the third trimester of pregnancy weighs more heavily in the balance than an embryo in the first trimester of gestation.[19] In 1927 the German Court took the view that as a general matter, the fetus is an interest less worthy of protection than the endangered pregnant woman. The argument is ingenious. The judges compared the statutory penalties for abortion with those for homicide and concluded that because those for abortion were lower, the code itself conveyed an implicit social judgment that "death and serious bodily harm are more serious evils than the loss of the fetus' life."[20] It may be true that the legislature took the acts of killing humans to be more egregious than the acts of killing fetuses, but there may be reasons for this judgment other than the relative weights of persons born and unborn. The lower punishment for abortion may reflect an awareness that killing a fetus is often the consequence of agonized decision-making and not the product of malice, premeditation, and deliberation. That the element of culpability is lower warrants a reduced punishment even if the interests damaged are of comparable value.[21]

For nearly a half century, spanning the innovative decision in 1927 to the enactment of the new Code in 1975, the claim of lesser evils was known in German law as the rule of extra-statutory necessity (*übergesetzlicher Notstand*).[22] Though it was a firm principle of the German legal system, it failed to find its way into the statutory law until the legislature adopted a comprehensive revision of the Criminal Code.[23] By looking at some concrete cases, we shall attempt to probe the features of the new theory of justification.

In 1951 the Supreme Court of the Federal Republic faced the question whether a German officer was guilty of battery and crim-

[19] *Cf.* Roe v. Wade, 410 U.S. 113 (1973).

[20] 61 RGSt. at 255 (maximum penalty for abortion, five years; but ten years for someone who performed an abortion for a fee, StGB 1871, §219).

[21] Compare the mitigating punishment for a mother's killing an illegitimate child. StGB §217 (penalty from six months to five years). German scholars interpret the reduced penalty as a legislative determination of reduced culpability. See §4.5.4 B *supra*.

[22] The term enjoys international currency. See 3 Jiménez de Asúa, Tratado de Derecho Penal 1069–71 (3d ed. 1965) (discussion of *la justificación supralegal*).

[23] StGB §34.

inal intimidation for ordering the physical beating of German soldiers under his charge in a Soviet prisoner of war camp.[24] The defendants sought to invoke the principle of extra-statutory necessity by arguing that his purpose in beating the soldiers was to get information about who was stealing supplies in the camp. In the defendant's view, the livelihood of all the prisoners was at stake and therefore he was justified in using harsh measures to suppress the stealing. The trial court found three distinct defects in the claim and rejected the defense; the Supreme Court affirmed.

The three reasons the defense did not apply were, first, that the risk of the harm to the inmates of the camp was not sufficiently imminent to warrant the use of physical brutality to detect the thieves. The Supreme Court regarded the issue of imminence as a factual matter, properly relegated under German law to the trier of fact. Secondly, the use of physical intimidation did not appear to be the cheapest means available to rescue the interests of the prisoners from the dangers of thievery. The trial court was convinced that in view of the defendant commandant's relationship with the Soviet authorities in charge of the camp, he could have secured the safety of the inmates by less costly means. And, thirdly, the defendant's case did not meet the subjective requirement clarified in the case law shortly after the 1927 abortion case. He did not engage in a process of "conscientiously" balancing and weighing the competing interests.[25] This unusual requirement is presumably designed to insure that people do not casually second-guess the legislative judgment about prohibited conduct.

Subsequent cases demonstrate a willingness to recognize the claim of lesser evils as well as to discipline the issue with tightly hewn requirements. In a 1959 case, the Supreme Court upheld the acquittal of two defendants who had locked up their mentally ill mother; the justification for the confinement was that this was the most suitable form of care under the circumstances.[26] Though this case is treated as a matter of extra-statutory necessity, it does not,

[24] Judgment of the Supreme Court, July 12, 1951, 1951 NJW 769.
[25] See note 16 *supra*.
[26] Judgment of June 16, 1959, 13 BGHSt. 197.

strictly speaking, represent a choice between conflicting interests. The primary issue was whether, in the absence of a court order, the defendant could make a determination about appropriate coercive measures in caring for their mentally ill mother. The Court held that a court order of guardianship was not required.[27] In a 1968 case the Supreme Court upheld a physician's breaching his duty of confidentiality to a schizophrenic patient (which breach is a crime under German law)[28] by reporting the patient's dangerous state to the authorities in charge of issuing and revoking driver's licenses.[29] The interest of public safety was held to outweigh the physician's statutory duty of confidentiality.[30] The Court might properly have been more concerned about the issues that defeated the claim of the commandant in the prison camp case. Doubts might have been raised about whether the risk of an accident was imminent and whether cheaper means were available to avoid the risk of unsafe driving. Apparently the lesser significance of the harm caused (breaching the duty of confidentiality), rendered it easier to make out a claim of justified necessity.

A 1974 case is illuminating, for it reveals the way in which a recurrent American issue is framed differently under German law. The case arose in a special procedure available in German law to compel prosecution after the prosecutor's office has decided not to file charges.[31] The complainant's husband was killed in an accident; the body was taken to the morgue and, on suspicion that the decedent was intoxicated at the time of the accident, the officials in the morgue took a blood test. Because the test established the decedent's intoxication and by implication his contributory fault in

[27] There was a problem of lesser evils implicit in the case and therefore it is cited as an example of necessity as a justification, Schönke-Schröder-Lenckner §34, note 2, at 450. But the narrow issue analyzed by the court was whether the defendants, acquitted at trial could recover for the costs of the defense. This they could only do if their innocence was "proven." StPO §467(2). The court held that this was the case and awarded the expenses.

[28] StGB 1871, §300; now StGB §203 (1).

[29] Judgment of the Supreme Court, October 8, 1968, 1968 NJW 288.

[30] The physician's duty itself was interpreted to serve the common good as well as personal privacy. *Id.* at 290.

[31] StPO §172.

the accident, the complainant was denied a pension. She sought to have the officials prosecuted for violating §168 of the Criminal Code, which prohibits *inter alia* desecrating a corpse or taking a corpse or parts of it out of the possession of the rightful possessor.[32] It is not at all clear that taking the blood test satisfied the definition of the offense,[33] but to bolster its conclusion that the prosecution was not warranted, the court argued that the taking was justified under the principle of extra-statutory necessity. The interest in determining whether the complainant was entitled to a pension outweighed the value of respecting the corpse. The case reveals the extent to which issues of justification lurk in the interstices of numerous crimes. These are issues that could be readily resolved in interpreting the definition of the offense.

The issue of involuntary blood tests is more familiar to American lawyers in the context of determining whether a search warrant is required for a body search.[34] Analogous arguments of justification come into play in determining that the interests of law enforcement permit exceptions to the Fourth Amendment requirement that, whenever practicable, a magistrate should decide whether a search should be executed.[35] It is doubtful, however, that the search of a dead body would raise an issue of constitutional dimension in the United States.

The 1975 Criminal Code brought the defense of lesser evils under legislative control for the first time in its long history. In addition to the details of the justification already crystallized in the case law, §34 of the new code contains two noteworthy points. First, it is not sufficient that the harm avoided simply outweigh the harm caused. The former must "essentially" or "substantially" outweigh the latter. This provision differentiates the German rule

[32] Judgment of the High State Court (*Oberlandesgericht*), in Frankfurt, November 11, 1974, 1975 NJW 271.

[33] StGB §168 (requiring at minimum the taking of "parts of the body" (*Leichenteile*)).

[34] Schmerber v. California, 384 U.S. 757 (1966).

[35] *Id.* at 770 ("the officer . . . might reasonably have believed that he was confronted with an emergency, in which the delay necessary to obtain a warrant . . . threatened 'the destruction of the evidence.' ").

from the analogous Soviet provision,[36] the Model Penal Code,[37] and the rules of several American states,[38] all of which require that the harm avoided simply be greater than the harm caused. Other new statutes, adopted in the United States,[39] follow the German pattern and require that the benefit of the deed "clearly outweigh" the injury the statute seeks to suppress.

Secondly, the German provision contains a unique qualification, not found in other legislative versions of the issue, which requires that the "act be an appropriate means"[40] to avoid the risk. This qualification harks back to the older German rationale of the justification, which was rejected in the 1927 abortion case. The sensible interpretation of this qualification is that it excludes the justification of killings like the killing and consuming of the cabin boy in *Dudley & Stevens;*[41] even if this killing might have spared the lives of three men, the taking of "innocent life" is not an "appropriate means" of averting the risk of starvation. This interpretation of the German qualification seems all the more compelling by contrast to the Model Penal Code which lacks a comparable provision and which, as the commentary to the code suggests,[42] would apply even in cases of taking innocent life. Utilitarians have no reason to regard the taking of innocent life as categorically forbidden. Yet some German commentators say that the additional qualification in the German Code is superfluous.[43] The additional sentence is supposedly not necessary to exclude the killing of the innocent, for these killings fall beyond the scope of justified conduct, whether there be a clause on the "appropriateness" of conduct or not. The logic of this argument is baffling, for if balancing interests is the only standard for justifying conduct, one is

[36] Ugol. kod. (RSFSR) §14.

[37] MPC §3.02.

[38] E.g., Pa. Cons. Stat. Ann. tit. 18, §503; Hawaii Penal Code §302.

[39] Tex. Penal Code §9.22; N.Y. Penal Law §35.05(2).

[40] StGB §34 (*ein angemessenes Mittel*).

[41] Regina v. Dudley & Stephens, 14 Q.B.D. 273 (1884).

[42] MPC §3.02, Comment at 10 (Tent. Draft No. 8, 1958).

[43] Schönke-Schröder-Lenckner §34, note 46, at 463 (and authorities cited). *But cf.* Jescheck 269 (maintaining that the "appropriate means" fulfills an important independent purpose).

led ineluctably to the conclusion that killing one person is justified to save three.[44]

The more sensible way to interpret the qualification of "appropriate means" is that despite the nominal connection between utilitarianism and balancing interests, the German legal system stands opposed to a utilitarian theory of law. None of the leading commentators seriously considers the possibility that killing the innocent would be justified in order to save a greater number of lives. Indeed it is surprising that the German legal theory ever brought the notion of *Recht* into the same matrix as conduct furthering the greater social good. No one could plausibly maintain that the constitutional dictate of due process amounted simply to maximizing utility. It is equally implausible to maintain that the highest values of the German legal tradition—the maintenance of *Recht* and of a *Rechtsstaat*—turn simply on the choice of the greater good under the circumstances. The principle of "appropriate means" signals absolute restraints on pursuing utility maximization. These restraints are implicit in the rule of law and in principles of *Recht*.

§10.2.3. The Emergence of Necessity as a Justification in Anglo-American Law. The history of the claim of necessity in the common law bears some resemblance to the course of development in German legal history. At an early stage, the English courts recognized that the destruction or jettisoning of property would be justified in order to save human life and other overriding values.[45] The courts also worked out the principle that landowners were required to tolerate justified intrusions and further, that they were entitled to damages for harm suffered.[46] The precedents carrying this development are to be found, as in German law, in the field of tort liability. Though German theorists have traditionally main-

[44] Apparently the argument is that a comprehensive system of balancing would lead to the conclusion that the killing was not justified. Schönke-Schröder-Lenckner §34, note 46, at 463. This seems highly dubious. The balancing will come out right only if one adds sufficient makeweights (e.g., upholding basic values of the society) to generate a predetermined result.

[45] Mouse's Case, 77 Eng. Rep. 1341 (1608).

[46] Vincent v. Lake Erie Trans. Co., 109 Minn. 456, 124 N.W. 221 (1910).

tained that conduct justified under one body of law is justified for all purposes, there is little evidence to suggest that this assumption shared in the history of the common law.

Although some writers maintain that necessity is a common-law defense,[47] there is no case in the Anglo-American reports comparable to the 1927 German abortion case. There is no explicit recognition of the claim of necessity as a justification as a general limitation on the punishability of all offenses. So far as the defense exists in Anglo-American law, it is to be found in the interstices of particular offenses, with a wide variety of arguments deployed to support the claim. There are cases, for example, in which the courts rely on theories of contract interpretation to justify the mutiny of seamen under hazardous conditions.[48] Other cases rely on theories of overriding natural rights or constitutional rights to justify nominal statutory violations.[49] An English case trades on statutory language in order to justify an abortion to save the mother from serious emotional injury.[50] So far as there is a leading case in the field, it is the conviction in *Dudley & Stevens*,[51] which stands squarely opposed to the claim of justification by necessity in larceny as well as in homicide cases.

The emergence of necessity as a justification in Anglo-American law is being wrought by legislation rather than by pathbreaking judicial decisions. The recommendation of the Model Penal Code has found explicit reception in Pennsylvania,[52] Hawaii[53] and Texas.[54] Other versions of the defense are to be found in codes

[47] See Williams, *The Defence of Necessity*, 6 Current Legal Prob. 216 (1953); Hall 425–27; LaFave & Scott 381–83. *But cf.* Glazebrook, *The Necessity Plea in English Law*, 30 Camb. L.J. 87 (1972).

[48] United States v. Ashton, 24 F. Cas. 873, 874, No. 14,470 (C.C.D. Mass. 1834) (the seamen "contract only to do their duty and meet ordinary perils . . .").

[49] State v. Jackson, 71 N.H. 552, 53 A. 1021 (1902) (natural right to protect one's children and to keep them out of school when ill); Cross v. State, 370 P.2d 371 (Wyo. 1962) (constitutional right to protect property from marauding moose).

[50] Rex v. Bourne, [1938] 3 All E.R. 615 (Cent. Crim. Ct.).

[51] 14 Q.B.D. 273 (1884).

[52] Pa. Cons. Stat. Ann., tit. 18, §503;

[53] Hawaii Penal Code §302.

[54] Tex. Penal Code §9.22.

recently adopted in Colorado,[55] Delaware,[56] Kentucky,[57] Illinois,[58] New York,[59] and Wisconsin.[60] The reason that the burden of innovation has fallen on state legislatures is that lawyers in the common-law tradition do not share the German principle that nominally criminal conduct must also meet the criteria of a transcendent notion of wrongdoing. The positivist philosophy that has prevailed in Anglo-American law for the last two centuries leads to greater deference to the legislative command. The principle *nulla poena sine lege* is taken to apply to criteria of justification as well as to the elements of the definition.

Though there is an impetus to recognize a justification of necessity in Anglo-American law, the rationale is different from the German principle that wrongful conduct, interpreted as a transcendental legal standard, is an implicit element of every offense. The rationale appears rather to derive from two considerations that are of particularly great concern in the Anglo-American perspective on law. The first principle is that the criteria of punishable conduct are so multifarious that a certain amount of discretion should be exercised by trial and appellate judges in filling out the details of the legislative prohibition. The legislature cannot envision the full range of cases in which someone might be motivated to commit larceny, destroy property, or engage in such peccadilloes as violating the truancy laws. To work out the details of the prohibition, the courts should decide in particular cases whether the defendant's conduct furthers an interest "greater than that sought to be prevented by the law defining the offense charged."[61]

The second consideration supporting this delegation of authority to the courts is that the ultimate purpose of the law is to further the general welfare. In the criminal law, this means that rational judges should encourage welfare-maximizing conduct. If a

[55] Colo. Rev. Stat. §18–1–702.
[56] Del. Code tit. 11, §463.
[57] Ky. Rev. Stat. §503.030.
[58] Ill. Ann. Stat. c. 38, §7–13.
[59] N.Y. Penal Law §35.05(2).
[60] Wis. Stat. Ann. §939.47.
[61] MPC §3.02.

particular violation in fact contributes to the common good, then it is supposedly irrational to subject the conduct to punishment. Starting from these utilitarian premises, the drafters of the Model Penal Code could see no reason why killing the innocent should be exempt from the privilege. In a case like *Dudley & Stevens,* killing one person would issue in a net saving of life, and therefore the act of killing furthers the general welfare. The only problem, as the commentary to the code suggests, is whether "fair means" are employed in selecting the person to be sacrificed for the sake of the others.[62]

This utilitarian rationale for the privilege of furthering the greater good muddles an important distinction. One question is whether the actor furthers the greater good in violating the prohibitory norm. The second question is whether the court furthers the greater good by recognizing the conduct as justified. In conflating these two questions, commentators assume that in a case like *Dudley & Stevens,* the impact of the decision will be limited to other situations in which shipwrecked sailors or miners buried in a cave-in must decide whether to sacrifice one of their number so that the rest may survive. If that were true, then the acquittal of justified conduct would generate a set of guidelines that, when followed in future cases, would indeed further the greater good. But there is no reason to make this assumption about the limited impact of the case. Acquitting in cases of justification may have a deleterious effect in undermining the general commitment to norms against stealing, killing, and harming others. A sensitive utilitarian account would have to consider these effects, and yet the standard wisdom of Anglo-American writing is that the privilege of lesser evils finds its warrant in the "reason of public policy" that "the law ought to promote the achievement of higher values."[63] The problem is that there are no data to support the conclusion that we further the greater or the lesser value by recognizing the principle of necessity as a justification. The only support for this claim is the specious argument that acquitting one

[62] See note 42 *supra.*
[63] LaFave & Scott 382.

person who promotes a "higher value" will lead others to follow suit.[64]

Our exposing the weakness of this utilitarian argument is not aimed at undercutting the claim of necessity as a proper justification. There may be good reasons for recognizing the claim without resorting to speculations about what sort of judicial behavior will promote the general welfare. The defendant's conduct might be justified on the grounds of promoting the greater value even if the jury's acquitting him is not so justified. To work out a justification of this sort we are required to introduce general principles about the sort of conduct that is right and proper and therefore justifiably exempt from criminal liability. The reasoning would then proceed along the lines suggested by the 1927 German abortion case. The major premise would be that the defendant's conduct should not be regarded as criminal if he did the right thing under the circumstances. The question of what was "right" under the circumstances might then properly turn on a balancing of competing interests. Our point is simply that the major premise, which would lead either to the legislative or judicial recognition of the privilege, is not itself clearly justified by utilitarian considerations. The premise that rightful conduct should not be punished finds its warrant in the general principle that the criminal law should sanction conduct only if it is incompatible with the norms of proper behavior in the society. This point is admittedly expressed more easily in German and Soviet jurisprudence, but the gaps in Anglo-American legal terminology should not inhibit our perceiving this general truth about criminal punishment. Though we can justify imposing tort liability on those whose conduct is right and proper, we intuitively balk at punishing someone whose conduct is justified under the applicable social canons of proper conduct.

§10.2.4. Limitations on the Privilege of Necessity. It is obvious that furthering the greater interest cannot always generate a justification for violating a legislative prohibition. If it could, any citizen's judgment of the social welfare could undermine the pro-

[64] Compare the analogous critique of the utilitarian theory of excuses, §10.3.5 *infra*.

cess of democratic decision-making. Stealing from the rich and giving to the poor might be justified, even though the legislature had already determined the proper redistribution of wealth in the society. Blowing up a pipeline to protect the environment might be justified, even though the legislature had already made a judgment about the relative merits of economic and ecological interests. All that it would take to justify these nominally criminal acts would be the concurrence of judge and jury that the individual second-guessing the legislative judgment made the "correct" assessment of the competing social interests.

What would be awry in delegating this authority to individual citizens, judges, and jurors is that in a democratic system of government, the legislature is supposed to strike the balance between competing meritorious interests. It is the body of elected officials that should set the rate of progressive income taxation and determine the relative weight of economic and ecological interests. Accordingly, there must be some provision for distinguishing between cases in which the individual properly overrides the legislative judgment and those cases in which deference is required. If the issue is violating a traffic regulation in order to get a sick person to the hospital, it seems that the individual judgment should prevail. If the issue is blowing up a pipeline in order to save the Alaskan tundra, it seems fairly clear that the individual judgment of the social welfare must defer to the decisions of the democratically elected legislature. The problem is devising a general theoretical account for classifying cases as closer to one of these extremes than the other.

The fact is that there are two tests abroad in the law, both designed to solve the same problem. One test expresses the orientation of positivist jurisprudence; the other, of the place of justifiable conduct within a system of transcendent legal norms. The positivist standard, as expressed in the Model Penal Code, is simply that the privilege of necessity depends on implied legislative delegation. If a legislative purpose to exclude the justification "plainly appears,"[65] then the court is powerless to recognize the defen-

[65] MPC §3.02(1)(c).

dant's assessment of the competing interests as a ground for acquittal. A legislative purpose to exclude the justification would be inferable from a detailed system for justifying conduct of a particular sort. The best example is abortion. If the legislature has specified three grounds for justifying an abortion, it follows from the relatively detailed nature of the scheme that the legislature implicitly rejected other grounds for justified abortion.[66] On the other hand, if the legislature has not entered the field at all, the court may regard itself as implicitly authorized to work out the details of justified conduct. The question is whether the legislature has preempted judicial authority by seeking, itself, to determine the contours of justified conduct.

When we grasp the extent to which the Model Penal Code's theory of justification is a function of implied legislative delegation, the power of the German analysis comes into sharper focus. On the assumption of the 1927 abortion case, namely, that the legislative function is limited to specifying the definition of the offense, there is no way that the legislature can preempt judicial authority over the criteria of wrongful conduct. The ideology of positivist and democratic jurisprudence is that all law—all norms of legally wrongful conduct—derives from legislative commands. It follows that there is no transcendent standard of legally wrongful conduct and the judges are, in principle, powerless to override the legislative judgment. The German theory is not bound by these restraints. Even if the legislature has entered the field and laid down specific criteria for justifying, say, abortion, the possibility remains that the courts might recognize additional criteria for the justified violation of the legislated definition. Thus German theory is put to the test of devising an alternative standard for working out the relative domains of legislative and individual competence to assess what the law requires.

To solve this problem of allocating competence, the German approach to necessity as a justification contains the restriction that the individual may interpose his judgment of rightful conduct only when he confronts an impending, imminent risk of harm to a le-

[66] MPC §3.02, Comment at 6 (Tent. Draft No. 8, 1958).

gally protected interest.[67] Risks must be imminent as well in cases of excused conduct in order to insure that the individual's reaction is the consequence of overwhelming pressures rather than calm deliberation.[68] Yet the point of justified conduct is that it may be freely chosen as the correct alternative under the circumstances. Therefore we must seek an alternative account of the requirement of an imminent risk as a qualification on justified conduct. The thesis that we shall develop is that the standard of imminence provides a solution to the problem of limiting the competence of individuals to override legislative judgment about the social welfare.

The significance of limiting the privilege of necessity to cases of imminent risk is that the individual cannot pick the time, the place, or the victim of his judgment about what the law requires him to do. If an accident victim lies bleeding on the sidewalk and it is necessary to take someone's car to get him to the hospital, the range of car owners who might suffer the intrusion is limited. The situation of imminent risk prescribes the parameters under which an individual can assert his view of rightful conduct. This limited range of competence stands in contrast to the free-ranging legislative competence to determine when the social welfare requires that conduct be prohibited. Every socially justified prohibition benefits some people and harms others, yet it is within the legislative competence to make these judgments that impose uncompensated costs on some people. The legislature is empowered, in short, to pick the victims of the common good. Yet these are not the costs that we wish private individuals to impose on each other, even if the private judgment of social welfare is correct. Thus the requirement of imminent risk insures that the stage be set before the individual play his part in furthering the common good.

The Model Penal Code appears to be indifferent to this important value that individuals not be able to pick the victims of socially justified conduct. There is no requirement of "imminent risk" in the Code's formulation of necessity as a privilege. Every-

[67] StGB §34 (*eine gegenwärtige, nicht anders abwendbare Gefahr*).
[68] StGB §35 (same phrase).

thing turns on implied legislative delegation. Yet as the code has been adapted by the courts and several state legislatures,[69] the requirement of imminent risk has asserted itself. In Kroncke v. United States,[70] the defendant sought to justify the stealing of draft cards on the ground that interfering with the Selective Service would shorten the war in Vietnam and thus save endangered human lives. The Court of Appeals rejected the defense and asserted a version of the requirement of imminent risk. The defense of necessity applies, the judges reasoned, only if the action was undertaken to avoid a "direct and immediate peril."[71] A more tolerant view of the defense would be incompatible with the basic obligation in a democracy to resort to legitimate political means as a way of furthering the common good. Thus the court intuitively recognized the limitation of imminent peril as a more sensible standard than legislative intent as a restriction on the range of justified conduct.

This limitation of the claim of lesser evils is fully warranted, but there is another limitation found in the American statutes that is questionable. It is common for the newly drafted statutes to condition the defense on the defendant's not bringing about the risk later invoked to justify his conduct. There are two versions of the limitation. The Model Penal Code provides that if the actor "was reckless or negligent in bringing about the situation requiring a choice of harms or evils" and then commits an offense to avoid the greater evil, he is liable only if the offense is subject to being committed recklessly or negligently.[72] Thus if the actor negligently starts a forest fire and then destroys property to check the spread of the fire, he is liable for the destruction if, in the particular jurisdiction, the destruction of property is an offense that can be committed negligently. This form of the limitation appears plausible, but it represents a transfer of the negligent act from conduct that

[69] E.g., Del. Code tit. 11, §463 ("to avoid an imminent . . . injury which is about to occur . . ."); Colo. Rev. Stat. §18–1–702 (same language as Delaware); Ky. Rev. Stat. §503.030 ("imminent . . . injury").

[70] 459 F.2d 697 (8th Cir. 1972).

[71] *Id.* at 701.

[72] MPC §3.02(2).

may not be a crime to another that was justified under the circumstances. If in the previous example, negligent arson was not an offense but negligent destruction of property was, the negligent setting of the fire would not be a crime. And though the subsequent act was the right thing to do under the circumstances, the actor would be liable for the negligent destruction of property. Suppose there were two different actors: *X* negligently sets the fire, and *Y* blows up a house in order to check the fire and save the town. It would be irrational to impute the negligence of *X* to *Y* and hold the latter liable for "negligently" blowing up the house. It is not clear, then, why it should matter whether the acts of *X* and *Y* are collapsed into the deeds of one person. The rule is irrational as well from a utilitarian point of view. For if someone negligently starts a fire and the interests of the community require further destruction, he should have every incentive to destroy the property and check the fire. This would be true whether or not the original act of setting the fire is punishable. Nonetheless, several states following the Model Penal Code in their legislative revisions have adopted this provision.[73]

Some states have gone even further and added a clause requiring that the accused be "without blame in occasioning or developing the situation."[74] Thus if the accused gets drunk and injures himself and has no means for getting medical aid but driving to the hospital, he would not have a justification for driving while intoxicated.[75] And in our previous example of negligently starting a fire, the actor would be guilty of intentional arson for blowing up a house in order to check the fire. There are two ways to account for this highly dubious limitation of the defense. It might be

[73] E.g., Hawaii Penal Code §302 (2); Pa. Cons. Stat. Ann. §503(b).

[74] Ill. Ann. Stat. c. 38, §7-13; *cf.* N.Y. Penal Law §35.05(2) ("through no fault of the actor"); Colo. Rev. Stat. §18-1-702 ("through no conduct of the actor"); Del. Code. Ann. tit. 11, §463 ("through no fault of the defendant").

[75] See Butterfield v. State, 317 S.W.2d 943 (Tex. Crim. App. 1958) (facts as stated in the text; claim of necessity rejected). The Texas legislature apparently considered this result unjust and therefore enacted a defense of lesser evils without regard either for the limitation of the Model Penal Code or the more radical exclusion of antecedent fault. Tex. Penal Code §9.22. See Searcy & Patterson, *Practice Commentary* in Tex. Penal Code §9.22, at 261 (Vernon 1974).

thought that some hedge was necessary against persons deliberately creating a situation in which they would be able to commit an offense under the justification of lesser evils. But this aim hardly warrants excluding the defense in all cases in which the actor is to blame for bringing about the risk of injury. The more plausible explanation is that legislators are ambivalent about whether the claim of lesser evils negates the wrongfulness of the act or the actor's culpability. So far as justification of lesser evils is considered an excuse, then it makes sense to require that the actor be free from blame in the entire transaction.[76] This is a good example of the way in which confusing the criteria of justification and of excuse can generate bad law.[77]

German jurisprudence rejected this limitation from the very beginning in the 1927 abortion case.[78] Yet the Civil Code does provide that if the actor brought about the risk, he should compensate the victim for the loss incurred.[79] This is a sensible compromise that should commend itself to other legal systems.

§10.3. *The Theory of Excuses.*

Interposing a claim of excuse concedes that there is a wrong to be excused. The claim challenges the attribution of the wrongdoing to the actor. If the excuse is valid, then, as a matter of definition, the actor is not accountable or culpable for the wrongful act. The focus of the excuse is not on the act in the abstract, but on the circumstances of the act and the actor's personal capacity to avoid either an intentional wrong or the taking of an excessive risk. Insanity

[76] Compare the analysis of reasonable mistake, §9.2.3 *supra*.

[77] For a good critique of intermingling criteria of justification and excuse, in this context as well as others, see Robinson, *A Theory of Justification: Societal Harm as a Prerequisite for Criminal Liability*, 23 U.C.L.A.L. Rev. 266 (1975).

[78] Judgment of March 11, 1927, 61 RGSt. 242, 255.

[79] BGB §228, sentence 2. See note 14 *supra*.

and involuntary intoxication are paradigmatic excuses. Duress and necessity are regarded as excuses in some legal systems, but not in others. As we have already seen, mistakes in perception and mistakes about legal prohibitions often function as excuses.[1] There are other exotic, potential excuses, such as excessive self-defense in a state of shock and the conflict of duties. In our preliminary discussion, we shall assume that all of these claims negate the actor's personal accountability; later we shall examine various doctrinal moves either to disregard a particular claim of excuse or to reclassify the claim as a matter of justification. In our study of mistake of law, we already noted both of these phenomena: (1) denial of the excuse altogether and (2) redefinition of the issue either as a denial of the required intent or as reliance on an unlawful governmental order.

Our initial task is to examine the embarrassingly elementary question: Why should anyone ever be excused for unjustifiably violating the law? If excuses are required as a matter of justice to the individual, we should be able to articulate more clearly what the underlying theory of justice is. A sound theory of excuses would account not only for the claims recognized in most Western legal systems, but it would also generate an explanation for our not recognizing some recurrently asserted excuses for wrongdoing, such as conscientious civil disobedience and social deprivation.

§10.3.1. Excuses, Character and Desert. In a case of justified conduct, the act typically reflects well on the actor's courage or devotion to the public interest. If he disables an aggressor in order to save the life of another, his conduct speaks well for his courage; if as a police officer he disables a felon seeking to escape, his conduct testifies at least to his devotion to duty. Justifications require good reasons for violating the prohibitory norm; someone who chooses to act on these reasons is likely to deserve respect and praise rather than blame.

The distinguishing feature of excusing conditions is that they preclude an inference from the act to the actor's character. Typi-

§10.3. [1] See §9.1 *supra*.

cally, if a bank teller opens a safe and turns money over to a stranger, we can infer that he is dishonest. But if he does all this at gunpoint, we cannot infer anything one way or the other about his honesty. Typically, if a driver knowingly runs over someone lying in the roadway, we might infer something about the driver's indifference to human life. But we cannot make that inference if the choice open to the driver was going over a cliff or continuing down the incline and running over someone lying in the roadway. Similarly, if someone violates a legal prohibition under an unavoidable mistake about the legality of his conduct, we cannot infer anything about his respect for law and the rights of others. The same breakdown in the reasoning from conduct to character occurs in cases of insanity, for it is implicit in the medical conception of insanity that the actor's true character is distorted by his mental illness. Whether this is the best way of looking at insanity is a matter that will concern us later.[2]

An inference from the wrongful act to the actor's character is essential to a retributive theory of punishment. A fuller statement of the argument would go like this: (1) punishing wrongful conduct is just only if punishment is measured by the desert of the offender, (2) the desert of an offender is gauged by his character—i.e., the kind of person he is, (3) and therefore, a judgment about character is essential to the just distribution of punishment. It might be objected that if punishment should be inflicted according to the type of person the actor is, then we should examine the full range of the suspect's deeds—not just the attributability of a single wrongful act. The limitation of the inquiry to a single wrongful act follows not from the theory of desert, but from the principle of legality. We accept the artificiality of inferring character from a single deed as the price of maintaining the suspect's privacy. God might judge people on the full range of their life's work, but the law does not arrogate this function to itself. The issue in the legal inquiry is not whether, all things considered, the actor is wicked, but whether a single instance of wrongful conduct warrants the inference that the actor deserves punishment. Dis-

[2] See §10.4.4 *infra*.

ciplining the inquiry in this way restricts the range of relevant information, but it secures the individual against a free-ranging inquiry of the state into his moral worth.

If we accept this legalistic limitation on the inquiry, then the question becomes whether a particular wrongful act is attributable either to the actor's character or to the circumstances that overwhelmed his capacity for choice. It is critical that we keep these two sources of explanation distinct. We begin to interweave the two when we argue, for example, that the defendant's background of deprivation excuses his wrongdoing.[3] It goes without saying that a person's life experience may shape his character. Yet if we excuse on the ground of prolonged social deprivation, the theory of excuses would begin to absorb the entire criminal law. If we seriously believe that disadvantage causes crime, then we should have to argue that excessive advantage—witness Loeb & Leopold, Mitchell & Ehrlichman—also induces criminal behavior. The argument leads us into the cul-de-sac of environmental determinism. Now it may be the case that all human conduct is compelled by circumstances; but if it is, we should have to abandon the whole process of blame and punishment and turn to other forms of social protection.

The arguments against excusing too many wrongdoers are both moral and institutional. The moral or philosophical argument is addressed to the problem of determinism and responsibility in the standard cases of wrongdoing. It is difficult to resolve this issue except by noting that we all blame and criticize others, and in turn subject ourselves to blame and criticism, on the assumption of responsibility for our conduct. In order to defend the criminal law against the determinist critique, we need not introduce freighted terms like "freedom of the will." Nor need we "posit" freedom as though we were developing a geometric system on the basis of axioms. The point is simply that the criminal law should express the way we live. Our culture is built on the assumption

[3] See Bazelon, *The Morality of the Criminal Law,* 49 S. Cal. L. Rev. 385, 394–98 (1976) (favoring a broadened test of insanity that would accommodate "disadvantaged" backgrounds); *cf.* Morse, *The Twilight of Welfare Criminology: A Reply to Judge Bazelon,* 49 S. Cal. L. Rev. 1247 (1976).

that, absent valid claims of excuse, we are accountable for what we do. If that cultural presupposition should someday prove to be empirically false, there will be far more radical changes in our way of life than those expressed in the criminal law.

The institutional response to excusing too many people is to counter with surrogate means of social control. If society is to remain safe and orderly, there are inherent limits on excusing dangerous persons, say, on the ground of social deprivation. If these persons are excused under the criminal law, they will be confined under civil commitment statutes.[4] Of course, this institutional argument does not tell us precisely where to draw the line between those who should be excused and those who should not. But it does highlight the political limits of excusing harmful and dangerous acts in a society concerned about self-preservation.

The only way to work out a theory of excuses is to insist that the excuse represent a limited, temporal distortion of the actor's character. Social deprivation and particular forms of social interaction might conceivably fashion a person's character to be heedless of the rights of others. If that should be the case, the influence of experience would be too pervasive to constitute an excuse. The circumstances surrounding the deed can yield an excuse only so far as they distort the actor's capacity for choice in a limited situation. The moral circumstances of an actor's life may account for some of his dispositions, but explaining a life of crime cannot excuse particular acts unless we wish to give up the entire institution of blame and punishment.

§10.3.2. **Excuses and Voluntariness.** Another way to approach the rationale of excusing conditions is to start with the premise that law should punish only in cases of voluntary wrongdoing. Excuses arise in cases in which the actor's freedom of choice is constricted. His conduct is not strictly involuntary as if he suffered a seizure or if someone pushed his knife-holding hand down on the victim's throat. In these cases there is no act at all, no

[4] See the argument by the plurality of four Justices in Powell v. Texas, 392 U.S. 514 (1968) (no constitutional requirement to recognize chronic alcoholism as an excuse). See §6.4.2 *supra*.

wrongdoing and therefore no need for an excuse. The notion of involuntariness at play is what we should call moral or normative involuntariness.[5] Were it not for the external pressure, the actor would not have performed the deed. In Aristotle's words, he "would not choose any such act in itself."[6]

The normative conception of involuntariness must be sharply distinguished from physical involuntariness. The distinction does not come easily, for our language systematically blends the two in one set of terms. When we are speaking about "circumstances overpowering the will" or "vitiating the will" or the actor's having "no choice" but to act as he does, we might have either physical or normative involuntariness in mind. If someone puts a knife in the actor's hand and forces it down on the victim's chest, the actor's will is overpowered. But we might also say that her will is overpowered if she testifies falsely for fear of being killed.[7] There is a rhetorical point in this confusion: by assimilating the case of normative voluntariness to the paradigm of physical involuntariness, we express the conclusion that the actor should not be held accountable for an "involuntary" act.

If a judgment about voluntariness in the normative sense is not a matter of physical description, how do we go about deciding whether the conduct is voluntary or not? The assessment of voluntariness in the normative sense depends in a curious way on the competing interests as in cases of justification. So far as the balancing of interests bears on justification, conduct is justified only so far as the benefit of the conduct exceeds the cost. Yet conduct may be perceived as morally involuntary even though the cost is substantially greater than the benefit gained. For example, if an actor kills in order to avoid mutilation of his body, threatened by a third party, he inflicts a harm greater than the mutilation that otherwise would occur. His conduct could not be justified on

[5] Note that the French distinguish usefully between *la contrainte physique* and *la contrainte morale* (physical compulsion and moral compulsion). 1 Bouzat & Pinatel §262, at 343. These concepts correspond to what we mean by physical and normative involuntariness.

[6] Aristotle, Ethica Nicomachea 1110^a (W.D. Ross trans. 1925).

[7] See Regina v. Hudson, [1971] 2 All E.R. 244 (Crim. App.).

the ground that he furthers the greater good. Nonetheless, he may have a perfectly sound claim of duress based upon involuntary conduct. Yet if the gap between the harm done and the benefit accrued becomes too great, the act is more likely to appear voluntary and therefore inexcusable. For example, if the actor has to blow up a whole city in order to avoid the breaking of his finger, we might appropriately expect him to endure the harm to himself. His surrendering to the threat in this case violates our expectations of appropriate and normal resistance to pressure. Yet as we lower the degree of harm to others and increase the threatened harm to the person under duress we will reach a threshold at which, in the language of the Model Penal Code, "a person of reasonable firmness" would be "unable to resist."[8] Determining this threshold is patently a matter of moral judgment about what we expect people to be able to resist in trying situations. A valuable aid in making that judgment is comparing the competing interests at stake and assessing the degree to which the actor inflicts harm beyond the benefit that accrues from his action.[9] It is important to remember, however, that the balancing of interests is but a vehicle for making a judgment about the culpability of the actor's surrendering to external pressure.

The notion of voluntariness adds a valuable dimension to the theory of excuses. That conduct is involuntary—even in the normative sense—explains why it cannot fairly be punished. Indeed, H. L. A. Hart builds his theory of excuses on the principle that the distribution of punishment should be reserved for those who voluntarily break the law.[10] Of the arguments he advances for this principle of justice, the most explicit is that it is preferable to live in a society where we have the maximum opportunity to choose whether we shall become the subject of criminal liability.[11] In ad-

[8] MPC §2.09.

[9] This point is developed nicely in Judgment of November 11, 1932, 66 RGSt. 397, 400: "[O]ne can formulate the general proposition that excusing a serious crime, such as perjury, requires a more significant and persistent invasion of bodily integrity than required for excusing a lesser crime." *Cf.* Welzel 180; Jescheck 362.

[10] H. L. A. Hart, Punishment and Responsibility 22–24 (1968).

[11] *Id.* at 23–24.

dition, Hart intimates that it is ideologically desirable for the government to treat its citizens as self-actuating, choosing agents.[12] This principle of respect for individual autonomy is implicitly confirmed whenever those who lack an adequate choice are excused for their offenses.

The connection between voluntariness and excuses helps us as well to cure a weakness in the theory that the point of excusing conditions is to check the normal inference from conduct to character. The claim was that determining a wrongdoer's desert depends on perceiving the kind of character he or she has. If the act of theft implies a character trait of greed, then we have grounds for blaming and punishing the theft. This argument is unconvincing unless we assume, with Aristotle,[13] that people choose to develop the kind of character they have. Indeed we assumed that this was true in contrasting character with factors beyond the actor's control, such as genetic makeup and psychological condition. Yet it is difficult to maintain that all our vices are traceable to prior acts of choice and that therefore character is ultimately linked to a way of life we are free to perpetuate or reject. A weaker defense of the relationship between character and desert is that even if individuals are greedy or aggressive, they can discipline these traits and that their failure to do so makes them accountable for the manifestation of their flawed predispositions in criminal conduct. This weaker argument blurs the difference between character and physical impediments, such as blindness or impotence, against which people might fairly be expected to take protective measures in their interaction with others.[14] To avoid this reduction of character to another form of pressure, we are led back to the psychologically dubious view that the genesis of character lies in voluntary choice. The only way to navigate between the Scylla of reductionism and the Charybdis of psychological naiveté may be to abandon the theory of character and rest the entire theory of ex-

[12] *Id.* at 23 ("Criminal punishment differs from the manipulative techniques of the Brave New World . . .").

[13] Aristotle, *supra* note 6, at 1103^{a} to 1106^{a}.

[14] Compare the analysis of moral dimension in mitigating punishment for homicide on grounds of provocation, §4.2.1 *supra*.

cuses on the injustice of punishing unavoidable violations of the law.

Whether we start with the theory of character or of involuntariness, we are led to understand why civil disobedience is not and ought not to be recognized as an excuse. It may be morally proper to paint signs on military airplanes in order to protest an unpopular or unjust war. It may be morally proper for a reporter to protect her sources even though she is held in contempt of court for doing so. Yet these acts of conscience do not provide an excuse for violating valid legal prohibitions. And it is not clear that they should. Unlike cases of excusable conduct, these acts of protest are not attributable to the distorting effect of surrounding circumstances. Rather they spring from the foundation of the actor's character. With their acts of moral witness, Berrigan, Gandhi—and let us not forget Orville Faubus—told the world where they stood in their essential beings. Though a conscientious civil disobedient might say, "I cannot do otherwise," the compulsion of conscience has little in common with the compulsion of circumstance. The claim that one lacks a choice is a way of saying that one's integrity requires a violation of the law. Far from being involuntary, acts in the name of conscience are voluntary in the deepest sense. They spring from the foundation of a person's character. Far from being attributable to circumstances, they represent a commitment to transcend all secular influence for the sake of a higher truth.

One can go a step further and argue that society not only has the right and the authority to punish civil disobedience, but it has the obligation to do so. Punishing the disobedient expresses our respect for his autonomy and his capacity to reject conventional moral and legal authority. The surest way for society to discredit a political protestor is to treat him as insane or otherwise not responsible for his protest.[15] For the disobedient, the price of being taken seriously is being held accountable for deliberate violation of the law.

One further word about the concept of involuntary conduct.

[15] *Cf.* H. Morris, On Guilt and Innocence 38–50 (1976).

The concept of involuntariness readily fits the situation in which an actor surrenders to external pressure, but it seems more strained in English to regard mistakes as raising problems in the voluntariness of conduct. If someone violates the law as a result of an unavoidable mistake about the legality of his conduct, there is nothing compelling or forcing him to act as he does. Apparently the Greek idiom of involuntariness could more readily accommodate mistakes, for Aristotle had little trouble treating ignorance as the basis for denying the voluntariness of acting by reason of ignorance.[16] Yet contemporary English usage leads us to think that voluntariness is a problem of self-control, not of choosing to do wrong. This is one reason why we filtered off the problem of mistake for consideration in a separate chapter.

§10.3.3. **Compassion and Mercy in the Theory of Excuses.** It is often argued that there is no particular need to recognize excuses within the law, for if the law is harsh and insensitive to the actor's capacity to avoid the violation, we can rely on the good sense, "conscience and circumspection of prosecuting officers"[17] to find a way to mitigate the severity of the rules.[18] If prosecutors fail to exercise their discretion properly, then we can always fall back on the jury's capacity to subvert the law; and if that should fail, we can properly rely on the pardoning power of the executive to bring justice to the criminal law. This way of thinking has a powerful grip on Anglo-American legal thought, and yet it is rife with serious political and moral issues that rarely meet with the scrutiny they deserve.

The critical difference between excusing within the law and

[16] Aristotle, *supra* note 6, at 1110[b] (as contrasted with acting "in ignorance," e.g., while intoxicated).

[17] This phrase was coined by Justice Holmes in Nash v. United States, 229 U.S. 373 (1913), and repeated by Justice Frankfurter in United States v. Dotterweich, 320 U.S. 277, 285 (1943), to justify strict liability for marketing adulterated drugs.

[18] See Glazebrook, *The Necessity Plea in English Criminal Law,* 30 Camb. L.J. 87, 118 (1972); United States v. Barker, 514 F.2d 208, 236 (D.C. Cir. 1976) (Bazelon, J., concurring) ("There are many 'escape valves' in the law which permit largely unreviewable discretion for certain officials to mitigate harshness caused by the law's inability to meet its highest ideals, including the ideal of punishing only the free choice to do wrong").

excusing in the administrative processes extrinsic to the law lies in the sentiment that motivates the excuse. Excuses are motivated by compassion for persons caught in a maelstrom of circumstance. The underlying sentiment is that if any one of us were forced to act at gunpoint or to steal in order to survive, we would do the same. If we recognize our essential equality with the accused and identify with his situation, then we cannot but feel compassion and excuse his all-too-human transgression.

Executive intervention in the criminal process might be an expression of compassion, but the posture of having power over the violator typically transmutes the sentiment into an expression of mercy. The difference between compassion and mercy is moral as well as political. Compassion is expressed between equals. Rather than surrendering a right to punish, the person expressing compassion recognizes that he has no right to begin with. Excuses based on compassion do not derogate from liability; they go to the question whether there is a sound basis for imposing liability. Mercy is expressed from a superior to an inferior. The posture of superiority is determined by the assumption of a right subject to enforcement at the superior's discretion. Portia's appeal to Shylock to show mercy toward Antonio presupposed that Antonio was liable on the bond. Presidential or royal clemency presupposes that the beneficiary is liable under the law. The exercise of prosecutorial discretion presupposes an administrative option to hold the subservient party to the strict letter of the law.

The implications of this distinction are far-reaching. Compassion is directed to the particular act that arguably generates liability. The claim of duress or necessity as an excuse focusses exclusively on the incident and circumstances that induced the violation. Mercy is appropriate only when the subservient recipient, viewed in his entirety, deserves it. No one argues that Shylock should have compassion for Antonio because Antonio had lost his head and entered into a foolhardy transaction. The argument is always that it would be heartless to enforce an admittedly valid bond. The assumption is that Antonio was a good and devoted citizen and that, viewed in his moral entirety, he should not suffer the strict enforcement of the law. When Antonio's friends petition

Shylock for mercy, the reply by the outcast in Venice is sound: Why should he grant mercy to a man who had ridiculed him and indeed not even recognized his humanity as a Jew?[19] The response has nothing to do with the circumstances of the bargain, but with the question whether Antonio, as the man subject to Shylock's power, is in fact a moral and decent man—a man for whom "the quality of mercy is not strained."

That mercy is directed to the moral worth of the whole man or woman carries serious political implications. If mistake of law, necessity and other excuses are left to prosecutorial discretion and executive clemency, is there any reason why the administrative decision should be limited to the particular transaction generating liability? If the actor is formally liable under the law, the appropriate question is likely to become whether the suspect, viewed in his entirety as a human being, warrants prosecution or freedom. Politically unpopular defendants and those with criminal records are unlikely to be the beneficiaries of administrative grace. If there is a political campaign to crack down on political radicals or organized crime, the expression of mercy will invariably be adjusted to the political needs of the moment.

The limited focus of compassion has much to commend it. If the issue is whether a publisher of pornography is excused for not being able to anticipate the Supreme Court's latest decision on obscenity, we need only ask whether this person under the particular circumstances should have been able to perceive the wrongfulness of his conduct. The publisher's background and the political pressures of the moment are irrelevant. Yet if the question is framed as a matter of prosecutorial discretion, a good administrator will obviously consider all the circumstances bearing on whether the prosecution is in the "public interest."

In view of the irreducibly political nature of prosecutorial discretion, it is surprising that so many contemporary observers regard the recent legitimation of the institution as a beneficent feature of American law. For example, Ronald Dworkin argues that the prosecutors should have stayed their power against con-

[19] W. Shakespeare, The Merchant of Venice, act III, scene 1.

scientious opponents to the Vietnam war.[20] The argument essentially is that many draft evaders had good reasons for thinking that the higher law of the Constitution permitted resistance. If Dworkin is right in this claim, then the appropriate argument should have been that the resisters had a sound excuse of mistake of law, not that prosecutors should have exercised discretion on their behalf. Certainly not all resisters deserved an exemption from punishment. It should matter whether the particular evader was conscientiously and unavoidably mistaken about the constitutionality of the war. It would be far preferable to focus on that narrow question than to turn the matter over to the political judgment of administrative officials.

It is beyond the present inquiry to subject prosecutorial discretion to the critique that it deserves. The issue is particularly difficult to discuss, for many proponents of discretion regard all instances of judgment and interpretation as discretionary. Therefore they are inclined to believe that discretion is inherent in the charging process; if discretion lurks in the nature of things, there is nothing to be discussed at the level of principle or policy. Rather than tackle that semantic briarpatch, I have limited myself to the simple point that the analysis of excuses is more disciplined when the excuse is incorporated in the law than when it is left to administrative discretion. The source of the discipline is the sentiment of compassion and its focus on whether there is an adequate basis for claiming power over the allegedly excused actor.

§10.3.4. Do Excuses Amend the Law? The single most difficult point in the theory of excuses is the relationship between excuses and the norms that govern our conduct. The nature of a justification is that the claim is grounded in an implicit exception to the prohibitory norm. The "right" of self-defense carves out a set of cases in which violation of the norm is permissible. When the principles of justification are rendered concrete in particular cases, the result is a precedent that other people may properly rely upon in similar cases. If a court recognizes a privilege, based on necessity, to shoot a rabies-stricken dog in order to protect children in

[20] R. Dworkin, Taking Rights Seriously 206–22 (1977).

the neighborhood, the result modifies the norm against the destruction of property. If deadly force is adjudged permissible against a threatened rape, the norm against homicide is *pro tanto* contracted. In similar cases arising in the future, similarly situated actors may rely on these recognized privileges in planning their conduct. The only requirement for claiming the precedent is the general legal rule that the new case may not be significantly different in its relevant facts.

Excuses bear a totally different relationship to prohibitory norms. They do not constitute exceptions or modifications of the norm, but rather a judgment in the particular case that an individual cannot be fairly held accountable for violating the norm. This fundamental difference means that cases acknowledging that conduct in a particular situation is excused do not generate precedents that other people may rely on in the future. This is obvious in cases of mistake of law, for the judgment of the court serves to advise the public of the rule in question, and therefore in the future there is even less excuse for ignorance of the particular law. The same inverse relationship holds, in a way worth explaining in some detail, in cases of excuses based on threats and the overwhelming pressure of circumstances.

Suppose a jury acquits a prison inmate who escapes from jail in order to avoid a homosexual rape.[21] The instruction required a finding that the inmate "had no choice" but to escape in order to avoid the rape. Now the question is whether inmates in the future may rely on this judgment of acquittal in contemplating whether to escape. The fact is that they cannot, and the reason is important. Excuses apply on behalf of morally involuntary responses to danger; they acknowledge that when individuals merely react rather than choose to do wrong, they cannot fairly be held accountable. If an inmate were to study the record of acquittals in escape cases and then wait for the right circumstances to accrue, his decision to break out of jail could hardly be termed involuntary. Planning, deliberating, relying on legal precedents—all of these are in-

[21] For a good example, see People v. Lovercamp, 43 Cal. App. 3d 823, 118 Cal. Rptr. 110 (1974).

compatible with the uncalculating response essential to "involuntary" conduct. If an individual seeks to rely on a precedent as a factor motivating his decision, his escape would appear to be less attributable to the threat of rape, and more to the promise of future immunity in the courts. Conversely, a string of convictions in escape cases would make a subsequent escape appear to be even more the product of desperation and fear. If the convict fears punishment and nonetheless escapes to avoid an impending rape, one senses more acutely that his conduct is the involuntary response to the terror of the situation.

Thus in the field of excuses, precedents have an inverse effect on the excusability of similar conduct in the future. So far as acquittals imply a promise of immunity, those who rely on the supposed promise will have a more difficult time making out their claims of involuntary conduct. A judicial record of disregarding excuses, in contrast, lends greater credence to those who subsequently claim that they are not fairly to blame for yielding to the pressure of circumstances. This inverse correlation brings out the radical difference between claims of justification, which do create precedents that others may rely on in the future, and claims of excuse, which do not. Decisions on justifying circumstances modify the applicable legal norm. Decisions on excuses, in contrast, leave the norm intact, but irreversibly modify the factual background of succeeding claims of excuse.

Excuses have this peculiar quality, for they occupy a hiatus between two concepts of law. Law in the narrow sense consists solely of the norms prohibiting conduct and laying down the criteria of justification. Law in the broad sense encompasses the total set of criteria that affects the outcomes of particular cases. In the ring between these two circles of law, one finds the criteria of excuses as well as other conditions—such as criteria of immunity and the statute of limitations—that affect the outcome of particular cases.

The theory of excuses presupposes that we cultivate this field that lies between the norms of the law and the question of liability. That is where the concepts of attribution and personal accountability take root. If we collapse the two concepts of law, then we must uproot the claims of excuses from their natural habitat and replant them in the shade of administrative discretion. There is no doubt that one can achieve individualized justice in less visible processes of prosecutorial discretion, jury nullification and executive clemency. But every legal system, one would think, should be committed to bringing the question of excuses out into open ground where the claims on our compassion are public and subject to reasoned argumentation.

§10.3.5. The Utilitarian Theory of Excuses. The entire exposition of excuses in the preceding sections is subject to a radical critique. The argument is that one need not resort to notions either of compassion or of mercy to account for the excuses recognized in the law. There is a good utilitarian explanation for defenses based on involuntary conduct. The argument is that involuntary conduct cannot be deterred and therefore it is pointless and wasteful to punish involuntary actors. This theory, which we shall call the theory of pointless punishment, carries considerable weight in current Anglo-American legal thought. It is invoked as a normative standard for pruning back the felony-murder rule[22] as well as to account for recognized excuses. And yet, as we shall show here, the argument is nothing but a fragile construct of logical fallacies. Why it fails to topple is a matter of considerable interest in understanding contemporary legal thought.

Jeremy Bentham first devised the argument as part of his attack on Blackstone's conventional theory that excuses were based on a "defect of will."[23] The principle that punishment should not be inflicted pointlessly derives from the main premises of the utilitarian theory of punishment. These premises are, first, that punishment is justified only so far as it furthers the general good, primarily by deterring others from harmful conduct; and, secondly, that if punishment does not contribute to the general good, it inflicts pain without a commensurate benefit and therefore is wrong.

[22] See §4.4.5 *supra*.
[23] 4 Blackstone 20.

If punishment is pointless in a particular class of cases, it inflicts pain without a commensurate benefit and therefore should not be permitted.[24]

These principles are coherent in themselves. Fallacies emerge, however, as soon as we try to apply them to account for exemptions from punishment in cases of insanity, involuntary intoxication, infancy and mistake. When spelled out fully, the account deriving from Bentham goes like this. Consider an actor, A_1, who appears to be insane. Should we punish him or not? Let us consider whether the punishment will have an effect on other insane people, A_1, A_2, . . . A_n, who will learn of this judgment and might be influenced. Upon inspection we discover that other insane people are not subject to being deterred, and therefore punishing A_1 can have no desirable effect in the future. It follows that punishing A_1 would be pointless and therefore insane persons as a class should be exempt from the scope of the criminal law.

In order to make this argument as attractive as possible, we should accept a few of the critical assumptions that buttress the thesis. One of these assumptions is that the only relevant social benefit in punishing insane persons is the general deterrence of others. There is no consideration of the benefit derived from isolating the dangerously insane. Nor is there any consideration of other utilitarian benefits of punishment, such as channelling aggressive energies into the orderly processes of the criminal law. The second assumption is that punishment ordinarily has a deterrent impact. If it did not, the utilitarian would be the first to question the desirability of forcing even sane people to suffer in penitentiaries. These two assumptions are not so difficult to accept. The more problematic points await our attention.

At the core of the argument of pointless punishment we find the assumption that if punishing an insane defendant has a deterrent effect, that effect would be registered exclusively in the responses of other insane persons. The general form of this assumption is that in order to assess the deterrent efficacy of pun-

[24] J. Bentham, Introduction to the Principles of Morals and Legislation 173–75 (La Fleur ed. 1970).

ishment, we must define a class of potentially deterrable persons. That class should be defined by identifying the critical features of the case at bar and extrapolating on the basis of these features into the indefinite future. Thus if an involuntarily intoxicated person is called to account for a criminal act, his claim would be that intoxicated persons cannot be deterred and therefore involuntary intoxication should be regarded as an exemption from punishment. Voluntary intoxication would not get similar treatment, for punishing in these cases would arguably deter people from getting themselves into a non-responsible stupor. Thus by assuming that the relevant deterrent impact must be measured in a line of cases just like the case at bar, one can account for the common excusing conditions of the criminal law.

The same premise of infinite replication is invoked not only to uphold the law, but to change it. For example, if an inadvertently negligent wrongdoer is called to account, he might well argue that punishing him would be of no avail. Other inadvertent people could not be guided by his example and therefore his suffering would be useless. This is a surprisingly popular argument against punishing inadvertent negligence.[25]

Bentham assumed that if any insane person were punished, the precedent would be interpreted as a case of punishing an insane person. Why is that self-evident? Suppose that the insane actor killed by strangling his victim with a rope. Perhaps the case would be understood by the public as an instance of strangulation. Punishing one strangler would thereby strengthen the general inhibition against strangulation. What prompts us to think that the only fact that the public would be interested in is the accused's insanity? Indeed, if the defense of insanity were abolished, the question would not be litigated at trial. There would be no expert witnesses on the issue, no instructions, no discussion on appeal. It is not clear how the public would even learn that the suspect was arguably insane.

But let us assume that the public routinely identifies with the

[25] See, e.g., Williams 122; Comment, *Is Criminal Negligence a Defensible Basis for Penal Liability*, 16 Buffalo L. Rev. 749 (1967).

potential excuses in every case, regardless of whether the issue is heard at trial. Thus we are able to extrapolate to a class of similarly situated people who have to be deterrable in order to justify punishment in the case at bar. Even if this is possible, the argument of pointless punishment harbors an insupportable assumption. How do we know that the impact would be limited to the class of people who would identify with the grounds of excuse? Take a case of inadvertently negligent vehicular homicide. We have concluded that the class of potentially deterrable people are those similarly defined, namely, as drivers unmindful of the risk to others. This class of people is by definition undeterrable (they are not mindful of the risk and therefore they cannot be influenced), but there are other, closely related classes of people who might be deterred by punishing an inadvertently negligent driver. These are:

(1) those who drive recklessly, mindful of the risks, but who believe they might be able to deceive a jury into believing that they were inadvertent of the particular risk that materialized.

(2) those who drive with the knowledge that they occasionally daydream, and who would be stimulated by the example of prior punishment to check their tendencies to let their mind wander while driving.

(3) those who have never been inadvertently negligent and would have additional incentive to remain alert and attentive while driving.

(4) those who engage in other activities, such as hunting and filling prescriptions, and who would be goaded by the prior case of punishment to remain attentive.

The list could be multiplied to include many other concentric classes of people who might be influenced by a single case of punishing an inadvertent driver who causes harm. The point is that there is no reason at all to assume that the potential deterrent effect would be limited just to people who are defined by the prominent features of the case at bar. If punishment deters at all, it is just as likely to have a spillover effect in closely related cases as it is to be limited to those who look just like the defendant who is punished.

The same critique obviously applies in cases of insanity. The list of potential deterrables should include all those who might kill and then seek to dissemble insanity, those at the borderline of sanity, those who are sane but would contemplate killing in the same manner as did the insane actor. There is no way to say a priori that some people should be excluded from the category of potential deterrables. The problem is ultimately empirical, not logical, and we simply know too little about the effects of punishment to say who can be deterred and who cannot be.

Without empirical support, the argument of pointless punishment hardly generates a rationale for the existing excusing conditions in the law. If the argument collapses in theory, one wonders why it is so tenacious in practice. The fact is that the utilitarian theory of excuses incorporates an appealing mode of instrumental reasoning. The contemporary legal mind finds it more persuasive to relate questions of justice to the long-range goals of the legal system. It is better to argue that the felony-murder rule should not be extended "beyond any rational function it is designed to serve"[26] than to face the question of justice to the accused as the ultimate issue in the case. This form of legal instrumentalism thrives on pervasive skepticism whether normative issues are subject to rational inquiry. Yet if we were appropriately skeptical about the pretensions of the argument of pointless punishment, we might recognize that excuses derive primarily from commitment to do justice in the particular case. We might then be prepared to cultivate the theory of excuses not as levers for maximizing efficiency, but as an expression of compassion in the criminal process.

§10.4. *A Comparative Survey of Excuses.*

Most legal systems have a literature on necessity, duress and intoxication as problematic cases in the theory of criminal liability.

[26] People v. Washington, 62 Cal. 2d 777, 783, 402 P.2d 130, 134, 44 Cal. Rptr. 442, 446 (1965).

All legal systems, so far as I know, recognize insanity as an excuse or exemption from punishment. Yet the approach to these issues is remarkably varied. The German legal system, for example, takes a maximalist view on the range and variety of excusing conditions; the Soviet Union takes a minimalist view rejecting all excuses except insanity. Anglo-American and French law find themselves at points ranged between these two extremes.

There are two distinct impulses impelling legal systems toward minimalist theories of excuses. The first is a frank desire to abolish consideration of the issue altogether. So it is often argued with regard to mistake of law, duress and, recently in the United States and England, with regard to the insanity defense. Alternatively, the impulse is to recognize the issue but under another rubric—perhaps as a justification, perhaps as an issue going to the susceptibility of the actor to sanctions in general. The first impulse to deny the excuse is substantive; the second, nominal, with some possible substantive effects brought on by repackaging the issue under a different label. That there are these diverse sentiments intersecting in the theory of excuses requires that we remain attentive to ambiguity. We shall try to be clear about whether the negative posture of a legal system toward an excusing condition is substantive or nominal.

§**10.4.1. Necessity.** The earliest thinking about excuses appears to be the recognition that the necessity to save one's own life prevails over the positive law. The claim of *se defendendo* has its roots in this theory of necessity. In the early seventeenth century, Francis Bacon formulated a sophisticated view of necessity that continues to illuminate the issues.[1] He pinpointed two cases of ongoing concern. The first is the case of the starving thief and the second, of the inmate who breaks out of a burning jail.[2] The difficulty with Bacon's account of acquitting these two actors is the failure to distinguish clearly between necessity as an excuse and necessity as a justification. Bacon's cases are overdetermined in the

§**10.4.** [1] F. Bacon, Elements of the Common Lawes of England (1630), published in 13 Collected Works 131 (Montague ed. 1831).

[2] *Id.* at 160.

sense that they might be rationalized on either ground. They are justified in the sense that saving life is more important than either petty property interests or the social interest in confining prisoners. They are excused in the sense that the starving thief and the inmate act under overwhelming pressure.

In another case Bacon claims that drowning another man is justifiable, if necessary for self-preservation. This point is made in discussing the famous hypothetical case of two shipwrecked sailors struggling to gain control of a plank.[3] If either drowns the other, Bacon would describe the killing as justifiable. Unfortunately, Bacon lacks a theory to explain why the killing is privileged—if that is what he meant by "justifiable." If he had focussed on the one party defending the plank against the other, then he might have invoked self-defense as rationale for justifying the forcible expulsion. But he did not make clear whether the slayer's position of relative security mattered in labelling the killing justifiable.

Over a century later, Immanuel Kant addressed himself to the more difficult version of the plank case in which the swimmer ousts the occupier from the plank.[4] Dislodging the occupier and thus causing his death cannot be justified as repelling an aggressor; it is a patent violation of the categorical imperative against killing the innocent. It is clearly wrong. But Kant reasoned that though the killing was punishable in principle, it should not be punished. The overwhelming pressure, the instinct to save one's life—these factors did not render the deed less wicked, but they did suggest that it would be unjust to punish the actor for his wicked deed. Bacon had rested his conclusions on the ground that stealing under starvation was not larceny and killing another sailor at the plank was justifiable. The cultural advance in Kant's reasoning was conceding that the deed was wrongful and a violation of duty, but arguing that a violation of duty was not conclusive on the issue of legal liability.

Several stages of development followed Kant's insight. First, the notion of self-preservation broadened into the standard of

[3] *Ibid.*

[4] I. Kant, Introduction to the Science of Right 52–53 (N. Hastie trans. 1887).

irresistible force or overwhelming pressure, which made the concept of necessity applicable to a wider range of cases.[5] Secondly, a more adequate account emerged to explain why necessity negated the punishability of the necessitated act. Only the first of these issues received much refinement in the 1871 German Criminal Code, which provided that there was no criminal act "if the actor acted in a case of necessity (for which he was not at fault) to save himself from an imminent risk to his life or limb or to the life or limb of a dependent."[6] The second was resolved in the early twentieth century when German scholars began to distinguish clearly between the justificatory and the excusing dimensions of necessity.[7] The provision of the Criminal Code was interpreted as an excuse, the justificatory defense was left to the creative hand of the courts.[8]

A few cases decided in the 1920s reveal how generously the excuse of necessity was applied in practice. In one case, the accused killed his father who had allegedly assaulted and terrorized the family for a long period of time.[9] The threat from the father on the occasion of the killing fell below the threshold required for self-defense; nonetheless the defendant was acquitted on grounds of personal necessity. The Supreme Court affirmed the acquittal. In another case, the defendant burned down a house that he had received from the local housing bureau.[10] Defending against the charge of arson, he claimed that the house was collapsing, that it posed a risk to life and limb, and that the only way of getting the housing bureau to assign another house to the family was to burn the first one down. He was acquitted, and again the Supreme Court affirmed. That the Supreme Court endorsed these acquittals is remarkable, particularly because in neither case does it appear that the defendant averted the risk of harm with the least costly, most reasonable means available.

[5] A. von Feuerbach, Lehrbuch des peinlichen Rechts §91, at 179 (14th ed. 1847).
[6] StGB §54.
[7] See Goldschmidt, *Der Notstand, ein Schuldproblem*, 1913 Österreichische Zeitschrift für Strafrecht 129, 224.
[8] See §10.2 *supra*.
[9] Judgment of July 12, 1926, 60 RGSt. 318.
[10] Judgment of January 23, 1925, 59 RGSt. 69.

The French Code of 1810 contains a single provision on excusing conditions, but the language of the code could lend itself to interpretation as a theory of necessity as an excuse.[11] Section 64 provides simply that there is no crime "if the actor was insane at the time of the deed or if he was compelled by an irresistible force." The notion of "irresistible force" is interpreted broadly to encompass *contrainte morale*—or cases in which the actor cannot be fairly expected to resist.[12] But still there is a problem in applying the provision to cases of "internal pressure" such as that in the case of the starving thief. When a French court encountered the problem of thievery by a starving mother in the late nineteenth century, the judges found an alternative theory to account for their impulse to acquit.[13] The trial court in Château-Thierry reasoned that the mother's purpose of acquiring food for herself and her starving child meant that her taking was not motivated by a "dishonest purpose"[14] as required by the definition of larceny.[15]

There is still considerable controversy in French law about the meaning and import of "irresistible force." There is one school of thought that favors treating necessity exclusively as a justification, namely, as a claim of lesser evils.[16] And some writers take §64 to be applicable solely to cases of duress or at least to cases of external force.[17] But the conceptual distinction between duress and necessity has never been beyond question, and in fact under the

[11] Note the rule in Code Pénal §65 requiring all excuses to be authorized by statute.

[12] Merle & Vitu 609 (conceding that judicial recognition of *contrainte morale* is rare); 1 Bouzat & Pinatel §268, §269, at 348–50 (limited application of the doctrine.)

[13] The reported opinion does not mention Code Pénal §64. *But cf.* G. Vidal, Cours de Droit Criminel 379 (9th ed. by J. Magnol 1947) (saying that the court relied upon §64 as well as the rationale reported in the text.).

[14] The technical term in the definition of larceny is that the taking be *frauduleusement*. Code Pénal §379.

[15] The acquittal was affirmed by the Court of Appeals in Amiens, April 22, 1898, [1899] Recueil Sirey II.1.

[16] Merle & Vitu 448–52; 1 Bouzat & Pinatel §294 to §298, at 367–71 (classifying necessity as a *fait justificatif* along with self-defense, but the discussion interweaves criteria of excuse with the principle of lesser evils; *id.* at 372). *But cf.* G. Vidal, *supra* note 13, at 377–79 (stressing necessity as an excuse, ignoring the element of lesser evils).

[17] Stefani & Levasseur 310–12.

new German Code, the two excuses receive unified regulation under a single provision.[18] After we canvass various approaches to necessity and duress, we shall return to the French Code and its potential for generating a similarly unified theory based on the analysis of pressure that one cannot be fairly expected to resist.

Though the English theory of excuses received early elaboration in Bacon, the path of development proved to be much different from German and French law. Hale ridiculed the idea that starvation might excuse the theft of food. Attacking "Jesuitical casuists" in France who were allegedly advising "apprentices and servants to rob their masters,"[19] Hale concluded that stealing to avoid starvation should be punished by death.[20] Blackstone followed Hale on this point but consoled himself with the belief that in England it was "impossible that the most needy stranger should ever be reduced to the necessity of thieving to support nature."[21]

If this chilling reception were not enough, the ascendant utilitarian theory of punishment in the nineteenth century further inhibited the development of excusing conditions. The new mode of argument was whether criminal punishment could and should deter specified forms of conduct. Macaulay had argued that the "mere fear of capital punishment which is remote, and which may never be inflicted at all, will never prevent [a person] from saving his life."[22] But Stephen retorted: "Surely it is at the moment when temptation to crime is the strongest that the law should speak most clearly and emphatically to the contrary."[23]

[18] As to French law, see Vidal, *supra* note 13, arguing that §64 can be extended to include a claim of necessity analogous to StGB 1871, §54. According to LaFave & Scott 381, duress is a response to human threats; necessity, to natural phenomena. *But cf.* the German case of a boy who killed his father and interposed a valid claim of necessity, *supra* note 9. There is obviously no trans-cultural conceptual distinction between the two defenses.

[19] 1 Hale 54; *but cf. id.* at 611 (recognizing the excuse of necessity on behalf of an inmate who escapes from a burning prison).

[20] *Ibid.* (but noting the possibility of the King's mercy).

[21] 4 Blackstone 32. *But cf. id.* at 30, 187 (discussing duress and *se defendendo* as excuses).

[22] Macaulay, *Introductory Report upon the Indian Penal Code* (1837–38), in 7 Macaulay's Works 456 (Lady Trevelyan ed. 1866).

[23] 2 Stephen 107.

Thus Stephen concludes that duress should not be an excuse at all.[24] This follows directly from the utilitarian theory of excuses: when the criminal sanction cannot influence behavior, it should not; when it can, it should. Thus the style of argument that Bentham introduced to rationalize the system of excuses is now deployed to argue against any excuse based on surrendering to the pressure of circumstance. If compassion for human weakness is lost in the process, we are hardly consoled by Stephen's concession that "The criminal law is a system of compulsion on the widest scale."[25]

A year after the publication of Stephen's *History of the Criminal Law,* the Queen's Bench in Exeter heard the case that would shape the Anglo-American theory of excuses for nearly a century. In Regina v. Dudley & Stephens[26] two sailors were indicted for the murder of a cabin boy at sea. Having been lost at sea in an open boat with no food for eight days and no fresh water for twenty-four days, the defendants killed the emaciated boy and consumed his body. On the fourth day after the killing they were rescued and brought back to England. According to a special verdict of the jury, the defendants killed the boy when there was "no sail in sight, nor any reasonable prospect of relief."[27] And further, "there was no appreciable chance of saving life except by killing some one for the others to eat."[28] The boy was not consulted, nor were lots drawn or any other means of chance used to determine which of the sailors would be sacrificed.

This case has gained considerable attention in the German, French and Anglo-American literature; it is a textbook example of the wrongful killing of an innocent person that might properly be excused on grounds of necessity.[29] Yet the judges of the Queen's

[24] *Cf.* F. Stephen, Digest of the Criminal Law §42, at 35–36 (7th ed. by H. Stephen & H. L. Stephen 1926) ("threats of future injury . . . do not excuse any offence").

[25] 2 Stephen 107.

[26] 14 Q.B.D. 273 (1884).

[27] *Id.* at 275.

[28] *Ibid.*

[29] Simonson, *Der "Mignonnette"—fall in England,* 5 ZStW 367 (1885); Merle & Vitu 450 n.6; 1 Bouzat & Pinatel §299, at 372 n.3.

Bench in 1884 found it difficult to assess the special verdict on any grounds except whether the sailors had a right to kill or whether it was permissible to kill under the circumstances. Framing the issue in this way, they readily concluded that the killing was wrongful and therefore murder. As Lord Coleridge reasons in his opinion: "[If] the broad proposition [advanced is] that a man may save his life by killing, if necessary, an innocent and unoffending neighbor, it certainly is not law at the present day."[30]

Of course we might agree that it is categorically wrong to kill innocent people, but it does not follow that the defendants could not be excused for their wrongdoing. As to the possibility of an excuse, Lord Coleridge has only this poignant comment: "[A] man has no right to declare temptation to be an excuse, though he might himself have yielded to it, nor allow compassion for the criminal to change or weaken in any manner the legal definition of the crime."[31]

The judges condemned Dudley and Stephens to the gallows, but hinted in their opinion that it might be appropriate for the "Sovereign to exercise [the] prerogative of mercy. . . ."[32] In fact the Crown did thereafter commute the sentence to six months imprisonment,[33] which is what the judges presumably preferred despite their high moral stand against "temptation." Yet one wonders why, if no one should have compassion for those who yield to pressures to which anyone might yield, the Queen should display mercy. And if it was appropriate to commute the sentence to a nominal term, why should the judges not have mitigated the penalty themselves, or indeed why should they not have recognized a complete excuse?

The key to Lord Coleridge's unwillingness to countenance an excuse of necessity is his fear that the "legal definition of the crime" would thereby be changed.[34] This is a familiar argument

[30] 14 Q.B.D. at 286 (criticizing Bacon).

[31] *Id.* at 288.

[32] *Ibid.*

[33] *Id.* at 288 n.2.

[34] *Id.* at 288.

against excusing conditions. The fear is that the public will always interpret an acquittal as a vindication of the deed.[35] In a highly publicized case, like *Dudley & Stephens*, the judges are likely to be even more than usually concerned about public misapprehension. The way to avoid the public's misunderstanding of the law against homicide is to enlist a different agency of government, namely, the Crown, to excuse the defendants indirectly.

The rejection of excusing conditions and the concern for the social impact of the judgment both express a utilitarian philosophy of criminal justice. The excuse of necessity is rejected because, in Fitzjames Stephen's words, it is at the "moment of temptation" that the law "should speak most clearly and emphatically to the contrary."[36] The orientation toward the public and their likely responses to an acquittal reflects the instrumentalist view of decision-making that has now become so familiar.

If Lord Coleridge could embrace utilitarian thinking on these points, one wonders why he recoiled against the prospect of justifying the killing on the grounds of lesser evils. If in fact the killing of one emaciated boy appeared likely to save the lives of two men, then the killing furthered the greater good. In his *Digest* and in his *History*, Fitzjames Stephen had begun to work out the claim of lesser evils. There may be cases, he wrote, "in which the expediency of breaking the law is so overwhelmingly great that people may be justified in breaking it."[37] As examples of this doctrine of "choice of evils" he lists (1) running down a small boat when it is "the only possible way of avoiding a collision with another ship" and (2) sacrificing the life of a child in birth when necessary to save the life of the mother.[38] Stephen concludes that "in neither of these cases would an offense be committed."[39]

The only impediment to applying this doctrine in *Dudley &*

[35] *Ibid.* ("such a principle once admitted might be made the legal cloak for unbridled passion and atrocious crime").

[36] 2 Stephen 107.

[37] *Id.* at 109.

[38] *Id.* at 110.

[39] *Ibid.*

Stephens would be qualms about killing the innocent, but utilitarians do not recoil at the idea of killing as an absolute evil. It all depends on the competing interests at stake.

It is clear that Lord Coleridge was aware of Stephen's view of lesser evils as justification. Coleridge apparently had great respect for Stephen and appears relieved to report that "we have the best authority for saying that [Stephen's theory of expediency] was not meant to cover" the case at hand.[40] That good authority was Fitzjames Stephen himself, who had communicated privately with Coleridge about the outcome of the case.[41] Yet in fact, as Stephen wrote later, the only qualm he had about justifying the killing was that, according to the jury's verdict, the likelihood of death at sea without consuming the boy was not sufficiently great.[42]

The passion of Lord Coleridge runs to a different principle. Though utilitarian in his posture toward excuses and influencing future behavior, Lord Coleridge takes a high moral stand about the unqualified evil of killing the innocent. "[T]he absolute divorce of law from morality," we are told, "would be of fatal consequence."[43] And that absolute divorce would occur "if the temptation to murder in this case were held to be an absolute defence of it."[44] Coleridge did not reject the principle of lesser evils because the probability of death at sea was not sufficiently great. He rejected the idea, root and branch, and delivered himself of a passionate opinion on the Christian duty to die for the sake of principle.

The outcome of the case is Kantian at the level of justification and utilitarian at the level of excuses—the worst possible combination for Dudley and Stephens. It is not surprising that the decision pleased no one. German writers, who would agree that the killing of the innocent can never be justified, condemn the judgment for failing to examine more carefully whether the wrongful killing was excusable.[45] Contemporary utilitarian writers condemn the judg-

[40] 14 Q.B.D. at 286.

[41] See F. Stephen, *supra* note 24, at 37 n.2 (referring to Coleridge's statement, Stephen wrote, "I authorized this statement . . .").

[42] *Ibid.*

[43] 14 Q.B.D. at 287.

[44] *Ibid.*

[45] See note 29 *supra*.

ment for failing to recognize the defense of lesser evils.[46] The effect of the judgment on the defense of lesser evils is now being overcome by legislation, particularly in the United States.[47] But the effect on the theory of excuse is still being felt in the common-law world. The Model Penal Code contains no excuse other than duress, which is defined narrowly to require a threat of unlawful force against the defendant.[48] And in case after case, judges recapitulate the concern of the Queen's Bench that an acquittal in a case of personal necessity would have undesirable social consequences.[49]

One area of recurrent prosecution that lends itself to the excuse of personal necessity is the range of prison escapes in response to unsanitary conditions or threats of personal harm. A good example is State v. Green, decided in 1972 by the Supreme Court of Missouri.[50] The defendant inmate had suffered a series of homosexual rapes by fellow convicts. He sought help from the guards, who ignored his pleas. On the day of his escape, four other convicts told him they would rape him that evening. There was no available protective confinement other than the disciplinary "hole." As you or I would have done under the circumstances, Green went over the wall. Upon being caught, he was charged with escaping from a state institution, convicted and sentenced to an additional three-year term. At trial, he sought to introduce evidence pertaining to the threatened rapes, but the trial judge ruled that the evidence was immaterial. The Supreme Court affirmed, over a vigorous dissent.

The majority in *Green* assumed that the only plausible defense was the claim of lesser evils as a justification for the escape. Yet the claim can be made out only by balancing the considerations

[46] Williams 741–45; MPC §3.02, Comment at 9–10 (Tent. Draft No. 8, 1958).

[47] See §10.2, at notes 52–60 *supra*.

[48] MPC §2.09. *Cf.* S. Kadish & M. Paulsen, Criminal Law and its Processes 570 (3d ed. 1975) (pointing out the gap in the Code's coverage). For a sound critique of the conceptual confusion in the Model Penal Code, see Comment, *Justification: The Impact of the Model Penal Code on Statutory Reform*, 75 Colum. L. Rev. 914, 922–24, 960–61 (1975).

[49] See cases cited notes 51–52 *infra*.

[50] 470 S.W.2d 565 (Mo. 1971), *cert. denied*, 405 U.S. 1073 (1972).

for and against the escape. In *Green,* this process of balancing came out the same way as it had in all other appellate opinions in this line of cases. When the judges start toting up the considerations on both sides, they are readily convinced that the need to maintain prison discipline is the most important value in the balance and therefore, the escape, which undermines discipline, always comes out to be the greater and not the lesser evil.[51] Sometimes the judges reject the defense outright, sometimes after examining the competing interests.[52] In either event, of all the cases appealed, there appears never to have been a reversal on grounds that the escape was justified.

The defendant in a case of necessitated escape has a far better chance of acquittal if he can direct the court's attention away from the problem of prison discipline and focus instead on his personal predicament. If he can successfully frame the issue as a problem of excuse rather than justification, he has a far better chance of success—not with the utilitarian writers, but with the judges who have a greater sense of compassion. Judge Seiler dissented in *Green* on the ground that the excuse of duress could properly be extended to cover cases of criminal conduct in reaction to threats

[51] People v. Richards, 269 Cal. App. 2d 768, 778, 75 Cal. Rptr. 597, 604 (1969) (referring to "the destruction of the general discipline of the prison"); People v. Noble, 18 Mich. App. 300, 303, 170 N.W.2d 916, 918 (1969) (court feared a "rash of escapes all rationalized by unverifiable tales of sexual assault").

[52] See Dempsey v. United States, 283 F.2d 934 (5th Cir. 1960) (defense rejected on behalf of escapee who was a diabetic and claimed that he escaped to get a needed shot of insulin); People v. Whipple, 100 Cal. App. 261, 279 P. 1008 (1929) (defendant sought to defend his escape on the ground that prison conditions were intolerable; defense rejected); State v. Palmer, 45 Del. 308, 72 A.2d 442 (Ct. Gen. Sess. 1950) (defense of the necessity rejected in escape case, the court stressing "[s]ound reasons of public policy," *id.* at 310, 72 A.2d at 444); State v. Cahill, 196 Iowa 486, 194 N.W. 191 (1923) (defense of necessity rejected in case of escape from allegedly intolerable solitary confinement); Hinkle v. Commonwealth, 23 Ky. L. Rep. 1988, 66 S.W. 816 (1902) (possibility of defense rejected even though defendant argued that he escaped for fear of being shot); State v. Davis, 14 Nev. 439 (1880) (possibility of justifying escape from allegedly intolerable conditions rejected); People v. Brown, 70 Misc. 2d 224, 333 N.Y.S.2d 342 (1972) (defense of lesser evils held inapplicable to case in which convicts held guards as hostages in order to protest prison conditions).

rather than in compliance with them.[53] In a case tried in 1971 in Sacramento, California, the defendants successfully argued that the defense of duress applied to their case and they were acquitted.[54] In several recent appellate decisions, judges have sensitively begun to fashion an excuse for inmates caught in a situation of great personal danger. In *Lovercamp*, which is likely to become a leading case favoring acquittal, the California Court of Appeals reasoned that the courts should direct their attention away from the problem of justification and the weighing of competing interests and attend instead "to the individual dilemma."[55] In the prison escape cases, the court reasoned, the central question is whether "the act of escape was the only viable and reasonable choice available." The court hedged its recognition of an excuse by various conditions, including avoidance of injury to innocent persons and surrendering upon reaching a position of safety from the imminent threat.[56] These rules are doctrinal approximations of necessity as an excuse, and thus they are but transient limitations in the continuing effort of the common law to refine criteria for fairly holding people liable for their wrongful acts.

§**10.4.2. Duress.** The claim of duress has traditionally had a firmer footing in the theory of criminal liability than the related claim of necessity. Though text writers in the common law have resisted recognition of the excuse,[57] the courts have been more compassionate.[58] The only legal system we have considered that does

[53] 470 S.W.2d at 568.

[54] People v. Cooper, No. 38602 (Sacramento County Super. Ct. Aug. 11, 1971), discussed in Note, *Duress and the Prison Escape: A New Use for an Old Defense*, 45 S. Cal. L. Rev. 1062 (1972). According to the latter report, defense counsel argued at trial that because the inmates feared for their lives, the case should be treated as one of duress under Cal. Penal Code §26 (8), 45 S. Cal. L. Rev. at 1062–63.

[55] People v. Lovercamp, 43 Cal. App. 3d 823, 827, 118 Cal. Rptr. 110, 112 (1974); *accord:* People v. Harmon, 53 Mich. App. 482, 220 N.W.2d 212 (1974).

[56] 43 Cal. App. 3d at 832, 118 Cal. Rptr. at 115.

[57] 1 Hale 40 (limited excuse recognized in wartime if accused is intimidated by the enemy); 2 Stephen 107 (opposed in all cases); Williams 751 (recognizes that excuse exists but considers it a conceptual anomaly).

[58] E.g. Rex v. Crutchley, 172 Eng. Rep. 909 (1831) (charge of malicious destruction of property); State v. St. Clair, 262 S.W.2d 25 (Mo. 1953) (robbery); Regina v. Hudson, [1971] 2 All E.R. 244 (Crim. App.) (perjury).

not recognize duress or coercion as a distinct defense is the Soviet Union.[59]

LaFave & Scott explain the defense as an instance of the general principle of lesser evils.[60] If the defense is not available in homicide cases,[61] it might often be true that the actor under duress asserts himself on behalf of the greater interest. If his life is threatened and he commits a wrong less serious than homicide, then the principle of lesser evils would seem to cover the case. But if the principle of lesser evils implies that the conduct is justified, a little reflection shows that this view of the defense leads to unacceptable consequences.

Suppose a terrorist group kidnaps an heiress (call her Patty) and threatens to kill her unless she robs a bank with them. They wait at the door as Patty goes inside. If we should say that her conduct is justified, two important systemic conclusions would follow. [62] First, the teller would not be entitled to resist the robbery; and, secondly, other persons would be entitled to come to her assistance. It might even follow that the rest of the terrorist band, waiting at the door, would not be guilty as accessories, for even under the Model Penal Code there are serious problems in holding accessories liable for the justifiable behavior of another.[63] These systemic implications are obviously counter-intuitive. Even though we might recognize a personal excuse on behalf of Patty, we should want the bank personnel to be able to resist and we should certainly wish to convict the terrorist band of bank robbery. [64]

Duress is a paradigmatic example of an excuse. It is so regarded

[59] See Kurs (GP 1968) at 320 (physical compulsion negates conduct, but psychological compulsion not an excuse). Some cases of duress might be treated as claims of justification under Ugol. kod. (RSFSR) §14 (lesser evils).

[60] LaFave & Scott 378–79.

[61] This was the rule of the older cases, e.g., Arp v. State, 97 Ala. 5, 12 So. 301 (1893); State v. Nargashian, 26 R.I. 299, 58 A. 953 (1904). *But cf.* p. 831 *infra.*

[62] See §10.1.1 *supra.*

[63] See §8.7.3 *supra.* Note the accessories could arguably be held as principals acting through Patty as their agent. Regina v. Bourne, 36 Crim. App. R. 125 (1952) (defendant guilty of buggery for having forced his wife to copulate with a dog).

[64] LaFave & Scott may think that resistance is permissible against force justified on the ground of lesser evil. MPC §3.11(1) holds to the contrary.

in France[65] and Germany.[66] The Model Penal Code treats the issue of duress outside the chapter on justification and takes the controlling criteria to be whether the actor is "coerced" by threats to the point that a "person of reasonable firmness in his situation would have been unable to resist."[67] In an important English precedent decided in 1971,[68] the court made it clear that the underlying issue in duress is the involuntariness of the defendant's act. A young girl named Hudson had committed perjury for fear that a friend of the defendant would "cut her up." The man she feared was sitting in the courtroom as she testified. The problem in the case was whether the threat was sufficiently imminent to excuse the perjury, but the Court of Appeal ruled that this was a matter for the jury to decide. In explaining the defense of duress, the court stressed that there was a ground for acquittal "if the will of the accused [was] overborne by threats of death or serious personal injury so the commission of the alleged offense was no longer the voluntary act of the accused."[69] Some writers may balk at metaphoric language about the "will's being overborne" by threats, but this indeed is one effective way to state the true ground of the excuse.

If duress in fact functions as an excuse, there should be no impediment to invoking the excuse to any wrongful act, including homicide. This has long been the posture of German law.[70] And now the Model Penal Code recommends the same principle for the United States.[71] Several states have already adopted sweeping provisions on duress with no explicit exception in homicide cases.[72]

These statutes have yet to be interpreted by the courts. And two recent decisions in England—one by the House of Lords and the other by the Privy Council—indicate how controversial the matter

[65] Code Pénal §64.
[66] StGB 1871, §52; StGB §35.
[67] MPC §2.09.
[68] Regina v. Hudson, [1971] 2 All E.R. 244 (Crim. App.).
[69] *Id.* at 246.
[70] See Judgment of July 12, 1926, 60 RGSt. 318.
[71] MPC §2.09.
[72] E.g., Del. Code Ann. tit. 11, §431; Hawaii Penal Code §231; Pa. Cons. Stat. Ann. tit. 18, §309; Tex. Penal Code §8.05.

of duress in homicide cases still is. In both cases the defendant was convicted of murder after a ruling that evidence of duress was inadmissible. In *Lynch* the defendant was guilty of aiding and abetting homicide by driving a known IRA terrorist to the place where he and two other men killed a constable.[73] In *Abbott,* on appeal from Trinidad and Tobago, the defendant held the victim while an accomplice stabbed her.[74] Three of the five Lords hearing *Lynch* voted to reverse; but in *Abbott,* decided a year later, the panel of Lords hearing the case was slightly different. One of the dissenters from *Lynch* joined two new judges to affirm the conviction; two Lords from the majority in *Lynch* entered a stinging dissent.

The only distinction offered by the majority in *Abbott* was that it mattered whether the defendant aided and abetted the homicide or actually participated in the killing. Thus the Lords revived points in the theory of complicity that Anglo-American lawyers thought had long since ceased to matter.[75] The issue, of course, was simply whether the defendant should be entitled to offer evidence on the issue and have it decided by the jury. It may be true that holding the victim during the fatal assault is worse than driving the murderers to the scene of the crime. And it would follow that a higher degree of external pressure should be necessary to excuse direct involvement with the killing. But once the principle is admitted that duress can excuse complicity in murder, it hardly makes sense to rule as a matter of law that no degree of threatened harm could excuse a direct killing.

If there is an explanation for the holding in *Abbott,* it is the posture of the majority toward the theory of duress. First, the majority balks at thinking of duress as an excuse for wrongdoing; they suggest that duress brings an act "within the law."[76] Secondly, the conception of duress focusses simply on the side of pressure exerted on the defendant, without considering the rela-

[73] Lynch v. Director of Public Prosecutions, [1975] 1 All E.R. 913 (H.L.).
[74] Abbott v. The Queen, 63 Crim. App. R. 241 (1976) (P.C.).
[75] See generally §8.5 *supra.*
[76] 63 Crim. App. R. at 246.

tionship between the threat to the defendant and the act he must commit. Building on this latter misconception, the majority thought that much worse cases—multiple killings and wartime atrocities—would have to be excused if any case of direct killing was excused.[77] This is a false *reductio ad absurdum*, for if the cost in human lives is sufficiently high we could properly expect someone to resist threats to his own life.[78]

§10.4.3. The Synthesis of Duress and Necessity. The new German code unites the claims of duress and necessity in a single excuse. The provision is worth quoting in full:[79]

> If someone commits a wrongful act in order to avoid an imminent, otherwise unavoidable danger to life, limb, or liberty, either to himself or to a dependent or someone closely connected with him, the actor commits the act without culpability. This is not the case if under the circumstances *it can be fairly expected* of the actor that he suffer the risk; this might be fairly expected of him if he caused the danger, or if he stands in a special legal relationship to the danger. In the latter case, his punishment may be mitigated in conformity with §49(1).[80]

The critical concept facilitating this synthesis is the notion of *Zumutbarkeit*—which is translated in the italicized passage as a criterion of what "can fairly be expected" of the suspect. This standard is the die from which all the terms of the provision are cast. Determining when a risk is sufficiently great to be resisted requires an inquiry about what can be fairly expected of the actor under the circumstances. The code mentions two factors that inform our decision of what we fairly expect from another. If the actor brings the risk on himself, he may be expected to endure the risk; and if he occupies a special office, such as that of police officer or soldier, more may be expected of him than from ordinary citizens.

The doctrine of *Zumutbarkeit* permits German law to transcend

[77] *Ibid.*

[78] *But cf.* Judgment of January 14, 1964, 1964 NJW 730 (recognizing duress as an excuse for the mass murder of Jews in White Russia).

[79] StGB §35(1) (emphasis added).

[80] On the terms of §49(1), see §8.6 at note 2 *supra*.

the particularities of threats in cases of duress and locate duress in a broader normative theory of fair social demands. Like the standard of reasonable care under the circumstances in Anglo-American law, the doctrine has remarkable versatility in German law.[81] It applies as an excuse for taking impermissible risks[82] as well as for intentional wrongdoing. In the context of duress, the Model Penal Code comes remarkably close to the German standard with its emphasis on the force that "a person of reasonable firmness in [the] situation would have been able to resist."[83] French law relies on the analogous standard of *contrainte morale*. The slight reorientation required to expand the concept of duress is to shift one's focus away from the "threat" and the "coercion" and toward the act that is impelled under the circumstances. The question should not be whether the actor can be fairly expected to resist human threats, but whether he can fairly expect to abstain from an act that seems required under the circumstances.

An expansion of duress in Anglo-American law would provide a vehicle for solving the cases of prison escape to avoid homosexual rape. It would also accommodate cases where saving one's own life necessitated the killing of others. Of course, it would do none of these things on a wholesale basis. The question is whether under

[81] See generally, Henkel, *Zumutbarkeit und Unzumutbarkeit als regulatives Rechtsprinzip*, Festschrift für Mezger 249 (1954). The doctrine emerged in the recent decision by the German Supreme Court to invalidate StGB §218a, permitting abortion on demand during the first trimester, as a violation of the constitutional right to life, Grundgesetz §2(2), Judgment of the Constitutional Court, February 25, 1975, 39 BVerfGE 1. Though the state is required to penalize abortion, the legislature may constitutionally recognize categories of permissible abortion on the ground that in some circumstances, carrying the fetus to term is *unzumutbar. Id.* at 48–51.

[82] The leading case is the Judgment of March 23, 1897, 30 RGSt. 25. A coachman knew that one horse in his team had the habit of swishing his tail over the reins. He knew of the risk that the reins might get tangled and he would lose control of the coach. He reported this danger to his employer but was apparently told to continue using the same team of horses. The feared event occurred, to the injury of a bystander. The defendant was acquitted of negligent battery and the Supreme Court affirmed on the ground that although the risk was excessive and wrongful, the employed coachman could not fairly be expected to disobey his employer and risk losing his job.

[83] MPC §2.09.

the concrete circumstances of the act, the particular person could be fairly expected to resist.[84]

§10.4.4. Insanity. The definition, administration and ramifications of the insanity defense express the deepest concerns of the Anglo-American legal culture. Vested with significance that goes beyond its practical impact, the issue of insanity requires us to probe our premises for blaming and punishing. In posing the question whether a particular person is responsible for a criminal act, we are forced to resolve our doubts about whether anyone is ever responsible for criminal conduct. And if some are responsible and some are not, how do we distinguish between them? Is it a matter for the experts or is it a question of common sense? If it is for experts, why do they persistently disagree; if it is a matter of common sense, why is the issue so difficult to resolve?

The recognition that a verdict of not guilty by reason of insanity typically leads to civil commitment raises a host of other issues. If the practical question is not freedom or confinement for the accused, perhaps we should not think of insanity as a defense at all, but rather as a device for sorting out suspects for different modes of treatment. The successful raising of the issues would no longer appear to be a defense but rather "a direction to punish but not to punish criminally."[85]

As a result of this incessant discussion of insanity, its meaning and its function, the English-speaking world has acquired a sophistication about crime and mental illness that Continental scholars could properly admire. If carving out the excuse of mistake of law refined German criminal law, then insanity is the question on which common-law criminal theory has come into its own.

Rather than summarize the vast literature and case law on insanity, we shall attempt to isolate some basic themes and draw

[84] On the problems and dangers of relying on a standard abstracted from the peculiarities of the accused, see Fletcher, *The Individualization of Excusing Conditions,* 47 S. Cal. L. Rev. 1269, 1290–93 (1974).

[85] Packer 134. The significance of this point was considered earlier in assessing whether insanity negates culpability. See §7.3 *supra*.

comparisons with Continental approaches to the claim of insanity. Most of these questions can be explored more deeply by consulting the cited literature.[86]

A. Is Insanity a Condition or an Excuse? There is a fundamental conceptual and functional difference between treating the insane as a class exempt from criminal punishment and treating insanity as an excuse for a particular act. The first trades on the analogy between insanity and infancy; the second, on the analogy between insanity and duress. The distinction between these two conceptions of insanity has profound implications. If insanity is an excuse, then it comes to bear on liability only if it is first established that the act of the accused is wrongful. If the allegedly insane defendant killed another in a barroom brawl, a good defense or even a reasonable doubt of self-defense should preclude consideration of insanity. If, in contrast, insanity is a condition akin to infancy, it would be appropriate to raise the issue at the very outset of the case. The claim of insanity would function as a challenge to the criminal jurisdiction of the court. A determination of insanity would justify the court's assuming an administrative role and ordering civil commitment. Most observers would probably agree that insanity is a subsidiary issue, appropriately considered only as excuse to a wrongful act.[87] But those who draw the analogy between insanity and infancy[88] may have a different view.

The conception of insanity as an ongoing condition carries additional procedural implications. If the actor is affected by insanity at the time of the act, his condition remains presumptively constant at the time of the trial and the verdict of not guilty. At common

[86] For good coverage of the field, see A. Goldstein, The Insanity Defense (1967); H. Fingarette, The Meaning of Criminal Insanity (1972); LaFave & Scott 268–95; Goldstein and Katz, *Abolish the Insanity Defense—Why Not?* 72 Yale L.J. 853 (1963).

[87] Note the jury instructions adopted in Brawner v. United States, 471 F.2d 969, 1008 (D.C. Cir. 1972) ("You are not to consider this defense unless you have first found that the Government has proved beyond a reasonable doubt each essential element of the offense").

[88] Packer 134; 1 Hale 30. It is also common in the Soviet literature to treat insanity in the same category of analysis as infancy. E.g., Kurs (GP 1972) at 192. Both issues pertain to the "subject of the offense." *Cf.* Merle & Vitu 617–32, grouping infants and the insane under the category of *L'aptitude à la sanction.*

law the Crown had *parens patriae* power over lunatics and children and thus there was neither a substantive nor a procedural problem in administratively committing an acquitted "lunatic" to a hospital for the safety of the public.

The general drift of history runs from thinking of insanity as a general condition to thinking of insanity as an excuse for a particular act. It is fairly clear that prior to the nineteenth century, lunatics—like witches—were thought to be a special class of people. They were thought possessed, compared to brutes and "wild beasts" and treated as generally incapable of evil.[89] The image of the insane began to change in the nineteenth century and by the time of M'Naghten's Case in 1843,[90] the conception of insanity as a particularized excuse had taken hold. In his speech to the House of Lords after the acquittal of Daniel M'Naghten, Lord Chief Justice Tindal commented on the general practice at the time of instructing the jury to find whether "at the time of doing the act the accused knew the difference between right and wrong."[91] This generalized inquiry continued to treat insanity as an undifferentiated moral incapacity. A weak-minded person might grasp that some things are wrong, but not others. Therefore, as Tindal, L.C.J., reasoned, the apt question for the criminal law is not whether the actor knows the difference between right and wrong in general, but whether he knows that a particular act is wrong.[92]

[89] See Platt & Diamond, *The Origins and Development of the "Wild Beast" Concept of Mental Illness and Its Relation to Theories of Criminal Responsibility,* 1 J. of Hist. of Behavioral Sciences 355 (1965) (noting that the "wild beast test" was not formulated in those precise terms until the eighteenth century).

[90] 8 Eng. Rep. 718 (1843).

[91] *Id.* at 722–23. *But note* that Tindal, L.C.J., himself had instructed the jury in M'Naghten's trial to find "whether at the time [of] the act . . . the prisoner had or had not the use of his understanding, so as to know that he was doing a wrong or wicked act." *Id.* at 719.

[92] Though Tindal, L.C.J., explicitly disavowed the generalized inquiry whether accused knew the difference between right and wrong, the *M'Naghten* test is still called "the right-wrong test" and criticized as though the test inquires simply whether the accused knew the difference between right and wrong. See Durham v. United States, 214 F.2d 862, 870, 869–72 (D.C. Cir. 1954). For example, the passage from I. Ray, Medical Jurisprudence of Insanity 32 (1838), quoted 214 F.2d at 870 n.22, supports rather than detracts from the *M'Naghten* test.

Thus this speech to the Lords (whence we derive the famous *M'Naghten* test) confirmed the ascendant practice of treating insanity as an excuse bearing on the actor's accountability at a particular moment for a particular act.[93]

M'Naghten also marked the culmination of another trend in understanding insanity, a trend related to, but logically independent of the transition from insanity as a condition to insanity as an excuse. For centuries lunacy was treated as a condition discernible to the untutored eye. If a person's behavior was bizarre, if it was like that of a person possessed, then he or she was insane. There was little that experts could say about the subject. But the conception of insanity began to change when, for example, "insane delusions" began to constitute a form of legal insanity.[94] Delusions come and go; and their onset may not be visible to the untrained observer. At some point in the nineteenth century, insanity ceased to be a matter of common discernment and became an issue on which counsel from medical experts was indispensable. How this transition occurred is not clear, but we do know that by the time of *M'Naghten* the medical conception of insanity was ready for absorption into the law. Amending the instructions he gave in M'Naghten's trial,[95] Tindal, L.C.J., concluded that insanity must be based on a "disease of the mind." In a revealing

[93] The full test is stated 8 Eng. Rep. at 722: "it must be clearly proved that, at the time of the committing of the act, the party accused was labouring under such a defect of reason, from disease of the mind, as not to know the nature and quality of the act he was doing; or, if he did know it, that he did know he was doing what was wrong."

Compare the version of the test currently employed in California, Caljic §4.00: "Legal insanity . . . means a diseased or deranged condition of the mind which makes a person incapable of knowing or understanding the nature and quality of the act, or makes a person incapable of knowing or understanding that his act was wrong."

[94] In the Trial of James Hadfield for attempting to assassinate the King, 27 How. State Trials 1281 (1800), Thomas Erskine argued effectively that insanity did not require a "total deprivation of reason" but that intermittent delusions should suffice. *Id.* at 1311–14. The Court directed an acquittal for Hadfield on the condition that he be committed. *Id.* at 1354–55.

[95] See note 91 *supra*.

admission, the Lord Chief Justice said that when the facts are well established, "the question becomes substantially one of science only."[96]

The two themes that intersected in *M'Naghten* are of continuing concern. We have yet to abandon the notion that insanity is a condition rather than an excuse, and the question of the extent to which the issue is "scientific" is even more perplexing. Though we have moved in the direction of treating insanity as an excuse for wrongdoing, we remain ambivalent about the issue. This is evident in the practice of automatic commitment after jury determination of insanity (or even a reasonable doubt as to insanity). It is only in recent years that we have begun to question the practice of automatic commitment. The current mood is insistent on a supplementary hearing to determine whether the acquitted defendant is sufficiently dangerous to himself or others to be justifiably committed.[97] It remains to be seen, however, whether these hearings will become an arena of dispute or a ritual preceding routine orders of commitment.

B. Is Insanity a Scientific Issue? If people once knew a lunatic when they saw one, that sense of confidence in identifying the criminally insane has long since disappeared. There may be nothing in the accused's behavior that reveals his incapacity. Thus the investigation of insanity has come to presuppose expert diagnosis. With the application of expertise to the issue of guilt or innocence, the nagging question has become whether the ultimate issue of criminal responsibility can be reduced to a scientific inquiry.

There are three distinct senses in which insanity might be thought to be a medical or scientific issue. First, the notion of "insanity" might be thought to be a diagnostic category like "psychosis" or "paranoia." Today, however, it is readily conceded that insanity is a legal and not a medical category. Secondly, the information necessary to analyze insanity—namely, whether the accused suffers from a "defect of reason" or a "disease of the

[96] 8 Eng. Rep. at 723.
[97] See §7.3.2 at note 29 *supra*.

mind" might be thought to be medical data accessible to scientific investigation. The appropriate analogy would be to establishing blood alcohol content in assessing whether the accused was subject to the influence of alcohol at the time of a deed. The data are scientific, but the inference from the data is a matter of judgment and interpretation. The analogy is not entirely apt. For there is considerable disagreement about whether particular diagnostic categories—such as the "sociopathic personality"—constitute a "mental disease or defect."[98] Thus even the basic categories of the insanity test are affected by legal dispute and potential tension between judges and the experts.

Thirdly, insanity might be reduced to a scientific question if it is officially defined so as to minimize the relevance of moral judgment. This was implicitly the ambition of the *Durham* test, adopted in 1954 by the Court of Appeals in the District of Columbia.[99] The test reduced the question of insanity and non-responsibility to a determination whether the act was "the product of a mental disease or defect."

Durham identified the moral issue of accountability with the seemingly scientific issues of diagnosis and causation. As with other arguments reducing value to fact, the affirmation of the fact carries more power than it should. The judges administering *Durham* soon discovered that psychiatric affirmation of the facts of disease and of causation "unduly" influenced the jury on the suppressed issue of value—namely, whether the accused was fairly to blame for a criminal act. The response was to convert the supposedly neutral issues of fact into legal issues beyond the competence of psychiatric expertise. This occurred first with the concept of

[98] This controversy came to the fore in Blocker v. United States, 288 F.2d 853 (D.C. Cir. 1961). In 1957 the staff at St. Elizabeth's hospital made a policy decision to regard a "sociopathic personality" as a "mental disease." On this episode and its impact on the *Blocker* case, see Becker, *Durham Revisited: Psychiatry and the Problem of Crime: Part II,* Psychiatric Annals, September, 1973, at 12, 16–17.

[99] Durham v. United States, 214 F.2d 862 (D.C. Cir. 1954). Note that the court concluded its opinion by saying that under the new test, "juries will continue to make moral judgments . . ." *Id.* at 876. But it was not clear which of the terms in the *Durham* test would invite moral judgment.

"mental disease"[100] and finally with the concept of "causation."[101] Whatever the initial reductionistic ambition, the courts eventually returned to the issues of value implicit in judgments of insanity. By 1972 the disaffection from the pseudo-science of *Durham* was complete, and the Circuit Court of Appeals was prepared to formulate a new set of instructions on insanity that would be patently more judgmental.

The problem in 1972[102] was whether the judges would swing to the opposite extreme and adopt a test that required jurors to assess whether the accused was suffering from a mental disease to the extent that he could not "justly be held responsible"[103] or that "he ought not to be held responsible."[104] Eschewing this extreme, which arguably burdened the jury with an unstructured moral inquiry, the Court adopted the highly conventional test proposed by the Model Penal Code.[105] This latter test, which is fast becoming the dominant rule in the United States, conforms to the definition of insanity used in Germany since 1871[106] and which is codified as well in the Soviet Union.[107] All of these tests consist of the following elements:

1) a recitation of relevant categories of "mental illness,"[108]

[100] McDonald v. United States, 312 F.2d 847, 850–51 (D.C. Cir. 1962) ("mental disease or defect" as "any abnormal condition of the mind which substantially affects mental or emotional processes and substantially impairs behavior controls").

[101] Washington v. United States, 390 F.2d 444 (D.C. Cir. 1967). For a good discussion of the development from *Durham* to *Washington,* see Becker, *supra* note 100, at 12–30.

[102] The issue was posed in United States v. Brawner, 471 F.2d 969 (D.C. Cir. 1972).

[103] This was the alternative proposal to MPC §4.01 (Tent. Draft No. 4, 1955). See 471 F.2d at 986–87 n.24.

[104] This was the language proposed by the Royal Commission on Capital Punishment. See *id.* at 986 n.23.

[105] MPC §4.01.

[106] StGB 1871, §51; StGB §20.

[107] Ugol. kod. (RSFSR) §11.

[108] *Brawner* requires a "mental disease or defect"; StGB §20 lists the following specific conditions: "a diseased mental disturbance, a deep disturbance to consciousness (*Bewusstseinseinstörung*), weak-mindedness or a serious mental defect";

2) a statement linking the "mental illness" to a particular deficiency in the execution of the criminal act,
3) a definition of two types of deficiency in executing the criminal act:
   a) a cognitive deficiency: e.g., not "appreciat[ing] the wrongfulness of the act;"[109]
   b) a volitional deficiency: e.g., not being "able to conform [one's] conduct to the requirements of the law."[110]

It is curious that after the tortuous history of the insanity defense in the United States, the courts and legislatures should gravitate toward a mode of inquiry that has long prevailed on the Continent.[111] This is particularly odd in view of important procedural differences in the adjudication of insanity in the United States and, say, in Germany. Though a more detailed comparative procedural analysis is required, I will mention two differences that might lead one to expect a different test of insanity in common-law courts. First, German law, as well as other Continental systems, recognizes the prosecutor's right to appeal a finding of insanity at trial. Not only is the state entitled to a trial *de novo* at the first level of appeal,[112] but even after the trial *de novo*, the state can appeal errors of law (including mistaken analysis in the trial court's opinion) to the Supreme Court. One might expect the absence of this prerogative in the common law to lead to a narrow, safer definition of insanity.

---

the Soviet test requires "a chronic mental illness, a temporary disturbance of mental activity, weak-mindedness, or any other diseased condition."

[109] *Brawner* requires a finding that the accused "lacked substantial capacity to appreciate the wrongfulness of his conduct"; StGB §20 requires that the actor be "incapable of seeing the wrong he has done"; the Soviet provision requires that the actor "not be able to account to himself for his actions."

[110] *Brawner* requires the actor "lacked substantial capacity to conform his conduct to the requirements of law"; StGB §20 requires that the actor be "incapable of acting according to his perception" that the conduct is wrong; the Soviet provision requires that the actor "not be able to control his actions."

[111] Note that the French Code lacks a definition of insanity; Code Pénal §64 requires simply that the actor be in a "state of insanity at the time of the act." The literature suggests that insanity (*démence*) consists primarily of diseases bearing on the capacity of self-control. Merle & Vitu 619–20.

[112] StPO §§312–327 (*Berufungsinstanz*).

The second procedural difference should have the opposite effect. The insanity defense arises in a common-law trial only if the accused is sufficiently sane to stand trial.[113] German law employs a system of compulsory legal representation,[114] one implication of which is that the insanity of the accused is not a reason for suspending the trial. It follows that common-law courts hear the insanity defense only in a subset of cases, while German courts hear the claim in all cases. It should follow (but does not), that American courts would fashion a standard of insanity oriented to forms of psychological aberration less serious than those that disable the defendant from standing trial.

In light of these differences, how do we explain the tendency of American thinking about insanity to dovetail with established Continental formulae? Perhaps the procedural differences simply offset each other. But another explanation might be that the resolution of concrete cases is less important than the ideological importance of the insanity test in conveying our conception of personal responsibility. The negative implication of the insanity test is that "all others are sane and responsible." The message that the law conveys on that issue is critical. Thus if the common test of insanity in Germany, the Soviet Union and the United States conveys a shared Western conception of personal responsibility, the procedural differences among the systems pale in significance.

C. The Movement To Abolish the Insanity Defense. Raising the ideological dimension of the insanity test invites us to consider the surprisingly large movement in the United States and England to limit the inquiry into insanity to evidence negating the mental element required for conviction. Thus if insanity negated the intent, knowledge, or recklessness required for conviction, it would lead to any acquittal; if not, it would be irrelevant. This is not the place to investigate all the arguments supporting this movement, but it is of some value to chart the diverse strategies taken by its proponents.

[113] For a critique of this practice implicitly favoring the Continental alternative, see Burt & Morris, *A Proposal for the Abolition of the Incompetency Plea*, 40 U. Chi. L. Rev. 66 (1972).

[114] StPO §140.

Virtually all the arguments are grounded in skepticism. Sometimes the skepticism is directed to the substantive issue; sometimes, to the possibility of satisfactorily proving or disproving insanity at trial. Substantive skeptics doubt whether there is coherent difference between the wicked and the sick.[115] The irony is that this camp consists of some people, like Lady Wootton, who regarded wickedness as irrelevant or impossible and therefore wish to treat us all as though we were sick—incapable of evil. At the other extreme, there are skeptics, like Thomas Szasz,[116] who take the issue of personal accountability so seriously that they wish to regard everyone as sane.

The claim that wickedness is impossible or irrelevant is a variation on the standard theme of environmental and psychological determinism. The thesis is a tired one; and the evidence on its behalf, largely a matter of a priori reasoning. What is so surprising is that these skeptics wish to retain the forms of the traditional criminal law. Even if insanity were not an excuse, there should still be trials, and the state should not take custody of anyone without proving that "a prohibited act has been committed."[117]

This formal attachment to the criminal trial, stripped of all issues of responsibility, blame and punishment, leaves one puzzled. If only "an act in violation of the law" must be proved, the question is why? What is the theory of political authority that justifies the state's intervention against someone who has committed a blameless act? If the source of the authority is social protection, why should the state wait until the dangerous offender injures an innocent victim? The frequently offered reply is that the act furnishes good evidence of social dangerousness. That may be true, but surely there must be other equally probative tests of dan-

[115] B. Wootton, Crime and the Criminal Law 46 (blame associated with wickedness, wickedness with sin, and sin with theology): *id.* 73 ("the impossibility of keeping a line between the wicked and the weak-minded now seems to be officially admitted"). To the same effect, see K. Menninger, The Crime of Punishment (1968); State v. Lucas, 30 N.J. 37, 82, 152 A.2d 50, 74 (1959) (Weintraub, J., concurring).

[116] T. Szasz, Law, Liberty and Psychiatry 123–37 (1963); T. Szasz, The Myth of Mental Illness (1961).

[117] B. Wootton, *supra* note 117, at 56.

gerousness. If the requirement of a "criminal" act is retained despite equally probative statistical tests, one suspects that the theorist might be hedging her bets. It would be good if a system of sanctioning without blame could trade on the principles of justice and respect for individual autonomy once characteristic of the criminal process.

The reciprocal skepticism, eloquently expressed by Thomas Szasz,[118] is that we are all responsible and blameworthy for our criminal acts. Mental illness is a myth, or at best a construct useful in therapeutic contexts. Whether these radical claims are true is an empirical matter, turning on whether we can find case studies that would reveal patently uncontrollable human reactions. Now we may in fact misuse the concept of mental illness as a way of dehumanizing and dispensing with threatening personalities. It is much easier to deal with sickness than with hatred and evil. But it hardly follows from these abuses that everyone is always in control of his conduct. And therefore, pending examination of the data, one should be skeptical about this branch of substantive skepticism.

The widely shared sentiment of procedural skepticism responds to the image of protracted trials, conflicting testimony by partisan experts and the sheer burden of trying to assess whether a particular individual lacked capacity to be held accountable for a criminal act. There are no doubt procedural problems and reforms possible. But it is curious to argue from these problems to the conclusion that the defense ought to be abolished. Would anyone wish to abolish the issue of duress because it might be difficult to establish whether the accused was fairly capable of resisting pressure exerted against him? That procedural skepticism should even enter the debate presupposes that insanity is an issue *manqué;* it is extrinsic to the main concern of establishing liability, and therefore if litigating the issue is too troublesome we should dispense with it. Procedural skepticism is influenced by substantive skepticism, specifically by the branch that doubts whether there is a coherent concept of responsibility. If there is no distinction, then

[118] See note 116 *supra.*

of course any effort to establish it at trial would seem, paradoxically, like the ranting of fools.

There is another argument that resembles the strategy of the procedural skeptic, namely, the claim that the defense is often "abused." But if the defendant has an unequivocal right not to be convicted if he is incapable of controlling his conduct, we would never speak of his "abusing"' that right. It is only tenuous rights that are abused. We never speak of abusing the right to counsel, but some claim that the privilege against self-incrimination is abused. Therefore the argument of "abuse" takes us back to the substantive issues of personal rights and governmental authority. The inescapable question is whether convicting the blameless is acceptable in a society committed to respect for individual autonomy.[119]

My view is that it is not acceptable. The criminal law expresses respect for the autonomy of the sane as much as it shows compassion for the insane. The line between the two may shift over time. Our theories of sanity may change. But the line remains. If the criminal law is to be an institution expressing respect as well as compassion, its institutions must be able both to punish the guilty and excuse the weak. These two sentiments depend on each other. Compassion is possible only so far as punishment is the norm. Punishing wrongdoing is possible only so far as we have a concept of accountability for wrongdoing. Respect for autonomy and compassion for the weak are too important to our culture to be easily shaken by the skeptics.

§10.4.5. Intoxication. The issue of intoxication is buffetted between two conflicting principles. One principle is that if someone voluntarily gets drunk and then commits a crime, his prior fault in getting drunk should deprive him of the claim that he was not responsible for his drunken acts. Thus one frequently finds statutory provisions, in the United States as well as in Continental codes,[120] holding that self-induced intoxication is not a defense to

[119] It is worthy of note that two efforts to abolish the insanity defense have been declared unconstitutional. See Sinclair v. State, 161 Miss. 142, 132 So. 581 (1931); State v. Strasburg, 60 Wash. 106, 110 P. 1020 (1920).

[120] For a good historical survey of the problem, see Hall 529–44. *Cf.* Merle & Vitu 620; Ugol. kod. (RSFSR) §12 (intoxication no defense).

any crime. But the period at the end of this provision is in fact only a semicolon. For it is obviously unjust to hold that an intoxicated actor is responsible for all crimes that he might commit as a result of drinking excessively and taking the risk of irresponsible conduct. His fault in rendering himself non-responsible at the time of the violent act is constant, whether he commits a burglary, a rape, or a murder. To bring the scope of his liability into line with his culpability in getting drunk, the law seeks a compromise. There has to be some accommodation between (1) the principle that if someone gets drunk, he is liable for the violent consequences, and (2) the principle that liability and punishment should be graded in proportion to actual culpability.

German law and American law reveal two different approaches to reconciling these conflicting principles. German law includes intoxication along with mental illness as a basis for denying the capacity to be held accountable for a wrongful act.[121] Deference to the conflicting principle of liability for the risk implicit in getting drunk is found in a special section of the Code, which is here translated in full:

§330a. (1) Whoever intentionally or negligently becomes intoxicated through the use of alcohol or other intoxicating substances is punishable up to five years in prison, if while in that intoxicated condition he commits a wrongful act and if by virtue of the intoxication is not responsible for that act (or his non-responsibility is a possibility).

(2) In no event may the punishment be greater than that for the wrongful act committed in the state of intoxication.

The concept of negligence underlying this provision is negligence as to the risk of committing a crime while intoxicated. If the suspect takes adequate precautions against committing a crime while intoxicated, there is no negligence. If, for example, he hires someone to supervise his conduct while he is intoxicated and the hired person unexpectedly fails to restrain him, there would be a good case against liability. If he gets drunk in a bar and while in a state of non-responsibility he throws a bottle at a valuable mirror, he is not punished for the wrongful act of intentionally destroying the

[121] Schönke-Schröder-Lenckner §20, note 16, at 262.

property of another; rather he is punished for the wrongful act of creating a risk that he would behave non-responsibly and intentionally destroy property.

A few points are worth noting about the requirement that the actor commit a wrongful act while intoxicated. If someone assaults him while he is drunk and he responds in self-defense, his act is not wrongful and therefore he is not liable under §330a. If he commits an act that is not wrongful under the code—say, he negligently destroys property in the pub—he is not liable.[122] Thus the theory of the provision is not simply that he negligently take the risk that he might do some harm. The requirement of a wrongful act while intoxicated is an important limitation.

Indeed the limitation suggests that the theory underlying the provision is not simply one of negligently endangering other persons. If risk-taking were the essence of the crime, there would be no concern about the wrongfulness of the intoxicated act and indeed it would be hard to explain why the subsequent act should be required at all. One could think of the offense by analogy to the principle of accessorial liability in the wrongful but excusable acts of another.[123] By getting drunk the actor becomes an accessory, as it were, in his own wrongful, but excusable act. This is not the prevailing understanding of the crime, but the prevailing theory of risk-taking fails to account adequately for a wrongful act as a condition of liability.

The compromise crafted by the common law is entirely different. The approach is to permit evidence of intoxication to reduce the crime to a lower degree, but not to admit evidence of self-induced intoxication if it would result in a total acquittal. The California Penal Code incorporates this compromise by stipulating that intoxication is admissible only to negate a "particular purpose, motive, or intent" that is necessary "to constitute a particular species or degree of crime."[124] When the particular purpose, motive, or intent is undercut by proof of intoxication, the effect is not to

[122] StGB §301 requires an intentional destruction of property.

[123] See §8.7.3 *supra*.

[124] Cal. Penal Code §22.

deny liability, but merely to reduce the offense to one of a lower species or degree. The clearest cases falling within this analysis are crimes defined by committing one offense with the ulterior intent of committing another. Examples are: assault with intent to rape or kill, and burglary, which is defined as breaking and entering with the intent to commit a felony. The general understanding is that intoxication is admissible in order to negate the ulterior intent (to rape, to commit the felony inside the house), but inadmissible to negate the intent required for the base crime (the intent to assault, the intent to break and enter).[125]

This general understanding is expressed by invoking the concepts of general and specific intent. The general intent is the intent accompanying the base offense; the specific intent goes beyond the base offense to reach further unrealized objectives. This distinction glides well through the sea of crimes defined by the pattern "assault with intent to. . . ." Yet the distinction scrapes bottom as soon as we consider more compactly defined offenses, such as murder and larceny. Though malice does not represent an unrealized goal that goes beyond the act of killing, the courts treat it as a form of specific rather than general intent.[126] This view facilitates a compromise between the rigors of denying the relevance of intoxication and allowing it to undercut all liability; in this respect, the classification is functionally sound.

Larceny is a more difficult case, for the intent required, namely, the intent permanently to deprive the owner of his property, does not serve to raise a base offense to a higher order of liability. If that intent is effectively refuted, the defendant should be able to extricate himself from all levels of liability. The charge of larceny could be reduced to the lesser, included offense of criminal trespass, but it is difficult to argue, in the language of the Califor-

[125] E.g., Avey v. State, 249 Md. 385, 240 A.2d 107 (1968) (admissible to negate intent to kill in prosecution for assault with intent to kill); People v. Ruiz, 265 Cal. App. 2d 766, 71 Cal. Rptr. 519 (1968) (admissible in burglary case to negate ulterior intent to commit felony).

[126] People v. Conley, 64 Cal. 2d 310, 411 P.2d 911, 49 Cal. Rptr. 815 (1966) (intoxication as the basis for the claim of diminished capacity); State v. Clark, 102 Ariz. 550, 434 P.2d 636 (1967) (intoxication admissible to negate malice).

nia statute, that the difference between trespass and larceny is one of "species or degree." Also, it is perfectly plausible to think of an intoxicated actor killing intentionally, but without malice. It is more difficult to think of intoxication negating the intent required for larceny yet leaving intact the intent required for criminal trespass. Thus in the context of larceny and other theft offenses, it becomes more difficult to find the appropriate middle ground in which to recognize the exculpatory effect of self-induced intoxication without allowing intoxication to function as a total excuse.

The distinction between general and specific intent is frequently litigated, for the simple reason that the courts tend to employ these terms as though they had a meaning beyond their function as devices for seeking a compromise verdict. The difficulty with taking the term "specific intent" seriously is that the same term is employed in a variety of contexts that have nothing to do with intoxication as an excuse.

Sometimes, the term "specific intent" is used simply to refer to a well-defined intent, such as the intent "permanently to deprive the owner of his property"[127] as opposed to the unclarified intent implicitly required for assault, rape or breaking and entering. In the totally different context of criminal attempts, the term "specific intent" functions to distinguish purposely causing a result from merely causing it knowingly, recklessly, or negligently. It is often said, for example, that attempted murder requires a specific intent to kill,[128] not merely reckless conduct that knowingly entails a high risk of death.

It is not surprising that counsel would repeatedly press precedents from three distinct fields in an effort to classify an intent as "specific" for the purposes of intoxication as an excuse. Sometimes the courts accept these arguments and admit intoxication as exculpatory evidence in larceny cases.[129] Assault with a deadly

[127] See Caljic 14.03 (larceny requires "the specific intent permanently to deprive the owner of his property . . .").

[128] Merritt v. Commonwealth, 164 Va. 653, 661, 180 S.E. 395, 399 (1935) (a person "cannot be guilty of murder unless he has a specific intent to kill . . .").

[129] See State v. Gover, 267 Md. 602, 298 A.2d 378 (1973).

weapon invites a similar process of transplanting precedent. If assault is defined as attempted battery, and attempts require a "specific intent," it is plausible to argue that assault with a deadly weapon requires a "specific intent" and that intoxication should be admissible to negate that intent. If the intent is disproved, the result is not a reduction to a lower offense, but an outright acquittal. The California Supreme Court recently decided two cases in an effort to fend off this argument and to preserve the principle of compromise verdicts in cases of intoxication.[130]

There should be a better way to solve the problem of intoxication than by moving the counters called "general" and "specific" intent. The Model Penal Code recommends that intoxication should be admissible so far as it negates "an element of the offense."[131] The difficulty with this approach is that it allows too much to turn on whether the legislature happens to define assault and rape to include elements of knowledge and intention or whether those elements are taken to be only implicitly required. The Model Penal Code itself defines rape without adverting to a required mental state.[132] Yet rape obviously requires at least knowledge that the actor is engaged in sexual intercourse with a woman. Would it follow from the Code's language in defining rape that "knowledge" is not an element of the offense and therefore that intoxication is inadmissible on the issue? This ambiguity could be corrected by a more explicit definition of rape, but that leaves open the question whether self-induced intoxication ought to be a complete excuse in rape cases. The common-law distinction between general and specific intent provides a better guide to that issue than the simple model of negating the mental state required for the offense.[133]

[130] People v. Hood, 1 Cal. 3d 444, 462 P.2d 370, 82 Cal. Rptr. 618 (1969); People v. Rocha, 3 Cal. 3d 893, 479 P.2d 372, 92 Cal. Rptr. 172 (1971), *accord:* Parker v. United States, 359 F.2d 1009 (D.C. Cir. 1966).

[131] MPC §2.08(1).

[132] MPC §213.1(1).

[133] The courts consistently deny the relevance of intoxication in rape cases and the grounds always are that the required intent is general and not specific. E.g., Frank v. State, 118 So. 219 (Fla. 1960); State v. Ramirez, 84 N.M. 166, 500 P.2d 451

The problem is how we should break away from the confusing doctrines of general and specific intent and yet preserve some social response to rape and assault induced by intoxication. The best solution we have surveyed is the compromise worked out in the German Code. A separate crime of negligent intoxication leading to criminal behavior pinpoints the social danger of improperly using alcohol and drugs, yet retains the principle of culpability as a requirement of liability.

§10.4.6. Inconsistent Duties. The German literature recognizes an additional excusing condition that has little to do with the theme of external pressure and internal incapacities underlying the issues of necessity, duress, insanity and intoxication. Some situations arise in which it appears that no matter what one does, one will violate a legal duty. When there is a genuine conflict of duties, we might be tempted to say that whatever one does is justified and right. But German theorists resist this option because the act might violate an absolute duty, such as the imperative against killing the innocent. Thus the preference is to consider inconsistent duties as a supplementary ground for excusing wrongful behavior.[134]

There appear to be two variations of the problem. In one situation the choice is between affirmatively killing innocent persons and doing nothing, which would effectively result in the death of more innocent persons. To take a hypothetical example, suppose a railroad switchman notices that a train is bearing down on a group of children playing on the tracks. The only way he can avoid the accident is to switch the train onto a second track, but that would probably cause a collision and kill the engineer driving the oncoming train. Under the circumstances, it appears highly likely that fewer people would die if the train were shunted onto the second track. That would appear to be the right thing to do, except that switching the train would be an affirmative act of killing an in-

---

(Ct. App. 1972); State v. Haywood, 2 Wash. App. 109, 466 P.2d 859 (1970) (indecent liberties). The result in these cases is supported by the additional consideration that the act of raping generates a reliable presumption of intent to rape. See the *Frank* case, cited *supra*, at 222.

[134] Jescheck 376–80; Welzel 184–86.

nocent person, while letting the train roll on would be simply a failure to save the lives of the children. The former is, in the view of many, strictly forbidden,[135] while the latter is wrong only if there is an overriding duty to act.

There is one approach to this problem that holds that killing innocent persons by affirmative action is flatly forbidden; whether the killing results in a net savings of life is considered irrelevant. Yet there is an opposing view, which holds that it is right to act in such a way as to minimize the death of innocent persons. According to this latter view, the switchman would not only be entitled, but he would be obligated to switch the train to kill fewer people. Thus there is an inescapable conflict between the moral duty not to kill and the utilitarian duty to act in such a way as to minimize suffering.

This exact problem arose in a German case of the late 1940s—one of the many in which the post-war courts grappled with the problems of accountability for criminal acts encouraged by the Third Reich. In this case a group of physicians were indicted for intentionally killing hospital patients. Their defense was that they were carrying out orders to perform euthanasia on mentally ill patients and that further, they did so only because they believed that they could save many patients by falsely warranting that the patients were curable. They believed, presumably on reasonable grounds, that if they did not participate in the killings, loyal members of the party would do so, with a much higher toll of innocent lives.[136] This is a familiar rationale for complicity with evil, and the appellate court in fact remained unpersuaded that this argument undercut the physicians' culpability for intentional homicide. The court was willing, however, to recognize a special exemption from punishment that was extrinsic to the actor's moral guilt.[137]

Commentators have subsequently argued that this case should be analyzed as a problem of culpability under the rubric of incon-

[135] Recall the discussion in *Dudley & Stephens,* text at notes 29 and 30 *supra.*

[136] Judgment of March 5, 1949, I Entscheidungen des Obersten Gerichtshofes für die Britische Zone 321. *Cf.* Judgment of July 23, 1949, 2 *id.* 117.

[237] On the implications of this decision for the burden of persuasion, see §7.3.3 *supra.*

sistent duties. There was admittedly a duty not to kill; but there was also a duty to act in such a way as to save lives. The only reason we might recognize a conflict of duties in the case of either the railroad switchman or the German physicians is that we are unsure of our moral premises. Neither Kant nor Bentham would see these problems as a conflict of inconsistent duties. For Kant as well as for Catholic moralists, the only relevant duty would be the categorical imperative not to kill—which means not to kill directly by affirmative conduct. For Bentham and other utilitarians, the only relevant duty would be the obligation to minimize suffering, regardless of whether the suffering resulted from an act or from an omission. If we see a conflict between these duties, it is because we cannot decide whether to follow Kant or Bentham. If whatever the actor does in these situations is free from culpability, it is because the moral conviction of the legal system is an equipoise. With the culture torn by conflicting moral premises, we cannot decide whether to demand that people adhere to one or to the other.

The second instance cited as an example of inconsistent duties is the failure to render aid where the actor is duty-bound to render aid to two people and he must choose between them. A father can save but one of his two drowning children; a physician can minister to but one of two dying patients. The argument that there is a breach of duty to the neglected child or patient would go like this. Suppose the physician chooses to save *A* rather than *B*, does he thereby fulfill a personal duty to *A*? If we say yes, it follows that he has a duty to save *A* even if he chooses to save *B*. Therefore if he does aid *B*, he breaches his duty to *A*. If we say there is no duty to save either *A* or *B*, then the physician is free to let them both die—an unacceptable result. One could escape this dilemma by formulating the duty in this special case as the duty to aid one or the other. Even if we rejected that option and insisted that there was a conflict of duty to the neglected party, the wrong in the breach would be different from the first case of killing the innocent. In these cases of failing to render aid, the problem arises from the peculiarity of affirmative duties, namely, that it is possible to be duty-bound to perform logically incompatible acts.

Neither the first nor the second type of case has anything in common with other excusing conditions. Acquitting people caught in these conflicts is not an expression of compassion for human weakness. The first type of case is the consequence of the moral uncertainty of the legal system, not of the moral weakness of the actor. The second is a logical peculiarity of duties to render aid. Thus it might be preferable to treat the category of inconsistent duties as a special category of exemption, rather than as a case of excused wrongdoing.

§**10.5.** *The Theory of Necessary Defense.*

The theory of self-defense, defense of others and defense of property is torn by its conflicting and uncertain premises. Is the defense an excuse based on the necessity of preserving life and limb? Or is it a justification based on the premise that thwarting aggression is the proper thing to do? If it is a justification, is the rationale a variation of lesser evils, or is there a totally independent foundation for the defense? These uncertainties in the basic structure of the defense generate ongoing disputes about (1) the degree of permissible force in particular situations, (2) the duty to retreat, (3) the right of third parties to intervene and (4) the permissibility of resisting excused aggression. These disputes pervade Continental legal systems as well as the common law. Our first task is to explicate the conflicting models of the defense that fuel these debates.

First a word about terminology. To provide a common basis for discussing problems in diverse legal systems we shall use the term "necessary defense" to encompass the specific categories of defense now recognized in Anglo-American law. Both German[1] and Soviet law[2] recognize a general privilege of "necessary de-

§**10.5** [1] StGB 1871, §53; StGB §32.
[2] Ugol. kod. (RSFSR) §13.

fense" as contrasted with the detailed regulation of self-defense, defense of others and defense of property in contemporary American legislation.[3] The broader term "necessary defense" more readily applies to the circumstances of Anglo-American law than the term "self-defense" would carry over to German and Soviet law.[4] Later we shall see that the breaking down of necessary defense into specific categories carried significance in the evolution of the common law.

§10.5.1. Necessary Defense as an Excuse. The first model of the defense is properly a theory of excuse rather than a claim that the use of force is right and proper. It has its origins in the common-sense view that a person sometimes has "no choice" but to kill his adversary. If his back is to the wall, if it is his life or his adversary's, the human response is to kill rather than be killed. Of course, the notion of involuntariness in these cases—of there being no choice but to kill—is not a matter of strict physical involuntariness. In a weak sense, the defender does "choose" to kill his adversary. Stressing the element of involuntariness is but our way of making the moral claim that he is not to be blamed for the kind of choice that other people would make under the same circumstances.

This theory of necessary defense runs parallel to a theory of necessity as an excuse. It is not critical that the slain party be viewed as the aggressor in the fray. Even in an unclarified chance melee, the party retreating to the wall would be able to invoke the defense. The critical perspective is not how the fight started, but the pressures bearing on the defender at the time that he kills or uses other protective force.

A number of important rules follow from this conception of

[3] MPC §3.04 (defense of self); §3.05 (defense of others); §3.06 (defense of property). This basic scheme is widely followed in the newly revised state statutes. See, e.g., Ill. Ann. Stat. c. 38, §§7-1 to 7-3; N.Y. Penal Law §§35.15 to 35.25; Tex. Penal Code §§9.31 to 9.43.

[4] The French term *légitime défense* is also encompassed by the broader term. The French Code treats the defense as an aspect of the law of homicide and battery, Code Pénal §§328, 329.

the defense. First, it is clear that appealing to force presupposes that the defender first retreat, appeal for help or use other options available to him. Further, the scope of the defense is likely to be limited to saving one's own life or limb. It is unlikely that protecting property would be seen as the kind of case where the defender has "no choice" but to kill. Additionally, it follows that third persons would not be able to intervene on the defender's behalf, unless perhaps they were close relatives. These positions coalesce in a minimalist conception of the defense. Where the overriding issue is the involuntariness of the response, one can expect no more.

French, German and English law all recognized this version of the defense at one stage of their development. The defense of *se defendendo* rendered homicide excusable,[5] it presupposed a duty to retreat to the wall[6] and it was limited to the preservation of self and closely related persons.[7] Sixteenth- and seventeenth-century Continental legal sources conceived of the defense in the same way.[8] Early French, like early English, practice relied on the royal pardon as the vehicle for granting the excuse.[9]

§10.5.2. Necessary Defense as a Variation of Lesser Evils. The second model of necessary defense is founded on the principle that it is right and proper to use force, even deadly force, in certain situations. The source of the right is a comparison of the competing interests of the aggressor and the defender, as modified by the important fact that the aggressor is the one party responsible

[5] 3 Coke 55; 1 Hale 479–87; Foster 275; 1 Hawkins 113; 4 Blackstone 184.

[6] 1 Hale 479; 4 Blackstone 184 ("no other possible (or, at least, probable) means of escaping from his assailant").

[7] 1 Hale 474 (recognizing *se defendendo* as between master and servant, husband and wife, child and parent). These same categories are incorporated in Cal. Penal Code §198(3), except that the legislature thought these restrictions should apply to justifiable as well as excusable homicide.

[8] For the German background, see Constitutio Criminalis Carolina §§139, 140 (1532); *cf.* Schröder, *Die Notwehr als Indikator politischer Grundanschauungen,* Festschrift für Maurach 127, 128–29 (1972); G. Vidal, Cours de Droit Criminel 352 (9th ed. by J. Magnol, 1949) (discussing the theory of excuse in the Criminal Ordinance of August, 1670).

[9] *Ibid.*

for the fight. This theory of the defense appears to be a straightforward application of the principle of lesser evils. The problem is that if we simply compared the interests of the two parties, we should never be able to justify the defender's killing the aggressor—at least where only his life is threatened. If it is one life against one, it is hard to see why we should favor either party to the fray.[10]

The factor that skews the balancing in favor of the defender is the aggressor's culpability in starting the fight. As the party morally at fault for threatening the defender's interests, the aggressor is entitled to lesser consideration in the balancing process. His interests are discounted, as it were, by the degree of his culpability. The extent to which his life is discounted determines whether the defender may use deadly force to defend against rape, serious bodily harm, loss of irreplaceable property and even, possibly, the loss of less important interests. The underlying premise is that if someone culpably endangers the interests of another, his interests are less worthy of protection.

This framework of thought lends its characteristic imprint to disputed points in the law of self-defense. It leads to the conceptualization of retreat as a problem of balancing the loss to the defender (his honor, increased risk of harm) against the benefit to the aggressor (saving his life). Whenever the problem of retreat is put in these terms, the inference comes easily that the defendant must favor life over honor. Thus, the practical difference between the two models is expressed first in the range of interests subject to protection by deadly force. If the aggressor's life is sufficiently depreciated by his culpability, one can imagine the defense's extending to serious bodily harm and valuable chattels. As there is no self-evident way to accord weight to conflicting interests, there is no way of specifying the precise importance of culpability in discounting the interests of the aggressor. The entire approach de-

[10] The comparison is even more subtle if we look at it from the perspective of risk. The defender faces the risk of death; in response he imposes certain death on the aggressor. The cost of his act is clearly greater than the benefit of avoiding the risk of death.

mands sensitivity to the conflicting values and to the moral significance of culpability.

A further difference between the two approaches is expressed in the rights of third parties to intervene on behalf of the threatened party. A theory of excused defensive force generates, at most, a right on behalf of close relatives who feel compelled to intervene.[11] A theory of justified defense, in contrast, generates a universal right of intervention coextensive with the defender's own privilege. If the exercise of force in necessary defense is not a concession to human weakness, but a judgment about the right outcome in a particular struggle of conflicting interests, any one should be able to assert the right to act on behalf of the superior interest. No matter who slays or disables the aggressor, the act of defense will vindicate the superior interest in the situation.[12]

This theory of necessary defense should seem familiar to Anglo-American lawyers, for it is the dominant (though not the only) theory of defensive force at work in our system. We take necessary defense to be a privilege rather than an excuse.[13] The tendency is to extend the privilege to third parties. And thus it seems uncontroversial for Glanville Williams to claim that "self-defense can be regarded as a part of necessity [i.e., lesser evils] that has attained relatively fixed rules."[14] The required balancing of interests of the defender against those of the aggressor is expressed in the unquestioned assumption that defensive force must be reasonable and proportionate to the threat.[15] Though deadly force

[11] See note 7 *supra*. *Cf.* StGB §35 (limiting necessity as an excuse to "persons standing in a close relationship").

[12] This emphasis on the objective rectitude of the defense should not obscure the requirement of a justificatory intent. See §7.4.2 *supra*.

[13] See statutes cited note 3 *supra*. *But cf.* the confusion between actual defense and putative defense, which reflects an inability to carry out the logical implications of a theory of justified defensive force. Comment, *Justification: The Impact of the Model Penal Code on Statutory Reform*, 75 Colum. L. Rev. 914, 917–21 (1975).

[14] Williams 733.

[15] LaFave & Scott 391; Caljic §5.30 (self-defense against assault); Ashworth, *Self-Defence and the Right to Life*, 34 Camb. L.J. 282, 296–97 (1975); *cf.* Kadish, *Respect for Life and Regard for Rights in the Criminal Law*, 64 Calif. L. Rev. 871, 886–88 (1976) (noting possible limitations on the principle of proportionality).

might be necessary to avert a minor assault or a petty theft, it is clearly disproportionate to the threat and therefore impermissible.[16]

Of the foreign legal systems under study, only the French system endorses necessary defense as a justification based on the balancing of competing interests.[17] What, then, is the model that prevails in German and Soviet legal theory? Theirs is a third model, once important to the common law, and now harder to grasp in its philosophical premises.

§10.5.3. Necessary Defense and the Vindication of Autonomy. The third model of necessary defense takes as its premise that the significant feature is not the conflict of interests, but the unilateral violation of the defender's autonomy. If a person's autonomy is compromised by the intrusion, then the defender has the right to expel the intruder and restore the integrity of his domain. The underlying image is that of a state of warfare. An aggressor's violation of our rights is akin to an intrusion of foreign troops on our soil. As we are inclined to believe that any community has the absolute right to expel foreign invaders, any person attacked by another should have the absolute right to counteract aggression against his vital interests.

This theory of necessary defense has taken hold in various legal systems at various stages of history. The right to kill manifest thieves breaking the close confirms early appreciation for the value of personal autonomy.[18] In 1532, legislation recognized that the killing of manifest thieves, robbers and other assailants was justifiable, and not merely excusable homicide.[19] In the following century Sir Edward Coke wrote that "no man shall (ever) give way to a thief, etc., neither shall he forfeit anything."[20] John Locke sup-

[16] For cases where the use of force was necessary to prevent theft but was held to be unreasonable, see State v. Metcalfe, 203 Iowa 155, 212 N.W. 382 (1927); Commonwealth v. Emmons, 157 Pa. Super. 495, 43 A.2d 568 (1945).

[17] See, e.g., Merle & Vitu 440; 1 Bouzat & Pinatel §290, at 363; *but cf.* Geyer, note 24 *infra.*

[18] Recall the dispute about whether killing manifest thieves was a private act of justice or the exercise of a privileged defensive force, §1.3.1 at notes 11–15 *supra.*

[19] 24 Hen. VIII, c. 5 (1532).

[20] 3 Coke 55.

ported the same theory of an absolute right to protect one's liberty and other rights from encroachments by an aggressor.[21] Among the various accounts for this theory one finds the common theme that the act of aggression puts the aggressor outside the protection of the law. Locke, for example, speaks of the aggressor's being in a "state of war" with the defender.[22] The argument is that the aggression breaches an implicit contract among autonomous agents, according to which each person or country is bound to respect the living space of others. The intrusion upon someone's living space itself triggers a justified response.

Though John Locke's theory of defensive force may not be compelling today, there are two important areas in which Anglo-American law still responds to the principle of autonomy. The first is the defense of one's home or "castle" from outside intrusion, and the second is the claim often made, but typically unfounded in the law, that everyone has an absolute right to prevent the commission of a felony.[23] The link between necessary defense and the protection of personal autonomy took hold in German thought in the nineteenth century[24] and today the connection is so powerful that opponents have difficulties undoing it.[25] Though the German commitment to autonomy reflects a liberal theory of law, Soviet jurisprudence has adopted many of the same principles for totally different reasons. The theory of autonomy generates maximum scope for the privilege and thus encourages private parties to maintain the social order by injuring or killing aggressors.[26] Thus one can come to Coke's conclusion that "no man shall ever forfeit

[21] J. Locke, Treatise of Civil Government 14 (Sherman ed. 1937).

[22] *Ibid.*

[23] Note the breakdown of this argument in Blackstone's analysis, *infra* note 42.

[24] One of the first systematic statements of the theory was Berner, *Die Notwehrtheorie,* 1848 Archiv des Criminalrechts 547; *but cf.* the opposition expressed by A. Geyer, Die Lehre von der Notwehr 39–42 (1857) (favoring use of deadly force only to save life; citing other writers in accord).

[25] On the unsuccessful campaign to incorporate the principle of proportionality in the 1975 criminal code, see Fletcher, *Proportionality and the Psychotic Aggressor: A Vignette in Comparative Criminal Theory,* 8 Israel L. Rev. 367, 381–83 (1973).

[26] See the recent decree encouraging a broader use of defensive force as part of the "struggle against crime." Decree No. 11 of the Plenum of the Supreme Court of

anything," either because the principle of autonomy is intrinsically appealing or because adopting it may serve the goal of deterring anti-social conduct.

There are several other features of this theory of the defense that we should examine before we turn to its implications for specific controverted issues in the law of self-defense. First, it is important to see the defense as informed by a trans-positivistic value of autonomy. The case law does not specify the contours of autonomy; rather the concept of autonomy tells us what the case results should be. As a concept beyond the law, it functions as a premise from which the courts seek to deduce results, much as the concept of "property" once functioned, and as the notion of "privacy" now shapes the thinking of so many people on current constitutional issues. Secondly, in contrast to necessary defense as a variation of lesser evils, the aggressor's culpability appears to be irrelevant; what counts is the objective nature of the aggressor's intrusion. This disregard for the moral blameworthiness of the aggressor matches our intuitions in cases of warfare. My assumption is that most people defending their country from foreign attack regard it as proper to be indifferent to whether the invaders have been brainwashed to the point of insanity or whether they are acting out of needs that make their conduct understandable and even blameless. Defending one's living space is not to punish the intruder for his culpable conduct, but to nullify an objectively hostile intrusion by an enemy.

If culpability is not the touchstone, then we encounter difficulties determining when a physical threat constitutes "aggression." One thorny patch is the cluster of attacks that threaten the vital interests of the defender, but are not instances of human conduct by the alleged aggressor. For example, if a driver suddenly has a heart attack and his car careens out of control, can a threatened pedestrian treat him as though he were an aggressor? The pedestrian might be able to divert the car over a cliff or cause it to

the USSR, December 4, 1969, [1970] Bulletin of the Supreme Court of the USSR, no. 1, at 15 [in Russian]. On the political significance of this decree, see Schröder, *supra* note 8, at 135–36.

crash into a nearby building. Does he have a right to defend himself if the driver is not only free from blame, but his attack is in no sense his own act? Of course, the theory of necessity as an excuse might support an acquittal if he should respond, but the more difficult question is whether the defensive conduct should be treated as right and proper. That issue requires that one confront the question whether the concept of aggression presupposes purposive conduct, or whether any threatening event will do.[27]

This issue becomes acute in assessing the rationale of abortion. The question is whether the fetus can be seen as an aggressor intruding upon the sanctity of the mother's body. The brunt of Thompson's influential article on abortion[28] is precisely that the fetus is an unnatural intruder, much like a person in need of kidney dialysis who would be parasitic on the mother's kidneys. The view that the fetus is a "wrongful aggressor" is a tempting metaphor for those seeking to justify abortion. The only question is whether extending the notion of aggression in this way is consistent with our intuitions in other cases in which the threat derives from the body, but not the act of another being. Is a person falling on me the same as a psychotic's attacking me? It seems odd to say that the two attacks are of the same moral quality. The issue in this context is not culpability, but the significance of human action in treating another person as a wrongful intruder. This might well be the proper distinction to draw from Holmes' famous aphorism: "even a dog distinguishes between being stumbled over and being kicked."[29]

A further problem in construing the concept of aggression is whether the notion turns on the phenomenon of a physical attack

[27] The German literature is ambivalent on the boundaries of the "attack" required for necessary defense. It is often said that any danger emanating from human conduct (*Verhalten*) is sufficient for an attack, Jescheck 252, Stratenwerth 135, but Welzel goes so far as to include risks triggered by a stomach cramp. Welzel 85. *Cf.* Schönke-Schröder-Lenckner §32, note 3, at 429 (noting that the question whether an attack presupposes a human act need not be decided, for, as the authors contend, an attack not based on a human act would not be wrongful).

[28] Thompson, *A Defe·se of Abortion,* 1 J. Phil. & Pub. Affairs 47 (1971).

[29] Holmes 3.

or whether any unjustified violation of the defender's rights counts as an instance of wrongful aggression. German and Soviet theorists extend the concept of necessary defense to the protection and vindication of virtually all the rights and interests recognized by the law. A 1963 Bavarian case goes so far as to treat the improper sequestering of a parking space as an "attack" generating a right to respond with defensive force.[30] Even though German and Soviet theory extends th notion of autonomy to include all of one's rights, the formal criterion of legitimate force is still linked to the core notion of an "attack" or "encroachment" (*Angriff, posjagatel'stvo*).[31] Of course, we do not ordinarily think of the violations of rights, such as the right to a parking space, as an encroachment akin to a physical attack. Thus the task of German and Soviet legal theory is to explain how the violation of a right is tantamount to a physical intrusion. The link between the two concepts is forged, particularly in German theory, by invoking the medium of a Legal Order that is threatened by every violation of private rights.[32] The Legal Order (*die Rechtsordnung*) is the set of private rights writ large. The violation of one person's rights betokens a threat to the rights of all. This way of thinking is not so different from investing private harms with public significance. In the German instance, the metaphysics of rights serves to interweave the notions of violating rights, attacking the Legal Order and physically assaulting a private person.

§10.5.4. Disputed Points in the Theory of Self-Defense. The value of having articulated these models of necessary defense is that now we are in a position to assess discrete doctrinal disputes as part of the broader tension among conflicting theories of liability.

A. The Duty To Retreat. We have already noted that the first

[30] Judgment of the High State Court (*Oberlandesgericht*) in Bavaria, January 22, 1963, 1963 NJW 824.

[31] StGB §32(2); Ugol. kod. (RSFSR) §13.

[32] Schönke-Schröder-Lenckner §32, note 1, at 429; Jescheck 251 (noting, however, that the protection of the legal order does not imply that necessary defense bears the quality of punishment); Schmidhäuser, *Über die Wertstruktur der Notwehr,* Festschrift für R. Honig 185, 193–94, 198 (1970).

two models of necessary defense readily support a duty to retreat prior to killing the assailant. The rationale of excuse leads to this result, for it is only if the defending party has no reasonable alternative that his killing is excused. The rationale of lesser evils leads to the same conclusion, for if the choice is between the actor's honor and the aggressor's life, contemporary sentiment would obviously favor saving the aggressor's life. The approach implicit in the third theory of the defense is entirely different. The basic maxim underlying the German conception of the defense is: *Das Recht braucht dem Unrecht nicht zu weichen* (Right need never yield to wrong).[33] If a defender is obligated to retreat, he is obligated to give way to the forces of *Unrecht* or the Wrong. The issue is not balancing the value of autonomy against the value of the aggressor's life, but whether the defender enjoys autonomy to begin with. If so, then the notion of autonomy entails a right forcibly to reassert one's rightful position. This way of thinking may seem strange to those of us fearful of absolutes, but the principle of autonomy implicitly influences common law as well as Continental thinking about the duty to retreat.

German law rejects the duty to retreat in all cases, except attacks by children and the deranged.[34] The latter exception may derive from doubts about whether necessary force, rather than lesser evils, is the appropriate vehicle for gauging permissible force against non-culpable aggressors. In any event the pure theory of

[33] This maxim was apparently first invoked by Geyer, *supra* note 24, at 557, 562. Since then it has become part of the "prevailing theory" of the German theory of necessary defense. See Schönke-Schröder-Lenckner §32, note 1, at 429.

[34] Stratenwerth 138; Samson in SK StGB §32, note 21, at 258; Jescheck 257. The rationale for this duty is disputed. One argument is that defender must retreat whenever he can do so without sacrificing his honor or otherwise damaging his interests. Judgment of the Supreme Court, October 2, 1953, 5 BGHSt. 245, 248; Welzel 87. The alternative theory, more in keeping with the principle of defending personal autonomy and the Legal Order, is that attacks by the insane, children and other non-responsible aggressors do not undermine the Legal Order. See Schmidhäuser, *supra* note 32, at 196 (an attack subject to defensive force presupposes that the aggressor "share the values of the Legal Order"); Samson in SK StGB §32, note 21, at 258. The latter theory leads to the reclassification of attacks by the insane as cases of lesser evils and necessity as an excuse, rather than necessary defense. Schmidhäuser 348.

the defense, based upon the defenders' upholding the Legal Order, seems now to apply only against responsible aggressors.[35]

Anglo-American law has undergone several stages in the evolution of its posture toward the duty to retreat, particularly in cases of deadly force. Prior to the nineteenth century, the excuse of *se defendendo* coexisted with the justification recognized in the Statute of 1532.[36] The former implied a duty to retreat; the latter, the principle of autonomy and the right not to "give way to a thief."[37] In the course of the nineteenth century, the distinction between justifiable and excusable homicide lost its procedural manifestations,[38] and thus the impulse was to fashion a single body of principles covering cases of both *se defendendo* and justifiable homicide. But if there was to be only one law of necessary defense, the question was whether it would incorporate the duty to retreat from *se defendendo* or follow the principle of autonomy implicit in the law of justifiable homicide.

Nineteenth-century case law was divided,[39] as might be predicted, but the weight of authority appeared to favor the principle of autonomy. This commitment to autonomy was expressed in the recurrent line of the opinions that if the defendant was "in a place that he had a right to be," then he had the right to stand his ground and vindicate his autonomy.[40] Yet the notion of defending

[35] The case of the person attacking under mistake is problematic under Schmidhäuser's theory, see note 34 *supra;* for the mistaken aggressor, in contrast to the psychotic aggressor, "shares in the values of the Legal Order." *Cf.* the discussion of putative defense in §10.1.2 *supra.*

[36] See note 19 *supra.*

[37] See the theories of Coke and Locke, notes 20–22 *supra.*

[38] On the forfeiture of goods linked with excusable homicide, see §5.1.1 *supra.*

[39] *Compare* Beard v. United States, 158 U.S. 550 (1895) (approving a broad right of necessary defense by a "true man without fault" in a "place where he has a right to be") *with* Allen v. United States, 164 U.S. 492 (1896) (limiting *Beard* to its facts, namely, the defense of habitation and its surrounding area; retreat required in all other cases). For other cases supporting the former view, see note 40 *infra;* for examples of the latter view, see Pond v. People, 8 Mich. 149 (1860); Commonwealth v. Drum, 58 Pa. 9 (1868). See generally Beale, *Retreat from Murderous Assault,* 16 Harv. L. Rev. 567 (1903); Perkins, *Self-Defense Reexamined,* 1 U.C.L.A.L. Rev. 133 (1954).

[40] See e.g., Runyan v. State, 57 Ind. 80 (1877); People v. Gonzales, 71 Cal. 569, 12 P. 783 (1887); Fowler v. State, 8 Okla. Crim. 130, 126 P. 831 (1912). *Cf.* Erwin v.

personal autonomy remained limited to the privilege of repelling aggression to tangible interests.[41]

As early as the eighteenth century, however, Blackstone had laid the foundation for a view of defensive force that would eventually displace the principle of autonomy from the Anglo-American conception of necessary defense. Blackstone rejected Locke's analogy between warfare and necessary defense on the ground that in civil society "the king and his courts are the *vindices injuriarum* and will give to the party wronged all the satisfaction he deserves."[42] Joseph Beale picked up this theme in the early twentieth century with his claim that the function of the law is to provide redress for the violation of rights, but not to protect and approve the vindication of rights jeopardized by the aggression of others.[43] According to this view of necessary defense, the private use of force is tolerated only because the state fails in its task of providing protection against aggression. If the privilege of necessary defense is derivative of the state's monopoly of force, then the regulation of the defense invariably reflects the interests both of the aggressor and the defender. If the latter can save the life of the former by retreating from the conflict, the greater social good requires him to withdraw. Blackstone's view of the state as the vindicator of our rights leads us to the denial of personal autonomy as a relevant premise in the theory of self-defense. This leaves the field clear to consider the problem of retreat from the standpoint of the competing interests at stake.[44]

Though the case law remains conflicted, the future might well

---

State, 29 Ohio St. 186 (1876) ("true man who is without fault" not required to retreat). For contemporary expressions of the same doctrine, see People v. Shields, 19 Ill. App. 3d 1080, 311 N.E.2d 212 (1974); People v. Collins, 189 Cal. App. 2d 575, 11 Cal. Rptr. 504 (1961).

[41] Compare the German view discussed at note 30 *supra*.

[42] 4 Blackstone 180–81, 185.

[43] Beale, *supra* note 39, at 581.

[44] The "derivative" theory of necessary defense is criticized in the Soviet literature, Kurs (GP 1970) at 349; Piontovsky, Theory of the Offense in Soviet Criminal Law 425 (1961) [in Russian]. Though the Soviet policy may be deterrence of crime, the rationale of this critique is that necessary defense is an "inalienable right." See Decree of the Supreme Court, *supra* note 26, at 17.

be reflected in the Model Penal Code's recommending the duty to retreat as the norm,[45] with exceptions acknowledged in particular cases.[46] Several states have already adopted this recommendation,[47] and more are likely to do so in the future. It is always possible, however, that our sentiments about private violence will shift and that we will begin to think, with Soviet jurists, that the maximum use of defensive force effectively deters crime.

The principle of autonomy survives in cases in which the defender is assailed in his home,[48] on the surrounding land,[49] and even at his place of work.[50] The special position of someone attacked in his private quarters continues to express our respect for personal autonomy, but it is harder to understand extending this theory to one's place of work.[51] If, in general, there should be a duty to retreat rather than kill, the same preference for life should prevail whether one is attacked at work or at play. This exception to the general duty to retreat is best understood as the survival of a compromise in the effort to reconcile the principle of autonomy with the criteria of *se defendendo*.

B. *Rights of Third Parties.* Thinking of necessary defense as

[45] MPC §3.04(2)(b)(ii).

[46] The primary exception is cases of defense in one's "dwelling or place of work." *Id.* §3.04(2)(b)(ii)(1). See notes 48-50 *infra*.

[47] Conn. Gen. Stat. §53a-19(b); Hawaii Penal Code §304(5)(b); N.Y. Penal Law §35.15(2)(a); Pa. Cons. Stat. Ann., tit. 18, §505(b)(2)(ii); Texas Penal Code §9.32(2). The typical provision requires the defendant to retreat if he can do so "with complete safety"; Texas requires the defendant to retreat only "if a reasonable person in the actor's situation" would do so.

[48] State v. Johnson, 261 N.C. 727, 136 S.E.2d 84 (1964). As to statutory recognition of this exception, see, e.g., Hawaii Penal Code §304(5)(b)(i); N.Y. Penal Law §35.15(2)(a)(i).

[49] The leading case is Beard v. United States, 158 U.S. 550 (1895).

[50] See, e.g., Brown v. United States, 256 U.S. 335 (1921) (defendant was superintending excavation work for the post office when he was attacked; he "was at a place where he was called to be, in the discharge of his duty." *Id.* at 344); State v. Francis, 252 N.C. 57, 112 S.E.2d 756 (1960) (defendant assaulted by aggressor as he tried to remove the latter from his, the defendant's, store).

[51] Note that the exception for places of work and business was omitted from N.Y. Penal Law §35.15(2)(a)(i).

an excuse limits the options of third parties to intervene; thinking of the defense as a variation of lesser evils should generate a universal right to intervene and further the greater good. Grounding the defense in the principle of autonomy leads to the same result of universal intervention, but there is a puzzle as to why it should. So far as the analogy with warfare between states is compelling, the right of intervention is not so easily explained. There is no general right of states in the international community to come to the defense of states attacked by others. The state rendering aid must be invited by the defending state to come to its defense. Yet the assumption in civil society is that all persons in the legal system have a right to come to defend the autonomy of the person attacked. This right is not generated by a sense that it is right and proper that the interest of the defender should prevail, as is the case when the conflicting interests are balanced and assessed. The rationale seems to be that an attack against one is an attack against all: the autonomy of the individual is identified with the sanctity of the Legal Order. Yet, suppose that a homeowner resisting aggression wished to do it in his own way. Would third persons nonetheless be entitled to intervene? The law says "yes," but apart from the metaphysics of the Legal Order the rationale remains elusive.

C. The Culpability of the Aggressor. One important difference between the two theories of justified force is that the variation of lesser evils turns on the actor's culpability, while the principle of autonomy focusses exclusively on the defender and his autonomy. Under the latter as well as the former theory, the aggression must be unjustified; if the intruder has a right to use force, resistance is impermissible. The problem cases are those in which the aggression is wrongful but excused—say, by insanity, duress, necessity or mistake. The hallmark of German[52] and Soviet

[52] This is the prevailing rule. See Schönke-Schröder-Lenckner §32, notes 19–21, at 433. *But cf.* H. Mayer, Strafrecht: Allgemeiner Teil 204 (1953) (necessary defense permissible only against intentional and culpable attacks); compare the problems raised by the duty to retreat from excused aggression, note 34 *supra*.

theory[53] is a virtual consensus supporting necessary defense against excused aggression.

The position of Anglo-American and French law is not so clear. Several commentators prefer to analyze attacks by non-responsible actors as a problem of lesser evils.[54] Unless we assume that the life of a child or psychotic aggressor is worth less than a "normal" adult life,[55] the principle of lesser evils fails to justify the killing. The Model Penal Code defines unlawful aggression to permit necessary defense against excused aggression,[56] but virtually all the states adopting the Code have dropped the prolix definition undergirding this coverage.[57]

D. The Problem of Proportionality. There are two requirements for the exercise of necessary force: (1) that the means chosen be the minimal force necessary under the circumstances; and (2) that the force not be unreasonable or disproportionate relative to the interest defended. Even if it is necessary to use deadly force to prevent a petty theft, the principle of proportionality forbids it.[58] Blackstone expressed the principle of proportionality when he reasoned that no act "may be prevented by death unless the same, if committed, would also be punished by death."[59] This equation cannot be taken too seriously, for it implies that jurisdictions abolishing capital punishment would also have to prohibit the use of deadly force in necessary defense. The enduring point in Black-

[53] Kurs (GP 1970) at 356–57; Piontovsky, *supra* note 44, at 426–27. *But cf.* Slutsky, Conditions for Negating Criminal Responsibility 48–49 (1956) [in Russian] (taking the same view as expressed by H. Mayer, *supra* note 52).

[54] Hall 436 n.85; Williams 733; 1 Bouzat & Pinatel §287 at 362. *Cf.* Schmidhäuser, *supra* note 32, at 196.

[55] Note the critique by Löffler, *Unrecht und Notwehr,* 21 ZStW 537, 541 n.7 (1901) of those "who regard it as modern to depreciate the life of the insane."

[56] MPC §3.11(1).

[57] Ill. Ann. Stat. c. 38, §7-1, Comment No. 3 (unlawful force is "criminal or tortious"); Wis. Stat. Ann. §939.48(6) ("either tortious or expressly prohibited by criminal law"). *But cf.* Pa. Cons. Stat. Ann. tit. 18, §501 (defining "unlawful force" in conformity with MPC §3.11(1)).

[58] See note 16 *supra.*

[59] 4 Blackstone 181; the quote follows Blackstone's rejection of Locke's analogy between self-defense and warfare.

stone's claim was not that deadly force is the equivalent of capital punishment, but rather that the use of deadly force must be justified by severity of the crime threatened.

The wholehearted embrace of the principle of proportionality in the common law accounts for the carving out of rules for the use of deadly and non-deadly force and the breakdown of necessary force into the distinct privileges of defense of the person, defense of habitation and the defense of property. The impetus for a similar analysis of necessary force has been wanting in German and Soviet law, for these systems start on the assumption that all legally protected interests are entitled to the same degree of protection.[60] In German theory, in particular, this view of the defense is closely connected with the commitment to personal autonomy and upholding the Legal Order.

This emphasis on autonomy as an absolute value has generated the most difficult single problem in the German theory of necessary defense. In 1920, the German Supreme Court ruled that the general principle of vindicating the Legal Order would justify shooting and killing an apple thief on the run if that was the only way to stop him.[61] This problem of proportionality or reasonableness has haunted German theory ever since.[62] Despite the consensus that killing apple thieves is inhumane, German legislators failed to write any limitation of proportionality into the new Criminal Code.[63] Soviet theorists have made some tentative forays in the direction of recognizing a limitation that would require that parties defending themselves sometimes suffer an intrusion rather

[60] For a detailed listing of the interests protected under the doctrine of necessary defense, see Schönke-Schröder-Lenckner §32, note 5, at 429–30.

[61] Judgment of the Supreme Court, September 20, 1920, 55 RGSt. 82.

[62] For a review of efforts to solve the problem in the draft codes of 1925, 1927 and 1937, see Fletcher, *supra* note 25, at 382.

[63] For an analysis of the background to this legislative decision, see *id.* at 386. Some writers regard it as important that StGB §32, as well as StGB 1871, §53, provides that necessary defense has a legitimating effect only if it is "required" *(geboten).* It is argued that necessary defense is not "required" if the likely harm is disproportionate to the likely benefit. Lenckner, *"Gebotensein" und "Erforderlichkeit" der Notwehr,* 1968 GA 1.

than vindicate their rights.[64] But in recent years, they too have gravitated to a position hostile to the rule of proportionality.[65]

The premises for the Soviet and German views may have little to do with each other. Soviet jurists favor the maximum social response against aggression and even claim that killing an aggressor is a moral duty as well as a right.[66] The best explanation for the German commitment to autonomy is not that it is right to shoot fleeing apple thieves, but that it is the orchard owner's decision to make. It should be his choice, traditional German theorists might argue, in much the same way the United States Supreme Court argues that people should be free to choose whether to use and sell contraceptives or abort fetuses in the first trimester of pregnancy.[67] To grant a sphere of independence from state control is not to make moral judgments about what should be done, but rather to recognize the individual's competence to make the final moral choice.

The autonomy underlying an absolutist theory of necessary defense resembles other doctrines of absolute right—the right to use one's property as one chooses or the right to enforce a valid contract. Yet the exercise of rights obviously conflicts with the rights and interests of others. Legal systems differ in their strategies for accommodating conflicting rights. The preference of common-law theory is to qualify the contours of rights with a stan-

[64] The Fundamental Principles of Criminal Legislation §13, enacted in 1958, provided that the limits of necessary defense are exceeded when the defense is "clearly out of conformity to the character and the dangerousness of the attack." This phrase was adopted in Ugol. kod. (RSFSR) §13. It is not clear whether the limitation refers to the requirement that the defensive response be "necessary" or that it be "reasonable" and "proportionate."

[65] See Kurs (GP 1974) at 189–91; Kurs (GP 1970) at 369, 371; Tishkevich, Conditions and Limits to Necessary Defense 22–24 (1969) [in Russian]; Shavgulidze, Necessary Defense 111 (1956) [in Russian]. *Cf.* the 1969 Decree of the Supreme Court, *supra* note 26, at 18 (point 3) (criticizing trial courts for mechanically applying the criteria of permissible force without considering special factors that would yield a more flexible right of defense).

[66] Kurs (GP 1972) at 210. ("For all citizens, necessary defense is not only a right, but a moral duty").

[67] Roe v. Wade, 410 U.S. 113 (1973).

dard, such as the pervasive concept of reasonableness, that incorporates the interests of others.[68] Continental legal theorists regard it as important to affirm the nominal absoluteness of rights even though the exercise of the right might be restricted in practice. A contractual obligee has the right to refuse counter-performance if the obligor has fallen short of his contractual duty.[69] But the courts hold that the right is "abused" if exercised against someone who has in effect rendered "substantial performance."[70] Thus Continental jurists rely on the doctrine of *"abus de droit"*[71] and *Rechtsmissbrauch*[72] as a way of taking rights seriously but not so seriously as to ignore competing claims of justice.

The doctrine of "abuse of rights" has provided German jurists with a way out of the quandary generated by basing necessary defense on the principle of autonomy. In the Bavarian decision, holding that the use of force to secure a parking space was an exercise of necessary defense, the court added, significantly, that the right of defense was abused because "the harm inflicted was disproportionate to that threatened by the attack."[73] This case is widely cited to support the growing consensus that the doctrine of abuse of rights limits the exercise of necessary defense.[74] This doc-

[68] For an insightful comparative analysis on this point, see Eörsi, *Rechtsmissbrauch und funktionsmässige Rechtsausübung in Westen und Osten,* 6 Zeitschrift für Rechtsvergleichung 30 (1965).

[69] BGB §326(1).

[70] Palandt, Bürgerliches Gesetzbuch §326, note 3(a), at 356 (33d ed. 1974).

[71] See P. le Tourneau, La Responsabilité Civile 522–30 (2d ed. 1976).

[72] The doctrine is considered in German law as an aspect of the general principle of "good faith and fair dealing" (*Treu und Glauben*), BGB §242. *Cf.* Swiss Civil Code (ZGB) §2 (explicitly referring to *Rechtsmissbrauch*). See generally J. Esser, Schuldrecht 32–43 (3d ed. 1968).

[73] 1963 NJW at 825.

[74] Jescheck 258; Welzel 87; Stratenwerth 139–40; Samson in SK StGB §22, notes 22, 23, at 258 (concurring in the result but rejecting the rationale of *Rechtsmissbrauch*); Schönke-Schröder-Lenckner §32, notes 50, 51, at 441. Another technique for approaching the problem of proportionality is to exclude necessary defense altogether in cases of protecting minor interests. This view finds support in the German as well as in the Soviet literature. *Id.* note 49, at 441; Oetker, *Notwehr und Notstand,* 1 Festgabe für R. Frank 359–61; Kurs (GP 1972) at 212–13 (minor attacks not socially dangerous).

trine may enable German lawyers to have their right[75] and curtail it too, but the contradictory style of reasoning conceals a serious problem. The 1975 Code purports to create an absolute right of necesary defense. If judges limit this right by invoking the doctrine of "abuse of rights," the resulting convictions may violate the constitutional rule, *nulla poena sine lege.*[76] The argument is that curtailing the privilege creates a new category of punishable acts, and the only response, it would seem, is to rely on the unpersuasive distinction between enacting a new prohibitory norm and removing the privileged exception to an existing norm. Of course, this argument does not inhibit legislative reform but it does suggest limits to reaching the result by covert and contradictory reasoning.

The point of relating these specific doctrinal disputes to underlying theories of self-defense is to demonstrate that issues such as the duty to retreat are but the revealed signs of deeper ideological clashes. The way to resolve these disputes is not to read the sign in isolation but to probe for hidden values that shape our thinking. It may not be easier to resolve the issue if we see what is at stake in contrasting the principle of autonomy with the principle of lesser evils. It may be that we can function well only if following one theory on the issue of resisting excused aggression and another on the issue of proportionality. But if our composite model is a hybrid one, and we know that it is, then at least we understand why our principles are unstable and subject to unending debate.

The discussion of necessary defense recapitulates, in method, the recurrent theme of this book. In our study of the relationship between harm and just punishment, we similarly found three promi-

[75] Ongoing devotion to the absolute right of necessary defense is reflected in the effort to circumvent the effects of the European Convention on Human Rights, art. 2, which purports to limit necessary defense to the protection of human life. The claim is that the convention regulates only relationships between the state and its citizens, but not the private use of force among citizens. See Schönke-Schröder-Lenckner §32, note 62, at 444–45. For a critique of this argument see Stratenwerth 140.

[76] See Kratzsch, §53 *StGB und der Grundsatz nullum crimen sine lege,* 1971 GA 65.

nent theories—the objective, personal and social theories of wrongdoing. As in the discussion of necessary defense, these conflicting patterns or theories aid us in understanding the tension and instability implicit in our doctrines. They enable us to see that doctrinal disputes are not arid and aimless fights about narrow doctrinal points, but rather a stylized struggle over basic issues of principle. The search for the underlying dynamic of legal discourse illustrates our deeper methodological commitment. In order to reflect upon the criminal law we must move beyond enacted law and accepted doctrines. In order to refine the law we must reflect upon claims of justice in subjecting fellow citizens to condemnation and imprisonment as criminals. We can rethink the burden of persuasion, complicity, conspiracy, omissions, the theory of mistake and much more, but to do so we must commit ourselves to the pursuit of justice in exercising the coercive power of the state.

The process of rethinking the criminal law does not generate definitive answers. It affirms a commitment to a quest, not a specific set of answers. But the quest cannot be a solitary undertaking. It requires a community of committed theorists and it demands unflinching critics.

Table of Cases

Index

Index